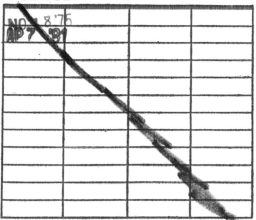

# BEYOND
# BELIEFS

## Ideological Foundations of American Education

**NORMAND R. BERNIER**
University of Wisconsin–Milwaukee

*and*

**JACK E. WILLIAMS**
University of Wisconsin–Milwaukee

PRENTICE-HALL, INC., Englewood Cliffs, N.J.

*Library of Congress Cataloging in Publication Data*

BERNIER, NORMAND R.
    Beyond beliefs.

    Includes bibliographies.
        1. Education—United States—History.   2. Educa-
tion—Philosophy—History.   3. United States—
Intellectual life—History.   I. Williams, Jack E.,
joint author.   II. Title.
LA212.B47          370′.973          72-10037
ISBN   0-13-076067-6
ISBN   0-13-076059-5 (pbk)

Printed in the United States of America

10   9   8   7   6   5   4   3   2   1

Prentice-Hall International, Inc., *London*
Prentice-Hall of Australia, Pty. Ltd., *Sydney*
Prentice-Hall of Canada, Ltd., *Toronto*
Prentice-Hall of India Private Limited, *New Delhi*
Prentice-Hall of Japan, Inc., *Tokyo*

To our teachers—

**Margaret Lindsey**
**Frederick Kershner, Jr.**
Teachers College, Columbia University
**Bernard Mehl**
The Ohio State University

If a man seriously desires to live the best life
that is open to him, he must learn to be critical
of the tribal customs and tribal beliefs that are
generally accepted among his neighbors.

Bertrand Russell


Loyalty to petrified opinion never yet
broke a chain or freed a human soul.

Mark Twain

# CONTENTS

FOREWORD   ix

INTRODUCTION   1

Chapter 1
THE NATURE OF IDEOLOGY   19

Man and His Communities   /   Culture, Ideology, and Personality   /
Cultural Diversity   /   Ideology and Citizenry   /
Characteristics of Ideology   /   Ideology and Anomie   /
Ideologies and Institutions   /   Ideologies and Sentiment   /
Ideological Efficacy   /   Ideological Dissonance   /
Ideology and Language   /   Ideology and Perception   /
Conclusion   /   Suggested Readings

Chapter 2
SCIENTISM   60
The Ideology of the Behavior Modifier

Introduction   /   Science and Religion   /   Scientific Methodology   /
Science and Technology   /   Scientism and Puritanism   /
Technology and the Labor Market   /
Scientism, Psychology, and Education   /
Scientism, Violence, and Social Control   /
Scientism and Social Issues   /   Conclusion   /   Suggested Readings

Chapter 3
**ROMANTICISM   120**
**The Ideology of the Artist**

Introduction   /   The Modern Crisis   /
Romanticism: The Ideology of Rebellion   /
Romanticism and Revolution   /   Religious Antecedents   /
Secular Antecedents   /   Romanticism and the Middle Class   /
Romanticism and Individualism   /   Melancholic Romanticism   /
Romanticism and Nature   /   Cultural or Romantic Nationalism   /
Utopian Romanticism   /   Romanticism and Schooling   /
Conclusion   /   Suggested Readings

Chapter 4
**PURITANISM   188**
**The Ideology of the Moral Exemplar**

Introduction   /   Puritanism as an Ideology of Revolution   /
Puritanism and the Demand for Formal Schooling   /
The Individual and the Community   /
Puritanism and Reform Movements   /
Puritanism and Economic Development   /
The Decline of Revolutionary Puritanism   /
Puritanism—Secularized and Democratized   /
Puritanism and Social Darwinism   /
Puritanism and the American Dream   /
Puritanism and Freudianism   /   The Virtues and Vices of Puritanism   /
Conclusion   /   Suggested Readings

Chapter 5
**NATIONALISM   236**
**The Ideology of the Patriot**

Introduction   /   The Meanings of Nationalism   /
National Communities: Citizenries and Nationalities   /
The Principle of National Self-Determination   /
The Emergence of National Consciousness   /
The Issue of American Unity   /   Nationalism and Schooling   /
The Teacher and Americanism   /   Conclusion   /
Suggested Readings

Chapter 6
**PROGRESSIVISM    290**
**The Ideology of the Facilitator**

Introduction   /   Progressivism: An Eclectic Ideology   /
The Doctrine of Progress   /   Progressivism and the Enlightenment   /
Progressivism and Pragmatism   /   The Progressive Movement   /
The Progressive Movement and Education   /
The Politics of Progressivism   /   The Critics of Progressivism   /
Factionalism in Progressive Education: Child-Centered, Creative
Expressionism; Social Reconstruction; and Life Adjustment   /
Neo-Progressivism: Issues and Education   /   Conclusion   /
Suggested Readings


Chapter 7
**EDUCATIONISM    335**
**The Ideology of the Professional**


Introduction   /   Assumptions of Educationism   /
Characteristics of Educationism   /   Historical Antecedents   /
Educational Conflicts   /   The Threat to the Art of Teaching   /
Aims of Education—An Overview   /
The Citizenship Aim of Education   /
The Emergence of Professionalism   /
Professionalism, Unionism, and Control   /   Conclusion


Epilogue
**A FINAL WORD: A PERSONAL VIEW    391**


**INDEX    409**

# FOREWORD

Examining American society from an ideological perspective, as Normand Bernier and Jack Williams have done in *Beyond Beliefs*, seems to me to be an extremely productive approach for students, teachers, and others, to understanding the peculiar constraints and freedoms of American culture. Further, it provides a particularly useful tool for young people, whose most difficult task today is understanding the many belief systems being offered—or imposed—by friends, parents, teachers, church, and mass media, and determining what they do believe, and how they might want to modify those beliefs. In the process of sorting out some of the more prominent ideological threads of Western society, Bernier and Williams offer a method that views ideological conflict and confusion as inherent in the society, rather than as a merely personal problem. Young people often suffer great confusion in the process of arriving at a personal belief system, and seeing the confusion as normal can be very helpful.

It is no criticism of this study to say that it presents versions of the ideologies considered that are less than pure. Obviously, an ideology is a rough correspondence of belief shared by many, and shaped in individual cases by the idiosyncrasies of the believer. A description of an ideology is shaped also by the ideological learnings of the observer, however objective he may attempt to be. An ideological system, then, as it is received by individuals, is full of inherent conflicts, confusions, and distortions. Often individuals further complicate their problems by incorporating inconsistent beliefs as they consciously or unconsciously go about integrating aspects of ideologies they encounter. This book can help make the decisions concerning what beliefs to adopt and what ones to reject a more conscious and orderly process. This book will not eliminate ideological confusion. But it is a far better approach to the subject than the prevailing "social problems" viewpoint, which merely dissects particular manifestations of ideologies in conflict. Bernier and Williams help people locate the source of the conflict, not only "out there," but also within themselves, and thereby help people weigh and integrate a consistent belief system.

But although they personalize the study of ideology in the class-room, the authors have left the final step—integrating a personal ideology—out of their book as beyond its scope. An introduction cannot accomplish that either, but it ought to contribute something more than praise; I would like to offer some considerations for constructing a personal ideology that permits revision as experience unfolds, rather than rigid rejection of new ideas. A belief system with these characteristics is necessary for the fullest development of one's individuality. The worst consequence of ideological extremism has nothing to do with substantive beliefs, but rather with the closing off of opportunities to experience other ways of knowing. There are even now many more ideologies than those explicated here, and new ones will emerge as people continue to respond to cultural change. Rather than totally rejecting these systems (as some ideologies require), one should be able to select the positive elements from many ideological systems. In the case of the youth countercultures, for instance, which is in the authors' view a manifestation of Romanticism, one should be flexible enough to consider whether or not to adopt facets of belief as concern for the environment, and emphasis upon interpersonal honesty, regardless of one's feelings about political and sexual revolution.

This process of selecting from diverse ideologies those aspects that contribute to the development of one's own unique individuality involves decisions that affect the three important areas of human endeavor—work, personal relationship, and leisure. First, we must all find meaningful work, which utilizes our skills and understandings in ways which are not damaging or destructive. Ideologies have a profound effect on our decisions in this area. In grossest terms, today Puritanism leads us to the factories, and Romanticism to the rural commune. Second, we must work out the nature and extent of our intimate relationships with family, friends, and lovers. Again, ideology is of critical importance as to how we make these decisions—whether we will adhere to conventional role patterns, or whether we will seek degrees and kinds of intimacy unknown to our parents. Third, we must utilize our leisure time. Leisure is more than non-work; how we choose to spend our free time is directly related to what we believe are the possibilities and purposes of life.

*Beyond Beliefs,* and the analytic approach to ideology that it encourages, can assist people in deciding how to lead these three aspects of life. One schooled in this approach is likely to respond positively to change rather than shrinking from it; and since change is inevitable, it makes sense to be willing to embrace the best of it.

RICHARD H. DAVIS
*Dean, School of Education*
*University of Wisconsin–Milwaukee*

# INTRODUCTION

The 1960s inspired the visionary, awakened the dreams of youth, and excited the imagination of a world that recently had emerged from phantom atomic shelters. With the renewal of the search for the milennium, however, there came no abatement in the fears that had first been generated when impotent men unleashed atomic power. Cynics continued to parade their doubts while fatalists popularized their despair.

While some men unshackled themselves from the earth's gravitational tug and walked smugly upon the surface of the moon, others raged because of the futility of their attempts to alter the course of an unpopular and indecisive Asian war. As a majority of Americans basked anxiously in the sunlight of their newly acquired affluence, some of their fellow citizens wandered in despair and anger because they could not unravel the Gordian knot of economic success.

While heroic leaders and dedicated crusaders joined forces to create a just society, other frightened men stalked them with guns or scorned them with ridicule. Most Americans, however, hoped quietly that gradual change would remove the unjust accumulation of institutional biases. They had not yet adjusted to the unexpected realization that their "American Dream" had been a nightmare for some of their hardworking and honest fellow citizens. Meanwhile some sincere reformers, too impatient to bargain for evolutionary change, demanded the immediate removal of unjust social practices. Conflicts raged and good men searched for solutions while a few weak and ignorant advocates of brutality and oppression hungered for a bloody confrontation.

The events of the past decade revealed that Americans hold a diversity of values and convictions. While the deeds generated by their differences unveiled appalling injustice and numberless violations of our sacred democratic charter, they also served to illustrate to a doubting world that many Americans continued to cherish a belief in liberty, a hope in equality, and a dream of fraternity.

The conflicts, however, also revealed that the centripetal forces of national institutions, especially the public schools, had not succeeded in removing the ideological differences among the citizens of the United States. Americans boldly reflected the refreshing but volatile pluralism that had remained camouflaged during previous decades. Inasmuch as the value of democratic processes evaporates when men apathetically avoid revealing their value differences, the ferment of the sixties served as an affirmation that the individualism inherent in the concept "freedom" continued to flourish in the oldest democracy on earth.

Although Americans had been trained to view ideological differences from a narrow political perspective—generally expressed in terms of the left-right continuum—the actualities of American life during the decade of the sixties disclaimed such a simplistic rubric. A simple-minded view of foreign ideological intervention in American life could no longer account for the ideological conflicts that raged across the country. The fact that Americans were unaware of the diverse ideological systems that were endemic to the American soil, however, served to compound their fears. While the United States had provided a nourishing ground for the healthy development of various ideological systems, these differences in belief systems were not readily apparent to most Americans during the frigid, oppressive nights of the Cold War. With the easing of tensions among the Great Powers and an involvment in an unpopular war which awakened the conscience of Americans, differences at home emerged to reveal a surprising ideological diversity.

With the advent of the seventies, America began a long overdue examination of itself. Many questions remain concerning the future direction of the United States, and they must be answered, for the direction we take will be largely determined by our willingness to look courageously at ourselves. The crises through which we have lived can serve us as we attempt to set a course for our future as citizens of a global village. If we are lucky, the seventies will be a decade of thought and dialogue after a decade of struggle and confrontation. This text is written to assist the teacher, the future teacher, and the concerned layman in analyzing the ideological fabric called Americanism. It is designed to provide an overview of American ideological emphases and their educational implications.

The remainder of this introduction furnishes the reader with an examination of some of the major dangers which confront American civilization. Although this *porte-cochère* may seem unduly pessimistic to some readers, we feel that the urgency of the need for an ideological reassessment, especially by teachers, justifies this tone. We cannot afford to unleash upon the schools teachers who act without thinking, who advocate change without understanding, or who support the status quo without sensitivity. The present decade requires that our teachers possess a keen understanding of their individual assumptions and of their nation's belief systems. Without such understanding, our country will flounder in the quagmire of the doubt which the previous decade left as its legacy.

We live in an age in which government tends to be the resolution of the force generated by the volatile aspirations of impatient men as they crash against the bland exigencies of massive technocracies. The previous decades witnessed the unprecedented centralization of political and economic power as well as the unrelenting demand for the actualization of the eighteenth-century dreams of liberty, equality, and fraternity. Unwilling to accept narrow political definitions of this revolutionary slogan, men and women, especially the youth among them, have embarked upon a crusade to destroy the icons of cultural sanctions. Liberation has become the byword of a generation and a multitude of organizations have emerged demanding equality of opportunity for individuals who have been the victims of prejudicial treatment. Language patterns and the arts reflect the exhilaration of deliverance from cultural constrictions. Advocates of genetic control prophesy that man will free himself from congenital limitations and will someday duel victoriously with the Angel of Death. Citizens read their daily newspapers awaiting announcements of new feats and discoveries. We can bathe in the illusion of man's omnipotence while observing precocious spacemen unconvincingly and hesitantly frolicking on the moon's surface.

The present era, however, frustrates the man who seeks simplicity in nature, fellowship in community, and repose in permanence. The ultramodern technocracies confound their citizenries with a slithering anomie that convinced Alvin Toffler to coin the phrase "future shock" in order to identify this new strain of the virus of alienation. With exhausting commitments which extend into distant lands, America's burgeoning technocratic society witnessed during the previous decade a growing malaise at home. The temporary loss of faith in the nourishing utopian dreams which had propelled the United States throughout its history created a moral crisis of enormous proportions.

The previous decade was often a painfully disillusioning time. The cosmopolitanism and affluence promised by urbanization degenerated easily into violence and urban blight. Cultural, racial, sexual, and religious differences often became the sources of economic and social isolation. The sometimes heroic attempts to remove inherited institutional patterns of prejudice were repeatedly followed by the inept pampering characteristic of benevolent paternalism. Social legislation designed to remove poverty and establish equality of opportunity generated a massive bureaucracy more noted for its incompetence, petty bickering, and officious meddling than for any real achievements. Yet poverty continues to be endemic to technological progress and the promises of social justice frequently remain unfulfilled.

To the expanding middle class—the class expected to reap the benefits of the affluence generated by the Promised Land of technological progress—the abundant milk and honey were often sour and bitter. Re-

peatedly admonished that they should be grateful for the fruits of progress, they were cajoled by political manipulators into obedience, taunted
by immature rebels with the false promise of freedom without responsibility, and confused by the fact that they did not experience the world
in the bland and debased ways in which some of the Brahmins of the
mass media affirmed were customary and proper. Their hope for creative
pursuits of knowledge in leisure hours was crushed by the endless pursuit
of the luxuries that pass for necessities in an affluent society.

The age in which man tapped innumerable sources of potent energy
was also an era in which a sense of hopelessness and helplessness gripped
him as he pondered his future.

The anxiety-ridden pace of life which characterizes modern societies
offers a frightening alternative to our violent past. The grim prophecy that
the life patterns generated in modern technocracies are merely samples
of the civilization of the future does little to shore up man's faltering faith
in his destiny.

To some readers the foregoing description of the immediate past
may seem excessively pessimistic. Indeed, the twentieth century has awakened man to magnificent possibilities and has witnessed the unleashing
of creative forces in almost every realm of human existence. The humanizing possibilities, for example, inherent in recent discoveries in the fields
of genetics, medicine, communication, and transportation are incalculable.

In order to utilize meaningfully and fruitfully the numerous products
of his creation, however, man must retain control of his destiny. Recent
history is not encouraging to those individuals who view man's freedom
to choose as an essential ingredient of a humanistic civilization. As man
gradually gains greater control over his environment and his own nature,
he faces the hideous possibility that he may design himself and his freedom into extinction. Indeed, the rapid changes which have enveloped
man's technocracies have generated ominous forebodings.

Because of the fears generated by population increase, the world
faces the stern reality that training will replace education. The hideous
imagery devised by the Malthusian prophets of doom and popularized by
the sensation-seeking mass media has increased the demand for discipline
and obedience at the expense of creativity and individuality. When population increases are viewed as a population explosion, the tentacles of
political constraint increase their hold upon the individual.

As a result of the confusion generated by an increase in scientific
data falsely labeled a knowledge explosion, individuals destined to be
trained and educated within formal educational institutions may never
enjoy the excitement of dialogue among cosmopolitans and generalists,
because the provincialism of their specialization will limit and perhaps
inhibit meaningful communication among scholars. Isolated and over-

specialized researchers falter in their anxious search for the solutions to man's existential dilemma.

With the fears, anxieties, and confusion generated by the increases in population and in knowledge, men may intensify the fragmentation of their identities to avoid the nagging malaise which results when an individual's behavior does not reflect his values. Human beings who expend their energies in attempting to preserve an equilibrium on the merry-go-round of rapid cultural change run the risk of destroying their individual valuing powers. They may come to sense that their opinions and actions are irrelevant if not valueless. Such an estrangement could ring the deathknell on man's democratic experiment and on mankind's chances for survival. In the name of necessity, efficiency, progress, and expertise, men, in their confusion, may surrender their basic right of intellectual, emotional, aesthetic, and spiritual self-determination.

The threat against man's freedom has augmented at an enormous rate. Within the foreseeable future, for example, bewildered individuals could willingly relinquish their decision-making power in politics to a cadre of experts because other confused men will have convinced them that the basis for governmental actions lies in highly secret and complex information which cannot be shared.

Similarly, men could find that they implicitly have abandoned their freedom to express their humaneness because they have structured a social system which inhibits spontaneous behavior. Perhaps in a future technocracy of experts a Good Samaritan will need a Ph.D. before legally practicing caring for his fellow men and only a psychiatrist will be allowed to wipe away the tears of a frightened, lonely, or despairing child. In such an Orwellian world a housewife will be expected to receive a Household Engineering Certificate while a future mother will be required to take courses in a childrearing program and to do a semester of fieldwork in a day care center before qualifying for a Parenthood Certificate. In an age of specialization, men often forget that humanness continues to be more functional for man than all the specialist techniques devised by him.

Although the aforementioned nightmare has yet to be fully actualized, we have moved closer to it during the twentieth century. Science has been politicized by becoming a tool of national governments. Specialists have been segregated from one another because of their political affiliation as well as by the fragmentation of knowledge. Secrecy and isolation have become a way of life for many experts. Thousands of individuals, for example, worked diligently as part of a program labeled the "Manhattan Project" without knowing that they were involved in constructing an atomic bomb. Indeed, the citizenry through its Congress allocated funds for such an endeavor without any knowledge of their use.

Throughout the twentieth century gòvernment acts were repeatedly justified by political leaders who referred to unopened secret files in order to legitimize their deeds. When a nation is at war, secrecy is vital and democratic dialogue is often abridged, but when a state of war becomes chronic —as it has in the twentieth century—the curtailment of democratic dialogue becomes a way of life. Modern language usage in on Orwellian Newspeak fashion continues to reflect the democratic assumptions of past ideological battles, but many "free men" wonder if they are free.

While many citizens are horrified to read reports about bystanders who ignore the cries for help by victims of violence, others are shocked to hear of charges of negligence directed against an individual who attempted to assist a victim of misfortune. When men need insurance policies to protect themselves from their own charitable acts, the laws are not only cruel but pathetic.

Modern man increasingly relies upon institutions rather than upon his neighbors. The "highway patrol" and the "welcome wagon," as well as the "welfare system," often have replaced the concerned motorists and neighbors. When men depend for charity upon institutions rather than upon their fellow men, they will learn also to serve their institutions rather than their fellow men. Institutions easily can become ends rather than means. In such an anti-human social system, individuals become expendable cogs in a bureaucratic machine; they learn that power is to be gained by becoming parasitic to bureaucracies and by imitating the all-powerful institutional ways. They will become bureaucratized, dehumanized, and insensitive toward human existence.

During the decade of the sixties a new Romantic movement emerged to challenge the excesses of the national cult of Scientism. Romanticism, of course, existed as an ideological force in the United States from its inception; indeed, many of the Puritan colonists were Utopian Romanticists seeking to establish a "New Jerusalem" in the American wilderness. Only in the 1960s, however, did Romanticism emerge as a mass movement to challenge the assumptions that pervaded the modern nation-states.

Spreading outward from such romantic colonies as Greenwich Village in New York and the Haight-Ashbury section of San Francisco, Romanticism served as a bandwagon for frantic ideological readjustment. Originating as a lonely voice echoed by rebels such as Allen Ginsberg and Jack Kerouac, twentieth-century Romanticism became a massive movement dedicated to liberating man from the excesses of technological efficiency. Enhanced by the idealism of the Freedom Riders in the South, the Free Speech Movement at Berkeley, and the beautification of America programs, Romanticism increasingly challenged the "gray flannel" way of life. With the inauguration of President John Kennedy, announced by the writings of the great American poet, Robert Frost, a New Camelot was unveiled with new social frontiers to conquer. Romanticism combined with National Scientism in a rare and short-lived *entente cordial*. But the smoke that emerged from the defective wiring system in the podium from which the poet spoke served as a prophetic sign for the violence which was to follow in America.

As the decade of disillusionment unfolded, numerous Romanticists either turned revolutionary, escaped through psychedelic drugs, or sought beauty and liberty through eccentricity. Others sought to relieve their romantic malaise through communal living, encounter marathons, introspection, or religious revivalism. Still others retreated to the safe haven of Scientism.

Social problems, viewed as new frontiers to conquer at the onset of the decade, increasingly came to be viewed as too complex to be fully comprehended or resolved. The asault upon racism was often withstood by legalistic manipulations. Black nationalist leaders emerged, and organizations such as the Black Panthers seemed to be directed by desire for a mutual vendetta involving themselves and agencies of the federal government. The monies allocated to remove poverty from the face of America produce few changes and the goal of beautifying America came to seem shallow as Americans were increasingly warned that the ecological balance had been destroyed and that life could become extinct in the foreseeable future. The call for beautification turned into a call for survival.

Although a large segment of the population saw in the space adventures and moon landings an escape from "incurable" world dilemmas, Americans on the whole were awed but not inspired by these extraterrestrial goings-on. A sense of powerlessness gripped the American people during the decade of the sixties and expressed itself in ways that shook the foundations of the young republic.

Violence spread from a distant tragic land, Vietnam, to American cities and college campuses. Americans polarized; some purchased weapons to defend their homes while others spread rumors of an impending bloody revolution. Inflammatory rhetoric became a way of life. The over-thirty generation, often called the silent generation, was singled out to pay the price for the silence of the fifties. Trapped in a mythical generation gap, the over-thirty generation was subjected daily to verbal accusations that they had created the problems in which America floundered. Not aware that the phrase "generation gap" was symptomatic of a greater ideological phenomenon, some political leaders joined in the verbal tirades.

A generation not only had witnessed the assassination of three of its respected and, to many, beloved leaders, but also was horrified to see its youth dying in an unpopular war abroad and in a frightening rebellion at home. Conflicts raged. With an escalating war, minority discontent, campus unrest, and an exasperated, often bewildered government, the situation bordererd on catastrophe. The tenuous calm which followed the first spring of the new decade seemed to result from disillusionment and despair rather than from hope or resolution. The young nation, with its reputation for vigor, humor, and confidence to the point of brashness, began to loose its youthful countenance. A nation that was renowned for its laughter could not be seen to smile.

The great American issues—such as legal and illegal drug abuse, air and water pollution, personal and institutional racism, rightist and leftist extremism, the centralization of power, and the inability of political leaders to control the multitude of government agencies—remain unresolved. A nation with unmatched power in a world of political chaos, with untold wealth in a world of poverty and with a democratic dream in a world where freedom is in short supply has suddenly found that its role is no longer clear. Yet hope has not faded. The United States has always based its goals upon expectations of the future rather than upon traditions of the past or complaints of the present. Vision, not memories, motivated and continue to motivate the young republic. Indeed, the nation's fallen heroes, the Kennedy brothers and Martin Luther King, Jr., had transmitted a legacy of reassurance. Their hopes and dreams remained to inspire others as Americans continued their search for a unifying national purpose—in Walter Lippmann's terms, a public philosophy.

Within such a volatile environment, other drastic changes were occurring in the United States. Major institutions, struggling against the onslaught of the inexorable forces of technological progress, attempted to redefine their purposes and tasks. The demise of the three-generation extended family, for example, was followed by an increasing tendency to raise doubts about the nuclear family which had replaced it and to experiment with the one-generation family of the peer commune.

In the name of liberation, old institutions were challenged by new modes of living. Hippie communes, homosexual churches, group marriages, and encounter groups made their appearance. Also, in the name of corporate efficiency, styles of business life were altered. America became a land of gypsy workers who increasingly were required to change geographical location to meet the exigencies of corporate expansion and production. The laws of the land reflected these social changes. Divorce, abortion, and civil rights laws were altered to coincide with the new values tht were emerging in America. Cigaret advertising was banned from the airwaves while debates continued concerning the legalization of marijuana. Sexual mores changed faster than the laws designed to regulate them.

Churches seeking relevancy through ecumenism often experienced a sense of normlessness which resulted in an increasing number of ex-members. Indeed, in an era when change was exponential in nature, an individual's personal history could best be told in terms of his ex-friends, ex-mates, ex-memberships, ex-beliefs, ex-values, and ex-principles. For many Americans the chameleon was replacing the eagle as the national emblem.

America, as always, was on the move; but as it sped into the future its citizens wondered increasingly about their goals and about the trust-worthiness of their leaders. The national government suffered from a credibility gap—which some attributed to mass media and educational institutions, thus making these institutions also less creditable. For those who sought accountability, the debunking sociological theorists C. Wright Mills and Herbert Marcuse had provided a visible target in what Mills called the Power Elite. The belief in a Power Elite ruling over the nation led many Americans to forsake their cherished belief in the democratic process. The sense of powerlessness which accompanies the conviction that a military-industrial complex rules the nation expressed itself through apathy as well as violence. Other skeptics, such as Jacques Ellul, rejected the concept of a Power Elite but reaffirmed their own powerlessness by arguing that the Establishment was a complex bureaucratic technocracy which moved in its own way and at its own pace, and which individual men or groups of men could alter only marginally if at all.

In the midst of the ideological ferment of the sixties, schools gen-erally remained open, dispensing formal education to the children and youths of the day. Struggling to prevent fast moving events from entering the classroom, schools continued, in many cases, according to preestab-lished programs and schedules. History, of course, will judge whether such an approach was fatal or medicinal for the ailing nation. While some schools attempted to deal with existing social problems—through occasionally successful sex education, drug abuse clinics, generation and racial encounter sessions, ecumenical dialogues, community exchange pro-grams, and ecological field trips—others weathered the storm quietly, and still others tightened existing programs and controls to protect themselves from the onslaught of zealous reformers. Regardless of which course of action the schools took, criticism of American education became a popu-lar pastime.

The educational endeavor, of course, received its share of the blame for the crises which divided America. Popularizers of educational prob-lems such as Jonathan Kozol, Paul Goodman, and Edgar Friedenberg, became instant spokesmen for those individuals who wanted to alter public schooling practices. Whereas in the fifties the severe criticisms of the educational endeavor had come from such men as Max Rafferty, Admiral Rickover, and Arthur Bestor, whose main concern was with the lack of mental or moral discipline within the schools, by the 1960s many

Americans held that the schools and their teachers were responsible for America's social failures. The reasons for the school systems receiving the blame for the society's failures are numerous; many are legitimate.

First, many of the issues which divided America in the sixties and which continue to divide Americans relate to schooling practices. Racial conflicts in America often make their appearance in schools, so that institutional and personal racism is inevitably an educational issue. Busing, the teaching of ethnic identity, the call for racially balanced school faculties, and the threats of race "wars" in schools located in transitional communities undergoing population shifts are educational issues which result from society's racial conflicts and which also serve to aggravate racial tensions.

Drug use, sex education, changes in dress and language mores, underground newspapers, and calls for schools to become agents of social change are major issues confronting American teachers. These educational issues reflect the ideological conflicts in American society. Since violence has erupted in some high schools and on college and university campuses, the call for law and order in society is often combined with a call for discipline in schools and universities.

Secondly, criticisms often have been directed at schools because the goals of schooling and the functioning of society are viewed as inextricably interwoven. In the field of education there is a continuous debate over the aims of the educational endeavor. It is easy to see why this controversy should be so persistent, for it is an unalterable fact that the preservation of society rests ultimately upon the effectiveness of the education or the training of the citizenry. Teachers are political agents by the very fact that they serve in an institution which is structured to politicize and acculturate the children and youth of the nation.

In a totalitarian state the centralization of power and the absolutist quality of the values adhered to by the power group may conceal the conflicting views concerning the role of the school and the nature of the education which "ought" to take place therein. In such a society, teachers are provided with clear-cut goals. If they disagree with these imposed goals, they must choose between leaving the teaching profession or endangering their lives.

Conversely, in a democratic society where differences of opinion compete freely, educational issues are perpetually being questioned. In a pluralistic society, the phenomenon of selecting educational aims assumes complex proportions. Cultural plurality leads to eclectic aims for education. In a plural and democratic society, schools cannot be structured to please everybody. Indeed, American public education has been a target of criticism since its inception. Of course, ideological sanctions impose limits upon the range of alternative aims. Understanding these sanctions is a necessity for all teachers, and the authors of this book hope that it will assist in developing such an understanding.

In the United States, where education is characterized by some decentralization and local control which permits public involvement in educational planning, and where the citizenry believe that schooling affects attitudes and behavior as well as the economic and social mobility of individuals, the school is inevitably a center of controversy and political pressure. Within such an environment, an observer would anticipate that diversity, innovation, and fluidity would characterize the educational endeavor. Unfortunately, such expectations are seldom realized. The educational system throughout the United States remains—with the exception of funding, materials, and student population—frightfully uniform. Without a national curriculum or national control, the United States has evolved a national school system characterized by an uncanny degree of uniformity. Because of such homogeneity, as well as because of the school system's resistance to rapid change, educational issues often become major social issues.

A third major reason why schools have been the victim of the wrath of the citizenry, especially when allocating tax monies, can be traced to a lack of sophistication on the part of its teachers and school administrators in dealing with ideological changes in the society. Many well intentioned and dedicated young teachers—loaded down with educational baggage consisting of analyses of theories of teaching and learning, sociological studies concerning school populations, and the ever-present eclectic philosophies of education—become disillusioned in their first teaching situation because they are unable to actualize desired reforms within their classroom or school. Experienced teachers also often face insurmountable obstacles when they seek educational reform. The tragedy here does not rest upon the fact that the schools are open to criticism, or upon the fact that parents and pressure groups are or are not involved in education programs. *The major cause of educational atrophy is due to the rigidity of institutionalized programs which are based upon outmoded ideological assumptions.*

For example, the curriculum of most high schools in the United States has remained relatively stable, with minor additions and deletions, over the last fifty years. Proposals developed to remove the unsound fragmentation of knowledge have received minimal acceptance. Chemistry, physics, and mathematics are generally taught as separate entities, just as history, economics, and civics are taught in separate time compartments. In addition, attempts to add "subjects" such as philosophy and anthropology to high school curricula generally have failed or have been trivialized. Or consider the fact that attempts to change the hours of the school day as well as the length of the academic year meet with dogged resistance, despite the fact that the major rationale for the preservation of existing school hours is rooted to an agrarian society that no longer exists in most of America.

Given this sort of imperviousness to change, many well informed, well intentioned, and highly committed individuals increasingly are seeking to innovate education outside the existing public educational system. Thus, various educational experimentations—free schools, storefront schools, community schools—are in the process of educating children and youth. Such educational innovation is refreshing and often worthy of support. However, the fact that many such programs were developed because of a lack of faith in the public school system is tragic. Indeed, the once inaudible voice calling for the abolition of public schools and compulsory attendance laws is growing louder. In an age of rapid technological change and increased social complexity such a call is not only dangerous but, if listened to, could be fatal.

What is more, the rigidity of educational institutionalism increasingly is making schools of education and teachers therein seem irrelevant. In some situations, student teaching hours and community involvement programs have been increased. Yet the expected changes which these alterations were to actualize are not forthcoming. In fact, many "experimental programs" simply have become mini-bureaucracies characterized by bickering and political infighting as well as a source of cheap labor for projects top heavy with administrators.

In order to develop schools which are both viable and susceptible to innovation and educational reform, the ideological foundations of educational programs must be studied critically. Unless the ideological forces which sustain existing educational programs are understood, reform will remain a myth.

This book is based upon the belief that intellectual exploration is a relevant and necessary adjunct to *all* school and community involvement. Understanding the factors that influence peoples and their perceptions as well as the forces that inhibit institutional change is a prerequisite to effective teaching and reform. To blame administrators, the public, teachers, or universities for the failures of the public school system may be soothing, but educational reform must go beyond criticism to understanding and action.

The authors of this text believe that ideas cannot be divorced from feelings. An individual's beliefs, judgments, and "philosophies" are attached to his fears, loves, hates, dreams, and visions. Thus, the focus of this book is on ideology. Ideologies—belief systems which bind "head and heart"—influence and are influenced by social systems. Ideologies open the door to certain changes and close it to others. To understand man's ideologies is to understand man.

The only valid education is one which liberates an individual from the shackles of belief devoid of thought or feeling. Man must move beyond beliefs to affirm his innate dignity. He must arrive at his beliefs through the arduous road of critical thinking and empathy. Education does not occur when beliefs are fed to man as pablum is fed to a baby. Nor does education occur when an individual rejects one value system for another because of propaganda or because the "new" system is in vogue. Much of what is called "liberation" is blind obedience to the subtle and not so subtle manipulation of charismatic leaders. Similarly, much of what is called "liberal" education is propaganda disseminated by institutions which reflect certain assumptions as though they were eternal truths beyond questioning. Free men are thinking men. Men who allow themselves to be *determined* by infant experiences, cultural or ideological forces, physical environment, or advertising and propaganda systems are not the foundation upon which a democratic society can flourish.

The authors of this book believe that all beliefs, dogmas, doubts, emotions, and goals should be critically analyzed, questioned, and then reanalyzed and re-questioned continuously. They also believe that man can make choices—moral and otherwise. Indeed, they believe that education in a democracy must be devised to assist individuals in the process of choosing.

As the numerous "power groups'" converge upon the school with their oftentimes antithetic proposals, the weary teacher, too often unprepared to deal with complex social issues, is tempted to resort to a "wait-and-see" attitude. Indeed, past history indicates that: "Not many teachers wish to personally fight the cause of freedom, to appear before school officials to respond to charges, or to become the object of local controversy and publicity. As a result, the teaching of political matters has, through the years, been formal, bookish, and often not very interesting." [1] Such an escape on the part of teachers could be a disaster to a society which is in the midst of profound social changes and which not only needs the advice of its teachers but which also must depend upon its teachers to resist the intemperate onslaught of extremist groups who would impose their "tunnel vision" interpretation of education upon the schools.

Especially important to future teachers are the recent expressions of teacher militancy and the increased activity of teacher organizations in community projects. Although this militancy and involvement may indicate a welcome commitment on the part of educators to participate as citizens in the democratic process, unless it is based upon clearly understood assumptions about their responsibilities as teacher-citizens it is not

[1] John Jarolimek, "Political Science in the Elementary and Junior High School Curriculum," *Political Science in the Social Studies* (Washington: National Council for the Social Studies, 1966), p. 241.

likely to be as productive as one would wish. Actions must flow from thought if they are to be constructive. No one could ask for less from those individuals who are assigned the task of educating the youth of the nation.

The image of the school and the teacher has changed markedly in the face of the recent cultural and educational conflicts. Mr. Peepers and sweet Miss Dove were replaced by Mr. Novak, Room 222, and rugged storefront schoolmasters. Teaching is no longer viewed as a profession for the timid. Indeed, some parents wonder whether they want their daughters and sons to join such an increasingly aggressive profession.

Teaching, of course, never was for the timid. The lives of Socrates, Jesus, and Abelard attest to this fact. Teaching always demanded courage, resolve, love, and commitment. It demands knowledge about individuals, societies, learning processes, and about oneself, as well as the ability to communicate this knowledge. The hopes of the world have always rested upon education. If mankind is to survive its own perfidy, its survival will be due to the success of its teachers. Teaching is an art which transcends training; it rests upon a faith in man and hope in his future. It is in this spirit that this book is written, and it is our hope that the reader will find within these pages the faith and vision which the authors believe is needed in performing the noble art of teaching, especially in an age characterized by disillusionment and cynicism.

The ideological systems selected for exploration in the following pages are Scientism, Romanticism, Puritanism, Nationalism, Progressivism, and Educationism. The selection is based upon value judgments concerning their relevancy. Other belief systems, such as Freudianism, Populism, Professionalism, Liberalism, and Conservatism, could have been selected for major analysis. The choice was rooted to the conviction that the ideological strands from the selected ideologies have significantly affected the nature of institutional life in the United States. Modernization, for example—along with its correlate, affluence—results from a combination of Nationalism, Scientism, and Educationism. While modernization and its ideological foundations dominate world politics, their particularized American expression results, in part, from Puritanism, Progressivism, and Romanticism. Secondly, the selection was based upon the belief that American education has assumed its twentieth-century countenance as a result of the ideological systems analyzed. Thirdly, the authors believe that the belief systems selected not only influenced America's past and present but will continue to exert a significant pressure upon American life.

Before reading this text, the reader should heed a word of caution. Ideologies are multi-faceted and complex. The following pages represent an *exploration* of some influential ideological systems. Such an exploration is viewed by the authors as a beginning for future dialogue and further study. This book represents but a probe into the complex belief systems which influence the American way of life and which make up Americanism.

Americanism is a manifold and intricate ideological fabric composed of various ideological threads which are, in some cases, mutually exclusive. Americanism implies cultural and ideological pluralism as well as ideological and cultural synthesis.

Athough individual Americans invariably reflect a particular ideological emphasis, they often conclude erroneously that their orientation represents the totality of Americanism. In some cases they view their particular belief system as the repository of all truth and goodness. A major purpose of this book is to dispel the simpleminded notion that Americanism represents any particular belief, goal, or tradition. Americanism is not a mono-belief system characterized by unity, logic, simplicity, or precision. It is complex and rarely if ever reflected comprehensively in the goals or actions of particular individuals or groups. Cultural and ideological pluralism is endemic to the United States. It is our hope that an attempt to unravel the fabric of Americanism will reveal this colorful plural countenance. In fact, the pejorative label "un-American," if utilized at all, should be reserved for those individuals and/or groups who reject the value of cultural and ideological diversity. To attempt to characterize a particular ideological or cultural system as unAmerican is to reveal ignorance concerning the foundations of American loyalty.

Our attempt to unravel the ideological fabric labeled Americanism should not be distorted into a mechanism for identifying particular personality types or simplistic belief systems as uniquely "American." Americanism has influenced all Americans; although some individuals may reflect the particular ideological orientations or emphases analyzed in this book, closer examination of these same individuals also will reveal the influences generated by American pluralism. Ideological subsystems, as we will be discovering continuously in our analysis, cannot be isolated or separated easily.

The fact that ideological subsystems cannot be separated or isolated from other belief systems or subsystems and cannot be uprooted from the volatile soil of the nonrational qualities of human nature should not serve as an excuse for avoiding the exploration of intranational ideological differences. Indeed, the conflicts that have raged throughout the United States in recent years are rooted, in part, in the intranational ideological differences that are reflected in Americanism. For this reason it is our conviction that the ultimate solution to violent conflict will rest upon an understanding of the ideological roots of disunity. To avoid analyzing such volatile belief systems because they are not susceptible to the dispassionate and unitary logical analysis of philosophical systems is to consign scholarship on principle to the realm of irrelevance and blandness.

The ideological categories analyzed in this book are not always mutually exclusive. Puritanism, for example, shares various elements with Progressivism, just as, in modern nation-states, Nationalism and Scientism serve as mutually enhancing ideologies. The categories are utilized because they represent major cognitive and affective orientations. Although the ideologies thus represented prevent any simplistic, systematic inquiry, they serve as meaningful and relevant bases from which to view education in the United States.

If individuals who read this book increase their awareness of the fact that some conflicts among human beings result from sincere ideological differences, we will have achieved our goal. Disagreement between and among individuals need not imply malevolence, ignorance, or dishonesty. Lack of consensus is *not* less noble than agreement.

This book offers *a* way (not *the* way) of viewing differences and similarities in the ideological fabric labeled Americanism. It should serve the teacher as the *beginning* of his or her exploration into the mysterious world of ideology and education.

While we assume full responsibility for the intellectual wanderings within this book and the errors which may have found their way into our enthusiastic search, we wish to express our gratitude to some of the individuals who directly influenced our thinking. Although we believe that learning can occur without teachers, we do not believe that an individual can achieve the maximum of his potential without the patient, sensitive, and rigorous help of an artist-teacher. Without the inspiration of a teacher who can reflect his unique style in his every observation and in his every assertion, a student cannot discover his own uniqueness and style. It is fitting, therefore, that we acknowledge our indebtedness to three outstanding practioners of the art of teaching by dedicating this book to them. To these three great teachers, Dr. Bernard Mehl at The Ohio State University, and Drs. Margaret Lindsey and Frederick Kershner, Jr., at Teachers College, Columbia University, we express our unwavering admiration and affection. These three creative artists not only have influenced our intellectual explorations but also have helped us to search beyond the mere acquisition of knowledge to discover the inherent aesthetic nature of the teaching art.

Without the comforting support of those individuals who share our endeavors, this book would not have been written. Without the patient caring of our families and intimate friends, our explorations would be meaningless. Dr. Bernier expresses his gratefulness to his mother, brothers, and sisters and to Jean Judge and Ann for their continuous encouragement. Similarly, Dr. Williams expresses his appreciation to his devoted wife Darlene, to his sons David and Mark, and to his parents. We recognize that we have been fortunate in the fact that in the midst of the frantic changes that we have endured, the love of our intimates has remained a persistent comfort.

Our often erratic intellectual wanderings, of course, were patiently tolerated by those individuals who forced us to continuously question our assumptions, our values, and our styles. To them, our students and colleagues, we also express our appreciation. We acknowldege gratefully the assistance of our typist Mrs. Shirley Laszewski. Finally, we also wish to express our gratitude to Mr. Arthur Rittenberg, Vice-President, Prentice-Hall, Inc., for his support and encouragement and to Mr. Philip Rosenberg, for his superb editorial suggestions.

*Chapter 1*

# THE NATURE OF IDEOLOGY

### Man and His Communities

In the course of his sojourn on earth, man has lived in diverse social groupings—families, neighborhoods, clans, tribes, clubs, gangs, religious sects, nations, and international unions and leagues. Clearly, man cannot live alone; just as clearly no "society" can exist without individuals. As John Dewey observed: "*Social* cannot be opposed in fact or in idea to *individual.* Society *is* individuals-in-their-relations. As individual apart from social relations is a myth—or a monstrosity." [1]

When man's groupings are small and characterized by geographic proximity among individuals—as in extended families, clans, gangs, and villages—the relationship among the members will be based, in most cases, upon "face-to-face" contact. The cohesion of such primary groups, rests upon this direct interaction among the members. A sense of order, security, and collective, participation results from the feeling that an individual has a rather clearly defined status and function to fulfill in a system of reciprocal exchanges. Inasmuch as such groups, labeled communities, [2] also include the feeling that the social grouping is both physically and psychologically a necessary condition of life, conflicts concerning such issues as individualism, conformity, anomie, and social mobility seldom arise.

Because the offspring of human beings cannot fend for themselves for a relatively lengthy period after their birth, some form of social group-

---

[1] John Dewey and John C. Childs, "The Underlying Philosophy of Education," in *The Educational Frontier,* ed. William N. Kilpatrick (New York: Appleton-Century Company, 1933), p. 291.

[2] Comprehensive descriptions and analyses of contrasting societal typologies have been developed by Robert Redfield (folk-urban), Ferdinand Tönnies (Gemeinschaft-Gesellschaft) and Howard Becker (sacred-secular). Robert Redfield, "The Folk Society," *American Journal of Sociology,* LII (January 1947) 295; Ferdinand Tönnies, *Community and Society,* trans. and ed. Charles P. Loomis (New York: Harper & Row, Publishers, 1963); Howard Becker, *Through Values to Social Interpretation* (Durham, N.C.: Duke University Press, 1950).

ing is necessary for the survival of the species. The gregarious instinct in man is a survival mechanism.

In addition to providing the basic physiological necessities for survival, communities also serve as acculturating agencies for the young. The education and training necessary to accomplish the tasks of preparing the neophytes for their future roles and responsibilities are performed informally by adults (or initiated members in the case of clubs and gangs) who serve as teachers by virtue of their adulthood or prior assimilation. Many primary groups officially acknowledge the successful completion of the acculturation processes by providing rites of passage through which the young or uninitiated pass into adulthood or membership

Man's communities, however, vary in size, degree of cohesion and diversity, geographic proximity of members, and complexity. Often the size, geographic extent, and complexity of the community prohibit direct communication among the members. Yet even within such secondary groups there may exist the basic elements of community—the feeling of kindredness, the feeling of participation, and the feeling of psychological dependency. Indeed, the intense community feeling may be reflected by the intimate language utilized by the group members. Thus, an international Marxist refers to his colleagues as "comrades" while a German refers to his nation as "the fatherland" and a Roman Catholic refers to his priest as "Father."

In such extended communities, which are not primary groups but within which the members reflect a spirit of kindredness, a knowledge of behavioral expectations, and a feeling of psychological dependency, other factors—namely, culture and ideology—create this community spirit. These factors are sustained and creatively expanded by the formal and informal educational and training institutions. Teachers within such communities will be expected to reflect the cultural and ideological elements adhered to by the majority of the members of the community or by the power elite which rules it.

In most cases the teachers will meet the expectations because effective cultures and ideologies inhibit the process of questioning the assumptions upon which expectations are based. Although totalitarian organizations are characterized by external controls to enforce compliance to the dictates of the leader or leaders, *all* extended communities exert compliance by members through the inner psychological controls implanted by the culture and/or ideology. Few Americans, for example, need to be convinced of the "evils" of cannibalism. Similarly, few Americans question the legitimacy of the American Revolutionary War or the desirability of democracy and progress.

In all cases, cultures and/or ideologies *influence* the ways in which people think, perceive, and behave. In many cases, however, cultures and/

or ideologies *determine* the ways in which people think, perceive, and behave. Formal educational systems and propaganda networks combine with less formal educational agencies, such as family and peer groups, to influence the ways in which an individual structures his "reality."

### Culture, Ideology, and Personality

The pervasiveness of culture in influencing thinking, perception, and behavior has been observed by numerous social scientists as well as amateur people-watchers. A Biafran tribesman's concerns, perceptions, and behavior differ from those of an English aristocrat. The differences are due in part to the fact that the cultural and ideological matrices in which each of them learns affect their personality development. The affirmation that culture as well as ideology influences personality development and behavior does not preclude the fact that all human beings possess similarities. Both the Biafran tribesman and the English aristocrat need emotional aesthetic, and spiritual stimulation to be fully functioning human beings. Furthermore, the assertion that culture and ideology influence or determine human development does not mean to imply that individual differences are obviated. While our Biafran tribesman approaches "reality" in a Biafran way and our English aristocrat in an English aristocratic way, the two individuals nevertheless differ from all other members of their respective culture groups. By their influence upon personality, culture and ideology serve to create similarities among people as well as to increase their differences from others. John Schaar observed:

> Since no social environment is composed of factors selected in a purely random fashion (i.e. there is a pattern of culture), it follows that each society presents its members with stimulus *patterns* which encourage the emergence of only certain kinds of needs, emotions, goals, and attitudes. Therefore, variations among social patterns will be reflected in differences in the beliefs and attitudes held by individuals in those societies.[3]

Two general models for viewing cultural and ideological influences upon character formation are the Freudian model and the dramaturgical model. The former, viewing character as indwelling, focuses upon the childhood experiences within a cultural and ideological network, reveals a belief in infant determinism, and emphasizes psychosexual development. A small sector of the Freudian faction, for example, has proposed that the toilet training of children determines their adult behavior and that national collective attitudes may result from such training. Such a "toilet tissue" interpretation of history has not received overwhelming support.

---

[3] John Schaar, *Loyalty in America* (Berkeley: University of California Press, 1957), p. 10.

All observers of human nature, however, would agree that childhood experiences influence adult behavior and that a child's environment determines, in part, the nature of those experiences. Head Start, Upward
Bound, and numerous other compensatory educational programs are designed, in fact, to "equalize" the opportunity for learning by manipulating
a learner's environment.

The second approach, the dramaturgical model, focuses upon manifested behavior and identifies social character as the life style applied
to the roles individuals assume in a society. Thus each society is viewed
as evoking instrumental roles and particular plots. David Riesman's classic
study, *The Lonely Crowd,* in which he analyzes the other-directed personality that is emerging in American society, exemplifies such a dramaturgical analysis.[4] In the dramaturgical model, the interactive behavior
of individual members is viewed as reflecting their group character. Such
an approach may focus upon the nature of the roles, the style, and/or
the thespian qualities which individuals bring to such roles. For example,
each society employs specified courting dramas. In the United States,
generally, marriage is preceded by an announcement of formal courting,
advertised by the transfer from the male to the female of a precious gem,
a diamond, which is worn by the fiancée on a ring on the third finger of
the left hand. If perchance she should return the precious gem to the male,
she signifies thereby that romantic love has expired. Other life dramas also
assume particularized expression because of culture and ideology. The
ways of welcoming newborn children, the passage into adolescence (usually formally declared in the United States by the acquisition of a permit
to move a passenger vehicle from one locality to another), and the ways
of bidding goodbye to the departed members are culturally and ideologically defined. The role of Scientism as an ideological force in the United
States, for example, is revealed in the following passage, which focuses
upon its centrality in the "dramas" experienced by Americans:

> In America today the rituals performed by the medical profession and
> sanctioned by scientific methods have truly sacred status. Babies are born
> in hospitals and their coming is preceded by elaborate purification cere-
> monies that drive away or wash away unseen threats to their health.
> (The ceremonial ablutions of surgeons make particularly effective film
> sequences.) Men and women who wish to be married *must* present them-
> selves to a functionary of the science and there give their blood for his
> examination. If signs in the microscope augur ill, neither priest nor
> politician is powerful enough to perform a fully legal marriage for the
> couple. At death, a man *may* have his priest to absolve him, and his
> family or friends to mourn him, but he *must* have a doctor to pronounce

[4] David Riesman, *The Lonely Crowd* (New Haven: Yale University Press,
1963).

him dead and to explain in the language of science why this man had to die.[5]

## Cultural Diversity

The fact that a culture may produce a modal personality which more closely resembles more individuals in a group than any other modal personality construct has been accepted by numerous anthropologists, especially in reference to isolated, nonliterate, and relatively static societies. The existence of such shared culture, however, has been questioned by other scholars, especially in reference to modern national groupings. Robert Bierstedt, for example, questioned the existence of such patterns in "civilized societies." Noting that such groups differ from primitive societies in that they are characterized by literacy, history, cultural diversity, frequency of cross-cultural contacts and are extended spatially and temporally, he concluded: "Thus it is sometimes possible to speak of 'pattern of culture' and of cultural integration in the case of the nonliterate situation; it is seldom, if ever, possible to do so in the same sense in the case of the literate." [6]

This issue is especially relevant with reference to large modern mass national societies such as the United States. These societies result, in part, from the interaction of a variety of groups which differ in "cultural antecedents" as well as in economic status. In such societies, what pass for social consensus and national culture in fact may reflect merely the "way of life" and the beliefs of a select power group or a dominant but nonetheless minority socioeconomic class. The way of life of the United States senatorial families, for example, differs markedly from that of a significant portion of the American populace. That many men and women who live in the poverty-stricken areas of Appalachia or in the stratified urban ghettoes scattered throughout the United States identify with the members of the Rockefeller, Kennedy, or Ford families implies that other factors besides cultural similarity preserve social cohesion within large industrial societies.

Just as a variety of cultural traits may exist within a particular nation, so there may be marked similarities between comparable social types from different national groupings. Because of technological factors which alter the environment and define the nature of work specialization, indivi-

[5] Solon T. Kimball and James E. McClellan, Jr., *Education and the New America* (New York: Vintage Books, 1962), p. 169.

[6] Robert Bierstedt, "The Limitation of Anthropological Methods in Sociology," *The American Journal of Sociology,* LIV, No. 1 (July 1948), 27.

duals in locations far removed from one another and in different countries may spend most of their days in similar tasks with similar behavioral expectations. Indeed, a Soviet engineer and an American engineer may *share* a perceptual framework that differs significantly from that of their fellow nationals. Regardless of these similarities in daily life, however, both citizens most likely would be loyal to their nation-state and would, in a crisis, identify more readily with their own nationals regardless of social and economic differences.

Many cultural variations may exist within a nation-state. Diverse groupings such as economic classes and age groups may reveal such distinguishing features. James Coleman's study of the adolescent society is particularly significant in this regard, especially in relation to the formal educational process.[7] Indeed, in modern mass societies, cultural quasi-uniformities are not perceived in a similar fashion by members of the society belonging to different subgroups.

Cultural integrity is not a characteristic of large, industrial nation-states. The fact that the Soviet Union and the United States could remain relatively stable politically while possessing various cultural groupings, religious groupings, and economic classes reveals that other factors account for social cohesion. These other factors—ideologies—are major forces of social cohesion. Ideologies reveal the social character of a people and have largely replaced culture as the basis of social cohesion. Ideological communities have become the basis of social life in technological, mass societies.

### Ideology and Citizenry

Common experience remains crucial for orienting the modern citizenry, as it was among preliterate people, but the nature of the commonality has been altered in the industrial nation. Common experiences as ideologies become participation (ideally, lifetime participation) in organizations which exist to indoctrinate and discipline the faithful. Behavior performed under the animus of such ideology is subject to a heightened will, the very stuff of societal purpose. If there is to be discipline for citizens as such, there must be a vital citizenship ideology.[8]

This observation by Leonard G. Benson emphasizes the extent to which ideologies serve to preserve cohesion within extended social groupings, which may include smaller groupings that differ significantly from one another in cultural, economic, and religious makeup. The role of

---

[7] James S. Coleman, *The Adolescent Society: The Social Life of the Teenager and Its Impact on Education* (New York: The Free Press, 1962).

[8] Leonard G. Benson, *National Purpose: Ideology and Ambivalence in America* (Washington: Public Affairs Press, 1963), p. 83.

ideologies in sustaining group cohesion is revealed by the ideological elements which serve as the ideational basis for the we-feeling, role-feeling, and dependency-feeling which were previously noted as essential elements of communities. These ideological elements—individual identity, authority, and group solidarity—are related to the functional flexibility of an ideology and its ability to preserve cohesion in a group characterized by diversity. As David Apter observed, "I am inclined to the view that ideology helps to perform two main functions; one directly social, binding the community together, and the other individual, organizing the role personalities of the maturing individual. These functions combine to legitimize authority." [9] In the ideology of Nationalism, for example, the government as an agent of the national group is viewed as the authority which seeks to preserve the liberty, security, and equality of the populace. In the ideology of Scientism, the community of scientists is viewed as the authority which preserves health, progress, and order, and thus protects individuals against the unseen, destructive forces of nature. In Puritanism, the Elect are viewed as the authority which will protect the community and the in- dividuals within it from the forces which would otherwise destroy its purity, unity, and authenticity. In all cases individuals are viewed as having a function to perform and a role to assume. Similarly, the ideologies serve to bind the peoples together in a fraternity of will dedicated to such goals as equality, liberation, purity of soul or environment, and progress.

Although national citizenship ideologies are pervasive in the twentieth century, other ideologies, often transnational, also exert pro- found influences upon peoples. Indeed, the experiential gap among peo- ples, labeled by various titles—generation gap, credibility gap, and educational gap—oftentimes amounts to the differences between groups adhering to different ideological strands. Thus a hippie suburban adoles- cent, while culturally similar to his business executive father, may differ markedly from him in ways of knowing, perceiving, and behaving. While the father may think with Aristotelian efficiency, perceive with the eyes of corporate acumen, and behave according to *Reader's Digest* articles, the son may think with elusive Zen universal Oneness, perceive as an oppressed social critic, and behave according to recent Allen Ginsberg and Alan Watts articles. The difference between them is not cultural but ideological—the differences between an emphasis upon Scientism and an emphasis upon Romanticism. Of course, the father and son will not be totally different ideologically. Perhaps both will agree to the legitimacy of the American Revolutionary War, the injunction to love thy neighbor as thyself, the belief in the dignity of the individual, and the need for

---

[9] David Apter, "Ideology as a Cultural System," in *Ideology and Discontent*, ed. David Apter (New York: The Free Press, 1964), p. 18.

progress. Their differences result from the fact that the ideological strands in the United States are diverse, making some degree of selection possible.

### Characteristics of Ideology

The term "ideology" was introduced by Destutt de Tracy in 1796. References to the essence of the concept implied by the term, however, are found throughout the history of human thought in the writings of numerous philosophers. In the *Republic*, Plato alludes to the concept in his well known Allegory of the Cave. He describes the human condition as one in which men are chained in a cave, their eyes firmly transfixed to the wall in front of them. There is a fire behind them, so their view is limited to the perception of their own shadows upon the wall. Having always lived in this manner, they assume that the shadows represent reality. When some prisoners are liberated and see the sunlight at the opening of the cave, they suffer great agony while adjusting to the "truth." Upon their return to the cave with their newly acquired wisdom, they suffer the rejection and ostracism of their former companions who have remained confined in the cave. Generally, mankind waits until after the burial of its visionaries and missionaries before extending them the praise and honor they truly deserve.

Plato's allegory can be related in many ways to the concept of ideology. Those who adhere to an ideology, especially those who are fanatic in their beliefs, are perceptually imprisoned. Like the prisoners in the cave who confuse shadows with reality, they quite easily confuse their own ideological perception with "truth," and may even believe their perceptions are universally shared. Those individuals who, to some degree, transcend their ideology and move beyond beliefs will be viewed as a threat by the ideologists who remain confined and no doubt will be subjected to the wrath of the fanatics.

The allegory also illustrates the difficulty of equating social consensus with reality. Obviously those entrapped in their own ideologies cannot serve as reliable resource persons in the search for "truth." Inasmuch as the men who transcend ideologies generally are few in number, the will of the majority does not always serve as a reliable guide to understanding "reality." Indeed, it was a majority vote which demanded the death of Socrates, an archtype of the transcending spirit.

The writings of Francis Bacon (1561–1626), a precursor of the eighteenth-century Enlightenment philosophers, also provided insights for individuals who searched for liberation from ideological enslavement. In *Novum Organum*, his classic study on nature and understanding, Bacon described "four classes of idols which beset men's minds" and obstruct comprehension: Idols of the Tribe and Idols of the Cave are found in human nature and are the prejudices of the tribe and the individual, respectively.[10] Idols of the Marketplace are misunderstandings resulting from the tyranny of words. This problem—the "ill and unfit choice of words"[11]—is further complicated by the fact that words must be used to define words. And finally, the Idols of the Theater, errors ensuing from a rigid adherence to systems, result from "the various dogmas of philosophies, and also from the wrong laws of demonstration."[12]

As early as 1600 Bacon anticipated the emergence of the scientific age. He condemned the static, deductive logic of the Aristotelian philosophers and emphasized the importance of empirical data, experimental method, and practical application. With his approach, he avowed, "knowledge is power." Mankind could, he believed, not only understand nature but also master it. His faith in this precursory Enlightenment mentality, however, prevented him from acknowledging the importance of the deductive method in science. In addition, it convinced him that certainty could be achieved in an inductive proposition when the "facts" of sense data were arranged properly. More importantly, from an ideological perspective, his faith prohibited him from the realization that Scientism itself could also be an Idol. Indeed, if Bacon returned to earth today, he might well add the Idols of the Research Laboratory to his previously developed list.

Although the term "ideology" has assumed a diversity of meanings, pejorative as well as descriptive, it generally refers to an integrated pattern of ideas, system of beliefs, or a "group consciousness" which characterizes a social group. Such a pattern or system may include doctrines, ideals, slogans, symbols, and directions for social and political actions. Ideologies also include objectives, demands, judgments, norms, and justifications, and in this sense they are value-impregnated systems of thought which may be perceived as sacred.

Ideologies may be dogmatic or flexible. They may be supportive of the status quo or may include demands for a new social order or a radical alteration of the existing system. In fact, Utopian belief systems directed toward overthrowing existing social systems may be subsumed by the term "ideology" if such a system characterizes the group consciousness of an existing social group.[13]

Besides being characterized by rhetorical aspects which appeal to

[10] Francis Bacon, *Novum Organum*, in *The English Philosophers from Bacon to Mill*, ed. Edwin A. Burtt (New York: Random House, Inc., 1939), p. 34.

[11] Bacon, *Novum Organum*, p. 35.

[12] Bacon, *Novum Organum*, p. 35.

[13] For an analysis of the differences between ideologies and Utopias, see Karl Mannheim, *Ideology and Utopia: An Introduction to the Sociology of Knowledge* (New York: Harcourt, Brace, Jovanovich, Inc., 1936), pp. 192–204; for a critique of "Mannheim's Dichotomy," see William E. Connolly's *Political Science and Ideology* (New York: Atherton Press, 1967), pp. 62–63.

the emotions and which may be directed toward developing self-confidence or self-glorification, ideologies include elements which may be based upon faith as well as upon empirically tested assumptions or explanations.

Because ideologies are mixtures of faith and reason, hopes and wishful thinking, self-awareness and vanity, they may include distorted representations of "facts." The misrepresentation of facts, however, need not imply intentional deception or intent to disguise basic motives or goals, for such misrepresentation may result from a we-group's specific perspective of reality. Nigel Harris admonished: "To say that this perspective is specific is not to say that it does not adhere to the ordinary criteria of truth and falsehood, but rather that it is related to only one committed viewpoint." [14] Ideologies, however, *may* include elements which have been devised to camouflage actualities and to deceive members of a social grouping or individuals within an "outgroup." Although such intentional deception may be included in an ideology, the sense of the term "ideology" as it is used in this book is by no means primarily pejorative.

Ideologies are products of collective life and serve, in part, as a "language system" within a social group. Because they are the belief systems of a group, they do not depend upon any one individual for their survival. They exist because man is a social animal. Their significance for individuals, therefore, rests upon man's associative characteristics; they have meaning for the individuals who hold membership in a group precisely because they are belief systems shared and held in common by members of a collectivity.

The term 'ideology" may be distinguished from the more comprehensive and all-inclusive term "culture" on the grounds of the particular foci which it assumes. Because they have greater specificity, ideologies draw from cultures or cultural elements for their content. Whereas the term "culture" relates to the individual as well as the associative aspects of man, ideologies focus primarily upon the social. As Harris noted: "Ideologies are differentiated by the feature that they provide us with organization for *social* experience, that is experience comprehensible only in the context of a society rather than in the context of an isolated individual or the relationship of inanimate objects." [15] Of course, man's associative and individual elements cannot, in fact, be separated.

A diversity of ideologies may exist within a cultural framework and may be based, for example, on such noncultural groupings as economic class, religious sect, occupational or social status, and age grouping. Similarly, ideologies may have cross-cultural membership and may serve to develop and sustain cohesion within a group characterized by cultural diversity.

[14] Nigel Harris, *Beliefs in Society: The Problem of Ideology* (London: C. A. Watts and Co., Ltd., 1968), pp. 22–23.
[15] Harris, *Beliefs in Society,* p. 41.

### Ideology and Anomie

The importance of ideologies in sustaining individual emotional health in modern mass societies cannot be denied. Each social group must provide its members with norms which they can utilize to evaluate and judge their behavior. Ideologies thus serve as a *conscience collective,* a referent, which individuals carry within them and which provides them with security when dealing with social situations. When such a *conscience collective* is absent or weak, a society suffers from *anomie,* a social condition similar to the individual condition referred to as alienation. In an anomic society, individuals often feverishly seek for a "security blanket" to protect themselves from the normlessness of their society. Sociologist Emile Durkeim, (1858–1917) documented this phenomenon. He postulated that increased suicide rates were due to the sense of normlessness which resulted from the rapidly changing values created by sudden alterations in socioeconomic conditions.[16]

In severely anomic societies, disillusionment, apathy, mass movements, high suicide rates, and social withdrawal may prevail. The German nation during the Weimar Republic, for example, suffered from an anomic condition which resulted from its defeat and humiliation in World War I. This anomic condition produced a devastating temporary "cure" for Germany, the perverse norms of Nazism. The ideology of the Third Reich served as a hideous *conscience collective* in Hitler's attempt to unify the "Arian" members of the German people and thus surmount anomic conditions.

While political scientist Robert E. Lane affirmed, "In the nation-state some identity diffusion and a touch of anomie is necessary for democracy to survive," [17] other scholars such as Erich Fromm and Sebastian DeGrazia have warned that anomie is destructive to human growth and creativity. Both anomie and extreme community identity (ethnocentrism) prevent the development of the essential elements of humanness.

Although individuality can be crushed by we-ness, it also can be destroyed by normlessness. The importance of ideology, therefore, cannot be underestimated, especially during periods of profound technological change. The altering of man's technological environment results in changes in institutions which may in turn affect the value systems on which they rest. Rapid changes in value systems may create anomie. With the length of time between inventions and their mass dissemination

[16] Emile Durkheim, *Suicide: A Study in Sociology,* trans. John A. Spaulding and George Simpson (New York: The Free Press, 1966).
[17] Robert E. Lane, *Political Ideology: Why the American Common Man Believes What He Does* (New York: The Free Press, 1962), p. 22.

decreasing, and with inventions increasing at an exponential rate, one can foresee the continuation of rapid technological changes, and thus continuous ideological crises. In such a rapidly changing society, the psychological needs of individuals can best be served by flexible ideologies. On the other hand, such ideologies also may encourage individuals to simply drift with or adjust to technological change. While static ideologies will tend to produce defensive antisocial institutional patterns and rigid behavioral expectations, they also may create the dialogue necessary for preventing the naive and unexamined social explorations of amoral technocrats and thoughtless social reformers.

The malaise of the 1960s, for example, while due to numerous social, political, economic, and national as well as international factors, was rooted in part to the breakdown of the ideology of political Nationalism. Such a faltering ideology could not totally withstand crises because the freely given loyalty of men cannot be sustained when ideologies falter. Not only did nation-states such as the United States, France, Northern Ireland, Pakistan, and the Soviet Union undergo profound ideological crises, but other social systems such as the Roman Catholic Church and the International Marxist Party also underwent ideological shifts. Whether such social systems can withstand the ideological crises brought about in great measure by the changing technological basis of civilization will depend upon their functional flexibility. If the ideologies are not adjusted to the "new realities," then emerging ideologies increasingly will assert themselves and eventually will replace the old ones.

When ideologies falter, the inner gyroscope by which individuals determine their behavior often loses its bearing. Individuals increasingly violate what have become poorly defined norms or transgress clearly defined norms that are inapplicable to current realities. The poorly defined norms that are shrouded in the numerous state Blue Laws, for example, are remnants of a previous age that serve to merely confuse the public rather than to inhibit it. In addition, the numerous state laws in the United States which seek to regulate the sexual behavior of married couples are either unknown, ignored, or ridiculed. Anachronistic laws serve to increase a sense of normlessness as law itself becomes neutralized. Similarly, the clearly defined laws and ideological forces against the use of psychedelic drugs proved to be "unenforceable" at the meeting of the Woodstock Nation and other ad hoc quasi-citizenries.

Generally, ideological breakdowns are accompanied by calls for law and order, loyalty oaths, and more external controls, such as increased police forces, narcotic agents, and wire tapping. When ideologies are vibrant and relevant to individuals' lives, external controls are needed only for a few renegades. When ideologies are static and anachronistic, however, external controls are needed for large segments of populations.

Although the classroom cannot be accurately labeled a social system which rests upon an ideology, the rules and regulations established there *can* serve as either a cohesive or a devisive force. Despite the fact that "face-to-face" contact is the basis of the class cohesion, a sense of norm-lessness can develop, and it can be quite disruptive. The teacher who, for example, alters rules and regulations continuously, as well as the teacher who attempts to impose rules and regulations which are not "relevant," may create a sense of anomie in the classroom. Anomie in a classroom will result in individual alienation and "unsocial" behavior. At this point disciplinary action, the school's brand of law and order, will become the basis for social order. When schools resort to hall guards, intercom-monitoring, and extensive restrictions, they may be described as social systems lacking ideological vitality. Unless it becomes ideologically relevant, the public school will be challenged by alternatives—community schools, free schools, or no school at all.

### Ideologies and Institutions

Athough ideologies are not necessarily coterminous with cultures and political boundaries, cultural factors and political considerations often determine the nature of an ideology. Obviously, ideologies are learned; the learning, however, may result from overt training or covert manipulation. Robert E. Lane discussed these types of indoctrination:

> Loosely speaking, there are three ways in which a father lays the foundation for his son's political beliefs. He may do this, first, through indoctrination, both overt and covert, as a model for imitation so that the son picks up the loyalties, beliefs, and values of the old man. Second, he places the child in a social context, giving him an ethnicity, class position, and community or regional environment. He also helps to shape political beliefs by his personal relations with his son and by the way he molds the personality that must sustain and develop a social orientation.[18]

Of course, an ideological perspective may change in the course of an individual's life. Even in the face of such changes, however, many adults will continue to adhere to the ideological system as it was taught to them by their parents. When an ideology has undergone severe alterations, an inherited belief system may serve to inhibit the social progress of an ambitious traditionalist. A segregationist, for example, will increasingly remove himself from the mainstream of the emerging American ideology as the country moves toward the fulfillment of its commitment to freedom and equality for all the citizens.

[18] Lane, *Political Ideology*, p. 268.

In addition to what he learns from his parents, a child is subject to other formal and informal ideological training. The environment provides him with ideological training as he observes dress, holidays, monuments, and nonverbal behavior. Seeing a policeman in uniform perform his task or viewing a military parade, for example, may serve to educate a child about the nature of authority in a society. Hearing adults whisper in a church may educate him about expected behavior within the meeting house of his religious group.

Besides the aforementioned ideological training, a child will be exposed to major socializing and politicizing institutions which are dedicated, in part, to communicating the national ideology to the young. Of course, the peers he encounters in these institutions may serve as counterideologists. The Romanticists (often confused with Revolutionaries) on the college campuses, for example, periodically undermine the college's unalterable dedication to Scientism.

Institutions which control the formal education and training of the children and youth in a nation will profoundly influence the selection of ideological content as well as the emphases, style, and rate of dissemination. Of course, such institutions may, consciously or unconsciously, distort the beliefs which compose an ideological system, with potentially dire social consequences. Most public schools in the United States, for example, hav failed to focus upon the contribution of ethnic minorities in teaching American history. Such an exclusion distorted the ideological prism through which Americans view themselves, and thus helped to produce a racial crisis which caught many Americans by surprise. Similarly, whereas the heroes of Scientism have been focused upon and eulogized—Louis Pasteur and Madame Curie readily come to mind—romantic innovators such as Robert Owen have been virtually ignored. Even such spokesmen for Scientism as Wernher Von Braun have been avidly quoted while romantic spokesmen such as John Lennon have been ignored if not ridiculed by the Brahmins of the social system.

While all American schools serve to inculcate the American brand of Nationalism, Scientism, and Puritanism, some schools also serve to inculcate local, regional, or international belief systems. For example, the Scopes trial in Tennessee in 1925 reflected a conflict between regional and national ideological bents. Similarly, some religious groups, such as the Amish, have been unable to bridge the ideological gap between their particular religious tenets and the requirements of national school policies. Most private schools, however—such as the parochial schools and the military academies—serve to inculcate the national ideology even while giving primary attention to the inculcation of religious or parapolitical ideologies. Thus international religious beliefs and sectional belief systems are meshed with national beliefs. The recent move to establish community schools to inculcate Afro-Americanism resembles, in part, the parochial school movement. The question remains, however, whether Afro-Americanism can or should mesh with the ideology of American Nationalism.

Social systems always establish institutions to protect their existence. That the public school systems reflect the social setting in which they are situated should not surprise an informed observer. George Count's perennial question, "Dare the Schools Build a New Social Order?" generally has been answered in the negative. Indeed, the criticisms of schooling in the 1960s and the calls for relevancy rarely have been demands that the schools change the social order but rather that they reflect it more accurately. Relevancy is a term that applies to adjustment, not to revolution. Formal schooling—institutionalized education—has not been, is not, and most likely will never be revolutionary in goal. Indeed, teachers who transcend the cultural and ideological forces within their societies will often be penalized for their transcendency: Jesus was nailed to a cross, Socrates was given hemlock, and Abelard was castrated.

In an age of rapid technological change and the resultant ideological shifts, institutions must not lag behind the exigencies of the time if they are to remain viable. The closest a public school system can come to being a revolutionary system is by remaining ideologically static, for ideological irrelevancy can be a seedbed for revolution. As most educationists finally have discovered, it is less disruptive for schools to reflect the changing views on fashions and patterns of curricula, than for them to insist upon unpopular traditions.

Formal schooling often has lagged behind other socializing agencies. Unlike the mass media, which keep a close watch on changing societal needs and desires—a necessity in the competitive marketplace—the school systems all too often structure their programs upon ideological considerations which are no longer *au courant*. For example, the perennial school programs emphasizing the importance of thrift may be viewed by some as anachronistic in an age characterized by a consumer economy. Similarly, the public school's hesitance, in some quarters, to deal with issues of sex education, in an age when television, magazines, and books deal openly and somewhat sophisticatedly with sexual concerns, may be viewed as outdated. The public schools generally have been reluctant to discard the ideological roots which guided them in the past; hence the often heard accusation that they are irrelevant—that is, not relevant to the popular ideological trends that characterize American civilization today.

The youth of technological societies increasingly are developing *ad hoc* ideologies to help themselves adjust psychologically to rapid social changes as well as rapid intellectual changes—processes which have ac-

celerated at an increasingly rapid pace. Of course, such transitional ideologies often do not serve their function of providing the community needs
of those who devise them.

The issue of ideological relevancy, however, is not clearly defined.
The term "relevance" does not stand alone; it must be attached to a prep-
ositional phrase signifying "relevant to something, someone, or some-
place." What is relevant to one person or group may not be relevant to
another, so that there always must be proponents of one ideological perspective or another who could criticize the schools for being irrelevant.
George D. Spindler, a leading American anthropologist, analyzed the
transforming of the American culture and concluded that there was a
gradual movement away from the traditional American values of puritan
morality, work-success ethic, individualism, achievement orientation, and
future-time orientation, toward the emerging American values of sociabil-
ity, relativistic moral attitude, consideration for others, hedonism, present-
time orientation, and conformity to the group. He further noted that the
transformation had gained momentum since the world wars and concluded that "different groups operating in the context of relations between
school and community, educator and public, occupy different positions
on the value continuum, with varying degrees and mixtures of traditional
and emergent orientations." [19] He diagrammed his conclusion as follows:

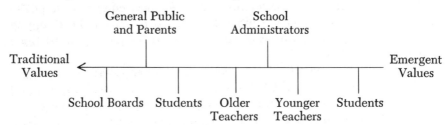

Thus conflicts concerning sex education, the teaching of Afro-American
history, dress codes, and school newspapers result, in part, from the fact
that the American public reflects ideological differences. The schools and
the teachers are observed closely, and they must continuously assess their
educational programs to ensure that they arrive at a functional balance
between traditional and emerging values if they are to withstand the ideological onslaughts of concerned citizens. More importantly, teachers must
ensure that schools operate according to ideological realities. Robert E.
Lane's admonition is especially relevant to teachers:

> Ideologies have consequences. The ideologies of a society shape its social
> and political institutions; when ideologies and institutions are more than
> normally out of phase, one may expect trouble. When men act without

[19] George D. Spindler, "Education in a Transforming American Culture,"
*Harvard Educational Review,* XXV (1955), 146.

beliefs to justify and give meaning to their acts, they are coerced, confused, or moving like automatons through social routines, and like automatons, are easily led to do something else.[20]

Certainly some schools in America encourage the development of automatons by structuring school policies and procedures which contradict the democratic ideological charter which governs the vision of the society.

### Ideologies and Sentiment

Although ideologies are less comprehensive than cultures and not necessarily coterminous with them, they are distinguishable from philosophies, policies, or theories. Ideologies are less abstract and more sentimental than philosophies. Thus men willingly have given their lives for Americanism; indeed, some men, such as the astronauts and cosmonauts, endanger their lives for scientific advancement as well as for national honor. On the other hand, few men offer their lives in consumate devotion to pragmatism or logical empiricism. The very nature of philosophy in the Western world is rooted in the attempt to control the "underbelly" of feeling which most concepts possess. Where philosophies convey the tone of the rational, ideologies reveal a strong emotional flavor. Indeed, the often heated struggles between the Western nation-states and the Soviet Union and its allies have been struggles between the ideology of Corporate Capitalism and the ideology of Marxist-Leninism. Recently the reckless and sometimes bloody conflict between the Establishment and the adherents of the counterculture (that is, the counter-ideology) on college campuses revealed the growing hostility between the adherents of opposing ideological systems, Scientism and Romanticism.

A central characteristic of ideologies, as was previously noted, is their quality of serving as a bond between and among individuals. Individuals within such ideologically based we-groups place sentimental value upon their membership and assume moral obligations, which may be perceived as sacred, to perpetuate, enhance, and defend the community and the ideology which binds it. Although such ideological communities may not satisfy man's need for intimacy, they provide him with emotional sustenance by serving to channel his loyalty.

Ideologies, therefore, serve as the bridge between a man's loyalty and his community. Morton Grodzins wrote: "When you scratch a man you touch loyalty. For man means society. And society—social structure of every sort—rests upon loyalties; upon attitudes and actions directed at supporting groups, ideals, and institutions. Loyalties sustain and are sus-

[20] Lane, *Political Ideology*, p. 268.

tained by mutual rights and duties, common beliefs, and reciprocal obligations—all essential ingredients of community life." [21] Because ideologies
function as symbols of the collectives which adhere to them, they tend
to become objects of loyalty. Men willingly defend their ideologies as
they would the members of their communities or a geographic possession.

Besides serving as the cohesive force for a we-group, ideologies also
relate to the processes of developing an individual's identity. Man is a
"carrier" of numerous ideologies and his personality matrix will reflect
those which significantly influence him. Indeed, individuals may perceive
an ideology as an extension of themselves. For example, an attack upon
Americanism may be viewed by some Americans as a personal attack
upon them. Ideologies are the children of men and they are often defended as though they were progeny.

Inasmuch as ideologies also include symbolic systems, attacks upon
certain symbols will also produce violent reactions. To some Americans
the American flag represents Americanism (to others, however, it may
represent the military-industrial complex), which in turn represents the
American people. Burning a flag, therefore, may produce the same effect
as physically striking an individual's child. Similarly, an attack upon the
dress style of hippies or other Romanticists may be viewed by them as an
attack upon their ideology of liberation and thus an attack upon a community dedicated to freedom. To ridicule a man's ideology is to ridicule
a man's community. To ridicule a man's community is to ridicule the man.

By providing an individual with a social identity, ideologies also
serve to furnish him with goals and norms. As was noted previously,
normlessness creates alienation. Ideologies, therefore, serve to stabilize an
individual's processes of making judgments by furnishing rules and providing the comfort of knowing that these rules are shared by other
individuals within the community.

Besides serving as symbols and representatives of a community,
ideologies also may serve to distinguish individuals from others. Men are
often judged by the ideologies they hold rather than by their character.
Thus ideologies often create anti-ideologies as we-groups create outgroups. Ideological families that tend to become exclusive ingroup identity
systems often create outgroup hostility. In this sense, ethnocentricism and
prejudice may be correlates of an ideology.

Ideologies also furnish the individual with a referent for selecting
among the stimuli which impinge upon his senses, thus helping him bring
order to his perceptual world. Although such an ordering creates the
conditions for stereotyping and other generalizations, it also serves to

[21] Morton Grodzins, *The Loyal and the Disloyal: Social Boundaries of Patriotism and Treason* (Chicago: The University of Chicago Press, 1956), pp. 5–6.

give an individual a sense of security. Immanuel Kant, the founding father of German idealism, emphasized the necessity of such security when he rejected the belief forwarded by the English empiricists that direct sense experience was a form of knowledge. He also rejected the skepticism of Hume by admitting that "things-in-themselves" did exist in the world. Yet the knowledge of such "objective things," he believed, depended upon the "subjective" judgment and understanding of the observer. Even the order of the world was imposed by the observer, and the imposition of such order was a psychological necessity to protect the individual's sanity. The human mind thus functions as a filter and designer, selecting and structuring the data of the world.

Some ideologies are viewed as mutually incompatible. The perennial American education dilemma concerning the hiring of a Marxist teacher and the requirements of loyalty oaths is due, in part, to the institutional struggle to protect a view of the American national ideology. Indeed, the American fear of Marxism is the product of two major ideological battles—the defense against an opposing national ideology ( Russian Marxism) and the defense against an anti-national class ideology ( International Marxism). Similarly, Scientism by its focus upon experimentation and progress has created outgroups of such individuals as astrologists, illiterates, and the Amish religious community, just as the Establishment ( the military-industrial complex which represents the forces of Scientism) is viewed as the outgroup by Romanticists. Although ideologies may include tolerance as an integral element, they tend to create their own brand of heretics. Indeed, the changing character of a civilization's heretics reveals the nature of the dominant ideologies. During the Medieval period in Western Europe, for example, the Roman Catholic Church controlled a network of educational and propagandistic institutions. Through its control the Roman Church implanted a Catholic perspective upon all major institutions. Regardless of economic class, ethnic origin, or geographical area, the overwhelming majority of people in the Western world perceived and behaved according to the inner dictates of the "Roman Catholic perspective." Those individuals who failed to internalize the perspective or who rejected it were isolated, outcast, or ordered to recant—often assisted in the process through various means, not the least of which was execution. Thus the Jew in Catholic Spain or the Albigensian in Catholic France suffered because of his ideological "error." Gradually the Roman Catholic Church lost her control over the major communication networks. As such competing ideological forces as the insurgent nationalistic movements developed, the "Roman Catholic perspective of the world" was corroded and replaced by such national perspectives as "French," "Spanish," "English," and "German." With the emergence of national ideological systems, religious heretics became less significant. Gradually political heretics became the *causes célèbres.* While heroes such as St. Dominic, St. Bernard, and St. Ignatius were being replaced by Oliver Cromwell, Tadeusz Kosciuszko, and Denis Diderot, "heretics" such as the Count of Toulouse (leader of Albigensians), Joan of Arc, and Jan Hus were replaced by Quisling, Pétain, and the Rosenbergs.


### Ideological Efficacy

The effectiveness of an ideology in creating and maintaining group cohesion will depend, in part, upon its functional flexibility. It must be diffuse enough to capture the loyalties of diverse people who may significantly differ from one another, and yet concrete enough to serve as a symbol for the group. Benson identified the functional flexibility of modern ideologies when he wrote: "In the case of the modern industrial nation, a vital ideology must bind the individual to some social system, riveting his allegiance to a set of non-rational values but not preventing him from thinking critically in the spheres of technical, creative, or scientific competence." [22] Generally, a functional ideology permits its adherents to attach the ideology to other ideologies. Furthermore, there exists a phenomenon of legitimization whereby ideologies support and legitimize one another. For example, nonnational ideologies such as Scientism mesh with national ideologies and both gain mutual support.. Arguments for the establishment of nation-states, especially in areas where tribal societies continue to flourish, often are based upon the claim that nation-states will provide the technological means to elevate the standard of living. Thus modernization is the offspring of both Nationalism and Scientism. Various groups find that they can adopt the national ideology and still claim that their particular belief system supports and expands it. Similarly, national ideologies reveal goals which are expressed by various intranational groups. For example, the members of the John Birch Society claim that their particular belief system is an expression of American Nationalism—Americanism. Similarly, members of various antiwar groups that have emerged in recent years in the United States claim that they represent the essence of Americanism. Indeed, the American ideological system is designed to permit such diversity in most cases.

Numerous ideological systems provide for such alliances of beliefs and cross-ideological fertilization. Some Afro-American nationalists, for example, have combined their Afro-American ideology with the Muslim faith and thus become Black Muslims. *The Autobiography of Malcolm X* offers a moving account of the psychological journey of a sensitive man's

---

[22] Benson, *National Purpose*, p. 72.

conversion to the Black Muslim ways.[23] Other Afro-Americans have combined their ethnic ideology with Christianity. The "Black Christian Nationalism" movement exemplifies this latter synthesis.

Ideologies, therefore, are not characterized by a systematic rational development; but rather, they include diverse elements which may *not* be mutually supportive in principle but which are synthesized as a result of internal as well as external pressures upon a collectivity. Of course, such combinations may create contradictions and conflicts. Americanism, for example, includes a belief in individual freedom and equality. Such ideals, however, are also utilized to justify class differences in the economic domain. Are political equality and economic inequality compatible bedfellows? Americanism generally affirms that they are compatible; Marxism affirms that they are not mutually supportive. Similarly, the conflict between national brotherhood and the competitiveness basic to a capitalistic economic system is often viewed as ideological dissonance.[24]

Although ideologies may be—in fact, must be flexible—they generally serve to define the operational boundaries for the collectivity. Ideologies resemble cultures in that both serve to limit the alternatives available in human behavior. This fact, however, does not prevent, ideologies and cultures from providing the wellspring for man's creative capacity. Both cultures and ideologies serve to expand man's horizons as well as to place directional signals which channel the way in which he will pursue his goals. William E. Connolly rightfully observed:

> The dominant value and belief system limits the types of groups that can be organized, constrains the range of issues that will be raised in the political arena, control the extent to which alternatives considered within each issue area will deviate from the *status quo*, and defines the possible procedure by which the public issues can legitimately be resolved.[25]

Indeed, when they are functional, ideologies set boundaries upon alternatives considered in making ethical choices. For example, the matrix of American ideologies prevents certain issues from arising. When Sputnik was propelled into space by the ideological competitor of the United States, Americans did not suggest that we could close the missile gap by sending human beings into space in untested rockets. The American ideological principle which affirms the importance of the individual

[23] Malcolm X, *The Autobiography of Malcolm X* (New York: Grove Press, Inc., 1966).

[24] For criticisms of economic ideological elements which emphasize competition and individual gain and their relationship to community cohesiveness, see John Dewey, *Individualism: Old and New* (New York: Minton, Balch, and Co., 1930); Erich Fromm, *The Art of Loving* (New York: Harper & Row, Publishers, Inc., 1963); and Sebastian de Grazia, *The Political Community: A Study of Anomie* (Chicago: The University of Chicago Press, 1966).

[25] Connolly, *Political Science and Ideology*, pp. 27–28.

prevents scientists from experimenting with human beings wthout concern for life. The Nazi ideology unfortunately did not contain such a tenet and, as was discovered, human beings were utilized with impunity in Nazi scientific experimentation. It should be noted, however, that ideological rhetoric may not reflect behavioral reality. As a consequence of the American ideological commitment to capitalism, a tax-supported medical program will be labeled "medicare," not socialized medicine. Likewise, as a result of the influence of Progressivism, few teachers would rhetorically defend rote memorization or advocate a disregard for a child's needs and differences; yet an observer may seriously doubt that the classroom behavior reflects the Progressivist rhetoric.

By serving to develop compliance habits and by defining legitimate activities, ideologies can assist in creating a *security* community which will be coterminous with the ideological community and which will minimize the probability of armed conflict between community members. Moreover, ideologies usually permit enforcement in those cases when noncompliance exists. Thus each ideological group possesses guardians who watch over the behavior of community members.

Any attempt to absolutely and finally delineate a belief system would of necessity end in failure, for ideologies require mysterious ambivalence if they are to remain flexible enough to attract the loyalty of numerous individuals. Scientism must house both the biologists and the nuclear physicists; Romanticism must house the voluntarily impoverished members of a hippie commune as well as the affluent "gurus," Alan Watts and Allen Ginsberg . Similarly, Americanism must appeal to such diverse groups as the John Birch Society, the Civil Liberties Union, the Zionists, and the Daughters of the American Revolution.

Although the Biblical admonition that "man cannot serve two masters" is relevant to a discussion of ideologies, in many cases man *can* serve two ideologies—or more—if they are not viewed as mutually exclusive. The process of ideological formation generally encourages diversity. Not only do diverse interpretation of ideologies flourish, but cross-fertilization of beliefs from diverse social groupings will produce syncretism—"that is the conjoining of disparate elements from different groups of beliefs without the logic of each source being permitted to work itself out in the form the original group conceived." [26] The process of syncretism reveals that ideological consistency may vary and that social groups may differ in the degree of unity their ideologies reveal.

Although, as we have seen, some ideologies are viewed as mutually exclusive, many of them, given the proper circumstances, turn out to be mutually supportive. Indeed, in some situations American Marxists may

[26] Harris, *Belief in Society,* p. 101.

support the United States government and tenets of Americanism if circumstances dictate. The process of syncretism, whereby various ideological threads are combined without the logic of their roots, explains why ideologies are not easily discussed or explained. Americanism, for example, has integrated within it Puritanism, Scientism, and Romanticism. It also includes the internationalism of Christianity, the sectionalism of "Confederate loyalty," and the localism of ethnic neighborhoods. Because of the process of syncretism, phrases such as Romantic Nationalism, Puritan Romanticism, Scientific Progressivism, and Scientific Romanticism have had to be devised. The American Catholic, the American Socialist, the hippie millionaire, and the young Puritan executive have managed to merge what could be viewed as conflicting ideologies into functional identities. Of course, the degree to whch an individual is successful in meshing ideological strands may depend upon his cunning and his patience. Any attempt to precisely analyze the beliefs of such individuals would frustrate the most patient of ideological analysts.

In large complex technological societies such as the United States and the Soviet Union, a variety of ideologies will coexist, for ideologies attach themselves to religious, ethnic, economic, and political communities. As Harris noted: "Within any complex society, a number of different tendencies will coexist, perhaps posed within a common terminology that derives from a dominant ideology." [27] Ideological agencies, however, will be assigned the task of assuring that the terminal community (i.e., the nation-state) will be preserved. Thus citizenship ideologies will remain dominant, so that although schools, for example, have the option of dealing with ethnic ideologies (e.g., Afro-Americanism), religious ideologies (e.g., Roman Catholicism), economic ideologies (e.g., Socialism), they are required to teach the citizenship ideology which is supportive of the existence of the nation-state.

### Ideological Dissonance

Central to the efficacy of an ideology is the requirement that it adequately represent the nature of the community which adheres to it. Otherwise, the ideology will generate inconsistencies and may result in cleavages within the community. Although viewed as brotherhood religions when they serve their function of developing and preserving social cohesion, ideologies also may serve as fratricidal sects when they produce schisms by misrepresenting the collectivity. William Connolly's observation is worthy of note:

[27] Harris, *Belief in Society,* p. 43.

If one's ideology portrays a large gap between the existing situation and one's vision of the possible and desirable, the resulting discontent is likely to issue in agitation to close the gap. If the ideology one accepts portrays a rough convergence between the actual, the possible, and the acceptable ideal, then one's political life is likely to remain relaxed and quiescent; whatever "troubles" one has are likely to remain latent or to find expression in extra-political ways. Furthermore, if the accepted ideology in fact "fits" the socio-political environment, it can effectively guide and channel one's actions. If it seriously distorts the real situation and seriously misreads the real option open, then it is likely to encourage action or inaction with pernicious effects.[28]

The assertion that ideologies are the belief systems of social groups does not imply that such beliefs are internalized or understood by all members of the collectivity, for individuals may participate in only portions of a belief system. However, the majority of people who belong to the social grouping, or the ruling elite who dominate it, will reflect the specific ideology in their verbalizations and will utilize it as they would the group's language. The ideology must effectively serve the group.

Although some members of a social grouping may be excluded from ideological norms and rules without disrupting a social system (as in the case of slaves in pre-Civil War America), if the ideology is directed to all people and the actual practices violate ideological assumptions, social disruption will result. If men are taught that they are to be treated as equal regardless of race, religion, or national origin, while the actual practice opposes this ideal, social disruption will occur. Similarly, if the laissez-faire and rugged individualism arguments are utilized to defend a capitalistic system which increasingly requires "other-directed" individuals and which increasingly comes to be based upon a corporate society characterized by "socialistic legislation," individuals will become disillusioned. Ideological elements cannot be taught and continuously violated without repercussions. The educated American and Soviet citizen—both of whom have inherited revolutionary traditions based upon ideological commitment to equality, liberty, and fraternity—will demand that these ideological ideals be implemented. Thus, within the last decade, the Soviet Jew and the American Black have expressed their dissatisfaction with the dissonances between ideals and reality.

Besides the danger that ideological ideals may conflict with projected realities, there is also the danger that ideological symbols of identification may cause cleavages if they incorrectly identify the collectivities. For example descriptive terms such as "Christian," "Anglo-Saxon," or "affluent," when applied to the American nation, may generate disintegration because they misrepresent the total collectivity. The ideological stances of the Ku Klux Klan and other nativistic movements, for example, contain

[28] Connolly, *Political Science and Ideology*, p. 121.

within them the elements of violence and disintegration. Because of their divisiveness in view of the total makeup of the American citizenry, they endanger the unity of the American Republic and thus are fundamentally unAmerican. Dissonance also occurs within other less political ideological systems—e.g., the conflict between the call for "spontaneity" and the "contrived techniques" for creating openness within some segments of the Romantic movement; or the conflict between the Puritans' admiration for schooling and hunger for knowledge and their periodic demands for censorship.

Sectional ideological conflicts continue to exist within this immense nation-state. Even though political cohesion may be achieved through forms of federalism, ideological battles will persist unless consensus exists as to the meaning of local autonomy, states' rights, or federal control. The historical struggle to establish federal aid to education programs in the United States, for example, reveals that sectional differences have produced varying interpretations of "equality of educational opportunity" and "national authority." Indeed, federalism and its implication of states' rights gradually have been corroded by the centripetal force of federal expansion. The Confederate flag, however, continues to serve as a symbol of states' right as well as of a now defunct confederation. To minimize the importance of this symbol by referring to it as a quaint remnant of a bygone age would be disastrous, for it symbolizes a particular ideological focus in Americanism. While it can fly along side the American flag, it also may be pitted against it.

Besides the continuous sectional differences, other differences, sometimes appearing primarily sectional in design, reflect other conflicts in the American ideology. For example, local control of education has remained an American ideal, even though it is in conflict with Supreme Court decisions calling for the implementation of the principle of equality of educational opportunity through integration. The future of this major ideological conflict remains unclear.

If the symbol matrix of an ideology, the object of loyalty, is characterized by precision, then the elements which are perceived as disloyal will increase. In a pluralistic society, group, or club, the potential conflicts among loyalties, is great, especially if the ideational configuration which symbolizes them is precise. If Americanism is defined as "God-fearing," for example, numerous atheists will be excluded from psychologically participating in the community despite their adherence to the American political creed. Similarly, if the adherents of Scientism narrowly define the "scientific method," numerous existential explorers will be excluded from the scientific community, just a numerous educators will be forced into the role of an outgroup if educationists strictly define educational research as quantitative.

Although expressions of loyalty toward persons or things tend to be more focalized than loyalties expressed toward ideologies, the latter form of loyalty must be based on some clearly perceived tenets—often slogans. To be functionally flexible, an ideology must be specific enough to be distinguished from competing belief systems and must contain norms which can serve as guides to an individual's actions while not limiting itself in such a way as to exclude numerous potential believers because of "minor" individual differences.

Ideologies, as noted previously, must provide individuals with norms for judgments and behavior. Sebastian de Grazia postulated that ideologies serve as "attendants" for adults. Noting that human beings suffer from a separation anxiety, he concluded that religious and political ideologies serve as inner attendants or guardians. They provide individuals with a sense that a ruler—a god, a nation, a king, or a church—protects one and guides one in making important personal and group decisions. Especially in the sphere of ethical behavior, functional ideologies serve to provide man with a referent for making moral choice. Robert E. Lane warned:

> . . . a forensic ideology cannot survive without a strong moral component in which there are specified evils, villains, exploiters, usurpers, devils on the one hand, and somewhat vaguer restitutions, reforms, heroes, and salvation on the other. This morality, rather than logic, is what holds an ideology together, and without it the whole thing tends to disintegrate into a series of piecemeal and pragmatic adjustments to changing circumstances and demands.[29]

### Ideology and Language

> "When I use a word," Humpty Dumpty said, in rather a scornful tone, "it means just what I choose it to mean—neither more nor less." "The question is," said Alice, 'whether you *can* make words mean so many different things." "The question is," said Humpty Dumpty, "which is to be the master—that's all." [30]

The haughty Humpty Dumpty is incorrect. He is not the master over words, for words, language, and perception assume meanings and relevancy within an ideological perspective. Often without his knowledge, Humpty Dumpty would use terms which reflect the ideology of the wonderland around him.

Because ideologies are not static, the meanings of terms are affected by their uses within particular social groupings and in different historical

---

[29] Lane, *Political Ideology,* p. 344.
[30] Lewis Carrol, *Alice in Wonderland* (New York: Washington Square Press, Inc., 1960), p. 190.

periods. Locality and temporality affect language, for as Samuel Johnson observed, words are the "daughter of earth."

The sociologist Karl Mannheim, in his classic study *Ideology and Utopia,* stressed the importance of the collectivity and its ideological framework on an individual's communication and thinking processes. He observed that the individual is not the sole determiner of his mode of thinking. The individual, he emphasized, "speaks the language of his group; he thinks in the manner in which his group thinks. He finds at his disposal only certain words and their meanings." [31] This observation is especially relevant in viewing political and sociological terminology. For example, the English term "nation," the French "*nation,*" the German "*nation*" and the Italian "*nazione,*" are not as synonymous as bilingual dictionaries would have us think, for national ideologies and national cultural elements affect their uses and determine, in part, their meanings. Culture and ideology determine and influence the meanings of terms. Concepts such as "philosophy," "education," and "freedom" carry different meanings in the United States, the People's Republic of China, and Saudi Arabia. Similarly, concepts may convey different meanings within a pluralistic nation. Terms such as "draft evader," "welfare," and "right on" convey meanings which cannot be accurately described by consulting the standard English dictionary.

Because of the variety of meanings which a term or phrase may take on as a result of cultural or ideological forces, teachers must cautiously select the terms they use to describe individuals or events. For example, the terms "colored" and "Negro" in reference to Afro-Americans were used during previous generations and within certain sections of the United States without question. Within recent years, however, a growing number of individuals interpret such terms as desparaging. Of course, the user of these terms could claim that such an intent did not motivate his use of them, and in many cases this defense is correct. However, in effective communication, the intent of the speaker must be combined with an understanding of the communication framework of the listener. In fact, the term *communication* implies shared meaning.

Because ideologies are dynamic and change with time, the meanings of concepts also change. Some terms include meanings which are distinguishable one from another in different historical periods. Terms are products of antecedents and trends and concrete historical realities, so that the meanings of terms such as "Progressivism," "Radicalism," "Marxism," and "Americanism" today differ significantly from their meanings in 1940. Indeed, the ideologies noted in this text have changed meanings and implications since their inception.

[31] Mannheim, *Ideology and Utopia,* p. 3.

Teachers must deal with ideologically loaded terms carefully. Many false statements have been attributed to individuals because of the lack of understanding of changing meanings. While ideological frameworks change, often the words utilized in them remain the same. Terms removed from their historical context may be misleading if contemporary meanings are attributed to them. Because nouns and adjectives do not reveal temporality and locality, the use of "old" words in referring to new situations may easily lead to ambiguity and misunderstanding. Terms such as "democracy," "capitalism," "loyalty," "education," and "beauty" have changed meanings continuously. Often heard attempts to defend corporate capitalism by referring to Adam Smith or to defend the existing form of American government by calling upon Thomas Jefferson are sometimes ludicrous. Likewise, individuals who want to impose their religious convictions upon their fellow citizens often defend their position by alluding to the "religious view of our founding fathers," failing to distinguish between the theism of Puritanism, the deism of Jefferson, and the agnosticism, if not atheism, of Thomas Paine. Dead heroes have been made to defend many practices which they would abhor. In consulting our ancestors, teachers must note carefully the ideological differences between them and us.

The meanings and definitions of terms, therefore, depend upon the "realities" perceived by the individuals utilizing them. Such "realities" are not always accurate views of events—in fact, one may well doubt whether there ever are accurate views of events, inasmuch as every one sees the world through one ideological lens or another. Indeed, distorted perceptions of events influence the meanings of terms as much as the events themselves. On this score we may note that the mythology that has developed concerning the generation gap results, at least in part, from the "distorted perceptions" of observers who misinterpret language because of differences in usage.

The difficulty in communication is further compounded when terms are proffered as descriptive in nature but also assume a normative aspect. Social psychologists Theodore Newcomb, Ralph Turner, and Philip Converse focused upon this element of communication in reference to the characteristic of group norms when they wrote:

> For example, such bald and merely definitional statements as the following refer merely to cognitions, without evaluations: murder involves the death of one person by intention of another; theft involves the transfer of one person's belongings to another without mutual consent. But it is virtually impossible to think of murder or theft without becoming evaluative: both are bad.[32]

[32] Theodore M. Newcomb, Ralph N. Turner, and Philip E. Converse, *Social Psychology: The Study of Human Interaction* (New York: Holt, Rinehart & Winston, Inc., 1965), p. 235.

The *raison d'être* for such a phenomenon lies in the fact that properties of objects are rarely neutral in terms of cultural and ideological values. Thus, individuals often prematurely evaluate the properties of objects without viewing them from different perspectives, so that when a term is utilized to describe "what is" as well as what "ought to be," the "is" may appear to be an "ought." (For example, consider the use of the word "natural": as a statement of fact it means merely that some event occurs without human intervention, but it is often taken to imply a judgment of approval.) Conversely, it frequently happens that a statement of judgment is mistaken for (or is passed off as) a statement of fact, as when a teacher announces that so-and-so is a great poet. In an age influenced by the ideological forces of Scientism, the danger of developing a moral system based on what "could be" rather than what "ought to be" cannot be ignored. In educaton, for example, issues such as the use of tranquilizers to calm the emotionally tense child must be resolved by weighing "oughts," "is," and "could," not by blandly assuming that the technological ability to use drugs in this way makes the practice desirable. Similarly, should a child be taught to read at the age of one if means are discovered for teaching reading at that age? Because of the influences of Scientism and Educationism, if such a possibility becomes a reality, the forces calling for its implementation would be powerful.

Because of ideology, terms such as "Americanism,' "Socialism," "Indian," "Negro," and "Communism" are expressions which often portend to be descriptive but which are utilized to convey normative meanings. Few Americans will *describe* Communism. Most will *condemn* it.

Included within the aforementioned limitations and sources of misunderstandings in language usage is the fact that some terms convey evaluative meanings which are pejorative in nature, and the move from lexicography to condemnation may not be detected easily. Such terms as "effete," and "Prussian" contain disparaging allusions when utilized by certain individuals. The term "bohemian," for example, may be utilized to describe an individual because of his provenance, or it may be utilized to describe an individual who behaves in a manner contrary to common conventions. Such phrases as "German measles" and "Jew's apple" reveal subtle and negative allusions. Others, such as "Harp," "Kike," "Frog" and "Nigger" are direct and vicious.

Ambiguity of terms may profoundly affect individuals and their society, for some concepts "are instruments of orientation and action, norms of behavior, and guides toward personal and social attitudes." [33] An individual's way of life, his perceptions and the degree to which he sustains or develops a personal identity are affected by the degree of

[33] Yehoshua Arieli, *Individualism and Nationalism in American Ideology* (Baltimore: Penguin Books, Inc., 1966), p. 2.

clarity conveyed by the concepts which he utilizes to pattern his life. Henry D. Aiken, observing that there exists a relationship betwen words and symbols and a man's way of life, asserted: "It is for this reason that the task of clarifying such golden words as 'liberty,' 'justice,' 'democracy,' 'person' and 'love,' is essential to the well-being of any people whose way of life is expressed in terms of them. For if they are unclear or confused or inconsistent, then the way of life is so also." [34]

The ability to make meaningful distinctions between the factors which influence individuals will affect and be affected by the process of defining and labeling. Individuals whose processes of identifying individuals, events, and beliefs are dulled by terminological ambiguity also suffer from dullness of sensitivity to subtle and not so subtle differences between such factors. Stereotyping, for example, is a form of generalization which results in part from an individual's dullness of sensitivity. Ambiguity of language intensifies individual insensitivity.

Ambiguity may serve an ideological purpose by sustaining social cohesion, binding individuals together who would disagree if precision were achieved. Commenting on the way in which ambiguity in communication can serve to generate social cohesion, Gregor Sebba, observed that imprecision of meaning in such phrases as "the American way of life" and "disarmament" enables splinter groups to form coalitions; ". . . if there are fundamental cleavages within the body politic," he admonished, "any search for a precise meaning of the symbol will bring these cleavages to the surface and produce open dissension." [35]

The issue which Sebba identifies raises fundamental questions. First, can coalitions based upon terms which convey possibly antithetic multi-faceted meanings survive when events force cleavages to the surface? And could such cleavages have been avoided through careful and continuous attempts to deal with "realities" rather than with terms which produce pseudo-consensus? Secondly, does the search for precise meanings follow as well as precede disintegrating phenomena in a society? And thirdly, does fruitful dissent in a democratic society imply clarity of concepts? If one answers these questions in the affirmative, the need to clarify terms which include multi-faceted meanings increases in importance. Without such analysis on the part of teachers, an Orwellian Newspeak could easily become the language of peoples. In *1984*, Orwell envisioned Newspeak as a language devised to meet the ideological needs of English Socialism (Ingsoc). He added:

[34] Henry D. Aiken, "Moral Philosophy and Education," in *Philosophy and Education* (Boston: Allyn & Bacon, Inc., 1959), p. 69.

[35] Gregor Sebba, "Symbol and Myth in Modern Rationalistic Societies," in *Truth, Myth, and Symbol,* ed. Thomas J. J. Altizer, William A. Beardslee, and J. Harvey Young (Englewood Cliffs, N.J.: Prentice-Hall, Inc., 1962).

The purpose of Newspeak was not only to provide a medium of expression for the world-view and mental habits proper to the devotees of Ingsoc, but to make all other modes of thoughts impossible. It was intended that when Newspeak had been adopted once and for all and Oldspeak forgotten, a heretical thought—that is, a thought diverging from the principles of Ingsoc—should be literally unthinkable, at least so far as thought is dependent on words.[36]

Although most observers would affirm that Oldspeak has not yet been replaced by Newspeak, ideologies have channeled thinking processes. For example, "Ministries of War" are called "Departments of Defense," and "newness" is equated with "best." What is more, technological progress is often automatically equated with improved human conditions. Recent ecological muckrakers have clearly disproved this assumption, which left its mark on the American ideological framework.

Ideologies and languages are inextricably interwoven. They influence each other and channel thinking processes and perception, thus affecting behavior.

### Ideology and Perception

Idcologics are similar to cultures in that they serve to channel perception. An individual, because of ideological forces, will see events, actions, things, and people within a certain frame of reference. For example, an individual carrying the American ideology will view a Marxist coup in a Latin American country differently from a coup in the name of democracy. Similarly, Puritans viewed the American Indians in a different manner than did the Rousseauean Romantic. Liberals and Conservatives perpetually argue concerning the rights and wrongs of political actions. Much of their discourse reflects an ideological bent which channels perception. Perceptions are not always accurate, but they are assumed to be by the perceiver, who bases his behavior on them.

Because of ideology, the same "facts" may imply contrary realities. For example, the Biblical passages in Ezechiel in which the prophet describes his encounter with cherubim is perceived differently by an agnostic UFO buff and a Biblical scholar. Ezechiel wrote:

Now as I behold the living creatures, there appeared upon the earth by the living creatures one wheel with four faces. And the appearance of the wheels and the work of them was like the appearance of the sea; and the four had all one likeness: and ther appearance and their work *was* as it were a wheel in the midst of a wheel. . . . And when the

[36] George Orwell, *1984* (New York: The New American Library, Inc., 1955), p. 227.

living creatures were lifted up from the earth, the wheels also were lifted up with them.[37]

To our latter-day UFO observer seeking historical evidence for the existence of "flying saucers," Ezechiel's description has implications unknown to a Biblical scholar. As Fischer and Thomas affirmed, "The same set of facts can be used differently by equally intelligent persons." [38]

In many situations and for a variety of reasons, facts may be difficult to attain. The process of identifying "facts" is further complicated by the problem of ideological definition. For example, should the percentage of individuals who fail to complete high school be labeled the dropout rate or the schooling-reject rate? Yet even when bland statistical facts can be attained and definitions can be agreed upon, the major issue remains—the issue of ideological meaning. Facts do not speak for themselves. Facts are simply facts; to acquire meaning they must be plugged into ideologies. For example, a decline in the school dropout rate may indicate the success of a stay-in-school advertising campaign, the increasing relevance of schooling, a decline in job market opportunities, or, simply, a different method used in arriving at the figure.

The ideological problems engendered while attempting to assess the "fact of the matter" are complicated further by such value-laden concepts as objectivity and subjectivity, rationalism and emotionalism. Often an individual ascribes the attributes of objectivity and rationality to individuals, magazines, and newspapers whose ideological perspectives mirror his own; likewise, those with whom we disagree often are branded subjective and emotional. This is especially important inasmuch as the dominant ideologies of Puritanism and Scientism, in contrast to Romanticism, apply a pejorative meaning to subjectivism and emotionalism. Although adherents to both Puritanism and Scientism would praise objectivity and rationality, they would strongly disagree about their meanings, for the one finds these qualities in the realm of religion, while the other looks for them in science.

An individual behaves according to the "realities" as he perceives them. Furthermore, if he understands his perception, he will begin to understand his behavior. Certainly some individuals inaccurately assess their perceptions and misjudge their interests. Yet an analysis of behavior based upon the belief that individuals do, in fact, understand their actions may be more productive than one that assumes unconscious, ulterior, or irrational motives. The admonition which William H. Whyte, Jr., directed toward human relations experts could be equally applicable to neo-

[37] "The Prophecy of Ezechiel," *The Holy Bible* (Chicago: The Catholic Press, Inc., 1952), Chapter 1.

[38] Louis Fischer and Donald R. Thomas, *Social Foundations of Educational Decisions* (Belmont, California: Wadsworth Publishing Co., Inc., 1965), p. 8.

Freudians, neo-Marxists, and anyone else who attempts to determine what another individual "really" means by his behavior. Whyte stated,

> Someday someone is going to create a stir by proposing a radical new tool for the study of people. It will be called the face-value technique. It will be based on the premise that people often do what they do for the reason they think they do.[39]

Since an individual behaves according to "realities" as he perceives them, it is necessary to understand those realities if one seeks to change the individual's behavior. The essential prerequisite to behavioral modification is perceptual change. This change in a person's perceptions is possible if one analyzes the ideology which channels his perceptions.

Past experiences provide the bases for perceptions of self and the environment. Frequent, stable, and important experiences further provide an "anchorage" for future perceptions, and thus they serve as points of reference in making judgments. Although "anchorages" provide stability within an individual's "realities," they also serve to classify people and objects, and such classifications may easily lead to oversimplification and stereotyping. Strong ingroup identity, for example, may provide "anchorages" which may lead to negative stereotyping and outgroup hostility.

"Perceived realities" and not "realities" affect an individual's behavior. Ideologies are like the lenses in the collective eyes of a group; they provide the individuals within the group with a way of looking at the physical and social environment around him. They provide him with an anchorage, a point of reference, in making selections and judgments about the "realities" he selects to see. Most teachers, for example, generally have refused to support teacher unionism and the American Federation of Teachers. A major factor in this rejection has been their identification with Professionalism. Although many social analysts, including C. Wright Mills (*White Collar*) and Myron Lieberman (*The Future of Public Education*), characterize the vocation of teaching as nonprofessional, teachers persist in allying themselves with a "professional organization," the National Education Association. (Their judgment, however, may be in the process of change. This is discussed in greater depth in Chapter VII.)

The differences between "perceived realities" and "realities" is also exemplified in views concerning social class. To clarify this discrepancy, social psychologists Muzafer Sherif and Robert K. Merton have developed the concepts *membership group* and *reference group*. An individual's *membership group* is determined by the "objective" conditions of his

[39] William H. Whyte, *The Organization Man* (Garden City, N.Y.: Doubleday & Company, Inc., 1957), p. 44.

reality. Such conditions might include his income, vocation, and property ownership. His *reference group* is determined primarily by his attitudes and behavior. Consequently, it would be very possible for an individual to be "objectively" lower class, while maintaining many middle-class values. The understanding of such a phenomenon should prevent teachers from automatically believing that lower-class families place little value on schooling. Indeed many lower-class individuals maintain a firm belief in middle-class values and may practice them even more faithfully than many "objectively" middle-class people.

Ideologies also serve to provide "attention areas" and interest areas for individuals. National ideologies, for example, influence perception in such a way that local issues often are viewed as irrelevant by the citizenry. An individual's daily life may be affected significantly by the decisions of local school boards, city councils, organizations of businessmen, or mayors. However, in an age of Nationalism, national and international issues often crowd these local issues outside the attention area of an individual. A flood in a distant state, for example, may minimize the importance of a local bond issue. National leaders have often arranged to announce unpopular political decisions at times when the attention area of the nationals was occupied by other important events, such as space adventures. Ideologies help to define certain issues, events, individuals, and objects as being relevant to the individuals who adhere to the belief system. Not only do attention areas influence individual behavior and feelings as well as thinking processes, but they also influence future deeds. As Harold Lasswell observed: "The focus of attention tends to influence expectations, demands, and identifications, and in turn to be influenced by the existing body of attitudes." [40]

Besides serving to provide an individual with explicit awareness of his membership within a group, ideologies also furnish him with a guide in predicting human behavior and thus the way he perceives it. An individual's expectations concerning others rest in part upon an understanding of the ideology which influences them. Knowing that an individual is a Marxist, or a hippie, or an American, or a Jew will influence our perception of him. Of course, such judgments may be inaccurate and may be the basis of stereotyping. Because of ideological pressures, however, men do judge others by their ideologies.

The process of decision-making also rests, to a certain extent, upon ideologies. Ideological systems, as previously noted, add a dimension to the valuing process by forming the ideational basis for judgments. Ideologies also add an emotional element which may predispose individuals or groups to behave in certain ways. For example, phrases such

[40] Harold D. Lasswell, *World Politics and Personal Insecurity* (New York: The Free Press, 1965), p. 147.

as "scientifically proven," "according to the Bible," "according to natural law," or "according to our leader" will influence an individual's judgment, for they may refer to legitimizing agencies within his ideological system. Abbie Hoffman is viewed as a reliable source of information concerning the American nation by numerous Romanticists, whereas those who adhere to Scientism may view him as an emotional, unreliable, misinformed, or uninformed observer. Few Americans will perceive him or his opinions in a neutral manner.

Finally, an individual's perceived self-identity will be affected by his ideology. If an individual belongs to a Puritan Church, it is *his* church, and someone who ridicules that church ridicules him. It is certainly naive to believe one can question an individual's ideology in such a way that there is "nothing personal" about it. The relationship between "group identity" and personal self-esteem is revealed by Carmichael and Hamilton when they write: "Black people must redefine themselves, and only *they* can do that. . . . There is a growing resentment of the word 'Negro,' for example, because this term is the invention of our oppressor; it is *his* image of us that he describes." [41] The legitimacy of their affirmation was revealed, in part, by James G. Martin's study of "Racial Ethnocentrism and Judgment of Beauty." In his 1964 study of interracial perceptions of female beauty, he concluded: "These data generally support the proposition that American whites and American Negroes share a common esthetic standard for judging beauty in the female face and confirm the thesis that Caucasian features are considered to be more attractive than Negroid features in American society." [42] The ideology of racism does affect perceptions. It is not surprising to read the sad and tragic observation made by the Black poetic philosopher W. E. B. Du-Bois. He exclaimed:

> It is a peculiar sensation, this double-consciousness, this sense of always looking at one's soul by the tape of a world that looks on in amused contempt and pity. One ever feels his twoness,—an American, a Negro; two souls, two thoughts, two unreconciled strivings; two warring ideals in one dark body, whose dogged strength alone keeps it from being torn asunder. [43]

Afro-Americanism as an ideological movement serves an important function in altering this Black identity crisis created by the ideological strands of racism in American society.

[41] Stokely Carmichael and Charles V. Hamilton, *Black Power: The Politics of Liberation in America* (New York: Random House and Alfred A. Knopf, Inc., 1967), p. 37.

[42] James G. Martin, "Racial Ethnocentrism and Judgment of Beauty," *The Journal of Social Psychology*, LXIII (June 1964), 60.

[43] W. E. Burghardt DuBois, *The Souls of Black Folk: Essays and Sketches* (New York: Fawcett Publications, Inc., 1968), pp. 16–17.

The problem of identity and ideology described by Carmichael and Hamilton was also encountered by Americans following the revolution. Having dissolved the political ties with England, many of the leaders of the new nation emphasized the necessity of creating a culture distinctively American. Noah Webster, a vigorous proponent of this ideal, stated,

> . . . a *national language* is a bond of *national union*. Every engine should be employed to render the people of this country national; to call their attachments home to their own country; and to inspire them with the pride of national character. . . . As an independent people, our reputation abroad demands that, in all things we should be federal; be *national*; for if we do not respect *ourselves*, we may be assured that *other* nations will not respect us.[44]

The relationship between ideological definitions, group identities, and an individual's self-perception is central to the learning process. The attempts of South Vietnamese soldiers to teach the Montagnards defense tactics utilizing modern weapons, for example, resulted in minimal progress. Later, American teachers were more successful. Part of the reason was the Montagnards' fear of being "used" by the Vietnam soldiers whom they mistrusted as a result of prolonged ethnic conflicts. A person will learn more effectively if trust exists between him and the teacher. Teachers educated in the ways of Scientism must be prepared to deal with students who may be disciples of a Romantic ideology and who will thus mistrust them as agents of the "Establishment." While most public schools serve to inculcate Scientism, the Romantic ideology, it is prudent to recall, is taught through the media, especially through musical recordings. Buffy Saint-Marie, Simon and Garfunkel, and Joan Baez are teachers of Romanticism. Ridiculing Romantic ideological heroes such as Bob Dylan may bring out the wrath of an adolescent group.

Similarly, because of the increasing influence of a Black ideology in certain communities, teachers in such communities must be prepared to understand the ideological framework of the children. A child who has internalized a Black ideology will perceive differently from one who has not. Teachers, especially in urban schools, must familiarize themselves with the forces which affect their students. Just as Americanism implies more than apple pie, so Afro-Americanism signifies more than chitterlings and Spanish Americanism implies more than tacos. By the same token, Romanticism involves complex ideas besides unusual dress codes, just as Puritanism connotes more than censorship. Indeed, the ecological movement gains much of its force and meaning from its taproots into the Puritan and Progressive ideological subsoil. Relativism, while focusing

---

[44] Noah Webster, "The Reforming of Spelling (1789)," in *Educational Ideas in America,* ed. S. Alexander Rippa (New York: David McKay Company, Inc., 1969), p. 150.

upon human differences, does not necessarily imply moral neutrality. Each ideological system is complex and each has served to furnish social groupings with a unique view of the world. While some men may view the ideological crises of the present as issues of semantics, those who understand the intricacies of ideologies will recognize that words symbolize and represent thought patterns which are rooted to the past but which are perpetually changing.

### Conclusion

Man cannot escape completely from ideology or culture. Both ideology and culture provide him with the intellectual, aesthetic, spiritual, and emotional bases to create and flourish. Without culture, the paintings of Picasso and Michelangelo would not be possible nor would the music of Bach and Beethoven exist. Without ideology, the Declaration of Independence, the paintings of Goya, or the music of Wagner would not exist either, for these creative works reflect the ideologies of their creators.

Although the elements of an ideological belief system are dispersed throughout the history of mankind, certain individuals emerge as representative exponents of specific ideologies. Charles Pierce, William James, and John Dewey, for example, achieved international prominence as theoreticians of pragmatism, the philosophical foundation of Progressivism. Similarly, Samuel Taylor Coleridge, Jean-Jacques Rousseau, and Henry David Thoreau are recognized for their contributions to the enhancement of Romanticism. As authors and lecturers these men performed as theoreticians in creating, clarifying, and defining the ideological systems by which men live and for which some men die.

In addition to theoreticians, ideologies require activists if they are to flourish and function effectively. In contrast to the theoreticians, activists are less concerned with the philosophical assumptions and intricacies of ideologies and more committed to implementing them. Rather than engaging in the literary enterprise or lecturing in the "ivy tower," the activists seek to propagate the faith by developing institutions, creating organizations, soliciting funds, organizing demonstrations, and distributing advertisements to popularize and realize the ideology. Joseph Stalin and Robert Owen exemplify this activist orientation in their attempt to implement the ideologies of Puritanism in the U.S.S.R. and Romanticism in New Harmony.

Some individuals have functioned successfully as both theoreticians and activists. For Progressivism, John Dewey not only wrote voluminously, but also aided in the development of experimental schools on university campuses. Nikolai Lenin, as a Puritan revolutionary adapted the theory of Marxism to the Soviet Union, participated in the revolution, and served as premier following the revolution. And John Humphrey Noyes furthered the ideology of Romanticism both by publishing the journal *The Witness* and by establishing the Oneida Community in New York.

The vast majority of individuals, however, are neither theoreticians nor activists in the sense that we have been describing; that is, they live below the level of historical scrutiny, and function to perpetuate ideological systems in their performance as average citizens in the everyday world of human existence. As such, they may be termed ideological agents —a category that would include teachers, parents, ministers, salesmen, union representatives, commune members, and politicians, among others.

The presence of the parodist magnifies the complexity of ideological analysis. In contrast to the theoretician, activist, and agent, the ideological parodist maintains minimal allegiance to any particular belief system. In David Riesman's terms, he is an *other-directed* individual who takes the cues for his ideology and its consequent behavior from individuals who comprise his more immediate environment. Motivated either by personal self-interest or by a desire for social acceptance, the parodist follows the dictates of authority figures or peer group members. He may be an adherent to Romanticism one week and Scientism the next. Depending on the situation, he may appear to be a counterculture hippie or a bureaucratic data processor. This type of parodist is quite common in an age where Scientism and Romanticism are major competing ideologies. To be accepted by his peer group the parodist may behave in a manner characteristic of the Romantic counterculture; yet to attain a teaching assistantship or receive the accolades of his professor, the parodist would gladly participate in the research of Scientism. Consequently, many people are shocked to discover a petty bureaucrat masquerading in hippie garb. To the purist, the parodist is a phony or a hustler; to the parodist, the purist is impractical and unaware.

People adhere to their ideologies with varying degrees of intensity. Most individuals under "average" conditions and in "normal" times are moderates when discussing or acting on their beliefs, whether they be adherents of Puritanism or of Progressivism. They live with their ideology and reveal a tpe of tolerance commonly stated as "live and let live." They seldom attempt to impose their views on others. Indeed, they seldom seriously question their own beliefs or the beliefs of others.

Within any ideological system, however, one may identify extremists. Extremists exemplify the characteristics of the authoritarian personality in their inability to tolerate ambiguity. They demand clearly defined limits, seek absolute certainty, and expect universal agreement. Having discovered their truth, they act as disciples and missionaries, imposing their ideologies on others. In Eric Hoffer's terms, the extremist is "the true believer—the man of fanatical faith who is ready to sacrifice his life for a holy cause." [45]

Although extremism usually is equated with Puritanism, it should be reiterated that every belief system has individuals of extreme ideological conviction. Progressivists, for example, can illustrate extremist tendencies in their demand for consensus and their absolutistic denial of absolutes. Progressive extremists have vociferously condemned many of the Romantic rebels and Puritan revolutionaries. Similarly, extremists of Scientism, an ideology usually known for its tolerance and rationality, have vehemently ridiculed mystics and theologians.

The preceding discussion of extremism, however, should not be construed as an unqualified condemnation of extremists. They have been responsible for many constructive transformations in social thought and societal institutions. Without extremists, perhaps slavery would continue to be an accepted practice and America would remain an English colony. Moderation may indeed be the mother of virtue, but it also can be a major supporting element of injustice. For it is difficult to determine if moderation is the result of an enlightened concern for consequences or a failure of nerve and lack of commitment.

While ideologies and cultures can limit man's vision, transform him into a bigot or a fanatic, and lead him into fratricidal conflicts, they also serve to give him meaning and to inspire noble acts of heroism, creativity and service to others.

Ideologies can be transcended, in part, by critical thought. An individual can move beyond ideologies to perceive "realities" from a philosophical perspective. While most men may choose to remain unthinking and unfeeling, others nourish their spirit. Men need not remain, as the prisoners in Plato's cave, encapsulated in a tunnel of vision or in an enclave of awareness defined by ideology. Men can learn cultural and ideological systems as well as languages other than those they inherited from their social environment. They may learn to transport themselves from one ideological system into another.

Also, men may carry themselves to the edge of ideological systems by questioning. Although the questions one asks are bound to be ideologically tainted, they can serve to broaden a man's perspective by liberating him from unthinking commitment and from unfeeling creeds.

Precisely because teachers are carriers of ideologies and are expected to transmit ideological "verities" to the children and youth of the communities in which they practice their art, they must guard against the

[45] Eric Hoffer, *The True Believer* (New York: The New American Library of World Literature, Inc., 1951), Preface.

form of ideocentrism which affirms that one's ideology is superior to all others. Teachers must also guard against ideological excesses. An individual may have a preference for a particular ideological position, but no ideology is fruitful if it is allowed to develop unchecked. Scientism, with its implied emphasis upon orderliness and rationality, may be destructive if permitted to reach the point of rigidity. Similarly, Romanticism, with its focus upon feeling and diversity, may prevent man from flourishing if permitted to reach the point of self-indulgence. Scientism *and Romanticism*, however, provide man with an ideational and emotional basis which more adequately takes into account his complex nature. A society needs both scientists and poets to flourish. Similarly, Nationalism without localism and internationalism can be distorted into a hideous, destructive, inhuman force, and the twentieth century already has witnessed the devastation produced by such an unchecked Nationalist ideology.

Ideological pluralism within a framework of some ideological synthesis is the best safeguard against destructive extremism. Indeed, it is because of the various ideological strands which compose the fabric of the eclectic beliefs labeled "Americanism" that the United States has been able to meet the exigencies produced by rapid change. In the conflicts which confront the nation today, various ideologists are attempting to obliterate counter-ideologies. The future of the Republic, however, will depend upon both pluralism and synthesis. The nature of the pluralism and synthesis will depend in turn upon the ability of the nation's teachers to withstand the assaults of extremists while conscientiously attempting to represent the diversity and unity inherent in Americanism. To affirm that teachers should withstand the onslaught of ideological extremists does not imply that teachers should rigidify an ideology. Indeed, the future is foreboding for those institutions which refuse to alter the ideological fabric.

All ideologies including one's own must be viewed critically. The lazy mind may assume that all is satisfactory with an ideology. The intelligent and sensitive person, however, will continue to wonder and probe the intricacies of ideological systems. He will fluctuate between optimism and despair, skepticism and commitment, detachment and involvement. Consequently, he will by necessity tend to walk alone in the world and suffer the condemnation and wrath of the ideologists, whether they be technocrats or modern Romanticists, Black Panthers or Klansmen. As Eric Hoffer stated: "In the eyes of the true believers people who have no holy cause are without backbone and character—a pushover for men of faith." [46] Yet, to move beyond beliefs is to move toward understanding the diversified human race. Robert E. Lane's admonition is worthy of remembering: "An ideological commitment gives men a sense

[46] Hoffer, *The True Believer*, p. 147.

of purpose and the criteria for appraising the justice of a society; but it poses a threat to the openness of society; it may make tolerance more difficult and adjustment to victory by the opposition harder to effect." [47]

The following chapters focus upon various ideological strands in the eclectic belief system labeled Americanism. While they are separated into particular systems for the purpose of analysis, the reader is cautioned to recall that the ideological systems described in each chapter are interwoven with each other as well as with others not included in this book and form the tweeter and the woofer of Americanism.

### Suggested Readings

APTER, DAVID, ed. *Ideology and Discontent.* New York: The Free Press, 1964.

BELL, DANIEL. *The End of Ideology.* New York: The Free Press, 1960.

BENDA, JULIEN. *The Betrayal of the Intellectuals.* trans. Richard Aldington. New York: W. W. Norton & Company, Inc., 1969.

BENSON, LEONARD G. *National Purpose: Ideology and Ambivalence in America.* Washington: Public Affairs Press, 1963.

CONNOLLY, WILLIAM E. *Political Science and Ideology.* New York: Atherton Press, 1967.

CORBETT, PATRICK. *Ideologies.* New York: Harcourt, Brace, Jovanovich, Inc., 1966.

DE GRAZIA, SEBASTIAN. *The Political Community: A Study of Anomie.* Chicago: University of Chicago Press, 1966.

HARRIS, NIGEL. *Beliefs in Society: The Problem of Ideology.* London: C. A. Watts and Co., 1968.

HOFFER, ERIC. *The True Believer.* New York. The New American Library of World Literature, Inc., 1951.

LANE, ROBERT E. *Political Ideology: Why the American Common Man Believes What He Does.* New York: The Free Press, 1962.

LASSWELL, HAROLD D. *World Politics and Personal Insecurity.* New York: The Free Press, 1965.

MANNHEIM, KARL. *Ideology and Utopia: An Introduction to the Sociology of Knowledge.* New York: Harcourt, Brace, Jovanovich, Inc., 1936.

[47] Lane, *Political Ideology*, p. 476.

# Chapter 2

# SCIENTISM
## The Ideology of the Behavior Modifier

### Introduction

In comparing the classic horror films of the 1930s with the science fiction spectaculars of the 1960s, the viewer becomes vividly aware of the rapidly changing image of the scientist and his working environment. The older image of the half-mad scientist in the cellar of an isolated castle offers a bizarre contrast to the latter-day sophisticated gentleman, bearer of numerous academic credentials and awards working with vast numbers of colleagues and research assistants in an expensive, sterilized laboratory supported by government funding.

Approximately one hundred and fifty years ago, Mary Shelley, the wife of the romantic poet Percy Bysshe Shelley and the daughter of the political philosopher William Godwin, wrote the classic science fiction novel *Frankenstein*. The theme of the novel is based upon the tale of the Greek mythological hero, Prometheus, who disobeyed the gods by giving fire to man and thus earned for himself the wrath of Zeus and eternal suffering. In Mary Shelley's tale, subtitled "A Modern Prometheus," the scientist Frankenstein is punished not only because he dared to create a monster but also because he failed to assume responsibility for its actions.

Responsibility becomes necessary with the loss of innocence. Whether the case be illustrated by the harsh tasks which followed the transgression of Adam and Eve, the proverbial guilt experienced at the loss of virginity, or the awesome threat to human existence unleashed by the discoveries of audacious scientists, the result is the same, for with the taste of sin there is no return to the simplicity of innocence. With the creation of the atomic bomb, science came of age and scientists lost their innocence. J. Robert Oppenheimer, one of the creators of the atomic bomb, confessed: "In some sense which no vulgarity, no humor, no over-statement can quite extinguish, the physicists have known sin and this is knowledge they cannot lose." [1]

[1] Quoted in J. Stefan Dupré and Sanford A. Lakoff, *Science and the Nation* (Englewood Cliffs, N.J.: Prentice-Hall, Inc., 1962), p. 105.

The "public be damned" stance of the scientific community which characterized its alliance with business at the turn of the century is no longer based on universally shared, socially acceptable assumptions. Indeed, the scientific establishment which has designed a significant portion of the environment which modern man inhabits has increasingly become aware of the social responsibility generated by such an ominous power. During the past decades this concern has been typified by the numerous research programs directed toward peaceful uses of atomic energy. Scientific forces also have been allied with governmental agencies in attempts to resolve the ecological nightmare generated by technological advancement.

The scientific frame of reference, however, continues to retain a secure hold upon the minds of men. Formerly an unpopular individual pursuit often condemned by the Brahmins of past social systems, the scientific mode of inquiry has become a massive, collective effort supported by all major social institutions and financed enthusiastically by governmental agencies. Formerly a social outcast and a martyr, the scientist has become the friend of social elites and the hero of the populace. From pinnacles of awe-inspiring power, his magnanimity oozes naturally to the "uninformed" or "ill-informed" but "well-intentioned" lay public who are destined to appreciate the rewards of technological progress. Indeed, twentieth-century man increasingly limits his perceptual world to the popularized and distorted "realities" supplied by the efficient but often debased scientific mode of observation. When such a mode of observing reality is shared by the members of a social group, it becomes an ideology labeled Scientism and reflects a formalism designed to control the forces of nature and the behavior of man.

### Science and Religion

Scientism has truly emerged victorious from its earlier, often embittered struggle with religion. The peaceful coexistence, if not mutual reinforcement, that presently exists between most theologians and scientists, however, gives little hint of the many controversies in their previous history. The ideological debates concerning supernaturalism and naturalism encompassed seemingly irreconcilable differences between faith and reason, revelation and empiricism, and spirit and matter. From early in the Colonial period, however, the scope of causal explanation grounded upon a supernatural rationale continued to decrease. Each new discovery in physics, astronomy, biology, and medicine seemed to diminish the importance of religious orthodoxy in questions concerning the functioning of the universe. Not even the Great Awakening, the religious revivals of the mid-eighteenth century, appeared to alter the seemingly inevitable triumph of Scientism over religion.

In public education the conflict between Scientism and religion emerged to gain national importance when John Scopes was brought to trial in Dayton, Tennessee, in 1925, for teaching Darwin's theory of evolution. The trial not only raised questions concerning academic freedom but also illustrated the continuing struggle between the ideologies of an agrarian culture—with its mixture of fundamentalism, absolutism, isolationism, populism, and slavery—and an urban-industrial culture, with its combination of relativism, pragmatism, imperialism, and Scientism. Scopes was found guilty—a concession to the declining agrarian culture—but his meager fine and suspended sentence reflected a quasi-recognition of the legitimacy of the emerging urban-industrial culture. Recent decisions of the United States Supreme Court concerning prayer in the public schools may be viewed as further evidence for the legitimatization of the emerging ideological patterns of Scientism as well as a reflection of the continuing process of the nationalization of schools in the United States. Both Scientism and Nationalism are necessary ingredients of modernization with its promise of affluence.

Disagreement concerning the place of religion and religious education in the public school curriculum continues. Rarely, however, do such issues deal with the conflicts between religious dogma and scientific dogma. God rarely enters the classroom. While the Ten Commandments are not displayed within public schools, the Periodic Chart of the Elements is readily exhibited. Few students in public universities would dare to explain to their sociology or education professor that a particular human characteristic results from original sin or from grace. Unfortunately, because of the anxiety generated by the desire to avoid legal problems and possible controversy, some teachers have forsaken their responsibility to teach *about* religion and its inherent value structure. The avoidance of issues dealing with the valuing process, however, does not reflect ethical neutrality. Rather, it serves merely to inculcate at best a relativistic and at worst an apathetic attitude toward morality.

Although religion and values are closely related in man's ethical systems, they are not necessarily bound togther. Teachers who are reluctant to deal directly with religion because of their interpretation of Supreme Court decisions fail to comprehend the subtle differences between religious dogma and morality. The difficulty in unraveling acceptable social values from sectarian religious convictions continues to be a major source of conflict within schools and serves to diminish the effectiveness of teachers in performing their task of preparing the children and youth for their role as moral agents.

Regardless of the potential conflict between religious dogmas and scientific assumptions, few teachers or students question their faith in science. Scientific assertions such as "plants turn toward the sun because of hormones" (rather than because of an act of divine providence), and "physical and mental problems may be cured by physicians and psychiatrists" (rather than by priests, magicians, and astrologers) rarely are challenged. Students are neither shocked nor dismayed to discover that the biological diagrams of the human body exclude the soul. When asked if they would seek the advice of a clergyman or a psychiatrist in order to assist an anxiety-ridden child, teachers invariably pick the latter, thus reflecting the degree to which Scientism has become the ideological frame of schooling. Indeed, some clergymen unhesitantly have armed themselves with the tools of their traditional foe and have become scientized. The degree to which the ideology of Scientism has replaced religion is exemplified by the fact that students and teachers who attempt to seriously challenge scientific assumptions with religious orthodoxy generally are viewed as ignorant, superstitious, fanatical, or all three.

To be sure, some individuals do become aware of the ideological dissonance between their religious tenets and scientific assumptions, but most people appear to adhere to a mixture of religious and scientific ideological assumptions without difficulty. Although there may be some individuals who deny the veracity of moon landing reports on the grounds that such feats would be contrary to God's will, the overwhelming majority of those individuals who label themselves religious in a traditional sense do believe in the accomplishments of space ventures, just as they believe that scientific pursuits will conquer cancer, manipulate genetic material, and, perhaps, create living beings.

The acceptance of Scientism within the religious creed became widespread, especially among the more educated, upper middle-class clergy of the late nineteenth century. The widely known and influential minister, Henry Ward Beecher, in a book entitled *Evolution and Religion* (1885), asserted that evolution was simply "the deciphering of God's thought as revealed in the structure of the world." [2] Beecher's attitude concerning evolution has been applied to nearly every scientific endeavor. In this sense, both the aerospace engineer and the priest are viewed as "carrying out the work of the Lord," either with His permission or with His tacit approval. A superb example of this mutual enhancement occurred when earth-orbiting astronauts read verses from Genesis to the multitudes watching television. In addition to being vindicated, Galileo has been sanctified.

From a secure position, the scientist no longer reflects a virulent distaste for his traditional foe, religion. With benevolent condescension

[2] Henry Ward Beecher, *Evolution and Religion* (n.p., Fords, Howard and Hulbert, 1885), pp. 45–46.

and scholarly curiosity, scientists now observe silently those rugged religionists who persist in believing that faith and revelation are valid and reliable ways of knowing. Indeed, the conflict between the two traditional antagonists has virtually disappeared as all major educational institutions have become havens for the scientific endeavor.

In any discussion of science and religion, the elements of ideological congruency may be of greater significance than the elements of dissonance. Although chastised by many religionists, Charles Darwin envisioned just such a congruency when he wrote of his insights on evolution: "There is grandeur in this view of life, with its several powers, having been originally breathed by the Creator into a few forms or into one." [3] Darwin's concept of God is an example of the brand of Deism generally maintained by adherents of Scientism. From this perspective, God is a superb mathematician and a master technician. Although this conception of God differed greatly from the one espoused by many religious leaders of that era, it did encompass a major element in the ideologies of both Scientism and religion—namely, a belief in *order*, whether natural or divine. As the eminent mathematician and philosopher Alfred North Whitehead rightfully asserted, the concept of order was

> the greatest contribution of medievalism to the formation of the scientific movement. I mean the inexpugnable belief that every detailed occurrence can be correlated with its antecedents in a perfectly definite manner, exemplifying general principles. Without this belief the incredible labours of scientists would be without hope. [4]

### Scientific Methodology

The belief in an ordered universe, although present in ancient Greek thought, was first fully developed by the Scholastic philosophers, who encompassed it within a framework of natural law. Natural law was viewed as perfect, absolute, and eternal; as St. Thomas Aquinas explained:

> Every law framed by man bears the character of a law exactly to that extent to which it is derived from the law of nature. But if on any point it is in conflict with the law of nature, it at once ceases to be a law; it is a mere perversion of law. [5]

With ideological modifications, this attitude toward natural law was echoed for centuries in the thoughts and deeds of various ideological

[3] Charles Darwin, *The Origin of Species and the Descent of Man* (New York: Random House, Inc., n.d.), p. 374.

[4] Alfred North Whitehead, *Science and the Modern World* (New York: The New American Library of World Literature, Inc., 1962), p. 19.

[5] St. Thomas Aquinas, Summa Theol., 1 2, Q. xcv, art. ii.

groupings. The Puritans incorporated natural law into a theory of pre-destination; Romanticists envisioned it as an ideal for structuring human existence; and Nationalists utilized it to sanction the rights of individuals and deny the divinity of kings (who, ironically, had used it previously to legitimatize dynastic *etatism*). From the seventeenth to the twentieth century natural law served as a philosophical basis for prediction in the ideology of Scientism. By combining the medieval concept of linear causality with an atomistic theory of reality, scientists developed a methodology that promised to unravel the intricate mysteries of the universe and to unify St. Augustine's City of God with his City of Man. As a First Cause, God may have created the universe and imposed His laws in nature, but it was man who would disclose this order and thus control his own destiny. Supernaturalism, with its beliefs in divine intercession, the working of miracles, and the dispensation of grace, was viewed as a metaphysical irrelevance that mankind was destined to discard. "The proper study of Mankind is Man," admonished the English poet Alexander Pope, whose assertions embodied the optimism of the Enlightenment's faith in science:

> Nature and Nature's laws lay hid in night;
> God said, Let Newton be; and all was light.[6]

Although learned men presently acknowledge the naivety inherent in such a mechanistic view of reality, the consequences of such a belief continue to influence our way of life. Indeed, the accomplishments during the seventeenth century, an era Whitehead so aptly termed the Century of Genius, included not only the works of Sir Isaac Newton, but also those of William Harvey, Robert Boyle, and Anton van Leeuwenhoek. Nevertheless, this mechanistic view of the universe, constructed upon a model of deductive logic, contained assumptions that could not be verified with the mathematical certainty upon which it was founded. In fact, science had substituted one form of metaphysics for another.

Acceptance of the so-called "laws of nature" and the assumption of inherent order are beliefs that result from an act of faith—a process usually considered antithetic to science. As early as the mid-eighteenth century David Hume, the Scottish philosopher, questioned the certainty of empirical knowledge. Foreshadowing the beliefs of twentieth-century science, Hume sensed that "order" was a metaphysical assumption, the validity of which is grounded in previous experience. Causal relationships (*A* causes *B*) are hypothetical rather than necessary; and they exist in mental habits, not in the world itself. Consequently, the validity of inferences formulated from empirical data (the inductive process) is probable,

---

[6] Alexander Pope, "An Essay on Man," II, 2; and "Epitaph Intended for Sir Isaac Newton."

not absolute, and is grounded in the previous experiences of mankind. In the words of Hume,

> Objects have no observable connexion together; nor is it from any other principle but custom operating upon the imagination, that we can draw inference from the appearance of one to the experience of another.[7]

The meaning of Hume's insight can be illustrated by considering the assertion, "The sun will rise tomorrow." The statement says nothing about the laws of nature; indeed, it does not even express a fact, but rather a probability. The validity of the assertion, of course, would be considered highly probable if compared to previous experience. Similarly, the validity of any assertion of causality is founded upon the pragmatic belief in order —that is, predictions based upon hypothetical constructs of causal relationships have "worked." Thus, the belief in order, exemplified in the statement "the future resembles the past," remains a motivating force for the scientific endeavor.

Latter-day scientists, of course, accept the cautious skepticism of Hume and do not assume either that external reality is totally knowable or that the ordering perceived by man is, in fact, "real." The twentieth-century scientific revolution brought about by quantum theory and the principle of indeterminacy has shattered the scientific concept that external reality can ever be fully observed and known. Adherents of Scientism, termed *scientians,* believe, however, that the failure to observe an ordering in the universe results from man's limitations rather than from the lack of an external ordered reality. Uncertainty must characterize all scientific propositions, for all scientific propositions rest upon probabilities rather than actualities. In their zealous belief in "order," however, scientians invariably ignore the contingency of their observations and forget that the proof that man's observations are accurate reflections of external reality ultimately must be in the form of philosophical propositions.

Scientism rests, therefore, upon the assumption that reality is or can be rationally ordered by man and that such an ordering implies predictability through the empirical testing of phenomenon by methods designed to secure objectivity and control. Creative scientists, of course, escape from the limited methodological framework of Scientism in order to produce creative hypotheses. Creative leaps of insight, however, precede the scientific method and are not incorporated within it.

A second major metaphysical assumption of Scientism is the belief that events are atomistic and repeatable. That is, they are atomistic in the sense that "causes" can be isolated from "effects" and that the most

[7] David Hume, "A Treatise of Human Nature," in *From Descartes to Kant,* ed. T. V. Smith and Marjorie Grene (Chicago: The University of Chicago Press, 1940), pp. 674–75.

appropriate "cause" is the one immediate to the effect. Although scientists recognize the contingency of statistical laws and accept the concept of polymodal causality, Scientism is rooted in the belief that events can be isolated, analyzed, and recorded, and that reliable inferences can be derived from such observations. What is more, Scientism holds that general propositions may be reliably devised from a limited number of occurrences. Adherents of Scientism readily utilize such propositions to guide their behavior and often minimize the fact that such statements are inherently contingent.

To be aware of the aforementioned assumptions at the root of the scientific method is to be cognizant of the tenuousness of scientific studies. Such an awareness also explains the skepticism of philosophers such as David Hume. Educators have often been duped by their blind adherence to propositions which were devised through scientific methods. For example, I.Q. tests devised to measure the intelligence of an individual in a specific geographical location, or from a particular socioeconomic strata, or ethnic culture, were and tragically continue to be utilized to test individuals regardless of environmental differences. To be sure, such practices violate some aspects of the scientific method, but the fact remains that I.Q. test scores are often legitimized by claiming that they rest upon scientific principles. Many self-fulfilling hypotheses have been devised by such assumptions, and many children have been falsely labeled by "scientifically" devised tests. The fact that some teachers continue to utilize some of these tests as definitive measurements of intelligence is an educational travesty.

The scientific endeavor also is based upon the belief that objectivity can be attained in controlled experimentation. Indeed, in an age dominated by the ideology of Scientism there is a strong tendency to equate "objectivity" with scientific methodology. It is worthwhile to remember, however, that the term "objectivity" cannot be divorced from its ideological implications. Inasmuch as the concept of objectivity generally has implied the necessity of universal agreement and conformity, it can be used to legitimize political actions. In the era dominated by Puritanism, for example, the term "objective" was attributed to those who adhered to the "literalness" of the biblical scriptures as determined by the theocratic magistrates. Roger Williams and Anne Hutchinson, among others, were branded subjectivists and suffered the fate of social ostracism. Similarly, in an age of Scientism those individuals who fail to adhere rigidly to the methodological tenets of science may have their endeavors pejoratively termed "subjective," thus relegating them to an inferior status. Although Theodore Roszak may have exaggerated the relativity of perception, he acknowledged the importance of ideological analysis when he wrote: "Science rests itself not in the *world* the scientist beholds at any particular time, but in his mode of *viewing* that world. A man is a scientist not because of what he sees, but because of *how* he sees it." [8]

Since all observation ultimately implies a human observer operating either directly or through his mechanical extensions, all scientific propositions must of necessity reflect the existence of the subjective observer. Indeed, to ignore the existence of the observer is to deny an important component of environmental reality. Despite the fact that the attempt to achieve a pure objectivity in observation cannot be achieved by man, such attempts and the precautions which they necessitate have resulted in significant achievements in scientific research. When objectivity becomes a social norm, however, its mythological basis is lost, and foolish men seek fruitlessly to denude themselves of their emotions. Their resultant behavior is not only ineffective but also ludicrous.

Although Scientism is rooted to the methodological patterns of scientific inquiry, it reflects the exaggerated emphasis upon scientific assumptions and processes which characterizes the style of the technocrat who diligently and uncreatively attempts to master the contingent by prescribed methodological paths and by aping the creative scientist. As Wylie Sypher observed:

> Techniques precede and often support science, but during the nineteenth century science became identified with the use of a certain method that was adaptable to the technological imperative, associated as it was with a naive ideal of "objectivity," a naive materialism, a naive logic of induction, a naive reliance upon observation, a compulsion to discipline the mind by making it "accurate." [9]

A creative scientific theorist, such as Einstein, provides philosophical elements which are incorporated in the ideology of Scientism and which serve ultimately as restrictive formalism for the less imaginative technocrat. When Scientism is applied to perceptions of the human condition it invariably serves to restrict human behavior by denying the wonderful as well as inhibiting the unpredictable.

Throughout the history of philosophy one can discern methodological and ideological differences between the humanities and the sciences. Within this century these differences have been intensified with the emergence of such behavioral sciences as sociology and psychology. Citing successful achievements in the physical sciences, proponents of Scientism have argued that research in the behavioral sciences should be patterned after the models of scientific methodology. Those individuals who have

    [8] Theodore Roszak, *The Making of the Counter-Culture: Reflections on the Technocratic Society and Its Youthful Opposition* (Garden City, N.Y.: Doubleday & Company, Inc., 1969), p. 213.
    [9] Wylie Sypher, *Literature and Technology: The Alien Vision* (New York: Vintage Books, 1971), p. 10.

resisted such an approach generally cite the inherent limitations of scientific methodology when applied to the complexities of human existence. They maintain that valid insights for the understanding of man and his world can be discovered in the study of literature and/or history. On the university campus, these conflicts often have escalated to such a degree that faculty decisions on matters of employment, merit, and tenure are influenced by the methodological approach utilized by the scholar in question. With the increasing acceptance of the ideology of Scientism, such decisions generally favor the "scientific" scholar.

The acceptance of scientific methodology as the only legitimate form of knowledge has been magnified with the increasing pervasiveness of Scientism. Consequently, the validity of research increasingly is viewed as being dependent upon the utilization of empirical studies, computerized techniques of data gathering, statistical analysis, and control of environmental variables. From this ideological perspective, the value of the endeavors of such medieval researchers as St. Augustine and St. Thomas Aquinas is diminished, if not ridiculed, and brilliant formulations like Rousseau's *Emile* fail to meet the criteria demanded for truths concerning the nature of child development. In fact, the findings of Sigmund Freud and Karl Marx (both of whom believed they were engaged in scientific enterprises) today are considered exceedingly unreliable unless they are subjected to verification within the framework of modern scientific methodology. Being in the position to define truth, the elite of Scientism has attained the degree of prestige and power formerly accorded priests and bishops. Indeed, the immense change in the status of Scientism is realized when one recalls that less than four centuries ago Bruno was burned at the stake, Galileo was forced to recant his scientific findings, and Copernicus was condemned and ridiculed so vehemently that he refrained from publishing his findings.

Obviously it would be naive, if not ridiculous, to reject completely the reliability and validity of scientific methodology. The immeasurable number of scientific discoveries and technological developments serve as undeniable evidence for the triumph of scientific man in the modern age. Indeed, such accomplishments generally are equated with the idea of progress and are used as the criteria for measuring the degree to which a culture is deemed civilized.

Perhaps it is rather ironic that many of the most ardent opponents of Scientism, the Romanticists, have condemned the ideology while living in the comfortable environment that science and technology have provided. This is especially true of many modern Romanticists who have migrated from the urban, industrial society to the pastoral or pseudo-pastoral life of rural America. They continue to benefit from the material rewards of Scientism, yet believe they are living in harmony with nature despite the fact that farming as a hobby is significantly different from farming as a vocation.

Surely most critics of Scientism also must acknowledge the fact that science and technology have contributed greatly to what mankind historically has considered "the good life." The purpose of criticism, therefore, is not to deny this fact, but to question man's ability to move beyond beliefs, to transcend Scientism—to seek "the better life."

## Science and Technology

The term "technology" was devised by Johann Bechmann in Germany in 1772, the term "scientist" by William Whewell in England in the early nineteenth century. Although these dates do not reveal any significant chronological pattern, they are indicative of differences in social sanction. The terms *science* and *technology* conventionally have been equated with theory and practice, with technology viewed as the practical application of scientific theory. Perhaps the distinction could be further clarified by considering the terms *science* and *technology* analogous to the concepts *intellect* and *intelligence* as defined by the noted historian Richard Hofstadter. "Intellect," he states, "is the critical, creative, and contemplative side of the mind. Whereas, intelligence seeks to grasp, manipulate, reorder, adjust, intellect examines, ponders, wonders, theorizes, criticizes, imagines." [10] The scientist uses intellect; the technician, intelligence. In this sense, then, technology is dephilosophized science.

The ideology of Scientism could not have emerged as a major social force without the contribution of the child of science, technology. The significance of Galileo's theory on the acceleration of falling bodies may never have been recognized, for example, without the discovery of the vacuum pump, an event that occurred more than a decade after Galileo's death. Similarly, the medicinal value of penicillin was known for decades prior to World War II, but the social importance of the drug could not be realized until the technical discoveries related to the war provided the means for its preservation and mass production.

Just as scientific theories are enhanced by the practical application of technology, so technological discoveries promote the proliferation of scientific theories. Leeuwenhoek's technical improvements of the compound microscope, for example, eventuated in many new theories concerning cell growth and development. Similarly, the development of the

---

[10] Richard Hofstadter, *Anti-intellectualism in American Life* (New York: Alfred A. Knopf, Inc., 1963), p. 25.

high intensity vacuum tube and the transistor resulted in an enormous proliferation of scientific theories regarding the electronic media. Thus, science and technology are inextricably intertwined—each serves to enhance the other. It is through technological systems that the "gifts" of science are mass produced and shared by large numbers of people; it is through the effective and systematic application of scientific principles that technological empires are constructed. Technological progress in turn serves to generate a proliferation of scientific theories. Cooperatively, science and technology have produced in man an unwavering faith in Scientism.

Modern man's ever-increasing dependency upon technology and his aspiration for technological advancement create an obsessive, idolatrous belief in the omnipotence of science. This technolatry enhances the belief in the gospel of objectivity as a tool for resolving human problems. Gerald Sykes, in a searching article entitled, "A New Salvation, a New Supernatural," observed the ethos that results when people are technicized. "This technical skill," he wrote, "is not content to remain technical; it develops religious pretensions, and attempts to convert others to its kind of salvation. Its pragmatic faith is more convincing today to most people throughout the world than older faiths of religious revelation or social teamwork or political ideology, in spite of all outcries to the contrary." [11]

The ideology of Scientism could not have emerged as a dominant social force in America without the assistance of other significant ideological elements. Citizens of Greek antiquity, for example, certainly had the intellectual capability for the development of Scientism. Indeed, the insights of Plato and Aristotle continue to excite the minds of modern men. Yet the mentality of ancient Greece emphasized unity, harmony, and moderation. Greek culture was founded upon a respect for contemplation and the beauty of nature, creating a Weltanschauung that gave birth to philosophers, poets, and artists. In contrast to the values expressed in Greek antiquity, American culture generally has emphasized individualism and competition; it has demanded that nature be conquered and has rewarded activism, efficiency, and practicality. These values represent substantive elements in the ideology of Scientism; yet they also can be found in the other ideological systems that comprise American thought. Consequently, such ideologies as Puritanism, Educationism, Progressivism, and Nationalism have enhanced, to a great degree, the growth of Scientism in America.

---

[11] Gerald Sykes, "A New Salvation, A New Supernatural," *Technology and Human Values* (Santa Barbara: Center for the Study of Democratic Institutions, 1966), p. 11.

### Scientism and Puritanism

The image of the God-fearing Puritan Fathers who settled in the American wilderness generally obscures the reality of their interest in realms of knowledge other than Holy Scripture. Many of their endeavors, for example, significantly stimulated the growth of science and technology. Puritans comprised the vast majority of the membership of the distinguished scientific society known as the Royal Society of England which had been established in 1660. John Winthrop, Jr., the Puritan son of the famous governor of the Massachusetts Bay Colony, was elected as an "original" member of the British scientific fellowship. Fellows of the Royal Society included Roger Williams, William Byrd, and Cotton Mather, a Puritan who, in 1721, defied an edict in the colony and allowed his family to be inoculated against smallpox by a Boston physician. Indeed, his support of inoculation propelled an anti-inoculation zealot to throw a bomb into his home. Although the bomb did not explode— a failure of technology that must have pleased Mather in spite of his principled support of technological achievements—this incident serves to illustrate the odd fact that this supporter of witchcraft trials was also ridiculed for his defense of a major advancement in medical science. For Mather, the defense of inoculation did not preclude the usual Puritan zeal to combat Satan; indeed, Cotton's father, Increase Mather, the founder of the first known scientific society in America, the Boston Philosophical Society, observed smugly that "known Children of the Wicked One" were often also opponents of inoculation. The fact that these Puritan zealots could defend both witchcraft trials and inoculation should give us, the children of technology, reason to pause.

In addition to the aforementioned support of scientific pursuits by many of the colonial Puritans, a more subtle relationship can be observed between the ideological elements of Scientism and Puritanism. As noted previously, both science and the Puritan religious ethos include a focus upon the importance of rational order. Furthermore, the ideologies of Puritanism and Scientism emphasize a sober commitment to rigidly controlled behavior, a strict devotion to discipline and literal truth, and an individualism that is often indifferent to the authority of tradition.

While some qualities of Puritanism are compatible with Scientism, the emergence of Scientism has served to diminish the influence of religious forces within society. The unique focus upon the coldly rational aspect of religious thought which characterized the Puritan faith was not shared by most religions. Because of the highly emotive quality of most religious expression as well as the tendency toward religious dogmatism, the adherents of Scientism generally viewed religion as an antithetical belief system. Religious faith and superstition were increasingly equated by the defenders of Scientism. Indeed, religious excesses such as the Crusades and the Inquisition are paraded in front of would-be skeptics as proof of the inhumanity of religion.

In contrast to the devastating image of religious oppression and its ancillary discouragement of scientific exploration in areas that related to religious dogma, adherents of Scientism display the scientific marvels of the technological age such as polio vaccines, space travel, and improved means of producing and processing foods. Their arguments are convincing. Their data, however, does not prove—except perhaps to other adherents of Scientism—that science is a more humanizing force than religion. Man's sufferings have continued unabated. His existential malaise and sense of alienation have perhaps increased in the last hundred years. While individual lives are being saved through heart transplants and antibiotics, other human lives are being lost because of acute emphysema and mercury poisoning occasioned by the excrement of the technological robot man has created. Similarly, the numerous murders that resulted from religious persecution and religious extremism can hardly be equated to the incredible loss of life occasioned by unleashed technological power. Even during periods of peaceful coexistence between the great technological empires, the great nation-states often fail to provide human beings with the kind of environment which is conducive to aesthetic and spiritual growth. The warmth of religious communities offers a tempting ideological alternative to the sometimes alienating coldness and normative confusion generated by technological progress.

Although the argument that religious and political forces have served to inhibit scientific progress is valid, it should not be forwarded without the realization that scientific progress has also been inhibited by scientific dogmatism. Most significant scientific discoveries have been ridiculed and discarded by many established leaders of the scientific world. Both the ether theory of energy transmission and phlogiston theory of combustion have been rejected after having been considered valid scientific formulations. In fact, the mechanistic view of Newtonian physics has been not only discarded, but also condemned for the restrictive influence it produced. Scientific dogmatism is similar to political and religious dogmatism, for it serves to inhibit rather than enhance ideological expansion and creative human expression.

The previous assertions have not been forwarded to convince the reader that scientific exploration or technological improvements are detrimental to man. Such a goal would be folly. They merely serve to illustrate that the ideology of Scientism is not without its extremism. Indeed, as Whitehead so aptly observed, "During the medieval epoch in Europe, the theologians were the chief sinners in respect to dogmatic finality. During the last three centuries, their bad pre-eminence in this habit passed to the men of science." [12]

In an age of pragmatic faith, it is necessary to reaffirm that man's search for happiness does not rest upon his creations but rather upon himself. That faith in science has achieved the popularity of a universal faith illustrates that it is potentially inhibitive to human intellectual freedom. Often the faiths of man's past have been discarded without sufficient intellectual exploration, while the assertions of scientists and technocrats are accepted without question. The difference in the credibility of pronouncements from Houston Control and biblical admonitions depends upon one's criteria of validity and reliability. Such criteria are rooted to ideological systems and depend upon ideological assumptions for their justification. To move beyond beliefs man must realize that scientific facts are similar to all other types of assertions—that is, they are beliefs substantiated by ideological frameworks.

Historically, the gradual emergence of Scientism has accompanied an alteration in the Puritan ethos. For decades the New England Primer and the maxims of *Poor Richard's Almanac* as well as the *McGuffey Readers* served to inculcate the Puritan virtues of the Protestant ethic. As the nation became increasingly industrialized, the agrarian Protestant ethic, which was rooted to colonial America and which served to sustain the young nation through the process of nation-building, was urbanized and formed the foundation upon which the American industrial state would rest. The virtues of hard work, purity, frugality, and honesty which served as the ideals for a young Republic were taught in the emerging public school system as ideals to support the industrialization and geographical expansion of the United States. Although these Puritan virtues were discerned in the lives of biblical prophets and taught as religious values during the colonial age in America, they were increasingly secularized as the nation evolved. Biblical prophets were replaced by inventors and business magnates as exemplars for the puritan virtues.

The secularization of Puritanism served as nourishment for the ideology of Scientism. History books increasingly served as sources for the inculcation of the secularized Puritan virtues adhered to by the saints of Scientism. The names and dates of inventions and inventors were memorized by students and brilliant inventors like Thomas Edison as well as visionary technocrats like Henry Ford became national heroes. This facet of our training has been so deeply engrained that adults often recall with ease the names of inventors while they remain befuddled

[12] Alfred North Whitehead, *Adventures of Ideas* (New York: The New American Library of World Literature, Inc., 1933), p. 149.

when questioned about the characters and convictions of such great literary artists as William Shakespeare, Charles Dickens, and William Faulkner.

The obsessive concern for Scientism has served to distort some sginificant educational innovations. The realization that public schools often have failed to teach for cultural pluralism, especially in relation to intranational racial and ethnic minorities, resulted during the 1960s, in the rapid proliferation of ethnic history courses. Often these courses were remarkable for their banality because curriculum designers failed to understand that the ideology of Scientism is not meaningful for or relevant to many cultural groupings. To approach history from an Afro-American perspective by focusing upon such irrelevancies as the invention of the potato chip and the mop handle is to rob the Afro-American culture of its richness and its uniqueness. To seek within the history of ethnic minorities for technological feats merely betrays a failure to appreciate the possibilities inherent in cultural and ideological pluralism. It also reflects ideological chauvinism for it presupposes that advancement in civilization is to be measured by technological progress—an assumption which, in the light of the ecological crisis and the military tragedies of the twentieth century, should be reconsidered. As Everett Knight so aptly admonished, "The horror of the concentration camps marks not an increase in human viciousness, but an increase in technical and organizational efficiency." [13]

The fact that the inventor and the technocrat serve as national heroes in modern technologically advanced nation-states not only reveals the importance of Scientism but also betrays its emphasis. Scientism is the ideology which supports technology and enhances the importance of the practical methodologists. Lewis Coser rightfully noted that the technocrat rather than the scientist is the central hero of Scientism when he wrote: "The hero of the young American interested in science is more often Thomas Edison than Willard Bibbs, Eli Whitney than Mendel, Von Braun than Einstein." [14]

### Technology and the Labor Market

The American agrarian society was characterized by a closely knit extended family, patriarchal in structure and designed for cooperative work shared among the members. Such families were situated in isolated,

[13] Everett Knight, *The Objective Society* (New York: George Braziller, Inc., 1959), p. 110.
[14] Lewis A. Coser, *Men of Ideas* (New York: The Macmillan Company, 1965), p. 302.

homogeneous communities in which roles were clearly defined, norms were seldom questioned, and transgressions were harshly condemned. The growth of commerce and trade influenced the agrarian family but generally did not alter its structure. Some of the children, upon reaching adulthood, left their homes as Colonial America moved westward, but for the most part the sons remained with the family and served as apprentices while daughters prepared for motherhood. Since education was family centered and craft oriented there was a little need for an extensive system of formal schooling.

Between the years of the first Patent Act of 1790 and the War of 1812, however, events occurred which profoundly influenced the future development of the United States. Within these decades the roots of rapid technological growth emerged as America witnessed the beginning of the glorious yet painful process that would be known as the Industrial Revolution. In 1790, Samuel Slater introduced the factory system for the production of textile materials. Eli Whitney's "jig" (1798) for the production of interchangeable parts and Oliver Evans' steam machinery (1804) further promoted the development of the factory system, while Robert Fulton's steam ship (1807) provided the transportation necessary for the expansion of trade.

The nineteenth century witnessed the extension of mass production and the immense growth of the factory system as well as the continuing decline of craftsmanship and agriculture. With the demands for a readily accessible pool of labor to operate the burgeoning industrial system, urbanization and massive immigration occurred and the dreams of a Jeffersonian democracy were shattered. In a very real sense, the Industrial Revolution was indeed a revolution. In contrast to the American Revolution of 1776, which served to formally sanction a power structure already existent in America at that time, the Industrial Revolution vastly altered many of the norms and institutions of the society. Political and economic power shifted from the landed aristocracy of the South to the industrialists of the Northeast. The extended family structure was replaced by the nuclear family, and the society became increasingly secularized. Man's technology rather than nature would serve as the referent for his behavior, and his concerns would focalize unrelentingly upon the problems generated by his seemingly unmanageable tools. Technology must be watered by the labors of men for it to blossom and Scientism provides the rationale for such labors.

The school system, of course, was greatly affected by the industrialization of America. The idea of compulsory education had been instituted in America by the Puritans in the mid-seventeenth century and had declined in influence with the emergence of the commercial and business ethic. The renewed interest in compulsory education occurred approximately one hundred and fifty years after the decline of the Puritan state. This renewal of interest in compulsory education resulted largely from the humanitarian zeal of educationalists such as Horace Mann, the father of American public education, from the need to "Americanize" the newly arrived immigrants, and from the requirements of a rapidly growing industrial system.

Educationists, as will be noted in Chapter 7, developed an elaborate ideological system to sustain their belief in formal public education, and thus served the technological society by developing a rationale for the schooling which such a society needed. Nationalists and patriots also enhanced the growth of public schooling by demanding that the newly arrived by migration and by birth be trained to defend the American Republic. In addition to the moral and value training which the educationists and patriots viewed as necessary aspects of schooling, they agreed with the defenders of Scientism in the need for schools to prepare individuals to "fit" in an industrialized and urbanized social system.

Schools assisted in the process of training the petty bureaucrats and the semi-skilled and unskilled workers by teaching the three Rs, and by inculcating the students with the values upon which the factory system was based. As work was moved from the bench of the craftsman to the assembly line of the factory, values were altered. Creativity was destroyed by the conformity of mass production, and self-discipline was replaced by the time clock and pay according to piece rates. In schools, teachers prepared the students for such a world through various means such as the recording of absenteeism and tardiness. Indeed, a cursory review of "grade cards" today, especially in elementary schools, reveals that schools continue in the task of preparing students for the labor market. For example, besides recording the level of achievement in the three Rs and other "subjects," grade cards include information about the attitudinal predispositions of the students. These lists often include such items as "the effective use of time," "relation with peers," "respect for authority," "ability to follow directions," "neatness of work," and "reliability in performing assigned tasks." Regular attendance continues to be stressed and tardiness to be recorded.

Because of the influence of Scientism—with its assumption that advances in civilization are rooted to the feats of the specialists rather than to the observations of the generalists—public school programs increasingly have been designed to meet the society's demand for specialists. Youth are often forced to declare vocational interests at an early age in order to compete in the rigorous academic programs designed for specialists. Of course, curricular offerings today appear to be designed for the generalists because of the increase in electives and the freedom to choose. Indeed, public school administrators are eager to point out that today's students are provided with greater choice in course offering than was customary in the past. In the name of freedom to choose among alternatives, however, general and common education has been shattered, for rarely do students share similar curricular experiences. With computerized programming, the possibilities to individualize educational programs is increased and thus general and common education is virtually destroyed.

The liberal arts gradually have assumed a secondary position in formal education, and the preservation of offerings such as literature and music appreciation is due mainly to attempts to preserve an educational smorgasbord rather than to convictions about the need for a liberal education. Students faced with the rigors demanded by increased specialization are more or less forced to "choose" those course offerings which best serve their narrow vocational interests. Thus the aspiring chemist must select educational experiences which will enable him to compete effectively in college courses. The freedom-to-choose ethos that pervades many educational programs is, in fact, a disguise of the reality that credentials denoting intense specialization are required for success in the computerized age.

While serving some of the needs of a technological society, early and intense specialization also creates conditions for the disruption of such a social system. The failure to provide all the children and youth with shared general education serves to increase the ideological gap among the citizenry. Indeed, the revolts of the sixties was able to take so many Americans by surprise precisely because Americans as a whole did not share common problems and were not educated to perceive the general conditions which faced their nation-state. Specialization had furnished the nation with competent bridge builders but had failed to awaken within them the sensitivity to resolve social problems which were producing potential demolition experts.

The school serves two major functions in reference to the society's labor needs. First, as noted previously, it helps to prepare students, especially ideologically, to serve as functionaries in the world of work. Secondly, it serves to protect the labor market from an influx of unneeded workers. Schools are temporary alternatives to work. At the turn of the century less than 10 percent of the children who entered elementary school completed their secondary education. The remainder "dropped out" to join the working force. Technological developments during the twentieth century, however, have eliminated a vast number of work options previously open to "dropouts." As farming and manufacturing became increasingly automated, the need for unskilled and semi-skilled workers dractically declined. Unable to be assimilated in a corporate system that increasingly relies upon automation, and prevented from effectively beginning entrepreneurial ventures, the young and not-so-young are faced with either unemployment or schooling. By remaining in school, many individuals are placed in the position of lengthening their economic dependency and thus are forced into prolonged childhood.[15] This trend is expected to continue as labor market figures reveal a decreasing need for individuals below the age of thirty-five.[16]

Technology helps to structure living patterns which its supporting ideology, Scientism, then serves to legitimize. Because of technological change, the extended family, which was formerly the cornerstone of Western civilization, has been replaced by the nuclear family. And change is so rapid that already the nuclear family, barely established, also is undergoing extreme alterations. Whether the peer commune which is emerging throughout the United States eventually will replace the nuclear family remains to be seen. There is little doubt, however, that the future course of man's social history will be significantly influenced, if not determined, by technology. For centuries social reformers attempted to alter the basic structure of social systems. Now such alterations have been actualized almost spontaneously within a few decades because of the effect of Scientism with its claim to ethical neutrality and objectivity. The fact that technology and its ideological defense has succeeded in altering the primary group structure of man should suffice to prove that the ethical neutrality of Scientism is a myth.

The increase in college enrollment reflects not only an oversupply of labor but also the increasing demand for credentials in order to function in a technological society. Job discrimination because of credentials is a pervasive reality. While most Americans would agree that discrimination because of race, sex, or national origin is a violation of the Bill of Rights, few would agree that credential discrimination violates an individual's civil rights. Yet credentials certifying the completion of educational programs are routinely required for many jobs that require little actual educational preparation. Inasmuch as Scientism rests upon the ideas of professionalism and qualification, the technological system which it supports necessitates the utilization of various forms of credentials in job placement. But despite the fact that the society is indeed more complex, the degree to which credentials are actually required for job performance far exceeds their need.

Scientism is also served by the fact that training requirements for many jobs have been raised while the actual skills needed for the per-

[15] For a brilliant cultural and historical analysis of childhood, see Philippe Aries, *Centuries of Childhood* (New York: Random House, Inc., 1962).

[16] Howard R. Bowen and Garth L. Mangum, eds., *Automation and Economic Progress* (Englewood Cliffs, N.J.: Prentice-Hall, Inc., 1966), pp. 62–81.

formance of these jobs have not been changed significantly. This is certainly not a recent development, but the rapid pace of technological change has made it more apparent. Throughout the history of the industrial revolution, master craftsmen raised the requirements for apprentices when labor supply surpassed demand. Such actions eventually were challenged by open revolt. There are indications that such a revolt is again in process as members of racial and ethnic minorities are demanding the removal of "standard criteria" in job placement, college admissions, and pay increments. Their criticisms are often valid, for such standards generally assume their relevancy from the ideological perspective of Scientism and not from actual measurements of achievement.

Graduating students in the field of education will confront the reality that credentials are increasingly added to job requirements. Until recently, a two-year certificate in education would suffice in obtaining a teaching position. As supply increases and surpasses demand, however, school systems and perhaps teacher associations will increase the requirements for job placement. Of course, labor market demands are similar to credential qualifications because the latter are often contrived to reflect the former. Smaller class sizes and decreased teaching load could serve to bridge the gap between teacher supply and teacher demand. Faced with an increasing taxpayers' revolt, however, such means of alleviating the job crisis is not forthcoming.

In an agrarian society where Puritanism reigns, unemployment is attributed to laziness. In a technological society, unemployment is attributed to lack of qualifications. "Dropouts" are viewed as people who have failed to qualify themselves for future job opportunities. Recent court cases, however, indicate that "years of formal schooling" as a basis for job placement increasingly is viewed as discriminatory. Educationists, of course, having a vested interest in the process of certification, reject this contention.

Closely related to the credential orientation of a technological society is its emphasis upon professionalism. From its inception during the medieval period, the concept of professionalism has implied the necessity of public service, social sanction, and formal schooling. Within the previous decades, as a result of technological influences on the labor market, numerous occupations have been professionalized. Beauticians assume the title of cosmetologists, janitors become maintenance engineers, and undertakers are titled morticians. Besides the relabeling ("upgrading") of preexisting occupations, technological advancement continuously creates new professions. Recent developments in nuclear science, space technology, and computer programming have generated hundreds of new professions. These developments illustrate the mutual relationship between formal schooling and professionalism; that is, an increase in formal education creates new professions and the proliferation of new professions creates a demand for more formal education. When professionalism prevails, schooling is required not only for employment but also for job advancement. It would be difficult to determine the number of individuals who could identify with Willie Loman, in *Death of a Salesman*, as he witnessed young "educated" executives bypassing him in job promotions. The days during which individuals were hired and promoted because of an "honest face," "hard work," or "seniority" are swiftly passing into history.

The increasing power of the education system in a technological society is rapidly being acknowledged by a wide variety of groups. Minority groups, with a new emphasis upon ethnic or racial pride and often faced with failure in "WASP" schools, are demanding community control, different admission standards, and a revised curriculum. Publishing companies, aware of increasing college enrollments, are utilizing the acceptance of paperback books, teaching "hardware," and the "publish or perish" ethos to become an important part of what is now termed "the knowledge explosion." In liberal arts schools, members of departments (e.g., sociology and economics) who have hardly been on speaking terms with the educationists are now "building bridges" to the education departments as money for research and development and a variety of projects is now flowing in the direction of education. Teachers also have recognized their importance and are demanding higher salaries and "better working conditions." And the university, rather than being seen as an institution that threatens the basic values of the business enterprise (e.g., on the grounds of its "ivy towered impracticality" and "leftist leaning sympathies"), is increasingly accepted as a partner with business and government in the development of technology.

The American emphasis upon science and technology was further enhanced by the successful launching of the Russian satellite, Sputnik. This event combined with the renewed anticommunism of the 1950s served as a major political force for increasing government spending in areas of technology. The fact that a technological feat such as the launching of an earth satellite could serve as a major force in reordering national priorities reflects the degree to which the great nation-states are locked into a competition which is fought out on the battlefields of Scientism.

The launching of Sputnik also served to legitimize the debunkers of Progressivism in education. Critics such as Hyman Rickover, James Conant, Robert Hutchins, and Max Rafferty, while differing on numerous issues, generally agreed that progressive education failed to inculcate either mental or moral discipline and that public schooling was failing to serve the needs of the nation-state. The call for a return to "subject matter" was echoed by the scientians who sought qualified specialists to operate the rapidly emerging cybernetic system.

Scientism, because it rests upon the importance of methodology and the centrality of order, is a conservative ideology that depends upon the support of authority. The permissiveness which characterized much of Progressivism was anathema to the technocrat, and the critics of Progressivism were avidly supported by the defenders of the technocratic society. The critics of Progressivism were, in part, correct in their attack upon the permissiveness which resulted from the ideology of Progressivism. The traditional authoritarian pyramid associated with the "little red schoolhouse" had been virtually eliminated, being replaced by the authority of social consensus. In other words, the basis of authority had shifted from the individual to the group. Progressivism served, in part, as a major impetus toward the development of the organizational man—the rugged collectivist.

Despite the fact that the permissiveness inherent in Progressivism was rejected by the defenders of the technocratic society, other aspects of the progressive ideology were supportive of Scientism, for Scientism and Progressivism turn out to be compatible bedfellows. Although progressive education has been part of the movement labeled by Professor Morton White as a revolt against formalism,[17] it did not reject the methodological basis of the scientific method. Indeed, the "scientific method" is one of the most revered concepts of John Dewey's philosophy. Dewey's belief in the desirability of "organized intelligence" in problem solving and his view that truth can be empirically verified by "intersubjective consensus" were consistent with the emerging mode of scientific enquiry—that is, investigations by groups of specialists serving as scientific research teams for governmental agencies. Dewey's view of "intersubjective consensus" could, if applied to social ethics, easily degenerate into a rationale for developing the bland "other-directed" personality vividly described by David Reisman. Progressive education easily evolved into consciously planned programs for the development of social consensus, just as its pragmatic emphasis upon the social, practical, and useful stands in natural contrast to emphases on the individual, the theoretical, and the aesthetic in designing educational programs. Thus Progressivism remains consistent with the demands of Scientism, despite the fact that its bastard child, the life adjustment curriculum, with its focus upon controlled self-expression, often fails to furnish the rigors demanded of the scientific method. Yet the life adjustment program, directed toward the "middle 60 percent" of the student population, was

[17] Morton White, *Social Thought in America: The Revolt Against Formalism* (Boston: Beacon Press, 1961).

designed to provide the type of salesmanship personality that would comply with the consumer-oriented, technological society.

### Scientism, Psychology, and Educationism

Prior to the influence of Scientism upon psychology in the late nineteenth century, the philosophical beliefs concerning man's psyche generally reflected the Platonic view in the version which came down to us after it had been christianized by medieval churchmen. The mind and the body were viewed as separate entities, one of a spiritual nature and the other material. Even the seventeenth-century Rationalist philosophers, such as René Descartes and Gottfried Wilhelm von Liebniz, utilized this dualism between the mind and body as a basic assumption of their epistemological theories. They concurred with the medieval churchmen in the belief in a God who serves as a necessary agent to unify the separate entities. Indeed, without God, the body and the soul could not remain united or functionally interrelated. Thus, from this perspective, the "village idiot" and the "village atheist" were often viewed as closely related.

Out of this metaphysical dualism there emerged the development of faculty psychology. The mind, according to this school of thought, is divided into different faculties—the intellect, the will, and the emotions. The traditional curriculum reflected the belief that these faculties could be trained by including the rote memorization of classical literature in addition to biblical proverbs and *Poor Richard's* secular moral maxims. Not only do faculty psychologists believe that the faculties can be trained, but they often believe that such training can be transferred from one area of learning to another. The reading of classic Greek literature, for example, could develop discipline, logic, and prudent judgment that then could be transferred into other areas of learning or into daily habits. Some religious schools taught, for example, that abstinence from certain foods on certain days could serve to train the will to resist illicit temptations of the flesh. On a more mundane level, the memorization of Latin noun declensions could, perhaps, prevent an individual from forgetting his umbrella.

During the latter decades of the nineteenth century the study of faculty psychology generally was forsaken as scholars turned to Scientism for answers concerning human behavior. The scientization of psychology was largely the result of the influence of Charles Darwin, whose theory of evolution profoundly affected the thoughts of the early theoreticians of experimental and behavioral psychology. Theoreticians such as G. Stanley Hall, William James, and John Dewey rejected the introspective approach of previous psychological theories and attempted to establish laws of human behavior which could be observed and experimentally verified. Their efforts were further enhanced by the endeavors of Edward L. Thorndike, who operationally defined many of their theories and formulated a variety of tests by which the theories could be quantified. In addition, Thorndike's doctoral dissertation entitled *Animal Intelligence* provided a major impetus for relating the study of animal behavior to that of man. In contrast to those who believed mankind to be qualitatively different from animals, Thorndike, reflecting the influence of Darwinian theory, asserted,

> Among the minds of animals that of man is the chief, but also kinsman; ruler but also brother. . . . Nowhere more truly than in his mental capacities is man a part of nature. Amongst the minds of animals that of man leads, not as a demigod from another planet, but as a king from the same race.[18]

The behavioral approach associated with Scientism lacks the elements of supernaturalism and rejects the aforementioned dualism between mind and body. Indeed, recent research in the area of behavior modification often begins with a denial of the existence of the mind, or equates the mind with behavior. Reflecting the sentiments of John B. Watson, an early advocate of behavioral psychology, Gilbert Ryle, a philosophical exponent of modern behaviorism, wrote:

> To talk of a person's mind is not to talk of a repository which is permitted to house objects that something called "the physical world" is forbidden to house; it is to talk of the person's abilities, liabilities and inclinations to do and undergo certain things, and of the doing and undergoing of these things in the ordinary world.[19]

Thus, the behavior modificationist is not interested in any processes possibly occurring "in the mind"; he is concerned, however, with controlling and quantifying behavior, inasmuch as it is possible to observe only the precipitating environmental conditions and the consequent behavioral responses.

The concept of behavioral modification emanated from the alteration of the Darwinian theory of evolution by the proponents of a scientific approach toward psychology. Darwin had noted that physical survival in the process of evolution was dependent upon a body's adaptation to its environment. In the emerging field of psychology, Darwin's assumptions concerning physical adaptation were applied to the mind so that mental

[18] Edward L. Thorndike, "The Evolution of the Human Intellect," *Popular Science Monthly*, LX (November 1901), 65.
[19] Gilbert Ryle, *The Concept of Mind* (New York: Barnes and Noble, 1949), p. 199.

health came to be viewed increasingly as dependent upon the mind's adjustment to the social environment. When this emphasis is combined with the view that the mind and behavior are quite similar, the role of the modern behavioral psychologist is clarified. He seeks to modify the behavior of an individual by adjusting him to his environment, or to manipulate the environment in order to readjust (control) the behavior of the individual. The scholarly social historian Merle Curti explained:

> . . . the ability of any organism, including man, to survive rested on its capacity to maintain an evershifting equilibrium or adjustment with its environment. To maintain this equilibrum, either the organism or the environment had to be "adjusted"; . . . The selection of blind or random impulses that worked most effectively in achieving the equilibrium became the basis of learning. Mind was, so to speak a function of the adjustment of the organism to its environment. The impulses or movements by which the organism adjusted itself to its shifting environment became fixed in habit systems. . . .[20]

Accepting this ideological pattern of thought results in viewing psychologists as behavior modificationists. Indeed, teachers are viewed as behavior modifiers, so that the ideal teacher, according to such a frame of reference, would be a behavioral psychologist. Teaching within the framework of Scientism is viewed as the science of manipulating individuals to achieve certain preconceived goals. The manipulation is to be performed according to positive (preferably) reinforcement of a learner as he accomplishes a certain preestablished set of operationally defined goals. This results in the fixation of habits which can be repeated endlessly or whenever the manipulator so desires. The process is labeled "operant conditioning" by its advocates and, when utilized for political ends, "brainwashing" and "menticide" by its opponents.

The intimate relationship between psychology and education certainly is not a recent development. Indeed, Plato's philosophy of education was directly related to his elaborate theories about the human psyche. Thus, one would anticipate that the scientization of psychology would have direct consequences for educationists.

At the turn of the century, with an increasing number of individuals involved in public schooling, Scientism promised the efficiency to surmount shortages of finances, facilities, and school personnel. As Thorndike, foreshadowing the arguments of current proponents of Scientism, asserted:

> Experiments measuring the effects of school subjects and methods seem pedantic and inhuman beside the spontaneous tact and insight of the

[20] Merle Curti, *The Growth of American Thought* (New York: Harper and Brothers, 1943), p. 558.

gifted teacher. But his personal work is confined by time and space to reach only a few; their [experimental] results join the free common fund of science which increases the more it is used, and lives forever.[21]

In addition, the scientization of education was viewed as a means of legitimizing the relatively recent growth of Educationism, thus enhancing the professionalization of education and granting educationists the respect and prestige they so eagerly sought. As with other professionals, educationists would then have a definite field of specialization and knowledge.

The scientific movement in education assumed diverse emphases. Generally it was rooted to the study of psychology rather than to the analysis of pedagogy although the recent concern for accountability increases the demand for scientizing pedagogy. Researchers such as G. Stanley Hall, Alfred Binet, and Edward Lee Thorndike were not educationists but social scientists concerned with the psychological nature and learning patterns of man. In 1883, Hall advanced the analytical study of psychology by opening a research laboratory at Johns Hopkins University. Later, test designers such as Binet, Thorndike, and Lewis Terman, devised diverse tests for quantitatively measuring mental ability and/or educational achievement. In his *The Principles of Teaching Based on Psychology* (1906), Thorndike revealed the centrality of Scientism in his view of education. Observing that testing is an essential ingredient in teaching, he wrote:

> Just as the scientist, though he has made his facts as accurate and his argument as logical as he can, still remains unsatisfied until he verifies his conclusion by testing it with new facts, so the teacher, after planning and executing a piece of work as well as he can, must "verify" his teaching by direct tests of its results and must consider uncertain any result that he cannot thus verify.[22]

Contemporary adherents to Scientism, the most notable being B. F. Skinner, would enthusiastically concur.

The testing and "mental health" movement in the United States gained importance during the world wars. Faced with an urgent need to classify and select inductees within the armed forces, the government extensively utilized various forms of quantitative testing. This military need generated various testing agencies and served to develop testing specialists. Schools, colleges, and business agencies now readily uitlize their services, and mental testing has become an integral part of the educational environment. A major function of the growing number of

---

21 Edward L. Thorndike, "Educational Diagnosis," *Science,* XXXVII (January 1913), 142.
22 Edward L. Thorndike, *The Principles of Teaching Based on Psychology* (New York: A. G. Seiler, 1906), p. 257.

counseling services within schools today is to administer and utilize diverse forms of testing.

The testing movement further enhanced the scientific study of children and encouraged the process of sorting and selecting individuals according to their "innate" abilities and academic achievement. This resulted in the currently expanding field of exceptional education and the ranking of individuals and schools according to national norms—a procedure that hastens the increasing nationalization of formal schooling. More recently, diverse aspects of human nature have been subject to the research of social scientists. With the advent of scientific management techniques in business and industry and the influence of Progressivism, numerous vocational guidance services have been developed and tests measuring personality factors, character traits, and social attributes have been popularized.

In the past, teachers were expected to serve as moral exemplars, but were not expected to understand or unravel the mysteries of the soul; that task was in the domain of clergymen. With the emergence of the "social ethic," however, psychology became a popular science and "mental illness" became a scientific problem.[23] The schools increasingly, and often unwillingly, have assumed the responsibility not only for the student's intellectual growth but also for his emotional maturity—the development of the "whole child." With the increasing emphasis upon personality development and upon the "social ethic" of the organization man, teachers are held accountable for the degree to which their students adjust to the demands of the corporate state. Accountability necessitates predictability, and thus schools have devised intricate patterns of testing to determine the potential which rests within their charges. Because of the influence of the Ideology of Scientism, such testing has become increasingly viewed as "objective" and as a basis for planning a child's future.

This view of the teacher and of the learning process raises a myriad of questions, especially among teachers who adhere to a humanistic perspective. Of course, the analytical testing movement within the field of psychology does not represent the total field of that behavioral science. Indeed, it results from a particular orientation which is viewed with suspicion by less thoroughly scientized psychologists. Perceptual psychologists, for example, reject the statistical model of mental health which the analytical psychologists utilizes. Similarly, designers of rational

---

[23] William H. Whyte, Jr., *The Organization Man* (Garden City, N.Y.: Doubleday & Company, Inc., 1956), p. 7. According to the author, the social ethic is the representative value structure of the modern, corporate society and encompasses the following propositions: "A belief in the group as the source of creativity; a belief in 'belongingness' as the ultimate need of the individual; and a belief in the application of science to achieve the belongingness."

theoretical models of mental health reject the objective testing designs of the analytical psychologist and arrive at divergent conclusions about the nature of mental health. If, for example, a psychologist begins with a "rational," theoretical model such as Freud's oedipal complex, Erikson's psychosexual development, or Marx's concept of alienation, he could conclude that all men either are or are not mentally ill and thus shatter the findings of the adherents to statistical models which generally fail to discuss the qualitative aspects of mental health. Erich Fromm, for example, fearing mass conformity and "robotism" in modern society, discussed the possibility of an entirely mentally ill citizenry:

> To speak of a "sane society" implies a premise different from sociological relativism. It makes sense only if we assume that there can be a society which is *not* sane, and this assumption, in turn, implies that there are universal criteria for mental health which are valid for the human race as such, and according to which the state of health of each society can be judged.[24]

Generally, Fromm's concept is rejected by the adherents of Scientism, for his absolutism is too general and precludes careful, systematic, methodological analysis. Adherents of the ideology of Scientism invariably view human nature as a malleable entity which can be decisively influenced by the environment. In contrast to the Puritans, the adherents of Scientism hold that man's nature rests not within himself but in the hands of those who manipulate his environment. Enamored of environmental determinism, scientians often scoff at the voluntarists who believe that man possesses a free will.

### Scientism, Violence, and Social Control

The asumptions inherent in Scientism and the technological system which they support generate social action and humanistic rebellion. Because Scientism emphasizes the "rational" and the logical ordering of reality, as well as the rule of law, its relationship to social ferment and violence is often denied. Indeed, the ferment and violence which it produces are invariably blamed upon Romanticism or other ideologies. While rebellion and revolution against a technological society are Romantic or Puritan in perspective, their intensity and orientation are rooted to the form of Scientism which legitimizes the institutional activities within the social system. A few illustrations should suffice to reveal the symbiotic and dialectical relationship between Scientism and social ferment and violence.

[24] Erich Fromm, *The Sane Society* (New York: Fawcett World Library, 1966), p. 21.

First, Scientism accentuates reason, law, and order. It seeks to control the unpredictable forces within society as well as the volatile emotions of men by encouraging the application of principles derived from the natural sciences to the study and control of man. Although this orientation may result in *de facto* repression, it does not necessarily imply deception or devious intent. Indeed, the popularity of Scientism results from its promise of improving the life of man through practical and rational systems of control.

The emotional, aesthetic, and spiritual aspects of man, however, cannot be ignored or significantly curbed without destroying the tenuous balance that exists in man. Some scientists and many technocrats invariably misunderstand the perfidity of man and the intensity with which he will protect his "nature." The promise of riches, immortality, or peace do not suffice to convince most men that their spontaneity or passion should be scientifically controlled. Many human beings would prefer to die rather than to be deprived of the right to err. When Scientism becomes prevalent and exaggerated, reason, predictability, and empirical studies rob men of passion, mystery, and mythology. The paradox of this situation is that, although Scientism may serve to enrich man's qualities of passion, mystery, and mythology, it serves simultaneously to curb their expression. The blandness and habituation which such a perspective eventually forces upon society create rage and discontent because some men will always believe that "existence" and "living" are not synonymous, and that existence without passion is death. Thus when Scientism becomes excessive, some men come not only to doubt the power of reason but also to detest it. Bland individuals and institutions drive passionate human beings into rebellion. Men seeking inspiration and liberation join forces against the stupefying exigencies of technology, and their social awareness inflamed by their discontent becomes social action.

A second major reason why Scientism is rooted to individual discontent and social ferment is its integral faith in the ability of man to manipulate the environment for his own betterment. It is an ideology which offers the hope of salvation on earth and ignores or ridicules the realm of the supernatural. Whereas religionists often diffuse discontent by promising happiness in a future life—a line of argument which prompted both Marx and Freud to denounce them as pushers of ideological opiates—Scientism, with its pragmatic and materialistic emphasis, is expected to deliver its promises in *this* world. In contrast to some ideologies, such as Puritanism, which avoid prophecies of joy by warning that life is essentially a vale of tears, Scientism promises a world replete with comfort, safety, and leisure. Its paradise will emerge, advocates of Scientism emphasize, when men learn to rationally control their environment and themselves.

Like all other ideologies, however, Scientism never completely fulfills its promises. Disillusionment forces dissatisfied men to seek a faith elsewhere. When the affluence and comfort promised by Scientism fail to produce the expected ancillary fulfillment, its adherents begin to view it as an ideological trick rather than a treat. Because the "Promised Land of Scientism" includes anomie, ulcers, and anxiety, its inhabitants from the affluent middle class invariably produce rebels who rage and seek alternative ideologies. In the 1960s, while the affluent middle-class adherents of Scientism in the United States were mounting a crusade to open the gates of their kingdom to the poor and cultural minorities, some of their children were escaping from their midst and seeking refuge in the ghettoes of poverty or in the bleak rural lands recently vacated by rugged individualists.

Unkept promises and unfulfilled dreams are the greatest sources of human rage and violence. Scientism roots its promises to the empirical domain. When empirical evidence reveals that man's increased control over his fellow man and over his environment has not produced the expected comfort and peace, then men in despair seek to change the world in which they live. Their dissatisfaction becomes monumental and highly volatile when their technological paradise increasingly limits their personal freedom and threatens the life support systems of nature.

The greatest ferment generated by excessive Scientism appears among the youth, especially within their institutions—the schools and universities of the country. The Free Speech Movement which emerged at Berkeley in 1964 served as a vanguard for student criticism and activism that continues to shock and exasperate some members of the academic community and "taxpaying" citizens throughout the country. Many alumni who participated in goldfish swallowing, panty raids, and fraternity pranks are dismayed to see their children demanding institutional changes through such means as "sit-ins," massive marches, and the destruction of property. Yet the social action emanating from the schools and universities is integrally related to the extension of Scientism and its influence in defining youth.

Scientism and the technological civilization which it supports tend to develop a social class system based, in part, upon age. Not only does Scientism attempt to prolong childhood by encouraging youth to remain within schools—and thus dependent upon institutions or parents or part-time work for support—but it also bars them from the work force by demanding that they obtain academic credentials which it takes an increasing amount of time to obtain. Thus, both automation and specialization serve to prevent youth from becoming economically independent. Of course, childhood cannot be artificially prolonged indefinitely. Individuals in their twenties and thirties will not accept the role of a child.

Like their working parents in previous decades, they rebel against a second-class citizenship. Rather than striking against their employers, however, they attack the educational systems in which they are forced to "work."

Dissatisfaction with a social system always expresses itself most vehemently against those institutions in which the hopes of the people rest. When the Roman Catholic Church, for example, failed to meet the expectations of social reformers, the ferment was expressed in churches. Martin Luther, the great Protestant reformer, posted his announcement of revolt upon the church door of the cathedral at Wittenberg. What is more, the Protestant Reformation witnessed numerous acts of vandalism against churches and church-owned property. Similarly, during the great Industrial Revolution and the resultant revolt of the workers throughout the industrialized world, the factories were the center of protest. The emergence of unionism was characterized by illegal sit-ins within factories, massive arrests of workers, vandalism against corporations, and attacks upon corporate representatives and union organizers. During the age of industrialization, the factory and business worlds were the centers where men placed their hopes for a better life. With the advent of the technological society, with its specialization, professionalism, credentialism, and other-directedness, the educational system has become the hope of a people who seek to better their lives economically, aesthetically, and socially. The schools and universities, therefore, are the centers in which the dissatisfactions with the technological society are expressed. The decade of the 1970s should witness, no doubt, an increasing emphasis upon reform in schooling.

A third major reason why schools, especially universities, have become the center of ferment is related to the close relationship which exists between the "military-industrial complex" and university research. Not only do research projects for government agencies occupy an increasing portion of professorial time, thus decreasing their involvement in the teaching and learning program, but this research often involves politically relevant programs. The type of research which was coordinated with military agencies caused many individuals to question the perennial academic claim that the university was an apolitical institution and that its professors were detached seekers of truth. Demonstrations on campus have not been directed toward the departments of Romance languages or fine arts, but rather against the ROTC programs, interviewers for war materials producers, and mathematics and science departments. Some of these demonstrations resulted in confrontations between students enrolled in the fine arts or liberal arts programs and students preparing for careers in engineering or the sciences. Students in the field of education, accustomed to the belief that teachers should remain politically neutral and concerned about their future vocations, often failed to involve themselves in these political confrontations.

Issues of "law and order" within the society are related to Scientism, for Scientism legitimizes the acts of institutions and the supporters of institutions. As a powerful social religion, Scientism is a conservative force but is not specifically aligned with either political conservatives or political liberals. Both liberals and conservatives who support the existing system and who defend institutional acts as legitimate are, in fact, adherents of Scientism. Indeed, some liberals who perpetually seek to increase the influence and extension of government agencies over the lives of the citizenry are actively forwarding the ideology of Scientism, whereas some political conservatives who stress the importance of free choice are often rugged individualists who seek to diminish the influence of Scientism upon the lives of the people. Thus neither political liberalism nor political conservatism can be categorized automatically upon the Scientism-Romanticism continuum. Nevertheless, technicians and engineers tend to be more politically conservative than scientists, and physical scientists tend to be more politically conservative than social scientists.

The ideology of Scientism has contributed greatly to the ever-increasing institutionalization of American life. With their burgeoning growth and centrality of position, institutions rather than individuals are viewed as the essential elements in the development of civilization. Consequently, Americans tend to regard demands for institutional loyalty as legitimate. Scientism, because of its mutual relationship with institutional life, has also gained respect and power, so that personal behavior is increasingly subject to scrutiny while institutional actions are accepted at face value and seldom investigated.

The decisions of the Brahmins of modern civilization are invariably legitimized by adherents of Scientism. Like the adherents of classicism during the reign of the Académie française who accepted the rules of aesthetic expression devised by that body, adherents to Scientism today invariably accept as unquestionable truth the arguments of scientists and technocrats on such issues as pollution, space exploration, and military defense.

Personal violence is generally more acceptable and expected in a society in which primary relationships are central. The Homeric heroes and the medieval knights participated in personal violence and often received the praise of their contemporaries. Likewise in the United States, the era of the "Wild West" was an age of personal acts of heroism and violence. Law and order was instituted and maintained by the personal, only vaguely institutionalized power of the sheriff. The fastest gun was respected and the fact that it often was placed in the hand of someone barely distinguishable from a juvenile delinquent did not diminish the fact that personal heroic acts were noble.

In a technological society with a massive impersonal bureaucratic system, such individual acts of violence come to be viewed as primitive and are not to be tolerated. The deeds of individuals are scrutinized more closely than the deeds of groups. National guardsmen, members of a football team, and bomber crews are more immune from criticism than a solitary policeman, a boxer, or a soldier killing an enemy with a bayonet.

Similarly, personal bigotry is held to be more inhuman and less tolerable than institutional racism. An individual act of prejudicial treatment on the part of a teacher against a child because of his race would receive quick and severe criticism, whereas the fact that college admission requirements as well as standardized tests are sometimes culturally skewed to the disadvantage of certain racial minorities often causes little concern.

The dehumanization and oppression of man, in whatever form they occur, invariably are legitimized through intricate systems of beliefs which rest upon claims of ethical necessity or objective neutrality. Rarely does one depend upon claims of military superiority or perfidy to legitimize political evils. The most hideous crimes committed by men have been defended either in the name of "the good" or on the basis of "objective truth." Devil worshipers and emotionalists do not seem to be desirable allies in the perpetration of massive crimes, so it is God and reason that invariably are proclaimed allies by aggressors. Slavery, for example, has been defended wherever it appears on the basis of morality (e g , the colonization of the African continent was legitimized by arrogant and stupid moralizations about the "white man's burden") or objectivity (e.g., the enslavement and genocide perpetuated by the Nazi regime of Germany was rationalized, in part, by claims that research revealed the superiority of the Aryan race). The devil can quote not only scripture but scientific journals as well!

Although the oppression that results from moralization and the claim that God requires certain deeds to be accomplished by his loyal followers has been the scourge of man, the form of oppression that results from the ideology of Scientism portends to be of even greater destructiveness to human life. In the distopias written by authors who are opposed to Scientism we get a glimpse of the subtle and insidious means that could be utilized to oppress individuals. George Orwell's *1984*, for example, does not simply represent a repressive system of a foreign power or a hpyothetical dictatorial regime, but rather reflects certain assumptions about a highly developed technological society which transcend political intrigue. A major quality of Orwell's distopia is the fact that in the world of 1984 human beings are virtually incapable of rebellion because of the overwhelming power of oppression generated by the application of technology and the limitations placed upon thought by the ideology of Scientism. For example, through the scientific manipulation and distortion of language, the generation of unorthodox opinions is rendered virtually impossible. In modern nation-states, technological application of principles of learning are utilized to correct political deviants. The political heretic is often subject to the same kind of treatment that is provided to those who are judged to be emotionally disturbed. In some nation-states, for example, political heretics are judged mentally ill rather than criminal and are benevolently furnished treatment to remove their antisocial ailment. Brainwashing or menticide rather than incarceration serve as a means of preserving latter-day fascist regimes.

The danger inherent in the application of the principles of Scientism, with their claim to objectivity and ethical neutrality, is a very real one today. Indeed, many rebels think that the Orwellian distopia is already in its incipient phase, and certain technological innovations and ideological developments during the twentieth century add credence to their fears. The manipulation of communication networks and thought patterns during the Great Wars reached a massive scale; and during the Cold War era which followed World War II, scientific explorations in the field of psychology revealed the frightful possibilities of mind control.

The popularization of recent developments in the science of psychology has served to generate a myth about psychiatry and mental illness. The currently popular conviction that psychiatry is based upon scientific and objective facts has been debunked by Thomas Szasz who perceives inherent danger in the massive acceptance of scientific psychology. He warned:

> Rulers have always conspired against their subjects and sought to keep them in bondage; and to achieve their aims, they have always relied on force and fraud. Indeed, when the justificatory rhetoric with which the oppressor conceals and misrepresents his true aims and methods is most effective—as had been the case formerly with tyranny justified by theology, and in the case now with tyranny justified by therapy—the oppressor succeeds not only in subduing his victim but also in robbing him of a vocabulary for articulating his victimization, thus making him a captive deprived of all means of escape.[25]

The uses of technology for social control have increased significantly during the previous decade. Wiretapping and computerized filing, for example, are valuable means of observing and controlling the activities

[25] Thomas S. Szasz, *Ideology and Insanity: Essays on the Psychiatric Dehumanization of Man* (Garden City, N.Y.: Doubleday & Company, Inc., 1970), p. 5.

of the citizenry. Partly as a result of a divisive and unpopular war in Indochina, national lists of subversives and suspects have increased exponentially. The fact that a significant portion of the population is viewed with suspicion reveals ideological absurdity as much as it reveals organizational efficiency.

The increase in mass movements and urban and college unrest during recent years has also served as an excuse to develop sophisticated technological means of controlling social actions. Modern sophisticated technology and specialized tactical squads are utilized to detect ideological deviants and to control crowds in a manner which makes the rational individual approach of Sherlock Holmes seem inept.

With the increased efficiency of managerial and monitoring systems, schools and colleges have been able to utilize identification cards and fingerprinting as effective means of social observation and to employ police agents and monitoring devices to observe controversial individuals.

These examples of the use of technology are not furnished to illustrate intentional tyranny or to question the ethical stance of political leaders. Indeed, these activities may represent the work of honorable and well-intentioned men who do not harbor the lust for power or the ambition of tyrants. They may merely reflect the ideological perspective of Scientism which is based upon the belief that social order is always more desirable than chaos and that the ability to predict future events, including those generated both by collective acts and by individuals, should be maximized. Adherents ot the ideology of Scientism invariably perceive information to be of inherent worth and often ignore questions concerning the morality of eavesdropping and the invasion of privacy by affirming that their intents are not tyrannical. The issue of data collection itself as a moral problem is often avoided by the adherent of Scientism. In the name of efficiency, progress, and ethical neutrality—the ideological elements of Scientism—individuals may relinquish their rights of privacy and their freedom of action. Of course, whereas most adherents of Scientism may believe in their objectivity and may not accept the arguments concerning their role in the centralization of political power, other men are not so innocent. Tyrants often have utilized the ideology of Scientism to support their personal ambitions. Hitler, for example, utilized technology and "objective" research to fulfill his conscious totalitarian goals.

As previously noted, ideologies function as binding forces, covert in nature. They also limit individual freedom by channeling perception and thus providing fewer alternatives for action. Scientism thus provides a rationale for a controlled society in the fashion of Aldous Huxley's *Brave New World* and B. F. Skinner's *Walden Two*. Law and order in these worlds are not maintained by external legal codes written by politicians, nor are they enforced by police agents. In the utopia of Scientism, assuming the acceptance of the ideology and the behavioral compliance to its dictates, law and order are based upon scientific principles discovered by scientific experts and managed by trained technicians through genetic control, operant conditioning, and psychological or chemical processes.

Scientism offers an alternative to a police state in which overt oppressive measures sustain social order through threat and fear. It offers the possibility of sustaining social cohesion through the psychological threat of treating deviance as a form of mental illness. Thomas Szasz observed: ". . . mental health and illness are but new words for describing moral values. More generally, the semantics of the mental health movement is but a new vocabulary for promoting a particular kind of secular ethic." [26] Mental illness has replaced the concepts of sin and criminality, thus removing the possibility of moral choice as a basis for antisocial action. In such a therapeutic state the psychiatrist rather than the priest or the court justice assumes the role of determining who is to be "re-educated." Students who violate school or social rules within such a therapeutic environment will not be viewed as a criminal, nor will they receive physical punishment or be incarcerated; rather, they will be assisted by guidance counsellors or psychiatrists through a process of "therapy" to correct their antisocial behavior. In such a world it will become increasingly difficult to blame "unfair punishment" on the politics, ineptitude, or personal hatred of those individuals administering the "cure" inasmuch as these individuals are, according to the ideology of Scientism, "scientists," who are by definition apolitical in the performance of their duties. As "scientists," they are considered to be qualified, objective, and detached from their personal feelings or sentiment.

The therapeutic approach to removing ideological deviancy is gaining acceptance and legitimacy. The terms "mentally ill" and "sick" have gained popularity and are now commonly applied to alcoholics, homosexuals, truants, prostitutes, hippies, political extremists, drug users, lawbreakers, and all persons viewed as incorrigible or eccentric. Suggestions for "treatment" for such ideological deviants have included compulsory therapy and mandatory confinement in sanitariums. Indeed, some adherents of the ideology of Scientism have conducted scientific studies to develop tests to administer to children in order to identify those children who are predisposed to "abnormal or antisocial activity." Preventitive detention logically follows from such an orientation.

Of course many of the developments that have resulted from the application of scientific principles to the study of human life are less

26 Szasz, *Ideology and Insanity*, p. 36.

violent and hideous than previous means of removing ideological deviancy. The harshness with which the Puritan perspective viewed emotional illness has been painfully documented. While some religionists viewed bizarre behavior as a sign of the wrath of an angry God or as the deed of Satan, others, especially the volitionists, dealt with psychological alienation by resorting to admonitions derived from the Protestant work ethic. The idle mind was viewed as the devil's workshop or, in the latter-day language of the Freudian, as the id's liberator. The humanization of the care of the psychologically alienated resulted in great measure from the efforts of such individuals as the frail teacher Dorothea Dix, who in 1841, on a field trip to a Massachusetts House of Correction with her Sunday school class, was shocked to discover that the mentally ill were treated as criminals. Her unrelenting dedication to changing the condition of treatment of the mentally ill is a monument to self-sacrificing commitment. Such humaneness is definitely more apparent in a therapeutic clinic than it is in an inquisitional court or in a festering prison.

The issue remains, however, that the therapeutic approach to human differences may limit human freedom more than inquisitional courts or prisons ever could. To label an individual mentally ill could quite conceivably, for example, undermine genuine and legitimate disagreements about life styles and political views and may result in bland conformity. The currently popular tendency to label individuals who disagree with prevailing social and educational fads as reflecting personal insecurity and psychological alienation is not only ludicrous and sophomoric but also dangerous. It serves to limit ideological alternatives. Such inept browbeating not only reflects impotent authoritarianism but also constitutes a glaringly inappropriate extension of the ideology of Scientism. Unfortunately, the therapeutic approach to deviance is strengthened by having a self-proving mechanism which renders it peculiarly immune to criticism. Those who would question the movement toward a therapeutic state are themselves engaging in a questionable act, and those who argue that man is becoming less civilized because of his growing inability to accept or tolerate individual differences may find their arguments treated as merely symptomatic of mental degeneration.

Rebels of the past would not find comfort or support within such a therapeutic world. The teachings of Jesus, for example, would have been virtually negated if he had been hospitalized rather than crucified.

The ultimate consequence of the application of scientific psychology to ideological deviance is to add scientific credence to conformity. Would the reader prefer being classified, if no other choice existed, as a public sinner, a criminal, or mentally ill? If the first two choices seem preferable, the therapeutic state is already upon us, for it reveals the fear of the label "mentally ill" and, consequently, the propensity to avoid deviancy as defined by the ideology of Scientism. The fact that this means of social control and the ancillary fear of violating society's standards is accompanied by the persistent doubt about one's own sanity occasioned by rapid social changes and questioning of personal values that accompanies such a change is an American tragedy. The thought that some Americans may live in terror of mental illness while propelling themselves into the arms of psychiatrists should serve to horrify even the most rabid defender of Scientism.

For many individuals, the ethos of Scientism with its educational application, behavior modification, raises the frightening spector of the dystopias of *1984* and *Brave New World*. In these novels, George Orwell and Aldous Huxley attempted to extend the ideology of Scientism to its logical conclusion. One hopes that their works reveal their prejudice in favor of the ideology of Romanticism and their rejection of Scientism, rather than an accurate portrayal of the future.

## Scientism and Social Issues

### METHODOLOGY

The increasing technological complexity in modern nation-states creates numerous social problems. Indeed, attempts to analyze technological implications create discord and confusion. Research findings concerning the effects of television, for example, are conflicting and are utilized by various groups to forward their views on social change. Is television the manipulative tool of a powerful, socioeconomic elite, is it a medium which caters to mediocrity and the mundane tastes of a mass audience, or is it a neutral agent, non-ideological in nature? Will television eventually replace the teacher or will it free the teacher to maximize student-teacher interaction? Does violence on television serve to increase actual acts of violence? Did television help create and exaggerate the pervasiveness of the counterculture? Critical questions such as these have not been fully answered, and such answers as have been forwarded tend to reflect the ideological perspective of the researcher.

Answers to these questions are further complicated by the nature of scientific research dealing with social phenomena. Scientific methodology, as previously noted, tends to focus upon isolated events and immediate causality. As a result, researchers who utilize the scientific methodology tend to ignore or minimize the long-range consequences of technological change. Indeed, the perennial dialogue concerning the effects of technological progress invariably confines itself to immediate consequences. Ecological prophets of doom, for example, have focused

upon the fact that only short-term effects were considered when technological discoveries were unleashed, and the most vociferous pessimists
among them proclaim the imminent end of the world as a consequence
of such short-range considerations.

Similarly, recent discoveries such as thalidomide, DDT, and cycla-
mates initially were viewed as beneficial to man. Indeed, their short-term
effects were useful, but later findings revealed that their long-range consequences were damaging. Analyzing and understanding the long-range
effects of technological change is a critical task, for the social consequences generated by technological advancement should not be minimized. The automobile, for example, has served to alter the courting
habits in the United States. Likewise, the oral contraceptive has changed
the premarital sexual patterns of numerous young couples. Does the oral
contraceptive "cause" sexual "promiscuity"? Will it serve to redefine the
moral sanctions relating to sexual behavior? Was the invention of the
oral contraceptive a morally neutral act?

The moral consequences of technological change are numerous and
pervasive. Indeed, future social historians may discern a direct line between the emergence of situational ethics and technological advancement.
Technology creates its own imperatives, and these imperatives can evolve
into moral sanctions and ethical guides. Although this assertion does not
necessarily imply technological determinism, it does reveal the profound
influence which technology exerts upon man's value systems. If these
influences are allowed to remain unanalyzed, then they do indeed become
determiners which force man to adjust. Without analysis, man becomes
merely an extension of various technological hardware.

The long-range effects of technological advancements are so numerous and subtle that they can never be fully understood. Indeed, the
ultimate questions concerning man and his relationship to his tools are
philosophical in nature and can be answered only within the context of
man's view of the meaning of life. The ethical questions which are at
the root of man's relationship to his inventions will become a paramount
concern in future decades as man learns to manipulate his own genetic
makeup. If he obtains the power to determine the intellectual potentiality of his offspring, should he do so? What will be the consequences?

Research in areas having obvious social consequences demonstrates
the significance of ideological analysis. For example, both the individual's
social and/or political bias and the value orientation of the society influence the selection of subject matter deemed worthy of research. The
researcher's bias will determine, in part, whether he studies the harmful
effects of marijuana or of alcohol; the racism of suburbanites or the
low motivation of minorities; the power of the super-rich or the wasteful-
ness of welfare recipients; the incompetence of administrators or the

dissent of students; the prejudices of employers or the lack of work skills among the poor. The individual's selection of the research topic is also determined, in part, by the value orientation of the society as manifested in the financial support accorded the research endeavor. The complexities inherent in technological advances have made the problem of funding increasingly important, especially for those who engage in expensive research in the physical sciences. The increasing necessity of economic support intensifies the problems of those researchers who are proponents of vast social reforms or whose work is of a controversial nature, inasmuch as the funding institutions generally have a vested interest in maintaining the status quo. These factors may or may not affect the validity of the findings, but they do indicate the ideological nature of research.

Adherents to the ideology of Scientism naturally advocate the utilization of the rigid tenets of scientific methodology in both the physical sciences and the social sciences. For those who research in areas of social concern, however, such a proposal raises complex questions. If scientific methodology is allowed to dictate the types of solutions to be sought, it also will tend to define and limit the problems to be studied. Problems that appear too difficult to quantify and measure—problems with many complex variables and contingencies—thus may be dismissed as "poetry" or treated superficially. How would a researcher, for example, approach the study of the influence of love, charisma, esprit de corps, and machismo on human behavior? To satisfy the methodological requirements of Scientism, such concepts would have to be operationally defined before they could be studied. But is this possible? Similarly, would a more holistic and historical approach to research be of greater significance to the understanding of human behavior than the scientific approach, which tends to emphasize attitude surveys and rigidly controlled, if not contrived, experimental situations? One need only read some recent educational research to conclude that triviality is often the price one pays for scientific verity! [27]

The utilization of language presents another major difficulty to individuals engaged in research, especially in the social sciences. As noted in Chapter 1, the ideological implications inherent in language can create numerous conflicts among individuals and groups who are dealing with issues considered controversial. Although researchers in the physical sciences escape this dilemma, in part, by using mathematical equations and symbols, researchers in the social sciences are continually faced with value-laden terms that may have various connotations dependent on one's ideological perspective. The label "culturally deprived," for example,

---

[27] For an insightful discussion concerning social science research, see C. Wright Mills, *The Sociological Imagination* (New York: Grove Press, Inc., 1959).

was changed to "culturally disadvantaged" and then to "culturally distinct" as the ideological nature of the terms became apparent.

During periods of intense social conflict an awareness of and a sensitivity to the ideological nature of language is especially crucial for even a modicum of understanding. Within the preceding decade, for example, student protest and racial conflict generated an avalanche of social research and raised the banner of "law and order." The civil rights movement and the "riots" in the cities were viewed as attacks upon the "law and order" of American society. Indeed, the numerous slogans calling for loyalty to the system and for "law and order" were often inept disguises of racism. Seldom, if ever, was the call for "law and order" viewed as a demand to prevent stock frauds, industrial pollution, income tax evasion, price fixing, or false advertising.

"Law and order" is obviously related to a person's ideologically determined perception of force and/or violence. The American Revolution, for example, could be perceived either as a liberation movement to free the American people from the oppressive force of the English monarchy or as a violent insurrection against the legal order of a legitimate government. Leaders of liberation movements become fathers of their countries while leaders of insurrections receive jail sentences or death penalties. In political situations, one must remember, the issue of the legitimacy of violence is largely determined by victory or defeat; or, "might makes right" in the very real sense that right is largely a legal concept and the victors are the ones who write the laws.

With its emphasis upon methodology and predictability, Scientism is rooted to the human desire to control the environment and to rationally order man's perceptual world. For decades social scientists utilizing carefully designed hypotheses have been attempting to objectively analyze and predict human behavior. In the 1960s their cause was taken up by activists who, motivated by the faith of true believers and armed with the "hard data" generated by the social scientists, attempted to rationally implement social changes. Government agencies, relying upon the findings of selected social scientists, joined them in attempting to engineer social changes. For the most part the only discernible result was the disillusionment caused by the loss of faith in Scientism which followed the failure of the promises of social reconstruction. Many individuals of politically powerless minorities became increasingly critical of being treated as subjects of experimental studies. This attitude was magnified by the frustration that resulted from the awareness that previous studies seemingly have had little effect in changing social conditions. Dr. Kenneth B. Clark expressed this painful truth when he testified before the Commission on Civil Disorders in 1967. Noting the similarity between this study and the previous studies of other riot commissions, he stated, "I must again in candor say to you members of this Commission—it is a kind of Alice in Wonderland—with the same moving picture re-shown over and over again, the same analysis, the same recommendations, and the same inaction." [28]

Certainly not all scientific studies have demonstrated such numbing agreement. Indeed, many studies generate conflicting findings and many eminently qualified experts disagree with each other. Such conflicts have cast further doubts upon the objectivity claimed by Scientism. In fact, it often appears that some individuals utilize scientific studies to legitimize preexisting convictions, just as Marxists use history and theologians use biblical scriptures to justify their beliefs.

The ideology of Scientism, of course, remains as a major influence upon thinking and perceiving. Social scientists continue to seek means to rationally understand the patterns and processes which they perceive in human behavior. The development of the field of cybernetics has enhanced the confidence of the adherents of Scientism, as well as their faith in their ability to rationally predict and thus design man's future. This faith becomes all the more tenable because of the fact that prediction and forecasting often produce previews that are tantamount to assignments in the sense believers in Scientism readily falter into an acceptance of scientific determinism—that is, a belief that findings derived through scientific analysis are binding upon their behavior. Unlike the Puritan determinism of the Calvinist tradition, however, scientific determinism generally reflects a faith in man's salvation and a confidence in an ultimate resolution of the human dilemma. If man cannot perfect man, perhaps he can perfect the environment which determines him. Thus R. Buckminster Fuller, the author of *Operating Manual for Spaceship Earth,* concluded his blueprint for survival with a resounding affirmation of his faith in man's technology:

> Man has ever-increasing confidence in the computer; witness his unconcerned landings as air transport passengers coming in for a landing in the combined invisibility of fog and night. While no politician or political system can ever afford to yield understandably and enthusiastically to their adversaries and opposers, all politicians can and will yield enthusiastically to the computer's safe flight-controlling capabilities in bringing all of humanity in for a happy landing.[29]

Fuller's faith in man's ability to design his future is reflected cautiously by the father of cybernetics, Norbert Wiener. Analyzing the social applications of Cybernetics, he asked:

[28] *Report of the National Advisory Commission on Civil Disorders,* Otto Kerner, chairman (New York: Bantam Books, Inc., 1968), p. 483.
[29] R. Buckminster Fuller, *Operating Manual for Spaceship Earth* (New York: Pocket Books, 1970), p. 120.

Can't one imagine a machine to collect this or that type of information, as for example information on production and the market; and then to determine as a function of the average psychology of human beings, and of the quantities which it is possible to measure in a determined instance, what the most probable development of the situation might be? . . . We may dream of the time when the *machine à gouverner* may come to supply—whether for good or evil—the present obvious inadequacy of the brain when the latter is concerned with customary machinery of politics.[30]

When the rationally ordered, systematized, and atomized production systems are effectively producing myriads of hypnotizing gadgets for a populace conditioned by a popularized consumer ethic, the subtle ideological system of Scientism becomes pervasive. Once rooted within the social fabric, Scientism propels man to seek rational means to remove the unpredictable from his social systems and from the human personality. Through the application of cybernation—that is, the combination of automation and cybernetics—the possible dominance of man by his inventions becomes an ominous reality. Although such a fear may reflect an irrational technophobia, the fact that technological advancement has served to improve the means of surveillance and control over large segments of populations serves as a warning of the misuse of technology by political elites.

## WAR

In 1961 President Eisenhower expressed apprehension about the increasing power of what he labeled the "military-industrial complex." This acknowledgement of the problem was of greater significance than the insight or profundity of his remarks, for it served to popularize the notion of a power elite. Historically, Scientism and the military establishment have been inextricably interwoven. As Bertrand Russell observed: "The practical importance of science was first recognized in connection with war: Galileo and Leonardo obtained government employment by their claim to improve artillery and the art of fortification. From their time onwards, the part of the men of science in war has steadily grown greater." [31] In 1798 a strikingly similar merger occurred in America. Eli Whitney applied his theory of interchangeable parts, the basic principle of mass production, to the manufacturing of firearms for the federal government. A half century later Samuel Colt, using a similar process, produced the Colt revolver (the "six-shooter"), an important factor in the United States' victory against Mexico.

[30] Norbert Wiener, *The Human Use of Human Beings: Cybernetics and Society* (New York: Avon Books, 1969), p. 244.
[31] Bertrand Russell, *A History of Western Philosophy* (New York: Simon and Schuster, Inc., 1945), p. 493.

During World War I many areas of technology were either created or improved. Significant developments, for example, occurred in photography, clothing, aircraft, gun powder, tanks, machine guns, dehydrated foods, dyestuffs, optical equipment, and storage batteries. During World War II, technological advances included amphibious equipment, radar, aerosol bombs, jet aircraft, sonar, rockets, and, of course, atomic energy. In a sense World War I was a chemist's war, World War II a physicist's war. With the recent developments in bacteriology, ecology, and biochemistry, perhaps World War III, if it occurs, will be a biologist's war—a possibility that might at long last prove to be "the war to end all wars," but in a sense far different from what President Wilson had in mind. For many individuals, including some of the political leaders of the major powers, this Armageddon appears to be a possibility, and they seem to be making reasonable efforts to avoid a confrontation which could result in a total war, for technological development has reached a point at which victory would mean little more than defeat.

Scientism creates its own process for resolving differences among nations. Unfortunately, peace is not the implied alternative to the elimination of "traditional" wars. Wars, like many other endeavors of man, reflect the ideological framework in which they are planned. The competitive wars of nation-states may become as antiquated as the heroic wars of Homer and the religious wars of the crusaders. In fact, there appears to be a trend toward a continual series of minor "wars." Such "Orwellian wars"—usually labelled "police actions," a term that implies the necessity of planned, controlled development—reflect the ideological ethos of a highly developed technology. "Police actions" are intentionally limited in scope and isolated geographically. Generally, they are encounters between the technocratized army of "developed" nations and guerrilla warriors of "underdeveloped" (Third World) nations. For example, in the "Six Day War," Israel, a rapidly developing technological society with a highly trained militia, easily demolished the less skilled army of the predominately agrarian Arab countries. Neither the United States nor the Soviet Union has unconditionally supported their Near Eastern allies, and both "Great Powers" strongly emphasize order and negotiations. As a consequence of the "Six Day War" and the continuing cold war in the Near East, the Arab cultures will become increasingly more technological. In the words of Marshall McLuhan, "War, in fact, can be seen as a process of achieving equilibrium among unequal technologies, a fact that explains Toynbee's puzzled observation that each invention of a new weapon is a disaster for society, and that militarism itself is the most common cause of the breaking of civilizations." [32] In an effort to attain some modicum

[32] Marshall McLuhan, *Understanding Media: The Extensions of Man* (New York: McGraw-Hill Book Company, 1964), p. 344.

of self-determination or self-preservation, an underdeveloped nation tends to identify with and to emulate the characteristics of its enemy. It is from this perspective that McLuhan observed: "War is a sizeable component in the educational industry, being itself a form of education. War as an accelerated program of education—compulsory education for the other part—is obvious the moment that it is mentioned." [33]

In 1967 a group of professional scholars allegedly met at Iron Mountain and issued a report stating that war was an inseparable feature of the economic and social system of the United States. The report stated that although peace was an ideal for which mankind yearns, it is in the waging of war, or the preparation for war, that man gains and maintains his technological affluence. The report indicated,

> The relationship of war to scientific research and discovery is more explicit. War is the principal motivational force for the development of science at every level, from the abstractly conceptual to the narrowly technological. Modern society places a high value on "pure" science, but it is historically inescapable that all the significant discoveries that have been made about the natural world have been inspired by the real or imaginary military necessities of their epochs. The consequences of the discoveries have indeed gone far afield, but war has always provided the basic incentive.[34]

Subsequently the report was considered by many to be a hoax, written perhaps by the economist John Kenneth Galbraith. Yet the controversy stimulated by the report was indicative of the plausibility of its thesis and the possibility of its eventual realization. It was from a reaction to a similar ideological perspective that Mohandas Gandhi had concluded that collective violence (or war) could be prevented only by man placing his full faith in the hand loom.

The conformity of nations to the ideology of Scientism has been noted recently by many authors, such as Marshall McLuhan, John Kenneth Galbraith, and Jacques Ellul. Several examples of this phenomenon might be cited, but the adequate development of this thesis is beyond the scope of this chapter. Cold War hostility, after peaking with the viciousness of the Joseph McCarthy era, has gradually abated. Government representatives have placed their emphasis upon negotiations and peaceful coexistence. Both super powers, the United States and the Soviet Union, are adherents of Scientism who have economically committed themselves to the research and development of space programs and defense systems. Indeed, the great gulf that separates the capitalist and the socialist ideol-

[33] Marshall McLuhan and Quentin Fiore, *War and Peace in the Global Village* (New York: Bantam Books, Inc., 1968), p. 124.

[34] *Report from Iron Mountain on the Possibility and Desirability of Peace,* with introduction by Leonard C. Lewin (New York: Dial Press, Inc., Macdonald and Company Ltd., 1967), p. 2.

ogies is coming to be bridged by the ideology of Scientism which both powers share. Thus many observers have noted that the Soviet Union is becoming more "capitalistic" while the United States is becoming more "socialistic." Nikita Khrushchev, the shouting, shoe-pounding, working-class leader of the Soviet Union was replaced by the well-mannered, temperate, white-collar, organization men, Leonid Bresnev and Alexei Kosygin—men whose life styles are somewhat similar to that of the President of the United States. Russian heroes and emissaries, like those of the United States, are astronauts, technocrats, and plant managers, not urban and rural proletariats. And finally, perhaps the best indication of the emerging ideological congruency between the Soviet Union and the United States is revealed by the disillusionment of the American radical leftists when they discovered that the citizens of the Soviet Union care more about space travel and colored television than about Marx's concept of alienated labor.

Obviously, it is premature to offer any conclusive statement concerning the ultimate consequences of technological progress. Yet the paradox for mankind rests in the possibility that the ultimate consequence may be either salvation or extermination.

### POLLUTION, POPULATION CONTROL, AND DRUGS

Technological pollution has become a major social issue in recent years. It is an issue which relates directly to man's ability to control his technology. To date, attempts at control appear to be half-hearted or inept. To be sure, the technological system has produced devices which are designed to control pollution—for example, afterburners which decrease the pollution caused by the systems to which they are attached. Yet the production of this anti-pollution device may generate its own pollution as a by-product. Thus pollution is merely transferred from one location or form to another. In brief, if technology rather than man is the cause of pollution, then technological "progress" will increase pollution and cannot possibly diminish it. If such is the case, the reasonable solution to the problem of pollution may be to limit technology. However, with our vast commitment to technology and our inability to restrain the "progress" of our vast corporations, as well as our unwavering faith in the ability of science to resolve all of our ecological issues, the conscious decision to limit technological advancement appears remote. Although solutions such as collecting trash and banning smoking in public areas serve to diminish our fears (as well as to trivialize the issue of pollution), they reveal man's inability to deal realistically with his new tools. Thus the utilization of ecological issues in schools as a means of inculcating the middle-class-Puritan values of cleanliness and frugality serves to popularize a sometimes naive view of a potentially volatile crisis. Man's view of his technology is shrouded in mythology, and it appears that he desires to project onto it the omnipotence that he once reserved for his god, for this sort of projection has proven to be a time-tested mechanism for avoiding responsibility.

Historically, religious "fanatics" have often prophesied the end of the world. Prayers and submission to the will of God were believed to be the means of salvation. The ideology of Scientism, however, rejected such elements and focused upon activism and control. Nature, according to Scientism, is viewed as a challenge to man, and civilization is defined as the ability of man to harness nature, control destiny, and provide solutions to all problems. Recently, however, individuals adhering to the ideology of Scientism have spoken with a quasi-religious fervor concerning the apocalyptic doom of man. Stunned by the massive problems generated by technological expansion and population explosion, these scientians avow that man's sojourn upon the earth will soon end catastrophically. They have combined the belief in the necessity of control inherent in Scientism with the belief in man's inability to control his destiny inherent in Puritanism. Although their doubt may serve to generate a variety of solutions that are not ideologically one-dimensional, their fears may produce dire consequences, for Scientism combined with the call of necessity may produce vicious results. For example, when the Jews in Germany were defined as a "problem" by the Nazis, research and propaganda eventually concluded with the call for a "final solution." The dehumanized technocrats who operated the extermination camps were not Romanticists who sought transcendence (that is, they were not Nietzschean believers in the *Übermensch*), but rather adherents of Scientism who accepted the hideous "practical solution" which their ideology legitimized.

When Scientism is popularized, technological crises generate a call for scientific solutions and a faith in the decisions of technocrats. Will the final scientific solution to overpopulation, for example, entail the institutional management of marriage selection, compulsory sterilization, infanticide, or geriatricide. Perhaps Swift's "modest proposal" to solve both hunger and overpopulation by having parents consume their children would seem less outrageous when proposed during a period defined as a crisis. Of course, his cynical proposal reveals that extremism in the pursuit of a solution is a vice, and such extreme measures probably would appeal to few individuals even in the direst of circumstances. Frightfully effective measures, however, have been discussed by some concerned individuals during the recent decade. When issues previously considered taboo receive the legitimacy of public debate, especially when such a debate is aired nationally, they are popularized, and there is a tendency for popularized views to become public policies. This foreboding possibility was noted by Jacques Ellul. In analyzing the problems of pollution and overpopulation, he admonished: "These phenomena, which have assumed such proportions that they threaten the whole of city life, are of purely technical origin. Only vigorous and authoritarian measures of general control can solve these problems if they are to be solved at all. That is to say, appeal to dictatorial state action is indispensable." [35]

Education is viewed as a moderate evolutionary approach to resolving social issues. In the United States it is generally imagined to be a panacea for social ills. Groups with as widely diversified ideologies as the Students for a Democratic Society, the John Birch Society, the National Association of Manufacturers, and the AFL-CIO regard the schools as a means of inculcating "accurate" views about social problems and their solution. When used to instill a particular ideological perspective, however, education is interchangeable with propaganda. For example, within the ideological perspective of Scientism, sex education becomes a means of resolving the issue of "prolonged childhood." It serves as a form of human engineering and as means of "teaching" children to accept social realities and to behave properly according to social expectations. Courses in drug education also serve to inculcate the scientific view of the "drug problem" and to encourage students to avoid the use of illegal drugs while ensuring that they will not be unduly concerned about the drugs to which their parents may be addicted legally. While drug education courses in school focus upon the "don'ts of drug use," the mass media, serving as propaganda agency for the drug producing corporations, popularize the use of drugs to relieve both physical and emotional discomfort. Rather than focusing upon the causes of the discomfort, the drug-oriented technological system focuses upon the temporary relief of the discomfort. Indeed, both with antisocial drug addicts and with socially acceptable addicts we tend to think that the best way to prevent the use of one drug is by the use of another, as can be seen both in methadone maintenance programs and in the various preparations people employ to help them stop smoking.

Americans live in an increasingly drug-oriented society. To single out one drug while overlooking others merely reveals a bias that gives credence to the angry protest of the young users of illegal drugs. Paradoxically, simultaneously with our increasing concern about the use of illegal drugs by many of the young, other drugs (amphetamines) are increasingly being prescribed for hyperactive youth (hyperkinetic behavioral disturbance). In which situation is the issue of drug abuse more frightening?—when an adolescent endangers his life and health by taking illegal drugs, or when responsible members of society are cowed by the

[35] Jacques Ellul, *The Technological Society* (New York: Random House, Inc., 1964), p. 237.

scientific elite into letting scientists eliminate behavior of which they disapproved by administering the appropriate drug?

Bound by an ideology of Scientism, individuals may fail to acknowledge the socioeconomic factors involved in social problems. Starvation, for example, may be rooted to the improper distribution of wealth and goods rather than to overpopulation. Similarly, quality of life may not be antithetical to quantity, especially if one assumes an economy of abundance rather than scarcity. Obviously, in the resolution of any problem, efficiency, statistics, and human engineering—the elements of Scientism— should never be a substitute for love, concern, and human rights.

### LIBERATION MOVEMENTS AND YOUTH CULTURE

As discussed previously, the social activism of the 1960s broke the apathy and quietude that characterized the previous decade. Several of the resultant liberation movements, as they have been termed, have far-reaching consequences for technological growth and reflect the pervasiveness of the ideology of Scientism. Our contemporary liberation movements certainly are not inherently revolutionary. Participants in many of them do not seek to overthrow the power structure but to assume a role within it. Advocates of women's liberation, for example, appear to fit this description. They are attempting to shed the remaining remnants of a patriarchial, Victorian era and to assume an equal role with their male counterparts in the technological system. Their call for equal pay and equal job opportunity as well as their demand for funded day-care centers will serve to legitimize the labor demands of a technological society. Furthermore, their plea for day-care centers will serve to enhance the ideological emphasis on "formal education" from birth to death. Indeed, some research technicians have performed experiments to prove that prenatal learning is possible. In the ideological language of a technocrat, 'A technological society demands that its youth be educated by trained experts according to sound scientific principles, in environments that provide for the optimal growth of one's potential.'

If successful, the recent liberation movements generated by this country's various racial and/or ethnic minorities also may enhance the ideology of Scientism. Like the advocates of women's liberation, the activist members of minority groups generally have been quite critical of the schools. Their demands for greater discipline, improved reading programs, and personal accountability can be readily adapted to the framework of Scientism. Adherents to Scientism in both the public and private realms of society have established programs founded upon quantitative tests and measurements and behavioral modification. And many educationists, befuddled by their apparent failure and fearful of additional turmoil, have relinquished their possible role as artist-teachers and accepted, perhaps reluctantly, the promises of Scientism.

Just as the industrial society destroyed the extended family, so, it is feared in some quarters, proliferation of day-care centers which is already underway in our technological, will destroy, or at least radically alter, the nuclear family. Of course, those who fear the formal institutionalization of child-rearing are opposed to such developments and express concern about the growing lack of intimate relationships, love, and family loyalty. Unfortunately, from the ideological perspective of Scientism, their view is hopelessly reactionary, if not trite. Yet it was merely a few decades ago that communal childrearing was condemned as "unAmerican" and was associated with the "totalitarianism" of Plato's *Republic* or the communism of the Soviet Union.

The lessening influence and importance of the nuclear family structure, however, provides several significant opportunities for those who enthusiastically endorse Scientism. In the first place, children in day-care centers can be studied, tested, and manipulated. Such centers can rightfully be labeled "child study" centers. They also increase the opportunity for technocrats to rationally order childrearing practices.

Secondly, as Frazier, the scientific manager of B. F. Skinner's, *Walden Two,* pointed out, "The weakening of the family structure will make experimental breeding possible." [36] Test-tube babies, artificial insemination, compulsory sterilization, genetic control, and legalized (or even compulsory) abortions are elements that comprise the language of some eugenicists.

Although such programs appear as dreams to the most ardent supporters of Scientism, they evoke nightmares in the minds of humanists. The caste system proposed by Plato in *The Republic* easily could serve as an archetype for the cybernetic society of the future. Rather than by the ideas of wise guardians, however, the masses would be governed by the scientific knowledge of benevolent technocrats. To question such a possibility, humanists must transcend the arguments based upon feasibility, for to argue on the grounds of whether proposals will or will not work is to accept the ideological framework of Scientism. The question is not whether the proposals of Scientism will work, but whether or not such endeavors are worthy of attainment. Only by formulating the questions in these terms can one transcend the ideology of Scientism.

It has become quite fashionable to praise today's young people for their social sensitivity and knowledge, especially when they are compared

---

[36] B. F. Skinner, *Walden Two* (New York: The Macmillan Company, 1948), p. 137.

to previous generations. This advance generally is attributed to increased affluence and the advent of television. Although evidence tends to support this view, further analysis is required to gain an understanding of the meaning and possible consequences of this phenomenon. Increased affluence, combined with lessened demands for labor, has resulted in an accretion in college enrollments. In a sense, we are witnessing a growing new leisure class, removed from the anxiety of immediate economic pressures and detached from the problems of familial responsibility. In the words of many parents, "they didn't live through the Depression." As with all leisure classes throughout history, some individuals have pursued a life of hedonistic pleasures (including, in this case, drugs, surfing, and rock festivals) while others have adopted a pattern of social service which results from their humanistic attitude of *noblesse oblige*. Activated by this attitude of a sense of mission, many "liberated" youth have become involved in such government programs as the Peace Corp or VISTA, or have joined groups interested in a variety of liberation movements reflecting minority aspirations.

There is some validity, however, in the more cynical view that most students will "outgrow" this sort of idealism and become supportive elements in the mainstream of American life. Indeed, some social scientists now believe that the generation gap is largely a myth enhanced by the media. Yet it is certainly difficult to deny that youth are more intellectually critical and socially active today than they were several decades ago. This fact is recognized, with some consternation, by the conservative elements in the society and also by the "taxpaying citizens" who watch with displeasure as their "hard-earned money" is taxed to "support" campus revolutionaries. Both of these critical groups, however, tend to view education as some form of vocational training rather than as a foundation for a well informed, thoughtful, and active citizenry. Although this anti-intellectual attitude has prevailed throughout our history, it has received more public attention with the increase of campus unrest. Indeed, if one is aware of the differences between education and training, one can gain better understanding of the paradox in American education—the firm commitment of the American people to "education," yet their general distrust if not ridicule of the intellectual.[37] Even the radical activists who view the educational system as the "tool of the corporate, capitalistic establishment" must reassess his position when he realizes that the vanguard of dissent rests with those individuals who have been within the formal educational system for an extensive period. College students rather than the rural or urban proletariat form the core of the revolutionary and

[37] For an excellent analysis of this phenomena, see Richard Hofstader, *Anti-Intellectualism in American Life* (New York: Random House and Alfred A. Knopf, Inc., 1963).

rebel movements.[38] Of course, Karl Marx was aware that revolutions would be enhanced by the disenchanted bourgeoisie. When one is totally committed to activism he may not have time to read or think about the individuals who offer the slogans that guide his movement.

Historically, criticism and dissent have been associated with universities. Thus, one might anticipate dissent to increase with the growing enrollment figures. But this factor alone is insufficient to explain the change in American universities in recent years. Obviously, the war in Indochina has been an important contributing factor, and the influence of television on student dissent has yet to be fully determined, although clearly it is a major factor in the socialization process in modern technocracies.

Marshall McLuhan, one of the best known authorities on the electronic media, has been vigorously criticized for his superficial treatment of significant historical forces upon man's perception and his naivety concerning the ability of the political power structure to manipulate and control the media.[39] These criticisms certainly cannot be ignored. Even if warranted, however, it is difficult to totally reject his major theses, for many of his insights obviously have some degree of validity. For example, he claimed that the present generation of students, reared with television (a cool medium), demand personal involvement, in contrast to the previous generation reared with radio and the printed word (hot media). "Any hot medium," McLuhan explains, "allows less participation than a cool one, as a lecture makes for less participation than a seminar, and a book for less than dialogue." [40] Thus television is viewed more as a collage than a painting. The viewer is bombarded by sense stimuli and placed in the world that William James described as a "blooming, buzzing confusion." Although James was describing the holistic world view of an infant, the description is applicable to the experiences of a television viewer. Students, even at the primary level, have witnessed assassinations, floods, earthquakes, wars, riots, police brutality, and images of poverty and affluence.[41] On an individual basis, they have viewed homosexuals, hip-

[38] Thus any list of contemporary rebels will include the names of Stokely Carmichael, Jerry Rubin, and Mario Savio, in addition to many lesser known individuals on campuses throughout the country. The extent to which student activists alarm the country is apparent when one reads the FBI's "most wanted list."

[39] The writings of both Herbert Marcuse and C. Wright Mills present a position in opposition to that proposed by McLuhan. See, for example, Herbert Marcuse, *One-Dimensional Man* (Boston: Beacon Press, 1964), and C. Wright Mills, *The Power Elite* (New York: Oxford University Press, 1956).

[40] McLuhan, *Understanding Media*, p. 23.

[41] During the Depression, individuals have noted that it was easier to accept poverty when one realized that many fellow citizens were poor. Similarly, poverty may have been easier to accept prior to the advent of television. Television has brought the image and perhaps the expectation of affluence ("the good life") to many poor individuals, whose previous perspective had been limited to their poverty-stricken neighbors. Rising expectations as Alexis de Tocqueville noted, cause revolutions.

pies, women "libbers," black "militants," drug addicts, racists, and hypocrites. Many students are familiar with the identity not only of the president and various movie stars and sports heroes, but also of such men as Timothy Leary, Abbie Hoffman, H. Rapp Brown, George Wallace, and Fidel Castro.

When someone "over thirty" recalls his own childhood experiences, phenomena comparable to those represented by the names just mentioned were something he read about—if he was aware of them at all. Certainly one was more aware of Booker T. Washington or George Washington Carver than of W. E. B. DuBois or Harriet Tubman, individuals who suffered from the censor's pen for their ideology. Today, however, DuBois would have appeared on the television news, establishment control of television programming notwithstanding. In fact, news is inherently different from propaganda because of its unusualness and lack of total control. It is in this sense that McLuhan states that all real news is bad news. Of course, sensate experience or sheer awareness should not be confused with knowledge or wisdom—the elements of education. To be "acquainted with" or "aware of" racism is one thing; to be "knowledgeable about" it is quite something else. But even so, the fact remains that the increased sensate experience and awareness of students provides a rich and varied atmosphere from which the artist-teacher can elicit opinion and intellectually explore ideological patterns, thus resulting in more meaningful and relevant educational experiences.

Television has been criticized for a variety of reasons by various individuals and groups. "High culture" connoisseur have condemned it for catering to mass tastes. From their perspective, the "boob tube" results in mediocrity and triviality. Political activists and politicians on both the right and the left believe that television is a tool of the "other side"—that is, either the liberal, eastern establishment or the corporate power elite. Both groups believe the "other side" obviously lacks objectivity and intentionally distorts reality, thus producing a credibility gap. Moralists, of course, are concerned about violence, sex, and racism. The common element among critics, as McLuhan points out, resides in their consensus that television is degrading and corrupting.

Besides its overt impact on student awareness, television also indirectly influences the radio and film industries. With the advent of television the format of radio changed to primarily news and music programming. This change resulted in the establishment of radio stations whose primary function was devoted to "rock music," thus aiding in the creation of a "youth culture." The young also comprise the majority of individuals who attend the movies today. The vast change in the age of those who attend motion picture theaters is intimately related to the change in the subject matter of films.

The relationship of the movies to television perfectly exemplifies

McLuhan's claim that "Each new technology creates an environment that is itself regarded as corrupt and degrading. Yet the new one turns its predecessor into an art form." [42] Thus television has made movies an art form just as the printed word made dialogue an art form. The return of the classic films, with their heroes such as W. C. Fields, Humphrey Bogart, and the Marx Brothers, is one indication of this phenomenon. As further evidence, one could cite the subject matter of new movies, which is that of movies found previously only in "art" theaters, as well as the methods and technique, including fancy cameras angles, still shots, and quick cutting. Just as art forms were a leisure-class pursuit in the past, so are they today: movies have become an art form primarily for college students, the newly educated leisure class.

Today we face a grave danger that the mass of unexamined experiences available from television, radio, and movies, may be taken, especially by the young, as an alternative to education rather than as a valuable adjunct to it. Rather than replacing dialogue, intellectual exploration, and teachers, these media make liberal education under the direction of artist-teachers all the more necessary. This perspective is in stark contrast to the view of "education" advocated by adherents of Scientism, who tend to think of education in terms of fragmented subject matter, specialization, programmed instruction, operant conditioning, and managerial control. It should be noted, however, that, partly as a consequence of humanist criticism, the vocabulary of Scientism has adopted much of the terminology usually associated with humanism. Thus manipulation is described as "guidance," programmed learning is called "individualized instruction" (meeting individual needs and differences), obedience to pre-established methods is labeled "self-reliance" or "motivation," and attaining the answers to programmed questions is defended as "thinking" and "creativity." If we are to assess the current state of education, we must be on the lookout for this scientific doublethink.

### Conclusion

At the beginning of this chapter, an attempt was made to distinguish between the scientist and the technician, between science and technology. Developments during the twentieth century, however, have served to obscure these differences. This century has witnessed the immense growth of vast bureaucratic enterprises, characterized by an intricate division of labor and a corollary system of management. In addition, the enormous proliferation of technological developments has created many new occupa-

[42] McLuhan, *Understanding Media,* p. viii.

tions with roles and functions very difficult to define with such traditional terms as scientist and technician. Consequently, as Ellul has so aptly observed, "In every instance, it is clear that the border between technical activity and scientific activity is not at all sharply defined." [43]

The story of Frankenstein typified the general image of the scientist as a lonely individual, obsessed with his work and performing a complicated task based upon the principles of many scientific fields. Today, however, the "Monster" probably would be the product of a vast bureaucratic enterprise under the management of a committee comprised of the representatives of giant corporations. Research would be heavily subsidized by the government and the project would be listed, perhaps, with the Department of Defense in liaison with the Pentagon. Research also would be developed by privately operated "think tanks" and/or universities. As in an assembly line, each member involved in the production would develop only a minute part of the whole, with little knowledge of the completed project and little understanding of the highly specialized work of other members. If the finished "Monster" went berserk—through mismanagement of course—and turned on its creator, would responsibility lie with the corporate executive, the Secretary of Defense, the professor, the lab assistant, or the taxpayer? Here we envision the complex problem encountered during the Nuremberg trials, for vast bureaucratic structures are characterized by what C. Wright Mills termed "organized irresponsibility." No one or everyone is to blame. As James Conant, himself a scientist, admonished, ". . . if science were too individualistic and anarchic fifty years ago, the danger now lies in the opposite direction." [44]

The problem of resolving issues of individual responsibility and ethical judgement in the vast bureaucratic centers of scientific research is complicated by the technological naivety that serves to enhance man's faith in Scientism. This frequently expressed naivety is typified in the sentiments attributed to General David Sarnoff: "We are too prone to make technological instruments the scapegoats for the sins of those who wield them. The products of modern science are not in themselves good or bad; it is the way they are used that determines their value." [45] This cliché is fairly representative of current conventional wisdom regarding technological development, whether it be an improved magnifying lens or the hydrogen bomb. The lens is good if utilized in a microscope; it is bad if used to set fire to the science room. Similarly, the bomb is good if used to destroy the enemy; it is bad if detonated among allies.

Such an orientation hinders attempts to assess adequately the con-

[43] Ellul, *The Technological Society*, p. 8.
[44] James B. Conant, *Science and Common Sense* (New Haven: Yale University Press, 1951), p. 312.
[45] Quoted in McLuhan, *Understanding Media*, p. 11.

sequences of science and technology. In the first place, by putting total responsibility of technological usage on man, one directs the analyses away from an examination of technology itself and toward a criticism of man. Consequently, if the fruits of Scientism prove to be detrimental, man stands accused—either because of his nature or his mismanagement; the tools themselves are never questioned, much as primitive believers in the powers of a witch doctor attribute failures to some fault in the practioner rather than in the practice itself. Second, such a view, when discussing such technological instruments as atomic bombs and deadly nerve gas, assumes a dichotomous world comprised of allies and enemies. Without such a perspective such instruments would be of no value. Indeed, arguments for the necessity of these instruments are based upon such an assumption; and it is to the interest of those corporations or individuals whose socioeconomic position is enhanced by the development of such technological weapons to create an enemy even if one did not exist. Third, such a view assumes that technological instruments are extraneous to the nature of man rather than, as McLuhan aptly labeled them, "extensions of man." Such an assumption obscures the inevitable reciprocal relationship between technology and man. A hammer, for example, is in the purely physical sense an extension of a man's arm and hand and obviously is directed by him, but the man's use of the hammer effects the muscular development of his arm and perhaps even influences his psyche. Similarly, a rifle may make a man feel "ten feet tall," and in a very real sense it is an extension of his physical stature; indeed, out west it was labeled "the equalizer" because of the way it leveled differences in the relative sizes of adversaries. Fanatical adherents to Scientism, however, generally dismiss questions concerning such reciprocal influences, and as a result their perspective of both man and technology remains biased and confined.

In the field of education the consequences of this reciprocal phenomenon have been scarcely examined, but they raise a myriad of questions. Technological hardware, for example, serves as an extension of a student. What effect will this have on him? If a child raised by a wolf is frighteningly wolflike, what will a child reared among computers or television sets be like? What reciprocal influences occur with the usage of reinforcement techniques? Will the total effects be known immediately, or will it take decades for these technological chickens to come home to roost? [46]

From the issues raised in this chapter, it is obvious that Scientism, like all other ideologies, has its own language, symbols, values, saints, and sinners. According to Scientism, sinners—that is, ideological deviants—are

---

[46] For a story of a child reared without love and understanding, see Bruno Bettelheim, "Joey: A 'Mechanical Boy,'" in *Man Alone*, ed. Eric and Mary Josephson (New York: Dell Publishing Co., Inc., 1962), p. 437.

considered illiterate, irrational, mystical, emotive, traditional, and religious. They are usually found among the Romanticists, humanists, and fundamental religionists. The saints are probably best typified by the heroes of "man's greatest technological achievement in history"—the astronauts. Generally, they are WASPs—white Anglo-Saxon Protestants—from small towns in middle America who attended land-grant universities and specialized in the practical sciences. From the perspective of Sinclair Lewis, they are the sons of Babbitt. Their personality and performance is rather indicative of the interrelationship of Puritanism (their background) and Scientism (their vocation). They appear to be rather repressed, rational, and programmed with a sense of mission, discipline, and dedication.

The moon landings represent the logical extension of the origins of technology in this country. The aerospace programs stand as a shrine to the modern religion, Scientism, and like other shrines, this one is constructed in the midst of the poor who bear the burden of its creation and existence, just as in the past when the great religions created the medieval cathedrals, the Taj Mahal, and the pyramids.

Of course in the past the poor had to take pilgrimages to the shrine, but today television brings the cathedrals of Scientism into the home. This vicarious experience, however, lacked the passion and commitment of the personal involvement that accompanied true pilgrimages. The moon, for centuries the subject of romance, mystery, and folk wisdom, has been claimed by the ideology of Scientism. Yet the banalizing power of Scientism and television have managed to turn a potentially magnificent and awe-inspiring episode into a mundane, routinized, and boring event. Regardless of attempts to recapture the interest of the spectators through a lunar golf game and Madison Avenue techniques, the product has lost its sales appeal. As televised, the program is becoming little more than a commercial for technology. Millions of people will observe a romantic or tragic event, but few will remain transfixed by a commercial.

Few individuals could doubt the benefits secured by the tremendous accomplishments of science and technology. Indeed, dependency upon them approaches the level of a neurotic need and they are taken so much for granted that our dependency is noticeable only when we are without them. New discoveries are rapidly accepted and "progress" becomes commonplace. With the ideology of Scientism, there is general agreement with the adage "whatever the mind of man can conceive he will someday do." It appears that science fiction inevitably becomes fact. Indeed, the degree to which an individual or a culture adheres to the ideology of Scientism has become the standard by which modern man measures his level of civilization. Consequently, to be critical of Scientism places an individual in a position of being opposed to "progress" and, indeed, against civilization. For the true believers of Scientism, criticism implies a reactionary belief in the "good old days" or perhaps a longing to return to the age of the caveman and the jungle of the Noble Savage. Obviously, this is not *the* alternative; in fact, it is not even *an* alternative. At best, an individual can empathize with and perhaps retain a romantic attachment to the adventures of Huck Finn and the natural goodness of Tarzan.

This chapter was written with the assumption that mankind will continue to exist in an increasingly technological society. It is assumed also that technology influences the life of man and, more importantly, that man can influence technological development. Indeed, without the belief in man's ability to control his destiny, criticism would be not only cynical but also irrelevant.

If technological development has brought us the good life, the question still remains open as to whether man, with the aid of technology, can create a better one. Hope lies only in our ability to range beyond the narrow limitations imposed by the fanatics of Scientism. Otherwise, man is faced with the terrifying prospect expressed so cogently by Karl Mannheim. Fearing the absolute and total triumph of such ideologies as Scientism, he admonished: ". . . the complete elimination of reality-transcending elements from our world would lead us to a 'matter of factness' which ultimately would mean the decay of the human will." [47]

## Suggested Readings

Coser, Lewis A. *Men of Ideas.* New York: The Macmillan Company, 1965.

Ellul, Jacques. *The Technological Society.* New York: Random House, Inc., 1964.

Feigl, Herbert, and May Brodbeck. *Readings in the Philosophy of Science.* New York: Appleton-Century-Crofts, 1953.

Ferkiss, Victor C. *The Technological Man: The Myth and the Reality.* New York: The New American Library, Inc., 1969.

Galbraith, John Kenneth. *The New Industrial State.* New York: The New American Library, Inc., 1967.

McLuhan, Marshall. *Understanding Media: The Extension of Man.* New York: McGraw-Hill Book Company, 1964.

Mills, C. Wright. *White Collar.* New York: Oxford University Press, 1951.

Mumford, Lewis. *The Transformations of Man.* New York: The Crowell-Collier Publishing Company, 1956.

Reichenbach, Hans. *The Rise of Scientific Philosophy.* Berkeley and Los Angeles: University of California Press, 1951.

Roszak, Theodore. *The Making of a Counter Culture.* Garden City, N.Y.: Doubleday & Company, Inc., 1968.

[47] Karl Mannheim, *Ideology and Utopia: An Introduction to the Sociology of Knowledge* (New York: Harcourt, Brace, Jovanovich, Inc., 1936), p. 262.

SANTILLANA, GIORGIO DE. *The Origins of Scientic Thought.* New York: The New American Library of World Literature, Inc., 1961.

SKINNER, B. F. *The Technology of Teaching.* New York: Appleton-Century-Crofts, 1968.

WHITEHEAD, ALFRED NORTH. *Science and the Modern World.* New York: The New American Library of World Literature, Inc., 1962.

WHYTE, WILLIAM H., JR. *The Organization Man.* Garden City, N.Y.: Doubleday & Company, Inc., 1956.

WIENER, NORBERT. *The Human Use of Human Beings.* Boston: Houghton Mifflin Company, 1950.

## Chapter 3

# ROMANTICISM
## The Ideology of the Artist

### Introduction

While numerous strands are woven into the ideological fabric of social systems, two belief systems are always present in varying degrees. All social systems will reflect the "pull and tug" between these two countervailing ideological forces—Scientism, which was the focus of the previous chapter, and Romanticism, which is discussed in this one. Together they give scope to man's individual and associative needs. Whereas the absence of Scientism (also labeled Classicism, Technism, or Realism) would inhibit constructive collective action, the removal of Romanticism would result in social atrophy and the obliteration of human creativity. Without strands from these two ideological antinomies, social systems could not flourish and the humanization of *homo sapiens* would falter.

The ideology of Scientism expresses man's desire and need for logical order and unity; reveals his ability to reason, plan, and organize; and emphasizes his psychological dependency upon institutions. Scientism provides a rationale for planned evolutionary change as well as a defense for the externally imposed standards which legitimize the patterns of behavior that support the *status quo*. Scientism offers material progress and security. Wylie Sypher, noting the essentially methodological and cautious nature of Scientism, wrote: "The engineer (the applied scientist at his extreme) must master the contingent. The technologist dreads surprises; indeed, he must not be surprised. He predicts everything—and, in a sense, discovers nothing. Technism might be defined as a conquest without surprise—or perhaps a conclusion without risk." [1] Jacques Barzun concisely made a similar observation: "Man explores and is romantic; man wants repose and becomes classical." [2] Scientism offers predictability, reliability, and security; Romanticism implies surprise and risk because

[1] Wylie Sypher, *Literature and Technology: The Alien Vision* (New York: Random House, Inc., 1968), p. 8.
[2] Jacques Barzun, *Romanticism and the Modern Ego* (Boston: Little, Brown & Co., 1947), p. 197.

the romantic ideology exposes man's drive to express his uniqueness, his love of diversity and mystery, and his thirst for spontaneity, authenticity, and individuality. Rather than logic and scientific hypotheses, imagination and intuition design the life style of the romanticist.

Both Scientism and Romanticism, and the uneasy truce which exists between them, reflect man's continuous struggle to affirm his individuality and to construct and sustain orderly, complex social systems. Although both ideologies have existed wherever human social groupings have been formed, their particularized expression within a given social tapestry results from historical antecedents, cultural factors, environmental stimuli, and other ideological systems which intermingle with them. Thus, it is more accurate to speak of Romanticisms because social environments differ and produce psychological conditions which result in unique expressions of the romantic ideology.

All human beings reflect, at times, the rebellious nature of the romanticist and reveal the agonizing search for the wonderful rather than the acceptance of the probable. Moderate men sometimes dream of rejecting moderation. The child who dreams of escaping with a circus troupe or an interplanetary exploration team, the adolescent who hopes to join an experimental agrarian or urban commune, and the businessman who fantasizes about a South Sea adventure all reflect the romantic urge to reject the existing social system for a liberated and exotic life style. Indeed, most romantic literature and theater serve, in part, to satisfy, channel, and perhaps control the rebellious wanderlust that is rooted in man's individuality.

Although all human beings manifest some romantic elements, not all human beings are romanticists. Romanticism necessitates that its adherents assume an anti-status-quo stance and that they *actively* and *sincerely* struggle against the centripetal forces of socialization. All social systems invariably strive to moderate individual differences, but the adherents of Romanticism assume the role of diminishing or nullifying the homogenizing forces of socialization by accentuating the unique characteristics of individuals. The romanticists differ, therefore, from fantasy adventurers by behaving according to their rebellious aspirations. Their motto was expressed lucidly by a twentieth-century romantic spokesman, Jerry Rubin, when he admonished: "Do It!"

In some social systems, the strands of Romanticism and Scientism are meshed into the institutional patterns and are often barely distinguishable from one another. In modern societies, for example, religious sects sometimes succeed in bridging the discrepancies between Scientism and Romanticism. It is the small preindustrialized communities—the Gemeinschafts, to use Ferdinand Tonnies' term—that best illustrate the manner in which the struggle between the romanticists and the adherents of

Scientism may be institutionalized and moderated, for it is within such communities that the forces of Scientism and Romanticism form an *entente*. The importance of tradition, the clearly defined rules and roles, the simplicity of daily tasks, the rites of passage, and the patterns of cultural isolation served to preserve social cohesion—the pivotal concern of the partisans of Scientism. The romantic needs of individuals within such a social system, however, were often expressed easily because close individual and nonformal ties were encouraged, cross-role communication was enhanced by the lack of extensive and complex specialization, and the opportunities for personal heroic acts were maximized within the hostile natural environment. Also, the absence of rapid social change permitted relationships to form, ripen, and persist. The belief in magic and the reliance upon myths enabled individuals to transcend the bland exigencies of practical daily life. Dreams and imagination combined with colorful oral traditions to form a people's view of their history and served as a source of aesthetic and spiritual rejuvenation.

Institutions within preindustrial tribal communities reflected both Scientism and Romanticism: counter-institutions were not needed and were not developed. The frequently-noted power struggle between tribal shamans, the harbingers of Romanticism, and tribal leaders, reveals in part the institutionalized patterns for resolving ideological conflicts. While the tribal leaders reflected the practical demands and political exigencies inherent in Scientism, the shamans often presented an eccentric view of life revealed to them through magic, insight, and unrepressed emotions. Through elaborate ritualistic patterns, shamans moderated the pressures of matter-of-fact affairs placed upon tribal members and furnished them with the opportunity for transcendence or liberation. In numerous cases drugs were utilized to enhance the influence of the imagination over perception. Through elaborate rites of passage, often accompanied by heroic acts of individual perseverance, the youth within such groupings found an avenue for expressing their individual nonrational natures while gaining social acceptance. Both the rituals of the shamans and the rites of passage reveal an essential quality of Romanticism—the rejection of objective consciousness and the reliance upon subjective experiences as a source of knowledge and truth.

### The Modern Crisis

Today the tenuous *entente* between Romanticism and Scientism is endangered by a number of alterations in the emerging social patterns. Urbanization, industrialization, and efficient political centralization gradually have replaced small, isolated, and homogenized mini-communities with massive political and economic groupings. The warmth of tribal communities increasingly has been chilled by the cold wind of society.

With the centralization of political power, the forces of "law and order" as well as the elaborate institutional means of controlling human behavior come to exert an inordinate influence over individual life. Technological advancements such as the invention of "snooping devices" enhance the power of the social system. Even the humanitarian efforts to coordinate massive social programs may serve to nullify erratic human behavior that may be judged socially dysfunctional. Often the romantic needs of individuals are ignored or suppressed in order to achieve a highly functional and social service-oriented society. The forces of repression are not necessarily the result of fascistic aims or profit-oriented ambitions. A massive welfare system, for example, may serve to protect large numbers of innocent victims of poverty or illness, but it also may serve to diminish individual acts of benevolence as depersonalized social services replace individual and neighborhood cooperative charitable ventures. In the name of efficiency and order, the two harbingers of Romanticism, individual involvement and compassion, are often sacrificed. As Christopher Caudwell, a Marxist ideologist, observed with some justification: "The bourgeois, with each fresh demand he makes for individualism, free competition, absence of social relations and more equality, only brings to birth greater organization, more complex social relations, higher degrees of trustification and combination, more inequality." [3] Of course, latter-day Marxism produces similar results when it is combined with Scientism. The paradox at the root of the modern dilemma lies in the fact that humanitarian reform provides the impetus for increases in political centralization.

The massing of large numbers of peoples within extended social systems—especially when such systems were characterized by cultural pluralism—demanded efficient and effective means of socialization. Toward this end public school systems were developed and structured to enhance the sharing of common educational experiences by the children and youth of the citizenry. While such public school systems enhanced the experiential opportunities of students and teachers, they also served to diminish the opportunity to express individual acts of creativity. Thus individual and cultural differences often were sacrificed in attempting to prepare an informed public. In the name of the democratic process, the benevolent forces of Progressivism sometimes served to de-individualize school behavior. Within such an educational environment, Johnny would learn more about exotic foreign lands than he would about himself, for individuality was put down as firmly as rebellion—which is hardly surprising

[3] Christopher Caudwell, *Illusion and Reality: A Study of the Sources of Poetry* (London: Macmillan and Company, Ltd., 1937), p. 101.

inasmuch as individuality and rebellion were often held to be the same thing.

Besides the massing of individuals and power within maxi-social groupings, recent historical developments in the intellectual life of man have served to diminish his reliance upon the emotional and intuitive aspects of his nature. The exponential achievements brought about by the application of scientific principles and procedures, as well as the elaborate and complex systems of production, transportation, and communication which they have generated, have served to diminish the importance of knowledge derived from nonscientific sources. Revelation, insight, and intuition are often discarded as archaic and invalid sources of knowledge. This scientification of life has increased human alienation because it ignores the poorly understood but ever-present emotional, aesthetic, and spiritual needs of man.

The centralization of economic power ushered in by the Industrial Revolution and exponentially increased by the technological and computer revolutions, while increasing and extending the gift of affluence, also has restricted the opportunity for nonrational and creative self-expression. Because automation demands methodology and standardization, freedom can easily be forsaken in the name of affluence and progress. Northrop Frye accurately observed:

> Technology cannot of itself bring about an increase in human freedom, for technological developments threaten the structure of society, and society develops a proportionate number of restrictions to contain them. The automobile increases the speed and freedom of individual movement, and thereby brings a proportionate increase in police authority, with its complication of laws and penalties. In proportion as the production of retail goods becomes more efficient, the quality of craftsmanship and design decreases.[4]

Because of technological complexity, social change, geographical extension, specialization, and urbanization, national collectivities have experienced increasing anomie as their citizenries reveal the symptoms of future shock and alienation. Ethnic, religious, racial, age, and socioeconomic differences are emphasized in such a way that they militate against the formation of the group identity needed for healthy emotional life. When the "we-feeling" corrodes and anomie becomes acute, the citizens suffering from insecurity come to rely increasingly upon the "facts" presented to them by specialists and experts. The debilitating influence of excessive Scientism was reflected by Theodore Roszak when he wrote: "Under the technocracy we become the most scientific of societies; yet, like Kafka's K., men throughout the 'developed world' become more and

---

[4] Northrop Frye, *The Modern Century* (Toronto: Oxford University Press, 1967), p. 40.

more bewildered dependents of inaccessible castles wherein inscrutable technicians conjure with their fate." [5]

In modern mass nation-states, therefore, the marriage between the ideologies of Scientism and Romanticism has gradually eroded, with Scientism reaping the rewards from the separation. National institutions, especially schools, increasingly resort to indoctrinating the citizenry according to the principles of Scientism, and often the authoritarian personality becomes a goal model for the socialization process. In periods of profound cultural transition, this indoctrination into the belief system of Scientism may turn out to be more significant educationally and politically than the overt but often bland and watered-down indoctrination into the national political creed. Because Scientism rests upon the acceptance of the status quo, schools focus upon restraint and methodology rather than upon liberty and creativity. The individual's unfulfilled creative needs become a major source of social irritation, especially when education according to Scientism is combined with boredom. Widespread alienation, especially among the young, easily results in militant social activism. Thus the alienation of youth has created a movement that gains its character by rejecting whatever elements of Scientism the Establishment considers important. In analyzing the need to overcome the inability to act which characterizes alienation, Morse Peckham observed:

> The Romantic solution has always been cultural transcendence, the construction of a metaphysics or a way of making sense out of the world and the derivation of sets of values which are antithetical and dialectical in relation to the metaphysics and values of the existing culture. Cultural transcendence is in particular something to be achieved by denying the validity of the form of human behavior which currently has the highest status and is believed to be the area in which more important problems are to be found and the most important solutions are to be achieved, the area of human activity which is the ultimate source of human values.[6]

In recent years, the United States has witnessed a significant movement toward the bifurcation of its culture—or, more accurately, a disjunction in its ideological system. Indeed, because these cleavages characterize most highly technocratized nation-states, the United States, as the model of twentieth-century technological development, has often been accused of exporting cultural malaise throughout the world. Although America's recently revitalized cultural pluralism and her inadequately implemented democratic creed have been blamed for this schizophrenic development, the major cause of the emergence of "counter-

---

[5] Theodore Roszak, *The Making of a Counter Culture: Reflections on the Technocratic Society and Its Youthful Opposition* (Garden City, N.Y.: Doubleday & Company, Inc., 1969), p. 13.

[6] Morse Peckham, *The Triumph of Romanticism: Collected Essays* (Columbia: University of South Carolina Press, 1970), pp. 243–44.

cultures," wherever they have appeared, in fact can be traced to the excesses of Scientism demanded by burgeoning technocratized societies.

The bifurcation of American ideology, of course, is not complete. Indeed, recent developments appear to indicate that a re-meshing of the ideological fabric is occurring. While the Establishment—i.e., the collective adherents of the ideology of Scientism—reflects Scientism's often obsessive concern for modernization and its belief in a future designed by the fusion of technology, Nationalism, and bureaucratic impersonalism, the Establishment itself is not devoid of romantic elements. Similarly, while partisans of the counterculture focus upon individual qualities, express their distrust of institutions, and explore the worlds of the nonconscious and extranatural, they also seek to establish new institutions, to develop new legal systems, and to organize economic and professional unions. Thus it should be noted that poets and priests may be found in the Establishment while technicians, legalists, and authoritarian leaders exist in the world of the counterculture.

Of course, this mutual interpenetration of the cultural mainstream and the counterculture is often the result of the former's desire to exploit the latter. The American economic system with its rugged collective profiteering has amply utilized countercultural elements as a means of popularizing the consumer ethic. The music and clothing industries, for example, are greatly indebted to Romanticism. Indeed, the popularization of the counterculture by "Madison Avenue" has served to bring about a rapprochement between the partisans of Scientism and of Romanticism. Present developments seem to indicate the gradual institutionalization of the counterculture within the boundaries of the Establishment. The modern theater and mass media also have played a major role in helping to bridge the gap between these two ideological systems. Of course, the demassing of the counterculture does not imply the demise of Romanticism. Rather, it will serve to authenticate the romantic partisans who remain within the alien role when alienation is no longer a badge of courage or a popular symbol of identity.

While current socialization patterns, especially that of the adolescent, appear to indicate that the extreme disjunction between the Establishment and the counterculture may be moderating, authentic romanticists will continue to assert themselves and will be viewed by the majority of people as outcastes, vagabonds, hoboes, and bohemians. Even though the present fluid interchange between the two ideological forces of Scientism and Romanticism is making it increasingly difficult to distinguish authentic from synthetic hippies, the fact remains that Scientism and Romanticism are ideological antinomies and can never be fully meshed. The nature of the romantic ideology is based upon the fact that it stands in a rebellious position to the social order.

Each ideology provides its adherents with a language system. Such a language system is changeable, and numerous romantic terms are appropriated by the adherents of the Establishment, but the romantic dictionary still differs markedly from that of the partisans of Scientism. While Scientism furnishes us with such terms as *cybernetics, input* and *output, human component, comunication networks, behavior modification,* and *systems analysis,* the language of Romanticism includes terms which reflect the romantic cosmology—*communion, ripoff, hippie, cat, copout, authentic, oneness,* and *cool.* Often the romanticist's utilization of superlatives reflects the intensity of his subjectivism and expresses man's highest aims and dreams. In an age of rapid change however, terms are swiftly created and discarded, especially within language systems which are primarily oral. Lawrence Lipton in *The Holy Barbarians* furnished the reader a glossary of Hipster terminology. Although written less then fifteen years ago, many of the terms he noted are outdated.[7] Such terms as "chick," "gasser," "groovy," and "hipster" are no longer popular and would be looked upon with dismay by the more modern romanticists. As Kenneth Rexroth observed: "Only squares and elderly Communist bureaucrats in the minor Balkan countries used the term 'beatnik' after 1960."[8] To remain *au courant* in the world of Romanticism requires a great deal of linguistic agility. Of course, in addition to verbal communication, romanticists also rely upon a variety of nonverbal gestures and symbols—a particular handshake, a peace emblem, or a specific movement of the fingers or hand.

Each ideology also provides its disciples with its saints and priests. To the technocrat, Saint Von Braun and Saint Einstein are revealed in their sanctity by their high priests, Father Shepard and Father Armstrong. Their cathedrals rise majestically into heaven and serve to awe the faithful into unquestioning belief in the religion of Scientism. The romanticists also have their sanctified heroes—St. Robert Dylan, the melancholic poet, and St. Paul McCartney, who was by some said to have died even though he continued to sing with the Beatles. Their priests, Father Alan Watts and Father Timothy Leary, speak of strange exotic ways to escape from the debased pragmatism inherent in life within technological societies. The English visionary and poet, William Blake (1757-1827) furnished a litany for the followers of Romanticism in his list of Proverbs from Hell. Among them he included: "The road of excess leads to the palace of wisdom," "Prudence is a rich, ugly old maid courted by Incapacity," "No bird soars too high, if he soars with his own wings," "Prisons are built

---

[7] Lawrence Lipton, *The Holy Barbarians* (New York: Julian Messner, Inc., 1959).

[8] Kenneth Rexroth, *The Alternative Society: Essays from the Other World* (New York: Herder and Herder, 1970), p. 105.

with stones of Law, Brothels with bricks of Religion," "What is now proved, was once only imagin'd," "Always be ready to speak your mind, and a base man will avoid you," "Exuberance is Beauty," "The tygers of wrath are wiser than the horses of instruction," "Sooner murder an infant in its cradle than nurse unacted desires." [9]

### Romanticism: The Ideology of Rebellion

Romanticism is the ideology of the rebel. It is reflected in the life style and value system of the prophet, the visionary the bohemian, the cynical philosopher, the vagabond, and the disenchanted bourgeois. It necessitates a demand for critical disaffiliation, for romanticists reject all *imposed* restrictions and standards. Romanticists are rugged individualists, especially in the realm of ethics, and they are uncompromising and often vociferous in their demand for the right of self-expression. In rejecting all external commandments, they rely upon their imagination and intuition in their search for truth. Thus Romanticism as an ideology is lampooned both by the true believers in the status quo and by revolutionary zealots. Romanticists are not motivated by the forms of collective power nor do they react to the call of expediency, for their life style and their ethical stance necessitate that they avoid any form of authority which does not rest upon defiance—that is, any form of authority which rests upon institutional sanctions rather than upon charisma. Romanticists, therefore, by definition, must remain marginal to functional social systems as well as peripheral to organized social movements. Their marginality and consequently their alienation may be the result of choice or circumstances, but their rejection of all social systems is conscious and energetically propounded.

Romanticism is the ideology of defiance. Its targets are invariably the hypocritical pretensions of the Brahmins who rule social systems or who direct mass movements, as well as the styles, manners, and behavioral patterns imposed by institutions. Romanticism thus assumes a countenance which is antithetic to the norms and values of existing systems. It is dedicated to unmasking the dehumanizing and de-individualizing elements in all functional systems. Indeed, the attacks of these antagonists are often upon the fundamental metaphysical assumptions of their civilization. Thus José Ferrater Mora, observing the philosophical stance of the ancient Greek romanticists, the Cynics, wrote:

[9] William Blake, "The Marriage of Heaven and Hell," in Geoffrey Keynes, ed., *The Complete Writings of William Blake* (New York: Random House, Inc., 1957), pp. 150–52.

The Cynic could be ascetic or moderately hedonistic. It made no difference; all he sought to do was to survive in the universal shipwreck. To the rest of mankind, he said—he screamed—"You really believe in nothing, and it is vain that you try to hide it. Why struggle to preserve your empty conventions? Act as you feel, as you are; perhaps by doing so you will achieve the one thing for which, at bottom, you hope—to save yourselves." [10]

The rebellion of the romanticists against convention as well as their rejection of the taboos and philosophical assumptions which inform their society often result in social alienation and ostracism. Rebels become a dispossessed class characterized by economic and social insecurity.

Because romanticists, by definition, assume an antagonistic role against all or part of the social system in which they find themselves, Romanticism is an anti-ideology. It assumes its character in its opposition to a system and thus does not carry within its design any particular ideological assumptions except rebellion. To be sure, the ideology of Romanticism often includes particular utopian constructs, but such constructs will differ according to circumstances. The one constant feature of all romantic ideologies is the fact that the romantic "ideal" system is antithetic to the existing system and serves to weaken the hold of the status quo upon peoples. The status quo thesis defines the romantic antithesis. Romanticism, therefore, is a reaction against a tradition, a way of life, a form of social organization, or a system of beliefs. The dependency of the romantic ideology upon the Establishment is revealed by the fact that romanticists invariably define themselves by debunking the adherents of Scientism; Antigone *needed* Creon.

Often the romanticist's description of the Establishment is an oversimplified and distorted view. Such criticism can best be understood by an analysis of the ideological assumptions of Romanticism rather than by a detailed study of the Establishment itself. Although the romantic construct is often a caricature of the Establishment, like all caricatures it reflects elements of truth and often detects the most obvious flaws. During the latter part of the eighteenth century and early nineteenth century, for example, romanticists created a mythical view of the Enlightenment as well as a distorted image of the social patterns of their time. The restrictions imposed by literary academies as well as the limitations inherent in relying solely upon the intellect easily served as targets for the wrath of the romantic militants. Similarly, the excessive reliance upon the bland and often meaningless terminology which characterizes political and scientific discourse in modern nation-states serves to amuse the rebel.

[10] José Ferrater Mora, *Man at the Crossroads* (Boston: Beacon Press, 1957), p. 16.

Because of the romanticists' success in getting people to accept the romanticists' own definitions of their enemies, they enhance their position by forcing their targets to expend great effort simply in attempting to answer the romanticists' often dubious charges.

Romanticism rejects the ideologies of existing institutions because romanticists believe that institutions corrupt human nature. In contrast to the prevailing puritan sentiment of his time, the eighteenth-century French romanticist Jean-Jacques Rousseau asserted: "All things are good as they came out of the hands of the Creator, but everything degenerated in the hands of men." [11] "Man is born free," Rousseau explained; "and everywhere he is in chains." [12] This romanticist belief in man's natural goodness and liberty secularized the problem of evil, just as Machiavelli had secularized the problem of politics. In answering the theodicy question—that is, if God is good, why is evil present in the world?—the romanticist replies that evil is caused by the institutions of society. An early American romanticist, Henry David Thoreau, agreed with Rousseau in his disdain for institutions; "where there is a lull of truth," Thoreau asserted, "an institution springs up." Romanticists believe that all societies, especially functional ones, are corrupting and that everything possible should be done to weaken their influence.

Romanticism generally appears as a major movement during periods of profound social change and economic affluence. Beginning as minor political critics, romanticists extend their influence by increasing the dissatisfaction among the newly affluent classes. Their rhetoric and unorthodox behavior helps them to loosen the hold which Scientism has upon the minds of the citizenry. The sudden upsurge of influence of the romanticists during periods of social change appears to be due, in part, to the general malaise created by the rapid change of life styles occasioned by economic expansion.

In addition to the sense of crisis which often accompanies rapid change, the ancillary disparity between a society's ideals and reality also serves the rebel cause. Social systems during periods of affluence tend to loosen the puritanical moral codes which were devised during times of revolution and nation-building. The problem of moral dissolution is accentuated by the fact that former national leaders are presented to the people as quasi-mythological figures. Thus governments and government leaders of the past appear to be heroically ethical and saintly. The leaders

[11] *Emile; or, A Treatise on Education,* translated from the French of J. J. Rousseau, Citizen of Geneva, in 3 vols. (Edinburgh: Printed for J. Dickson and C. Elliot, 1772), I, 1.

[12] Jean-Jacques Rousseau, *The Social Contract, and Discourses,* Everyman's Library edition (New York: Dutton and Company, 1914), Book I, Chap. I, II, IV, p. 5.

of the present social order in comparison pale into insignificance, thus weakening faith in the political process and in the prevailing moral codes.

The loosening of the moral tone which accompanies affluence does not shock most romanticists, who tend to be libertarian rather than puritanical, rather, it arouses their wrath because of the hypocritical stance often adopted by social leaders faced with relaxing value systems. Inasmuch as the romanticists prize authenticity and openness, hypocrisy and civility make favorite targets for their animosity. Thus, during the ferment of the 1960s when the radical movement (a brief alliance between romanticists and revolutionaries) emerged, the stance of the political liberal often received their scorn. Landau and Jacobs wrote:

> The Movement rejects the careers and life styles of the American liberal too, for the Movement it is the liberal way of life and frame of mind that represent the evil of America. Those in The Movement feel that modern American liberals have substituted empty rhetoric for significant content, obscured the principles of justice by administrative bureaucracy, sacrificed human values for efficiency, and hypocritically justified a brutal attempt to establish American hegemony over the world with sterile anti-Communism.[13]

Recently, romanticists also have directed their attention to the gradual erosion of the valuing process as a result of what the sociologist Jacques Ellul labeled "technological anesthesia." Values continuously remain a central aspect of the romantic view of the world and are closely tied to the ideas romanticists espouse. To the romanticists, therefore, technological imperatives and the materialism that is implied in them are a threat to individuality and to the valuing process which adds moral freedom to the individual and upon which individuality rests.

While serving as gadflies of the established social system, romanticists are not necessarily social reformers. They seldom provide detailed plans for a reconstruction of society unless such a plan is Utopian in design and applicable to an elite segment of the population. In ancient Greece, for example, many of the Cynics, while continuously critical of their society, did not advocate the abolition of slavery. To the Cynics, as to most romanticists, liberation is a psychological phenomenon and not a social or political movement. They seek liberation of the "inner self," the authentic personality, rather than political freedom. Jesus, for example, did not assume the role of an antagonist against the political structure or against the institution of slavery. He was not a civil libertarian for, as he affirmed often, his kingdom was not of this world. Romanticists, therefore, often prove to be psychological eccentrics rather than civil libertarians. When they advocate liberation or revolution, they often do so within a

[13] Paul Jacobs and Saul Landau, *The New Radicals: A Report with Documents* (New York: Vintage Books, 1966), p. 4.

psychological context. They believe, in the words of a twentieth-century spokesman, Abbie Hoffman, in "revolution for the hell of it."

Romanticism cannot be classified automatically according to the conservative-liberal political continuum. Because of their historical or Utopian point of view, romanticists often express their criticisms of the present in terms of a call to return to a previous civilization, to establish a Utopian world of the future, or to return to the bosom of untainted nature. Their visions of the future and dreams of the past serve as fuel for their dissatisfaction, while the present social order functions as a target for their barbed wit and unrelenting scorn. The kind of ideal construct which they utilize to debunk the present social order will determine, in part, their individual political propensity, whether reactionary or radical, democratic or autocratic, feudal or republican, communal or totalitarian.

Although numerous romanticists have been allied with political liberalism, others have joined reactionary political forces. During the eighteenth- and nineteenth-century revival of Romanticism, this one ideology appeared in diverse political forms. A political liberal such as the poet Lord Byron supported the Carbonnari of Italy and fought and died in the cause of Greek liberation, while Utopian socialists such as Étienne Cabet and Charles Fourier philosophized and designed plans for communal ventures. Other romanticists, however, turned to a mythologized view of the past or to nature for ideals which they contrasted to their own debased societies. Conservative Romanticism was revealed in the love of the medieval past as expressed by Sir Walter Scott and Alexandre Dumas, and by the hunger for the simplicity of aboriginal life and natural beauty found in the works of such nature poets as Coleridge, Wordsworth, and Shelley. While a nobleman like Chateaubriand and a clergyman like l'Abbé de Lamennais [14] searched within the traditions of the past and within the bosom of the Roman Catholic Church for liberation, the English poet Shelley preached atheism. Many romanticists during their frantic careers reveal a capacity for ideological fluctuation. Coleridge and Wordsworth, for example, once suspected of alliance with Jacobin radicals in France, turned away in disgust at the excesses of the Reign of Terror and joined the conservative forces of their society. Of course, a conservative romanticist may be every bit as disruptive to the social order as a radical one.

[14] L'Abbé de Lamennais's life reflects the diverse expression of the romantic ideology. A fervent Roman Catholic, he energetically served the church. Dedicated to the search for truth, he developed a thesis based upon the principle that truth would be achieved by universal human consensus. Because universal human consent could not be practically achieved, he further concluded that the Pope spoke for all men, and thus was an infallible source of truth. The Vatican hierarchy, fearful of this concept of Papal Infallibility, admonished the priest to stop his preaching of this questionable doctrine. Faltering in his obedience, he reportedly exclaimed, upon receiving the news of the censure: "I will teach them what it means to defy a priest." He died a staunch advocate of democracy.

Indeed, during the twentieth century, the romantic movement has been notable for the political differences it contained. The excesses of the reactionary romantic Nationalism adhered to by the Nazi regime in Germany as well as the militant socialistic utopianism of a bourgeois hero such as Che Guevara and his band of followers represent the extreme political diversity inherent in Romanticism. During the recent revival of Romanticism in the United States, in the form of the so-called counter-culture, various ideological patterns have emerged. Some romantic true believers have joined Nazi-like bands of roving motorcyclists, while others have formed pacifist agarian communes patterned after the life style of pretechnological farmers; some have joined religious movements, while others have become disciples of Dr. Timothy Leary who advocates the use of drugs to achieve a form of transcendence. Still others have searched for grace by adhering to a puritanical religious ideology designed to match the simplicity of early agrarian Christians. While religious roman-ticists of one stamp establish halfway houses for the urban outcasts and adhere to austere rules of discipline, some of their romantic colleagues dis-cover their truth in secluded Buddhist temples or in bizarre rites of devil worship.

Philosophically, the rationale for the romantic ideology has been devised by divergent proponents of Romanticism. During the twentieth century, for example, the conservative individualist Ayn Rand, who founded the Objectivist movement, and Alan Watts, the father of Ameri-canized Zen Buddhism have written avidly about a romantic way of life.

Regardless of their stance, however, romanticists help to liberate others by providing alternatives to socially acceptable behavior and by their vociferous rejection of the ways of the "philistines" who rule their societies. Their stance causes them to be misunderstood by those who equate rebellion and revolution. Thus the poorly informed in the Soviet Union accuse their country's romanticists of being bourgeois revisionists, while in the United States romanticists are often labeled "Commies" or "fellow travelers."

Although some romanticists achieve liberation through highly un-orthodox behavior—often based upon a conscious attack upon the manners rather than the morals of bourgeois societies—others achieve liberation through the arts and various forms of creative expression. Both the eccen-tric vagabond and the creative artist serve to place into question the present social system, for through their behavior and works they illustrate alternative ways of perceiving, feeling, and behaving. By providing non-political alternatives within politically disillusioned social groupings, they disrupt the life stye of the supporters of the status quo and thus weaken the control that the social system exercises over individuals.

While encouraging and protecting the social deviant who may be a parasitic bohemian or a creative artist, Romanticism, is nevertheless an ideology of style rather than substance. It is not what is said, what is achieved, or what is attacked that forms the core of Romanticism, but rather how it is said, how it is achieved, or how whatever is attacked is attacked. By their style of expressing their discontent in nonrevolutionary ways, romanticists provide the opportunity for the liberation of the politically disaffiliated. Of course, the fact that Romanticism is an ideology of style rather than substance implies that the creative elements within the romantic framework may be accompanied by destructive, antisocial, and dysfunctional behavior.

While the existing social system and the Brahmins who direct it are targets for their scorn, romanticists also clash with the "masses" whom they see as a threat to individuality. Romantic rebels seldom find a home in mass movements and they rarely are egalitarian in spirit. As Hoxie Neale Fairchild observed: "The average intellectual radical devotes his life to clamoring for the rights of people who would make him extremely unhappy if he were forced to associate with them." [15] Often their love for "mankind" conceals their contempt for man—or at least for man as he appears in modern mass society.

Because they fear the detrimental influence upon the creative individual that may be exerted by the "masses," romanticists often turn their scorn against the ruled as well as (or instead of) the rulers. Although willing to identify with the politically disenfranchised or with cutural minorities, romanticists rarely sustain working relationships with them. The major target of their scorn, is hardly ever the oppressed or alienated but rather the gladhander or organizational man. They reject the call of public opinion and detest the individuals who become directors of programs designed to help others. Their concern for the downtrodden is overshadowed by their hatred of restrictions imposed by organized assistance programs.

### Romanticism and Revolution

Romanticism is the ideology of action rather than thought. As the romantic existentialist Albert Camus proclaimed, "With rebellion, awareness is born." In contrast to defining oneself through thought, as in Descartes' familiar dictum *Cogito ergo sum* (I think, therefore I am), the rebel is known through his deeds. Goethe has provided a perfect expression of this conviction in his famous tragedy *Faust*. Faust is studying the gospel according to St. John and he speaks: " 'T is written: 'In the Beginning was the *Word*.'/Here am I balked: who, now, can help afford?/The

---

[15] Hoxie Neale Fairchild, *The Romantic Quest* (Philadelphia: Albert Saifer, Publisher, 1931), p. 225.

Word?—impossible so high to rate it;/And otherwise must I translate it,/If by the Spirit I am truly taught." Rejecting both "Thought" and "Power" as replacements for the "Word", he suddenly is inspired and exclaims: "The Spirit aids me now I see the light!/'In the Beginning was the *Act*,' I write." [16] "In our daily trials," Camus asserted, "rebellion plays the same role as does the 'cogito' in the realm of thought: it is the first piece of evidence. But this evidence lures the individual from his solitude. It founds its first value on the whole human race. I rebel—therefore we exist." [17]

Inasmuch as Romanticism always rests upon the rejection of the existing social system, it rarely has to assume the defensive postures that are often necessary for those who offer constructive alternatives to existing social systems. This intellectual freedom from cognitive accountability explains, in part, the arrogant stance of the romanticists. While their criticism often strikes at the Achilles' heel of their target, they seldom have carefully reasoned out arguments or research data. They are identifiable by their wit and glibness rather than by their logic or intellectual depth. Their strength results from their passion rather than from their accuracy. Because, as the philosopher Hume observed, an idea without passion has no force, the romanticists sometimes outwit the Establishment, which must preserve a rational moderate stance. In an age when the mass media are in search of existing and salable news items, the passion and eccentricity of the romanticists provide the populace with interesting escapes from the tedious chores demanded of those who are assigned the task of pampering and nourishing the technological robot.

Although Romanticism is similar to the ideologies of revolution in its opposition to the status quo, it is not a revolutionary ideology. Indeed, the fact that romanticists have been labeled revolutionary and treated accordingly is little less than a major historical tragedy. Many innocent romantic disrupters have suffered the fate of revolutionary zealots. Unlike revolutionaries, however, romanticists do not seek to substitute one political system for another, for they prefer to weaken all political systems and remain disaffiliated from all groups which adhere to political ideologies. They tend to mock groups which wield political power and influence. Kingley Widmer accurately observed:

> The accusation that the rebel wishes to overthrow the social-political order may be righteous fear or a trick of those in power. For the rebel wishes to escape from the pattern of the dominant society, to bottom out, where the revolutionary wishes to take over society, to get on top. Where revolutionaries tend to be moral puritans seeking all power, rebels tend to be amoral libertarians mocking all power. Rebels, unless cor-

[16] Johann Von Goethe, *Faust*, Part I, Sec. 3.
[17] Albert Camus, *The Rebel* (New York: Random House, Inc., 1956), p. 22.

rupted into something else, can hardly be revolutionaries since they make absolute criticisms of authority and power and emphasize kinds of individual autarchy which can never be the aim of major social and political organizations.[18]

The tenuous *entente* between the revolutionary and the romanticist was readily revealed in the gradual bifurcation of the American radical movement of the mid-twentieth century. The romantic SDSer and his revolutionary counterpart, the Weatherman, eventually broke their alliance. Because romanticists tend to form brief alliances with revolutionaries, however, they often serve revolutionary causes by increasing the popularity of antigovernmental rhetoric. These alliances also create an inaccurate view of the size of revolutionary bands and thus produce inordinate government repression which often far exceeds the need. As repressive measures and defensive rhetoric increase, revolutionaries gain adherents. Unwittingly, therefore, rebels tend to increase the danger of violent political upheavals and the transfer of political power. Inasmuch as violent changes in power usually are accompanied by a temporary weakening of political control, the rebel's goal is partially achieved by such revolutionary overthrows. Rebels, however, prefer mutual exchange and influence rather than class conflict and violent revolution. They may view personal violence as an act of heroism, but they regard collective, impersonal violence as a tragedy. Romanticists, in fact, often become counterrevolutionaries when confronted by the harsh collective demands and uncompromising puritanical attitude of revolutionaries. Indeed, revolutionaries often reveal little patience with the barbed wit of the rebel. As Widmer observed, "[T]he differences between rebels and revolutionaries are not really very subtle; revolutionaries are those who, in contrast to the more plodding ways of long established authorities, *quickly* deny, condemn and destroy rebels." [19]

Even though romanticists are not revolutionaries, they are often attracted to them because of the zeal which accompanies revolutionary activities. Ralph Waldo Emerson, the American transcendentalist and romanticist, made this clear when he wrote:

> If there is any period one would desire to be born in, is it not the age of Revolution; when the old and the new stand side by side and admit of being compared; when the energies of all men are searched by fear and by hope; when the historic glories of the old can be compensated by the rich possibilities of the new era? This time, like all times, is a very good one, if we but know what to do with it.[20]

[18] Kingley Widmer, *The Literary Rebel* (Carbondale: Southern Illinois University Press, 1965), p. 21.

[19] Widmer, *The Literary Rebel*, p. 22.

[20] Ralph Waldo Emerson, "The American Scholar," in *The Selected Writings of Ralph Waldo Emerson,* ed. Brooks Atkinson (New York: The Modern Library, 1950), p. 60.

Despite the fact that romanticists may further revolutionary goals by idealizing their implementation, the revolutionary postulate that "the ends justifies the means" eventually causes the rebel to withdraw from revolutionary activities and to vent his scorn at his former allies. Beethoven, for example, wrote his masterful third symphony for Napoleon, the champion of the people. When he discovered, however, that Napoleon had proclaimed himself Emperor, Beethoven became outraged and changed the title of his symphony from "Buonaparte" to *Sinfonia Eroica— Composta per Festeggiare il Souvenire d'un Grand' uomo* (Heroic Symphony—composed to celebrate the memory of a great man). Because revolutionaries demand absolute loyalty and blind obedience as well as "party discipline" and individual sacrifice for a cause, the renegade rebel is often punished by the revolutionaries for his "revisionism." Some rebels may survive the revolutionary upheaval, often with physical and psychological scars, but their disillusionment with the cruel exigencies of revolution force them to withdraw into themselves, a Utopian dream, nature, or drugs. Romanticists of the eighteenth century, such as Wordsworth, Southey, and Coleridge, served as heralders for the French Revolution but with the cruel excesses of the Reign of Terror, they turned away from political affairs. Coleridge and Southey withdrew into a Utopian dream— Pantisocracy—while Wordsworth turned toward the peaceful world of pastoral simplicity. Other rebels suffered the loss of life. Thus Jesus of Nazareth, rejecting all political power, continued to be hounded by those who could not understand his romantic stance. The members of the Sanhedrin accused him in the court of Pontius Pilate. The accusation and the subsequent punishment were based upon the charge that the humble rabbi was fermenting revolutionary activity. His torturers prior to his execution joined Pontius Pilate in their inability to understand the non-political nature of the rebellion of Jesus and taunted him and ridiculed him as a burlesque king. The tragic tale of Jesus's life reaches monumental paradox when Barabbas, a revolutionary zealot, was granted a pardon and released rather than Jesus.

The paradox of this situation lies in the fact that although romanticists are not advocates of violent revolution, they may affect a society more significantly than revolutionaries. The bloody and often heroic struggle of early Christian rebels during the Roman Empire often caused greater anxiety to the emperors than did the barbarian hordes along the Empire's borders. Jesus and his band of followers affected the future of society more profoundly than did Barabbas and his revolutionary followers. Similarly, the works of Beethoven remain more vivid than the deeds of Napoleon. Creative artists may form the future of a people's history in ways that far exceed the accomplishments of military heroes. Indeed, romanticists often become symbolic saints for established revolutionary regimes or tradition-oriented social systems, serving in death to justify the use and misuse of power. Thus Che Guevara serves in death as a symbol and supporter of revolutionary goals, although it remains questionable whether Dr. Guevara ever would have successfully adjusted to the bureaucratic and puritan maze of Marxist Cuba. Like Lord Byron, the English poet and rebel, he died in a foreign land seeking the excitement and freedom of the struggle to liberate others.

In summary, however, it must be emphasized that rebels, to remain rebels, must remain politically powerless. Because romantic rebels believe that power corrupts, the intentional avoidance of power stands as a central and essential quality of Romanticism. It distinguishes the rebel from the revolutionary zealot and the clever opportunist.

A major reason why romanticists are confused with revolutionaries, beside the fact that they share a common hostility to the social system, is the fact that individuals who judge their behavior think in power terms. Those who are in power, or who seek power, often cannot comprehend the role of the rebel who seeks to remain disaffiliated while struggling to weaken the political power of others. Because the rebels' desire to diminish power is viewed by those in power as an attempt to transfer power, they have been exiled, hunted, mutilated, and killed. The "loss of power syndrome" which characterizes political opportunists is often combined with the dissatisfaction of bureaucratic functionaries who resent the inefficiency of the romanticists and perhaps secretly envy their freedom. Both syndromes serve to increase the insecurity of the rebel position, and explain in part why a living rebel is a threat and a dead one is a saint.

### Religious Antecedents

As was previously noted, Romanticism expressed itself in the role and activities of tribal shamans. It also appeared as part of the Greco-Roman and Judaeo-Christian heritage and forms a major part of the evolving traditions of Western civilization.

The development of Romanticism within the framework of Western history has assumed two major thrusts. First, within the Judaeo-Christian tradition, it has assumed a religious subjectivism often separatist in nature. Such religious subjectivism has revealed itself through revivalism, transcendentalism, naturalism, and pietism. Secondly, it has expressed itself within a secular framework designed to diminish the power of secular elites. In some cases, such as in the appeal of pantheism, the secular and the religious spirit combined.

The history of the ancient Hebrews reveals the profound influence of religious subjectivism upon their lives. Expressed through the voices of the prophets, who often adamantly rejected the practices popularized in the ancient centers of commerce, Romanticism served to curb the excesses of a legalistic people. Biblical beatniks like Ezekiel and Jeremiah uncompromisingly rejected the excesses of affluence and formalism and withdrew from their influence.

The ancient pharisees and sanhedrins—the targets of the scorn of the biblical romanticists—were continuously admonished about the dangers resulting from their acceptance of affluence and their turn toward materialism. Indeed, the persistent warnings to the Hebrews expressed by various prophets concerning the forthcoming destruction of Jerusalem reflect, in part, the romantic and puritan rejection of a social order based upon affluence.

Though critical of power elites, the ancient prophets did not seek revolutionary upheavals; rather, they withdrew from political life. Dressed in atypical garb, they often inhabited desolate desert or mountain regions. On occasion, however, they entered the commercial centers and warned against sin, corruption, and the whole prevailing state of affairs. Although respected by the multitudes and thus possessing significant potential political power, these prophets rarely assumed political positions and remained peripheral to the seats of political power. Indeed, some of them joined communal religious sects, such as the Essenes, and withdrew from public life.

In the second testament, both John the Baptist, the "voice crying in the wilderness," and the empathetic and gentle rabbi, Jesus of Nazareth, represent the romantic religious spirit. John the Baptist's denunciation of the ruling house of Israel for its immoderate affluence and liscentiousness cost him his life. King Herod of Antipas, whose wife was unable to tolerate John's accusations about the sexual immorality of the royal court, and whose daughter Salome danced a costly bargain, eventually succumbed to their pleas and beheaded the rebel.

Jesus also taunted the power elite. His sometimes immoderate attacks upon the Hebrew bourgeoisie, the pharisees, reflected his rebel nature. His hatred of hypocrisy is revealed in his charge that the pharisees were "whited sepulchers" and "vipers." The gospel according to his apostle Matthew is veritably a document of romantic ideology. Like his cousin John the Baptist, Jesus was continuously accused of revolutionary activities. Conversely, both were taunted by their followers for refusing to maximize their political power.

The prototype of the rebel in the Judaeo-Christian heritage is the Serpent in the Utopia of Eden. This notorious rebel, through his incessant prodding and socratic questioning, drove the quixotic Adam and Eve to commit the first recorded act of peaceful civil disobedience. Thus, they not only earned the privilege of knowing the difference between good and evil but also received the romantic badge of courage—alienation. Of course, their rejection of the operational rules of the benevolent and dictatorial agrarian society of Eden did not go unpunished. Banished from Eden, they were condemned to "sweat and tears." A similar fate, we are sometimes informed, awaits those who refuse to adjust to, and "drop out" of, the technological and computerized society. Whether the newly acquired knowledge gained by the Mom and Dad of mankind would have permitted them to adjust to the ethically antiseptic ethos of Eden remains an unanswered question. Suffice to note that to the classicist, their act represents a decline in human nature, whereas to the romanticist their rebellion represents a decided step forward inasmuch as it reflects an evolved expression of free will.

The Serpent who, depending upon one's ideology, either led them astray or liberated them from the banality of Edenic agrarian affluence also was punished. The power elite of the time condemned him saying: "Because thou hast done this thing, thou art cursed among all cattle and beast of the earth. Upon thy breast shalt thou go, and earth shalt thou eat all days of thy life." [21] The severity of the biblical condemnation would be repeated numerous times by other power elites who would persistently seek to silence the nagging dissatisfaction expressed by the rebels who were attempting to "liberate" their fellow citizens from the bland oppression of affluence. Numerous romanticists would, like the Serpent, "bite the dust."

Besides the Serpent, who, it should be noted, did not seek political advantage in his act, romantic poets also have singled out the malevolent firstborn son of Adam, Cain, as a romantic hero. After committing the heinous crime of fratricide and claiming no social responsibility ("Am I my brothers keeper"), he was condemned to roam the east side of Eden as a "fugitive and vagabond." Many latter-day "east-sides" have furnished a home for vagabonds and fugitives who deny social responsibilities and "cop out" or "drop out," an act viewed by most true believers as fratricide against their fellow human beings.

From the preceding illustrations the reader will note that numerous individuals, rather antithetic in behavior and value orientation, such as Jesus and Cain, are placed under the umbrella of Romanticism. Rebels are rebels because of their rebellion and not because of any particular value system. Thus, in the pagan Roman world a Jesus readily functioned as a rebel, whereas in the modern world, with its institutionalized Christianity, a rebel could assume an atheistic stance. The style and the role of an individual, rather than the issue which motivates him, determines whether he is a rebel. These illustrations also reflect the centrality of Romanticism in the roots of modern Judaic and Christian religions. Al-

[21] Genesis 3:14.

though not a revolutionary manifesto, the Bible is, in fact, an account of romantic ventures. In many ways it is a romantic manifesto and contains numerous accounts of man's successful rebellion against oppressive social systems.

Throughout Western European history, Romanticism continued to reflect a religious face. During the Middle Ages, for example, Romanticism found expression in the hedonistic but also spiritually oriented lives of the clerks and balladeers who preserved romantic mythology in poetry and song. Many of their romantic tales have been preserved and are included in Carl Orff's anthology, *Carmina Burana*. While balladeers and clerks devised the cult of the woman and the cult of the Madonna and thus popularized the concept of romantic love, other rebels sought refuge in communalism and adventure. While religious organizations such as the Benedictine and Franciscan orders served as communities for rebels who sought simplicity and communalism, the Knights of Hospitallers organized crusades for the more swashbuckling and wordly rebels.

During the sixteenth century, the gradual institutionalization and bureaucratization of the Roman Catholic church served to repress rather than liberate the rebelliousness of man, and rebels led what has been labeled the Protestant Reformation but could aptly be relabeled the Romantic Affirmation.

While the Protestant Reformation can be traced to various historical antecedents, its famous messenger, Martin Luther, fueled the religious ferment by posting his ninety-five theses of rebellion on the church door at Wittenberg in 1517. Although Lutheranism challenged the existing social order, it was relatively moderate when compared to numerous other religious sects such as the Anabaptists who sought christian primitivism. Because its target was the immorality of the highly centralized Roman Catholic church, sixteenth century religious radicalism often was democratic and puritan in character.

The spirit of religious Romanticism also spread within the Roman Catholic church and resulted in the creation of new religious organizations such as the puritan Capuchin order. Romanticism also was reflected in the lives of such famous mystics as the humble and ecology-minded St. Francis of Assisi and the intense Spanish Carmelite nun and poetess, St. Teresa. The persistent expression of Romanticism within religious ideological patterns reveals the close relationship between religion and the romantic spirit of man, for both inclinations rest upon faith rather than reason.

Puritan Romanticism gained importance in England especially among the seventeenth century newly emerging business class. With the reigns of James I (1603-1625) and Charles I (1625-1649) of the House of Stuart, however, the romantic aspects of the puritan ideology were doomed to be viewed as minor ideological elements in England. The failure of the Puritans in the political world of British life led them to Holland where they embarked upon a remarkable romantic migration in search of a land to establish a Utopia based upon the ideology of a Puritan theocracy. With the death of Oliver Cromwell, the Puritan Dictator of England, and the return of the Stuarts to the throne of England in 1660 the seat of religious Puritanism was moved to the New World and was destined to indelibly mark the incipient American character.

In the wilderness of colonial America, after the increasingly con-servative revolutionary puritans of the Massachusetts Bay Colony had founded Harvard College and introduced the concept of mandatory school attendance, protesting immigrants preserved the romantic thrust in the New World. The Anabaptists and Quakers, and individuals such as Roger Williams, "a windmill gone mad," and Ann Hutchinson struggled to preserve their form of rugged romantic individualism against oppressive institutionalized Puritanism and eventually sought refuge in lands sur-rounding the Bible State.

The romantic conviction that an individual possesses the right and the duty to behave according to his conscience entered into American ideology through Protestantism. While the romantic impulse in America was gradually being secularized, religious expression of Romanticism con-tinued through such communal ventures as those of the Dunkers, the Shakers, and the Mormons. In the Bible Belt of the South, within small communities throughout the United States, and among ethnic minorities, the spirit of religious Romanticism continues to be reflected in such practices as "speaking in tongues," "revivalism,' and "mass conversion." Indeed, the current rise in evangelical movements within diverse churches in the United States reflects the upswing in romantic subjectivism.

Although Romanticism has played a major role in the development of Western religious thought, the importance of Eastern religious ideas, as expressed in the Beat Movement in the 1950s, as analyzed by Alan Watts in the 1960s, and as promoted by various popular entertainers, cannot be minimized. While Zen and Yoga have become the "pantheism" of the intellectual avant garde of the countercultures, they also have spread among the middle class, no doubt aided by the fact that the United States was involved in an unpopular Asian war which tended to make interest and sympathy with Eastern folkways and religion into a marginal form of political protest.

Recently, other counterculture advocates have established religious communes in agrarian and urban areas. From Buddhist temples in large American cities to evangelical meeting houses, the spirit of romantic religious subjectivism is being expressed. The oddity of the religious spirit of some of these emerging evangelical Christians, especially in the context of a highly secularized society, and in view of their countercultural mode of life and dress, has earned for them the dubious title of "Jesus Freaks."

### Secular Antecedents

The secular expression of Romanticism is rooted in the Greco-Roman world. The first major expression of Romanticism in the ancient world is found in Greco-Roman mythology, where rebels are presented for man's admiration and emulation. Perhaps the most beloved and famous mythological rebel in Greek tradition is Prometheus, a favorite hero for romantic poets throughout the ages. According to Greek mythology, a gigantic race of Titans inhabited the earth prior to the creation of man. The gods, in fact, assigned these Titans the task of creating and equipping mankind. A Titan rebel, Prometheus, stole fire from heaven and presented it, with the gift of civilization and art, to the inadequately equipped human race. Because of his disobedience he was condemned to be chained forever to a rock on Mount Caucasus, where every day a vulture would tear at his liver and every night the destroyed organ would regenerate itself for the next day's torture. His adamant refusal to succumb to the will of the gods and his refusal to betray mankind have endeared him to man and he remains a hero for countless rebels.

The first major nonmythological expression of Romanticism in the ancient world is found in the lives and teaching of the philosophers labeled "Cynics" or "dogs." Their philosophy, Cynicism, emerged as the first major school of Romanticism within both the Greek and Roman civilizations during ages characterized by affluence and the extension of leisure time. Cynicism gained in importance and influence, especially as social systems stratified, interest in Greek and Roman politics subsided, and affluence became a way of life for a significant section of the population. Men like Diogenes roamed through the cities of ancient Greece with their bedrolls under their arms, and the Roman Cynic Demetrius, according to certain accounts, declined the offer of a large sum of money from the Emperor Caligula, saying, "It would have cost him his whole Empire to induce me to change my way of life." Like most romanticists, including the twentieth-century hippies and beats, the Cynics lived at a subsistence level in order to avoid the complications which the pearls of affluence would impose upon their lives. As Widmer noted: "The followers of Diogenes, then and now, may be the sour fruit in an overripe time, announcing that rottenness is all. The Cynic program announced most notably a philosophy of failure which also provided a devastating commentary on the fatuous successes of ages of counterfeit." [22]

The urge for simplicity and the rejection of affluence were impressively reflected in the life style of both the Greek and Roman Cynics. Indeed, the school of Cynicism is more noted for its adherence to a life style based on voluntary poverty than for its philosophical statements. In the true individualistic and rebellious spirit of Romanticism, Cynicism never did become an established formal school of thought. Unlike other philosophical systems, it remains unorganized and is best understood in the life style of its adherents.

The most famous spokesman for Cynicism and the most remembered *enfant terrible* of ancient Greece was Diogenes. Born at Sinope in Pontus, Diogenes did his teaching at games and festivals. He taught through didactics and through his life style. His eccentricities and asceticism as well as his continuous attempt to *épater le bourgeois* earned Plato's description of him as a Socrates gone mad. He would have prized that description for he believed that "Most men are so nearly mad that a finger's breadth would make the difference." [23] Kingley Widmer described him as "an anarchist when it came to political authorities, a libertarian when it came to social customs, and a cosmopolitan when it came to loyalties. . . . His dog's life, physically mean and rough, intellectually tough and biting, was an outrageous dramatization of radical awareness." [24] Diogenes called for simplicity, behavior according to nature, rejection of affluence, pacifism, and extreme individualism. He was critical of all systems and all ideologies. Much of his recorded behavior reflects the theatrical and anticonventional mode of teaching. Like the latter-day romanticists within the counterculture, he resorted to behavior that shocked the Establishment—in his case including defecating and masturbating in public. He slept in a vase-like object which normally was used as a casket.

Essential to Diogenes' teachings and central to the romantic ideology is the belief that happiness is best achieved by behaving according to nature. Like Rousseau, but perhaps in a more direct fashion, Diogenes called for the natural man to liberate himself from the chains of conventionality. As the historian Dudley observed: "He was a dog whom all admired, yet few dared go hunting with him." [25] Diogenes reportedly

[22] Widmer, *The Literary Rebel*, p. 4.
[23] Donald R. Dudley, *A History of Cynicism* (Hildersheim: George Olms Verlagsbuchhandlung, 1967), p. 21.
[24] Widmer, *The Literary Rebel*, p. 6.
[25] Dudley, *A History of Cynicism*, p. 37.

said of himself: "Other dogs bite their enemies, I bite my friends for their salvation." [26] Centuries later, Nietzche was echoing Diogenes' sentiments when he proclaimed, "To make the individual *uncomfortable*, that is my task." [27]

Other Cynics followed in the footsteps of Diogenes. Crates rejected wealth and dedicated himself to serving the poor. He was viewed by his contemporaries as a secular saint—a pagan St. Francis of Assisi. Known as the cheerful hunchback and noted for his physical ugliness, he traveled with his devoted and attractive wife Hipparchia. Their love story and freewheeling life style, which included giving their daughter in marriage for a month's trial—a practice which has its current counterpart in some Western nations—explains in part the lurid tales that are recorded about his life.

Through extensive utilization of diatribes, anecdotes, theatrics, and imagery as well as shock tactics, the Cynics taught their philosophy of rebellion and rugged individualism. Cynics were thus characterized by their *authenticity* rather than for their *sensitivity*. Men such as the unpredictable, caustic Diogenes and the Cynic Bion, who was remembered for his vulgar language, would not find comfort in latter-day progressive educational patterns which encourage gladhandism and group sensitivity sessions. Indeed, cynicism demands rugged psychic strength and self-sufficiency and rejects an environment designed to furnish psychic and physical comfort.

Cynicism does not appear in standard philosophy of education textbooks. But even though they are ignored in textbooks—a fact which would have been to their liking, for they wanted little to do with such establishment oriented phenomena as formal education—the Cynics did not go unnoticed by the Establishment. While most citizens probably ignored and rejected these odd men, some spokesmen for the Establishment hounded them. The Emperor Vespasian, for example, threw them out of Rome for fermenting dissatisfaction by teaching their disruptive creeds.

In a work entitled "Fugitivi," the second-century writer Lucian reflected some of the criticism directed against the Romanticists throughout the ages when he wrote:

> The whole city is full of this roguery. . . . The canine qualities they possess are barking, lasciviousness, theft, sexual license, flattery, fawning on any one who will feed them. . . . We shall soon see wholesale dissertion from the factories, when the workers realize how they have to

[26] Dudley, *A History of Cynicism*, p. 43.
[27] Friedrich Nietzsche, "Notes (1875)," in *The Portable Nietzsche*, ed. Walter Kaufmann (New York: The Viking Press, 1954), p. 50.

toil and labour from morning till night, and wear themselves out to earn a pittance for their drudgery, while these quacks and charlatans live a life of plenty, demanding like lords and readily getting what they ask.[28]

Although such an admonition may meet with the sympathy of the true supporter of the *status quo,* Widmer aptly observed that "The awesome fear that rebels, unless put down, will encourage vast numbers to throw off work and orderly life is more a condemnation of the society than of the rebels. . . . Surely a surplus of bearded bad poets is more desirable than a surplus of clean-shaven bad policemen, even to pietists of the conventional authorities." [29]

After the passing of the Greek and Roman Cynics, and of the empires that gave rise to them, Romanticism was preserved during the Middle Ages, as previously noted, in the mendicant orders and in the lives of rugged mystics. It was also reflected in the bohemian life style forced upon the Jews by a Christian society, and in the life style of the Gypsy who preserved a nomadic form of existence. It was also expressed in the lives of the troubadour and the wandering scholar, who by their subtle and not so subtle criticisms and their romanticization of chivalry and love reflected the weakening of state and dynastic control over individuals. They undermined the repressive social system by focusing upon individual love and the plight of the outcast. St. Jerome's admonition that the songs of poets are the food of demons is true—at least if the established order represents the will of the gods. The songs of the troubadours, many of which are extant, are examples of the oral tradition which is one of the essential characteristics of Romanticism. Romanticism is primarily a verbal ideology that is best expressed spontaneously in music and poetry, for it is through the song or the musical instrument that the romantic spirit of man is best communicated. In the twentieth century jazz has served as a medium for the ideology of Romanticism. In this sense, Marshall McLuhan's observation that "the medium is the message" is accurate.

As previously noted, the gradual emergence of modern nation-states was accompanied by a centralization of massive political power and resulted in the elaborate communication networks through which the ideology of Scientism was to be popularized. Romanticism, however, remained as a significant ideological force—although, at times, awkwardly limited in the range of resources at its command.

During the dynastic political era, the ideology of Romanticism continued to be expressed in the courts of the potentates. Manifesting itself in the role of the court jester, Romanticism set itself the important task of limiting the excesses of classicism and scholasticism in centralized social

[28] Dudley, *A History of Cynicism,* p. 143.
[29] Widmer, *The Literary Rebel,* p. 11.

systems. Often court jesters proved to be cunning and powerful political figures. From the times of the Pharaoh Pepi I to the present, jesters and comical debunkers of the established social order, from King Lear's fool to Lenny Bruce, have served to moderate the use of political power. Such debunkers, however, often served to preserve the social order by furnishing a comic relief for the dissatisfied within the social system. William Willeford, observing the role of the king's jester, wrote:

> In tolerating such jokes the king partly affirmed the royal power that the fool pretends to deny. Thus the office of the jester fulfills some of the same functions as the ritualized rebellion in which political subjects express actual and possible resentments against authority. The fact that the rebellion is allowed and even encouraged implies that the social institutions and the persons in power are strong enough to tolerate it; thus it serves the interests of authority and of social cohesion.[30]

The role of the court jester, of course, is not easily distinguished from that of the fool or the hero. They are all foolhardy and often behave in a manner that is to their personal disadvantage. The thin line between the fool and the hero is revealed in the trial and persecution of Jesus of Nazareth.[31] Both court jesters and fools reflect the romantic ability to resist external authority and control their own behavior. The fool can behave according to his impulses and can transgress the values and behavioral norms of the society in which he finds himself; indeed, he is not expected to behave properly. As noted previously, the Cynics often created a strawman and then utilized him as a target for their scorn. Court jesters commonly employed a similar technique, with the jester using his scepter or bauble (often made with a caricature of a human head) to conduct one-man conversations usually critical of the King.

The first modern romantic movements emerged in Europe at the end of the eighteenth and the beginning of the nineteenth century. Although the Renaissance had produced a creative flowering of art, it soon became the foundation for a stringent system of rules which regulated artistic endeavors and human social behavior. Associations of artists, such as the French Academy, founded in the seventeenth century, established laws concerning aesthetic expression, including regulations limiting the use of certain chords, modulation, and tonality. At the same time socialites devised lavish canons of etiquette and the courts of the nobility along with their imitators, the clubs of bourgeoisie, were patterned after ritualized modes of social behavior. It is during such periods of classicism

[30] William Willeford, *The Fool and His Scepter: A Study in Clowns and Jesters and Their Audience* (Evanston, Illinois: The Northwest University Press, 1969), p. 155.
[31] For a brilliant analysis of the character of the fool as expressed in Erasmus' *Praise of Folly* and in Shakespeare's *King Lear,* see William Empson's *The Structure of Complex Words* (Ann Arbor: The University of Michigan Press, 1967).

that social programmers like Amy Vanderbilt and Emily Post became relevant. The great French writer of the seventeenth century, Molière, vividly captured the absurd lengths to which the emerging middle class in France went in observing the precepts of classicism. Satirical dramas such as *The Bourgeois Gentleman, The Hypocrites,* and *The Bores* are monuments in the history of debunking middle-class literature, in comparison to which many of the current works in this genre pale to insignificance.

The inherent limitations in eighteenth-century classicism were vividly described by Jacques Barzun when he wrote: "It had supposed society to be static, emotions compressible, and novelty needless. It had selected what seemed to it best and truest and most eternal—monarchy, orthodoxy, courtly etiquette, mathematics, and rules of art and of morality so simple that their universality could be taken for granted." [32]

The first to challenge the coldly imitative view of the world presented by the eighteenth-century classical tradition were the children of the classical tradition, the enlightened philosophers. Not enamored of classical imitations and highly dedicated to the primacy of reason, intellectuals like Voltaire and Denis Diderot challenged the old cosmology, the absurdity of bourgeois manners, and the restricted dreams and visions of the aristocratic leisure class. They delved into "natural law" and revealed an unwavering faith in progress through science. While challenging the status quo, the debunking *philosophes* did not discard the Aristotelian epistemology which was fundamental to the existing social order. Their godchildren, however, did challenge, sometimes unwittingly, the old cosmology and epistemology. Thus, although both the *philosophes* and the romanticists rejected the old imitative way, they disagreed fundamentally with one another. Voltaire's critical reply that he would not crawl on all fours in order to fit Rousseau's view of man exemplifies the difference between the intellectual rebellion of the *philosophes* and the emotional liberation of the romanticists. Ayn Rand, noting their fundamental difference and the dilemma which it created, wrote: "Romanticists saw their cause primarily as a battle for their right to individuality and—unable to grasp the deepest metaphysical justification of their cause, unable to identify their values in terms or reason—they fought for individuality in terms of *feelings*, surrendering the banner of reason to their enemies." [33] "I feel; therefore I exist!" proclaim the romanticists.

A major occasioning force for the expression of the spirit of Romanticism was the French Revolution. The call to Liberty, Equality, and

[32] Barzun, *Romanticism and the Modern Ego*, p. 79.
[33] Ayn Rand, *The Romantic Manifesto* (New York: The New American Library, Inc., 1971), p. 70.

Fraternity reflects the emotive quality of Romanticism. Although the French Revolution gained its relevancy and its rationale from the Enlightenment, and its conceptions of natural law, rights of man, reason, progress, and belief in objective consciousness, the spirit of the Revolution was romantic in nature. John Halsted, observing the close relationship between Romanticism and the revolutionary events in Europe at the close of the eighteenth century, wrote:

> The Romantic era was one in which there was a widespread sense of crisis, a sense evident even before the outbreak of the French Revolution that the old order was coming to an end. And once the Revolution had broken out, the activities of intellectuals gained in urgency as fear of *political* disaster spread—fear of the Terror, of Napoleonic armies, of the chaos in internal and international politics as war continued for twenty-five years.[34]

The eighteenth and nineteenth century romantic movement not only supported political changes but it also stimulated various experimentations in social organization. Numerous communal ventures were attempted and while most of them failed to alter the life styles of most citizens, they served to provide non-revolutionary alternatives to the established order. The communal ventures of the disciples of the comte de Saint-Simon are illustrative of attempts to establish such social change. David Evans captured the ethos of a French commune:

> Some forty disciples set up a community at Menilmontant, 'dans la maison du Père,' where they tilled the soil to the singing of hymns, and with much ceremonial prepared themselves for the coming of La Mère. Bearded and long-haired like the bohemian Jeunes-France, they adopted a peculiar uniform, including a vest buttoned at the back to remind them that the individual is helpless without the cooperation of his fellow men. Enfantin himself wore a red toque rather like a Turkish fez, a tight fitting blue coat, and white trouser; across his chest he wore a ribbon with the words Le Père. The disciples 'abolished domesticity' and were romantically called to their meals by the sound of the horn, until in August, 1832 they were summoned to appear in court on the charge of being an illegal society and of 'outraging public morals.'[35]

The leaders were jailed for a year and the commune was never revived. The fate of these communalists would be shared by many utopian romanticists throughout history.

Although political changes and social experimentation characterized the eighteenth and nineteenth centuries, the term romantic movement generally serves to identify an aesthetic and literary tradition that

[34] John B. Halsted, ed., *Romanticism: Problems of Definition, Explanation, and Evaluation* (Boston: D. C. Heath and Company, 1965), p. 3.
[35] David Owen Evans, *Social Romanticism in France, 1830–1848* (New York: Octagon Books, 1969), pp. 24–25.

emerged in the eighteenth century. Creative romanticists throughout Europe and the United States liberated from the formal rules of classicism turned their genius toward concerns which classicists had judged to be unworthy of aesthetic focus. Concentrating on such subjects as nature, individuality, medieval legends, folk culture, mystery, mysticism, and love they unleashed their imaginations with gusto and passion and produced a flowering of the arts.

In England, Wordsworth and Coleridge published their *Lyrical Ballads* and announced the romantic age. While Wordsworth sought to capture the simplicity of rural life and the beauty of untainted nature, Coleridge wrote his haunting *Kubla Khan* and his spiritual ballad, *The Rime of the Ancient Mariner.* The three great English romantic poets, Percy B. Shelley, Lord Byron, and John Keats exemplified the triumph of literary Romanticism and revealed in their personal lives the close relationship between the romantic aesthetic tradition and social awareness. Sir Walter Scott provided in historical novels a romantic view of medievalism. *Ivanhoe* is his most famous tale.

In Germany the Schlegel brothers provided the leadership for a Romantic Movement, however, the masterpiece of romantic German literature remain's Goethe's *Faust* which he completed in 1832. Ludwig Van Beethoven exemplified the musical expression of both Romanticism and Nationalism.

The great romantic novelist, Victor Hugo wrote his ever-popular *Les Miserables* and *The Hunchback of Notre Dame* while his fellow French novelist, Alexandre Dumas, captured a romantic flavor in history and wrote *The Count of Monte Cristo* and *The Three Musketeers.* In Russia Pushkin and Gogol unraveled romantic themes while in the United States, James Fenimore Cooper romanticized the early history of the country in his "Leatherstocking Tales."

While Constable, Turner and Delacroix captured the romantic spirit in their paintings especially in their poetic views of nature, the gothic revival that accompanied the romantic movement was expressed in architecture as well as in literature. The British Houses of Parliament rebuilt in the nineteenth century stand as a rather austere monument to the Gothic revival occasioned by the spread of Romanticism.

The romantic movement in the arts is a major historical and cultural phenomenon that cannot be explored adequately within these pages. The interested reader is encouraged to avail himself of the numerous scholarly works which analyze this aspect of cultural and ideological history and to experience the romantic spirit by enjoying the literary and artistic works produced by romantic artists.

Romanticism has always been native to America. The Puritan Utopians who opened the land in the New World combined ideological strands of Romanticism and Puritanism. Their rebellion against the Old World was followed by the rebellions of other romantic dreamers. In the nineteenth century Utopian experiments, such as Robert Owen's New Harmony and Étienne Cabet's Icarian communities, attempted to implement European romantic schemes in the United States. Indeed, the continuous influence of Romanticism in the intellectual history of the United States is revealed in the Transcendentalist writings of such seers as Ralph Waldo Emerson, who popularized a self-reliance thesis, and Henry David Thoreau, whose life and writings argued powerfully for the moral validity of acts of civil disobedience.

The writings of Mark Twain also exemplified many essential elements of American Romanticism. The natural decency and integrity of Huck Finn, the youthful "noble Savage," continually encountered the hypocrisy and cruelty of a corrupting "civilization." Although the alienated Huck Finn was no rebel, the alluring portrayal of his life style posed a threat to establishment norms. Indeed, Twain's book, considered quite controversial, was banned from many public school libraries, lest the young be seduced to "light out for the territory." J. D. Salinger's *Catcher in the Rye,* with its hero Holden Caulfield depicted as a Huck Finn of modernity, suffered a similar fate.

Besides these American philosophers and literary figures, historians such as Francis Parkman and John Pendleton Kennedy mythologized and romanticized America's past. Kennedy's acounts of life on Southern plantations during the slavery era, however, also served to create a myth about the benevolence of the slavery system.

Many romantic ideas of the "Old West" were popularized in "dime novels," pseudo journalistic accounts of would-be cowboys, and the tales of Zane Grey. The American ideological adherence to violence as a means of resolving conflict, as well as the childish view that good and evil are easily distinguishable, result from the romantic faith in simplicity. In the twentieth century this combination of personal violence, hero-worship, and rugged individualism has been popularized in the detective stories of Mickey Spillane, updated in the 1960s by Ian Fleming's James Bond, a rugged individualist at home among the toys of Scientism.

During the 1950s Romanticism gradually spread outward from its various strongholds, some of which it had held for decades. From the romantic colonies in Greenwich Village, the Haight Ashbury sector of San Francisco, Carmel, California, Taos, New Mexico, Provincetown, Massachusetts, the Latin Quarter in New Orleans—the birthplace of the blues—to the bohemian colony that was established in the vacated camp grounds of the World's Fair in Chicago, the ideology of Romanticism eventually radiated across the nation and became a major social movement. The growth of Romanticism also unwittingly served to revitalize

Progressivism in education, which had floundered after its failure to withstand the attacks of the anticommunists and the "space race" disbelievers who saw in the fact that *Sputnik* beat John Glenn into orbit a thumping defeat for Progressive education in America. Besides helping Progressivism, it also helped in its early stage to create a Little Theater movement in the United States which served to rediscover such artists as the poet Edna St. Vincent Millay and the dramatist Eugene O'Neill.

Hipster communities thrived in the 1950s. The "California Renaissance" radiated across the country, and romantic spokesmen such as Allen Ginsberg and Jack Kerouac were avidly quoted by their disciples.

During the 1960s social Romanticism expressed itself through the Freedom Riders in the South and the Free Speechers on the Berkeley campus.

However with the failure of the tenuous *entente* between the Establishment and the Romantic spirit during the brief presidency of John Kennedy, the bifurcation of American culture became a major theme for pessimistic seers. Prodded by an unpopular war and social problems that seemed incapable of resolution, the rebel and revolutionary forces separated from the Establishment and from one another. While puritanical revolutionary groups such as the Black Panthers and the Weathermen accepted the necessity of violence and the overthrow of the government, rebels increasingly withdrew to agrarian communes and *ad hoc* "nations" such as Woodstock to resolve their ethical dilemma.

Like their eighteenth-century precursors, the heralders of the mid-twentieth-century romantic revival had been preceded by intellectual debunkers. Sociologists such as David Riesman, C. Wright Mills, and William Whyte, Jr., served to debunk the myth that the emerging Scientism, with its professionalism, bureaucratization, and technological progress, had produced a healthy, creative, democratic way of life. They revealed the innate danger of repression through affluence and progress and warned that the American dream could become an Orwellian nightmare.

Besides the debunking sociologists, the ethnic minorities also encouraged the emergence of a vibrant Romanticism. Barred from participation in the increasingly stratified social system, ethnic minorities developed belief systems, symbols of identity, language patterns, and institutions which differed (or diverged) from the life style of the assimilated middle class. Norman Mailer characterized the relationship between the Hipster and the Afro-American in his heady monograph, *The White Negro*. That emerging Afro-Americanism influenced the formation of the counterculture is revealed in the common use they make of similar verbal and musical expressions as well as in the importance they both place upon community. The call for a national cultural pluralism that would protect the ethnic identities of America's minorities also served to "liberate" the children of the assimilated classes to search for and create cultures and ideologies that diverged from those of their parents.

The twentieth-century neo-romantic revival has significantly "liberated" the arts. The works of Jack Kerouac, Allen Ginsberg, and Norman Mailer, for example, have broadened the meaning of aesthetic taste. The Polish stage director Jerzy Grotowski, the creator of the "Poor Theater," and Samuel Beckett, whose *Waiting for Godot* ushered in the Theater of the Absurd, have changed the conception of the dramatic arts. Social romanticists such as Alan Watts and Paul Goodman have attempted, with some success, to emancipate their readers from the tunnel vision of Scientism by continuously questioning the cosmological and epistemological bases of the American way of life. Dr. Timothy Leary, the *enfant terrible* of the romantic movement, has awakened an uncomfortable issue concerning the uses of drugs for psychic liberation in a society that increasingly resorts to drugs as psychic medication.

Perhaps the greatest accomplishments of twentieth-century Romanticism is to be found in the world of music. Composers and lyricists such as Robert Dylan (who reportedly selected this pseudonym in honor of the romantic poet, Dylan Thomas), the Beatles, the Rolling Stones, Simon and Garfunkel, and Joan Baez, to name but a few, have created a musical renaissance. Even the gradually dying art form of traditional musicals has been revitalized by such works as *Jesus Christ Superstar, Hair,* and Bernstein's *Mass.* In the area of classical music the twentieth century witnessed the exploration of new forms. The romanticist impulse was captured in the "primitivism' of Igor Stravinsky's *Le Sacre du printemps* (1913). Arnold Schoenberg, although closely aligned with the rationalism of neo-classicism, became an acknowledged composer for his experiments with twelve-tone works. Charles Ives' symphonies combined the romanticist's dreams of the past with the nationalist's concern for patriotism; and Karlheinz Stockhausen's electronic music united elements of Scientism and Romanticism.

Future generations undoubtedly will select and judge the contributions made by twentieth-century romanticists. Some of the popular romantic expressions will be discarded, while others will be added to man's aesthetic traditions. Only when such a judgment has been made will the sociological deviancy of the rebels of our time be viewed as interesting eccentricities which reflected inner genius at least as much as petulance.

### Romanticism and the Middle Class

The style of the rebel is designed, in part, to shock his greatest adversary—the middle class. Denouncing the "average man," hippies—

whether Cynics, eighteenth-century romanticists, or twentieth-century beatniks, have attempted to *épater le bourgeoisie*. This attitude has earned for the rebel the title of defamer and blasphemer. The famous American dancer Isadora Duncan, who is remembered for her eccentricities rather than for her creative genius, symbolized the exhilaration that accompanies rebellion. She was the target for puritan and nationalist hatred. Her public antics and flirtation with Russian revolutionaries provoked the puritan preacher Billy Sunday to condemn her as a "Bolshevik hussy who doesn't wear enough clothes to pad a crutch."

The following observations illustrate the similarity in style of rebels throughout history. Widmer observed that: "The Cynics were noted for their obscenity, in act as well as word, and they reportedly were willing to 'be natural' about fornicating and defecating, anywhere. Their notorious 'shamelessness' was both part of their lesson and part of a way of life." [36] Arnold Hauser, observing the eighteenth-century romantic movement known as the *Jeune-France*, commented:

> The bad manners and impertinences of the bohemians, their often child-ish ambition to embarrass and provoke the unsuspecting bourgeois, their frantic attempt to differentiate themselves from normal, average men and women, the eccentricity of their clothes, their headdress, their beards, Gautier's red waistcoat and the equally conspicuous, though not always so dazzling masquerade of his friends, their free and easy and paradoxical language, their exaggerated, aggressively formulated ideas, their invectives and indecencies, all that is merely the expression of the desire to isolate themselves from the middle-class society, or rather of the desire to represent the already accomplished isolation as intentional and acceptable.[37]

In all ages and countries young rebels mock conventions with beards, long hair, and outrageous behavior: Jean-Jacques Rousseau and Oscar Wilde in their bizarre costumes; George Sand smoking her cigars; and DeQuincey, Coleridge, and Poe with their reliance upon drugs. It was behavior such as this that earned the scorn of Goethe, who exclaimed that the rebels of his day wrote "as though they were ill, and as though the whole world were a hospital."

Today the same behavior patterns can be found among the spiritual descendents of these earlier rebels. As Jacobs and Landau observed, "In some measure, though, the modes of extreme personal behavior adopted by [the "New Radicals"]—their permissive view of marijuana or hallu-ciogenics like LSD, their matter-of-fact acceptance of sexual freedom and their habitual profanity—are part of their search for identity. That search assumes a rejection of everything connected with their old identity and

---

[36] Widmer, *The Literary Rebel*, p. 6.
[37] Arnold Hauser, "A Flight From Reality," in *Romanticism: Problems of Definition, Explanation, and Evaluation*, p. 74.

of the technological, bureaucratic values they see as dominant in American life.[38] As the French say, the more a thing changes, the more it remains the same.

The nature of the activities at such gatherings as the Woodstock Nation reflects in part a desire of rebels to shock the middle class with nudity, "obscene" language and gestures, and public sexual activity. The new rebel theater as well as current counterculture literature reveal a major preoccupation with the outrageous. In an age of mass media, much of the "shocking" behavior of the rebel is quickly popularized. The legitimate theater and press have helped to liberalize the codes of conduct and thus have legitimized within a relatively short period behavior that a few years ago would have been generally rejected. A symbiotic relationship exists between the liberalization of laws and the growth of the counterculture, but this phenomenon, while serving to decrease the bifurcation of the culture, adds to the difficulty of distinguishing between authentic and counterfeit hippies.

The antibourgeois stance of the rebel can be attributed to numerous causal factors. First, in the modern age, the bureaucratic functionaries and supporters of the technological systems are, in fact if not in name, members of the bourgeoisie. These highly visible supporters of the established order usually reflect its principles in their life style. The fact that they may be labeled a "silent majority" does not alter the fact that they are more or less effective defenders of the system.

Secondly, the bourgeoisie often behaves in ways that are easily caricatured. Its members tend to exaggerate social etiquette and to display their affluence in their attempts to imitate the referent group which served them as a role model while they were struggling to achieve their middle-class status. Emulation and imitation easily result in caricature and exaggeration. The attempts of the bourgeois ladies during the eighteenth century to imitate the nobility often proved ridiculous as they swooned and fainted in salons patterned after the palaces of the wealthy, and the *nouveaux riches* of today are no less easy targets of satirical mockery.

Thirdly, most rebels emerge from the middle class. Some eighteenth-century rebels such as Chateaubriand and Lord Byron are notable exceptions. Often the bourgeois rebels emerged after long arduous personal conflicts over bourgeois strictures. Thus, their attack upon the bourgeoisie may be, as some traditionalists have observed, an attack upon their own parents, and their rebellion may be in part an attempt to resolve the unfinished business of youth.

Fourthly, especially since the eighteenth century, the children of

[38] Jacobs and Landau, *The New Radicals,* p. 6.

the middle class have become members of a temporary leisure class who can roam freely without fear of want. Thus, they can afford to be critical of their social system and their bourgeois supporters. Because of the increase in leisure time, the youth seek newness and cultivate romantic rebellion for the excitement of it.

Like the Cynics, the rebels of today gain disciples among the middle-class youth, and like the Cynics who taught at festivals and games, their latter-day counterparts teach at their *ad hoc* nations and in their settlement districts.

In addition to the more obvious reasons for the rebel's shocking behavior, there is also a philosophical basis for such conduct. By shocking the middle class—the largest class supportive of the existing social system—rebels often succeed in calling into question the fundamental assumptions and inequities upon which their civilization rests. As Widmer observed:

> "Forbidden" language, used more or less seriously, serves not only to shock but to reemphasize natural functions and exalt "common" awareness. Done with skill, curses can provide defiant prayers, obscenity a poetry of outrage. Indeed, a literary rebel whose language does not achieve some such sort of violation in itself is neither very poetic nor very rebellious.[39]

Paradoxically, the antibourgeois literature of the rebel is most popular with the middle class. Indeed, the writings of Rousseau and Watts are barely meaningful outside of middle-class settings. The self-actualization syndrome of Rousseauean pedagogy has little relevance to the struggling working classes or to the wealthy managerial classes. Rarely does the rural dweller, the urban proletarian, or the aristocrat reveal an interest in such rebel eccentricities.

Wherever the rebel is situated, the struggle against the embourgeoisement of peoples during times of affluence is his major concern. Indeed, the greatest threat to Hippiedom is its popularization and subsumption by the bourgeoisie.

Among the numerous reasons for the popularization of the counterculture, undoubtedly the clearest and most significant is the massive increase in the size of the adolescent leisure class combined with an ideological admiration for newness and youth which serves to increase interest in the nonwork-oriented counterculture. Because of the importance and financial implications of the appearance of such a major new economic group in the market, Madison Avenue has mobilized its resources to sell its products on the youth market. Indeed, in the realm of economics, if not in the realm of religion, John Lennon of the Beatles was accurate when he observed, "We have more influence than Jesus

[39] Widmer, *The Literary Rebel*, p. 5.

Christ." Yet as Widmer noted, in a commercialized youth culture: "Rebellion, too, becomes a commodity." [40] The popularization of the counterculture has distorted the prism we use to identify authentic hippies, for eccentric and bizarre behavior need not imply rebellion, especially insofar as such behavior may be economically rewarding. Thus Rexroth admonished: "All you have to do nowadays is begin to growl and somebody in a pin-striped suit with real buttonholes on the cuffs shows up with a fist-full of foundation money." [41] Ersatz hippies are difficult to distinguish from authentic ones. Numerous young executives in hippie clothing are fleecing their unsuspecting authentic hippies for corporate profits.

If rebels are energetic and often creative geniuses, are the masses of youth associated with the Woodstock Nation and other quasi-citizenries also rebels? Are those popularity-seeking television personalities also rebels? Stylistically they appear to be authentic, but appearances can be deceiving.

Because the counterculture flourishes upon diversity and because Romanticism avows that uniqueness is always beautiful, social groupings based upon these premises cannot be highly selective in membership. Whereas those who adhere to Scientism or Classicism often reject rebels, authentic rebels usually cannot reject technocrats. What is more, the counterculture is not a highly integrated cultural network and thus within its haven there are numerous individuals who are not rebels. In the following paragraphs we will attempt to identify some of the counterfeit hippies who often resemble their authentic romantic companions.

A common pseudo-romanticist is the sycophant. This hanger-on, who is not particularly creative, liberated, or aware of his identify, is parasitic to the romantic movement. He generally does not "fit" anywhere and therefore joins any group which is not highly selective. Temperamentally he may be a technocrat, but, he usually refuses to develop a sophisticated specialization or to discipline himself; thus adherents of Scientism reject him. He is not particularly creative for he has not developed his imagination. He is an imitator *par excellence.* He apes what he believes are unique liberated characteristics developed in the counterculture. He may expend a great deal of effort and money in imitating the authentic hippie. Synthetic poverty does not come cheap! He is generally other-directed and thus he participates unthinkingly in the rites of passage—clothing styles, language behaviors, and psychic explorations —that initiate one into the counterculture. He experiences the world in an ersatz manner for he lacks the courage or the discipline to confront the existential questions which are fundamental to Romanticism. This

[40] Widmer, *The Literary Rebel,* p. 144.
[41] Rexroth, *The Alternative Society,* p. 22.

individual often confuses eccentricity with uniqueness and thus tends to be enamored of the grotesque. In an age when the mass media seek the unusual, this "counterfeit" often becomes the spokesman for the rebels.

Besides the sycophant, the "middle-class hustler" also claims the counterculture as a home. This exploiter is an adherent of Scientism and a supporter of the Establishment. However, he finds himself temporarily placed in the awkward position of enhancing his chances of success by imitating rebel behavior. For example, in large universities, segments of the university community often form liberal enclaves supportive and protective of hippies. Because these professors generally consider grades, written papers, examinations, and attendance as irrelevant if not damaging to personal growth, they are considered valuable allies for those who desire instant, unearned success. Such professors are especially popular with the clever middle-class hustler.

In his enthusiasm, the hustler adopts a mode of language and dress which reflects an organized disorderliness. His long hair and beard are especially well trimmed. One anticipates that he will be a particularly clever authoritarian parent or Establishment functionary.

The revolutionary is a third type of rebel fellow traveler. As previously noted, he is often confused with the rebel, for the two groups often utilize the same language (e.g., terms like "liberation" and "revolution"), and often share the same heroes (e.g., Herbert Marcuse and Che Guevara). The revolutionary true believer, usually a Maoist or an SDS Weatherman, allies himself with the counterculture because it provides him with the opportunity to preach his revolutionary doctrine. He continuously seeks converts. Although rebels are not especially susceptible to revolutionary rhetoric, they appear to be more promising than Establishment functionaries or present-day blue-collar workers. Of course, sycophants are prime targets for the revolutionary's rhetoric. Romanticist gatherings may provide him with an opportunity to create "disturbances" which serve to broaden the gap between the rebel and the defenders of the established order.

There are numerous other synthetic hippies, including stimulant seekers, escapists, clever hedonists, agents of the Establishment, and psychic tourists. Indeed, counterfeit hippies may outnumber real ones. Unfortunately, twentieth-century rebels have not been cleansed by history, so it is difficult to distinguish rebels from charlatans.

### Romanticism and Individualism

The romantic impulse in the United States is one of the few remaining threads in the American ideological fabric which is supportive of rugged individualism. Although Puritanism, as we shall see in the next chapter, is equated with rugged individualism, its major emphasis is communal in that Puritans emphasize individual and/or social reform for the enhancement of society. Consequently, their efforts generally result in the reinforcement of the power of the state. Similarly, the endeavors of Progressivists interested in social reconstruction generally result in increased legislation that further enhances the power of governmental agencies. Even the more romantic Progressivists, those interested in creative self-expression, envision creativity as a group activity within socially acceptable boundaries. Progressivism, when it forms an alliance with Scientism, removes the unpredictable and competitive forces which inhibit the operational efficiency of social systems.

Romanticists, on the other hand, cherish the unpredictable and the spontaneous, as well as individual creativity. Genius is their referent for moral and aesthetic action and they believe that it cannot be shackled by community or corporate needs, nor by the exigencies of economic planning.

Curiously enough, the romantic belief in rugged individualism often results in profit-making ventures. This unexpected relationship between Romanticism and the business world is reflected in F. Scott Fitzgerald's *The Great Gatsby.* As Nick Carraway, the young bond salesman discovered, however, Jay Gatsby's racketeering did not aid him in his attempts to achieve liberation. As early as the eighteenth century, some romanticists, after attempting utopian communal life, turned to the practical business world of the emerging industrial states. Their business ventures often proved successful because the individualism which led them into their sometimes heroic antisocial behavior also served them in an expanding capitalistic system. Romantic functionaries, for example, constructed the profitable French transport system while others established successful banking houses. A follower of the romantic social planner Saint-Simon, Michel Chevalier, for example, first devised a plan for the Suez Canal. Hippies, once assimilated into the business or educational world, are prone to become directors of programs and administrators rather than minor functionaries within them. Their individualism and middle-class origins propel them into leadership roles.

Even though they are not excessively interested in collecting consumer goods, authentic romanticists continue to exemplify the qualities of the rugged entrepreneur. Whether they be utopian communalists who sell farm products, print newspapers, or design hammocks, they approach their labor with business acumen. The limits which they may impose upon their profits is due to their distrust of economic success and the corruptibility of money rather than to hesitance to excel. Many latter-day entrepreneurs have established small business ventures such as organic food stores or boutique shops in urban centers. Others, with moral abandon, sell drugs at rock festivals.

Economic individualism, although popular in American economic folklore, is virtually nonexistent in the bulk of American economic life. The free enterprise system of the rugged business entrepreneur has been replaced by massive corporate capitalism. American economic life may have remained rugged but it has not remained individualistic. Hippies in the economic domain have thus become historical anachronisms.

Despite the loss of scope for economic individualism, Romanticism remains rooted in the cult of the individual. Emerson's essay on *Self-Reliance* typified this element: "Whoso would be a man, must be a nonconformist. He who would gather immortal palms must not be hindered by the name of goodness, but must explore if it be goodness. Nothing is at last sacred but the integrity of your own mind." [42] Believing that individual genius is the most reliable source of truth and that institutions corrupt, rebels resent all strictures that may be placed upon an individual's behavior. They are protestants and their spirit of individualism is not foreign to the bourgeois character prior to the advent of Progressivism. Indeed, their rugged individualism reflects, in part, the close relationship between the rebel and the bourgeois value system. Christopher Caudwell, an English Marxist, noted: "This is the bourgeois dream, the dream of the one man alone producing the phenomena of the world. He is Faust, Hamlet, Robinson Crusoe, Satan and Prufrock." [43] Indeed, the massive emergence of Romanticism in twentieth-century America may have resulted, in part, from the fact that the political national ideology continued to support romanticized, rugged individualism while the political, social, and economic system became increasingly controlled by progressive Scientism. The hippies are, in a sense, the children of an outdated American ideology popularized in literature and in the mass media, especially in the ever-present "family westerns" which often dominate television prime time.

The rebels see man as an organism with virtually limitless possibilities that have been inhibited by social systems. What prevents man from achieving his potential and revealing his inner beauty, according to the rebel, is not human nature but the social environment. Thus, though not social determinists, they believe that man must struggle against the debilitating social forces which inhibit him. Even the mystical search for transcendence or for experiencing Oneness with the Universe reveals an antisocial thrust insofar as it presupposes that transcendence

[42] Ralph Waldo Emerson, *Selected Prose and Poetry* (New York: Holt, Rinehart & Winston, Inc., 1950), p. 168.
[43] Caudwell, *Illusion and Reality: A Study of the Sources of Poetry*, p. 58.

is based upon highly individual effort, often connected with a process of psychological and social withdrawal.

The rebel's rejection of finite restrictions upon his behavior often leads him to a democratic vision entailing the romanticization of the common man. The great democratic manifestos such as the Declaration of the Rights of Man and the Declaration of Independence not only reflect the enlightened dreams of the rationalist but also reveal the spirit of Romanticism. Liberty rather than equality, however, motivates the rebel.

The alliance between Romanticism and rugged American individualism forms a major thread in the emergence of American belles-lettres. American Romanticism emerged with Ralph Waldo Emerson, Henry David Thoreau, and Mark Twain as its spokesmen. It was nurtured by the call of the West and mythological Western heroes, the discovery of gold, Utopian communal ventures, and national expansion. Emerson reflected the romantic hatred of institutions and the persistent American distrust of institutions when he affirmed: "I have little esteem for governments. . . . The less government we have, the better,—the fewer laws, and the less confided power." [44] The rebellious Thoreau, in a more direct fashion, wrote to his selectmen: "Know all men by these presents, that I Henry Thoreau, do not wish to be regarded as a member of any incorporated society which I have not joined." [45] American Romanticism, based upon the principle of self-reliance devised by Emerson and lived by Thoreau at Walden Pond, remains as a major force against government attempts at social planning. Legislation devised to control morality has been especially ineffective. Similarly, the calls for individual submission to a cause also have been weakened by the romantic thread. Writing in his Journal, Thoreau revealed the cautionary nature of his romantic views when he observed that individuals easily "capitulate to badges and names, to large societies and dead institutions."

Nowhere is the unpredictable and subjective force of individualism expressed more colorfully than in the conception of "romantic love." Emerging as a powerful belief in the Middle Ages, the concept of "romantic love" between a man and woman followed upon the heels of the cult of the Madonna. During the medieval period, the ideological base of romantic love was developed by the troubadours who elaborated the story of lovers pitted against an inhuman social system until it became a major theme in western literature.

Romantic love may be a highly disruptive phenomenon in regard

[44] Emerson, *Selected Prose and Poetry*, p. 203.
[45] Henry David Thoreau, "Civil Disobedience," in *The Works of Thoreau*, ed. Henry S. Canby (Boston: Houghton-Mifflin Co., 1946), p. 800.

to the commonweal for it affirms the right of self-determination. From a social perspective, it serves to undermine relationships which have been developed in terms of rational, political, and practical considerations as well as social need. The belief in romantic love not only has served as a major force in neutralizing the power which parents have over the marital future of their children (an incredibly powerful conservative force) but also undermines the power of institutions. Indeed, royal families until recently have operated in the marriage domain by ignoring the call of "romantic love," in order to satisfy political considerations. When a young king, however, rejects his throne to marry the woman of his choice, the rebellious nature of romantic love is revealed in a most politically disruptive manner.

Romantic love can serve, therefore, to undermine the political system, especially when it involves important political figures. The tragic Homeric tale of Paris and Helen of Troy reveals the highly disruptive force of "romantic love." The greatest social danger of romantic love is that it serves to weaken the loyalty bond between individuals and the state. Lovers are potentially disloyal to the state because their "heart" easily may challenge the dictates of external authority. Indeed, most dystopias would be incomplete without attempts to eliminate romantic love. Without love, individual rebellion is not possible; conversely, loving people are not easy to manage. A world in which love exists is an unpredictable one. The term "romance" therefore also implies individualism, rebellion, and self-assertion. Although melancholic self-destructive love is often at the root of the romantic dilemma, romantic love also serves as a decisive force in political developments. The romantic nature of love, however, prevents it from providing a realistic approach to organized social change.

### Melancholic Romanticism

Because rebels continuously debunk the creeds, styles, and manners of the adherents of the established social system, they are often ridiculed and shunned by the functionaries of the society in which they live. Because they relentlessly attempt to diminish the power of the leaders of the political systems, they are hounded, coerced, imprisoned, and sometimes banished or killed by the defenders of the established order. Although revolutionary groups may give them temporary haven, they too eventually reject the individualistic ways of the romantic rebels. Romanticism, therefore, is the cult of the outcaste, and rebels are doomed to remain vagabonds. As Emerson remarked, "For nonconformity the world whips you with its displeasures." [46]

[46] Emerson, *Selected Prose and Poetry,* p. 171.

Society's rejection of the rebels becomes for them a badge of courage or a symbol of identity. When the leaders of social systems curse or defile them, they are honored and authenticated. To vilify them is to elevate them in the judgment of their fellow vagabonds. Their rejection and subsequent social alienation often becomes the cohesive force which unites the dwellers of the land of Hippiedom. Centers of the romantic ideology, such as Greenwich Village in New York and the Haight-Ashbury section of San Francisco, overflow with aliens from the technological society—artists, deviants, addicts, hobos, criminals, and sundry social rejects.

Inasmuch as being cast in the role of alien by the social system is viewed by rebels as an assistance in their liberation—a psychic achievement—they often expend much effort and time in unraveling tales about their identity and their alienation. The *Confessions of Jean-Jacques Rousseau* as well as the tales of Henry Miller and the wanderings of Norman Mailer reflect a confessional desire to reveal the romantic soul. The poems and songs of the romanticists abound with affirmations about their plight and liberation. During the eighteenth century, such a liberation from the stricture of society was viewed as a symptom of artistic genius or, according to the romantic philosophers, August and Friedrich Schlegel, a synthesis and a new level of organization. To Charles A. Reich, the author of *The Greening of America*, Romanticism is Consciousness III, a level of consciousness higher than both Puritanism (Consciousness I and Scientism (Consciousness II). The tendency of romantic rebels to view their level of awareness as above that of the duped followers of social norms and regulations reflects their essentially elitist position and their rejection of egalitarianism. Viewing themselves as psychic elites, the rebels seek to alter the conceptions and perceptions of their less "enlightened" brethren. Like the biblical beatniks, the prophets of the Old and New Testaments, they assume the role of arrogant spiritual visionaries. The arrogance of the rebel is revealed in Thoreau's remarks to his friend concerning the sacredness of traditions. Affirming that he patterned his life in accordance with his own impulses, he rejected his friend's admonition that such impulses were rooted to his lower nature. "They do not seem to me to be such," Thoreau answered; "but if I am the Devil's child, I will live then from the Devil."

The social liberation which the rebels experience through alienation creates numerous problems for them. In their affirmation of individuality, they frequently forsake the comforts of community and thus their aloneness often turns to loneliness. Their right of individual self-determination often carries with it, when it is affirmed, the price of rejection. Their sense of social alienation as well as the psychological scars which it may produce are expressed painfully in their poems and in their journals.

Chateaubriand, the eighteenth-century Roman Catholic Byron and brilliant romanticist, wrote in his memoirs: "Why did I come into the world *in an age in which I am so out of place?* . . . Why was my lot cast amongst that crowd of mediocrities who looked on me as a madman when I spoke of courage, as a revolutionist when I spoke of liberty?" [47] Chateaubriand's ennui remained to taunt him throughout his life. Like their ideological godfather of the eighteenth century, Jean-Jacques Rousseau, most rebels who have not resorted to Utopian dreams suffer the pains of feeling misunderstood. Irving Babbittt observed ruefully: "When the romanticist is not posing as the victim of fate he poses as the victim of society. Both ways of dodging moral responsibility enter into the romantic legend of the *poète maudit*. Nobody loves a poet. His own mother, according to Baudelaire, utters a malediction upon him. That is because the poet feels so exquisitely that he is at once odious and unintelligible to the ordinary human pachyderm." [48] Caudwell also noted the antisocial quality of the rebel life: "He finds the loneliness which is the condition of his freedom unendurable and coercive. He finds more and more of his experience of the earth and the universe unfriendly and a restraint on his freedom. He ejects everything social from his soul, and finds that it deflates, leaving him petty, empty, and insecure." [49]

Although the alienation from the present social system which rebels experience leads some of them to "escape" into the past, into a Utopia, or into nature, others find relief by going into themselves while attempting to unravel the mysteries of their identity. In seeking to overcome the plight of their social alienation, however, their introspection often turns them into victims of their own pursuit and creates psychologically self-alienated individuals who cannot fathom or unravel their own identity. The cause of the social alienation, of course, lies in the conscious rebellion of the rebels and the impatience and "nastiness" of the leaders of the Establishment. Northrop Frye furnished an insightful observation about the oppressed rebel when he wrote:

> The combination of Bohemian and hobo traditions in the beat, hip, and other disaffected movements of our time seems to be part of an unconscious effort to define a social proletariat in Freudian instead of Marxist terms. . . . Creation is close to the sexual instinct, and it is in their attitude to sex that the two groups collide most violently, as each regards the other's views of sex as obscene. The Freudian proletarian sees established society as a repressive anxiety-structure, the basis of which is the effort to control the sexual impulse and restrict it to predictable forms of

---

[47] Quoted in Georg Brandes, *Revolution and Reaction in Nineteenth Century French Literature* (New York: Russell & Russell, n.d.), p. 164.

[48] Irving Babbitt, *Rousseau and Romanticism* (Boston: Houghton Mifflin Company, 1919), p. 366.

[49] Caudwell, *Illusion and Reality: A Study of the Sources of Poetry*, p. 59.

expression. His emphasis on the sexual aspect of life, his intense awareness of the role of the thwarted sexual drive in the cruelties and fears of
organized society, make him quite as much a moralist as his opponent,
though his moral aim is of course to weaken the anxiety-structure by the
shock tactics of "bad" words, pornography, or the publicizing of sexual
perversions and deviations.[50]

Although the rebels may experience some degree of communal
identity as a Freudian proletariat, their search for reality through introspection often creates numerous pitfalls—some of which can be fatal.
As Alex Comfort observed, "The classicist is running the perpetual risk
of forfeiting his responsibility—the romantic of forfeiting his sanity." [51]

The sense of existential aloneness, of metaphysical alienation, results in part from the rebels rejection of external referents. The rebel is
always thrown upon himself to make moral judgments. Lilian Furst
observed:

> In its extreme consequences individualism can result in the uncertainty,
> the moral relativism, the anxious soul-searching typical of the age of
> *Angst*. It is surely a significant comment on this development that the
> brand of satire so popular nowadays, instead of pillorying an eccentric
> victim against the background of an ordered society, in the manner of
> Pope and Keller, is aimed at a whole way of life.[52]

The search within the self, therefore, is an essential part of the rebel
who must rely upon his own judgments to determine his moral action.
Because of this rebellious moral attitude, the romantic ideology has
served to debunk the "up-down" perspective of human existence. The
rebel perceives the world in terms of an "in-out" frame of reference and,
therefore, dedicates himself to exposing that which is "in"—i.e., internal.
This, by the rebel's definition, is authentic and pure and noble for it
has been untainted by civilization—which is "out"—i.e., external. To the
rebel, the environment does not necessarily determine human action, but
an environment such as that of current civilization does tend to be corrupting. Most rebel journals serve to reveal the noble individual within
the setting of corrupting civilization.

Believing in the fashion of their nineteenth-century spokesman,
Victor Hugo, that "All systems are false; only genius is true," the rebels
in their moral individualism easily fall into moral relativism or moral
anarchy and its ancillary condition—anxiety and behavioral atrophy or
irresponsibility.

[50] Frye, *The Modern Century*, p. 79.
[51] Alex Comfort, *Art and Social Responsibility* (London: The Falcon Press
Limited, 1946), p. 28.
[52] Lilian Furst, *Romanticism in Perspective: A Comparative Study of the
Romantic Movements in England, France and Germany* (New York: The Macmillan
Company, 1969), p. 12.

The romanticist's loneliness is also closely related to his reliance upon feelings and imagination rather than upon reason and logic in communication. If two individuals wish to explain an idea or conceptual scheme to each other, they may effectively accomplish this task if they carefully define their terms and devise a symbol system which they agree upon. Indeed, the logical positivist philosophical school is based upon the conviction that symbols and concepts need to be clarified in order to ensure valid and reliable communication. The mathematician, for example, can communicate effectively with other mathematicians if they agree upon the basic constructs which underlie their mathematical systems. Ideas are communicable. Feelings, however, are not easily communicated because, by their nature, they are unique and individual. Although terms such as "love," "hate," and "fear" are utilized to express feelings, a human being never can be secure in knowing that his "feelings" of these emotions are understood by another. The romanticist's dilemma is compounded by the fact that he realizes that verbal communication of feeling cannot easily be relied upon. Thus, romanticists often rely upon nonverbal communication, which can prove to be disastrous in a society in which the socialization process is founded upon verbal communication. Music, of course, remains as a major medium for romantic communication. The language of the romanticist, whether verbal or nonverbal, often resembles scat singing in jazz in that it reflects deep human experience but communicates effectively to few people.

Romanticism has been labeled the cult of enthusiasm. Thus it is clearly tied to revivalism and sentimentalism. Inasmuch as rebels do not believe that emotions should be curbed, their eccentricities explode with myriad possibilities. Precisely because there is such a bewildering array of possibilities, the rebel strives for integration—for a sense of inner unity. Often this search leads him into a form of transcendence. While some romantic mystics such as Blake and perhaps Watts have arrived at momentary joyous peak experiences, others have turned away from their search in melancholy failure. Because most romanticists believe that man possesses infinite potentialities—potentialities which have been limited by civilization—they create a myth of a Utopian individualism but are rarely able to arrive at the ideal which they set for themselves. Thus some of them despair. Their tendency to think about imponderables and to delve the depths of human emotions which they can imagine but not feel often turns to melancholy despair and possible suicide.

The rebel's inability to adjust his identity to the social environment is replicated in his search for complete knowledge about the nature of the universe. But because the gap between his ideal and his reality can seldom be bridged, he continuously experiences *Ichschmerz* or ego-suffering. Relying upon his imagination to apprehend reality, he is often doomed to be a victim of distorted perceptions, some of which may assume grotesque proportions under the stimulation of drugs. The French poet Charles Baudelaire reflected this existential dilemma in a letter to his mother concerning his thoughts about suicide: "For me to kill myself is absurd, isn't it? And so you are going to leave your old mother all alone, you will say. My heavens! if, strictly speaking, I do not have the right, I believe that the amount of suffering I have undergone for *more than thirty years* would excuse me." [53]

The rebel's search for the natural goodness of man is as elusive as his conscious attempts to achieve spontaneity. While he often seeks to return to the natural state of man, he is perpetually inhibited by the fact that he has been weaned in civilization and thus nurtured in its corruption. The paradox of the corrupted man's search for innocence is never resolved by the rebels. While they may extoll innocence—as in Chateaubriand's description of the American Indian, Jean-Jacques Rousseau's view of the child, or Alan Watts' description of a serene Zen Buddhist priest—the fact remains that all these rebels have been nurtured by Western civilization and thus, by their own definitions, corrupted, making them rather unreliable sources of information concerning the innocence or the natural goodness of man.

The paradox of their enslavement by irreversible socialization processes may explain, in part, the fact that many romanticists have attempted to discard the distorted prism of their socialization by ingesting various forms of drugs. Beaudelaire, Berlioz, Poe, Coleridge, Alan Watts, and Timothy Leary all utilized opiates or stimulants to achieve a form of liberation from the chains of their socialization. Through such ersatz grace, they have sought to counteract what De Quincey in *The Confessions of an English Opium Eater* labeled the curse of *teadium vitae*. Like salvation, authenticity is elusive. Hoxie Fairchild stressed the importance to the romanticists of returning to one's authentic nature. "The romantic God, however, exists for the purpose not of transforming a weak and sinful creature into a being worthy of salvation, but of authenticating the natural goodness of man and lending divine sanction to his expansive impulses." [54]

The rebel's attempt to reveal his inner identity often manifests itself as weak emotionalism or sensationalism. However, this impression of

---

[53] Lois Boe Hyslop and Francis E. Hyslop, Jr., eds., *Baudelaire: A Self-Portrait* (New York: Oxford University Press, 1957), p. 170.
[54] Hoxie Neale Fairchild, "Romantic Religion," in *Romanticism: Points of View*, p. 208.

insincerity may often be due to the fact that the romantic wanderer must of necessity disclose his identity to others by looking at himself, and to accomplish this he must look at himself looking at himself. As might be expected, the romanticists' search within themselves to expand their consciousness often leads to increased self-consciousness rather than increased self-awareness. Like the proverbial centipede who could not walk when he concentrated on his many limbs, the rebel often cannot self-actualize because he is so busy searching for his identity.

Besides forcing him into inactivity, the rebel's search for self-knowledge may easily turn into guilt and despair, for as Adam and Eve discovered, knowledge creates responsibilities which may far exceed the agony imposed by ignorance. Thus the loss of innocence may be accompanied by the despair of disillusionment. What is more, self-knowledge carries with it the danger of loneliness. The eighteenth-century romantic poet Alfred de Vigny captured the flavor of this existential dilemma when he wrote: "I feel myself bowed down, O Lord, by the weight of a punishment which causes me a constant suffering; but as I neither know my crime nor the accusation brought against me, I reconcile myself to my prison." [55] With little relief from the obsessive urge for introspection, many rebels despair.

As an ideology that has been labeled a hotbed of decadence, Romanticism is perhaps more dangerous to its adherents than to the defenders of the established order. The men of feeling may reject social authority but rarely do they destroy it. On the contrary, all too often they are doomed to remain solitary wanderers who are more dangerous to themselves than to others. While the joyous rebellion of these unfulfilled dreamers is reflected in jazz, their melancholic failures are revealed in the blues, and somehow the last chapter in the lives of many romanticists seems to be the cry of the blues.

Perhaps the search for the natural goodness of man represents an element of reality distorted by unexamined ideological assumptions. Can the romanticist realistically blame institutions and/or society for the evil perpetrated upon himself and others? Is the belief in innate goodness a childish illusion? Must he succumb to the suggestion of the puritanical Sigmund Freud: "The time comes when every one of us has to abandon the illusory anticipations with which in our youth we regarded our fellow-men, and when we realize how much hardship and suffering we have been caused in life through their ill-will"? [56]

[55] Quoted in Brandes, *Revolution and Reaction in Nineteenth Century French Literature*, p. 20.

[56] Sigmund Freud, *Civilization and Its Discontents*, trans. Joan Riviere (Garden City, N.Y.: Doubleday & Company, Inc., 1958), p. 62.

### Romanticism and Nature

Although romanticists reject the "law-and-order" constructs designed by the classicists and rationalists, they do not discard the importance of order. Romanticism is not necessarily based upon the adherence to anarchy or absolute relativism, but it is based upon the principle that bland, man-made repetitive patterns imposed by classical standards distort the natural ordering of life, and that such a natural ordering should be reinstated. Victor Hugo, for example, contrasted the carefully trimmed gardens of the Palace of Versaille with descriptions of the rugged landscape of the New World and affirmed that beauty and order existed in the latter rather than in the symmetry and regularity imposed by man in the former. The eighteenth-century romantic movement was essentially a search for the hidden, beautiful nature of reality and a rejection of the distorted—that is, highly ordered—constructs imposed by reason, science, and social institutions. Similarly, Romanticism in the twentieth century repudiated the world view of technologists who would slavishly follow the dictates of science while rejecting creativity and innovation. In "Surrealism and the Romantic Principle," Herbert Read expressed the romantic view of the destructiveness of classicism when he wrote:

> Classicism is the intellectual counterpart of political tyranny. It was so in the ancient world and in the medieval empires; it was renewed to express the dictatorships of the Renaissance and has ever since been the official creed of capitalism. Wherever the blood of martyrs stains the ground, there will you find a doric column or perhaps a statue of Minerva.[57]

Kenneth Rexroth made much the same point when he wrote: "To suppose that one can have classicism without authoritarianism is like supposing that one can have braking power without friction." [58]

Inasmuch as romanticists believe that man's emotions and instincts as well as his imagination are valuable and reliable sources of knowledge concerning the natural order, they generally reject the forms of order perceived through rationalistic and scientific methodology. Because one's perspective of the beautiful and the ugly rests, in part, upon one's conception of order, the romantic artists often perceive beauty where a classicist would perceive ugliness. Similarly, the classical view of art is often rejected by the romantic critic, who views the highly ordered work of the classicist as a distortion of reality. The classical artists who painted

[57] Herbert Read, "Surrealism and the Romantic Principle," in *Romanticism: Points of View,* p. 95.
[58] Rexroth, *The Alternative Society,* p. 69.

children in the form of miniature adults exemplify this type of distortion by excessive order.

Because romanticists believe that true genius alone can determine beauty and order, and that the genius's instincts are his best tool for ascertaining the true nature of order, they reject the aesthetic judgments of most social critics. Although it results in a form of aesthetic relativism, this rejection also serves to liberate the arts from strictures imposed by the classical codes of standard-mongers.

Besides rejecting the rationalistic and classical perspective of art and thought, the romanticists also rejected the scientific way of analyzing reality. Although the scientists and the romanticists are very similar in that both attempt to unravel the mystery of reality through exploration and experimentation, they differ markedly in the tools which they bring to their research. The former seeks truth through objectivity, whereas the latter denies the existence of objective consciousness and relies upon the subjective personal experience of his instincts, feelings, and imagination. (Of course the technocrat, who is a slavish methodologist, differs from both the romanticist and the scientist in that he does not seek to discover but to replicate.)

The difference between the rationalist, the scientist, and the romanticist is revealed in the search for a "religious" basis for reality. The rationalist believed that through a rational ordering of scientific laws he could arrive at a systematic understanding of the intelligible scheme of the universe. Such rationalist deists have their counterparts in the followers of Pierre Teilhard de Chardin who seek through scientific analysis and mystical experience to discover the nature of the evolving cosmos. Their search is similar but their mode is different from that of the romantic pantheist who, through intuition and intense personal feeling, seeks to unravel the nature of the Universe.

Romanticists view life organically rather than from a mechanistic perspective, so that, insofar as they use science at all, they tend to rely upon the life science of biology rather than the mechanical science of physics for the heuristic models which they use to explain the nature of the universe. To the romantic researcher, the whole is greater than its parts and any attempt to dissect reality will destroy its nature; as Wordsworth exclaimed, "We murder to dissect." Thus Bruce Wilshire observed: "To the romantic, human life seems intrinsically purposive and goal-directed; a science which construed man as a body in space, as a machine within a machine, seemed not only false but dangerously demoralizing." [59]

Free will is an essential characteristic of man according to the

[59] Bruce Wilshire, *Romanticism and Evolution* (New York: G. P. Putnam's Sons, 1968), p. 11.

romantic philosopher, and constructs which destroy this essential quality are rejected by him. All forms of determinism—environmental, historical, childhood, genetic, cultural, or evolutionary—are rejected by the romantic philosopher because they contradict his basic conviction that man can transcend his externally imposed limits. As Jean-Paul Sartre, whose views fluctuate between those of a romantic rebel and those of a puritan revolutionary, noted, "This possibility of *rising above* a situation in order to get a perspective on it (a perspective which is not pure knowledge, but an indissoluble linking of understanding and action) is precisely what we call freedom." [60]

Both the technocrats and the romanticists energetically strive to change the world, but while the former view progress as a methodological and practical phenomenon designed in accordance with clearly stated propositions, the latter utilize as their referent for human advancement an organic view of mankind, a belief in free will, and an application of ideal constructs to daily life. Although Scientism and Romanticism have been combined periodically in an attempt to formulate a comprehensive view of man, such unions generally have proven disastrous, for the assumptions of the two ideologies are antithetic. In his "Discourse on the Moral Effect of the Sciences and Art," Jean-Jaques Rousseau compared science to a dangerous weapon in the hands of a child. Nature's secrets were a blessing, Rousseau claimed, and attempts to probe them by scientific means posed great dangers to mankind. Consistent in his obscurantism, he expressed joy at the fact that human beings are born without learning and that the acquisition of knowledge is a difficult and long process.

Wilshire explains the origins of this hostility to science when he points out that the romantics realized "that scientific knowledge with its power over nature had been used by man to change the world before he had determined what his real interests were; as if he had wielded a fabulous weapon but, unaware of the position of his own feet, had begun to hack them off." [61] To the romanticists, therefore, science not only served to distort reality by ignoring the poetic, nonquantifiable dimension of life, but also could be utilized to destroy man. Numerous science fiction distopias are in fact tales which illustrate man's struggle against the children of science—technological systems. They reflect in crisis proportions Thoreau's complaint that "We do not ride on the railroad; it rides upon us." Technology becomes the *bête noire* of man's search for happiness.

While some romanticists develop Utopian constructs and theories

[60] Jean-Paul Sartre, *Literary and Philosophical Essays* (New York: Collier Books, 1955), p. 235.
[61] Wilshire, *Romanticism and Evolution*, p. 11.

of the conscious evolution of the human race to sustain their belief in the perfectibility of man, others, believing that man has been perverted by civilization, search within nature for the romantic ideal. During the eighteenth century, romanticists viewed the city as a center of corruption —or, as Wordsworth labeled London, a "Wide Waste." Their contention was supported by the fact that the environmental blight which accompanied the industrial revolution was centered in the dense urban monstrosities generated by the factory system. As Wilshire noted, "There is an obvious feature in the romantics' championing of nature and in their attack on newly industrialized society. Landscapes were destroyed and replaced by factories, streams were being polluted, and towns blackened by soot and grime." [62] Indeed, the misuse of nature by civilizations oriented to technological development and affluence has been well documented and remains as a major argument in support of the romantic naturalist's denunciation of science and technology. The dehumanization of man that resulted from the precipitate leap into the industrial age generated movements aimed at altering the modern state of affairs. While some sought refuge in a return to nature and in devising utopian schemes, others, such as Karl Marx, avoided the romantic "escape" and sought through revolution a means of removing the excruciating social ills that accompanied the simultaneous rise of industrialism and urbanization.

The English romanticists of the eighteenth and nineteenth centuries set the tone for the return-to-nature movement. Viewing the cities as centers of the corruption and disorderliness that created alienation, they sought, through agrarian communal ventures and through their poetry, to discover the simplicity of the natural world. What is more, by seeking in nature for poetic inspiration, the romanticists overthrew the classicist's longstanding prejudice against utilizing nature as a basis for poetic concern. They also turned to nature to escape from the complex social relationships which limited man's spiritual development, for nature offered not solely an escape from the city but also an object of man's adoration. Shelley viewed the religion of Nature as the only immortal religious system and his fellow nature-worshiper, Wordsworth revealed his mystical soul as he listened to "the music of the seasons" and observed mountains and saw nature's "solemn temples." In his analysis of the nature mysticism of Wordsworth, H. G. Schenk noted:

> Moreover, it was Nature to which he had fled to soothe his *Weltschmerz* in the early 1790s: Nature, and Nature alone, had filled the spiritual void created by the shipwreck of his hopes in the French Revolution as well as by his disillusionment with Godwin's philosophy, and last but not least personal vicissitudes. Significantly, Nature—or the Universe, to which he

[62] Wilshire, *Romanticism and Evolution,* p. 20.

also attributed infinite wisdom—almost invariably appeared to Wordsworth in the shape of a beneficent goddess.[63]

Nature thus served the romanticist in his process of transcendence—that is, his struggle to spiritualize his individuality. Immersion in nature would serve for many romanticists as a religious, often pantheistic, experience. Keats exclaimed:

> To one who has been long in city pent,
> 'Tis very sweet to look into the fair
> And open face of heaven,—to breathe a prayer
> Full in the smile of the blue firmament.[64]

It was through a return to nature that the romantic naturalist struggled to remove the alienation which led others to Utopian experiments or to drugs. The nature poet believed that his individual identity and the natural world were one. Lord Byron in *Childe Harold* asked:

> Are not the mountains, waves, and skies, a part
> Of me and of my soul, as I of them?
> Is not the love of these deep in my heart
> With a pure passion? [65]

Yet, as with any ideology, Romanticism distorts man's vision of reality. The romanticists infatuation with nature, for example, prevents them from being aware of the sufferings of man resulting from nature's diseases, floods, tornadoes, and droughts. The economic security, materialistic comforts, and leisure enjoyed by so many American citizens (*including* many modern romanticists) were the results of Puritanism and Scientism—ideologies that viewed nature *not* as a god to be revered, but as a demon to be conquered, a challenge to man's capabilities. Indeed, to deny this obvious fact is to reject a major element of civilization.

Nevertheless, Romanticism, with its unwavering faith in the natural goodness of man, created the myth of the "Noble Savage," who embodied the uncivilized virtues so dear to the romantic imagination. The "Noble Savage" label was applied to various groupings—shepherds, Indians, South Sea Islanders, Africans, and children—in short, anyone who one could plausibly claim had not been corrupted by civilization. Indeed, in the twentieth century the "Noble Savage" took the unlikely form of urban dwellers who, because of economic deprivation or ethnic and racial identity, were denied access to the bourgeois civilization. Perceived by the adherents of the counterculture as free, sensitive, authentic, and oppressed, the racial and cultural minorities were avidly imitated by the

[63] Hans G. Schenk, *The Mind of the European Romantics* (New York: Frederick Ungar Publishing Co., 1967), p. 171.
[64] John Keats, Sonnet X from *Poems* (1817).
[65] George Gordon, Lord Byron, *Childe Harold's Pilgrimage*, III, LXXV, 1–4.

romantic children of the bourgeoisie—much to the puzzlement of the objects of this admiration. Men who have not possessed wealth often find it difficult to understand why it is so corrupting, just as those who have not experienced imposed poverty fail to understand its dehumanization. In their eagerness to find ideals, however, rebels often forget that poverty in theory is vastly different from poverty in fact.

Another candidate for the mantle of the natural and noble man has been the American Indian, who rebels often imitate in style and clothing. During the eighteenth century, tales related by travelers to the New World helped to popularize a whole mythology about the benevolent pastoral primitivism of the American aborigines. Some of the most popular descriptions of the American Indian were devised by writers who had not been to the Americas.

As one might expect, the European romantic image of the American Indian was not fully appreciated in the United States, especially among the descendants of the settlers in the Old West. In America, on the contrary, it was the Indian fighter, the cowboy, and the western trailblazer and settler who were to emerge as folk heroes and to serve as exemplars for romantic historical legends. Davy Crockett rather than Geronimo served as a model of the "natural man" for American children.

Romantic heroes abound in literature. Edgar Rice Burroughs' numerous tales about his noble white savage Tarzan, have served as the basis of numerous popular paperbacks and films. James Fenimore Cooper's *Leatherstocking Tales* with their romantic hero Natty Bumppo have reached generations of American children through American literature courses. Besides Tarzan and Natty Bumppo, American children have invariably been educated to the plight of the romantic hero through such literary characters as Mary Shelley's Frankenstein, Victor Hugo's Hunchback of Notre Dame. and Herman Melville's Billy Budd—all three of whom exemplify the tragic fate of rebels, with or without a cause, in that their innocent lives fell victim to the fear and cold-heartedness of what passes for civilization.

### Cultural or Romantic Nationalism

While the romantic idealization of primitive and simple peoples served to enhance the study of cultural differences and to expand the anthropological study of man, it also served as a basis for the development of cultural Nationalism. Thus the discovery of the "common folk" and the development of the mythology that was to accompany the search for their identity were put in the service of devious ends.

Given certain circumstances, romantic individualism develops naturally into romantic Nationalism. Beginning with a focus upon the importance of uniqueness and individuality, some romanticists turn toward cultural differences between groups and join forces with those dedicated to the preservation and creative expansion of cultural diversity. Their hatred of political institutions includes a rejection of political national groupings, nation-states. Rebels, therefore, are often allied with cultural minorities who seek cultural or political autonomy.

A second major reason why romanticists support cultural Nationalism is their admiration for the "simple folk"—that group of individuals within nation-states which has had the least contact with major institutions. Rebels distrust the defenders of objective consciousness—the intellectual and educational elite—and thus turn to the folk for knowledge about man. In their search for truth they rely upon the manners, styles, and mythology that characterizes the less formally educated. As Emerson affirmed: "Colleges and books only copy the language which the field and the work-yard made." [66]

The concern of some romanticists for history, tradition, folk mythology, "local color," and racial and ethnic differences as expressions of individuality leads directly to cultural pluralism. Viewing the development of cultures as organic growths, these romanticists contend that nature in all her workings reveals diversity, and that cultural pluralism is thus a reflection of the natural order of things.

Their search through the oral traditions of peoples, especially in folk music and national legends, creates a "renaissance" of national traditions. Such an investigation in the nineteenth century served to destroy the artistic reliance upon the Greco-Roman tradition and created an aesthetic dependency upon ethnic antecedents. Delving into the traditions of the "folk," romantic nationalists discovered semi-forgotten and rarely accurate "facts" which they developed into a cohesive force capable of being deployed by peoples seeking political autonomy.

The romanticist focus upon ethnic identity in the nineteenth century served to destroy the rational citizen-of-the-world model devised by the philosophers of the Enlightenment. As an ancillary consequence of this focus upon cultural differences, European civilization witnessed a renaissance of art based upon aesthetic cultural provincialism. Great composers such as Schubert and Wagner helped to awaken an ethnic identity in the German people by utilizing ancient mythology as the bases of their compositions. Similarly, the music of the romantic composers Smetana and Sibelius enhanced the spirit of Nationalism in Czechoslovakia and Finland. Dvořák, in addition to expressing the Nationalism

[66] Ralph Waldo Emerson, *Selected Writings*, p. 54.

of Bohemia, was influenced by the spirituals of Black Americans—an influence discernible in his ninth symphony, "From the New World."

By asserting that cultural differences should be enhanced and that minorities should be granted cultural autonomy, the rebel once again challenges the centripetal forces which characterize socialization within a technological society. Seymore W. Itzkoff affirmed that individual identity and creativity can best be achieved through cultural pluralism; in a debunking view of the technologized and urbanized American society, he bemoaned: "Too often man is made to feel that the only way he can exhibit his individuality is to resign from the 'organized system' to give up those prized securities and material advantages modern life has given him, become a hippie, a yippie, or an outcast on the Bowery." [67] Cultural pluralism is necessary, Itzkoff claims, because there is an inverse correlation between the size of social groupings and the development of meaningful values. "An individual man," he writes, "cannot freely assent to or identify with values that are purportedly shared by hundreds of millions of people; hundreds yes, perhaps thousands." [68]

The romantic vision expressed by Itzkoff is also reflected by John Collier in his article concerning the neo-monistic form of assimilation perpetuated by the United States government upon the American Indian. The romantic rejection of technology behind his argument is clearly revealed in the following passage:

> Individuals and groups who are different from the pulvarized, unstructured masses are to be pitied, and as in an earlier time to be scorned and hated. They are to be charitably saved from themselves through being made partners in the material and cultural dominance of the White, Western, economically affluent, socially atomistic, and spiritually featureless society which in this H-bomb epoch is being herded towards its own and the world's doom. Not guns or the lash or, in the main, not jails, are to be used in the grinding of human differences into the faceless deadlevel of White-decreed Western economic man; instead, that which Madison Avenue calls the "engineering of consent" is to be used.[69]

The call for romantic Nationalism or cultural Nationalism was especially potent in Germany where a centralized nation-state was late in forming. It was combined with a strong sense of national character and national history. Thus Wagner, in his operas, captured the haunting romantic call for a return to the roots of the German people, and even the romantic accounts of the Roman historian Tacitus were utilized to mythologize the German past: "No one in Germany finds vice amusing,

---

[67] Seymore W. Itzkoff, *Cultural Pluralism and American Education* (Scranton: International Textbook Company, 1969), p. 33.

[68] Itzkoff, *Cultural Pluralism and American Education*, p. 109.

[69] John Collier, "Pluralism and the American Indian," *American Indiogena*, XXII, No. 3 (July 1962), 205.

or calls it 'up-to-date' to debauch and be debauched. . . . Good morality is more effective in Germany than good laws in some places that we know." [70] The fact that such cultural identity can turn into ethnocentrism was exemplified by the emergence of Nazism in Germany. Utilizing the romantic mythology developed about the purity and nobility of Germany's primitive ancestors (and a distorted interpretation of Nietzche's superman, Zarathustra), Hitler devised an Aryan myth capable of supporting vicious and inhuman political measures. By combining political and cultural Nationalism, he developed incredible public support for diverse political acts. The bouquet of cultural pluralism easily turns into a basket of serpents! The excessive religious spirit that may form around cultural Nationalism was noted by Carlton B. Hayes:

> The intellectual constructs a speculative theology or mythology of nationalism. The imagination builds an unseen world around the eternal past and the everlasting future of one's nationality. The emotions feed the theological virtues of faith, hope and filial love; they arouse a joy and ecstacy in the contemplation of the national god, who is all-good and all-protecting, a longing for his favours, a thankfulness for his benefits, a fear of offending Him, and feelings of awe and reverence at the immensity of His power and wisdom; they express themselves naturally in worship. . . .[71]

Although Romanticism is supportive of cultural Nationalism and the enhancement of differences among nationalities, romanticists, are not necessarily chauvinistic or ethnocentric. Indeed, their emphasis may be international. Similar in spirit to the *Lieber Meister* of cultural pluralsm in the United States, Horace Kallen, some have sought the preservation of cultural differences because it is an inalienable right. In 1915 Kallen expressed his internationalism by calling for intranational diversity: "Its form is that of the Federal Republic, its substance a democracy of nationalities, co-operating voluntarily and autonomously in the enterprise of self-realization through the protection of men according to their kind." [72] His pluralistic dream is similar to that of the English poet Shelley who, in his introduction to "Prometheus Unbound," called for the decentralization of England into city-states where cutural revitalization could lead to a reawakening of creativity.

Thus the devastating form of romantic Nationalism that is identified with Nazism is a distortion of the romantic vision, for romanticists are international in spirit in that they reject political boundaries and demands

---

[70] H. Mattingly, trans., *Tacitus on Britain and Germany* (Baltimore: Penguin Books, Inc., 1951), p. 117.

[71] Carlton B. Hayes, *Essays on Nationalism* (New York: The Macmillan Company, 1937), p. 105.

[72] Horace Kallen, "Democracy Versus the Melting Pot: A Study of American Nationality." *The Nation*, C, No. 2591 (February 25, 1915), 220.

placed upon peoples by nation-states which limit their freedom. The ideology of Romanticism is cross-national and the recent revival of it has been an international movement. It is no accident that a rockfest like the one in Woodstock, New York, called itself the Woodstock Nation, for its participants saw the gathering as an alternative to the nation-state. What is more, the jet age has facilitated massive migrations of romantic internationalists. The more enlightened and most secure nation-states, such as Holland and Denmark, have made provisions to adjust to this romantic migration, but the less enlightened and politically more repressive states, such as East Germany and Greece, have attempted to prevent these new migrants from entering their particular national boundaries. That Greece, the home of the Cynics, should fear twentieth-century rebels is a sad commentary on the present condition of that ancient land.

### Utopian Romanticism

Social romanticists reject the social environment in which they live and seek, whether in the past, in nature, in the future, or in Utopian ventures, for means of liberating human beings from the destructive forces of "civilization." Although the Utopian romanticists exert little pressure upon the social systems which they reject, they offer colorful and visionary examples of ways to alter the alienating forces in stratified and stultified social systems.

In contrast to those romanticists who believe in the natural goodness of man and call for a return to nature because they hold a very negative view of social planning, the utopian romanticists believe in the perfectibility of man and try to design social systems to liberate man's perfectible nature. The writings of Rousseau contain elements of both perspectives. In his *Emile* we have an example of the ideology of a romantic rebel who wishes to return to the goodness of nature and escape the corruptibility of society; his *Social Contract*, however, is the work of a puritanical revolutionary who yearns for absolute order in a communal society. "If we have to combat either nature or society, we must choose between making a man or making a citizen. We cannot make both," Rousseau wrote.[73] Rousseau the romantic in a corrupt society believes in education for manhood; Rousseau the puritan in a just society, believes in education for citizenship.

Utopian romanticists differ from realistic Marxists not only in their rejection of collective violence as a means of achieving social justice but

[73] The *Emile* of Jean Jacques Rousseau, trans. and ed. William Boyd (New York: Bureau of Publication, Teachers College, Columbia University, 1963), p. 13.

also in the ends toward which they work. Where Marxists seek to alter the social systems they inhabit, utopian romanticists search outside of that system for salvation. David Evans has pointed out some of the consequences of this difference: "It is a striking paradox that whereas Marxism, the socialism of a universal man, makes its appeal to the working class, Saint-Simonism which is an engineer's or business man's socialism addresses itself pre-eminently to intellectuals and concerns itself with their function in society." [74] His observation is relevant to the communal movements of the mid-twentieth century, which have achieved a certain degree of popularity with the children and youth of the middle class but rarely have attracted the rural or urban poor or the disenfranchised and economically deprived members of minority groups. Hippie communalism is a bourgeois phenomenon. Whereas the oppressed see the issue of social justice as a matter of political cunning and revolution, to the romanticists it is a matter of dreams and love. Emerson expressed the romanticists' incredible naivety concerning politics when he stated, "The power of love, as the basis of a State, has never been tried." [75] On matters of politics, certainly Machiavelli's realism was more profound.

Utopian Romanticism does not imply a rejection of the rebel's belief in the importance and centrality of individual liberation. On the contrary, it is perfectly consistent with such a concern, for the Utopian rebel believes that within an ideally designed social system an individual will be able to actualize his true potential. Obviously, however, the attempt to combine individual freedom with the values of communal living can easily produce tensions which can disrupt the most visionary of communal ventures. The organizational struggles which commonly mar communal ventures result from the somewhat paradoxical nature of attempts to maximize individual freedom in the context of social system. Without a cohesive ideological bond, the paradox of communalism as a means of individual liberation can result in pathetic defeat. The relinquishment of individual liberty, however, may be the price one pays for such a bond; and, for romanticists in particular, this price is usually exorbitant.

Utopian romanticists have existed since the beginning of recorded history, turning toward Utopian communal schemes in order to avoid the debilitating forces imposed by the social systems in which they found themselves. Some of them have turned to the past in search of a previous golden age, whereas others have devised and actualized communal schemes to escape from the tentacles of their civilizations. Depending upon one's perspective, such an alternative way of life may be viewed as escapism or liberation. Arnold Hauser admonished: "What the roman-

[74] David Owen Evans, *Social Romanticism in France, 1830–1848* (New York: Octagon Books, 1969), p. 27.
[75] Emerson, *Selected Prose and Poetry*, p. 206.

tic clings to is, in the final analysis, of no consequence; the essential thing is his fear of the present and of the end of the world." [76] Bruce Wilshire, on the other hand, views Romanticism as an expression of realism: "We should not call a man an escapist who is trying to escape from what he thinks is a trap," he aptly observes.[77] Because Utopian romanticists see in the technological sterility of mass industrialized societies a destructive force which exerts negative pressure on the growth and development of humanness, they seek respite and liberation within visionary ventures. Some romanticists sought refuge in the ascetic solitary life; thus John the Baptist, St. Ambrose, and Henry David Thoreau sought liberation in mono-communities.

Besides solitary mystical unity with the universe, and secular communalism, Utopian Romanticism may express itself in terms of religious communal movements. Indeed, religious communalism has been one of the most powerful strains in the history of utopian Romanticism. Religious communes not only have outlasted secular ones, but they have flourished throughout man's history. The Essenes, for example, established communes on the shores of the Dead Sea during biblical times. The recently unearthed written records of these ascetic communal rebels have helped to clarify the codes of conduct which regulated their communities.[78] The early Christians also formed communes, especially during periods of persecution. Jesus and his apostles, for example, formed a gypsy commune in which all goods were communally owned.

Throughout the Middle Ages, monastic orders served to channel efforts at Utopian communalism. The fact that such communal ventures were designed with the conviction that the commune itself was but a way station in the journey to the City of God may have served to diminish intercommunal strife. With the rise of Protestantism, numerous communal religious ventures were attempted, many reflecting the intense and passionate belief in the supremacy of individual conscience and the rugged communal spirit of the Anabaptists.

The Amish, a pacifist religious people, have survived the onslaught of the technological age and have preserved an agrarian base for their isolated communities. This quiescent and undisturbing people recently have confronted the assimilative demands of a large technological nation-state. Seeking to preserve the influence and primacy of the family, the Amish believe that their youth should not be educated in formal institutions. Because this position is in violation of state school attendance laws

[76] Arnold Hauser, "A Flight From Reality," in *Romanticism: Definition Explanation, and Evaluation,* p. 68.

[77] Wilshire, *Romanticism and Evolution,* p. 10.

[78] Theodor H. Gaster, trans., *The Dead Sea Scriptures* (Garden City, N.Y.: Doubleday & Company, Inc., 1957).

in the United States, the firmness of their stand raises the issue of religious freedom versus obedience to the state. This strong-hearted people patiently awaited court decisions and revealed that they would emigrate to other lands if unable to practice the dictates of their creeds. Such a "forced" migration was averted by the 1972 Supreme Court decision affirming that compulsory school attendance laws did not need to be applied to the Amish people.

Numerous other religious communities, with diverse emphases, have been established during the nineteenth and twentieth centuries in the United States. The United Society of Believers in Christ's Second Appearing, popularly labeled Shakers, for example, was based upon an enforced celibate code, whereas the Oneida community, which eventually was changed from a religious order to a joint stock company, was based upon the doctrine of "complex marriage."

The recent revival of Romanticism during the mid-twentieth century has resulted in the creation of diverse religious communes which flourish especially in the western states of the United States. In Hawaii, for example, the Maui Zendo commune adheres to Zen Buddhism, while the Himalayan academy of Nevada is based upon belief in Yogism. The Family of the Mystic Arts stresses a fundamentalist Christian doctrine, while the "One World Family of the Messiah's World Crusade" focuses upon the oneness of mankind and the belief that flying saucers are manned by higher beings who will save humanity.[79]

Although romanticists are not environmental determinists, they have sought continuously to weaken the hold which civilized societies exert upon individuals. In some cases rebels began with grandiose plans for social reform and hoped for a universal liberation of man. At the conclusion of the eighteenth century, for example, European romanticists looked upon the French Revolution as the beginning of a new age, an age in which a liberated man would flourish in societies designed in accordance with the ideals of liberty, equality, and fraternity. Such grandiose plans were betrayed by unforeseen events. The French Revolution, for example, eventually resulted in a hideous Reign of Terror and the rise of Napoleon as emperor. During the twentieth century the romantic faith in social reform, as expressed in the rhetoric of the New Frontier, soon turned to bitter disappointment as the young President was assassinated. Violence perpetuated by young revolutionaries and overzealous defenders of the established order replaced the romantic dreams reflected in songs such as "We Shall Overcome." Racial conflicts,

[79] For an overview of recent communal ventures see *The Modern Utopian*, Vol. V, Nos. 1, 2, 3 (San Francisco: Alternatives Foundation, 1971), and Ron E. Roberts, *The New Communes: Coming Together in America* (Englewood Cliffs, N.J.: Prentice-Hall, Inc., 1971).

assasinations, a bitter pathetic war, and student rebellion served to accentuate the failure of social reform schemes. Numerous disillusioned twentieth-century rebels turned away from social action and focused upon controlled social reform; they turned toward secular and religious Utopian schemes in a search for the solution to man's dilemma.

Similarly, in the eighteenth century, the two famous English poets, Robert Southey and Samuel Taylor Coleridge, disillusioned by the excesses of the Reign of Terror, turned to Utopian plans. Working with a third rebel, Robert Lovell, they devised a plan for a "pantisocratic" community in the United States on the shores of the Susquehanna. Coleridge wrote of this "Pantisocracy":

> What I dared not expect from constitutions of governments and whole nations I hoped from religion and a small company of chosen individuals, and formed a plan, as harmless as it was extravagant, of trying the experiment of human perfectability on the banks of the Susquehannah; where our little society, in its second generation, was to have combined the innocence of the Patriarchal Age with the knowledge and general refinements of European culture; and where I dreamed that in the sober evening of my life I should behold the cottages of independence in the individual dale of industry.[80]

The kinds of Utopian plans proposed by rebels depend in great measure upon the nature of the social system in which they find themselves. Nineteenth-century Utopian plans, for example, were often socialistic in design—an obvious rejection of the growing and often brutal capitalistic economic systems that accompanied the emergence of large industrial states. In the twentieth century, Utopian schemes often reflect a rejection of the nuclear family and middle-class modes of behavior.

During the nineteenth century, numerous secular Utopian ventures were attempted in the United States. For example, Charles Fourier, a French philosopher and follower of Saint-Simon, designed a communal venture which was attempted in the United States. His communal plan was based upon phalanxes—that is, communes of 1,620 people in which individuals continuously rotated their work assignments. He argued that man possesses a "butterfly passion," by which he meant a need for diversity, and that such a scheme would serve to satisfy it. Popularized by a disciple, Albert Brisbane, phalanxes were established in the United States. One of them, Brook Farm in Massachusetts, included in its membership Ralph Waldo Emerson and Nathaniel Hawthorne.

Another major Utopian scheme was devised by Étienne Cabet. Called Icaria, this dream city was based upon the belief in common ownership, equality, and universal suffrage. In 1848 an Icarian commune was established in Texas. Eventually, after many unpopular decisions

[80] Quoted by Fairchild in *The Romantic Quest,* p .54.

as communal leader, Cabet was removed as president from one of his communes in the Midwest. His decision to limit women's hats to specific standard sizes was especially unpopular. He died outside his commune in St. Louis in 1856. Icarian communities eventually became joint stock companies.

Among the many communes in existence today, we can find some reflecting virtually all of the issues that twentieth-century society faces. From the scientific community pattern of Walden Two, a commune based upon the behavioral dream of B. F. Skinner, to the psychedelic commune of Milbrook, the home of the Neo-American Church which reflects the teaching of Dr. Leary, various communal forms have evolved. Some are organized for social service; Synanon, for example, attempts to rehabilitate drug addicts while Camhill Village is designed to teach mentally retarded children. Koinonia Farm in Georgia is designed as a self-help biracial brotherhood of farmers while Trivoli Farm in upstate New York is designed to house the homeless.

Throughout history Utopian movements have served as a safety valve through which creative and dissatisfied members of social systems can attempt to actualize their visions. Such movements also reflect the defects of particular social systems. Although communal movements have not profoundly or directly altered the American way of middle-class life, they reflect man's persistent search for means to actualize himself and to form meaningful social relationships. That such experiences often fail should serve as a sign of man's difficult struggle against the forces of alienation rather than as a lesson for resignation. The difference between fools and heroes, as previously noted, is not easily distinguished. Often it is the fool who perceives that which the reasonable man does not dare to observe.

### Romanticism and Schooling

A major contribution of romanticists, especially during the eighteenth century, was their influence upon educational developments. Romanticists during the eighteenth century vociferously rejected the conception of the child as a miniature incomplete adult or as a moral degenerate. In the former case, children were often treated according to the society's expectation concerning adults. Thus, they were often cruelly punished when they did not meet these rigorous expectations. But according to the romanticists, the child was not a miniature adult or a partially formed creature. Indeed, Wordsworth, reversing what was in his day a generally accepted attitude toward children, announced that "The child is father to the man."

Romanticists also helped to bring about the debacle of the puritan view that children were born evil and had to be "trained" into the ways of goodness. The importance of schooling to the Puritans derives from their belief that children had to be saved from the "old deluder Satan." The Puritan view of children, popularized in a latter-day form in William Golding's *The Lord of the Flies,* was adamantly rejected by the romanticists, who preferred, as in the poetry of Blake, to see children as fundamentally innocent. Inasmuch as romanticists believe that nature is noble and that individuals are corrupted by civilization, it followed that children were indeed superior to "civilized" adults. Some romanticists, taking a cue from the Bible ("Except ye are as little children, ye shall not enter into the kingdom of heaven"), tried to emulate the innocence of children; others saw in them paragons of wisdom. Thus Wordsworth exclaimed of a child of six: "Mighty Prophet! Seer blest!" Jerry Rubin, in a twentieth-century version of a similar theme, affirmed: "Babies are zen masters, curious about everything. Adults are serious and bored. What happened? Brain surgery by the schools." [81]

Idealizing both children and primitive peoples in general, because of their closeness to the pure and noble influences of nature, romanticists rejected the idea of schooling. Nature was the best teacher; schools were only the bastion of civilization. Jerry Rubin reflected the rebel's view of formal schooling when he wrote: "Schools—high schools and colleges— are the biggest obstacle to education in America today." He added: "Schools are a continuation of toilet training." [82] In the same vein, Emerson wrote:

> Meek young men grow up in libraries, believing it their duty to accept the views which Cicero, which Locke, which Bacon, have given; forgetful that Cicero, Locke, and Bacon were only young men in libraries when they wrote these books.
> . . . The book, the college, the school of art, the institution of any kind, stop with some past utterance of genius. This is good, say they,— let us hold by this. They pin me down. They look backward and not forward. But genius looks forward: the eyes of man are set in his forehead, not in his hindhead: man hopes; genius creates." [83]

To Emerson and numerous other rebels, "Things taught in college and schools are not education, but the means of education." Thus romanticists, like their Greek prototypes, do not establish formal schools. Rather, they educate informally wherever they gather. They do not focus upon issues

[81] Jerry Rubin, *Do It! Scenarios of the Revolution* (New York: Ballantine Books, Inc., 1970), p. 211.
[82] Rubin, *Do It!,* pp. 211–12.
[83] Emerson, "The American Scholar," in *Selected Writings,* pp. 49, 50.

of curriculum or class size or lesson plans. Nor do they seek to devise formal alternative school systems, for they do not believe in formal schooling. As Jacobs and Landau observed about the New Radicals: "They think the ivory-towered men of ideas have cheated them, lied to them, and that action and spontaneous experience will show them truth." [84]

The rejection of formal schooling by romanticists is especially important in view of the numerous educational experiments which have been made recently in the United States. Many of these experiments appear superficially romantic but in fact are neo-progressive attempts at formal education. An authentic rebel would advocate deschooling rather than school reform. Much of the current experimentation in education reflects the ideologies of Scientism and neo-progressivism and is oriented toward extending the influence of formal schooling. Thus, programs such as the preparation of day-care workers, community leadership workshops, and community organization programs are progressivist attempts to professionalize the society. Rarely are they supportive of the kind of rugged individualism that existed prior to the arrival of social and educational planners. Kingley Widmer accurately observed: "The inherent tolerance of formal institutions for rebels of intelligence and passion is quite limited, and a good many will inevitably be forced into either more fully counterfeiting the settled style—often to their own defeat—or into more bitterly nomadic and sporadic ways of life." [85] Institutional adjustment is not the forte of rebels, and an education which would require such behavior would betray their basic ideological assumptions. As Nietzche proclaimed, "The surest way to corrupt a youth is to instruct him to hold in higher esteem those who think alike than those who think differently." [86]

A second major reason why romanticists cannot readily develop and sustain formal schools is their rejection of reliance upon reason and science. Thus Coleridge stressed the importance of developing subjective consciousness in the education of children when he wrote:

> From my early reading of fairy tales and genii, etc., etc., my mind has been habituated *to the Vast,* and I never regarded my *senses* as in any way the criteria of my belief. I regulated all my creeds by my conceptions, not by my *sight,* even at that age. Should children be permitted to read romances, and relations of giants and magicians and genii? I know all that has been said against it; but I have formed my faith in the affirmative. I know of no other way of giving the mind a love of the Great and the whole.

[84] Jacobs and Landau, *The New Radicals,* p. 7.
[85] Widmer, *The Literary Rebel,* p. 82.
[86] Nietzche, "The Dawn," in *Portable Nietzche,* p. 91.

He added, criticizing the influence of Scientism:

> Those who have been led to the same truths step by step, through the constant testimony of their senses, seem to me to want a sense which I possess. They contemplate nothing but *parts*, and all parts are necessarily little. And the universe to them is but a mass of *little things*.[87]

Yet formal schools invariably are designed to enhance the influence of objective consciousness upon man. Only in the education of very young children is the focus upon romantic qualities, and it is precisely this focus that is currently under severe attack by the advocates of Scientism who desire to increase the efficiency of schooling.

In rejecting formal schooling romanticists do not discard education; rather, they seek alternatives to *formal* schooling.[88] Art provides one such alternative, and thus romanticists focus upon the educational value of artistic expression, especially the forms that emphasize feelings. Rock music is, in a sense, the mid-twentieth-century educational medium for the romanticists.

### Conclusion

Romanticism is the ideology of the young and in an age when youth is placed in high esteem and imitated, its ideology gains significant influence. Although public schooling continues to serve a vital function in vocational preparation and socioeconomic positioning, it has often failed to keep abreast of the ideological shifts that affect the young. The fact that teacher-preparing institutions often ignore the reality that music serves as a major medium of rebel communication reflects the inability of classicists and progressives to fully comprehend the extent to which they are engaged in a defense of the established order and are steeped in a social planning approach to human society.

With the rise of the youth subclass as a major economic class, the issue of Romanticism increases in importance. When ideological systems are attached to social class differences, the dangers of violent confrontation are accentuated. Whether the recent progressive attempts to involve students in decision-making processes at schools and universities will help to prevent a major class confrontation between the youth and the adult-controlled establishments remains to be seen. What is certain, how-

---

[87] Quoted in Fairchild, *The Romantic Quest*, p. 24.

[88] A romanticist alternative was discussed by Nietzche in his tribute to Schopenhauer. *Schopenhauer as Educator* (Chicago: Henry Regnery Company, 1965). When one compares Nietzche's proposal with those recently advocated by numerous neo-progressivists, the difference between the two ideological positions is clarified.

ever, is that Romanticism will increase in importance as affluence and anomie continue.

## Suggested Readings

BARZUN, JACQUES. *Romanticism and the Modern Ego*. Boston: Little, Brown & Co., 1947.

COHN, NIK. *Rock from the Beginning*. New York: Pocket Books, Inc., 1970.

DUDLEY, DONALD R. *A History of Cynicism*. Hildersheim: Georg Olms Verlags-buchhandlung, 1967.

EVANS, DAVID OWEN. *Social Romanticism in France, 1830–1848*. New York: Octagon Books, 1969.

FAIRCHILD, HOXIE NEALE. *The Romantic Quest*. Philadelphia: Albert Saifer, Publisher, 1931.

——————. *The Noble Savage: A Study of Romantic Naturalism*. New York: Russell & Russell, 1961.

FURST, LILIAN R. *Romanticism in Perspective: A Comparative Study of Aspects of the Romantic Movement in England, France and Germany*. New York: St. Martin Press, 1969.

HALSTEAD, JOHN B. *Romanticism: Problems of Definition, Explanation and Evaluation*. Boston: D. C. Heath and Company, 1965.

JACOBS, PAUL, and SAUL LANDAU. *The New Radicals: A Report with Documents*. New York: Vintage Press, 1966.

LIPTON, LAWRENCE. *The Holy Barbarians*. New York: Julian Messner, Inc., 1959.

McDOWELL, TREMAINE. *The Romantic Triumph: American Literature from 1830–1860. New York: The Macmillan Company, 1933.

PARRY, ALBERT. *Garrets and Pretenders: A History of Bohemianism in America*. New York: Dover Publications, Inc., 1960.

REXROTH, KENNETH. *The Alternative Society: Essays from the Other World*. New York: Herder & Herder, 1970.

ROSKAK, THEODORE. *The Making of a Counter Culture: Reflections on the Technocratic Society and Its Youthful Opposition*. Garden City, N.Y.: Doubleday & Company, Inc., 1969.

RUBIN, JERRY. *Do It! Scenarios of the Revolution*. New York: Ballantine Books, 1970.

SYPHER, WYLIE. *Literature and Technology: The Alien Vision*. New York: Random House, Inc., 1968.

WIDMER, KINGLEY. *The Literary Rebel*. Carbondale: Southern Illinois University Press, 1965.

WILSHORE, BRUCE. *Romanticism and Evolution* (New York: G. P. Putnam's Sons, 1968.

## Chapter 4

# PURITANISM
## The Ideology of the Moral Exemplar

### Introduction

During ceremonies commemorating various historical dates of national honor, numerous speakers extol the virtues of Puritanism. They associate the ideology with ideals of "our founding fathers" and the lives of a myriad of national heroes, and proclaim it to be the foundation upon which our national prominence rests. Noting signs of decadence, however, and fearing an impending decline and fall, these speakers urge a renewed commitment to the tenets of Puritanism lest our country suffer the fate of great empires of the past.

The ambiguity of the concept of Puritanism enhances the possibility of concensus but lessens the potential for understanding. The term Puritanism has been utilized to connote a variety of attitudes, many seemingly antithetical. Puritanism, for example, may mean rugged individualism or rigid, hierarchical authoritarianism; principled, moral commitment or fanatical intolerance; an adherence to anti-intellectual, theological dogma or a tough-minded, stubborn literalism regarding truth. H. L. Menken once defined Puritanism as "that haunting fear that somehow, somewhere, someone is happy." [1] To understand these apparent contradictions, one must view Puritanism as an ideology—that is, as a total perspective—rather than as a single narrow doctrine. Without this approach the student of Puritanism may single out only one element of the ideology and assume that it serves as the rationale for a great variety of actions. Individualism, for example, means one thing in the classical laissez-faire philosophy of John Stuart Mill, but quite something else in the Puritan concept of Covenant espoused by Cotton Mather.

The pejorative label of "puritane," first used in 1564, was applied to those who attacked what they believed to be the "popish abuses yet remaining in the English Church." [2] Collectively, the term encompassed

---

[1] Quoted in Clarence J. Karier, *Man, Society, and Education* (Glenview, Illinois: Scott, Foresman and Company, 1967), p. 15.

[2] Herold E. Sterns, ed., *Civilization in the United States* (New York: Harcourt, Brace, Jovanovich, 1922), p. vi.

a variety of religious groups that supported the Protestant Reformation, including the Separatists, Quakers, Antinomians, and Anabaptists. In referring to an ideological position, however, the term Puritanism is generally used to designate the belief system promulgated by those who established the Massachusetts Bay Colony in 1630. These individuals were Calvinists, as were the Huguenots of France, the Dutch Reformed community of Holland, and the Presbyterians of Scotland.

Calvinism from its inception had appealed primarily to the middle and upper-middle classes. Its adherents included some noblemen, especially in France, and many clerics, newly educated professionals, craftsmen, and *nouveau riche* merchants. Although the Puritans who established the Bay Colony in New England were Calvinists who advocated change within the established church, the Pilgrims who established the Plymouth Colony were separatists. In contrast to the Calvinists, the Pilgrims tended to be agrarian rather than bourgeois, and their generally lower-class origin tended to be reflected in egalitarian political views. In the New World, however, the Puritans of both schools, far removed from their brethren in England, eventually formed an alliance and adopted a creed increasingly independent from that of the mother country.

The Puritans of Bay Colony adhered to the essential elements of the Calvinist creed which were expressed in the Five Points adopted by the Synod of Dart in 1619. Thus they acknowledged the existence of a foreordained plan determined solely by God. Within this plan, salvation was possible only for the chosen. Once selected, nothing could prevent their salvation.

On the face of it, it seems that the concept of election and pre destination could well serve as a rationalization for human apathy or a life of hedonistic pursuits. Inasmuch as salvation rests outside human will, the individual is left free to function as he pleases. The town drunk as well as the village prostitute could be among the chosen while the chief magistrate and the local cleric might be damned. In fact, however, these possibilities were vehemently denied by the adherents of middle-class Puritanism, who staunchly repudiated the possibility of such divine unfairness. As Ralph Barton Perry stated, for the Puritans, ". . . God, though supreme, is a constitutional and not a capricious ruler. Salvation is an orderly progression in which those intellectual and moral attainments which fit a man to be saved are adopted by God as the antecedents of salvation." [3]

Nevertheless, despite the fact that Calvinistic election was not held to confer on its possessor absolute impunity to act in any selfish, antisocial

[3] Ralph Barton Perry, *Puritanism and Democracy* (New York: Harper & Row Publishers, Inc., 1964), p. 69.

way he chose, Calvinist leaders did use the doctrine of election to secure a certain kind of political leverage. Thus John Knox, an ideologist for Calvinism, warned in 1554 that a prophet of God possessed the right to teach treason against a king. (A similar belief is expressed by Marxists when they claim that the proletariat are the "chosen of history.") Such a stance, rooted to the Puritan view of elitism, truth, and inevitability, can easily become the seedbed of revolution. Of course, when the doctrine is institutionalized after the revolution has been successfully completed, as in the Bible State of colonial America, it can serve to legitimize the actions of the power elite. John Winthrop, the first governor of the Massachusetts Bay colony, for example, in his defense against charges that he had exceeded his authority as a magistrate, warned his dissatisfied citizenry that liberty applied solely to acts that were just, good, and honest, and that liberty was best expressed in one's voluntary submission to just rule. Many twentieth-century revolutionaries and power elites have utilized such a puritan argument as a rationale for their deeds.

The belief that God was not a capricious being and that his elect can be identified by their deeds was utilized during the emergence of America's industrial state. Secularized Puritanism viewed the successful businessman—that is, the individual who succeeded in his God-appointed calling—as the favored of God. This theme was popularized by Horatio Alger, the Unitarian minister who left the ministry for a literary career. In his novels, such fictional heroes as Ragged Dick and Tattered Tom exemplified the nobility inherent in those who move from rags to riches. The theme of business success as a sign of God's grace and its ancillary admonition that work was a virtue helped to legitimize the amassing of large fortunes during the industrialization of America. The unemployed and poor were viewed as not only lazy but also sinful, inasmuch as they obviously had not heeded their calling. The theme also implied a bourgeois version of the aristocratic concept of *nobless oblige* in that it served to impress upon the super-rich the idea that, as Elect, they had responsibilities toward their society—a belief that resulted in philanthropic endeavors. Thus Puritanism not only served to enhance the church support by American millionaires during the early twentieth century but also encouraged the establishment of charitable foundations which continue to this day. Indeed, the Astors, Vanderbilts, Mellons, and Morgans not only attended churches but also built them.

Although the theme of the nobility inherent in the accumulation of wealth evolved primarily from the application of Darwinism to the socioeconomic realm, traditional religious beliefs also served to accentuate the emergence of the industrial state. As early as 1836 a clergyman, Thomas P. Hunt, captured this theme in his book entitled *The Book of Wealth; in Which It Is Proved From the Bible That It is the Duty of*

*Every Man to Become Rich.* Some clergymen not only justified the accumulation of wealth, but also equated financial rewards with moral superiority.

Although it appears to be paradoxical that a deterministic ideology should permit free choice, in actual practice this is often the case. Marxism, for example, views the inevitability of a proletariat victory as historically determined. The individual may choose, however, to join the forces of history or be swept away by the revolution. Similarly, although Puritanism held that God foreordained the order and values of the world and the ultimate truth of man's inevitable role, this belief placed an even greater demand on the individual to be cognizant of His design. One might expect little from a nonbeliever, but "chosen" people should *act* redeemed, and it is largely left to the individual to discover what acting redeemed entails.

To the dissenter or the creative spirit, however, this sort of individual freedom within a framework of determinism leaves much to be desired. Indeed, it is little more than obedience; like Adam, he can *accept* "good" or *choose* "evil," which does not give him much of a choice at all. Roger Williams, for example, was banished and persecuted for knowing "right" and refusing to choose it. He was, in fact, accused of sinning against his conscience. Dissent and creativity, concepts so admired by romanticists, demand in Nietzchean terms a transvaluation of values. To counter the ideologues of determinism, Nietzsche proclaimed, "Nothing is true; everything is permitted. Here we have real freedom, for the notion of truth itself has been disposed of." [4] Similarly, Jean-Paul Sartre asserted that with the death of God all things are possible.

Although it seems readily apparent that, given the social biases of the Puritans, some individuals were more apt than others to be believed to be "chosen," in fact the Puritans tried not to let themselves forget that ultimately individual salvation was known only to God. Consequently, the self-righteousness that accompanies a belief in one's own sainthood encounters the uncertainty that results from the impotence of man's finitude. This ambivalence creates a need for continual self-examination and self-criticism. This aspect of our Puritan heritage explains, in part, the continual conflict in America between the arrogance of moral superiority and the humbleness of soul-searching. Americans not only fear failure but also question success.

Puritan literature often reflects this ambivalence between elitism and humility. Puritans are similar to Romanticists in their insistence on writing autobiographies. They differ from the romantic literary exhibitionists, however, in that they emphasize their ethical struggle and

[4] Friedrich Nietzsche, *The Birth of Tragedy and the Genealogy of Morals* (Garden City, N.Y.: Doubleday & Company, Inc., 1956), p. 287.

moral failures. Puritan confessional diaries, such as John Bunyan's *Grace Abounding to the Chief of Sinners: Or, A Brief and Faithful Relation of the Exceeding Mercy of God in Christ, to his poor Servant Bunyan,* reflect a passionate spiritual struggle often morbid in its self-effacement. Even the practical secular Puritan, Benjamin Franklin, revealed in his autobiography his dilemma in developing the virtue of humility by eliminating pride: "even if I could conceive that I had completely overcome it," he lamented, "I should probably be proud of my humility." [5] A debased latter-day version of the puritan confession is revealed in the popular "confession magazines" which are written to titillate unimaginative puritans through hideous stories about the price of transgression.

The self-effacement which characterized the colonial Puritan elite's view of itself also was expressed about their society. In 1679 a Synod under the direction of Increase Mather met in Boston to report on the civic health of their society. The Synod's findings, published in a document entitled *Necessity of Reformation,* reviewed in an apocalyptic fashion the degenerate condition in which their society floundered. This puritan image of the individual spiritual struggle against a "sick society" continues to influence Americans. Twentieth-century synods now labeled "national commissions" continue to be formed to investigate the condition of American civilization. Whether the commissions are called to analyze racism, or sexual mores, or violence in the United States, their messages are invariably apocalyptic and moralistic. They warn Americans about the dire condition produced by their degeneracy. It is important to stress that this sort of self-effacement usually is expressed by the Brahmins of the society or their representatives. The documents, written by Establishment representatives following severe social crises, serve as a rationale for increased government involvement in the socioeconomic domain and prepare the general public for the necessary social changes as predetermined by the Brahmins.

In contrast to the quietism and pious acquiescence of other Protestant sects such as Lutheranism, Puritanism was militant and activist. Where Lutheranism tended toward faith, chiliasm, and a priesthood of all believers, Puritanism relied on individual effort and an enlightened, reasoned interpretation of God's word. As the Puritans saw it, Lutheranism was merely a way station on the road to the beliefs of Quakers, Antinomians, and Anabaptists; it would result in unrestrained sectarianism and social disorder, perhaps anarchy. Puritanism thus attempted to retain a moderate religious position between religious emotionalism and fanaticism on the one hand and rational secularism and naturalism on the other.

[5] Julian W. Abernathy, ed., *Autobiography of Benjamin Franklin* (New York: Charles E. Merrill Company, 1918), p. 114.

## Puritanism as an Ideology of Revolution

In addition to the intellectual antecedents of puritan thought, one must consider the social context from which Puritanism developed and eventually became a mass movement. In the words of Michael Walzer, Puritanism served as an "ideology of transition" from the old social order to a new one: ". . . it met the human needs that arise whenever traditional controls give way and hierarchical status and corporate privilege are called into question." [6] In this sense, the Puritans were similar to the Jacobins and Bolsheviks in the past or the Maoists, Castroites, and Black Muslims of the present. In order to establish a new social order and prevent the repetition of the "mistakes" and "decadence" of the previous one, it was necessary to create a new man. Once purity is achieved within the individual, he is then ready to project this purity, battle the enemy, and create a new social order. This concept was exemplified in John Milton's eulogy of Cromwell: "A commander first over himself; the conqueror of himself, it was over himself he had learnt most to triumph. Hence he went to encounter with an external enemy as a veteran accomplished in all military duties. . . ." [7] In like manner, Malcolm X describes his conversion after falling victim to the influence of the devil in the form of the white man. It was only after attaining purity within that he went out to save his brothers and shape the world. The words of Cotton Mather, as well as those of Lenin, Mao, Castro, and Elijah Muhammad, describe the purity of the new man with such terms as sobriety, austerity, perseverance, discipline, and diligent work.

The discontentment of middle-class Puritans in England resulted generally from the Enclosure Acts, the Acts of Supremacy and Uniformity, and the growing conflicts between the merchants and craftsmen —events that marked the disintegration of the corporate agrarian feudal order. The Enclosure Acts not only evicted many lower-class peasants but also deprived many middle-class furniture craftsmen of a lumber supply. The Acts of Supremacy and Uniformity re-emphasized royal authority over episcopal hierarchy and demanded a uniformity of worship, thus alienating the Puritan clergy. And, finally, the actions of Charles I and the Stuart policies in general resulted in more stringent control over guilds and craftsmen, thus providing a milieu more sympathetic for middlemen traders and merchants, at the expense of craftsmen.

Discontentment alone, however, is insufficient to generate a mass

---

[6] Michael Walzer, *The Revolution of the Saints: A Study in the Origins of Radical Politics* (Cambridge: Harvard University Press, 1965), p. 312.

[7] As quoted in Walzer, *The Revolution of the Saints*, p. 315.

movement. As Eric Hoffer has pointed out, "Those who are awed by ther surroundings do not think of change, no matter how miserable their condition." [8] Thus, in addition to discontentment, individuals or groups must have a sense of power, a feeling of hope, and a belief in the future. On the eve of their "exodus" to the Massachusetts Bay Colony in 1630, this attitude was expressed by the theologian John Cotton as he blessed the Puritans with words that retain historical relevance: "When God wrappes us in his ordinances and warmes us with the life and power of them as with wings, there is the land of Promise." [9]

The Puritans actually spoke of their movement as an "exodus" to the land of promise, an obvious analogy to the Israelites leaving Egypt. In more modern history, we have seen Marcus Garvey's attempt to generate a "back-to-Africa" movement, Elijah Muhammad's wish to establish a Nation of Islam, and even Martin Luther King's vision of a land of freedom and equality espoused in his "I have a Dream" speech. As Hoffer stated, "Every mass movement is in a sense a migration—a movement toward a promised land; and when feasible and expedient, an actual migration takes place." [10] For the Puritans, the "land of Promise" would provide the opportunity to create a Utopia of the Saints, a home for what Vernon L. Parrington titled the "Oligarchy of Christian Grace." It is necessary to emphasize that for the Puritans the "land of Promise" was indeed a presently existing land, not a Kingdom of Heaven divorced from the realities of everyday existence. Puritanism was an attempt to eliminate the dualism of St. Augustine by synthesizing the City of God and the City of Man. As Perry stated, "The Puritan's other-worldliness was not a withdrawal from the world, but a living *in* the world in accordance with other-worldly standards." [11]

Puritanism, of course, is only one ideological approach to the frustration and anxiety man encounters in his sojourn on earth; obviously there are other alternatives. Some individuals may turn to nostalgia, searching for peace and satisfaction in "the good old days." Others may attempt to detach themselves from the world, seeking pious quiescence in monasticism or mysticism. And still others, especially those members of lower socioeconomic strata, turn to God or chiliasm, submitting to fate and awaiting the millenium. These alternatives, however, are viewed as forms of weakness or escapism by the tough-minded, activist, moralistic Puritans. Similarly, it was the fatalistic religions that emphasized withdrawal, pacifism, and chiliasm that drew the condemnation of Marx when

[8] Eric Hoffer, *The True Believer* (New York: The New American Library of World Literature, Inc., 1951), p. 17.

[9] Quoted in Vernon L. Parrington, *The Colonial Mind: 1620–1800* (New York: Harcourt, Brace, Jovanovich, Inc., 1927), I, 27.

[10] Hoffer, *The True Believer*, p. 28.

[11] Perry, *Puritanism and Democracy*, p. 304.

he termed religion the opiate of the masses. Recently, youthful revolutionaries have leveled similar criticism at members of the counterculture, for whom "opium" has become the religion of the masses. Many of the more militant, youthful revolutionaries condemn the escapism of drugs and mysticism. Hedonism or radical individualism have little to offer to the collective discipline required of an exemplary community of saints committed to the implementation of a new social order. This mission was best defined by the oft-quoted statement of John Winthrop, the first theocratic magistrate: ". . . wee shall be as a Citty upon a Hill; the eyes of all people are uppon us. . . ." [12]

The moral exemplarism implicit in the ethos of Puritanism is an extremely important aspect of the ideology. For although Puritanism may tend toward self-righteousness and arrogance, it also demands perfection and excellence from individuals regardless of their station in life. The admonishment Eleazar Mather expressed to parents would be equally applicable to clergymen, teachers, master craftsmen, and magistrates: "Precept without Patterns will do little good. You must lead them to Christ by Examples as well as Counsel; you must set *your-selves first*, and speak by Lives as well as words. . . ." [13] In colloquial form this is generally stated: "Put your own house in order before telling someone else how to run his." Like charity, revolutions begin at home. They must be indigenous, and cannot be exported. Thus the revolutionary governments of both the Soviet Union and Communist China have utilized most of their energy *within* their own countries—as is notable in their lack of imperialism.

Obviously, the question as to whether one's own house is in order is open to argument. If it is, a missionary view of manifest destiny can develop very easily. Apparently, however, puritans do not often find that their house is in order, for they rarely move on to developing arguments about manifest destiny. On the contrary, manifest destiny, when it appears, generally has been the result of classical laissez-faire liberalism and economic expansionism. In fact, the historian Edmund Morgan atributed the demise of the Puritans primarily to the lack of missionary zeal directed toward the unregenerate. With the exception of Thomas Hooker, the Puritan ministry directed their words to the saints and their offsprings rather than to sinners and heathens. Morgan said:

> The Puritan minister, then, tried to convert two kinds of people: hypocrites who had been admitted to membership by mistake and the children

[12] John Winthrop, "A Model of Christian Charity," in *Puritanism and the American Experience,* ed. Michael McGiffert (Reading, Massachusetts: Addison-Wesley Publishing Company, 1969), p. 32.
[13] Quoted in Edmund S. Morgan, *The Puritan Family* (Boston: Trustees of the Public Library, 1944), p. 57.

of the godly who enjoyed membership though not converted. Not a word about the mass of men who remained in the outer darkness.[14]

### Puritanism and the Demand for Formal Schooling

Although the Puritans placed little emphasis on missionary work, they were intent on "saving" themselves from satanic influences. Once established, any mass movement requires agencies and institutions to indoctrinate the young with the values of the new community and to provide the training for the future leaders in the new social order. To accomplish this goal, the Puritans, with a disproportionate number of university-educated clergymen among their original members, established Harvard College only six years after landing in the New World in order to prevent leaving "illiterate Ministry to the Churches, when our present Ministers shall lie in the Dust." [15] In addition, from 1642 to 1671 all the New England colonies, with the exception of Rhode Island, had written statutes providing for tax-supported educational facilities, thus establishing cultural and legal precedents for the common school movement. It should be noted, however, that early legislation emphasized compulsory education but not compulsory attendance—that is, it was compulsory for the state to provide education but not compulsory for the citizens to avail themselves of it. Both religious and vocational training remained primarily a family responsibility. As with the recent innovations of driver's education, sex education, Head Start, and day-care centers, formal schooling replaces family responsibility either through familial abdication or societal judgment regarding familial competence in dealing with such matters. From the extended family of the colonial period to the nuclear family of modernity, the importance of schooling has increased with the correlative decline of family structure and influence.

From the ideological perspective of Puritanism, the process of education is an extremely difficult one.[16] In contrast to the natural goodness of man espoused by Romanticism and the moral neutrality (*tabula*

---

[14] Morgan, *The Puritan Family*, p. 97.

[15] Of the newly arrived immigrants prior to 1646, one hundred had received degrees from Cambridge and thirty-two from Oxford. There was one university graduate for every forty or fifty families. See Richard Hofstadter, *Academic Freedom in the Age of the College* (New York: Columbia University Press, 1955), p. 82, and p. 83, where the passage quoted here is to be found.

[16] As discussed previously, Puritanism is an ideology of revolution (albeit a revolution of Christian "saints"). Consequently, many of the elements of Puritanism are shared by a variety of revolutionaries, including Maoists, Castroists, Bolsheviks, and Jacobins; and to a more moderate degree by a variety of groups classified as reformers and militants.

*rasa* or blank slate) assumed by Scientism, Puritanism assumes the inherent evilness of man. Consequently, strict discipline is not only a moral necessity but also an exceedingly difficult task in asmuch as it goes contrary to man's nature. Subscribing to many of the maxims of medieval Christianity and the Old Testament, Puritanism adhered to the biblical Proverbs: "Foolishness *is* bound in the heart of a child; *but* the rod of correction shall drive it far from him" (Proverbs 22:15); "Train up a child in the way he should go: and when he is old, he will not depart from it" (Proverbs 22:6). Certainly adherents of Puritanism may prefer persuasion over force, but they would also agree with the words of Cotton Mather: "Better whipt than Damn'd." [17]

Puritans loved their children, but they loved them for what the children could be, not for what they were. They viewed them in a fashion similar to the way that they viewed themselves—the banished children of Adam worthy of eternal damnation. Puritan parents incessantly were warned that a permissive attitude toward their children could cost them their salvation. Subjected to comparisons to vipers and rattlesnakes, Puritan children were harshly educated. Besides severe corporal punishment for transgressions, they were bombarded with a barage of frightening reading material. A required reading text for the colonial children was Michael Wigglesworth's *Day of Doom, or a Poetical Description of the Great and Last Judgement, With a Short Discourse about Eternity.* They were often required to memorize this gruesome text in which God admonished them:

> You sinners are, and such a share as sinners, may expect;
> Such you shall have, for I do save none but mine own Elect.
> Yet to compare your sin with their who liv'd a longer time,
> I do confess yours is much less, though every sin's a crime.
>
> A crime it is, therefore in bliss you may not hope to dwell
> But unto you I shall allow the easiest room in Hell. . . .[18]

When compared with modern elementary school reading materials, Puritan texts appear not only grim but also quite difficult to read and comprehend. In contrast to the romanticist and progressivist view of childhood, Puritanism viewed the child as a miniature adult. An individual was expected to be responsible for himself early in life and to be ready to confront a world that was cruel and demanding. Both Satan and Death lurked in the shadows of the hostile wilderness and Puritans of any age must be prepared lest they fall victim.

The corruption of man is not the result of institutions, as claimed

---

[17] Quoted in Morgan, *The Puritan Family*, p. 57.
[18] Michael Wigglesworth, "The Day of Doom," in *Educational Ideas in America,* ed. S. Alexander Rippa (New York: David McKay Company, Inc., 1969), p. 48.

by Rousseau and the romanticists, but is the consequence of the fall of Adam. As the Puritan textbook, *The New-England Primer,* stated, "In Adam's Fall We sinned All." [19] It is only by means of institutions that social order can be maintained and anarchy prevented. Children may be born in ignorance and sin, but with the religious education provided by Puritan educational institutions they may come to know the word of God and be better prepared to resist the omnipresence of Satan. Contrary to the Socratic dictum equating knowledge with virtue, Puritanism considered them separate entities and demanded that both be taught. To prevent knowledgeable men from being immoral and moral men from being ignorant, it was necessary for an individual to know both the three Rs and the Scriptures. According to the tenets of Puritanism, teachers are expected to be scholars and moral exemplars, a combination that persists as a puritan ideal to this very day. The emphasis, of course, is skewed toward morality. Consider, for example, how many teachers are released for intellectual incompetency compared with the number terminated for "corrupting the morals of youth." One of the most publicized cases illustrating this point occurred in 1941 when Bertrand Russell, the eminent English philosopher and mathematician, was refused a position as a mathematics professor in the College of the City of New York because of his previously published views regarding sexual mores.[20] The decision to reject Russell typifies the puritan's concern for morality, a concern that overshadows his faith in academic knowledge. Although secular modernity prevents a literal interpretation of Cotton Mather's words, his sentiments concerning teachers and education remain relevant:

> Consider it as their chief interest, and yours also, that they may so know the Holy Scriptures as to become wise to salvation. . . . Certainly, it is a nobler work to make the little ones know their Savior than know their letters. The lessons of Jesus are nobler than the lessons of Cato.[21]

Puritans wished to retain the best of both worlds: their minds were in the Renaissance, their souls in the Reformation.

In addition to the moral dimension, Puritanism is generally eulogized in public school textbooks for being the ideological antecedent of religious freedom, individualism, and democracy. Certainly these elements are present. They must be defined, however, within the totality of the ideology. Religious freedom meant freedom to worship as a good Puritan as opposed to worshiping as an Anglican, a Catholic, or a variety

[19] Paul Leicester Ford, ed., *The New-England Primer* (New York: Teachers College, Columbia University, 1962), p. 25.

[20] For a full account of the case, see Bertrand Russell, *Why Am I Not A Christian,* ed. Paul Edwards (New York: Simon & Schuster, Inc., 1957).

[21] Cotton Mather, *Bonifacius: An Essay Upon the Good* (Cambridge: The Belknap Press of Harvard University Press, 1966), p. 83.

of separatists, including Antinomians, Quakers, and Anabaptists. In fact, it was the separatists, the enemy within, that the Puritans most feared. Radical separatists had literally interpreted Luther's mandate of a "priesthood of believers." The consequences of such belief could be either a piety tending toward apathy or an arrogance inducing disorder and anarchy; both would result in the dissolution of the covenant. Thus Puritanism accepts the literal truth of the scriptures only if read "properly" according to "right" reason, and a learned ministry and teachers were a necessity to accomplish the important task of educating people to this correct reading.

The individualism stressed in the Puritan ideology is in no sense a doctrine of worldly egalitarianism. Although everyone was equal in the eyes of God, some were obviously more equal than others in the eyes of man. The sentiments expressed by John Winthrop make this point clear: "God Almightie in his most holy and wise providence hath soe disposed of the Condicion of mankinde, as in all times some must be rich some poore, some highe and eminent in power and dignitie, others meane and in subjeccion." [22] This view was reflected in, and reinforced by the educational system. A variety of schools were established, including dame schools, writing schools, Latin grammar schools, and colleges, each type designed to prepare the individual for his predestined station in life. University degrees served as prerequisites for civil and ecclesiastical appointments, thus preserving theocratic (political and religious) power for the educated. As a speaker at an early Harvard Commencement stated, without the college "the ruling class would have been subjected to mechanics, cobblers, and tailors; the gentry would have been overwhelmed by lewd fellows of the baser sort, the sewage of Rome, the dregs of an illiterate plebs which judgeth much from emotion, little from truth." [23]

This sentiment, stated in the blunt, straightforward style characteristic of Puritanism, may appear quite harsh to the modern American who has been influenced by populism, Jacksonian democracy, and the American dream. Yet if the statement were moderated with a temperate, sophisticated style, would it not express the honest educational philosophy of many individuals today? For those who seek social reform through education, this attitude is quite disheartening. Yet the fact remains that, historically, the educational system has functioned more to preserve the established order than to significantly alter it.

The puritan conception of a community formed by voluntarists who

[22] John Winthrop, "A Modell of Christian Charity," *The Winthrop Papers* (Boston: Massachusetts Historical Society, 1931), II, 282.
[23] Quoted in Perry Miller, *The New England Mind: The Seventeenth Century* (New York: The Macmillan Co., 1931), p. 84.

remain free to disengage themselves from their social system, as well as their belief that an elect few possesses the right to dictate to others continue to be promulgated in a secularized form in America today. A cursory examination of political and educational literature invariably reveals that many politicians and educationists view themselves as an elect group who must decide what should be done onto those other individuals who do not occupy such key roles. A frightening number of Americans express confidence in the actions of a perceived "power elite" and are fearful of the actualization of the slogan "Power to the People." Like their colonial forefathers, numerous Americans today reflect the Puritan distrust of the "common folk" while expressing democratic platitudes. Although populism prevails in some sectors of the United States, many Americans reject a belief in the democratic process. Contrary to what is commonly believed, American schools have not necessarily taught a faith in democracy; on the contrary, it often seems that they have taught the citizenry the subtle language in which to couch their lack of faith in their own ability to rule themselves.

When the puritan sense of the importance of preserving hierarchical differences among individuals and groups within society is attached to an emphasis on racial and ethnic differences, the result may be social suicide. The combination of elitism and racism serves as fuel for revolution. Needless to add, the defense of social position based upon racial or ethnic identity not only reveals that a meritocracy does not exist but also indicates that individuals within the power structure are unable to legitimize their position except by deception.

The inherent weakness of puritan arguments that success, whether earned or granted by God, implies merit lies in the fact that it legitimizes hierarchical systems regardless of their roots. Hard work and dedication may have served to propel certain individuals into key social positions, but their children are often accorded similar positions solely because of their birth. The often heard argument that capitalism provides the opportunity for individuals to excel in proportion to their efforts and their abilities is somewhat superficial in view of inheritance laws, socio-economic interaction patterns, and differences in learning environments. Indeed, when one analyzes the family lineage of the Puritan elect, the reality that "blood" rather than merit often determined an individual's salvation and social role becomes apparent.

Puritans throughout the ages have argued for just social systems in which the meritorious would be rewarded. Because of this orientation, puritans are not enamored of the concept "equality." Where colonial puritans viewed man's inequalities as a result of God's decision, latter-day puritans speak of genetic predispositions, but the anti-egalitarian implications are the same in both cases. Rejecting environmental determinism, puritans invariably claim that inequalities between men cannot be removed and that a social system should be structured to ensure that each individual is able to actualize in his proper place. Puritans in education invariably have supported the separation of students according to their intellectual ability. They have viewed homogeneous grouping as a means of limiting the potential of the "gifted" while frustrating the handicapped.

Of course, although puritans believe that individuals should be placed within an hierarchical scheme within society, they do not advocate the mistreatment or unfair treatment of social inferiors. Believing that either God or nature has defined the potentialities of individuals, they generally structure a social system designed to protect the "less fortunate."

### The Individual and the Community

Puritanism sees the issue of individualism from a perspective similar to that to be found in Ferdinand Tönnies' *Gemeinschaft* or Plato's Republic. Every individual has a "calling" in life which he is expected to fulfill as his contribution to the ultimate perfection of the community. Failure is attributed to the individual's weakness in his adherence to the values of Puritanism or to his misjudgment regarding his calling. For example, a teacher who failed to instruct his pupils either lacked proper diligence and industry or was mistaken in thinking he had a calling to teach. In his failure, he disgraced not only himself but also his community and God. Consequently, he will suffer personal humiliation, community condemnation, and God's wrath. In modern educational theory this is termed "accountability"—with a vengeance. Puritanism translates the modern romantic slogan "each individual should be allowed to do his own thing" as "each individual is obligated to do the *right* thing." Every individual is indeed necessary and important, but his necessity and importance are defined within the context of community. Thus, Puritanism stresses individualism yet castigates individuals who are considered to be dissidents, vagrants, and incompetents.

In any hypothetical construction of a community, roles are carefully delineated. Each individual has a function to fulfill and every function is considered of equal worth, reflecting no hierarchy of prestige. It is within this context that Puritanism views the "callings" of individuals, including the separate and distinct roles of men and women. Few Puritans, for example, would deny that a woman's place is in the home. This role is not viewed as denigrating to women, for motherhood is a most noble calling. The importance of these ideals was clearly illustrated in the writings of Governor Winthrop. When Mistress Hopkins, the wife of the governor of Connecticut, was declared insane, Winthrop explained, "For if she had attended her household affairs, and such things as belong to women, and not gone out of her way to meddle in such things as are proper for men whose minds are stronger, etc., she had kept her wits, and might have improved them usefully and honorably in the place God had set her." In addition, Winthrop blamed the husband of Anne Hutchinson for her dissidence, claiming he had failed to instruct her properly, being "a man of a very mild temper and weak parts, and wholly guided by his wife." [24]

The puritan's sense of calling is just one of the many ways in which his beliefs about covenant (community) and moral commitment create a demand for censorship and restrictions on individual freedom. If an individual believes he is an inhabitant of a "chosen" community, or more importantly, if he is attempting to "create" a chosen community, it is necessary to promote "good" and to eradicate "evil." In fact, even minor attempts at social reform generally require restrictions on individual freedoms.[25] Many legislative achievements of the New Deal resulted from the acknowledgment that the pursuit of individual self-interest did not necessarily promote the common good or the public welfare. Similarly, recent concern about automobile safety and ecology has resulted in legislative restrictions or guidelines. Concepts such as compulsory union membership and labor-management arbitration imply individual restrictions for the collective good. And such institutions as the Peace Corps and VISTA are formed in an attempt to create a societal commitment on the part of individuals seemingly engaged only in their own self-interest. All these communal actions in some way illustrate the same puritan sense of the necessary subordination of the individual to the community as we see in John F. Kennedy's statement, "Ask not what your country can do for you—ask what you can do for your country."

Puritans persistently have been accused of censorship and the mistreatment of dissenters. Roger Williams, a victim of Puritan scorn, accused them of punishing individuals for following their conscience. John Cotton's response to Williams' accusation, entitled *The Bloody Tenent, Washed,* denied that allegation: "I doe not therefore say (as the Discusser reporteth me) that after once or twice admonition, then such Consciences may be persecuted, but that if such a man after such admonition shall still persist in the Error of his way, and be therefore punished, He is not persecuted for cause of Conscience, but for sinning against his own

24 Both quotations appear in Morgan, *The Puritan Family,* p. 10.
25 For a brilliant analysis of this phenomenon, see Alexis de Tocqueville, *The Old Regime and the French Revolution,* trans. Stuart Gilbert (Garden City, N.Y.: Doubleday & Company, Inc., 1955), Chap. III, Part 3.

Conscience." [26] According to John Cotton truth was knowable and the rejection of truth indicated that an individual was violating his own conscience. Within such a framework, individuals are never punished for ignorance but for perfidy; as the Puritan sees it, ignorance of God's law is no excuse for one can never really be ignorant of God's law once responsible members of the Puritan community have told one what it is. Obviously, the outcome of such a belief in objectively knowable truth may be exceedingly similar to that forwarded by all totalitarian systems. John Cotton's stance reveals the degree to which the Puritans accepted the implications of their assumptions and explains, in part, why they have been often described as narrow-minded fanatics.

In imposing censorship, communal or state authorities restrict an individual's freedom for the common good, or, in some situations, for the good of the individual himself. Covert censorship results from the simple necessity of making choices. Cultural pluralism, geographical provincialism, economic scarcity, and ignorance of alternatives are just a few of the numerous reasons that account for covert censorship. In this sense, cultural groups, publishing companies, school boards, families, and teachers censor books, films, magazines, ideas, attitudes, and clothing styles. This is obviously true in a situation when commitment to a choice precludes any alternative choices. A school board, for example, cannot buy all the textbooks in a specific area, nor can a family subscribe to all the avaliable magazines. Adherents to Puritanism, however, demand and actively support overt censorship. These individuals openly and consciously choose not only to accept one form but also to reject another. Puritans on the right generally demand censorship in areas relating to sex and patriotism, while those on the left are concerned about the censorship of racial and ethnic prejudice. The libertarian mentality, it seems, has never been able to deal effectively with the problem of being tolerant of intolerance. This issue was raised in writings of Herbert Marcuse, the hero of modern left-wing Puritanism.

Arguments by libertarian opponents of censorship generally are based upon the "principles of democracy" or the "rights of the individual." (For a fuller discussion of libertarianism, liberalism, and Progressivism, see Chapter 6.) Yet the fundamental issue is not one of abstract principles; it is basically one of ethical judgment. The libertarian probably does not care to argue that the reading of "evil" books will not result in an increased number of "evil" people, for to do so would be to imply the corollary that the reading of "good" books will not increase the number of "good' people—a conclusion which those who believe in

[26] John Cotton, "The Bloody Tenant, Washed," in *Tensions in American Puritanism,* ed. Richard Reinitz (New York: John Wiley & Sons, Inc., 1970), p. 112.

culture and education find unacceptable. Thus he is forced to deny either the existence of, or the importance of, any distinction between "good" and "evil." Insofar as the arguments against censorship depend upon such a blurring of moral distinctions, the puritan will have nothing to do with them. Where puritan censorship tends to drive "evil" underground, the libertarian position allows for open discussion and confrontation on the intellectual marketplace. This is precisely what the puritan finds objectionable, for he sees no virtue in definitions of freedom which give evil a chance to compete freely with good—especially because, as we have seen already, he does not have the faith in human nature that would make him confident in the ultimate triumph of the good.

Obviously, the puritan view of community is antithetical to the libertarian mentality typified by the great nineteenth-century liberal John Stuart Mill. From his classical, atomistic, laissez-faire point of view, society is comprised of freely choosing individuals, each pursuing his self-defined interest. The freedom of the individual should be restricted only when it impinges upon the freedom of another, or, in the words of the colloquial expression, "Your right to move your fist ends where my nose begins." Government thus is allowed to function as a restrictive force only insofar as its restrictions permit the free pursuit of individual self-interest. The fear of a government's overstepping the bounds of this limited function led Thomas Jefferson and other enlightenment theorists to proclaim that the best form of government was the one that governs least.

Major difficulties obviously arise within any ideological position when its fundamental assumptions are called into question. For atomistic, laissez-faire libertarianism, these difficulties are especially noticeable with issues that involve a conflict of rights. For example, an individual's right to be served in a restaurant conflicts with the owner's right to refuse the service. Similarly, problems arise with freeway construction, urban renewal, medical examinations and treatments, and abortions. In the area of education, such issues as busing, religious ceremonies, loyalty oaths, and school integration continue to raise problems involving conflicts of rights. In fact, compulsory education itself is an infringement upon the rights of the individual. Although a majority of Americans agree with the sentiment expressed in the Jeffersonian crusade against ignorance, the legality of compulsory education continues to be questioned by a variety of groups. Attempts to resolve such conflicts in a democratic framework usually result in definitions of justice as "the greatest good for the greatest number." This utilitarian resolution, however, fails to take full account of the grave dangers produced by what

Alexis de Tocqueville described as *the tyranny of the majority*. "The authority of a king," Tocqueville explained, "is physical and controls the actions of men without subduing their will. But the majority possesses a power that is physical and moral at the same time, which acts upon the will as much as upon the actions and represses not only all contest, but all controversy." [27] Too often the slogan "the majority also has rights" is raised only in response to minority demands. Recent surveys indicating the failure of majority support for various aspects of the Bill of Rights and various Constitutional amendments should not be very surprising when judged on the basis of actual experience. For although these documents were intended for all Americans, very few individuals would ever have occasion to use them, and thus might fail to fully appreciate their necessity. What is shocking and alarming, however, is the failure of the educational system in its attempt to create an educated citizenry, a citizenry who would acknowledge the necessity of such rights on the basis of educational enlightenment. To aid in this basic acculturation, American history and civics must be viewed as living processes, not ancient facts to be memorized and quickly forgotten.

Just as there are those who complain that the rights of the minority are emphasized, so there are those who complain that there is "too much democracy," too many rights for individuals. Yet others avow America is in the hands of a power elite, and there is much evidence to support their view. Yet even they should remain cognizant of the dangers inherent in a more purely democratic form founded upon the actual self-interests of any majority. If reactionaries judge too quickly the selfishness of man, romanticists judge too quickly his benevolence. Those who speak for the "silent majority" or "the people" are quite often shocked, if not appalled, when "the people" speak. On this point the words of Tocqueville remain tragically prophetic: "If ever the free institutions of America are destroyed, that event may be attributed to the omnipotence of the majority, which may at some future time urge the minorities to desperation and oblige them to have recourse to physical force. Anarchy will then be the result, but it will have been brought about by despotism." A democratic state fails not because of impotence but "almost always by the abuse of its force and the misemployment of its resources. . . . Anarchy is almost always produced by its tyranny or its mistakes, but not by its want of strength." [28]

Adherents of modern liberalism (Progressivism), with their roots in the ideas of the Enlightenment philosophers, generally speak with a

[27] Alexis de Tocqueville, *Democracy in America,* trans. Phillips Bradley (New York: Random House, 1945), I, 273.
[28] Tocqueville, *Democracy in America,* I, 279.

vocabulary that lacks such words as "evil," "sin," and perhaps even "immoral." They discuss "problems," "mismanagement," and "restructuring the institution," and seek "mutual understanding" and "dialogue." The "system" is at fault. In stark contrast, those who adhere to Puritanism are aware of the evil facet of human nature and condemn sinful action with strong judgment and without hesitation. Puritans on the right "know" that welfare recipients cheat the government, customers steal from stores, workers are lazy, and young people disrespect those in authority; in similar fashion, Puritans on the left "know" that government officials lie, merchants overcharge their customers, and capitalists exploit the masses. Both agree, to paraphrase Pogo, that we have met the enemy and it is *him*. It is the individual, not the system, that is at fault. Consequently, neither is in principle opposed to dictatorial government, although they may oppose particular dictators. Likewise, support for the doctrines of free speech, freedom of the press, and academic freedom depends upon who is speaking, writing, or teaching. Puritans on both sides emphasize and admire the power and the responsibility of the individual (of their own particular persuasion, of course) to a greater degree than does the liberal, who tends to act by structuring institutions and establishing programs with relatively little consideration given to the individuals involved.

Liberalism (Progressivism), with its belief in human goodness and reasonableness, places an emphasis on natural, evolutionary social change. Order may be attained, maintained, and changed through rational discourse, compromise, and consensus. Puritans, in contrast, suffer anxiety about human wickedness and irrationality and fear the dangers of social disorder. Yet they also are cognizant of the extreme means necessary for bringing about social change. Perhaps the difference is vividly exemplified if one compares the Puritanism of John Brown and the abolitionists with the liberalism of the Supreme Court during Chief Justice Warren's tenure and various Presidential commissions. Brown and the abolitionists "knew" that racism existed, that it was evil, and that decisive action was necessary; and, they "knew" this a century ago.

Purist in attitude and perfectionists in action, puritans strive to live moral lives in the midst of spiritual decadence and material corruption. And their belief in moral superiority and the necessity of commitment commonly results in confrontation. These factors necessitate faithful vigilance and perpetual training. Consequently, Ralph Barton Perry characterized Puritans as "moral athletes." Placing an emphasis on will at the expense of judgment and upon justice at the expense of mercy, puritans are narrow-minded in moral choice. Judgment without will is certainly vacuous, but will without judgment is blind. Likewise, mercy without justice is maudlin, but justice without mercy is brutal.

### Puritanism and Reform Movements

Although not limited to a repressive attitude toward human behavior, Puritanism does encompass a staunch moralistic orientation to human nature. Puritans through the ages have attempted to protect men from themselves and have sought to control vice through the legislation of morality. They would prefer personal repentance and individual moral regeneration to legislation, but they realize man's innate weakness. The Prohibition amendment to the United States Constitution, for example, was a victory for the puritanical advocates of the use of laws to control the corrupted or at least easily corruptible nature of man.

Attempts to curtail the advertisement of tobacco products, the control of legal and illegal drugs, and antipollution legislation reflect in part, the puritan strain in American life. The arguments utilized to justify legal restraints on water and air pollution, smoking, drug use, and the addition of chemical additives to foods are generally rooted to a call for the return to purity, cleanliness, and social responsibility—the three principles of puritan morality. Often the reform crusaders issue dire warnings of a forthcoming apocalyptical disaster—a form of rhetoric characteristic of puritan verbal behavior.

Puritanism, of course, may express itself within a religious or secular framework, and the calls for reform may focus upon God, morality, health, or social necessity. Carry A. Nation, the "Madwoman of Kansas," for example, led a religious crusade against John Barleycorn. Inspired by a passage drawn from Isaiah ("Arise, shine, for thy light is come, and the glory of the Lord is risen upon thee"), she battled the dispensers of alcoholic beverages with a moral arrogance that matched that of the Biblical prophets. Recent concern about drug use and pollution also reveals a puritan zeal although they are couched in secular, usually scientific language. Population control advocates as well as drug control proponents often reflect the moral indignation of an elect and reveal that they believe that most adults are incapable of making reasonable judgments about their behavior. Of course, the apocalyptic threat in this case is put forward in statistical and scientific jargon.

The puritan's moral indignation and urge to reform society and to control human behavior for the good of the community have helped to bring about significant social changes. Without the influence of Puritanism, reform would be virtually neutralized. Sometimes, however, puritan zeal ends up producing only minor fads. During the mid-nineteenth century, for example, Sylvester Graham fought assiduously to provide his organic food faddist Grahamite followers with a nonadulterated bakery product and wound up with nothing more spectacular than the humble graham cracker.

Other puritan crusades in America have been rather more eventful, perhaps none so much so as the abolitionist movement which resulted in the Civil War and the abolition of slavery. The puritan spirit within the abolitionist movement showed itself in various ways. Lincoln's Gettysburg address expressed a subdued but intense commitment to the cause of social unity while the martyr John Brown, "decreed by Almighty God, ordained from Eternity," activated the puritan zeal of the revolutionary through his heroic violent rejection of oppression. While Harriet Beecher Stowe expressed in *Uncle Tom's Cabin* the moral indignation which served to inflame the rage of the North, the Battle Hymn of the Republic provided them with a puritan and Christian battlecry. Puritanism provided the North with a moral fusillade to fight a war which had resulted primarily from cultural sectional differences. The spiritualization of the Civil War was a major factor in its popularization and in its bloodiness. Northern soldiers not only fought for the "nation" but also viewed themselves as crusaders for a holy cause. As Jesus died to make men holy, they fought to make them free, while God's truth was marching on.

Moral fervor, righteous indignation, and passionate commitment characterize the ideology of Puritanism as it serves to instigate social reform. Such characteristics also distinguish puritan reformers from the progressivists who are concerned about social reconstruction. The following quotation by Wendel Phillips, the abolitionist, further illustrates the distinguishing characteristics, and if the terms "puritan" and "progressive" are substituted for Phillips' "reformer" and "politician," its applicability to our analysis is readily apparent:

> The reformer is careless of numbers, disregards popularity, and deals only with ideas, conscience, and common sense. He feels, with Copernicus, that as God waited long for an interpreter, so he can wait for his followers. He neither expects nor is overanxious for immediate success. The politician dwells in an everlasting NOW. His motto is "Success"—his aim, votes. His object is not absolute right, but, like Solon's laws, as much right as the people will sanction. His office is not to instruct public opinion, but to represent it.[29]

### Puritanism and Economic Development

In his classic study *The Protestant Ethic and the Spirit of Capitalism,* Max Weber theorized that the Calvinist doctrine provided the ideological foundation for the emergence of capitalism. Protestantism, especially

[29] Quoted in Richard Hofstadter, *The American Political Tradition* (New York: Random House, Inc., 1948), p. 138.

Calvinism, focused upon the sacredness of work, the necessity to plan for the future, and the centrality of such virtues as frugality, patience, and discipline. These virtues, according to Weber established the ethos for transforming an agrarian society into a commercial state. Weber's thesis, however, failed to explain the emergence of capitalism in countries predominately Catholic; and, it failed to acknowledge the significance of a community covenant in determining the direction of economic development.

Although the symbiotic relationship between American Puritanism and capitalism cannot be denied, the fact remains that Puritanism also presented a socialistic visage.[30] Puritans opposed the form of competition characterized by overpricing and rejected any economic system which was not based upon the centrality of social responsibility. Within the Bible State of Massachusetts, Puritan Brahmins supervised the economic marketplace and readily admonished businessmen to beware of unfair practices. They regulated prices, limited interest rates, established wage ceilings, and publicly whipped individuals who refused to work. The oft-noted case of Mr. Robert Keane, for example, typified the relationship between the theocracy and the individual in matters of business. Keane was emphatically admonished, harshly fined, and nearly excommunicated from the church for maximizing his profits. Obviously, such practices are more attuned to a socialized economy than to the classic model of laissez-faire capitalism.

Indeed, the emphasis on social responsibility theme far exceeds the emphasis on rugged individualism in the Puritan ideology. Although Puritans acknowledged that man stood alone before his creator and that his salvation was an individual issue, they were communal in their orientation. Perry Miller in *Errand Into the Wilderness* observed:

> Puritans did not think that the state was merely an umpire, standing on the side lines of a contest, limited to checking egregious fouls but otherwise allowing men free play according to their abilities and the breaks of the game. They would have expected *laissez faire* to result in a reign of rapine and horror. The state to them was an active instrument of leadership, discipline, and wherever necessary, of coercion. . . .[31]

This point is crucial to understanding the latter-day form of puritan expression in the United States. While one thread of the puritan strain enhances rugged business acumen, another stresses social responsibility

[30] For a discussion of the relationship between religion and economics, see R. H. Tawney, *Religion and the Rise of Capitalism* (New York: The New American Library, Inc., n.d.), and Max Weber, *The Protestant Ethic and the Spirit of Capitalism*, trans. Talcott Parsons (New York: Charles Scribner's Sons, 1958).

[31] Perry Miller, *Errand Into the Wilderness* (Cambridge, Mass.: The Belknap Press of Harvard University Press), p. 103. Copyright, 1956, by the President and Fellows of Harvard College.

and community welfare. Socialistic reformers often reflect the Puritan ideology in their emphasis upon a holistic view of society and upon the need to curb individual freedom for the welfare of the society. Puritanism as an ideological thread in the fabric of Americanism has served to enhance the centralization of governmental power and the development of welfare capitalism. Governmental wage stabilization and other economic controls reflect not only an advanced stage of technological development but also the communal element of Puritanism.

Although Puritanism has served as a major ideological support for the capitalistic system by viewing the business world as a calling and work as a means of fulfillment, it also has been utilized to support other economic systems. The values Weber viewed as inherent in Calvinism are the values that contribute to the development of industrialism, regardless of whether it takes the form of capitalism, socialism, or communism. One need only listen to the speeches of Fidel Castro or read the works of Chairman Mao to realize that the same Calvinist virtues are required to create the ethos and to develop the productive potential for the transition from a feudal, agrarian society to an industrial society of the communist type as for the transition to Western-style capitalistic industrialism. Three of the chapters in the "little red book" of Mao Tse-Tung, for example, are entitled "Building Our Country Through Diligence and Frugality," "Self-Reliance and Arduous Struggle," and "Discipline." In one chapter he states, "The principle of diligence and frugality should be observed in everything. This principle of economy is one of the basic principles of socialist economics." [32]

If the "Protestant Ethic" serves to enhance the emergence of an industrial state, whether that state will be capitalistic, socialistic, or communistic depends in part on the presence of a community ethos. If this ethos is present, the economy tends toward socialism or communism. Without such an ethos, each-man-for-himself capitalism is the consequence. The concepts of communal Puritanism, however, often are borrowed by advocates of public welfare and social control to initiate legislation which inhibits corporate competitive forces and used by the government during periods of economic crisis. Indeed, the gradual way in which Puritanism has emerged as a force for socialism based upon the puritan's sense of individual duty to the welfare of the community cannot be ignored. Even when it was utilized to support the capitalistic enterprise, it always included a view that the rich had a responsibility to their community. Puritanism has always attacked the hoarding of money, the idle rich, and the misuse of funds. Without a true sense of community, however, the corporate structure substitutes various philan-

[32] Mao Tse-Tung, *Quotations from Chairman Mao Tse-Tung* (Peking: Foreign Languages Press, 1966), p. 187.

thropic endeavors and foundations for genuine support of communal values.

## The Decline of Revolutionary Puritanism

With the decline of the revolutionary spirit, the social order of Puritanism acquired the characteristics attributed to liberalism. Within several generations the rigid Calvinistic Protestantism weakened and became secularized as the offspring of many Calvinist leaders became the leaders of Unitarianism; the next generation saw their children become Transcendentalists. As Calvinists had found their God in revelation, Unitarians found God in reason, and Transcendentalists found God in nature. Although the new religions retained the puritan focus upon the necessity of moral regeneration and the rejection of materialism and self-interest, they lacked the Puritan theism and rigidity. In the realm of politics, some revolutionary leaders are sainted (Lenin and Mao Tse-Tung), while others are denounced (Stalin in the deStalinized Soviet Union). Regardless of their ultimate fate, they eventually are replaced by men of moderate persuasions. In America, Franklin represented this general phenomenon: his religion was a pragmatic deism rather than a Calvinistic theism; on questions of morals he emphasized a practical, individualistic approach rather than an absolutistic, communal attitude; politically, he criticized the concept of theocracy and advocated a tempered form of democracy. In fact, shortly after Cotton Mather published his *Essays to Do Good*, Franklin, using the name Mrs. Silence Dogood, attacked a pillar of Puritan ideology, Harvard College, for its conspicuous display of affluence and its promotion of idleness, uselessness, and pretentious scholars. Thus, the newly emerging middle class was attacking its "betters" and the voice of democracy was making itself heard.

The failure of Puritanism as a revolutionary ideology can be attributed to several factors. First, simply because they are mortal men, revolutionaries tire and grow wearisome. As Marshall McLuhan quipped, "The price of eternal vigilance is indifference." [33] Others simply succumb to egotism and greed. The desertion rate continues to increase as the saints turn to hedonistic pleasures and, failing to resist satanic temptation, "sell out" to sinners. They sleep late, miss meetings, lust for the flesh, and go to the beach. Some even use the ideals of the revolution for personal gain; they sell revolutionary symbols, sing revolutionary songs, and write revolutionary books—all for private profit. Second, and inextricably intertwined with the first, revolutionary ideology demands a

[33] Marshall McLuhan, *Understanding Media: The Extensions of Man* (New York: McGraw-Hill Book Company, 1964), p. 30.

close, tightly knit community that remains partially detached from the community at large. Puritanism of the past was faced with frontier expansion, urbanization, and foreign trade, whereas the remnants of Puritanism in modernity encounter technocratization, increased affluence, consumerism, and leisure, all of which encourage the development of values antithetical to the puritanical ethos of production and work. It remains a rather ironic fact that the puritanical virtues of perseverance, thrift, and work create a social order that increasingly obviates these virtues. This phenomenon is partially the consequence of Puritanism's failure to consider environmental influences by concentrating entirely on individual virtue. As Perry Miller noted,

> . . . while the ministers were excoriating the behavior of merchants, laborers, and frontiersmen, they never for a moment condemned merchandising, laboring, or expansion of the frontier. They berated the consequences of progress, but never progress; deplored the effects of trade upon religion, but did not ask men to desist from trading; arraigned men of great estates, but not estates.[34]

In like manner, modern American puritans—Ralph Nader and Paul Ehrlich among others—admonish technocrats, capitalists, bureaucrats, and managers but seldom question the inherent value of technology, capitalism, bureaucracy, and management.

Finally, as an ideology of transition, Puritanism is a means of creating a new social order after the dissolution of a previous one. Once the transition is accomplished, however, the original spirit becomes irrelevant. As Maoists will no doubt learn, continuous revolution becomes an increasingly arduous, if not impossible, task. It suffers from the defection of the children of the revolutionaries. As Bay Colony parents discovered, neither the compromise Half-Way Covenant nor the Great Awakening prevented their children from leaving the theocracy. Even the secular puritan virtues, characterized in the maxims of Poor Richard and reiterated during the Great Depression, are rapidly becoming trite slogans to the children of affluence. Parents may continue to admonish their offspring about thrift, adding "you didn't live through the Depression"— which is, as the children well realize, precisely the point.

Life offers a different perspective to the children of the puritans-with-a-mission than it did to their parents. Puritan children face a world in which practical, nonspectacular demands are made of them. Lacking this sense of mission, such a child, as Perry Miller observed, "might wage a stout fight against the Indians, and one out of ten of his fellows might perish in the struggle, but the world was no longer interested. He would be reduced to writing accounts of himself and scheming to get a pub-

---

[34] Perry Miller, *The New England Mind from Colony to Province* (Boston: Beacon Press, 1953), p. 40.

lisher in London, in a desperate effort to tell a heedless world, 'Look, I Exist!' . . . His greatest difficulty would be not the stones, storms, and Indians, but the problem of his identity." [35] Miller's observation is especially relevant to understanding the plight of the children of the twentieth-century middle class in the United States. Their parents or grandparents, often immigrants from another land in search of liberty and economic security, joined in ethnic communities or labor fellowships and struggled valiantly against the forces of tradition which were exerted by advocates of the established order. Dedicated to the mission of achieving economic security and civil equality, they tackled the demon of prejudicial treatment in order to ensure that their children would attain the promises written upon the base of the Statue of Liberty and in the numerous "rags to riches" legends.

The depuritanization of society begins in puritan homes. Puritan parents struggling to gain economic, spiritual, and social security often protect their children from the harsh world of competition and injustice. Benefitting from the security earned by their parents' deeds, these children are prevented from sensing the joy of self-help and independence, two of the ideals taught by puritans. The children of puritans, therefore, are placed in the uncomfortable position of receiving the puritan ethic without the opportunity to actualize it. Those who struggle for affluence and achieve it deprive their children of the opportunity to engage in economic struggle, which is, for the puritan, a psychologically important phenomenon. Deprived of the experience of economic struggle and protected from the crushing effects of prejudice, the children of puritans attempt to undo the confusion of their own identity by joining, often with puritan zeal, the battle to overcome their sense of incompleteness. Romanticism and religious revivalism offer ideological havens for puritans without a cause. Their parents, of course, watch this process with dismay, wondering why their children seem not to want their share of the fruits of the parents' success. The answer, of course, lies precisely in the fact that the success is that of their parents, not their own. Faced with this paradoxical situation, many such parents found the goal desired more fulfilling than the goal achieved. Seeking to unravel the ideological nightmare that pervades their homes, many disillusioned puritan parents focus upon imaginary adversaries. Like colonial puritans, they look for the devil behind the failures of their struggle, but in today's version of the ideology the devil takes the form of the Communist menace, drug abuse, or permissiveness of schools. Only thus can they find a concrete reason for their failure to achieve happiness with the attainment of their goals.

[35] Miller, *Errand into the Wilderness*, p. 37. Copyright 1956, by the President and Fellows of Harvard College.

The so-called generation gap is essentially a conflict which results from ideological dissonance. Parents educated according to the ideology of Puritanism, for example, seek to instruct their children in a similar value system. Social realities, however, change rapidly, requiring ideological change. In a society in which the economic world is ruled by a consumption-oriented market, the political world by spectacular expenditure of funds, and the social world by codes of morality which are relaxing so rapidly that the changes are visible to the naked eye, Puritanism cannot be highly relevant. As Daniel J. Boorstin observed, "Puritanism . . . was not so much defeated by the dogmas of anti-Puritanism as it was simply assimilated to the conditions of life in America. Never was it blown away by a hurricane. It was gradually eroded by the American climate." [36]

Besides revealing ideological irrelevance, the generation gap also indicates that the ideological education is successful. The call for relevance is often a scream against one's own inability to cope with ideological dissonance. In this sense, the accusation that institutions and the older generation are irrelevant reflects the fact that the rage of youth derives at least in part from their personal struggle with their own defective ideological orientation.

Many adult Americans now view the Soviet Union and Communist China with some degree of admiration inasmuch as both countries continue to emphasize the puritan virtues of nation-building and production. The strict discipline imposed upon their children awakens a nostalgic memory and offers a welcomed alternative to the dissent and counter-cultural ethics developing in our consumption-oriented society. The view advocated in a bulletin to businessmen by motivational research expert Dr. Ernest Kichter, however, is rapidly being accepted by many modern American youth:

> We are now confronted with the problem of permitting the average American to feel moral even when he is flirting, even when he is spending, even when he is not saving, even when he is taking two vacations a year and buying a second or third car. One of the basic problems of this prosperity, then, is to give people the sanction and justification to enjoy it and to demonstrate that the hedonistic approach to life is a moral not an immoral one.[37]

To an American who continues to adhere to the tenets of Puritanism, these attitudes typical of a *Playboy* philosophy may appear unAmeri-

[36] Daniel J. Boorstin, "The Puritans: From Providence to Pride," in *Puritanism and the American Experience*, ed. by Michael McGiffert (Reading, Massachusetts: Addison-Wesley Publishing Company, 1969), p. 107.

[37] Quoted in William H. Whyte, Jr., *The Organization Man* (Garden City, N.Y.: Doubleday & Company, Inc., 1956), p. 19.

can; to an old Bolshevik or a Maoist, they are a counterrevolutionary example of the decadence of bourgeois capitalism. Yet dissent among the youth also appears to be increasing in the USSR, and perhaps succeeding generations of Chinese will consider the *Red Book* as trite and cliché-ridden as Franklin's writings appear to many American youth today. If there is nothing so powerful as an idea whose time has come, it is also true there is nothing so boring as an idea whose time is past.

### Puritanism—Secularized and Democratized

It is necessary to differentiate between the ideology of Puritanism exemplified by the members of the Massachusetts Bay Colony and the ideology of Puritanism illustrated in the writings of Benjamin Franklin. Whether authors eulogize or condemn Poor Richard, they generally agree that he became symbolic of the American character. Although a product of strict Puritan childrearing practices, Franklin was also a man of the Enlightenment. Diestic in religion and utilitarian in philosophy, he secularized and democratized the values of Bay Colony Puritanism. For the Puritans, "early to bed and early to rise" was God's will; for Franklin, it made you "healthy, wealthy, and wise." The religious Puritans believed God had destined some to be rich and others to be poor, some to rule, others to be ruled. But Franklin wrote a handbook describing how the poor can become rich and how followers can become leaders. With this development the communal covenant between God and man was replaced by the doctrine of atomistic, laissez-faire liberalism, the ideological foundation for emergent middle-class capitalism. Perhaps capitalism had not been willed by God, but it became increasingly acceptable as a dictate of Natural Law. No longer did each man work for the greater glory of God; it was now each man for himself. The rejection of communal spirit was reflected in the words of the classical economic theorist Adam Smith: "It is not from the benevolence of the butcher, the brewer, or the baker, that we expect our dinner, but from their regard of their own interest. We address ourselves, not to their humanity but to their self-love, and never talk to them of our own necessities, but of their advantages." [38] It is primarily in this regard for individual self-interest that incipient capitalism differs from communism. Both capitalism and communism stress what Weber termed the Protestant ethic, especially in their transitional stage. But in contrast to Smith's view of individual self-interest, Mao states that the Chinese citizen must "proceed in all cases from the interests of the people and not from one's self-interest or from

---

[38] Adam Smith, *An Inquiry into the Nature and Causes of the Wealth of Nations* (London: Methuen & Co., Ltd., 1961), I, 18.

the interests of a small group. . . ." [39] "All work done for the masses must start from their needs and not from the desire of any individual. . . ." [40]

The educational system played a significant role in the formation of the American character after the Revolutionary War. The secularization of Puritanism, reflected in the writings of Franklin, continued rapidly with the revisions of the *New England Primer.* The newer version of the puritan values was greatly reinforced as the schools adopted the books of William Holmes McGuffey and Noah Webster. These books served as fundamental texts for millions of Americans. In addition, the influence of Webster's dictionary was awesome. One can scarcely imagine the power and influence of the puritanical Webster, who was able to define the words not only of a new nation but of a nation with an increasing number of newly arriving, non-English-speaking immigrants. To even attempt to gain some understanding of this power and its ideological implications, try to imagine the difference between communist and capitalist definitions for such words as free enterprise, working class, God, freedom, and justice. How would the definition of love differ in a dictionary written by a puritan from what one would find in the dictionary of a romanticist?

In his *Almanack* (1732), Franklin actualized an earlier directive of Cotton Mather. In *Essays to Do Good* (1710), Mather had stated, "Let their copies be composed of sentences worthy to be had in everlasting remembrance—of sentences which shall contain the brightest maxims of wisdom, worthy to be written on the fleshly tables of their hearts. . . ." [41] The maxims of Poor Richard were illustrative of the thirteen virtues described in Franklin's *Autobiography* (1784). These virtues, considered necessary for the "arduous project of arriving at moral perfection," included temperance, silence, order, resolution, frugality, industry, sincerity, justice, moderation, cleanliness, tranquility, chastity, and humility. To assure a strict adherence to this code of conduct, Franklin maintained a daily checklist—an activity repeated in many modern school systems. [42]

Franklin's writings typify secularized Puritanism not only in content but also in style. In modern jargon, Puritanism emphasizes "telling it like it is," direct and to the point. As Mather often stated, a good Puritan is less interested in the "wisdom of words" than in the "words of wisdom." Although politically nonegalitarian, Puritanism has a message for everyone, regardless of his station in life, and the teacher should refrain from

[39] Mao Tse-Tung, *Quotations from Chairman Mao Tse-Tung,* p. 170.
[40] Mao Tse-Tung, *Quotations from Chairman Mao Tse-Tung,* p. 120.
[41] Mather, *Bonifacius,* p. 85.
[42] Benjamin Franklin, *The Autobiography of Benjamin Franklin* (New York: Random House, Inc., 1944), pp. 92–104.

pompous verbosity and "drive home a 'lively and affectionate' sense of the divine by shooting rhetorical arrows not over his peoples heads but into their hearts.'" [43] In comparison with the bland, sterile primary readers of today, exemplified in the Dick and Jane stories, the books of Puritanism would appear harsh and "value-laden." Yet questions of sin and salvation are extremely important ones, rarely bland or boring. When considering such questions, value judgments are not only inevitable but commendable.

In addition to moral maxims and yet related to them is the literary emphasis of Puritanism on biography. Stories relating to individual conversion, will, and achievement continue to maintain a significant place in American literature. *The Autobiography of Malcolm X* epitomizes the religious elements of Puritanism, while Booker T. Washington's *Up from Slavery* epitomizes the achievement elements. And the variety of books with the theme "How to Become . . ." describe the route to success, whether in the areas of politics, economics, or sex, in a style reminiscent of Franklin's checklist for moral perfection. Perhaps Kenneth Murdock best summarized the literary attitude of Puritanism: "Homeliness of imagery, simplicity of diction, and a constant emphasis on the values most easily recognizable by honest Englishmen of no pretensions to critical acumen characterized this style, and the influence of the audience in shaping it is patent." [44]

### Puritanism and Social Darwinism

The popularized version of puritan values received scientific legitimacy in the social Darwinistic writings of Herbert Spencer in England and William Graham Sumner in America. Charles Darwin's *The Origin of Species* was published in 1859. His evolutionary theory focused upon the Malthusian principle of overpopulation. Overpopulation, according to Darwin, resulted in a competitive "struggle for existence" in which the process of natural selection favored those individuals best fitted to the environment. As a result of the "survival of the fittest," to use Spencer's famous slogan, not only are these individuals more likely than the less well endowed to produce progeny to perpetuate the species, but their progeny are more likely to improve the species. Thus mankind has improved through the natural order of evolution. Expressing this theory

---

[43] Increase Mather, "The Life and Death of Mr. Richard Mather," in *Collections of the Corchester Antiquarian Historical Society,* No. 3 (Boston, 1850), p. 85.

[44] Kenneth B. Murdock, "The Puritan Literary Attitude," in *Puritanism in Early America,* ed. George M. Waller (Boston: D. C. Heath and Company, 1950), p. 92.

with his characteristic certitude, Sumner declared: "let it be understood that we cannot go outside of this alternative: liberty, inequality, survival of the fittest; not liberty, equality, survival of the unfittest. The former carries society forward and favors all of its members; the latter carries society downwards and favors all its worst members." [45] Similarly, Spencer in his sociology textbook states, "Not simply do we see that in the competition among individuals of the same kind, survival of the fittest has from the beginning furthered production of a higher type; but we see that to the unceasing warfare between species is mainly due both growth and organization. Without universal conflict there would have been no development of the active powers." [46]

With the advent of social Darwinism and its implicit concept of human progress, the socioeconomic facet of the American character was completed and remained relatively unchanged for decades. As Richard Hofstadter stated, "Sumner's synthesis brought together three great traditions of western capitalist culture: the Protestant ethic, the doctrines of western capitalist culture; the Protestant ethic, the doctrine of classical economics, and Darwinian natural selection." [47] The Protestant ethic supplies the *modus operandi*, the ethos of laissez-faire taken from classical economics eliminated communal restraint, and Darwinism provided the scientific legitimacy for the success of the individual, both economically and, to some degree, socially. Whether the successful was "chosen" by God or "selected" by nature became an academic question debated by theologians and social theorists, but the fact that the rich deserved their success was generally agreed upon. The wealthy industrialist Andrew Carnegie described the fruits of what he termed the natural law of competition:

> . . . while the law may be sometimes hard for the individual, it is best for the race, because it insures the survival of the fittest in every department. We accept and welcome, therefore, as conditions to which we must accommodate ourselves, great inequality of environment, the concentration of business, industrial and commercial, in the hands of a few, and the law of competition between these, as being not only beneficial, but essential for the future progress of the race.[48]

Sentiments similar to those of Carnegie were expressed in a theological framework by the Right Reverend William Lawrence, who wrote:

[45] William Graham Sumner, "The Challenge of Facts," in *Essays of William Graham Sumner,* ed. Albert Galloway Keller and Maurice R. Davie (New Haven: Yale University Press, 1934), II, 95.
[46] Herbert Spencer, *The Principles of Sociology* (New York: D. Appleton and Company, 1895–1898), II, 240–41.
[47] Richard Hofstadter, *Social Darwinism in American Thought* (Boston: Beacon Press, 1944), p. 51.
[48] Andrew Carnegie, "Wealth," *North American Review,* CXLVIII (June 1889), 654.

". . . it is only to the man of morality that wealth comes. We believe in the harmony of God's Universe. . . . We . . . occasionally see the wicked prosper, but only occasionally. . . . Godliness is in league with riches." [49]

Additional scientific credence was provided by the eugenic theory developed by Darwin's cousin, Thomas Galton. Those individuals who survived the competitive struggle for existence not only had fulfilled the evolutionary laws of nature, but also could be viewed as genetically superior. The scientific theorists had discovered a pattern that bore striking resemblance to the Calvinist theological creed. Where Calvinists had viewed human failure as a consequence of inherent sinfulness in the Fall of Adam, eugenists defined it in terms of degenerate genetic makeup. Success, for Calvinists, had been predestined, chosen by God. In eugenic terms, success, if not written in the stars, was inscribed in genetic content. Both theories minimized the significance of environmental influences in determining human character and behavior.

The studies conducted in the early 1900s of the infamous families, the Jukes and the Kallikaks, became widely disseminated and continue to be reiterated in modern textbooks. For those individuals of the puritanical eugenic mentality, the studies proved conclusively that both evil and good were inherent in an individual from conception. Prostitutes, drunks, and criminals as well as lawyers, ministers, and captains of industry were born, not made.

This limited view of human character and social behavior caused even the scientific community to look askance at, if not totally reject, environmentalist theories such as those proposed by Jean Baptiste Lamarck, whose preDarwinian theory of evolution was based on the premise that parents are capable of transmitting characteristics acquired during their lifetime to their offspring. Although it is now quite obvious that acquired characteristics cannot be inherited, it is equally obvious that wealth can be. An affluent individual may have his finger amputated as a result of some misfortune occurring on his yacht. His offspring, born after the unfortunate event, would certainly have access to all his digits, and after his death he would also receive his yacht. This simplistic example illustrates the difficulty of directly relating physical science with social issues. In fact, recent scientific endeavors have revealed how closely environmental factors and genetic factors are related to each other, making it extremely difficult to determine which in fact are of greater importance. Birth defects, for example, may be the result of genetic factors. They may also be caused by a variety of poor environmental conditions

[49] William Lawrence, "The Relation of Wealth to Morals," *World's Work* (January 1901), I, 287.

affecting egg and sperm development prior to conception and fetal development during pregnancy.

The eugenic theory obviously enhanced the image of the wealthy and provided a rationale for attacking any social reformers attempting to alter the status quo through human intervention. Yet, paradoxically, it also provided the plan by which human intervention could be used to aid in the creation of a more perfect society modeled after the present one. The difference, obviously, is that the reformer wished to alter the environmental conditions; puritanistic eugenists worked to manipulate the individual. Adherents to the eugenic theory engaged in a variety of activities that resulted in the passage of state sterilization laws, as well as the formation of the American Breeders' Association, the Eugenics Record Office, and the National Conference on Race Betterment. Perhaps it is less than ironic that members of the Rockefeller family provide leadership in the present Planned Parenthood Association, and that the giant philanthropic foundations are involved in birth control programs as over-population has again become an important issue to the more affluent members of our society. Indeed, the position of many modern proponents of birth control echoes that of their ideological forefather Thomas Robert Malthus, an English clergyman and political activist, who rejected certain public relief programs on the grounds that they would encourage population growth. Believing that pain and suffering would control the rapid rate of reproduction among the masses, he admonished: ". . . it is necessary to be fully aware of the natural tendency of the labouring classes of society to increase beyond the demand for their labour, or the means of their adequate support, and the effect of this tendency to throw the greatest difficulties in the way of permanently improving their condition." [50]

After reading Darwin's *The Descent of Man,* William Jennings Bryan declared that Darwin's theories would "weaken the cause of democracy and strengthen class pride and the power of wealth." [51] This insightful expression of Populist sentiment illustrates the complexity of the ideological conflict eventually symbolized by the trial of John Scopes. Puritanism and Scientism had become allies in the formation of a powerful eastern, industrial establishment—Wall Street, the symbol of evil for agrarian interests and Populism. In an agrarian society, land was the measure of man; private property was equated with freedom. The nineteenth century, labeled by Charles Pierce as "the century of greed," witnessed the emergence of industrial man; money replaced land as the

[50] Thomas Malthus, "A Summary View of the Principles of Population," in *Three Essays on Population,* ed. The Population Council (New York: New American Library, Inc., 1963), p. 20.

[51] Quoted in Hofstadter, *Social Darwinism in American Thought,* p. 200.

measure of man. Needless to say, money was freedom. As a character in a Balzac novel proclaimed, "There is no scaffold, no headsman, for millionaires!" [52]

No doubt many individuals found striking similarities between the ruthless, competitive capitalism of the nineteenth century and the animal world of the Galapagos Island, the locus of Darwin's studies. Yet, few would defend utilizing "the law of the jungle" as a criterion for measuring man's degree of civilization. Proponents of social Darwinism, no doubt, would argue that they are obeying the laws of nature, and nature is perfect. Yet this rhetoric never prevented them from destroying nature and its resources with a rather ironic rationalization that this destruction, also, was in obedience to natural law.

Even if one acknowledges the legitimacy of scientific findings, the problem of ethical judgments remains unresolved. Scientific method may prove, with a high degree of probability, what in fact *is* the case. One leaves the realm of scientific endeavor, however, when one considers what *ought* to be the case. By using the scientific method, for example, it could be illustrated that if an infant received an insufficient amount of Vitamin D, he would probably become a victim of rickets. Whether he *ought* to have free food stamps or compulsory medical checkups, however, is a consideration pertaining to values, not science. Similarly, recent scientific findings have correlated smoking with lung cancer. Yet even if the individual accepts the validity of such evidence, he is left with a value choice. Philosophically, all attempts to equate "what is desirable" with "what ought to be desired" have proven futile. The value of human life transcends the realm of science.

### Puritanism and the American Dream

The Horatio Alger stories, beginning in 1867, popularized the "rags to riches" mythology of the American Dream. With such books as *Struggling Upward, Ragged Dick,* and *Mark, the Matchboy,* generations of youth were taught the secrets of economic success. Although Alger's secret included luck, a highly degenerate virtue for Puritanism, the remaining puritan virtues were quite clearly present in truly democratic form. Like *McGuffey's Readers,* these blatantly moralistic stories related the nearly limitless potential for upward mobility of all Americans, including "bootblacks," orphans, and the physically handicapped. In fact, these individuals were pictured as being in nearly advantageous positions, their handicaps providing them with added challenge and incentive. It

[52] Honoré de Balzac, *The Thirteen* (New York: The Macmillan Company, 1901), p. 64.

seemed difficult to pity them when they had so far to go and so much to gain.

In a rather paradoxical way, *McGuffey's Readers* also provided the rationale for the virtue of pious acquiescence for those who failed in upward mobility. In return for accepting their humble stations in life, the poor were partially romanticized. For example, in the story "The Poor Boy," the student is told,

> When he sees little boys and girls riding on pretty horses, or in coaches, or walking with ladies and gentlemen, and having on fine clothes, he does not envy them nor wish to be like them.
> He says, "I have often been told, and I have read that it is God who makes some poor, and others rich; that the rich have many troubles which we know nothing of; and that the poor, if they are but good, may be very happy; indeed, I think that when I am good, nobody can be happier than I am!" [53]

Certainly one function of a myth is to provide a unifying belief. Who but Abraham Lincoln could characterize and express the myth of the American Dream with such clarity and honesty. Speaking to an audience in Milwaukee, Wisconsin, Lincoln asserted,

> The prudent penniless beginner labors for wages awhile, saves a surplus with which to buy tools or land, for himself; then labors on his own account another while, and at length hires another new beginner to help him. This, say its advocates, is *free* labor—the just and generous, and prosperous system, which opens the way for all—gives hope to all, and energy, and progress, and improvement of conditions to all. If any continue through life in the condition of the hired laborer, it is not the fault of the system, but because of either a dependent nature . . . or improvidence, folly, or singular misfortune. [54]

Yet by the end of the century this dream was weakening. It had been attacked by muckraking journalists, debunking literary figures, social utopians, union organizers, and a variety of other disenchanted individuals, pejoratively labeled idealists, socialists, anarchists, communists, and visionaries. But, ironically, perhaps the greatest blow to the American Dream resulted from the success of the successful—competitive capitalism had become corporate capitalism. Farmers and craftsmen became factory workers, private accountants became bureaucratic functionaries, and entrepreneurs became corporate directors. By 1885 even Andrew Carnegie had to admit, "There is no doubt that it is becoming harder and harder as business gravitates more and more to immense concerns for a young man without capital to get a start for himself, and in this city especially,

[53] William Holmes McGuffey, *Newly Revised Eclectic Second Reader* (New York and Cincinnati: VanAntwerp, Bragg and Co., 1848), p. 40.
[54] Abraham Lincoln, *Collected Works* (New Brunswick, N.J.: Rutgers University Press, 1953–1955) IV, 478–79.

when larger and larger capital is essential, it is unusually difficult." [55] Carnegie then added, although one gets little sense of conviction from his words, that the new social order will provide an even greater incentive for social mobility than the old.

Certainly the chances of *Mark, the Matchboy* and *Ragged Dick* for any ultimate socioeconomic success has declined. The betting odds were described by Richard T. Ely in 1889: "If you tell a single concrete working man on the Baltimore and Ohio Railroad that he may yet be the president of the company, it is not demonstrable that you have told him what is not true, although it is within bounds to say that he is far more likely to be killed by a stroke of lightning." [56]

The American Dream, however, continues to persist, albeit in highly modified form. The concrete worker may not become the company president, but he may become foreman. More importantly to him, however, is that his children will receive an education. This, he believes, will guarantee them some modicum of social mobility. And, of course, to attain a degree one must practice perseverance, diligence, and industry—the virtues of Puritanism applied in a society where social mobility is increasingly determined by formal schooling.

The remnants of capitalistic Puritanism persist in the United States especially among the lower-middle-class, "blue-collar" workers. Having been taught the American dream and the virtue of hard work, blue-collar workers maintain a belief in competitive ethic. While often denying or failing to realize that the super-rich most often have gained their wealth through inheritance rather than hard work, they adamantly resent and reject suggestions which advocate the extension of welfare roles or a guaranteed annual income. Much of their resentment of socialistic legislation and their adamant support of Puritanism result from their uncomfortable position in the socioeconomic system. Unable to reach a stable and secure economic status, they struggle incessantly to avoid the nightmare of poverty and unemployment. Fearing that socialistic legislation will propel the poor into middle-class status—a position which they hope to attain by hard work—they reject legislation devised to assist the poor. Often accused of lacking charity or sensitivity concerning their less fortunate brethren, they are commonly the brunt of ridicule. The tragedy of their position is accentuated by the fact that their economic struggle if successful will liberate their children from extreme economic worry, and these liberated children will come to resent the values of their parents and will turn against them with accusations of "bigotry" and "ignorance."

[55] Andrew Carnegie, *Empire of Business* (New York: Doubleday, Page, 1902), p. 207.

[56] Richard T. Ely, *Social Aspects of Christianity* (New York: T. Y. Crowell and Company, 1889), p. 36.

The fact that these citizens—adherents of an ideology taught to them by the schools and the rhetoric of the Brahmins of the society—serve as a target of scorn for individuals seeking social reform is an American tragedy.

Indeed, the fact that many Americans believe that the economic inequalities in America result from the views and deeds of the blue-collar workers is not only a tragedy but a travesty. The travesty is most clearly discernible when we realize that the super-rich, who often viciously and unrelentlessly coerce political leaders to pass legislation to protect their personal wealth, throw elaborate parties to support the call of the poor (hence the development of the ideologically grotesque phenomenon known as "radical chic") and join in the pastime of ridiculing sincere but ideologically outdated blue-collar workers.

Puritanism, as defined by the residents of the Bay Colony, had been primarily a social and political ideology; only later did it become predominantly an economic matter. The heroes of the earlier form of Puritanism were upper-middle-class theocratic magistrates and theologians. These *Brahmins,* as some were later termed, included familiar names that continue to signify social power in this country. The offspring of generations of Winthrops, Dudleys, Bradstreets, Lodges, Saltonstalls, and Brewsters appear on the society pages of *The New York Times* and other "eastern establishment" gazettes. Heroes of later Puritanism, however, were wealthy, self-made, rugged individualists of lower-middle-class origins. Included in this group, some of whom eventually were labeled *Robber Barons,* were the families of Rockefellers, Morgans, Vanderbilts, Carnegies, and Fords. The Barons, with their combination of puritan virtues and technological pursuits, were praised by all levels of the educational system. Indeed, the heroic episode of the Golden Spike, uniting East and West, is long remembered by the vast majority of educated Americans and far overshadows the grim realities of railroad graft and labor exploitation.

The Brahmins, no doubt, would have been appalled with the original Barons, considering them greedy, crass, and ill-mannered. Thorstein Veblen, among others, wrote scathing attacks on the cultural ethos of the captains of industry. His terms "conspicuous leisure" and "conspicuous consumption" described several characteristic traits of these nouveaux riches as they attempted to translate their wealth into social prestige. Wealth alone, however, is not sufficient, for success. Prostitutes and Mafia members, for example, may have some degree of wealth, but they lack social prestige. To reach the plateau of aristocracy, one also needs "culture" and social legitimacy. Manners have always been an economic luxury; they are symbolic of "having arrived" economically. As the Barons were forging their empires with the virtues of Puritanism (in addition to fraud and graft), they had little time for the cultural trappings of aristocracy. Their endowments and foundations, however, helped support the prep schools and Ivy League universities that brought culture to their offspring.

Ideologies, especially in their early phase of development, can function to raise the spirit of men. They can provide the exemplary symbols and transcendent ideals that serve as catalysts to direct the actions of those who adhere to them. The ideology of Puritanism served this function for the original Bay Colony residents, just as its revised edition, the American Dream, provided a beacon of hope for the vast number of westward settlers and newly arriving immigrants. One certainly cannot denigrate this dream, so nobly stated on the base of the Statue of Liberty, any more than one can deny the importance of diligence, perseverance, industry, and self-reliance. Living in an age characterized by alienation, anxiety, and despair, any ray of hope is as welcome as a ship to the man lost on a raft at sea.

An ideology, however, also can serve as a rigid rationale for the preservation of the established order. Its elements can become trite clichés for those with power when confronted with legitimate demands for social change. To deny migrant farmworkers a minimum wage or the right to bargain collectively on the grounds that hard work will guarantee anyone economic success, or to attribute their poverty to a lack of character is insensitive, dehumanizing, and false. Yet for more than a century, elements of Puritanism have been used as slogans to evade societal responsibility and prohibit social change. Proponents of programs one would assume were necessary correlatives of industrial growth, such as workmen's compensation, unemployment compensation, social security benefits, welfare assistance, medicare payments, and, more recently, a guaranteed income, continue to encounter the deeply engrained shibboleths of Puritanism. One might anticipate this response from the less educated classes of society, but when such rhetoric is espoused by the more educated and affluent members of the society, many of whom were socially and/or economically subsidized throughout their life, it is both shocking and appalling. [57] As C. Wright Mills pointed out, "Nobody talks more of free enterprise and competition and of the best man winning than the man who inherited his father's store or farm." [58] Perhaps the greatest tragedy of the American Dream rests less with its intent than with the

[57] To gain an understanding of the extent to which our corporate welfare state approaches "socialism for the rich and free enterprise for the poor," see Michael Harrington's *The Other America: Poverty in the United States* (Baltimore: Penguin Books, 1963), and C. Wright Mills' *The Power Elite* (New York: Oxford University Press, 1956).

[58] C. Wright Mills, *White Collar* (New York: Oxford University Press, 1951), p. 36.

fact that many Americans have faithfully practiced the virtues of Puritanism, and yet have not shared in the rewards. For them, the American Dream is a nightmare.

Puritanism retains ideological significance in rhetoric, if not in actuality, within rural areas and small towns. Sinclair Lewis, in his widely read novels *Babbitt* and *Main Street,* was one of many American authors who portrayed the influence of Puritanism on the lives of small-town Americans. According to the puritan way of looking at things, the pluralistic culture and the extremes of wealth and poverty found in large urban centers symbolize moral degeneracy and materialistic decadence and represent a threat to the sanctity of the puritan virtues. Puritan parents in rural areas and small towns, who have witnessed the loss of their offspring to the cities, realize the truth in Thomas Wolfe's remark, "You can't go home again."

### Puritanism and Freudianism

One version of secularized Puritanism is cogently expressed in the writings of Sigmund Freud and his disciples. Both the Puritans and the Freudians saw life as consisting of predestined adversity and tension in a hostile world in which the individual's mental survival is achieved through his psychic adjustment to social conditions. Restructuring the social order was of little significance inasmuch as human freedom was founded upon the control of inner compulsions rather than upon the removal of external constraints.

In America, Freudianism became increasingly popular in the 1920s following the disillusionment of the upper-middle-class intelligentsia with the early Progressive movement. The conflicts within the movement resulting from World War I and the seeming insignificance of prior social reforms were some of the factors that shattered the ideals and dampened the spirit of the social reformers. For many of these individuals, some of whom had been ardent proponents of social activism, Freudianism provided a secular explanation for irrationalism and evil, a rationale for the failure of social reform, and a blueprint for the future. Agreeing with the puritans, they discovered that the enemy rested within—human nature was at fault. Social reform had been predestined to failure, for if the individual and his society were inevitably in conflict, as Freudians had proclaimed, then social change could be of minimal ameliorative value.

Such a view of "Civilization and Its Discontents," to use the title of one of Freud's more influential books, not only may lessen the necessity for making discerning judgments about different societies, but also may militate against developing or sustaining any enthusiasm for "improving" the existing social order. In fact, such a view often resulted in a tendency to preserve the status quo and implicitly condone the repressiveness of societal institutions, for the alternatives appeared to be the chaos of anarchists or the violence of revolutionaries. As Sigmund Freud admonished, "Civilized society is perpetually menaced with disintegration through this primary hostility of men towards one another." [59] Consequently, Freudians, whether they are political leftists or rightists, maintain allegiance to the forces of social order in the chronic conflict between civilization and repressed antisocial instincts.

Although the adherents to Freudianism were indebted to Darwin for many of their ideas concerning human nature and behavior, they did not share his belief in evolutionary progress. Freud's utilization of ancient Greek mythology and history to exemplify the psychological dilemmas of modern man is illustrative of his linear view of history. Social change was an obvious reality, but man's attempt to maintain his sanity was a continuing process. In contrast to the progressivists, adherents to Freudianism could never view history as proof of man's inevitable ascent from barbarism to civilization.

The analysis of many Freudians is grounded upon a very narrow psychological view of reality. As a consequence of this psychologizing, social issues are reduced to personal problems. The demands of revolutionaries and the criticisms of more moderate men tend to get lost in an intricate analysis of the individual psyche or simply to be dismissed as public exhibitions of private neurotic tendencies. Few Americans who consider themselves patriotic would perceive the actions of the American revolutionaries as merely public manifestations of the Oedipal conflict between father and son, for to do so obviously would be to diminish the significance of Independence Day.

Freudian psychologizing results in the search for the reality behind reality; that is, the individual seeks to determine the instinctual drives and unconscious motivations that determine his overt behavior. Adherents to the ideology of Freudianism perceive reality as a psychic world of predetermined causal relationships. By directing concern away from social issues and toward potential personal neurosis, the act of psychologizing results in the stabilization of social norms and institutions. Rather than questioning the legitimacy of the society, one questions the integrity and mental health of the individual. Social and intellectual criticism is stifled and dialogue is terminated. The potential for tyranny inherent in such a process was aptly observed by Philip Rieff:

> When social action is conceived as the precipitate of personal emotions, protest against society can be explained away as a neurotic symptom. It

[59] Sigmund Freud, *Civilization and Its Discontents*, trans. Joan Riviere (Garden City, N.Y.: Doubleday & Company, Inc., 1958), p. 61.

is here that psychiatry may play a significant role in an authoritarian ideology: by viewing an admittedly sick society in terms of that subtlest of all authoritarian images, the hospital.[60]

The Freudian concepts of human nature and personality theoretically democratized mental illness. By defining neurosis in quantitative rather than qualitative terms, the difference between the neurotic and the healthy individual was a matter of degree rather than kind. In terms of the Freudian constructs, everyone could be viewed as a potential mental patient. These constructs and definitions, however, did not prevent the belief in a hierarchial construct for judging mental health. Thus the theoretical democratization that could result in a tolerant and nonjudgmental attitude toward individuals was generally destroyed by the reality of the rather puritanical judgments of ardent Freudian disciples who usually considered themselves near the summit of the mental health hierarchy. Just as the puritans maintained beliefs in the universality of inherent sinfulness and the predetermined election of the saints, so the Freudians could believe in the universality of the innate potential for neurosis and a predetermined disposition for mental health among an elite group of individuals. In fact, Freud demonstrated these anti-egalitarian views in a seminar concerning the avoidance of war. In a statement strikingly similar to the sentiments expressed previously by the Puritan theocratic magistrates, Freud asserted:

> One instance of the innate and ineradicable inequality of men is their tendency to fall into the two classes of leaders and followers. The latter constitute the vast majority; they stand in need of an authority which will make decisions for them and to which they for the most part offer an unqualified submission. This suggests that more care should be taken with independent minds, not open to intimidation and eager in the pursuit of truth, whose business it would be to give direction to the dependent masses.[61]

The Rousseauean concept of the natural goodness of human nature appears extremely naive to the puritanical Freudian. The innocence and happiness of childhood, so idolatrized by the romanticists, is merely a fanciful image contrived by individuals suffering from a neurotic adulthood. Rather than striving to develop childlike qualities, the Freudian is more apt to criticize them as childish tendencies. A field trip to a local day care center certainly would not disclose noble savages. In fact, the Freudian observer notes that the behavior of young children displays egoistic pleasures, frustrated incest impulses, and competitive sibling rivalry.

[60] Philip Rieff, *Freud: The Mind of the Moralist* (New York: The Viking Press, 1959), p. 243.

[61] Sigmund Freud, "Why War?" in *Collected Papers of Sigmund Freud*, ed. Ernest Jones (New York: Basic Books Inc., 1959), V, 614.

### The Virtues and Vices of Puritanism

Karl Marx's pessimistic contention that capitalism contains the seeds of its own destruction could be equally applied to any ideological position. With Puritanism these seeds rest in their pursuit of virtue. Contrary to the belief expressed by the 1964 presidential candidate Barry Goldwater, extremism in the pursuit of virtue is (or certainly can be) a vice. Few things are attained or even pursued unless one pays a price for them, a maxim one would certainly expect a puritan to remember. For example, a zealous pursuit of covenant (or community) exacts a price in terms of the diminution of individualism. Roger Williams and Anne Hutchinson, among many others, paid that price. The puritan fears the possible disorder and chaos of individualism more than the potential tyranny and brutality of totalitarianism. In this respect, he would agree with Martin Luther, who claimed that "God would prefer to suffer the government to exist no matter how evil rather than to allow the rabble to riot, no matter how justified they are in doing so." [62] In his diligent search for absolute morality, the puritan quite easily risks the dangers not only of hypocrisy but also of pharisaism, the sincere belief that one is more righteous than one really is. Just as Captain Ahab needed Moby Dick, the saint needs a sinner. In his eagerness to brand another individual as sinner, the puritan tends to overlook his own sins. Because of his belief in his own salvation, because he views himself as one of the chosen people, the puritan often fails to hear potentially valid criticism, especially when voiced by a "heathen." "Chosen" people may provide the basic elements necessary to create a new social order, but they do not make pleasant neighbors. And finally, an obsessive emphasis upon the sinful nature of the individual crushes the human spirit rather than inspiring it and creates a climate of distrust that undermines the idea of community rather than adding to its strength.

Just as the mind of the censor is like that of the censored, so too is the ideology of the revolutionary like that of the reactionary. Both illustrate a sense of firm commitment with an emphasis clearly placed upon means rather than ends, for to such minds "ends" remain relatively vague and/or abstract. Consequently, phrases such as liberty, equality, and fraternity, or public good and salvation can be the clarion cries of both the revolutionary and the reactionary. In contrast to their obscurity concerning ends, their sense of "means" is often quite clear indeed: it is merely a question of will. Training of the will may be emphasized to such

---

[62] Quoted in Hoffer, *The True Believer*, p. 122.

a degree that it becomes an end-in-itself, resulting in the situation described by Perry: "The revolutionary forgets what he is trying to create, the reactionary what he is trying to keep." [63] In either situation, the individual may become the victim of his own distorted sense of commitment. Risking the danger of goal displacement, he may allow instrumental values to become terminal values, with the result that he will be crushed by his own distorted dedication. Vivid examples of such victimization and eventual self-destruction were portrayed in the characters of Captain Ahab in Melville's *Moby Dick* and Inspector Javert in Victor Hugo's *Les Misérables*.

Both absolute commitment and absolute tolerance result in nihilism. Each viewpoint places the individual in a position where he fails to make distinctions between good and evil. For the man of absolute commitment all issues become important points on which he must make judgments. For the man of absolute tolerance, there are no issues on which man can take a stand, for all actions are permissible. Consequently, adherents to either position fail to establish a hierarchy of human values. The man of commitment must remain aware of Nietzsche's dictum, "Convictions are more dangerous enemies of truth than lies." [64] The man of tolerance must remain aware that there is a difference between truth and falsity, knowledge and opinion.

Puritanism views man holistically and from a moralistic perspective. It is an ideology which combines the spiritual, aesthetic, and social aspects of man into a politico-economic framework. Viewing man as a moral agent regardless of his role in society and holding him accountable for all of his actions, it demands integration of the human personality. Because they also see man as innately weak or vicious, however, puritans call upon institutions or revolutionary tribunals to serve as agencies for limiting and controlling his behavior. And because they root all morality to individual behavior, puritans invariably fail to perceive the misdeeds of institutions or the degree to which institutions may influence the freedom of individual choice. For example, they blame traffic deaths on drunk or senile drivers rather than on poorly designed automobiles; they attribute the rise in "sexual promiscuity" to individual moral degeneracy rather than to the development of the oral contraceptive; and, they attribute the death of a heart transplant patient to a weakness of his own body structure rather than the transplant operation. Consequently, this aspect of Puritanism serves to enhance Scientism in that it directs one's perception away from the possible "evils" of technology and focuses upon the faults of the individual. Serving as watchmen against evil, puritans

[63] Perry, *Puritanism and Democracy*, p. 637.
[64] Friedrich Nietzsche, "Human, All-Too-Human," in *The Portable Nietzsche*, ed. Walter Kaufmann (New York: The Viking Press, 1954), p. 63.

perpetually search for individual transgressions and individual conscious malevolence while ignoring the debilitating influences which institutions may exert upon human beings. They rarely concern themselves with institutional patterns of aggression. Indeed, when puritan revolutionaries are successful, they often preserve the old political institutions in order to actualize their new ideological patterns.

Because puritans reject all forms of environmental determinism they reject all arguments which root man's behavior to the inexorable pressures of social systems. They hold all individuals, leaders as well as followers, accountable for their deeds. Thus puritans joined with humanists at the conclusion of World War II, in demanding that an international court prosecute Nazis for committing war crimes. Regardless of the social environment, commands of leaders, or the individual's role, puritans hold individuals accountable for their acts.

Puritanism is often viewed as a repressive and oppressive ideological system because of its focus upon seriousness, temperance, order, industry, and frugality. Indeed, when Puritanism prevails, individuals are continuously admonished to dedicate themselves to a goal and to sacrifice their personal interest to the interest of their social group. Because of the demand for obedience and self-effacement, puritans view personal aggrandizement and creative individuality as disruptive. When a social group adheres to Puritanism, transgressions are severely punished. Yet despite this harshness, individuals have willingly and joyfully served puritan causes, undoubtedly because the hardships which adherence to Puritanism usually entails is largely offset by the sense of personal fulfillment which can only be achieved through commitment. Puritans throughout history have viewed their daily work and personal sacrifice as serving to achieve a goal more important than their own personal welfare. Indeed, puritans often have given their lives in devotion to their cause.

Because of the interrelationship between personal sacrifice and a communal goal, the puritan virtues are increasingly ridiculed or ignored whenever a puritan society achieves its goal or a semblance of success. Societies which have passed through Puritanism into Progressivism, generally view social systems based upon Puritanism as undemocratic and oppressive. Of course, adherents of Puritanism view their social system as serving the good of all, rejecting progressive societies as anomic, selfish, and self-destructive.

Because of the puritan belief in the centrality of individual behavior and in the importance of institutions in protecting man from actualizing the inherent innate corruption of his nature, puritans continually fear degeneracy; puritans in colonial times, were warned repeatedly against becoming heathens like the Indians. This fear of degeneracy plays an important role in the political life of adherents of Puritanism for puritans rarely think that man at any given historical moment is elevating himself. Especially when times are good and struggles are few, the natural tendency to enjoy luxury is viewed by puritans as a sign of degeneracy. Puritans, therefore, can never achieve their goals, for whenever their revolutions are won, those puritans who remain true to the cause perpetually bemoan the loss of character. They tend to imagine the future in apocalyptic terms. Because they see in institutions and laws a means of checking man's corrupt nature, they persistently call for an increase in law and order. The fact that puritans when they reign increase the severity and numbers of laws also serves to diminish the effectiveness of legal sanctions. The numerous blue laws that reflect an attempt to regulate morality serve in fact to encourage their transgression. When laws become overly burdensome and when they are trivialized, they become less and less important in the lives of people.

American history reveals numerous examples in which the missionary spirit of Puritanism with its moralistic stance was utilized to legitimize political actions. Believing in the moral superiority of a democratic form of government, some Americans throughout the history of the Republic have called for the exportation of our governmental structure and our political creed. In 1899 William T. Harris, the United States Commissioner of Education, observed that the great powers were taking over territories of "uncivilized" peoples and added: "This fact causes every thoughtful American to look seriously to the question whether it is not a duty devolving upon us as a people to have our hand in this work of division to show that we can hold conquered nations for their own benefit—that we, in short can lift them toward self-government." [65] Manifest destiny and imperialism have been the result of the combination of classical laissez-faire liberalism and economic expansion with the moral exemplarism of Puritanism. Besides legitimating imperialism, the puritan spirit of moral superiority and its accompanying missionary zeal also served to legitimize diverse forms of manifest destiny such as the entrance of America in the world wars to "make the world safe for democracy" and diverse "police actions" to protect democracy by containing communism.

On the other hand, Puritanism also has served to encourage certain types of reform movement in the United States. Prohibition, woman suffrage, child labor laws, pure food and drug acts, pollution control, antismoking campaigns, antitrust laws, and campaigns for the protection of the consumer are but a few of the forms in which Puritanism has found

[65] William T. Harris, "An Educational Policy for our New Possessions," *Journal of Proceedings and Addresses of the National Education Association* (Washington: National Education Association, 1899), p. 72.

expression in America. Reflecting diverse ideological strands, these movements often revealed the rugged moralistic and missionary spirit of the
Puritan.

Although the forces of Puritanism continue to influence American
perceptions about moral choice, the Western world increasingly has been
affected by progressive thinking. The former bastions of puritan thought,
the organized religions, have themselves been progressivized. The ecumenical movement, for example, reveals a significant move toward Progressivism in religion. As a result of the progressivization of religion, men
deal with ethics rather than morality, with personality rather than character, with do's rather than don't's. Similarly, situational ethics serves as
a guide to moral choice rather than to eternal immutable laws. Morality
becomes a process rather than a system of law. Within such a value-
making system, individuals easily succumb to the hunger for direction,
so that a counter-force is generated whenever Progressivism becomes pervasive. Thus revivalism and dogmatism grow in their appeal as segments
of the major religions come to seek comfort in the haven of certitude.

Whereas Puritanism presents a clearly defined system of morality,
Progressivism tends to consider moral norms and behavioral expectations
in terms of social consensus or "scientific" analysis. In practical terms this
difference often comes down to the fact that puritan children tend to
develop feelings of guilt and a sense of failure, whereas progressive children are more likely to be beset by deep anxiety. Whether guilt or anxiety
is more damaging to child growth and development is a difficult question
to answer in any objective way. Indeed, if these are the only alternatives,
the choice may well seem not worth making.

### Conclusion

Puritanism is a highly functional but temporary ideology. It serves
to sustain individuals during periods of crisis and change. It is the ideology of instrumentalists for it serves to encourage the accomplishment
of difficult tasks by providing a rationale for self-sacrifice and hard work.

Its value as a motivating ideology was well illustrated during the
conquest of the West. While the West was opened by the rebel trail-
blazers, trappers, and scouts, the building of Western towns was a task
assigned to puritan settlers. Indeed, the violent struggle that characterized
the development of America's West was essentially a conflict between
romantic individualist and puritan communalist. The taming of the West
is essentially the defeat of the romantic gunslinger and heroic sheriff by
the town council and code of laws imported by puritan settlers from the
East. With the puritan farmers came judges, parsons, and schoolmarms,

and the rebels with their highly volatile personal behavior passed into American folklore. Of course, history records the numerous deeds of the rebels such as Kitt Carson, Billy the Kid, and Doc Holiday, but it barely mentions the quiet, persistent, dedicated, and rugged farmers and businessmen who cleared the wilderness and built the towns which within a hundred years had become large urban centers.

To the present day, Puritanism remains one possible response to adversity. When one's worldly situation appears to be in the state of deterioration and collapse, crumbling around him, what can be done? When heroic figures are found to have feet of clay, sacred symbols have become profane, and fundamental beliefs have been shaken, what can be done? When one's home has been destroyed, his family and friends have deserted him, and his worldly achievements have turned to dust, what can be done? Some would respond to these situations by becoming other worldly, seeking immediate gratification in a transcendant world of dreams, drugs, and mysticism. Some would respond by living their remaining life in resignation, or perhaps ending it in an act of suicide. Still others would seek refuge in a life of reason or contemplation, an aspect of monasticism. For Puritanism, however, the response would be one of "girding up the loins," or, in Lenin's phrase, "steeling the character." The puritan would assess the situation, pull himself together, and march onward. He may appear at first to have withdrawn from the battle, but if he does so it is only to recreate himself and return to battle a stronger and better man. And what applies to the individual in such a situation is equally applicable to a collectivity.

On both the individual and the collective level, Puritanism is a "bootstrap" philosophy used to unite the believers and prepare them to control their destiny. At its worst, it crushes the weak, castigates the dissenters, and humiliates the tender-minded; it is brutal and insensitive to the feelings of others. At its best, it provides the integrity, industry, and perseverance necessary for production and achievement; it is strong and forthright. It is more attuned to mass production than craftsmanship, to technology than science. Puritanism lacks the elements of Romanticism necessary for creativity, but it encompasses those elements required to "get the job done."

### Suggested Readings

FORD, PAUL LEICESTER, ed. *The New England Primer*. New York: Teachers College, Columbia University, 1962.

HOFSTADTER, RICHARD. *Social Darwinism in American Thought*. Boston: Beacon Press, 1944.

KENNEDY, GAIL, ed. *Democracy and the Gospel of Wealth.* Boston: D. C. Heath & Company, 1949.

MILLER, PERRY. *The New England Mind from Colony to Province.* Boston: Beacon Press, 1953.

MORGAN, EDMUND S. *The Puritan Family.* Boston: Trustees of the Public Library, 1944.

PARRINGTON, VERNON L. *The Colonial Mind, 1620–1800,* Vol. I. New York: Harcourt, Brace, Jovanovich, Inc., 1927.

PERKINSON, HENRY J. *The Imperfect Panacea: American Faith in Education, 1865–1965.* New York: Random House, Inc., 1968.

PERRY, RALPH BARTON. *Puritanism and Democracy.* New York: Harper & Row, Publishers, Inc., 1944.

REINITZ, RICHARD, ed. *Tensions in American Puritanism.* New York: John Wiley & Sons, Inc., 1970.

SANFORD, CHARLES L., ed. *Benjamin Franklin and the American Character.* Boston: D. C. Heath & Company, 1955.

TAWNEY, R. H. *Religion and the Rise of Capitalism.* New York: The New American Library, Inc., n.d.

TOCQUEVILLE, ALEXIS DE. *Democracy in America,* trans. Phillips Bradley. 2 vols. New York: Random House, 1945.

TYACK, DAVID B., ed. *Turning Points in American Educational History.* Waltham, Mass.: Blaisdell Publishing Co., 1967.

WALLER, GEORGE M., ed. *Puritanism in Early America.* Boston: D. C. Heath & Company, 1950.

WEBER, MAX. *The Protestant Ethic and the Spirit of Capitalism,* trans. Talcott Parsons. New York: Charles Scribner's Sons, 1958.

## Chapter 5

# NATIONALISM
## The Ideology of the Patriot

### Introduction

Modern man is a national creature who inhabits a world which has been segmented into various national geographic and ideational areas. Nationalism is a pervasive ideology in the twentieth century; its influence reaches throughout the globe and into the daily life of most earthlings. Indeed, most ideological systems, such as Scientism and Puritanism, take on national dimensions because Nationalism is the ideology which serves as the fulcrum for twentieth-century belief systems. So prevalent are nationalist sentiments that no less than 40 percent of the nation-states of the world have gained their independence or have been created since 1950.

The uses of the term "Nationalism" reveal that it is a word which includes a variety of meanings reflecting diverse phenomena. It has been utilized to describe, evaluate, defend, and condemn a multitude of social issues, and its meanings range from the eulogistic to the pejorative. Indeed, an analysis of the usages of the term "Nationalism" provides a clear example of how, in Dryden's phrase, people can "torture one poor word ten thousand ways." As K. R. Minogue aptly observed, "The very word 'nationalism' has the power of stopping thought." [1] Nationalism is Janus-like in that it can assume diverse forms when it appears within different social settings and historical periods, and when expressed in different languages and by different individuals. It can be juxtaposed with any belief, ideology, or political movement.

Because of the development and proliferation of nation-states combined with the shifting of educational control from nonpolitical to political agencies, the issue of Nationalism and its subjective expression, which takes the forms of loyalty and patriotism, has become a central concern of schools. Indeed, the development of loyal citizens is one of the most important aims upon which teachers are required to focus. The

---

[1] K. R. Minogue, *Nationalism* (New York: Basic Books, Inc., 1967), p. 16.

meaning of "loyal citizen" and "national loyalty," however, may rest upon any one of the variety of meanings attributed to Nationalism, and the possibility of confusion here has been an important source of conflict within the educational system. The perennial questions "What is an American?" and "Who is un-American?" can be answered only within the framework of the ideology of Nationalism.

### The Meanings of Nationalism

Generally, the term "Nationalism" has been utilized to describe phenomena that relate to a particular form of political and/or cultural grouping. It has been utilized to describe: (1) The ideology, theory, rhetoric, beliefs, and symbol systems which refer to the nation-state and/or nationality, and which may reflect a desire to absorb "the state and society into a community of will and purpose—the nation." [2] (2) A process whereby nation-states and nationalities are developed and sustained. In this sense it has been defined as a political movement to preserve national integrity or as a movement to form, sustain, and expand cultural solidarity. Nationalism may also refer to the process whereby a culturally "distinct" group seeks political autonomy, or the process whereby nation-states seek to develop and sustain cultural homogeneity. (3) The mental and/or emotional condition which is the psychological basis for national loyalty. In this sense it has been defined as "a condition of mind in which loyalty to the ideal or to the fact of one's nation-state is superior to all other loyalties and of which pride in one's nationality and belief in its intrinsic excellence and in its 'mission' are integral parts," [3] and as "a consciousness, on the part of individuals or groups, of membership in a nation, whether one's own or another." [4] Similarly, it may be viewed as a "unifying sentiment" or as a "feeling of solidarity" which forms the subjective basis of a national grouping of individuals.

In addition to the three definitions given above, Nationalism has been defined as a form of patriotism, as the acceptance of the state as an institutionalized means of resolving disputes, and as a process of establishing nationalities.

The meaning of Nationalism is further confused by the use of the term in a pejorative sense to imply an exaggerated emphasis upon the national grouping with a concomitant denigration of other social groups

[2] Yehoshua Arieli, *Individualism and Nationalism in American Ideology* (Baltimore: Penguin Books, Inc., 1966), p. 7.

[3] Carlton J. H. Hayes, *Essays on Nationalism* (New York: The Macmillan Company, 1937), p. 6.

[4] Study Group of Members of the Royal Institute of International Affairs, *Nationalism* (London: Frank Cass and Company, Ltd., 1963), p. xviii.

and the denial or limitation of the rights of individuals. Because of the exclusive and excessive emphasis upon one's nation implied in such a definition, this meaning of the term "Nationalism" suggests a condescending attitude toward other nation-states or other social groups which may compete for the loyalty of individuals. Thus Arnold J. Toynbee avowed: "Modern nationalism is the ancient idolatrous worship of collective human power raised to an unprecedented degree of intensity by the infusion into it of post-Christian fanaticism." [5] Pejorative definitions of Nationalism have been so popular of late that few citizens, especially the youth, wish to label themselves as nationalists. Indeed, the term is increasingly applied to political extremists who believe in fascism or who advocate racism.

Further compounding the disagreement on definitions is the fact that a variety of Nationalisms have and do exist. Nationalisms have been humanitarian, messianic, traditional, liberal, imperialistic, militaristic, and democratic.[6] Nationalism inspired the Freedom Fighters during the Hungarian revolution and propelled the Nazis into Poland. It motivated the Biafran rebels and served the Nigerian government with a rationale for crushing their revolution. It united East and West Pakistan and provided the momentum for the proclamation of the nation of Bangladesh. Nationalism created colonialism and destroyed it. In the totalitarian government of Nazi Germany, it was characterized by a fanatical opposition to Marxism and democracy, while in Soviet Russia, Lenin's theory of international socialism notwithstanding, it combined with the Marxist ideology. In the United States it combined with individualism and capitalism and serves separatists as well as the Brahmins of the political system. It inspires individuals who struggle for the preservation of ethnic differences in multi-ethnic nation-states as well as proponents of cultural homogeneity.

What is certain is that Nationalism has been praised as an expression of popular sovereignty and condemned as an ideological ally of fascism and militarism. It has been called the Anti-Christ, God's gift to man, and the measles of mankind. It can emphasize the dignity of the individual or it can suppress him in a collectivity which is indifferent to individual rights. It may be provoked by intranational as well as international or extranational developments. It may vary in form and intensity among

[5] Arnold J. Toynbee, "The Reluctant Death of Sovereignty," *The Center Magazine,* I, No. 3 (March 1968), 29.
[6] For an analysis of various kinds of Nationalism see Carlton J. H. Hayes, *The Historical Evolution of Modern Nationalism* (New York: The Macmillan Company, 1950); Max Sylvius Handman, "The Sentiment of Nationalism," *Political Science Quarterly,* XXXVI (1921), 104–7; and Louis Wirth, "Types of Nationalism," *American Journal of Sociology,* XLI (1935), 723–37.

nations, during different historical periods, and between social groupings or regions within a nation. By itself, Nationalism does not automatically fall on any part of the political left-right continuum; however, it is a social phenomenon and cannot exist by itself.

The term "nationalist" may be applied to individuals as divergent in their views as Woodrow Wilson, Abbie Hoffman, Fidel Castro, and Adolf Hitler. Both the President of the United States and the Black leader Stokely Carmichael are nationalists. A blanket condemnation of Nationalism means the rejection of the United States, the Woodstock Nation, ethnic pride, the right of peoples to determine their own destiny, and most aesthetic works created during the twentieth century. As Gladys Wiggin observed, "The nationalism of the twentieth century is a many-splendored thing. It is neither good nor bad in and of itself. Its manifestations can lead to good or bad results." [7]

In a general fashion, Nationalism may be viewed as an ideological thrust within a cultural community, a nationality, to achieve a degree of social and/or political autonomy (e.g., various forms of Afro-Americanism such as Black Pride, Black Capitalism, or Black Separatism), or as an ideological matrix within a political community, a nation-state, designed to achieve cultural homogeneity (e.g., the "melting-pot" type of assimilation which was utilized to characterize the United States in the heyday of immigration).

In an age of Nationalism, the national groupings (nation-states and/or nationalities) are viewed as *terminal communities* in that they are the most significant and extended social groupings in which a person may hold membership. They are characterized by comprehensive solidarity unmatched by any other type of grouping. Thus international alliances such as the North Atlantic Treaty Organization (NATO) or international forums such as the United Nations have not been able to attract the intense loyalty of peoples. Citizens of the United States continue to view themselves primarily as Americans (that is, citizens of the United States' rather than as NATOites, United Nationites, or, for that matter, Earthlings.

Most individuals within national groups are conscious or aware of their national membership, and although their emotional attachment to their nation may vary, they generally reveal a loyalty and a love for it. Of course, *most* earthlings belong to nation-states and *all* belong to nationalities, whether they be labeled tribes, ethnic minorities, or cultural communities. Cultural deprivation is a condescending myth perpetuated by individuals who perceive cultural differences in a hierarchical framework;

[7] Gladys A. Wiggin, *Education and Nationalism: An Historical Interpretation of American Education* (New York: McGraw-Hill Book Company, 1962), p. 7.

it is a code term by which the speaker indicates the pity he feels for members of other national communities who are "deprived" of the cultural benefits that accrue with membership in his own community.

Although some individuals, such as tribesmen within the heart of the Brazilian jungle, belong to a nation-state but are not aware of their citizenry, modernization has tended to increase national awareness. Leaders of nation-states expend large sums of money to ensure that their fellow citizens are conscious of their national identity. Indeed, public education was designed, at least in part, to create and preserve national consciousness. Unfortunately, international competition concerning national literacy levels does not reflect a universal hope that individuals will be enabled to enjoy the great literary and philosophical works; rather, it reveals a desire on the part of political leaders to increase the homogeneity of their societies and the efficiency of their propaganda networks by controlling linguistic symbolic systems.

National symbols are often expressed as adverbs and adjectives through which individuals, acts, and objects are nationalized by adding an identifying label ( e.g., the *American* inventor Alexander Graham Bell). National symbols, however, may be so clearly integrated within a culture that adjectival or adverbial modifications are not necessary. National symbols may assume diverse forms: flags, animals, political ritual, slogans ( e.g., *e pluribus unum*), personifications ( Uncle Sam), flowers, and oaths. Indeed, national symbols can relate to any aspect of a culture, physical environment, historical antecedents, or belief system. National symbolism may be as subtle as the name given one at birth or as direct as the cultural specificity of a universal ideology ( e.g., the American form of parliamentary republicanism). ( Indeed, so pervasive is Nationalism that dictionary definitions of individuals generally consider only three facts in identifying a personage: his birth and death dates, his occupation, and his nationality. Hence: Wolfgang Amadeus Mozart, 1756-91, Austrian composer; William Shakespeare, 1564–1616, English poet and dramatist. The fact of being Austrian or English apparently tells us more about a man than the fact of his having written *The Magic Flute* or *King Lear*.)

Although national symbols may reflect facts, they also may be based upon gross distortions, such as the concept "racial purity." Thus symbols assume diverse forms, including statement of facts ( or perceived facts), deliberate lies, admonitions, hopes, wishful thinking, and recollections ( often distorted), as well as statements about other groups which may serve to emphasize a nation's distinctiveness.

Nationalism, therefore, channels perceptions, beliefs, and interests. Indeed, the adjective "national" has been attached indiscriminately to most nouns. Natural splendors, for example, are often nationalized; the white cliffs of Dover are British, the Grand Canyon is American, and Vesuvius is Italian. Wildlife such as the lion and the eagle become national symbols while ancient monuments constructed prior to national awareness, such as the Taj Mahal, Cheops Pyramid, and Westminster Abbey become national shrines.

The deeds of men are recorded in histories and journals as the acts of nationals. Heroes become national heroes and saints represent their countries at the Heavenly Tribunal. The deeds of great scientists, artists, inventors, and athletes are viewed as national deeds and national honors. Astronauts and Cosmonauts are labeled by their country of origin and not as representatives of mankind. Indeed, national flags have been placed on the surfaces of the moon and Mars while the flag of the United Nations has remained on earth. International programs and awards such as the Olympic Games and Nobel Prizes serve as occasions for national competition.

In an age of Nationalism such as ours, international order must rest upon an "association of nations—just as the national community is composed of individual members, so the international community must be made up of nation members." [8] International political bodies rather than supranational bodies superior to their member nations characterize the international scene. Nations are supported not only by the belief that they cannot be segmented (they invariably claim to be "indivisible") but also by the view that ultimate political and economic rights rest with national groupings.

In an age of political Nationalism, the economic well-being of peoples is perceived as an integral part of the political structure of nation-states. Economic measures, such as those encompassed in the New Deal legislation in the United States during and following the international economic depression, were national in scope. It is in terms of *national* wealth that people, at least materially, perceive their chances of developing an advanced civilization. Movements to develop international regional economic communities such as the European Common Market and the American Alliance for Progress continue to be viewed by most people as means of increasing *national* wealth and *national* employment and as ways of improving the *national* life of peoples.

Although some forms of international cooperation, such as that expressed in the "International Goat Breeding Federation," may have little relevance to the national ideology of most national groupings, others, such as the "internationalism" of Marxist doctrine and the internationalism expressed by supporters of the United Nations, NATO, and the Warsaw Pact, may profoundly affect the actions of nation-states.

[8] Edward H. Carr, *Nationalism and After* (New York: The Macmillan Company, 1945), p. 41.

Because of virulent forms of Nationalism, some nations have attempted to geographically, ideologically and/or economically extend their power. Indeed, ultranationalism has served as a major cause of the two conflagrations which enveloped the world in the brief span of the twentieth century. Because of this form of excessive Nationalism, Nationalism has been incorrectly defined as an extreme form of patriotism. Patriotism, however, is not an ideology but rather an emotional attachment to a person, object, or group. It serves as the emotional underbelly of the ideology of Nationalism; it is the emotional element which combines with Nationalism, just as chauvinism or jingoism is the emotional counterpart to ultranationalism.

Nationalism is not automatically contrary to the preservation of individual freedom, nor is it necessarily opposed to internationalism. In a democratic and pluralistic society, intranational concord could serve as a sound foundation upon which to build an international peace. Just as the biological family may serve as a cornerstone of a nation-state or nationality, so nations may serve as the foundation for an international order. Indeed, if national groupings could be abolished, what form of social groups would serve as the basis for a world order? Kandel admonished: "The greatest obstacle to the development of international understanding lies in the failure to realize that the ideal of internationalism is not something that is in conflict with nationalism or something to be added to other aims of national education." [9] The international implications of intranational events (e.g., racial conflicts) as well as the intranational implications of international events (e.g., the Vietnam War) reveal that national and international issues are inextricably interwoven. Indeed, a nation that is unable to resolve its intranational conflicts, especially in relation to cultural, religious, and racial differences, is in no position to condemn or bemoan international discord.

### National Communities: Citizenries and Nationalities

The term "nation" is, as Carlton Hayes observed, "tantalizingly ambiguous." Its etymological root is the Latin word *nascor*, which means "I am born," or the term *natio* meaning "birth" or "race."

The term "nation" has been utilized in a general fashion in the past to identify a group of individuals who were said to belong together by reason of birth. Thus it has been utilized to describe social groupings such as a clan (e.g., the leader of an Irish clan was called "captain of his nation") or a tribe. Similarly, provenance served to identify groups

[9] I. L. Kandel, "Nationalism and Education," *The Year Book of Education* (1949), p. 45.

within medieval church councils and universities. The University of Paris, for example, included four nations identified as *France, Picardie, Normandie,* and *Germanie.* Such groupings, although referring to place or origin and/or language, did not imply a political social unit. It is fitting to note, that in such cases these labels identified subgroupings within a unitary whole such as a university or council; thus they served to symbolize and describe provincialism.

Even professional groups have on occasion been described as nations. Ben Johnson in *Sejanus* referred to physicians as a "subtile nation," while Samuel Butler used the term to identify lawyers. Eventually the term "nation" assumed an exclusively political meaning and reflected the idea of political power. Joseph de Maistre used the term to describe the king and the nobility; Montesquieu in *The Spirit of the Laws* used it to identify French lords and bishops.

With the rise of democracy the term "nation" increasingly was used to describe the citizenry of a democratic state—that is, the membership of a political collective. Thus the term "nation" labeled a people who were sovereign and whose governmental leaders were accountable to them. This shifting meaning reveals the close positive correlation between the rise of Nationalism and the rise of democracy.

The differences between the terms "state" and "nation" need be understood to clarify the differences between *étatism* and Nationalism, and between national loyalty and loyalty to the state or government leaders. The difference is psychologically significant to members of a political social grouping. As Minogue aptly phrased it: "The 'state' might be 'them,' but the 'nation' was 'us!'"[10]

Nationalism implies that the nation, the collectivity, is represented through the machinery of the state. The state is to fulfill the will of the nation (the people) and its government agencies exist to manage political activities for the people. Nationalism thus conceived provided new possibilities in the political and social domain—possibilities whch could be expressed in the form of totalitarianism, even though the rise of Nationalism was rooted historically to the rise of popular sovereignty. Totalitarianism in an age of Nationalism differs markedly from prenationalistic forms of dictatorship. Modern totalitarianism is not synonymous with *étatism.* For Nationalism to exist the citizenry must "feel" itself central to the political process. In totalitarianism this may be achieved by developing the myth that the ruler speaks for the people. Most if not all revolutions that have occurred since World War II are based upon the call of "Power to the People." When military regimes abridge constitutions and abolish elections, they generally argue that such actions were necessary to protect

[10] Minogue, *Nationalism,* p. 11.

the freedom of the people against an enemy who would use political debates and elections to destroy the will of the majority and the civil liberties of the minority.

So long as totalitarian regimes struggle, often with incredible cunning, to sustain the myth that the people rule themselves and that the dictator speaks for the people, democracies must defend themselves valiantly against national disintegration. The reasons for such a disintegration are numerous, but central to the dilemma is the fact that the democratic process encourages individuals to develop multiple loyalties which could become mutually exclusive. What is more, citizens are often encouraged to form loyalties to symbols of the collectivity rather than to the collectivity itself. Although the object of the nationalist's loyalty is the social group labeled nationality and/or nation-state—that is, "the people" —national loyalties are often indirectly expressed through an attachment to a symbol, creed, ideal, institution, or geographic area. Thus symbols of the collectivity become *ends* and loyalties remain fixed upon objects, institutions, or particular national leaders. When such attachments ignore the changing composition of the collectivity, they can inhibit collective identity and be highly disruptive.

This issue of disruptive pseudo-national loyalties is best illustrated by the loyalties directed toward political leaders. The state or "ruler" who represents the people is, in fact, merely an agent or synod of the people. If an individual places his supreme loyalty in a particular President, for example, he is probably an *étatist* rather than a nationalist—a position which bespeaks a misunderstanding of both Nationalism and democracy.

If, indeed, Louis XIV asserted that "L'état c'est moi," then loyalty expressed toward him or to the French dynasty which he represented was a personal loyalty or a state loyalty and not a loyalty to the national group. The shifting of a loyalty from the sovereign king or dynasty to the social group labeled nation and/or nationality is generally viewed as an integral element of the rise of Nationalism and democracy. Thus, Jeanne d'Arc and Martin Luther, although symbols of Nationalism, were not in reality nationalists or adherents of democracy as some latter-day nationalists often avow, but rather Christians who devoted themselves to a form of *étatism*. Although nationalized, they were not nationalists.

The nature of the loyalty directed toward a modern totalitarian ruler such as Hitler or to a democratic leader such as the American President should not be viewed as similar to the loyalty granted to a Caesar or a Henry VIII. In an age of Nationalism, dictators and democratic rulers are depersonalized to the extent that their assumed roles make them "symbols" of the national collectivity. What is more, their power is increased a hundredfold because of such a representative role. Ancient rulers, for example, often paid mercenaries to fight their battles, while today's presidents and dictators possess the power to conscript entire populations. Similarly, the pronouncements of leaders during ages of Nationalism are much more powerful than those of some of their ancient counterparts, for when a president or a dictator speaks, he speaks in the name of "his" people. Of course, in prenationalism days, some kings claimed to rule by divine right and to speak in the name of, and with the support of, God.

In an age of Nationalism and democracy, the people automatically assume the responsibility for the actions of their governments because their governments are powerless without their consent. In theory, all citizens should be held accountable for their government's deeds and voting should be viewed as a duty as well as a right. Unfortunately, democracies often fail to sustain the interest of citizens in the political process. Voting patterns in the United States, for example, reveal appalling citizen irresponsibility.

Because actions of governments are viewed as actions of the national collectives that they represent, the citizenry must be prepared to defend their government's commitments and deeds. Thus, in an age of Nationalism, wars are fought by the people and for the people. Needless to add, such wars are extremely vicious and differ markedly from some of the battles fought by mercenaries during prenationalism days. In wars before the rise of Nationalism, professional soldiers representing states fought for their leaders; today, citizen-soldiers representing their people fight for their group's existence or honor. Nationalism created the universal soldier.

The symbols utilized to identify a nation will determine, in part, the nature of national loyalty.[11] Expressions of loyalty toward persons or things, for example, will tend to be more focused than loyalties expressed toward ideals, ideologies, or institutions. In the latter case, loyalties are more diffused and abstract. The nature of the "national character" (the perceived identity of the people) also will play a role in determining, the nature of the national loyalty. If the national character is perceived with a high degree of specificity, so will the loyalty, whereas if the national character is defined vaguely, the loyalty directed toward it also will be somewhat amorphous. The issue of specificity and diffusion is especially relevant to the fact that man is a carrier of multiple loyalties which may be mutually supportive or mutually exclusive. Obviously, authoritarian personalities, who have difficulty dealing with ambiguity, are often un-

[11] For analyses of national loyalty see John H. Schaar, *Loyalty in America* (Berkely: University of California Press, 1957); Morton Grodzins, *The Loyal and the Disloyal: Social Boundaries of Patriotism and Treason* (Chicago: University of Chicago Press, 1956); and Harold Guetzkow, *Multiple Loyalties: Theoretical Approach to a Problem of International Organization* (Princeton: Princeton University Press, 1955).

comfortable in plural nation-states and often seek to define their nation in a way that is specific and concrete. Such Super-patriots, invariably define their nations with unwarranted precision, thus increasing the range of factors they perceive as disloyal. Thus, for example, if the national object clearly excludes certain ideologies, races, or cultural patterns, then loyalty to these excluded elements and national loyalty could not be mutually supportive. The symbols of national identity, therefore, may serve to disintegrate the national society. In a pluralistic society the potential conflict among loyalties, especially if the nation-state is symbolized in a precise manner, becomes great.

Conflicts between loyalties are among the most tragic experiences men can endure. The perennial tales of the disloyal lovers and the religious and political heretics attest to the centrality of loyalty to man's life. The essence of the conflict between competing loyalties is vividly captured in Guy de Maupassant's short story entitled "Ball-of-Fat" which focuses upon a forlorn harlot and her French traveling companions held captive by a Prussian officer who demands her favors in return for the freedom of his captives. Her patriotic refusal to perform her professional duties with a Prussian officer is met by various interpretations of loyalty from her freedom-loving fellow travelers. Their admonitions range from the argument that the need justifies the means, through calls for her to make the sacrifice for the greater glory of God, all the way to this excruciating and not so subtle bit of propaganda: "and you know, my dear, it would be something for him to boast of that he had known a pretty girl; something it is difficult to find in his country." [12] She succumbs to these rationalizations, and to the advances of the officer, but her fellow travelers, once freed, turn away from her. The "lady" vividly exemplifies Charles Merriam's assertion that: "We are involved in an intricate whirl of competing loyalties, alternately attracted and repelled by one and another, in an endless series of forming and dissolving interests, the nature of which is still but dimly comprehended." [13]

This complexity is attributable to the fact that national group loyalty may be rooted to nonnational groups such as classes, sects, religions, language communities, race, and other permanent or nonpermanent groupings. Inasmuch as man is a carrier of multiple loyalties which need not be mutually exclusive, national loyalties may combine with loyalties to extranational and intranational groups, and be strengthened by local patriotism or by international "humanitarianism." Crises, however, may create schisms in a formerly stable web of affiliations. Although various defini-

[12] *The Complete Short Stories of Guy de Maupassant* (New York: Blue Ribbon Books, Inc., 1903), p. 23.
[13] Charles Edward Merriam, *The Making of Citizens: A Comparative of Methods of Civic Training* (Chicago: The University of Chicago Press, 1931), p. 2.

tions of Nationalism indicate that the loyalty directed to the nation-state must be *supreme*, the fact of the matter is that when groups are inter-meshed, the concept of supremacy between them is virtually irrelevant unless a crisis causes them to be incompatible. Expressions of supreme loyalty to a local community or to a family need not imply disloyalty to the nation. Likewise, expressions of loyalty to an international community (e.g., the Roman Catholic church) or an ethnic group (e.g., Afro-Amer-ican) need not imply weakness of political national loyalty. Although, for example, Marxist doctrine calls for supreme loyalty to the proletariat class, such a loyalty has been combined successfully with national loyalty in the Soviet Union ever since Stalin changed the priorities from world revolu-tion to "socialism in one country." Similarly, the assertion of supreme loyalty to one's family or one's state in the United States is viewed as an expression of the "American way of life."

National political communities also are based upon political ideol-ogies or belief systems which define, in part, the behavioral expectations of the rulers and the ruled. The political credenda form part of the group consciousness and serve, if they are functional, to develop and sustain the *conscience collective* of the citizenry. Within such a community, "*the acceptance of the state as the impersonal and ultimate arbiter of human affairs*" must be shared by the citizenry, similarly the members of the citizenry who are obliged to accept, at least operationally, the norms which govern the relationships among citizens, between the state and citizens, and between citizens and extranational states.[14]

Although the term "nation," as noted above, often denotes a citizenry, it also may refer to a social group which is not politically inde-pendent and which may or may not be seeking to possess political sover-eignty—a nationality. Notwithstanding the fact that citizenries and na-tionalities may be coterminous, the nature of the bond which unites politically nonindependent nationalities is of supreme importance in un-derstanding Nationalism, especially as it is expressed in a politically sovereign nation-state such as the United States in which the peoples reflect a variety of ethnic origins.

John Stuart Mill in *Considerations of Representative Government*, defined a nationality as:

> A portion of mankind . . . united among themselves by common sym-pathies, which do not exist between them and any others—which make them co-operate with each other more willingly than with other people, desire to be under the same government, and desire that it should be government by themselves or a portion of themselves, exclusively.[15]

[14] K. H. Silvert, ed., *Expectant Peoples: Nationalism and Development* (New York: Random House, Inc., 1963), p. 19.

[15] John Stuart Mill, *Considerations on Representative Government* (London: Longmans, Green and Co., Ltd., 1926), p. 120.

The phrase "common sympathies," with its implication of the sharing of experiences, is generally viewed as a central element of nationality. Thus Karl Deutsch, finding an index of common sympathy in social communication, concluded that a nationality is a group of individuals who are linked together by "complementary habits and facilities of communication," which enable them to "communicate more effectively, and over a wider range of subjects, with members of one large group than with outsiders." [16] Deutsch sees culture as the factor in social behavior which develops, selects, and channels ideational elements and argues that "ethnic complementarity" or cultural unity is a function of communicative efficiency. The German term, *Volk*, for example, which closely resembles the concept "nationality" and is quite distinguishable from the concept *"Staat"* also relates to "ethnic complimentarity." The term *Volk* is a metaphysical construct referring to the "meta-entity" which produces those elements as art, language, customs, and personal creativity which provide a people with a distinct identity. The nineteenth-century French historian Ernest Renan utilized an ethereal approach like this when he defined a nation as a "soul" which is formed in the past and in the present and which is analogous to a "daily plebiscite." Other non-analytical definitions in terms of "spiritual unities," community of character, national mind, mental communities have been forwarded. The concept "collective personality" also has been used and will be analyzed in a subsequent section.

In summary, a nationality is a community—that is, an area of social living shared by members of a group who live together in physical proximity or in mental proximity. They share a common environment, either physical or symbolic, and can be identified by their shared "way of life." A nationality, therefore, reveals a degree of social coherence. It is a cultural community which is created through social learning.

A variety of cultural elements may be perceived as the basis of a national community. The elements regarded as the basis of a nationality —that is, those elements viewed as common to all its members—will vary among nationalities and will depend upon historical antecedents, existing myths, environmental stimuli, and the nature of the evolved national ideological and symbolic systems. They may be reflections of reality (e.g., language or religion) or they may be myths (e.g., purity of racial identity). Generally, however, the elements projected as the determinants of nationality will stress the *unique* and *shared* elements which serve to identify the nationals. Local traditions and geographical characteristics, for example, will be focused upon if geographical mobility is low. Similarly, nations which have emerged from long periods of foreign tutelage

[16] Karl W. Deutsch, *Nationalism and Social Communication: An Inquiry into the Foundations of Nationality* (New York: John Wiley & Sons, Inc., 1953), p. 71.

will tend to focus upon precolonial history as well as upon future development in order to establish the bases of national identity. Wars of independence, military, political, and/or cultural leaders who "liberated" the colectivity from foreign domination, as well as local customs and traditions may serve as symbols of the collectivity. All too often, as Kandel observed, "The heroes of the child are the heroes of the battlefield. . . ." [17] Nations such as France and England, on the other hand, have had relatively stable geographical boundaries for extended periods of time and therefore tend to focus upon past history, traditions, and language as the basis of their nationality. Nation-states which share a common language or a common form of government with other collectivities will tend to accentuate those elements of their own nation-state which are different and unique. Unfortunately, some of the unique elements thus focused upon may reflect merely the countenance of one segment of the population, so that national definition in the international scene results in a certain amount of divisiveness *within* the nation-state.

The nature of the elements of group identification will profoundly affect national behavior and the perceptions of the nationals. For example, perceptions of past history may influence the present and the future actions of nation-states. As Moskos and Bell have pointed out, "To control what people think they *were* is to some extent to control what they think they are, and it goes a long way toward controlling what they believe they are becoming and what in fact they may turn out to *be*." [18]

Although no particular factor can be isolated as the cause of national consciousness in general, essential to all nations in an age of Nationalism is the belief that such causes or basic factors do exist. As a result of historical antecedents, cultural factors, and intranational and extranational events, national ideologies will include various elements designed to accentuate claims for independence. Often such elements do not reflect existing realities and may generate cleavages rather than cohesion. The following items represent some of the most common elements of group identification that have been forwarded to reflect the perceived "objective" bases of a national collectivity:

1. National Recollections: past deeds, common history, cult of heroes.
2. National Mission: destiny, goals, aspirations.
3. Myth of Common Descent: racial, ethnic.
4. National Symbols: songs, emblems, holidays.
5. National Model Personalities: qualities, faults, differences from other people.

[17] I. L. Kandel, "Education, National and International," *The Educational Forum*, XVI (November 1951–May 1952), 154.

[18] Charles C. Moskos, Jr., and Wendell Bell, "Cultural Unity and Diversity in New States," *Teachers College Record*, LXVI, No. 8 (May 1965), 682.

6. National Dramaturgical Ways: thespian characteristics, style of roles.
7. National "Culture": literature, art, science, traditions, customs, manners.
8. National Institutions and Ideologies: political, social, economic, educational.
9. Land as a Group Possession: love of local, sectional, and/or national geographic area.
10. National Language.
11. National Religion.
12. Common Dangers: threat to nation from external or internal forces.

### The Principle of National Self-Determination

Inasmuch as political national communities and cultural national communities are not always coterminous, issues arise concerning the bases of the rights of individuals to declare their political independence. Despite the fact that political communities strive to develop and preserve cultural homogeneity, some cultural communities within nation-states strive for political autonomy. Throughout the world, cultural communities which constitute enclaves within citizenries continuously seek political independence. Conflicts between political communities and cultural enclaves are extremely brutal; some nation-states, such as Northern Ireland and Pakistan, have witnessed unrelenting struggles because of conflicts between political and cultural Nationalism.

Central to most national ideologies, among both established nation-states and nationalities seeking statehood, is one form or another of the principle of national self-determination. This principle affirms that (1) some national groupings of people have the right to possess their own unified territory and to establish or preserve a nation-state; (2) the nation-state has the right to regulate its affairs without foreign intervention and to utilize its territory as it sees fit; and (3) certain groups of individuals have the right to select from among existing political communities the community in which they will hold membership.

The doctrine of national self-determination can be traced to the principle of individual self-determination which the eighteenth-century philosopher Immanuel Kant viewed as a supreme political good. This Kantian principle of individual self-determination was nationalized by Johann Gottlieb Fichte, who argued that a free individual achieves his self-realization when he is absorbed into the societal whole. Other post-Kantian philosophers elaborated on Fichte by developing the thesis that self-realization through absorption into the societal body results from strife and struggle. Combined with Johann Gottfried von Herder's principle that diversity rather than uniformity characterizes the universe and results in the diversity of social groupings which should be preserved, the principle of national self-determination assumed its modern visage at the time of the French Revolution. As the scholar of Nationalism, Elie Kedourie, points out, "A nation, to the French Revolutionaries, meant a number of individuals who have signified their will as to the manner of their government. A nation, on this vastly different theory, becomes a natural division of the human race, endowed by God with its own character, which its citizens must, as a duty, preserve pure and inviolable." [19]

In addition to its sources in German idealist philosophy, the theory of national self-determination also can be traced from another source— Jean-Jacques Rousseau. This *enfant terrible* asserted that the "people" and not the "ruling class" is the nation and that the "people" have the right to determine their own national destiny and to develop and sustain their unique national character.

The American Revolution and the establishment of the Confederation and the Federal Union produced the first major expression of the principle of national self-determination in the Western world. The American principle of national self-determination was based upon the "natural rights" of a citizenry and not upon the claims of a unique and shared national ethnic identity. The American Declaration of Independence affirmed that individuals have unalienable rights and that governments are instituted to preserve these rights. The King of Great Britain, the declaration affirms, continually repeated injuries and usurpations, and because the British *brethren* have been "deaf to the Voice of Justice and of Consanguinity . . . these United Colonies are, and of Right ought to be, FREE AND INDEPENDENT STATES. . . ." The issues which are raised in the Declaration of Independence remain a major cause for concern In the twentieth century. If the inhabitants of ghettos believe that their *brethren* have failed to meet their needs and that the governments have violated their "natural rights," do they also have the right to declare their independence?

The principle of collective self-determination also can be utilized as a declaration of dependence and as a call for the preservation of the unity of a people who share or who are believed to share similar cultural orientations or ethnic characteristics. Such a call for dependence also is expressed in terms of a desire for "freedom." Fichte emphasized this ethnic orientation when he wrote:

> Our earliest common ancestors, the primordial stock of the new culture, the Germans . . . resisted the world domination of the Romans. . . . The descendants, as soon as they could do so without losing their freedom, even went so far as to assimilate the Roman culture, insofar as this was possible without losing their identity. . . . Liberty to them means this:

[19] Elie Kedourie, *Nationalism* (London: Hutchinson and Co., Ltd., 1961), p. 58.

persisting to remain Germans and continuing the task of settling their own problems, independently and in consonance with the original spirit of their race. . . .[20]

The particular form taken by the principle of national self-determination in any given case rests upon whatever criteria are chosen for demarcating the "nation" and identifying those individuals who possess the right to exert their independent "will." The principle, therefore, may be based upon any one of a variety of possible we-group identifications. On the whole, by the end of World War I, the principle of national self-determination largely had assumed a character which accentuated the importance of cultural distinction and included the claim that some culturally distinct peoples should obtain their political sovereignty. This emphasis became the *sine qua non* of the Peace Conference which followed the end of the war. President Woodrow Wilson, an advocate of the ethnic principle of national self-determination (outside the boundaries of the United States), incorporated this conviction in five of his Fourteen Points. The attempt to divide the map of Europe according to the ethnicity of peoples resulted in a form of political gerrymandering and the creation of irredentism, thus paving the way for Hitler's insistence on the right of an ethnic group to be politically united—an insistence which he enforced by annexing lands that included individuals of the German nationality.

The principle of national self-determination for ethnic groups has been both defended as an expression of democracy and condemned as a violation of the democratic ideology. John Stuart Mill, for example, asserted that an individual had the right to select the collectivity to which he is to belong, adding that "Free institutions are next to impossible in a country made up of different nationalities." [21] The opposing view was expressed by Lord Acton, who asserted that the combination of diverse nationalities in one state is an indispensable condition of a democratic state. "By making the state and the nation commensurate with each other in theory," he admonished, "it reduces practically to a subject condition all other nationalities that may be within the boundary." [22]

The principle of national self-determination which a people uses in assessing the nationhood of other nations is not necessarily the same as the principle they apply to their own social grouping. For example, although Woodrow Wilson accepted the validity of ethnic claims to national self-determination in Eastern Europe, he continued to affirm that the United States was an indivisible political entity. Indeed, all national

[20] Johann Gottlieb Fichte, "Address to the German Nation," in *The Dynamics of Nationalism: Readings in Its Meaning and Development*, ed., Louis L. Snyder (New York: D. Van Nostrand Co., 1964), p. 148.

[21] Mill, *Considerations on Representative Government*, p. 121.

[22] John Dalberg - Acton, Lord, "Nationality," in *The Dynamics of Nationalism*, p. 7.

ideologies, both in law and in practical application, generally include an insistence that their national political collectivity cannot be dissolved or segmented. Thus, regardless of a people's support for separatist movements elsewhere, they generally view any wish for national self-determination expressed by a group within their own national collectivity as an expression of excessive sectionalism and localism. Wars for national liberation that fail are labeled rebellions, sectionalist outbreaks, or civil wars. Traitors and Founding Fathers differ only in the outcome of their struggles.

Because of the upsurge in the popularity of theories of cultural pluralism, teaching about ethnic identity has become a major educational task within many schools attended by children of ethnic minorities. Courses such as Afro-American and Mexican-American history have been added to school curricula. Indeed, some private schools ("community schools") have been established primarily for the purpose of focusing upon the teaching of a particular ethnic culture. They are similar to religious schools in that they emphasize the teaching of a particular intranational group identity. Of course, such schools are viewed with suspicion by common school advocates and by Americans who view pluralism as a threat to national unity.

Teachers often show signs of confusion about the assimilative function of the school as it relates to the right of national self-determination. Indeed, some individuals avoid exploring the possibility that the teaching of cultural identity eventually may serve as a basis for a call for political separatism. Cultural pluralists who believe that their political nation is indivisible ultimately may encounter some ideological dissonance on this score when the ethnic identity they have encouraged in the name of pluralism manifests itself in a call for the dissolution of our plural society and its replacement by multiple ethnically uniform nation-states. Conversely, some of those who insist that the American school system should serve as a "melting pot" and that minority identity should *not* be focused upon in public schools, undermine the development of such national uniformity by rejecting various expedients proposed to achieve racial balance. Segregated schools, regardless of the reason they exist, have not, do not, and will not bring about a melting of racial or ethnic differences.

### The Emergence of National Consciousness

#### EUROPEAN ANTECEDENTS

Men always have belonged to groups which they could identify and label and to which they offered their supreme loyalty. Such groups, however, were not and are not necessarily national in design. Family, religion, neighborhood, and regional groups, as well as nonnational ideological communities may be characterized by "we-feelings" and comprehensive solidarity just as much as may national groupings. Indeed, national groupings as objects of supreme loyalty are newcomers in the social life of man.

Although, as we have seen the birth of modern Nationalism emerged in the eighteenth century in Europe, the roots of national consciousness extend into the primitive tribalism of modern man's aboriginal ancestors. Such "small-scale nationalism," as the historian Hayes labeled it, was a forerunner of modern Nationalism and revealed the group sentiment and "we-feeling" which were a subjective prerequisites for the existence of Nationalism. Indeed, Hans Kohn has traced the roots of modern national consciousness to the ancient Hebrews and Greeks. He noted that the ancient Hebrews put the ideational emphases on the concept of a chosen people, national Messianism, traditions and national aspirations, while the ancient Greeks stressed the importance of supreme loyalty to citizenry.[23]

After the collapse of the ancient Hebrew and Greek empires, nationalistic tendencies are discoverable in the political and cultural developments which began to appear in Western Europe as early as the twelfth century. The consolidation of dynastic states such as France and England formed the territorial bases for some of the modern nation-states and established a pattern for other peoples to follow. Besides providing a political structure to a geographical setting, dynasties also constructed governmental agencies, institutions, systems of law, and communication networks which would eventually assume a national countenance. Thus the development of monarchical *étatism* led to a form of national provincialism which, combined with the rise of the merchant class, the increase in the number of governmental bureaucratic functionaries who had a direct stake in the newly emerging political systems, and the increase in ideational materials produced by "court" ideologists, served to form a social basis for incipient Nationalisms. Similarly, the growth of national churches enhanced national consciousness.

The social and political unification of dynastic systems was accompanied by the development of linguistic and cultural homogeneity within certain social groupings. By the sixteenth century the vernacular languages, for example, had significantly replaced Latin. This form of linguistic particularism began to appear as early as the twelfth century and was accentuated by the increase in literary, governmental, and historical documents which focused upon the nation. The *Chansons de Geste*,

---

[23] See Hans Kohn's *The Idea of Nationalism: A Study in Its Origins and Background* (New York: The Macmillan Company, 1944), pp. 27–60.

the poems of François Villon in the fifteenth century, Petrarch's son-
nets, Dante's *Divine Comedy,* and "national" histories such as William
Camden's *Remains Concerning Britaine,* reveal a move toward a par-
ticularization of interests which would serve, in part, to destroy the remnants of medieval universalism and supplant the ecclesiastical society of
the Catholic Church as the central object of supreme loyalty. Men of
letters, historians, ethnographers, ideologists, artists, musicians, scientists,
and economic leaders increasingly performed the important social function of developing national cultural homogeneity and thus helped to
overcome the cultural isolation of mini-regional communities. Similarly,
social centers of cultural leaders which formerly had been localized in
the courts of rulers and universities now extended into national associations of men of letters, artists, promoters of knowledge (e.g., the *Académie
française,* founded 1635), and political associations. Such national associations replaced, to some extent, the cosmopolitan community of scholars
which operated, in part, within the ecclesiastical community of the Roman
Catholic Church. The secularization of society emerged as a national
movement.[24]

Thus the development of dynasties and monarchial *étatism* led to
the breakdown of the universalism of Christian Europe which had allowed cultural localism and provencialism to flourish. Combined with
economic and cultural factors, the growth of *étatism* gave birth to an
incipient form of national consciousness. Nevertheless, to a considerable
extent the medieval period remained universalistic in its outlook and its
loyalties in great measure continued to be directed toward the Church
and/or local communities.

The Enlightenment also had this universalistic quality, inasmuch as
the cosmopolitan philosophers of that era generally focused upon the
uniqueness of the individual and/or upon the elements which all men
held in common. They were truly humanists. Yet, the universalism of the
Enlightenment was to furnish one of the foundations for modern Nationalism, which emerged out of the ferment of the Enlightenment.[25]

The Puritan Revolution in the seventeenth century and the French
and American Revolutions in the eighteenth represented an increase in
national consciousness and the application of national ideologies to social
movements. These revolutions, which were characterized by a shifting of
sovereignty from the monarch or state to the people, resulted in the
establishment of the state as an agency of the people themselves and in a
shift in the object of loyalty from the monarch or state to the social

[24] For a concise and scholarly analysis of this process, see Florian Znaniecki,
*Modern Nationalities: A Sociological Study* (Urbana: The University of Illinois Press,
1952).
[25] See Kedourie, *Nationalism.*

grouping. With this shift of loyalty *étatism* became Nationalism. School curricula in the United States reflected this emerging national spirit, and textbooks such as the *New England Primer* were revised to include patriotic maxims, while Noah Webster's texts and, later the McGuffey Readers, furnished ample tales to accentuate national awareness.

The historical development of European Nationalisms has been characterized by two major thrusts toward the growth of national consciousness. Lucidly described by Kohn and labeled the "Kohn Dichotomy," these two thrust are (1) the political Nationalism that focuses primarily upon the rights of the citizenry; and (2) the cultural Nationalism that developed primarily as an expression of the spirit of Romanticism. While political Nationalism combined with Scientism, cultural Nationalism allied itself with the ideology of Romanticism. In the former case the state created the nation, whereas in the latter, the nation created or sought to create the state. The resultant contact between these two expressions of Nationalism led to power conflicts which further enhanced national consciousness and national patriotism.

In Europe, Napoleon, serving as a symbol and "godfather" of the emacipated French people, embarked upon wars which exported the doctrine of Nationalism and further enhanced the incipient Nationalisms of the peoples "liberated" by the "liberated" French army. Indeed, the process of exporting the ideology and its underbelly of feeling has characterized the colonial expansion of European powers throughout the nineteenth century, resulting in the creation of incipient Nationalisms throughout the globe. Louis Dupree in an essay concerning Nationalism in Afghanistan noted the following:

> Colonialism often provides a convenient stone for the whetting of nationalism. An educated, middle-level colonial administrative class can be the rock of dissension around which nationalists may rally their complaints of economic and political exploitation; the colonial administrators and their local servants also create the ideological rock upon which the founders of nationalism can build their church. When there is no colonialism from which such a unifying and centralizing administrative group can come, the extreme stubbornness of tribal and regional interests cannot easily be broken with the tools of xenophobia or with techniques of centralizing power learned abroad.[26]

Not all Nationalisms, however, are the result of exportation from Europe through colonial systems, nor are they necessarily a correlate to the establishment of statehood. Bolivian Nationalism, for example, did not accompany the establishment of the Bolivian state or its liberation from the Spanish colonial empire. Bolivian Nationalism was nurtured, in

---

[26] Louis Dupree, "Tribalism, Regionalism, and National Oligarchy," in *Expectant Peoples: Nationalism and Development*, p. 41.

part, by the anachronism of an elite who dominated the Bolivian masses within an independent state characterized by a feudal structure. Scientism served as an ideological vanguard for Nationalism in this case. Richard Patch observed: "The subjection of the great majority of the population *depended* on the non-existence of the nation; the power of the elite *depended* on non-adaption to the new forces tending toward democracy and mobility which modern technology, war, and mass communication made irresistible." [27]

During the revolutions and wars of the eighteenth century and after, the nationalization of armies, resulting in the creation of citizen-soldiers, served to increase the national consciousness of the citizenry. Revolutions and wars have provided the "communal experiences" which season developing national ideologies with a subjective emotional and collective flavor.

As national societies increasingly held sway over diverse areas of social life, a "self-perpetuating" system of national consciousness was set into motion. Through communication networks such as education systems and propaganda, the state, government agencies, and people were increasingly viewed as an integral whole, so that actions by the state or government agencies could plausibly be labeled actions of the people. Such shared perceptions were encouraged, developed, and sustained by the activities of political agencies which sought to increase the homogeneity and cohesiveness of the citizenry of nation-states. Thus through a variety of media of communication, such as journals, governmental agencies, national societies, and schools, the necessary social learning from which national consciousness is developed and sustained was assured.

What is more, the increase in the activity of a state in the economic and social life of its citizens also served to accentuate national consciousness. Although mercantilism may be viewed as an economic system which augments the power of the state rather than the welfare of its citizenry, it nevertheless served to form a basis for national economic systems. The nineteenth-century economic system of laissez-faire capitalism, with its "night-watchman" states, eventually gave way before the rise of political and cultural Nationalism which encouraged governments to augment their role in economic activity by providing ever-increasing regulatory and social services. As Carr observed: " 'Planned economy' is a Janus with a nationalist as well as a socialist face; if its doctrine seems socialist, its pedigree is unimpeachably nationalist." [28]

Modernization, which denotes man's increasing control over his physical environment through an increase in cooperation among indi-

[27] Richard W. Patch, "Peasantry and National Revolution: Bolivia," in *Expectant Peoples: Nationalism and Development,* p. 113.
[28] Carr, *Nationalism and After,* p. 54.

viduals of a society, and which includes the movement of industrialization, rationalization, secularization, and bureaucratization, is also closely allied with Nationalism in that the social tapestry which results from modernization is national in design. Modern large-scale industrial systems are national rather than international or provincial in scope. This symbiotic relationship between Scientism and Nationalism was noted by D. A. Rustow when he wrote: "Only societies, transformed into nations have shown themselves capable of attaining the more advanced forms of modernity, and only modernizing nations are likely to retain their identity in the present era of modernization." [29]

The forces of Scientism generally work against the liberation of ethnic minorities from the political nation-states which encompass them. For example, the Biafrans, the Afro-Americans, and the Northern Irish Roman Catholics who seek political independence because of their ethnic or religious identity often encounter the devastating argument that affluence and technological advancement rest upon the practical and legalistic characteristics of nation-states rather than upon the creativity derived from ethnic awareness. Tribalism, ethnicity, regionalism, religionism, and localism are invariably denounced as inhibitive to technological advancement.

Increasingly, newly liberated and emerging nations are characterized by their ideological imitation of the Great Powers. Their political leaders often ape the behavior patterns and governmental policies of "Westernized" or "Sovietized" systems as a means of indicating to would-be investors that they are stable political nations. Often supporters of regional or cultural national unions (e.g., Pan-Americanism, Pan-Africanism) view such alliances as means by which small agricultural nation-states will evolve into industrial giants.

Rapid modernization requires concentration upon the production of capital goods, and emerging nations increasingly view socialism as the most viable economic system for accomplishing this task. Thus modernization often combines Nationalism, Scientism, and socialism. Such a triadic pattern easily fosters political centralization, especially when centralization is encouraged by the Super Powers. Through massive economic assistance programs, the utilization of technical advising systems, and the "show of force" against revolutionary and romantic elements, the Super Powers encourage the political centralization of governments in emerging nations. Utilizing the economic and technical needs of newly formed nation-states as a pretext for ideological involvement in their programs of national development, the United States and the Soviet Union have indirectly confronted each other in their search for dependable allies.

[29] Dankwort, A. Rustow, *A World of Nations: Problems of Political Modernization* (Washington: The Brookings Institute, 1967), p. 31.

In summary, the six central movements which are viewed as enhancing the development of the ideology of Nationalism are (1) the establishment of monarchical *étatism;* (2) the development and expansion of cohesive national cultural communities; (3) the growth of popular sovereignty which was ushered in by the Puritan, American, and French revolutions, and the spread of its ideational correlate, the right of group self-determination; (4) the utilization and expansion of communication networks such as public education systems, armies, journals, and various other agencies and associations which serve to socialize individuals in national societies; (5) the exportation of Nationalisms through wars, revolutions, and the general process of international cross-fertilization of ideologies; and (6) the growth of modernization whereby the economic well-being of a people, technological progress and increased governmental involvement in the economic and social life of citizenries are viewed in terms of political national communities.

## AMERICAN NATIONALISM

Like all Nationalisms, Americanism has assumed a unique design and has changed in character throughout its existence. It has been perceived in a variety of ways by those who search for its nature. American Nationalism has been described in terms of individualism, democracy, Protestant tradition, an Anglo-Saxon racial unit, federalism, states' rights, laissez-faire capitalism, the "melting pot," and a variety of other phenomena—many of them antithetic.

Americanism is a complex matrix of ideologies which includes the ideological systems noted in this text as well as numerous other beliefs, some of which are the source of persistent controversy. Pivotal to the meaning of Americanism, however, are the beliefs concerning the national identity of the United States. The perceived American identity has emerged from the past in the sense that, as noted in the preceding section, European antecedents served as a major root source for American self-definition. The unique qualities of Americanism, however, emerged on the American soil.

At its inception the sociopolitical system named the United States did not reflect any distinguishable *unique* and *shared* cultural identity. The citizenry of the young Republic was not characterized by a *common* and *unique* language or religion, by a well-defined territory, or by memories of a previously shared dynastic state or descent. Those dominant strands which characterized the citizenry of the young Republic were also shared by the citizenry of the "Mother Country" (a relevant anthropomorphic expression) from which many of the early settlers emigrated.

Indeed, the severance of the ties with the British Empire was based not on a rejection of the ancestral traditions but on an application of them. Hans Kohn rightfully observed: "The Anglo-Americans fought England not because they felt themselves un-English but because they were English." [30] The American Revolutionary War, in fact, was a civil war within a relatively benevolent empire. Most American revolutionaries were not natives of the colonies seeking to overthrow a foreign government but rather English settlers seeking political independence from their brethren in England. American revolutionary leaders were not fighting for American Nationalism but for political and economic rights that they viewed as part of their English heritage. Indeed, the basis of American loyalty during the latter part of the colonial period reflected a devotion to both American and English traditions. Indeed, so paramount were local and regional loyalties that the Revolutionary War often was perceived as a conflict to protect localism.

Because Americans lacked the binding similarities and shared cultural identity of a unique nationality, American Nationalism was based upon the concept of a political community—a citizenry. Citizenry rather than nationality was the criterion of membership in the emerging American national community. Perhaps this explains why Americans rarely have recourse to concepts such as "fatherland" or "motherland" and why their national symbols have been either a brother (Brother Jonathan) or an uncle (Uncle Sam).

The distinguishing feature of the American citizenry—that is, the *rationale* of the American political community—was the "democratic creed," expressed within the framework of political federalism and based upon a futuristic dream that the United States would implement the creed and serve as a symbol of its successful realization. The Constitution of the United States with its Bill of Rights—the oldest written constitution in the world—stands as a concrete and symbolic representation of American political Nationalism.

Arieli, tracing the inception of the American national identity to the enlightened concept of the natural rights of man, observed: "With the spread of political democracy, the concept of American society as a system of liberty and equality became a dominant concept of national identity." [31] The concepts of "liberty" and "equality," however, are not easily actualized, for traditions, fears, and selfishness tend to inhibit their application. Indeed, the reconciliation of "equality" and "liberty" is difficult to achieve, inasmuch as the liberty of one person to accumulate wealth, for example, seems to imply his inequality with another man.

[30] Hans Kohn, *American Nationalism: An Interpretative Essay* (New York: The Crowell-Collier Publishing Company, 1961), p. 19.
[31] Arieli, *Individualism and Nationalism in American Ideology*, p. 341.

Alexis de Toqueville, the prophetic observer of the American way of life, believed that equality served as the cornerstone of the American political ideology. He derived this opinion from his vivid awareness of the differences between European and American social systems. Traditions within Europe had created a stratified class system based upon inheritance of wealth, or title; indeed, European history, especially from the mid-nineteenth century to the mid-twentieth, was marked by violent attempts to alter the stratified class structure of Europe. In 1892 Friedrich Engles, noting the lack of class consciousness in America, explained the difference between the American system and its European antecedent in the following terms:

> It is quite natural that in such a young country, which had never known feudalism and has grown up on a bourgeois basis from the first, bourgeois prejudices should be strongly rooted in the working class. Out of the opposition to the mother country, which is still clothed in feudal disguise, the American worker imagines that the bourgeois regime as traditionally inherited as something progressive, superior by nature, and for all, a nonplus ultra.[32]

Engles observation, when combined with the fact that Americans traditionally have rejected radical solutions to social problems, explains in part the perennial inability of Marxist or Maoist ideologies to take root in the American soil.

Most historians, however, have viewed liberty rather than equality as the basic theme of the American experiment. Alexander Meiklejohn echoed the historian Hans Kohn's view of American Nationalism when he wrote: "The man who fails to find in us a deep, consuming passion for freedom does not know what we are." [33]

Whether one agrees with Tocqueville or Kohn about the nature of the American ideology, there is little disputing that liberty rather than equality or fraternity served as the major ideological mover for social reform during the short history of the American democratic experiment. While the slogan "equality of opportunity" provided a rationale for rugged individualism, it also legitimized extremely unfair competition, especially during the industrialization of the United States. Americans, however, invariably have adhered to the ideal of equality of opportunity within a class system. Their struggles against inequalities such as those created by slavery and poverty were attempts to remove class stratification, a phenomenon perceived as a violation of an individual's *liberty*. Both the Civil War and the Civil Rights Rebellion of the 1960s were

---

[32] Karl Marx and Frederick Engles, *Selected Correspondence 1846–1895*, trans. Dona Torr (New York: International Publishers, 1942), p. 501.
[33] Alexander Meiklejohn, *What Does America Mean?* (New York: W. W. Norton & Company, Inc., 1935), p. 71.

attempts to actualize the promises of liberty. Americans continue to reveal their belief that freedom is a natural right whereas economic equality is an earned one. The colonial maxim that "All men are by nature equal, but differ greatly in the sequel" continues to serve as a rationale in support of the American socioeconomic system.

Although Americans rejected the principle of absolute economic equality, they did attempt to apply their egalitarian philosophy to other aspects of social life. Rejecting social and intellectual elitism, for example, Americans until the mid-nineteenth century opposed schooling and viewed "book larnin" as a type of pseudo-knowledge. The anti-intellectualism inherent in this form of egalitarianism receives popular support among American citizens since it is a common element that unifies the views of such diverse groups as radicals, know nothings, populists, and the business community. In addition, it appeals to the many educationists who promote a distorted view of John Dewey's belief that man learns through experience. The recent attacks upon the intelligentsia by some of America's political leaders are only public manifestations that emerge periodically to disclose a fundamental thread of American thought (or non-thought) that is distrustful, if not contemptuous of intellectualism. And while such anti-intellectualism serves to prevent any possible dictatorship of the intelligentsia, it also functions as fuel for the fire of political demagogues.

Because of their rejection of the "cultured gentleman" and their admiration for the practical common man, Americans have been ridiculed periodically for their anti-intellectualism and "cultural deprivation." The The romantic poet Charles Baudelaire, for example, referred to the United States as a "gas-lit barbaric country" and a "zoocracy," while Edgar Allen Poe labeled it "MOB."

Despite the fact that the national ideal of liberty was perhaps too abstract to serve as a symbol of national unity or identity, American Nationalism was not solely a legalistic, constitutional or political creed. The Constitution itself may be a magnificent document but it did not serve to inspire a people with patriotic fervor. Americans, therefore, have continuously sought to discover an ethnic basis for American Nationalism.

Although their search in some cases eventuated in ethnocentrism and jingoism—which helped to bring about a war against England (The War of 1812), Mexico (The Mexican War, 1846–48) and in the latter days of the nineteenth century, a war against the Spanish Empire (The Spanish-American War, 1898)—some of their attempts to find a cultural identity were perfectly in harmony with their democratic fervor. In order to succeed democratic Nationalism needed a cultural bases that differed from European antecedents. A republican form of government without a supportive cultural framework could not endure so Americans set out to redefine themselves soon after their successful revolution. Indeed, Noah Webster's admonition that "our national character is not yet formed" continues to preoccupy national historians and patriotic citizens.

Besides the democratic ideals basic to the founding of the young Republic, American Nationalism also assumed a number of other forms. In the first half of the nineteenth century, numerous attempts were made to develop a form of ethnic Nationalism. While Noah Webster designed his simplified spelling system to ensure that all the citizenry could achieve literacy, John Pickering devised a dictionary in which he identified five hundred words and phrases which were uniquely American. Noah Webster called for the creation of an "ASSOCIATION OF AMERICAN PATRIO-TISM FOR THE PURPOSE OF FORMING A NATIONAL CHARACTER." Webster's triology entitled "A Grammatical Institute of the English Language, Comprising an Easy, Concise, and Systematic Method of Education De-signed for Use of English Schools in America!" replaced the *New England Primer* as the basic textbook in American schools. By 1843, twenty million copies of his speller were sold and its fables, maxims, and manners be-came a major source for teaching Americanisms to the children of the republic.

Besides Noah Webster's contribution to American Nationalism, other Americans such as the historians George Bancroft and Francis Parkman provided a national view to America's past. In addition to developing a unique national memory by combining facts and myth and creating legendary heroes and legendary deeds, such as diverse portrayals of George Washington and David Crockett, American character also was particularized through the development of the national aesthetic tradition which emerged from the country's unique linguistic patterns. Daniel J. Boorstin admonished:

> An American counterpart of European belles-lettres, insofar as there was such a counterpart at all, did not appear until the American spoken lan-guage had acquired its special character. Then it, too, bore marks of the peculiarly American situation; it testified to the American rebirth of the vernacular, to American preoccupation with community, with the con-crete, the relevant, the here-and-now. Much of it, at its best and most characteristic, would be the *spoken* word cast into print.[34]

American authors such as James Fenimore Cooper, Nathaniel Hawthorne, and Herman Melville as well as essayists such as Ralph Waldo Emerson and Henry David Thoreau furnished the nation with a literary tradition. While the former helped to define a national type, the latter reflected a universalistic quality; rather than focusing upon a "national soul" or a "national duty," they focused upon an "Over-soul" and problems of civil

[34] Daniel J. Boorstin, *The Americans: The National Experience* (New York: Random House, Inc., 1965), p. 307.

disobedience. Both Emerson and Thoreau serve as godfathers for the American tradition of individualism.

Besides national histories and a national literary tradition which were scrupulously separated from their English counterparts in the public school curricula, schools focused upon the observance of national events (e.g., the signing of the Declaration of Independence and the ride of Paul Revere). Indeed, schools played an increasingly important part in the nationalization of the children and youth.

Educationists such as Horace Mann and Henry Barnard had successfully fought against the opponents of public schooling, with the result that in the Massachusetts Act of 1842, Massachusetts adopted a policy of compulsory school attendance—a policy which was replicated in other states. The compulsory teaching of Nationalism, however, had preceded the attendance law, for in 1827 Massachusetts law required that American history be incorporated in the curriculum. Within the schools, William Holmes McGuffey's *Eclectic Reader* was popularized and served to instruct children and youth about American political Nationalism.

Prior to the Civil War, an American character—in contrast to a British character—had emerged in the United States. Indeed, the nationally sponsored expeditions in the West by men such as Lewis, Clark, and Pike, as well as the rapid settlement of Western lands by Easterners and newly arrived immigrants, served as an amalgam for the formerly fragmented American national character. As Arieli observed, "The people did not give the land its name; rather the land made them a people. . . ." [35] Robert Frost in a remarkably similar fashion wrote: "The land was ours before we were the land's." [36] The shared experiences of the citizenry provided them with a destiny and thus an identity as well.

The American character, however, tended toward schizophrenia as a result of the solidification of sectional differences; indeed, sectionalism eventually emerged to challenge the nascent Nationalism. Sectionalism, of course, is a term which implies divisiveness within a national society. If the Civil War, the War for the Abolition of Slavery, or the War for Confederate National Liberation, depending upon one's perspective, had been lost by the Northern forces, then what is now labeled sectionalism would be viewed as Confederate Nationalism. Be that as it may, the Civil War resulted from numerous issues which are all more or less covered by the umbrella of sectionalism and which resulted from the fact that the political citizenry of the United States had produced a cultural bifurcation that manifested itself in the form of distinctive Southern and Northern

[35] Arieli, *Individualism and Nationalism in American Ideology,* p. 40.
[36] From "The Gift Outright" from *The Poetry of Robert Frost* edited by Edward Connery Lathem, Copyright 1942 by Robert Frost. Copyright © 1970 by Lesley Frost Ballantine. Reprinted by permission of Holt, Rinehart and Winston, Inc.

nationalities. The Civil War represents a vivid and tragic example of the struggle between political nationalists and cultural nationalists.[37]

The Northern defeat of the secessionist forces resolved, in part, the issue of Nationalism versus sectionalism. Although sectional differences would remain throughout American history as an irritant to national peace and unity, the massive influx of immigrants from Europe and the liberated Afro-Americans served as the major foci in attempts to resolve the perennial issue of America's national identity.

Because of the racial pluralism that characterizes the United States as well as the increased cultural pluralism generated by the arrival of large numbers of immigrants from Catholic and Eastern European countries, attempts to define the American national character according to cultural Nationalism became increasingly difficult. By 1850 one tenth of the American population was foreign-born, and Anglo-Americanism no longer served as an acceptable model for defining American Nationalism. Attempts to develop a cultural national identity often degenerated into nativistic movements. Because pluralism is a reality in America, efforts to limit the national character to a particular racial, ethnic, religious, or sectional identity are based upon ignorance or viciousness. Some of the dilemmas encountered because of distorted views of assimilation will be discussed in the following section.

Just as American "loyalists" had decided after their defeat of the Confederacy that Southern cultural identity would not become a basis for political independence, so they also sought to deculturalize the immigrants who were welcomed as cheap labor to America's shores. With immigration steadily climbing throughout the latter half of the nineteenth century, the "nation of many nations" faced numerous issues dealing with the task of assimilating its immigrants. From an annual total of 8,000 immigrants in 1824, the number increased to 1,100,000 in 1906. As the number of immigrants increased, the cultures which they carried with them were increasingly distinguishable from that of their adopted land. After 1840, for example, the Irish and German immigrants were predominantly Catholic and their loyalty was to be questioned by some factions within the United States—especially that of the Irish Catholics after the declaration of papal infallibility, and of the German-Americans as the war clouds of the "Great Wars" passed over the world.

The debates dealing with the "Catholic problem" have been replicated numerous times with other minorities. In 1889, a symposium held at the national convention of the National Educational Association reflected the intensity of the debate concerning the issue of public schooling

[37] See Kenneth M. Stampp, ed., *The Causes of the Civil War* (Englewood Cliffs, N.J.: Prentice-Hall, Inc., 1961) for numerous statements from various sources which reveal the nature of this cultural bifurcation.

and private education and perfectly exemplifies the conflicts generated by cultural pluralism. The symposium focused upon the question: "Should Americans Educate their Children in Denominational Schools?" The affirmative side of the issue was presented by Cardinal Gibbons and Bishop John C. Keane. The former called for religious education to counterbalance the "centrifugal motion of free thought" while the latter affirmed that Christians were the best Americans and called for denominational schools. On the negative side, Edwin Mead admonished Catholics to attend public schools because so many were essentially "foreigners." It may be true that the Catholic boy was ridiculed in the public schools, but, he replied, "Shall he then be fenced-in, or live it down like a man? So is the Irish boy ridiculed—'Paddy' is an epithet much oftener hurled than 'Catholic'—and the Chinaman, the Negro and the Jew. Shall they then be herded by themselves? Rather it is a reason why they should stay. The Jew at the head of the class must be reckoned with; in the Ghetto he is a starveling and a menace." [38]

In a speech ostensibly for the purpose of welcoming Cardinal Gibbons and Bishop Keane, John Jay revealed the doubts shared by many of this hearers about the compatibility between Roman Catholicism and Americanism:

> We welcome today to the field of free discussion before the sovereign citizens of the Republic, a Prince Cardinal and Right Reverend Bishop of that church which holds Pope Clement XIV to have been infallible. They are here, we understand, in charge of the Roman mission for the conversion of America, claiming like ambassadors from a foreign power to be governed by the edicts of their own sovereign, and claiming in addition, that the authority of the potentate whom they represent is supreme also in this land, and above all constitutions and laws.[39]

His disdain was further revealed in his specious argument that the Catholic belief that marriages unsanctioned by the Pope are invalid reduces "American wives to concubines, and children to the position of bastards. . . ." [40] Surprisingly, however, Jay proclaimed himself in favor of preserving the "ethnic qualities" which the immigrants brought to their adopted land.

America continuously doubted its power to absorb the millions of immigrants who came to her shore, and various attempts were made to restrict immigration and to redefine American Nationalism. The most

---

[38] Edwin D. Mead, "Has the Parochial School Proper Place in America?" *National Educational Association Journal of Proceedings and Addresses, Session of the Year 1889 Held at Nashville, Tennessee* (Topeka, Kansas: National Educational Association, 1889), p. 140.

[39] John Jay, "Public and Parochial Schools," *National Educational Association Journal of Proceedings and Addresses,* 1889, p. 159.

[40] Jay, "Public and Parochial Schools," p. 167.

hideous of these attempts were the nativist movements. Nativist groups such as the Ku Klux Klan and the Know-Nothing Party attacked as un-American those individuals who did not reflect their image of an American—and image which assumed that an American was a White Anglo-Saxon Protestant, a fuzzy replica of an Englishman. Thus they denied American nationality to those who for ethnic, social, religious, or racial reasons did not replicate the Anglo-Saxon type. Robert Owen, the communalist Utopian, rightfully observed that nativists were essentially un-American in that they did not place trust in the democratic process.

Nativism represents the desire of a militant dominant group, or of a segment of the dominant group, to "purge" a nation-state of an internal minority because of its "foreign" origin. American nativist movements have singled out Catholics, "radicals," and non-Anglo-Saxons as the internal minorities perceived as "unAmerican." The nativist movements have employed diverse forms of repression ranging from discrimination in job opportunities and housing, and exclusion provisions in immigration laws, to acts of violence such as those perpetuated against Chinese immigrants in California and against black people by the heinous Ku Klux Klan. These movements reject belief in a cosmopolitan nationality and lack faith in the principle that unity and diversity may coexist.

The history of American nativism reveals that it has remained a persistent element in our national throught, although it has varied in intensity, its character depending upon the conditions of the time. John Higham observed:

> Specific nativistic antagonisms may, and do, vary widely in response to the changing character of minority irritants and the shifting conditions of the day; but through each separate hostility runs the connecting, energizing force of modern nationalism. While drawing on much broader cultural antipathies and ethnocentric judgements, nativism translates them into a zeal to destroy the enemies of a distinctively American way of life.[41]

Nativism is inextricably interwoven with minority militancy. As Higham noted, "Every symptom of reviving nativism aroused a fiercer, more militant immigrant opposition. Through individual appeals to public opinion, through organizations, and through political pressure, the immigrants fought back." [42] Thus the nativist, despite the fact that he poses as the "defender of the American way of life," serves to create dissonance and to disrupt national cohesiveness.

Faith in the future of the Republic remains as a major quality of American national identity. The faith in the future of the latter-day

[41] John Higham, *Strangers in the Land: Patterns of American Nativism, 1860–1925* (New York: Atheneum Publishers, 1968), p. 4.
[42] Higham, *Strangers in the Land,* p. 123.

"chosen people" has combined with a faith in progress—political, social, aesthetic, and technological. Although this faith has served to sustain the United States throughout its numerous national ordeals, it also has combined with a messianic vision which was expressed in various forms. It served to motivate Americans toward the expansionist dreams expressed in the "Manifest Destiny" of westward expansion; toward "making the world safe for democracy"; and toward the exportation of the democratic ideology. The ideological expansionist dreams of the United States as well as its role as the agent of technological change throughout the world have led it into numerous foreign intrigues which have outraged the isolationists, befuddled the conservative, and dismayed the liberal.

International developments as well as internal conflicts have affected the features of American Nationalism, and have led to differing views of Americanism. Such differences became apparent in the wake of international conflicts such as the Mexican War and the Spanish-American War when both imperialists and anti-imperialists marched under the banner of American Nationalism. Similarly, the world wars brought to a focus the question "Who is an American?" and whether citizens perceived as nonAmerican because of their national origin were in fact unAmerican. During the two world wars, German-Americans especially were signaled out as suspects. The German language was dropped as an elective from many school curricula, sauerkraut was renamed "liberty cabbage," chopped meat became "Salisbury steak," and a popular type of sausage became the "hot dog," a name that would help people forget its origin in Frankfurt. Many German immigrants Americanized their names, and Fourth of July orators suddenly remembered that George III had been a German sitting upon an English throne.

The "American way of life" remains an ill-defined and elusive concept, although various symbolic representations of the national character serve to provide nationalists with concrete images. These symbols—ranging from monuments, legends, anthropomorphic representations of the collective, the cult of heroes, and slogans—either enhance or hinder national cohesion. Unless the symbols change with the changing nature of the collectivity, Nationalism and national consciousness will be threatened. For example, the Afro-American search for cultural identity in the 1960s revealed a failure of the symbolic system of American identity and will be analyzed in a following section.

The previous analysis has shown us that American Nationalism has been utilized to restrict the identity of the citizenry by basing it upon a particular ethnic, racial, or religious identity. Such a view is rooted in a belief that Americanism is a completed fact rather than a continuous process. It also reveals that patriotic rhetoric can be utilized to serve divisive and antinational ends.

### The Issue of American Unity

Besides legitimizing a national group's existence, Nationalisms also include beliefs about the nature of national cohesion and the processes through which it is developed and sustained. The issue of the nature of social cohesion is especially relevant in extended multi-ethnic and multi-religious nations such as the United States and the Soviet Union.

Nationalism implies that subnational political divisions, cultural diversity, and class differences are subsumed within a national framework in which national group consciousness is preserved and expressed through the national loyalty of its members. Whether local, religional, cultural, and class differences enhance national unity or are disruptive will be determined, in part, by the compatibility of national patriotism and class, ethnic, sectional, and religious loyalties, the degree of geographic mobility, the relationship between cultural groupings, class mobility, ideological patterns and their flexibility, and government policies.

The nature of the process of assimilating individuals into nation-states such as the United States is a central factor in determining the effectiveness of Nationalism in preserving social cohesion. Unfortunately, confusion prevails in this area. The confusion has been increased because prescriptive theoretical constructs of assimilation are forwarded as descriptive in nature and because similar labels are used to describe dissimilar assimilative processes while dissimilar labels are utilized to identify similar processes. The three major theoretical models of assimilation—Anglo-conformity, the melting pot, and cultural pluralism (a form of Romantic Nationalism)—have been utilized to describe a variety of actually existing processes or desired forms of assimilation.[43] Within each of these models antithetic views have been propounded.

The monistic model of assimilation, labeled "Anglo-conformity," has been utilized to describe the aim of preserving English traditions, the English language, and the English cultural patterns which were internalized by the early immigrants and transformed by them in the American setting, including the desire to preserve such divergent goals as "democratic traditions" and "racial purity." John Higham, viewing the ideological basis of American nativism, revealed the debilitating effect of the Anglo-conformity perspective when he wrote: "The anti-Catholic, anti-radical, and Anglo-Saxon traditions had opened channels through

---

[43] For variations of these processes see Nathan Glazer and Daniel Moynihan, *Beyond the Melting Pot* (Cambridge: M.I.T. Press, 1967); and Milton M. Gordon, *Assimilation in American Life: The Role of Race, Religion, and National Origins* (New York: Oxford University Press, 1964).

which a large part of the xenophobia of the late nineteenth and twentieth centuries would flow." [44]

An exaggerated form of monistic assimilation was forwarded by the Anglo-conformist, Madison Grant. Calling for an end to all immigration into the United States, he warned: ". . . we would still have with us an immense mass of Negroes and nearly as many southern and eastern Europeans, intellectually below the standard of the average American." [45] In addition to his suggested restriction upon immigration, a program to which he gave the frightfully Orwellian title of "Counsel of Perfection," he also called for intranational controls: "The proper extension to and use by these undesirable classes of a knowledge of birth control may be in the future of substantial benefit, and the practice of sterilization of the criminal and the intellectual unfit, now legally established in twenty-seven States, can be resorted to with good result." [46] Anglo-conformists, of course, are not all racial "purists." Although some, such as Madison Grant, adhere to such a one-dimensional view, others use the doctrine of Anglo-conformity as no more than a means of preserving some of the established cultural patterns adhered to by the first European immigrants, which they view as culturally superior. If this is not full-scale racism, it nevertheless has been denounced, and rightfully so, as "racism of culture."

The second assimilation model, the melting pot construct, also contains dissimilar views under the umbrella of its label. It has been utilized to describe or prescribe a form of assimilation whereby a variety of ethnic groups contribute a significant portion of their cultural elements to an emerging "national type." The melting pot construct, however, also has been utilized to describe a process whereby newly arrived immigrants gradually divest themselves of their ethnic identity and "melt" into the preexisting patterns of their "host nation." Israel Zangwill, in his drama *The Melting Pot,* revealed his belief in the emergence of an American "type" through the exclamation of his hero, David Quizano, who affirmed: "America is God's crucible, the great Melting Pot where all the races of Europe are melting and reforming! . . . Germans and Frenchmen, Irishmen and Englishmen, Jews and Russians—into the Crucible with you all! God is making the American." [47]

The "melting pot" view of assimilation implies, in a sense, a process of deculturalization. Julia Richman, a melting pot advocate, focusing upon the education of the immigrant child, warned in an address to the NEA General Assembly in 1905 that the flood of foreign-language publica-

---

[44] Higham, *Strangers in the Land,* p. 11.

[45] Madison Grant, *The Conquest of a Continent* (New York: Charles Scribner's Sons, 1933), p. 351.

[46] Grant, *The Conquest of a Continent,* p. 351.

[47] Israel Zangwill, *The Melting Pot* (New York: The Macmillan Company), p. 37.

tions inhibited the process of Americanization by retarding the learning of the "vernacular." Calling for an effort to bridge the generation gap between the Americanized child and his parents, she called upon teachers to visit homes and to teach the children to respect the heroism of the parents who left their native land to ensure that they would receive a free education in a land of freedom. The political and religious freedom which the adopted country furnished the immigrants did not, according to Miss Richman, extend to freedom of selecting cultures. Immigrant parents, she believed, "must be made to realize that in forsaking the land of their birth, they were also forsaking the customs and the traditions of that land; they must be made to realize an obligation, in adopting a new country, to adopt the language and customs of that country. They must be made to understand that the welfare of America demands the proper assimilation of all these conflicting foreign elements that are so generously admitted to our land." [48] With regard to those who desired to resist the melting pot, she warned: ". . . unless they readily and willingly take on Americanization in its best sense, the day will come when our government must close its gates to their compatriots who wish to follow. The sins of the earlier immigrants will be visited upon their cousins and wives and brothers who try to follow." [49]

Richman's version of assimilation was questioned by the sensitive social reformer Jane Addams at a convention in 1908. Calling for a cultural pluralistic perspective, she admonished:

> If the body of teachers in our great cities could take hold of the immigrant colonies, could bring out of them their handicrafts and occupations, their traditions, their folk songs and folk lore, and beautiful stories which every immigrant colony is ready to tell and translate; could get the children to bring these things into school as the material upon which culture is based, they would discover that by comparison that which they give them is a poor meretricious and vulgar thing.[50]

In addition to positing cultural amalgamation as a desirable goal, the melting pot thesis also was used to describe what was perceived as the inevitable result of the forces working upon the immigrants in their adopted land. That is to say, while some supporters of the melting pot thesis were arguing that cultural amalgamation *should* take place, others were announcing that it in fact was taking place and could not help doing

[48] Julia Richman, "The Immigrant Child," *National Educational Association Journal of Proceedings and Addresses of the Forty-Fourth Annual Meeting at Asbury Park and Ocean Grove, New Jersey, July 3–7, 1905* (Winona, Minnesota: National Education Association, Secretary's Office, 1905), p. 120.

[49] Richman, "The Immigrant Child," p. 120.

[50] Jane Addams, "Foreign-Born Children in the Primary Grades," *National Educational Association Journal of Proceedings and Addresses of the Thirty-Seventh Annual Meeting Held at Washington, D.C., July 7–12, 1898*), p. 102.

so. Of the latter, some followed Frederick Jackson Turner in seeing the American frontier as the crucible where the new American type was being formed, while other social analysts viewed the large industrial centers and the public school system as the cauldrons where ethnic differences would "blend and melt" to form a new national character.

On the other hand, Franz Boaz distinguished between mere acculturation and full assimilation which allows individuals to interact and communicate with other members of the national society. This sort of assimilation is both a cultural process and a social and psychological process, and Boaz was convinced that it was in fact not typical of the American experience. He wrote:

> Everybody will agree that American Whites, Negroes, and the native born Asiatics are members of the same nation, but they would hardly be called members of the same nationality, because of the social barriers between these groups and the consciousness that they are derived from races that continue to be distinct.[51]

In other words, the imparting of a culture even where there are pressures making for monistic acculturation does not necessarily result in assimilation in the sense of an increase in the ability to communicate or to share frames of reference. Even though a dominant nationality may successfully enculturate "foreigners," assimilation will not occur if the process is accompanied by prejudices or by rules which prevent the enculturated from participating as full members of the national society. Nationalization and enculturation are not sufficient for assimilation. Participation through social integration is required.

Both the Anglo-conformity and the melting pot models of assimilation were challenged by numerous individuals who desired the preservation of immigrant ethnic identity. Horace M. Kallen, an advocate of cultural pluralism, presented his views on assimilation in two articles which appeared in *The Nation* in February 1915. Warning that "there is a marked tendency in this country for the industrial and social stratification to follow ethnic lines," [52] he rejected Zangwill's melting pot solution and added: "As for Zangwill at best he is the obverse of Dickens, at worst he is a Jew making a special plea." [53] Rejecting the belief in the emergence of an "American type," he commented:

> The "American race" is a totally unknown thing; to presume that it will be better because (if we like to persist in the illusion that it is coming) it will be later, is no different from imagining that, because contemporary,

[51] Franz Boaz, *Anthropology and Modern Life* (New York: W. W. Norton & Company, Inc., 1962), pp. 89–90.

[52] Horace Kallen, "Democracy Versus the Melting-Pot: A Study of American Nationality," *The Nation*, C, Number 2590 (February 18, 1915), 194.

[53] Kallen, "Democracy Versus the Melting-Pot," p. 193.

Russia is better than ancient Greece. There is nothing more to be said in the pious stupidity that identifies recency with goodness.[54]

Deploring the moves toward the integration of the races, Seymour W. Itzkoff agreed with the pluralistic theme of Kallen's national orchestration of differences. He wrote: "What is being proposed by the integrationists is that the one largely undigested group in our society be freed to partake of the very malaise that affects us all." [55] His call for the preservation of black communities was convincingly expressed by Stokely Carmichael and Charles Hamilton, who wrote: "The racial and cultural personality of the black community must be preserved and that community must win its freedom while preserving its cultural integrity. Integrity includes a pride—in the sense of self-acceptance, not chauvinism —in being black, in the historical attainments and contributions of black people." [56]

The variety of opposing views concerning assimilation does not offer any clear-cut viable alternatives. Each theoretical construct carries with it inherent limitations. The assimilation models that stress the elimination of the ethnic cultural differences among the American citizenry provide as a basis for national cohesion the development of shared cultural elements which would serve as a common referent for effective intranational communication. Such models, however, may serve to threaten those individuals within the citizenry who include membership in ethnic cultural groupings as an important part of their self-identity. Attempting deculturalization with such individuals may serve only to rigidify their ethnic identity and thus may lead to intranational group conflict. It also drastically inhibits creativity and the learning process.

Conversely, assimilative models that emphasize the preservation of ethnic differences may serve to enhance cultural group identity and may reduce threat to individual identity, but they also endanger national cohesion by allowing the development of diverse symbol systems and points of reference which inhibit intergroup communication. The greater the difference between culture groups, the greater the difficulty in developing mutual understanding. Unless cultural fields overlap, effective communication cannot occur. What is more, models that are based upon preserving intranational group differences may result in the development of irreconcilable value systems and thus may ignore the needs of the total society. In his essay "Beyond Tolerance," Robert Paul Wolff, after admitting that cultural pluralism was "humane, benevolent, accommodat-

---

[54] Horace Kallen, "Democracy Versus the Melting-Pot: A Study of American Nationality," *The Nation*, C, Number 2591 (February 25, 1915), 219.

[55] Kallen, "Democracy Versus the Melting-Pot," Part 1, p. 129.

[56] Stokely Carmichael and Charles V. Hamilton, *Black Power: The Politics of Liberation in America* (New York: Random House, Inc., 1967), p. 55.

ing" and "responsive to the evils of social injustice," rightfully cautioned: "But pluralism is fatally blind to the evils which afflict the entire body politic, and as a theory of society it obstructs consideration of precisely the sorts of thoroughgoing social revisions which may be needed to remedy those evils." [57]

Because of the complexity of the issue and the emotions it arouses, one could debate the pros and cons of assimilation endlessly. When we turn, from theory and ideology to fact, however, we see that in actual cases the rapidity of assimilation of distinct minorities depends upon the national ideology, the color and physiognomy of the peoples involved (especially when amalgamation is not prevalent between races), settlement patterns, the similarities and differences between the "old" and "new" cultures, and the nature of the immigrants' movement into the society (individuals are more easily assimilated than groups). The *perceived* "character" of the outgroup" also will affect the assimilation process.

National ideologies differ in the manner in which they deal with the process of assimilation or the process of rejecting minority groups. In the United States, for example, approaches to assimilation have taken such forms as "Anglo-conformity" in language, the melting pot theory in culture, and pluralism in religion; America is also the home of such non-assimilative programs as attempts to transfer populations (the Back-to-Africa movement in the 1920s and the "incarceration" of Indians in reservations), the gradual extermination of some of the Indian nations, and the economic subjugation of some minorities such as Mexican-Americans and blacks.

Although Afro-Americans, Asiatic-Americans, American Indians, and some Spanish-speaking minorities have been urged by some Americans to accept the Anglo way of life, they have, in practice, been kept out of the melting pot through segregation and discrimination. Kyle Haselden stressed the fact that the Afro-American has been excluded from participating in the collective American national body when he wrote:

> To take the most pessimistic but still only slightly exaggerated view, the Negro has gained certain limited equalities in the past 100 years, but so far as his membership in the American family is concerned, he has merely exchanged his individual ghetto for collective ghetto. He can exercise the mobility which emancipation gave him, but as he does so the Negro finds that he is merely moving from one racial ghetto to another.[58]

[57] Robert Paul Wolff, "Beyond Tolerance," in *A Critique of Pure Tolerance* (Boston: Beacon Press, 1965), p. 52.
[58] Kyle Haselden, "Race—And the Divided American Soul," in *The Search For Identity: Essays on the American Character* (New York: Institute for Religious and Social Studies, 1964), p. 140.

True assimilation requires the removal of irreconcilable discrepancies through adjustment on the part of both the ethnic group and the national society. Assimilation implies, therefore, that *some of the American traditions must be obviated.* It also assumes that racial, cultural, or religious ideologies which reject coexistence with differing intranational belief systems and which are based upon a denial of equality of opportunity to other intranational groups must be challenged. Enforced race segregation as well as other forms of institutionalized racism are traditions which have been preserved on American soil, but they must be eradicated if assimilation is to be possible. Such institutionalized anachronisms not only violate the democratic credenda but endanger the survival of the nation-state. To claim to be an American nationalist while adhering to beliefs in racial inequality or race supremacy in any form is not only illogical but also reflective of gross ignorance as to the meaning of the terms "American" and "Nationalism."

Assimilation as an aim of education, therefore, is a *process* and *direction* rather than a goal or target. It is a process of meaningful interaction whereby individuals develop an awareness of the elements which they share in common. By the same token, although assimilation implies that meaningful interaction will result in a constantly increasing pool of shared experiences, it does not imply the removal of ethnic differences. As Chapman pointed out, "Assimilation is a multiple process, in which there are strictly speaking no assimilators or assimilatees, in which there are merely participants in assimilation." [59]

Assimilation also implies that access to national institutions should not be inhibted because of racial, cultural, and religious differences. Successful assimilation requires, therefore, that members of all racial, cultural and religious groups interact or be free to interact within all *national* institutions as equals.

While academicians as well as ideologists continue their debates concerning the merits of diverse assimilative models and processes, the public school systems of the nation must confront these issues daily. Waiting for an ideal model, if such can ever be contrived, is not a luxury which American teachers can enjoy.

### Nationalism and Schooling

In addition to the unintentional political and cultural nationalization of individuals, such as when children observe soldiers and political

[59] Stanley N. Chapman, "The Spirit of Cultural Pluralism," in *Cultural Pluralism and the American Idea*, ed. Horace M. Kallen (Philadelphia: University of Pennsylvania Press, 1956), p. 109.

leaders performing their duties or when they observe the processes of national institutions, formal education serves as a major means of developing national consciousness.

Public school systems are educational agencies which are established to sustain and expand Nationalism. As Gladys Wiggin observed: "In the twentieth century some of the educational symbols are a function of a force called *nationalism*. So pervasive is this force in determining the patterns of education that it is an unstated assumption in educational circles that an education system is expected to support nationalism." [60] Through such means as the teaching of national history, the native language (which may stress differences from a similar language spoken elsewhere), geography, folklore, national literature, customs, and the ideological bases of the national political and economic system, national character is formed and national loyalty is developed and sustained. Similarly, the use of national symbols (e.g., the Liberty Bell), symbolic gestures (e.g., saluting the national flag), and patriotic rhetoric (e.g., phrases such as "the Founding Fathers" and "the American way of life") serves to sustain national consciousness.

Indeed, the nationalizing process of assimilation stands as one of the central purposes of the public school system in the United States. Harry N. Rivlin was alluding to this neo-assimilative function of the school when he admonished:

> The children who present the great problem and challenge to today's schools may well be regarded as our new immigrants even though they are American citizens and may not be newcomers to their urban communities. The Southern Negro, the Puerto Rican, and the displaced rural family are immigrants because they have moved from a cultural setting with which they have been familiar to one that is markedly different. Even the Northern Negro and the Mexican-American present many of the social characteristics of the immigrants as they seek to escape from a population eddy in which they have been trapped for generations.[61]

The "new" immigrants claiming their rights as citizens of a democratic society increasingly are questioning the attempts of the schools to foster values, beliefs, and orientations which result from a monistic perspective of assimilation in American society. Indeed, the melting pot model has been rejected by many members of ethnic minorities who are searching for means of gaining the equality of opportunity promised them by the American political creed. Although scholars such as Seymour W. Itzkoff have rejected the notion that the school should "melt" the ethnic minorities within a "debased society," others have affirmed that

[60] Wiggin, *Education and Nationalism*, pp. 3–4.

[61] Harry N. Rivlin, "New Teacher for New Immigrants," *Teachers College Record*, LXVI, No. 8 (1965), p. 710.

the public school system in the United States has failed continuously in the twentieth century to fulfill its assimilative function. Thus Colin Greer, in "Public Schools: The Myth of the Melting Pot," avowed: "The public schools have always failed the lower classes—both white and black. Current educational problems stem not from the fact that the schools have changed, but from the fact that they continue to do precisely the job they have always done." [62]

The assimilative function of the school in the mid-twentieth century is faced with a threat to national cohesion which may far exceed the problems which confronted teachers in the past who sought to assimilate immigrants from other national societies. Indeed, the crisis in the 1960s is not unlike that of the 1860s at the end of the American Civil War. Ghettoism is similar to sectionalism in that it challenges rather than accepts the ideal of *e pluribus unum.*

Recent educational innovations resulting from the Bilingual Education Act with its culturally pluralistic implications, and the Economic Opportunity Program, with offshoots such as Project Head Start, the Job Corps, VISTA, and the National Teacher Corps, have been devised to assist those members of our society who have been described as the "new" immigrants. Whether such programs are directed to teaching children and youth who are labeled "culturally different," "socially disadvantaged," or "economically deprived," they are inextricably interwoven with the aim of developing and sustaining civic cohesion. National Assessment programs, government funding of compensatory programs, and Supreme Court decisions concerning the integration of public schools and the abolition of religious practices in public schools are important recent nationalizing forces. Indeed, attempts to nationalize American schools are deeply rooted in America's past, despite the fact that local control of public schooling has been the predominant American pattern. Latter-day federal involvement in education was foreshadowed as early as 1787, when the Northwest Ordinance was passed with its enforced provision for public education. Since then, the numerous attempts to establish a national university, the establishment of military academies, and the Morrill Act (1862) with its provision for land grants to state universities have all pointed in the same direction. National educational programs also were designed for reservation Indians as well as for natives of America's colonies during her ridiculous fling into imperialism.

To fulfill nationalizing tasks of American educational institutions, some individuals have advocated that the public school system in the United States should be a *common school system.* Educationists such as Horace Mann and Henry Barnard supported such an ideal and dedicated

[62] Colin Greer, "Public Schools: The Myth of the Melting-Pot," *Saturday Review* (November 15, 1969), p. 84.

themselves to realizing it. Lawrence A. Cremin, the historian of education, concluded his analysis of the development of the common school ideal in the United States prior to 1850 with four fundamental meanings which the ideal implied:

1. A common school was a school ideally common to all, available without cost to the young of the whole community.
2. A common school was a school providing students of diverse backgrounds with a minimum common educational experience, involving the intellectual and moral training necessary to the responsible and intelligent exercise of citizenship. It was careful to avoid in the process those areas which in terms of conscience would prove so emotionally and intellectually divisive as to destroy the school's paramount commitment to universality.
3. A common school was a school totally controlled by the common effort of the whole community as embodied in public funds.
4. A common school was a school completely controlled by the whole community (usually through its representatives) rather than by sectarian, political, economic, or religious groups.[63]

According to its advocates, the purpose of such a common school, Cremin noted, was to develop "a common core of sentiment, of value, and of practice *within which* pluralism would not become anarchy. They were seeking, in a sense, a means of constant regeneration whereby the inevitable inequalities arising out of freedom would not from generation to generation become destructive of its very source." [64]

The actualities of twentieth-century American society reveal, however, that the "inevitable inequalities" have, in many cases, been maintained from generation to generation and have served to perpetuate social inequalities. Colin Greer, denying the public school's success as a melting pot agency, affirmed that public schools have failed to remove the inequalities generated by differences in socioeconomic status. "School performance seems consistently dependent upon the socio-economic position of the pupil's family," he wrote; ". . . while American males born after 1900 spend more years in school than their nineteenth-century predecessors, federal and other estimates indicate no concomitant redistribution of economic and social rewards." [65] Although Greer may have overstated the causal relationship between socioeconomic position and school performance, he is quite correct in pointing to the schools' failure to remove social and economic inequalities generated by perceptions of racial and cultural differences.

The American educational tradition has emphasized the common

[63] Lawrence A. Cremin, *The American Comon School: An Historic Conception* (New York: Bureau of Publications, Teachers College Columbia University, 1951), p. 219.
[64] Cremin, *The American Common School,* p. 221.
[65] Greer, "Public Schools: The Myth of the Melting-Pot," p. 85.

school ideal, but actual patterns of public school education, both in the past and to this day, continue to violate the ideal. Racially segregated schools, for example, are not common schools. Whether such schools are the result of *de jure* or *de facto* segregation, they have not been funded equally, they have not been controlled by representatives of the whole community, nor have they provided common educational experiences for all children and youth. Far from reflecting the pluralism within the American society, racially segregated schools minimize the common experiences shared by individuals of different races. The fact that racial isolation in the schools has increased in some sections of the United States since the 1954 Supreme Court desegregation decision is an educational threat to national cohesion.

Similarly, public schools which are segregated according to socioeconomic levels also violate the common school ideal. A national common school system does not exist when some schools within agrarian communities or urban centers receive grossly unequal funding compared to that of other more affluent communities. Local or state funding based upon unequal abilities of the communities to sustain school taxes is an indirect means of sustaining a dual public educational system. This bifurcation produces an educational elite within the affluent communities who will fill the top positions in national institutions. This bifurcation of national schools results in a "caste" society which violates the democratic creed and which mitigates against national cohesion. What is more, this sort of elitism is totally inconsistent with American meritocratic ideals inasmuch as it is rooted only in socioeconomic position.

The failure of the public school system in the United States to effectively remove the inequalities of access to national institutions because of racial, cultural, and economic factors is not a failure of a common school system but a failure resulting from the fact that America does not have a common school system.

In order to successfully accomplish its nationalizing and assimilative functions in a pluralistic and democratic society, public schools must provide all students with the means of communicating effectively with their fellow nationals. They also must ensure that individuals of equal ability have equal access to all national institutions regardless of racial, cultural, and socioeconomic differences. *Quality* education in the United States necessitates that this adjectival modifier of education be prefixed by "e."

### The Teacher and Americanism

One task of teachers in the American public school system is to ensure that American children and youth will include the national collectivity as a significant part of their group identity. The nationalizing aim of citizenship education is an integral part of the more general aim of preparing individuals to participate in the democratic process. The members of the Joint Project on the Individual and the School noted this relationship when they wrote:

> The notion of some universal democratic man seems an abstraction of doubtful value. Actually there is no universal, supranational democratic culture in which he might be nourished. Consequently, it seems best to describe the democratic character in relation to the culture which embodies it. In an inquiry directed toward American education, the attempt should be to delineate an American character. This is not the same as a French or a Japanese democratic character, but presumably it is congenial to these and able to communicate with them.[66]

Although the democratic ideology is held to be a universally applicable belief system, cultural patterns as well as historical antecedents affect the manner in which it will be practiced. Thus John Dewey, in a speech to the general assembly of the NEA in 1916, referred to the relationship between American Nationalism and democracy when he affirmed: ". . . our nation and democracy are equivalent terms . . . our democracy means amity and good will to all humanity (including those beyond our border), and equal opportunity for all within." [67] The task of teachers in the United States, therefore, does not include only the teaching of the democratic creed and Nationalism; rather, it must extend to the teaching of a national democratic creed and a democratic national ideology.

The fact that one of the fundamental aims of American public education is the nationalization of children and youth so that they will identify with and express a loyalty to the national collectivity does not necessarily imply that the destruction of intranational group differences is held to be desirable. Tolerance within a democratic society should extend beyond the acceptance of individual differences to the recognition and encouragement of group diversity. To accept the former and reject the latter would be to deny the fundamental reality that a person's individuality is, in part, a reflection of his group identity.

Embracing the ideal of cultural diversity, however, should not blind us to the numerous educational problems it creates. Of these, one of the most difficult to deal with is the tendency to perceive intranational cultural differences as though they were ranked on some sort of hierarchial scale. People often equate differing from the cultural mainstream with being "culturally inferior" or "culturally deprived." When a majority in a

---

[66] Joint Project on the Individual and the School, *A Climate for Individuality* (Washington: American Association of School Administrators, 1965), p. 12.

[67] John Dewey, "Nationalizing Education." *Journal of Proceedings of the Fifty-fourth Annual Meeting of the National Education Association of the United States, New York, July 1–8, 1916*, p. 188.

society adopts such a duality of perception, discord and enmity almost inevitably follow.

When an individual or a group which is part of his "social identity" is threatened, he often responds with a self-defense mechanism which has the effect of limiting his range of perception. Whether the threat is physical violence or the psychological violence that follows in the wake of discrimination or prejudice, the result may be increased self-defensiveness and increased rigidity in behavior. What is more, when a cultural group is threatened, its members may react by idealizing the characteristics of the group and by insisting on its superiority over the threatening group. At one time or another most Nationalisms have had recourse to such idealizations; for example, the Nationalisms of nation-states such as France, Germany, and the United States, as well as the Nationalisms of intranational ethnic and racial groupings such as black nationalists, French Canadian nationalists, and Slavic nationalists have been shaped to a large extent by belief in the existence of a threat to the group's survival or honor. This perception of threat easily can lead to a kind of group paranoia, which makes it essential that schools be designed to minimize the conflict and distrust that pervades cross-cultural communication, especially when such communication is enforced by school attendance laws rather than by the desire to resolve conflicts. Similarly, schools must ensure that students are not penalized because of their ethnic identity.

Members of intranational cultural minorities often have been penalized by public school systems because of their cultural differences. That a student's socioeconomic position and cultural identity may affect his achievement in public schools has been substantiated by numerous studies Horatio Ulibarri admonished: "The schools have been complacent to a large degree in presenting only a small aspect of the American culture, namely, the middle-class values and orientations, as the sum total of the curricula in the schools." [68] The issue Ulibarri raises is central to citizenship education and Nationalism in that it relates to the issue of equality of opportunity which, in an age of modernization rests upon formal education. Further, the nature of the curricula also powerfully affects the symbols of identification which serve vital functions in sustaining or destroying national cohesion.

Three educational phenomena relate directly to the issue of national cohesion: testing, language patterns, and symbols of identity. Testing has served as a major institutional means of penalizing students because of ethnic differences. The inherent limitations in existing I.Q. tests, for example, must be recognized. Louis C. Bernadoni warned: "It is un-

---

[68] Horatio Ulibarri, "Teacher Awareness of Sociocultural Differences in the Multicultural Classrooms," *Sociology and Social Research* (October 1960), p. 49.

realistic to expect an intelligence test magically to be 'fair' to all cultures and accurately predict behavior for these cultures when the values affecting the definition of intelligent behavior vary drastically." [69] Combs and Snygg grovide an example of the dilemma of evaluating the results of intelligence tests when, in analyzing the results of an intelligence test administered to men from the mountain of Kentucky, West Virginia, and southern Ohio, they noted:

> An intelligence test in use at this station was composed of a series of five pictures with instructions to cross out the picture of each series that did not belong with the others. One set of five pictures showed a trumpet and four stringed instruments, a guitar, a harp, a violin, and a bass fiddle. Many of the men crossed out the harp because they had never seen one or because as they explained, "all the others are things in our band." . . . Presumably, had the mountain men made a test and administered it to the psychologist, the psychologist would have appeared rather dull.[70]

When a "culturally unfair" test is utilized as the basis for measuring intelligence and then segregating students within schools, an ancillary result of such testing will be the segregation of students according to cultural differences. If "culturally unfair" standardized tests are to be utilized by the public school system (a practice which should be reevaluated), it should be only in order to provide information concerning the degree to which a student's perceptions are similar to the perceptions of the individuals who constructed the measuring instrument. When they are utilized to measure intelligence, they often turn out to be the basis of a "self-fulfilling prophecy" whereby a member of a culturally different minority will be treated as intellectually inferior because of his cultural minority status and will perform according to the expectations of his teachers.

Testing results can serve a valuable purpose by revealing the communication threshold between the teacher and his students. *Testing should be viewed as a way of "measuring" that segment of an individual's perceptual world which overlaps with the perceptual world of the tester.* Used in this way, standardized tests can facilitate the teaching-learning process by revealing differences in perceptions. If the tester's perceptual world does indeed reflect the expectations of the major institutions within the national society, all students should have the opportunity to "grow" intellectually in that perceptual world inasmuch as their socioeconomic success will depend in part upon their ability to "see" the world as the "establishment" sees it. Of course, the student need not discard

---

[69] Louis C. Bernadoni, "A Culture Fair Intelligence Test for the Ugh, No, and Oo-la-la Cultures," *Personnel and Guidance Journal* (February 1964), p. 557.

[70] Arthur W. Combs and Donald Snygg, *Individual Behavior: A Perceptual Approach to Behavior,* rev. ed. (New York: Harper & Row, Publishers, Inc., 1959), pp. 95–96.

or diminish the perceptual world derived from his ethnic intranational culture, for a meaningful personal life depends to a significant extent upon the quality of his ethnic inheritance; but he should be given a full opportunity to participate in the perceptual world of the national community at large. Cultural differences are expressed in numerous ways. Although language differences offer perhaps the major source of conflict in the educational process, a variety of other culturally determined factors also may "interfere" with the learning process. For example, some cultural groupings do not value long-range goals and thus are not motivated by promises of rewards in the distant future. Similarly, some ethnic groups value nonverbal communication and are prone to discard complex verbal patterns as ostentatious. Whatever the differences, any attempt on the part of teachers to bring about the "melting" of subcultural differences through ridicule or coercion will fail. Attempts to assimilate individuals into a national "melting pot" cannot be based upon a process of deculturalization. *Attempts to accomplish the assimilative aim of public schools must be based upon a perspective of cultural enrichment if they are to succeed.* Attempts at deculturalization may result in a threat to personal identity and thus may serve only to increase ethnic group defensiveness. Such attempts also violate the fundamental task of the teacher—the liberation of human thought and feeling.

The importance of cultural elements such as language in the perceptual life of an individual was revealed in a study of some French-Canadian immigrants to the United States. Many children of French-Canadian immigrants, for example, were admonished by their parents and priests that "Loss of language meant loss of faith, and loss of faith meant loss of eternity." [71] For individuals who internalized such a directive, language loyalty was inextricably interwoven with their sense of identity. Any teacher who attempted to teach the American language by minimizing the importance of the French language could readily be perceived as a "tool of Satan." Perceptions are not always accurate, but they do affect judgments and behavior.

Paradoxically, bilingualism, which is sometimes viewed as cultural enrichment, is often perceived as "cultural deprivation" when it is rooted in intranational ethnic differences. While the "incorrect English patterns" of Charles Boyer were admired, the "incorrect English patterns" of Mexican-Americans are often denigrated. In their anxiety to teach the English language to non-English speaking minority group members, teachers often fail to recognize the cultural richness attached to an ethnic group's language. The Mexican-American who can speak Spanish and English,

[71] Herve-B Lemaire, "Franco-American Efforts on Behalf of the French Language in New England," in *Language Loyalty in the United States: The Maintenance and Perpetuation of Non-English Mother Tongues by American Ethnic and Religious Groups* (The Hague: Mouton & Co., 1966), p. 254.

regardless of his socioeconomic level, may surpass his mono-linguistic fellow nationals in cultural richness. As Caleb Gattegno noted:

> We can also surmise that those who miss learning another language or even another dialect of their native language would miss more than just a new skill. They would miss the experience of using themselves in different ways and discovering that nothing in them is destined to remain enclosed in one culture, in one way of being. The use of another language fluently displays the flexibility of one's mind, the coexistence of more than one culture in one's self, and of some of the mind's functionings.[72]

Not only do ethnic bilingualists have to struggle with a "handicap" in formal educational institutions, but those members of the national community who speak dialects other than so-called "standard" American also have suffered exceedingly from being labeled by the pejorative phrase "culturally disadvantaged." Linguistic differences within the same language are often viewed as the difference between what is proper and what is "substandard." Robert L. Politzer and Diana E. Bartley, viewing the variety of American dialects, admonished: "We know that from the linguistic point of view nonstandard dialects are coherent 'regular' systems of communication comparable to the standard dialect."[73] Inasmuch as language is a social tool and its *raison d'être* is communication, all dialects are "correct" and depend upon the social setting for their communication value. The public school has a responsibility to ensure that all children and youth will be able to communicate effectively with their fellow nationals. Such a responsibility should not imply removing his ability to communicate effectively with the members of his particular linguistic group.

Nationalism implies that all children and youth should be taught standard English because it is through standard English that they will gain "acceptance" in national institutions. Standard English, however, should be taught as *a* way of speaking and not as the *correct* way of speaking. The issue of differences between dialects should be viewed as linguistic differences and not as differences in cultural sophistication. Indeed, the public school teacher who is seeking to teach in those areas of the nation which are characterized by individuals who speak nonstandard English should prepare himself or herself to understand the relevant linguistic style.

All children and youth should be encouraged to become bilingualist and/or bi-dialectist. To teach a child or youth the nonstandard English

---

[72] Caleb Gattegno, "Notes Toward a Coexisting Self," *The* [New York] *Center* [for Urban Education] *Forum*, IV, No. 1 (September 1969), p. 14.

[73] Robert L. Politzer and Diana E. Bartley, *Standard English and Nonstandard Dialects: Phonology and Morphology*, Research and Development Memorandum, No. 46 (Stanford: Stanford Center for Research and Development in Teaching, 1969), p. 2.

uf an intranational minority as a second language is not to teach him incorrect English. It is to increase his communication ability. The perennial misunderstandings that occur between individuals utilizing different dialects is a major cause of the persistent "credibility gap" between intranational groupings.

A third major educational issue as it relates to assimilation in a pluralistic nation is the use of symbols. The nature of symbols and the meanings of terms undergo continuous change. Inasmuch as symbols have profound psychological effects, it is essential that teachers develop a sensitivity to the effects of symbols and an ability to understand the emotional implications attached to words and phrases.

Teachers should avoid utilizing ethnic slurs. They also should be prepared to understand the social and psychological implications of such terms and the relationship between labels and ethnocentrism. Similarly, teachers must be prepared to deal with terms which are *emerging* as ethnic slurs. For example, the term "colored" has been utilized in the past by both whites and blacks to describe the Afro-American minority, but recent Afro-American ideologists have rejected it because it implies, they believe, "cultural deprivation." Teachers must understand such social realities as the changing meanings of terms. For a teacher to argue that a descriptive term such as "colored" was socially acceptable in the past and therefore should continue to be utilized is to betray a lack of understanding of the psychological implications inherent in language usage as well as of the reality of language changes. Anachronistic terminology and symbolism not only are unsound pedagogy but also may be destructive to social cohesion. Teachers should be aware of such things as the negative image of the Afro-American portrayed in some school textbooks, should avoid using such materials, and should avoid conveying such attitudes themselves. As Jonathan Kozol pointed out in connection with one such text. "It is from reading a book like this over the course of twenty years that the Reading Teacher and thousands of other teachers like her might well come to believe that you would do a child nothing but a disservice to let him know that he was Negro. The books are not issued any more—but the teachers still are." [74]

Just as some descriptive terms should be discarded because of their native emotional impact in the present social order, so others must be clarified whenever they are utilized. To attempt to utilize the terms "Nationalism" or "patriotism," for example, without clarifying the specific meaning intended will lead to gross misunderstandings. Similarly, phrases such as "Black Power" and "Indian Power" are multi-faceted and their

[74] Jonathan Kozol, *Death at an Early Age: The Destruction of the Hearts and Minds of Negro Children in the Boston Public Schools* (Boston: Houghton Mifflin Company, 1967), pp. 69–70.

meaning should be examined in each context in which they appear. When a speaker utilizes the phrase "Black Nationalism," does he mean the political or the cultural form of Nationalism? If his meaning is not made clear, misunderstanding is quite likely to follow. Similarly, nonverbal symbols also must be analyzed and clarified. Does the American flag, for example, represent the American ideals, the collectivity, or the economic-military complex? Are those dissenters who are "destroying" the American flag rejecting the democratic process or a particular action of the government? Such questions should be analyzed by teachers because their responses to and perceptions of these issues will profoundly affect their pedagogical behavior.

Descriptive terms applied to particular segments of the population must be analyzed with full awareness of their psychological implications. Labels affect behavior. John C. Condon, Jr., admonished: "It is clear that when one tries to live up to a label he has given himself, he limits his activities to those the label has prescribed. It is possible, however, for persons to change the character of behavior of other persons and institutions by labelling them and then by acting on the label."[75] To affirm, for example, that some students suffer from economic deprivation should not imply that such students are also "culturally disadvantaged." Some ethnic communities, although plagued by poverty, in fact surpass more affluent communities in cultural richness. Stereotyping individuals according to socioeconomic class or ethnic group may decrease a teacher's ability to perceive cultural diversity. Ethnic differences among individuals who share the burden of poverty may have greater pedagogical implications than their shared poverty. To assume that poverty creates a similarity of perceptual fields in those individuals who are so burdened, is inaccurate and militates against the teacher's ability to understand the variety of culturally patterned behaviors. Conversely, ethnic identity does not imply that all members of the ethnic grouping share similar perceptions. Although socioeconomic position and ethnic identity affect behavior, other factors, such as childrearing patterns, family relationships, religious convictions, and ideological perspectives, also play an important role in shaping an individual's perceptual world. An individual's group memberships are elements of his or her identity, but they do not subsume his or her individuality. On the contrary, they are inextricably interwoven with it. Teachers must always deal with individual students as individuals and not as symbols of groups. The principle of individual differences serves as the best guide for understanding human behavior.

Just as teachers must ensure that all children and youth within the public schools develop an awareness and appreciation of shared national

[75] John C. Condon, Jr., *Semantics and Communication* (New York: The Macmillan Company, 1966), pp. 60–61.

elements, so they also must ensure that characteristics which identify only a segment of the national collectivity are not presented as though they were shared by all members of the collectivity. Such misinformation serves to disrupt rather than enhance national unity. It may be true, for example, that a majority of the American citizenry are theists, but assertions that equate theism with Americanism are inaccurate and divisive for they tend to inhibit the identification processes of atheists and agnostics who *are*, in fact, American nationals. Similarly, if the national collectivity is viewed as Caucasian, nonCaucasians will be prevented from sustaining or developing national group identity and will seek membership in another national grouping which does not humiliate them by exclusion.

Both old and new symbols of national identity must be reanalyzed continuously. Those symbols and descriptions which are inaccurate must be labeled as such and must be counterbalanced by accurate symbolism and description.

To affirm that national symbols must reflect the realities shared by all members of the collectivity also implies that omissions in the symbol system may be divisive. The pantheon of national heroes, for example, must represent the ethnic, religious, and racial pluralism in the United States. Similarly, the elements of the national heritage presented in schools must reflect the diversity of influences which have formed the present American social order. Historical accounts that trace all American institutions to European antecedents, for example, are not only divisive but also inaccurate.

### Conclusion

Diverse factors may provide bases for a national *society* as well as elements of national consensus, but in the final analysis the development of a national community rests upon the freely given loyalty of the citizenry. *Feelings cannot be commanded.* Loyalty, as a cognitive and affective expression of man devolves from a sense of group identity. Phrases such as "love it or leave it" or "America for Americans" not only are trite and unimaginative but also reveal a false conception of patriotism and national loyalty. Attempting to change what one sincerely believes to be wrong in the nation, far from being a sign of disloyalty, is often a sign of loving concern for one's country.

Although national cohesion depends upon an awareness of the "shared elements" within the national collectivity, such shared elements need not imply *consensus*. Consensus permits sharing, but it need not be the force of cohesion. Although ethnic origin, religion, and race are not shared elements in a pluralistic society, the American citizenry does share significant identifiable characteristics. The creeds as expressed in the Constitution and in the Declaration of Independence are essential elements of Americanism. The shared geographical space and its diversity also provide a basis for national identity. Similarly, the American dream, with its integral belief in the extension of liberty and equality, in the value of education, in progress, and in the creative powers of the individual provides meaningful basis for national identity. National symbols such as the flag, the Statue of Liberty, and the Liberty Bell serve as concrete representations of national shared beliefs.

Even though the search for intranational concord and international peace appears to be a "Penelope's web "—a process which goes on continuously without ever achieving its aims—nationalists continue to hope that it will be through Nationalism that such goals will be achieved. Like all ideologists, they often fail to recognize that any ideology driven to excess is destructive to man. The history of the twentieth century has revealed some of those excesses. It remains to be seen whether nationalists can direct Nationalism toward international amity and intranational brotherhood.

### Suggested Readings

ARIELI, YEHOSHUA. *Individualism and Nationalism in American Ideology.* Baltimore: Penguin Books, Inc., 1966.

CARR, EDWARD H. *Nationalism and After.* New York: The Macmillan Company, 1945.

CREMIN, LAWRENCE A. *The American Common School: An Historical Conception.* New York: Bureau of Publications, Teachers College, Columbia University, 1962.

CURTI, MERLE E. *The Growth of American Thought.* New York: Harper & Row, Publishers, 1951 (1st ed.) and 1964 (3rd ed.).

DEUTSCH, KARL W. *Nationalism and Social Communication: An Inquiry into the Foundations of Nationality.* New York: John Wiley & Sons, Inc., 1953.

DOOB, LEONARD W. *Patriotism and Nationalism: Their Psychological Foundations.* New Haven: Yale University Press, 1964.

GLAZER, NATHAN, and DANIEL MOYNIHAN. *Beyond the Melting Pot.* Cambridge: M.I.T. Press, 1967.

GORDON, MILTON M. *Assimilation in American Life: The Role of Race, Religion and National Origins.* New York: Oxford University Press, 1964.

HAYES, CARLTON J. H. *Essays on Nationalism.* New York: The Macmillan Company, 1937.

HERTZ, FREDERICK. *Nationality in History and Politics: A Psychology and Sociology of National Sentiment and Nationalism.* London: Routledge & Kegan Paul, Ltd., 1951.

KEDOURIE, ELIE. *Nationalism.* London: Hutchinson and Co., 1961.

KOHN, HANS. *American Nationalism: A Study in Its Origins and Background.* New York: The Macmillan Company, 1961.

MINOGUE, KENNETH R. *Nationalism.* New York: Basic Books, Inc., 1967.

TOCQUEVILLE, ALEXIS DE. *Democracy in America,* trans. Phillips Bradley. New York: Random House, Publishers, Inc., 1945.

ZNANIECKI, FLORIAN. *Modern Nationalities: A Sociological Study.* Urbana: University of Illinois Press, 1952.

*Chapter 6*

# PROGRESSIVISM
## The Ideology of the Facilitator

### Introduction

Few concepts in America have attained the degree of reverance accorded the idea of progress. Indeed, an attack upon progress would be a greater heresy than William James' denunciation of the "bitch goddess SUCCESS." Citizens may disagree about what specific phenomenon may in fact be labeled progress, or, more likely, they may differ about the proper method to be utilized to implement progress, but they generally agree that progress is a worthwhile and necessary ideal.

The idea of progress is especially cherished in this country because of its compatability with the "American dream." Lacking any traditional feudal caste system, America developed a reputation as the land of opportunity. Americans generally deny the existence of a rigid class system yet accept as inevitable a society structured in terms of hierarchal status. For the individual interested in upward mobility, the belief that "tomorrow will be better than today" is quite desirable, if not essential. As C. Wright Mills observed, "Notions of progress are congenial to those who are rising in the scale of position and income." [1] Adherents to the doctrine of progress readily affirm that if present conditions are less than favorable, they are at least better than previous ones, and it is only a question of time until the situation will improve. Thus, the belief in progress is a faith in the future, which also entails a rejection of the past and an acceptance of the present. The idea of progress would be meaningless to a peasant whose life style has not altered for generations, vile to the aristocrat whose society is becoming increasingly democratized, and threatening to the factory worker whose job is eliminated by automation.

Since the industrial revolution, the idea of progress has been closely related to and generally equated with technological development. Yet its implications encompass a much broader scope. As Charles A. Beard noted, the ". . . idea of progress is both an interpretation of history and

---

[1] C. Wright Mills, "The Professional Ideology of Social Pathologists," in *Power, Politics and People* (New York: Ballantine Books, Inc., n.d.), p. 546.

a philosophy of action." [2] As an interpretation of history, progress implies change and growth in a desirable direction; as a philosophy of action it assumes man's ability to control this change. The theory of progress entails belief in the potentiality of moral and/or social perfectibility.

The concept of progress was a significant element in Social Darwinism. As we saw in Chapter IV, Herbert Spencer and William Graham Sumner, using Darwin's theory of evolution, developed a social theory that served as a rationale for the competitive business enterprise of the nineteenth century. Adherents of Social Darwinism believed that it was indeed the "fittest" who survived the economic struggle for existence, and that mankind was destined to improve with each generation. Because the Social Darwinists felt that the law of natural selection led inevitably to progress they generally advocated a "hands-off" policy in the area of social reform. They argued that Darwinian evolution was a natural law—perfect, inevitable, and immutable—and that man's intervention into the workings of nature could result only in chaos. As a consequence of this "laissez-faire" belief, adherents to Social Darwinism generally were considered to be political conservatives.

Contemporary American political and economic conservatism should not be confused with the traditional concept of conservatism as it developed in the nineteenth century. Traditional conservatism generally entails one form or another of cultural elitism and focuses upon organic social relationships; it is grounded upon tradition rather than progress. Representatives of traditional conservatism include Edmund Burke, Henry Adams, Alexis de Tocqueville, José Ortega y Gasset, and George Santayana. Indeed, Peter Viereck, one of the leading spokesman for traditional conservatism, described modern American conservatism as "a petrified right-wing of atomistic *laissez-faire* liberalism." [3]

Although the sort of belief in progress manifested in Social Darwinism is largely associated solely with political or economic conservatism, the theory of progress itself does not automatically eventuate in conservative political and social ideas. Indeed, the immense popularity of the concept results, in part, from its compatibility with various political belief systems. Liberals, for example, generally emphasize the idea of progress in the realm of social reform. As Charles Frankel noted in his definition of the conventional view of liberalism,

> To hold the liberal view of history meant to believe in "progress." It meant to believe that man could better his condition indefinitely by the application of his intelligence to his affairs; it meant, further, to measure

[2] Charles A. Beard, Introduction to J. B. Bury, *The Idea of Progress* (New York: Dover Publications, Inc., 1955), p. xl.
[3] Peter Viereck, *Conservatism* (Princeton, N.J.: D. Van Nostrand Company, Inc., 1956), p. 19.

the improvement of man in secular terms, in terms of his growth in knowledge, the diminution of pain and suffering, the increase of joy, the diffusion and refinement of the civilized arts; and it meant that such improvement in the condition—and, indeed, in the nature—of man could be brought about by deliberately adopted legislative and judicial techniques which would gradually change the institutions that framed men's lives.[4]

Both radical and moderate social reformers have espoused the doctrine of progress. Socialists and romanticists such as Karl Marx and Robert Owen viewed progress within a closed theoretical system in which progressive development ultimately would reach a termination. The ends or goals of their systems are knowable and are held to be attainable. Moderate reformers, such as B. F. Skinner and John Dewey, however, have advocated an open system of social progress in which development is a continuing progress with flexible ends or goals which are determined, in part, by an experimental trial-and-error process. The focus in this case is upon the means of achieving the temporary and changing goals, rather than on one overriding goal.

Although Progressivism implies that progress is achieved through man's efforts, Progressivists do not necessarily reject the Darwinian conception of natural evolution. Some Progressivists—such as Julian Huxley and Pierre Teilhard de Chardin, for example—have developed theories which place man within a psychosocial evolutionary framework in which man can consciously influence the evolutionary process. Huxley, utilizing the phrase Evolutionary Humanism to describe his ideology, affirmed: "Quite apart from the practical function which he [man] performs in society and its collective enterprises, he can help in fulfilling human destiny by the fuller realization of his own personal possibilities. A strong and rich personality is the individual's unique and wonderful contribution to the psychosocial process." [5]

While some progressive "highbrows" adhere to the evolutionary and optimistic views of Teilhard de Chardin, progressive. "lowbrows" have attached the concept of progress to the "American Dream" and find comfort and vindication in the plethora of television series which emphasize a simplistic bourgeois view of change—a view that often unquestioningly assumes the inevitability of evolutionary progress. Others are comforted by periodic visits to the perennial local, national, and international expositions designed to popularize progress.

[4] Charles Frankel, *The Case for Modern Man* (Boston: Beacon Press, 1955), p. 36.
  [5] Julian Huxley, "The Humanist Frame," in *The Humanist Frame* (New York: Harper & Row, Publishers, Inc., 1961), p. 27.

### Progressivism: An Eclectic Ideology

Progressivism is the ideology most attuned to modern liberalism. Adherents to Progressivism are men of moderate persuasion—men of compromise whose ideological stance bespeaks an eclectic approach to life. Progressivism, therefore, shares elements with some of the ideologies discussed previously. Maintaining an optimistic faith in science and technology, Progressivism is compatible with Scientism. Indeed, progressivists generally attempt to apply the techniques of science to the solution of social problems, seeking in this way to furnish the material rewards of technology to an expanding number of individuals. They differ from adherents to Scientism, however, in their rejection of strict linear de-developments, the technique of Scientism, the progressivists employ a create what they term a "humanistic science." To accomplish this task, scientific methodology must be future-oriented and must include a concern for personal involvement and social responsibility. Rather than seeking to understand antecedent causes in order to be able to predict future developments, the technique of Scientism, the progressivists employ a future-oriented method by which the consequences of experimental social action can be verified they believe, with the same degree of precision attained by researchers in the physical sciences.

Progressivism forms an alliance with Romanticism in its disregard for the rigid formalism of institutional structures and its rejection of traditionalism as a basis of social norms. Progressivists, however, do not share the romanticist's desire to destroy institutions; they plan, instead, to improve or humanize them. Where progressivists believe that the validity of social norms can be determined by arriving at a concensus judgment concerning their consequences, romanticists believe in an ethical system which is rooted to rebellion and individual choice. According to progressivists, romanticists are impractical, socially irresponsible idealists. Similarly, progressivists place little value on Utopian schemes, especially when such plans are divorced from practical, systematically developed means. In addition, they differ from the romanticist in their fear of disorder, subjectivity, emotionalism, and unrestricted spontaneity; "law and order" and social responsibility must prevail over anarchy. Like the romanticists, they place an emphasis on creativity and freedom, but they believe that creativity must be rational and controlled—and freedom, as they are quick to point out, is not license. A. S. Neill, a hero of the progressivists, states this distinction clearly:

> . . . freedom in my school is, do what you like as long as you don't interfere with somebody else. . . . If a child doesn't want to study mathe-

matics, its nobody's business; it's his own. But if he wants to play a trumpet when other people are sleeping, that's everybody's business. That's license.[6]

Progressivists generally find the ideology of Puritanism attractive because it is moralistic and contains the elements of individual responsibility, order, and community. The rhetoric of the progressive President Theodore Roosevelt, in his puritanically titled document "A Confession of Faith," exemplified the similarity between the two ideologies: we are engaged in an "endless crusade against wrong. . . . [G]ird yourself for this great new fight in the never-ending warfare for the good for humankind. . . . We stand at Armageddon, and we battle for the Lord." [7] Similarly, John Dewey, writing in a way reminiscent of the Puritan Brahmins, stated:

> The world in which most of us live is a world in which everyone has a calling and occupation, something to do. Some are managers and others are subordinates. But the great thing for one as the other is that each shall have had an education which enables him to see within his daily work all there is in it of large an human significance.[8]

Ultimately however, progressivists reject the system of Puritanism, which they associate with dogmatism, extremism, and indoctrination. Instead, they stress persuasion, relativity, moderation, and reflective thought. Morality for the progressivist is situational and must be evaluated in a secular, social context. Thus for the progressivist moral issues lack the harshness and rigidity one generally associates with the principled absoluteness of Puritanism. As stated previously, progressivists seek group sanction for moral action and social norms, whereas the legitimacy of Puritan authority is based upon tradition and divinity.

The ideology of Progressivism has never appealed to the disillusioned, the cynic, or the radical; nor has it ever been viewed as a means of solving the universal and fundamental problems of man. Its approach is situational and piecemeal. During the rebellious decade of the sixties, the more disillusioned and radical youth rejected Progressivism as an ideology of social reform. The disillusioned turned "inward" to find comfort in exploring the "otherworld" thoughts of Zen and the romantic poets or the philosophical ideas of absurdity expressed by some existentialists. The radical youth, on the other hand, became disciples of puritans such as Herbert Marcuse and Mao Tse-Tung, or proponents of the

---

[6] Mario Montessori and A. S. Neill: "A Dialogue," *Redbook* (December 1964), p. 92. Copyright © 1964 McCall Corp.

[7] Theodore Roosevelt, "A Confession of Faith," August 6, 1912, in *Political Thought in America*, ed. Andrew M. Scott (New York: Rinehart & Co., 1959), p. 421.

[8] John Dewey, *The School and Society* (New York: McClure, Phillips; Chicago: University of Chicago Press, 1899), pp. 38–39.

ideals expressed by rebels such as Gandhi and Thoreau. Progressivism, however, is an ideology of moderation; in times of relative stability and affluence it functions as a comfortable perspective for the liberal mentality; in times of chaos and upheaval it often ceases to function at all.

### The Doctrine of Progress

The ideology of Progressivism is rooted to the historical development of the idea of progress. In his classic study *The Idea of Progress,* J. B. Bury affirmed that belief in the doctrine of progress originated in the sixteenth century and was popularized a century later. Elements of this doctrine, however, have existed throughout the history of mankind. As early as 500 B.C., the Greek philosopher Heraclitus developed a theory which saw reality as essentially a process of constant change, although the change he envisioned did not imply progress. Refuting the doctrine of permanence espoused by Parmenides, Heraclitus declared, "You cannot step twice into the same river; for fresh waters are ever flowing in upon you." [9] Less than a century later, the Greek poet Aeschylus developed a more complete doctrine of change, one which contained definite implications for a belief in progress. In his tragedy *Prometheus Bound,* Aeschylus, a scion of the landed nobility, expressed a sympathy toward Prometheus, a hero to the modern adherents of both Progressivism and Scientism. According to Aeschylus, the gods sent their messenger Hermes and their servant of justice, the Spirit of Sheer Force, to punish Prometheus for taking fire from the heavens. He was chained to a rock and every day an eagle attacked him and tore at his liver, which regenerated itself every night so that the torture could go on forever. The connection between Aeschylus's sympathetic interpretation of the Prometheus myth and the beliefs of modern Progressivists and technocrats has been pointed out by Werner Jaeger:

> The divine power of fire was for him [Aeschylus] the concrete image of civilization. And Prometheus was the civilizing genius who explores the whole world, who makes it subservient to his will by organizing its forces, who reveals its treasures and establishes on a firm basis the groping insecure life of man.[10]

There was no concensus, however, among the early Greeks concerning the value of progress. In the eighth century B.C., Hesiod, a poet the Greeks considered second only to Homer, implied a philosophy of re-

[9] As quoted in Giorgio de Santillana, *The Origins of Scientific Thought* (New York: The New American Library of World Literature, Inc., 1961), p. 50.

[10] Werner Jaeger, *Paideia: The Ideals of Greek Culture* (New York: Oxford University Press, 1965), p. 262.

gressive history in *Works and Days*. Having been a shepherd, Hesiod, sympathized with the peasants who toiled and suffered in the "Age of Iron." This fifth among the ages of man, an age in which "might makes right" and "evil triumphs," illustrated the continuing degeneracy of mankind. The "Age of Iron" resulted from unrestrained *hybris* (pride), a lack of respect for the gods, and the continuance of war. It represented a regression from the original age, the Age of Gold, in which men lived a life of leisure characterized by cooperation, tranquility, and justice under the reign of Kronos. (One can easily see the similarity between Hesiod's version of historical change and the biblical account of man beginning with the story of Adam and Eve in the Garden of Eden.)

In his condemnation of Prometheus, Hesiod represented a reactionary form of Romanticism. The conflict between his ideological position and that of Aeschylus a few centuries later retains relevance for the continuing dilemma of modern man, for they raised the question of whether freedom and the "good life" could be equated with increased technology and man's dominance over nature. Similarly, Socrates waged a continual intellectual struggle against the increasingly popular teachings of the Sophists who equated reality with change. Socrates, of course, maintained the view that change was illusory or irrelevant because the significant ideals of truth, beauty, and justice were immutable and eternal. In contrast to the Sophists, who in many respects could be considered the progressivists of ancient Greece, Socrates was concerned about ideals (ends) and the legitimacy of power rather than about the process (means) and the utilization of power. As Jaeger pointed out, Socrates raised a classic question that continues to perplex man, a question of special relevance to progressivists:

> Are religious scepticism and indifference, and moral and metaphysical "relativism," which Plato opposed so bitterly and which made him a fierce and lifelong opponent of the sophists, essential elements of humanism? [11]

### Progressivism and the Enlightenment

Although the *Weltanschauung* of the medieval period was generally antithetical to the Progressivist ideology, the ideas of the Franciscan Friar Roger Bacon anticipated the spirit of Progressivism. In one of his most important works, *Opus Majus*, he attempted to convince Pope Clement IV of the necessity of university reform. He advocated an increased emphasis on such secular studies as astronomy, mathematics, and chemistry, stating they not only were necessary for the betterment of

[11] Jaeger, *Paideia*, p. 301.

mankind but also were indispensable for an understanding of theology and the scriptures. Although Bacon's immediate influence was doubtful, his ideas foreshadowed the coming Enlightenment. He lived as a man between two ages and his views linked the old world with the new, the medieval with the modern. The difference between these two world views has been described by the historian Carl Becker:

> Since our supreme object is to measure and master the world, we can make little use of theology, philosophy, and deductive logic—the three stately entrance ways to knowledge erected in the Middle Ages. In the course of eight centuries these disciplines have fallen from their high estate, and in their place we have enthroned history, science, and the technique of observation and measurement.[12]

The ideas of the Enlightenment philosophers strongly influenced the development of the ideology of Progressivism. The Enlightenment view was expressed in the writings of the Frenchmen Montesquieu, Voltaire, Diderot, Turgot, and Condorcet; the Englishmen Locke, Hume, and Gibbon; the Germans Kant and Liebniz; and the Americans Jefferson, Paine, and Franklin.

In his *Discourses at the Sorbonne,* Turgot, in 1750, typified the Enlightenment perspective when he presented a view of progress that has remained popular among progressivists. He asserted that progress engenders

> . . . that leisure whereby genius, relieved of the burden of caring for primal needs, emerged from the narrow sphere where they confine it and directs all its energies toward the cultivation of the sciences; hence that more vigorous and more rapid advancement of the human mind, which bears along with it all parts of society, and which, in turn, receives new energy from their perfection [13]

As Becker stated, the fundamental faith of the Enlightenment consisted of the following four principles:

> (1) man is not natively depraved; (2) the end of life is life itself, the good life on earth instead of the beatific life after death; (3) man is capable, guided solely by the light of reason and experience, of perfecting the good life on earth; and (4) the first and essential condition of the good life on earth is the freeing of men's minds from the bonds of ignorance and superstition, and of their bodies from the arbitrary oppression of the constituted social authorities.[14]

The intense and dogmatic commitment of the Enlightenment philosophers to the belief in progress was typified by the tragic tale of

[12] Carl L. Becker, *The Heavenly City of the Eighteenth-Century Philosophers* (New Haven: Yale University Press, 1932), p. 17.
[13] As quoted in Leslie Sklair, *The Sociology of Progress* (London: Routledge and Kegan Paul, Ltd., 1970), p. 19.
[14] Becker, *The Heavenly City of the Eighteenth-Century Philosophers,* p. 102.

Marquis de Condorcet. While hiding from the reign of terror that followed the French Revolution, Condorcet authored an essay entitled "The Progress of the Human Mind." The essay described the inevitability of progress and the infinite potentiality of the perfectability of man. Shortly after his essay was completed, Condorcet was captured by the revolutionary authorities and committed suicide. The fact that he could write such an essay at all under these circumstances testifies to the unflappable optimism of some adherents to the doctrine of progress, for the faith has continued regardless of wars, concentration camps, and other examples of man's inhumanity to man.

In many ways, the progressivists continued the optimistic tradition of the eighteenth-century philosophers. With the suppression of prejudice and the elimination of superstition, they believed, an enlightened populace would discover universal agreement on every important issue. In similar fashion, Socrates had believed that no one does wrong knowingly. This equation of knowledge and virtue is certainly a noble belief, especially for those engaged in formal schooling. Yet events of the twentieth century have sobered even the truest of believers. Individuals with many years of formal schooling have supported, either covertly or overtly, some of the most inhuman behavior ever perpetrated upon mankind. Wars, racism, and poverty persist and have made it increasingly difficult to believe that evil is an accident or simply the consequence of ignorance. The ethics of relativity and situationalism espoused by many progressivists illustrate the moral vagueness and naivety of their ideology. John Dewey's statement that "growth itself is the only moral 'end'," for example, typifies the weakness of progressivist morality.[15] In contrast, C. Wright Mills, a sociologist greatly influenced by the progressivist ideology, admitted this weakness. In his attempt to deal with the profundity of moral issues, Mills expressed a toughminded perspective, but perhaps one more attuned to social reality:

> . . . as philosophy and politics show, there comes a point when any solution of any "value problem" becomes: Who can kill whom? Or in peaceful civilized countries: Who can have whom put in jail? That's tough for the philosopher, but that's the way things really are.[16]

The ideology of Progressivism took the Enlightenment faith in progress and fused it with Darwin's theory of evolutionary change which enhanced the ideas of naturalism and worldly progress. The Darwinian theory secularized and scientized the Calvinistic view of predestination and determinism. In contrast to the pessimism of inevitable toil and suf-

[15] John Dewey, *Reconstruction in Philosophy* (Boston: Beacon Press, 1948), p. 177.
[16] C. Wright Mills, "Pragmatism, Politics and Religion," in *Power Politics and People*, 168.

fering inherent in Calvinism, however, the doctrine of progress made necessity a virtue. "Newness" was equated with "goodness."

With the advent of the theory of relativity in the twentieth century, the ideology of Progressivism was fully developed. It encompassed a combination of intellectual elements derived from the eighteenth, nineteenth, and twentieth centuries. The concepts dear to the hearts and minds of Progressivists include: reason (intelligence), evolution, progress, relativity, process, adjustment, change, experience, citizenship, democracy, responsibility and law.

### Progressivism and Pragmatism

Pragmatism provided the philosophical foundation for the ideology of Progressivism. The word "pragmatism" as well as the words "practice" and "practical" are etymologically related to the Greek word *praxis*, meaning action. The term "pragmatism" was first utilized and its meaning developed by the mathematician Charles S. Peirce in his articles "The Fixation of Belief" and "How to Make our Ideas Clear," which appeared in the *Popular Science Monthly* in 1877 and 1878. Rejecting the philosophic and logistic formalism of the English empiricists and the subjectivism and absolutism of the German idealists, the pragmatists, including Peirce, William James, and John Dewey, developed a scientific philosophy founded upon an experimentally verifiable method of progressive inquiry. In the words of Peirce, the pragmatic method "is no other than the experimental method by which all the successful sciences . . . have reached the degree of certainty that are severally proper to them today. . . ." [17] Echoing this sentiment, Dewey declared that "the result achieved in science is a challenge to philosophy to consider the possibility of the extension of the method of operative intelligence to direction of life in other fields." [18]

Obviously, the pragmatists were enamored with the rapidly increasing developments in science and technology that had occurred in the nineteenth century. Indeed, they sought to develop a social and ethical model analogous to that of the physical sciences. The scientific method and attitude, they believed, could be utilized to ameliorate the problems created by the impact of immigration, industrialization, and urbanization. Dewey, in his book *Reconstruction in Philosophy*, developed a rationale

[17] Charles S. Peirce, "Pragmatism in Retrospect: A Lost Formulation," in *Philosophical Writings of Peirce*, ed. Justus Buchler (New York: Dover Publications, Inc., 1955), p. 271.

[18] John Dewey, *The Quest for Certainty* (New York: G. P. Putnam's Sons, 1960), p. 169.

which would justify philosophers in engaging actively in dealing with the problems of man. Previously Karl Marx had rejected the contemplative role of the philosopher when he penned his oft-quoted directive, "The philosophers have only *interpreted* the world, in various ways; the point, however, is to *change* it." [19] Taking the same approach, Dewey condemned the "spectator's view of knowledge." In contrast to the empiricists who saw the world of reality as existing outside of man and the idealists who placed the world within man, the pragmatists asserted that man and his world were inextricably intertwined. Consequently, man did not have the choice of escape or detachment from the world, for he was interrelated with it whether he wanted to be or not. He could either acquiesce or act for the improvement of the interrelated whole, for, as Dewey asserted, ". . . while saints are engaged in introspection, burly sinners run the world." [20]

In the philosophical framework of pragmatism, the "truth" of one's actions or ideas is determined not by antecedents, whether they be "causes" or *a priori* ethical prescriptions, but by practical consequences. In the words of William James:

> Grant an idea or belief to be true, it [pragmatism] says, what concrete difference does it make in anyone's actual life? How will truth be realized? What experiences will be different from those which would obtain if the belief were false? What, in short, is the truth's cash value in experiential terms? [21]

For James, the measurement of the "cash value" was a matter for individual determination. Thus he described his system as "radical empiricism." Dewey's concept of truth, or "warranted assertability" as he later termed it, was similar to that of James—that is, what is desirable, or what ought to be done, is judged by its consequences: ". . . standards and tests of validity are found in the consequences of overt activity, not in what is fixed prior to it and independently of it." [22] To exemplify this concept, the pragmatists often alluded to biblical text "By their fruits ye shall know them." In contrast to James's individualism, however, Dewey believed the consequences should be "publicly verifiable" and judged by an "intersubjective [collective] consensus."

Because pragmatism as a philosophy is oriented to problem solving and the resolution of human social ills, it does not deal with the ultimate questions of man's destiny. Concerned with goals that are attainable—

[19] Karl Marx, "Theses on Feuerbach," in Karl Marx and Friedrich Engels, *Basic Writings on Politics and Philosophy,* ed. Lewis S. Feuer (Garden City, N.Y.: Doubleday & Company, Inc., 1959), p. 245.
[20] Dewey, *Reconstruction in Philosophy,* p. 196.
[21] William James, *Pragmatism* (New York: The World Publishing Company, 1955), p. 133.
[22] Dewey, *The Quest for Certainty,* pp. 72–73.

that is, practical—pragmatists often have ignored the existential dilemma
of man. Indeed, the long-range effects of technological progress rarely
concerned them for they are oriented to achieving realizable goals.

The philosophy of pragmatism influenced, to some degree, the principles of modern institutionalized religion. Reacting against the rigid, dogmatic authoritarianism of many religious institutions, pragmatists called
for flexibility and tolerance. In *A Common Faith* Dewey emphasized the
possibility of being "religious" without adhering to a "religion." He argued
that religious ideals were not only pedantic but also abstract, divorced
from reality, and thus irrelevant. Dewey viewed "ideas and idealism" as
"hypotheses not finalities." They "are anticipatory plans and designs which
take effect in concrete *re*-constructions of antecedent conditions of existence." Criticizing the theologians, he contended ethicals problems result
from the fact that "moral and spiritual 'leaders' have propagated the
notion that ideal ends may be cultivated in isolation from 'material'
means. . . ." [23]

Certainly much of the criticism against American religious institutions was warranted. With few exceptions (such as Walter Raushchenbusch and the Social Gospel movement), members of the religious
community had remained silent and detached from pressing social issues.
During times of intense social ferment religious leaders or their followers
who assumed active roles in social issues seldom receive institutional
support. Indeed, the belief in the separation of church and state generally has served to dampen any manifestations of antagonism between the
institutional representatives of these social structures. In fact, institutionalized religion generally supports government policy and corporate interests either covertly or overtly. The majority of individuals engaged in
religious activities continue to preach individual moral uplift—the saving
of souls. It is true, of course, that man cannot live by bread alone; however, without bread he cannot live at all.

The philosophy of pragmatism, with its focus upon the interrelationship between man and his environment, the unity of thought and deed,
and the necessity of experimentation, stressed the need for social activism.
The emphasis on activism and the concern for practical consequences
provided the background for pragmatism's involvement in social change.
Yet such a philosophical position, in the hands of true believers, easily
can become an anti-intellectual dogma opposed to contemplation and
theory. Similarly, the belief that truth can be judged by its practical
consequences quite easily degenerates into a rationalization for unscru-
pulous behavior, a doctrine amenable to hustlers. And finally, the pragmatist's insistence upon a methodology of problem solving results in

[23] Dewey, *The Quest for Certainty*, p. 280.

focusing only upon those problems deemed capable of being solved. Consequently, metaphysical problems concerning the nature of man and the relationship of man to God are ignored because they do not fulfill the prerequisite criteria of pragmatic testing. Yet these metaphysical topics certainly are of importance to one's ideological perspective and profoundly effect one's behavior.

### The Progressive Movement

During the latter decades of the nineteenth century the laissez-faire version of Puritanism and Social Darwinism were increasingly challenged. Numerous individuals and groups with a variety of conflicting interests were united by a common thread of criticism against the "rugged individualism" of the Protestant ethic and demanded or acquiesced to the need for collective action. The assumption that the pursuit of individual self-interest would result in the "common good" was seriously questioned on the grounds that the competitive struggle for existence, as the Social Darwinists termed it, had produced disruption and discord rather than natural harmony. Consequently, the traditional belief in individual self-interest rapidly gave way to belief in collective self-interest; and the tenor of the times became "organize or perish."

Nevertheless, individual freedom certainly remained an ideal. The means for attaining this desired end, however, was now said to emanate from collective action. Unionism gained in strength with the success of the Knights of Labor and the American Federation of Labor. The farmers of the south and midwest, previously ardent supporters of individualism, sought collective aid in the formation of the Populist party as well as of the more moderate Patrons of Husbandry (Grange) and Farmers' Alliances. Even the business community, although espousing individualism and strenuously opposing the collectivization of labor, united in the formation of the National Association of Manufacturers and the American Anti-Boycott Association. With the process of merger and the creation of trusts, collective, corporate capitalism was emerging from the earlier entrepreneurial free enterprise system.

*The Gilded Age,* so named by Mark Twain and Charles Dudley Warner was a striking parallel to the "best of times, the worst of times" described in Charles Dickens' *Tale of Two Cities.* While the prosperous nouveaux riches were indulging in what Thorstein Veblen called "conspicuous consumption," an increasing number of poor were being crowded into the decrepit and rat-infested tenement houses of the cities. Thirty-five million immigrants had heeded the call of "give us your tired, huddled masses, yearning to be free" and settled in the ghettos of the urban areas.

ln addition to the vast number of immigrants, many rural laborers, displaced by increasingly mechanized farming, were massing in the cities in search of employment. Together, these two groups, many of whom previously had never seen a city, suffered from anxiety because of the diversity of urban culture, the degradation of poverty, and the alienation resulting from the increasing impersonality and bureaucratization of urban life.

The Progressive movement was an attempt to engender the political power necessary to challenge and curb the economic power of the entrepreneurial barons. The progressivists rejected the formalistic determinism of the natural law theorists and denounced the competitive, rugged individualistic world of the Social Darwinists. In contrast to the defenders of the established order, who generally asserted that time and nature inevitably would cure social ills, the progressivists believed that legal action and government intervention would be necessary for social progress. And, in contrast to the socialist critics of capitalism who advocated public ownership of industry, the progressivists urged public support for governmental control of the privately owned business enterprise—that is, state capitalism rather than state socialism.

The Progressive movement, as it emerged and developed in the northeastern states, was dominated by the descendants of the older, socially established upper- and upper-middle-class families. Their cultural background was similar to that of many of the abolitionists. Seymour Martin Lipset described both groups as "American Tory radicals . . . who as conservatives helped to democratize the society as part of the struggle against the vulgar nouveau riche businessman." [24] Threatened by the increasing economic power of the Barons, the progressivists sought to regain the power which their families traditionally had enjoyed. Describing this status conflict, Richard Hofstadter pointed out:

> Progressivism was a mild and judicious movement, whose goal was not a sharp change in the social structure, but rather the formation of a responsible elite, which was to take charge of the popular impulse toward change and direct it into moderate and, as they would have said, "constructive" channels—a leadership occupying, as Brandeis so aptly put it, "a position of independence between the wealthy and the people, prepared to curb the excesses of either." [25]

Much of the social involvement of the Progressives has been armchair activism. Being middle- and upper-middle-class college graduates, they generally avoided direct action and accepted the more conservative roles of their professions. Often, they were men and women of words and

[24] Seymour Martin Lipset, *Political Man* (Garden City, N.Y.: Doubleday & Company, Inc., 1960), p. 319.
[25] Richard Hofstadter, *The Age of Reform From Bryan to F.D.R.* (New York: Random House, Inc., 1955), pp. 163–64.

letters—lawyers, professors, and authors. As Hofstadter stated, ". . . the Progressive mind was characteristically a journalistic mind, and . . . its characteristic contribution was that of the socially responsible reporter-reformer." [26]

The facts necessary for informed judgment, an essential element of the progressivist mentality, were provided by the more notable and controversial progressivists, the muckrakers. They received their title from President Theodore Roosevelt, himself a progressive conservative, who criticized the writers for concentrating on the "vile and debasing" aspects of man and society. Comparing them with the Man with the Muckrake in Bunyan's *Pilgrim's Progress,* he stated,

> But the man who never does anything else, who never thinks or speaks or writes, save of his feats with the muck-rake, speedily becomes, not a help to society, not an incitement to good, but one of the most potent forces for evil.[27]

Fearing that the activities of the muckrakers would generate a "backlash," he added,

> Any excess is almost sure to invite a reaction; and, unfortunately, the reaction, instead of taking the form of punishment of those guilty of the excess, is very apt to take the form either of punishment of the unoffending or of giving immunity, and even strength, to offenders.[28]

The muckraking journalists provided the evidence essential to the problem-solving mentality of the Progressive movement. The journalistic endeavors of Lincoln Steffens, Ida Tarbell, and Ray Stannard Baker on the staff of *McClure's,* one of the most widely read muckraking journals, popularized the average middle-class citizen's distrust for big business and labor. The muckrakers ridiculed the theoretical "invisible hand" that was supposed to regulate private enterprise and unmasked the deceitful rhetoric of natural law economics. They exposed the graft and ruthlessness that created the economic power of the corporate titans. Exemplifying the progressivist approach to social problems, the muckrakers sought evidence of misconduct in all areas of human existence. Their scathing attacks were directed toward both business and labor, both political bossism and local ward favoritism, both corporate strikebreaking and the disruptive tactics of union organizing. They were especially harsh on those who demonstrated a disrespect for the law whether they be Barons, union organizers, or immigrants. As progressivists they sought harmony, legality, and honesty—they were moderate, Protestant puritans. As Richard Hofstadter so aptly observed,

[26] Hofstadter, *The Age of Reform,* p. 186.
[27] Theodore Roosevelt, in *The Progressive Movement, 1900–1915,* ed. Richard Hofstadter (Englewood Cliffs, N.J.: Prentice-Hall, Inc., 1963), p. 18.
[28] Roosevelt, in *The Progressive Movement,* p. 18.

Their criticisms of American society were, in the utmost reaches, very searching and radical, but they were themselves moderate men who intended to propose no radical remedies. . . . [T]heir chief appeal was not to desperate social needs but to mass sentiments of responsibility, indignation, and guilt.[29]

The election of President Wilson in 1912 enhanced the spirit of Progressivism. The American citizens had elected an intellectual, giving the intelligentsia and/or professionals a modicum of the prestige they so eagerly sought. The liberal reform dream was shattered, however, with America's entrance into World War I. Wilson's puritanical moralism shifted from matters of peace to the problems of war. His staunch advocacy of a "war to end all wars," a war that would "make the world safe for democracy," splintered the Progressive movement. Some of the progressivists, most notably John Dewey, espoused the cause of war. At first reluctantly but later enthusiastically, Dewey promoted America's entrance into World War I and condemned the pacifist position of such Progressivists as Randolph Bourne and Jane Addams:

> The ordinary pacifist's method is like trying to avoid conflict in the use of the road by telling men to love one another, instead of by instituting a rule of the road. Until pacifism puts its faith in constructive, inventive intelligence instead of appeal to emotions and in exhortation, the disparate unorganized forces of the world will continue to develop out-breaks of violence.[30]

The pragmatist philosophy focused upon the necessity of maintaining harmony in means-ends relationships. Democracy as an end-in-view could be achieved only by democratic means. Consequently, to the critics of Progressivism, Dewey's support of the war typified the shallowness and hypocrisy of the progressivists pragmatic morality. The progressivists had urged social reform while vociferously condemning those who believed that violence and conflict were necessary elements in achieving social change; yet many of these same Progressivists advocated war to solve international problems.

"War has always been the Nemesis of the liberal tradition in America," observed the historian Richard Hofstadter.[31] Indeed, the collapse of the Progressive movement following World War I has been repeated throughout the history of liberal political thought. The quasi-missionary mentality of progressive reformers has resulted in their acquiescence to or advocacy of imperialistic policies of government intervention into international affairs, the most recent example of which is the war in South-

---

[29] Hofstadter, *The Age of Reform*, p. 196.

[30] John Dewey, "Force, Violence and Law," in *Intelligence in the Modern World: John Dewey's Philosophy*, ed. Joseph Ratnu (New York: Random House, Inc., 1939), p. 495.

[31] Hofstadter, *The Age of Reform*, p. 272.

east Asia. If not actually promoted by liberals, such ventures have received their support, and often years must pass before liberals begin to desert the ranks of the hawks to become doves.

## The Progressive Movement and Education

The educational system at the end of the nineteenth century reflected the ideology of the Progressive movement. Responding to rapid changes in the social order, the schools functioned as a "socializing" influence with the immigrants and provided an alternative to the labor market. Between 1870 and 1900, enrollment in the public schools more than doubled and the number of high schools increased twentyfold. During the same period, the number of colleges doubled and the number of state normal schools increased from twelve to 175. In addition, the length of the school term was increased and many states passed legislation making school attendance mandatory.

Traditional forms of schooling had been influenced by the methods of Johann Pestalozzi and Johann Herbart, but their impact was to be far overshadowed in the twentieth century by John Dewey with his concept of progressive education. Dewey was born in 1859, the year Darwin's *Origin of Species* was published, and by the time of his death in 1952 he had published thirty-six books and over eight hundred articles.

Faced with the problems of ever-increasing urbanization and industrialization, Dewey reiterated a faith in the common school movement and viewed education as "the fundamental method of social progress and reform." [32] He and his progressivist disciples attacked the school system on many points. In the area of psychology, they rejected any form of mind-body dualism and its educational implications—the disciplining of the mind and the transfer of training. Rote memorization and mental exercises were to be replaced by the active involvement of the student in problems that were significant to him ("learning by doing"). Accepting a modified form of Rousseau's theory developed in *Emile* and G. Stanley Hall's phylogenetic recapitulation theory, the progressivists emphasized the necessity of studying child development. In contrast to the traditionalist's belief that the child was a miniature adult, the Progressivists believed the child to be a unique type of creature. The maturation of the child, theorized Hall, mirrored the evolutionary pattern of nature. Yet, as the progressivists added, each child brought to the learning situation a vast array of previous experiences, habits, and preconceived concepts

[32] John Dewey, "My Pedagogic Creed," in *Dewey on Education*, ed. Martin S. Dworkin (New York: Teachers College, Columbia University, 1959), p. 22.

that could be utilized to further his educational growth ("individual needs").

Education, as defined by Dewey, "is that reconstruction or reorganization of experience which adds to the meaning of experience, and which increases ability to direct the course of subsequent experience."[33] Unlike the strict behaviorists with their stimulus-response theories, the progressivists pointed out that the individual does not mechanically respond to stimuli; rather, he responds to stimuli according to his previous experiences ("individual differences"). Thus, for education to be meaningful ("relevant," in modern rhetoric), it must be related to one's actual experiences in a "present" context. Education was a process of growth, not a preparation for future life. As Dewey stated,

> . . . the educational process has no end beyond itself; it is its own end; and . . . the educational process is one of continual reorganizing, reconstructing, transforming. . . . Since in reality there is nothing to which growth is relative save more growth, there is nothing to which education is subordinate, save more education.[34]

The schools, it was thought, would provide the opportunity to create miniature communities formed from the students' cooperative engagement in the practical art of problem solving. This environment would furnish the opportunity for students to engage in the practice of American democracy and would stimulate the acculturation of an increasing number of immigrant children into the "melting pot." With an emphasis on harmony and cooperation, individual differences would be acknowledged but cultural differences and competition would be minimized if not eliminated. Dewey's "cultural pluralism," for example, did not imply cultural separation or isolation. "The dangerous thing," he said, "is for each factor to isolate itself, to try to live off its past, and then to attempt to impose itself upon other elements, or, at least to keep itself intact and thus refuse to accept what other cultures have to offer, so as thereby to be transmuted into authentic Americanism."[35] Dewey's "symphony" did not include the cultural distinctions that Horace Kallen's cultural pluralism implied, but in his 1916 speech to the NEA Dewey added: "The fact is, the genuine American, the typical American, is himself a hyphenated character . . . he is international and interracial in his makeup. He is not American plus Pole or German. But the American is himself Pole-German-French-Spanish-Italian-Greek-Irish-Scandinavian-Bohemian-Jew

[33] John Dewey, *Democracy and Education* (New York: The Macmillan Company, 1916), pp. 89–90.
[34] Dewey, *Democracy and Education*, pp. 59–60.
[35] Dewey, "Nationalizing Education," *Journal of Proceedings of the Fifty-Fourth Annual Meeting of the National Education Association*, p. 185.

and so on." [36] Dewey's remarks typify the progressivist view of assimilation and explain, in part, why latter-day progressivists have supported
educational programs that emphasize ethnic identity but have withdrawn
in dismay when such programs accompanied the call for ethnic or racial
separation.

According to the progressivists, the school would be a way of life
rather than a preparation for life, and thus would eliminate the distinctions between the individual and his environment, between the school
and the society. Thus interrelationship, the progressivists believed, would
increase the relevance of education and would prevent the inherent dualism of traditional education, in which "Pupils are taught to live in two
separate worlds, one the world of out-of-school experience, the other the
world of books and lessons. Then we stupidly wonder why what is studied
in school counts so little outside." [37]

Recent concern for the "culturally deprived" and/or the "culturally
disadvantaged" reflects the "social worker" mentality of the progressivist
ideology. In contrast to the "bad seed" assumptions of Puritanism and the
"inadequate I.Q." theories of Scientism, progressivists generally focus upon
the "inferior" environmental conditions that influence the children of
minority groups. Thus, cultural pathological models have replaced individual pathological models. The progressivist recognizes that the stulti-
fying aspects of ghetto life cannot be denied and that conditions imposed
by involuntary poverty should not be romanticized, but he falls easily into
the trap of cultural imperialism. To proclaim one's environment totally
superior to another is arrogance if not racism, and it subverts any possibility of cultural pluralism. As the outraged townspeople in *The Music
Man* insist, individuals are not evil, the pool room is at fault; a boy's
band would provide a constructive alternative. Minnesota Fats, however,
would never have accepted such a proposition.

Believing in change and progress, progressivists focus upon the
future rather than the past. Believing that the social structure is in a
state of constant flux and progress, progressivists generally see little value
in focusing upon the study of history or the classics of literature. Because
they see man's knowledge as rapidly changing and expanding, progressivists generally find it difficult to delineate any specific and common
body of knowledge worthy of extended study. Consequently, Dewey and
many of the progressivist educators espoused the belief that the major
function of education should be to teach students how to think. Dewey
defined "reflective thought" as the "Active, persistent, and careful consideration of any belief or supposed form of knowledge in the light of

[36] Dewey, "Nationalizing Education," p. 185.
[37] John Dewey, *How We Think* (Boston: D. C. Heath and Company, 1933),
p. 256.

the grounds that support it and the further conclusions to which it tends. . . ." [38] Furthermore, Dewey asserted, "The function of reflective thought is, therefore, to transform a situation in which there is experienced obscurity, doubt, conflict, disturbance of some sort, into a situation that is clear, coherent, settled, harmonious." [39]

The progressivist belief that education should promote "thinking" has created several difficulties. First an individual cannot simply "think" —he must think *about* something; and progressivists could never agree on what precisely one should think about. Second, the concept of thinking as defined by Dewey focuses upon problem solving and harmonious consequences. Such a narrow definition eliminates the type of thinking that creates doubt, instigates conflict, and enhances vision—a style of thought that is becoming increasingly rare in our overly organized, technocratic society. Problem-solving techniques may cause the trains to run on time, but they seldom question whether the trains should run at all and where they should go.

Although most progressivists (with the exception of those who have allied themselves with adherents of Scientism) generally realize that students cannot be evaluated except within a wholistic framework, they have not discarded the view that evaluation is an essential aspect of the educational process. Some progressives, especially those who adhere to a felt-needs curriculum, believe that individual learners can best judge their own progress and growth; such educators generally utilize diverse forms of self-evaluation. Others believe in a form of supervised self-evaluation— a process whereby a student is *assisted* in making an honest and accurate self-evaluation. Unfortunately, this process easily can degenerate into a subtly disguised form of teacher evaluation. A third popular progressive evaluation scheme is the attempt to evaluate the "whole student." It generally involves an evaluation process in which the student participates with other individuals in arriving at an assessment of his growth. Despite the fact that this progressive form of assessment is most reliable from a theoretical point of view, it offers numerous problems. A student, for example, who "fails" an evaluation in which his whole identity is "measured" is surely in worse condition than the one who flunks a math course. What is more, attempts to evaluate the whole child require an understanding of the intricate processes of an individual's growth, an understanding which is difficult if not impossible to attain and which requires probing into a student's private world—a violation of his right to privacy. Of course, progressive evaluations of the "whole child" consume an enormous amount of time and, with school conditions as they are, most teachers find themselves "forced" to write "standard

[38] Dewey, *How We Think*, p. 9.
[39] Dewey, *How We Think*, pp. 100–101.

evaluations" which closely resemble the products of traditional grading systems.

After John Dewey had furnished American education with a somewhat systematic and complex pedagogical philosophy, his general orientation to the educational process was popularized by William Heard Kilpatrick of Teachers College, Columbia University. Arriving at Teachers College at a time when it served as the most important center for the development of the ideology of Educationism, Kilpatrick exerted profound influence upon the educational world. His pedagogical creed, although rooted to Dewey's pragmatism, moved further into the child-centered approach to education. His "Project Method" was based upon student-designed goals and plans. Indeed, the establishment of goals, planning, and evaluation processes was viewed as the central aspect of the educational endeavor. Teachers were to serve as facilitators and resource personnel. Preexisting subject matter increasingly was rejected as inhibitive to the creative activity of the child. Followers of Kilpatrick ignored Dewey's scholarly attempts to develop a modernized curriculum that could serve both the learner and his society.

All progressivists agree that the learner should be actively involved in the instructional task. They disagree, however, as to the role and function of the student in this process and the nature of his needs. While some progressivists, for example, believe that professionals should design the educational programs after consulting with students and/or conducting research to ascertain their needs and desires, others have advocated an educational program that is completely designed by students and results from their "felt needs."

### The Politics of Progressivism

Many authors of historical analyses consider the Progressive and Populist movements as a unified whole. The differences between the two factions, however, are significant. While the populists generally were rural, blue-collar workers and farmers, the progressivists were urban, middle-class professionals. In contrast to the populists, many of whom maintained an agrarian mythology based upon a utopian view of the past, the progressivists espoused a cosmopolitan view oriented toward the future.

From the viewpoint of the traditionally defined liberal-conservative continuum, progressivists generally have been more liberal on social issues than the populists. They usually support the basic civil liberties as well as the "four freedoms." Even protests and demonstrations are considered valuable political tools if they are kept within the legal framework and are conducted peacefully. This attitude, however, usually results in a dilemma for both the progressivists and the more militant activists. As men of words and letters, the progressivists express the need for social change and provide the social legitimation for such change. When the call for change results in militant, direct action, however, the progressivist is faced with a critical choice. Fearing disorder and possible violence, he usually reverts back to the side of "law and order." Unlike the conservator of the established order who generally is consistent in his attitude and behavior, the progressivist is less predictable and the militant can never fully count on his continued support. Even many of the "muckraking" journalists attacked the militancy of the more radical activists and the "vices of the masses" as vehemently as they had attacked the excesses of the robber barons.

If progressivists are generally more liberal on social issues than populists, they are usually more conservative on political and economic issues. In areas related to politics the progressivists have emphasized "qualifications" and "standards," and thus their support of civil service reforms has replaced "spoil systems" appointments with a type of "meritocracy" that has resulted in the exclusion of many members of lower socioeconomic groups from government positions because they fail to meet the preestablished "qualifications." Similarly, in contrast to the more radical populists, the progressivists adhere to a moderate economic policy. The populists traditionally have viewed the world as divided into two economic factions —the "robbers and the robbed," the "parasitic non-producers and the producers"—whereas the economic perspective of the progressivists does not entail any concern for an equalization of status or wealth. As David Donald so aptly observed,

> They did not support radical economic reforms because they . . . had no serious quarrel with the capitalistic system of private ownership and control of property. What they did question and what they did rue, was the transfer of leadership to the wrong groups in society, and their appeal for reform was a strident call for their own class to re-exert its former social dominance.[40]

Progressivists generally would agree with Theodore Roosevelt's oft-quoted assertion: "We draw the line against misconduct, not against wealth." [41] Refusing to support any program advocating a radical redistribution of wealth, they have proposed economic programs that gear salary to "merit" and have advocated minimum wage requirements, unemployment benefits, and workmen's compensation.

[40] David Donald, *Lincoln Reconsidered* (New York: Alfred A. Knopf, 1956), p. 34.
[41] Theodore Roosevelt, "A Confession of Faith," August 6, 1912, in *Political Thought in America*, p. 421.

When analyzing the positions taken by progressivists on social, political, and economic issues, it is necessary to consider the fact that they usually are members of the middle and upper-middle classes and generally are engaged in the professions. Consequently, from a standpoint of self-interest, they tend to be concerned about issues of free speech, freedom of the press, and academic freedom. In a way, thy can "afford" to be liberal on such social issues as integrated housing and employment of minorities inasmuch as their own positions are not threatened. That is, their housing areas, situated in upper-income districts, are quite unlikely to be integrated either socioeconomically or racially. In like manner, they are less threatened than blue-collar workers by job insecurity. Politically, the professionalization of politics and public employment provided them with increased opportunity for advancement and the legitimization of a culturally skewed meritocracy. Economically, the progressivists could have little quarrel with a corporate-capitalistic system from which they had benefited—not as much, perhaps, as they desired, but enough to keep them from any consideration of radical change.

The progressivist generally considers himself an independent when it comes to political candidates and issues. Denying party allegience and believing he is "above politics" on social issues, he often wishes to vote for the "most qualified candidate." His stand on specific issues is one of "principle" and is determined only after thoughtful consideration by weighing the pros and cons of each issue. His decision generally reflects a moderate position, a desire to be "fair to both sides," and a concern for the "public good." In the European tradition of politics such citizens would be Social Democrats; in this country they have supported "liberal" third-party movements and comprise, for example, a majority of the members in the Liberal Party of New York. In national politics their conservatism has been expressed in their support of Hoover after the defeat of the Progressive Party's Robert LaFollette (who himself had bolted the GOP), Theodore Roosevelt, and Eugene McCarthy.

Certainly one of the most common characteristics of progressivists was their desire for planned change and social reform. Believing that such reform was compatible with progress, they sought social change "within the system." They reject not only the dogmatic rigidity of the conservatives' rugged competition and individualism, but also the inevitability of class conflict and proleterian revolution proposed by radical socialists. Social change was obviously necessary, but for the progressivists this change was to occur in an evolutionary manner through experimentation and directed by responsible men of reason.

The progressivists emphasized centralism and "social justice" as paternalistic alternatives to grass-roots power. Their programs, however, were too often condescending and tinged with guilt or self-righteousness.

For example, progressivist historians, political scientists, and teachers generally have fervently condemned political bossism, forgetting or failing to see that such a structure serves a function for many individuals outside the mainstream of the social order. As Hofstadter noted, "The immigrant, in short, looked to politics not for the realization of high principles but for concrete and personal gains, and he sought these gains through personal relationships." [42] The truth of this observation was cogently expressed by an immigrant as he related his attitude toward a ward boss: "I think that there's got to be in every ward a guy that any bloke can go to when he's in trouble and get help—not justice and the law, but help, no matter what he's done." [43] "Good" "clean," government as an alternative to "corruption" and "political bossism" too often represents a concern for "standards" and "qualifications" and an insensitive disregard for the representatives of those on the bottom of the socioeconomic ladder. What is more, their concern for harmony and order too often masked a squeamishness about the "masses" and a failure to recognize the power of the entrenched interests of the large industrialists.

The progressivists emphasized the need for government involvement in the solution of social ills. Their success, in part, enhanced the emergence of a corporate welfare state. The New Deal, the Fair Deal, the New Frontier, and the Great Society were promoted by progressivists who in turn reaped many of the rewards that resulted from such programs. Many of the progressivists were called upon to organize research projects, and to develop and administer new agencies and institutions. Progressivists as *professional innovators* working in teams with technocrats, often are subsidized by government and corporate agencies to engage in research and development (R and D). Many of these teams have formed "think tank" agencies that serve to develop experimental models for various types of social change. Such social "reforms" may include anything from creating models for future cities to developing intricate methods of riot control and public surveillance.

By using the progressivists' own pragmatic test, one may discover that many if not most of their programs are invalid; that is, they do not work. Of course, to the true believers among the progressivists, the failure of the experimental projects is attributed to reactionary attitudes of the public or to "mismanagement." Regardless of the failure, however, they believe that the solution to the problem is to be found through further experimentation, more funds, and more projects; and, of course, more qualified individuals in management.

The belief in the necessity of a stronger, more centralized govern-

---

[42] Hofstadter, *The Age of Reform*, p. 183.

[43] As quoted in Oscar Handlin, *The Uprooted* (New York: Grosset & Dunlap, 1951), p. 212.

ment taking an active role in the management of social reform has been popularized considerably since the heyday of Progressivism, and the idea that political power increasingly should be utilized to control economic power has received wide currency. This progressivist atmosphere encouraged the emergence of private welfare capitalism and the legitimization of governmental business regulation. The consequences of the progressivist-supported policy of increased governmental powers of regulation and control have included child labor laws, food and drug laws regarding inspection and regulation, protection of natural resources, income and inheritance taxes, unemployment benefits and workmen's compensation, minimum wage and hour laws, legally established health and safety standards, and the power of initiative, referendum, and recall.

One major dilemma resulting from the progressivist policy, however, has been its tendency to foster a coalition between a powerful government and the large corporations. The formation of such a coalition was analyzed by C. Wright Mills in *The Power Elite* and a warning concerning the danger of such a coalition was expressed by even such a moderate conservative politician as the late President Eisenhower. Behind these warnings lay the fact that Ivy League education (social power), established wealth (social and economic power), and government position (political power) have joined forces in many areas, giving rise to a potentially dangerous monopoly of power in the hands of a startlingly small elite.

### The Critics of Progressivism

The Progressive movement, as Morton White has pointed out, was a "revolt against formalism." [44] In many areas of human endeavor the progressivists were strongly influential in the destruction of rigid traditional beliefs. In law, Oliver Wendell Holmes, Jr., and Louis Brandeis viewed the legal structure as a means for the amelioration of social problems. They believed that the legal structure was not based on a static body of immutable principles, but was a changing process, interrelated with current social issues. In history and economics, Charles Beard, James Harvey Robinson, and Thorstein Veblen, rejecting chronologies and natural orders attempted to illuminate present-day phenomena by developing theories to account for human desires and actions in problematic situations. And in philosophy and education, Dewey attacked traditional views, roles, and functions because of their irrelevance to a society in a process of continous social change.

Their success in the "revolt against formalism can hardly be ques-

[44] Morton White, *Social Thought in America: The Revolt Against Formalism* (Boston: Beacon Press, 1947).

tioned. Indeed, critics from both the right and the left of the political spectrum agree that the progressivist influence has had a significant effect on our views concerning man and society. Critics on the right continue to attack the social activism of the courts and the "permissiveness" of both the legal structure and the educational institutions; they continue to decry the lack of "objectivity" in history and the loss of the "free-enterprise" spirit of economic policy. Critics on the left, while agreeing with many of the progressivist goals, generally have attacked the progressivists for their hesitancy and moderation on social issues and for their piecemeal approach and their squeamishness about conflict and violence. Critics from both the left and the right have ridiculed the progressivist tendency toward groupism and glad-handism. Perhaps the most devastating criticism of Progressivism has been directed toward their blandness—their inability to create enthusiasm and stimulate vision. "You grow," Randolph Bourne proclaimed, "but your spirit never jumps out of your skin to go on wild adventures." [45] To the charge of blandness is added the charge that progressivists place an excessive emphasis upon technique while failing to demonstrate an adequate concern for morality. By focusing on technique, progressivists form a powerful alliance with the technocrats of Scientism. Dewey's "scientific method," for example, generally has become a "how-to" cookbook in many science classrooms throughout the country. Its major thrust is not discovery but a simplified form of verification. Such a superficial approach to the problems of science, however, serves only to promote a naive faith in the ability of Scientism to solve all the problems of mankind.

Although Progressivism was a revolt against formalism, it focused its criticism upon the formalism that is rooted to tradition and ignored the formalism that results from the utilization of institutions to resolve human problems. Progressivist reformers, for example, continually organize action groups to deal with various problems. Their action groups, however, often become ends in themselves. They spend inordinate amounts of time in designing organizational patterns and in planning alternate reform programs. Generally concerned with the process of reform rather than actual achievements, progressivists reveal an almost saintly patience with program planning and a penchant for petty bickering. Robert's Rules of Parliamentary Procedure serves as a bible for progressivists, who are perpetually forming and reforming themselves in permanent or ad hoc committees, commissions, and agencies.

Although they focus upon the process of decision-making rather than upon its outcome, however, progressivists are not devoid of value commitments. Indeed, progressivists adhere to a complex value system from which they rarely deviate; they can be as uncompromising as puri-

[45] Randolph Bourne, "The Twilight of Idols," in *The Seven Arts* (October 1917), p. 10.

tans. G. K. Chesterton lucidly observed: "Nobody can be progressive without being doctrinal; I might almost say that nobody can be progressive without being infallible—at any rate without believing in some infallibility. For progress by its very name indicates a direction; and the moment we become doubtful about the direction, we become to the same degree doubtful about progress." [46] An imposed direction can be as limiting and repressive as an imposed goal.

Even though progressivist educators may reject the traditional teacher-centered educational process, they often continue to reveal the characteristics of the authoritarian personality. All too often, progressive educational programs featuring "freewheeling" student involvement in setting educational goals turn out in fact to be a subtle system through which a teacher utilizes his influence to achieve his own previously defined program. And what is true of the individual teacher is even more true of the institution he serves. Numerous progressive schools sustain a myth that students possess the ultimate democratic power to establish educational goals and school policies, whereas in fact the "important decisions" result from choices made by headmasters or teachers. Serving on a "policy committee" does not necessarily mean setting policy. Indeed, it may be a subtle way in which cunning autocrats neutralize opposition to their policies by legitimizing them with a "contrived consensus" achieved through clever manipulation.

This form of pseudo-democracy can be disastrous to a society which is struggling to actualize a democratic creed. Adults who have been educated within such an educational system easily may be convinced that their numerous committees, policy boards, and action programs are affecting government or institutional policies, when in fact they are only enabling autocratic leaders to more effectively make and implement the important decisions. Such involvement may serve to generate a sense of participation, but a sense of participation is no substitute for participation itself. So long as pseudo-democracy is served up as a soothing pap provided by individuals who are too authoritarian and officious to believe in the democratic process, the hope for genuine democracy will be under sentence of death.

### Factionalism in Progressive Education: Child-Centered, Creative Expressionism; Social Reconstructionism; and Life-Adjustment

As noted previously, America's involvement in World War I divided the Progressive Movement and shattered national unity. The quick pas-

[46] As quoted in Edgar W. Knight, *Progress and Educational Perspective* (New York: The Macmillan Company, 1942), pp. 115–16.

sage and zealous enforcement of the Espionage Act (1917) and the Sedition Act (1918), and the establishment of a large-scale, prowar propaganda agency, the Committee of Public Information, exemplified the government's intense effort to create unity from diversity. The noted psychologist J. McKeen Cattell was dismissed from Columbia University for his moderate antiwar position. One week later the eminent historian Charles A. Beard, having been harassed for condoning an antiwar speaker and expressing outrage at Cattell's dismissal, resigned from Columbia University. The Socialist leader Eugene Debs was one of countless individuals who received jail sentences for expressing antiwar sentiments and behavior. Such severe restrictions on civil liberties reduced President Wilson's "New Freedom" to a trite slogan.

The decade of the twenties witnessed the repudiation of both Wilsonianism and the Progressive movement. The American citizenry generally rejected both foreign intervention abroad and social reform at home. Wilson had linked the war with the Progressive movement, and when the war ended the Progressive movement ended. The practical idealism of the Progressivist had been shifted from peace to war, but failed to survive reconversion to peacetime conditions. While Ernest Hemingway's *Farewell to Arms* represented many Americans' disillusionment with war, John Chamberlain's *Farewell to Reform* depicted a similar sentiment with regard to social change. Warren G. Harding was elected president as the voters sought a "return to normalcy."

Social conservatism, political apathy, and economic prosperity characterized the Roaring Twenties. Superpatriotism, or nativism, was typified in the numerous hunts for communists, the dreadful activities of the Ku Klux Klan, and the executions of Nicola Sacco and Bartolomeo Vanzetti. The postwar hysteria for conformity was reflected in the passage of the Lusk Laws, requiring loyalty oaths from teachers in New York, and the prosecution of John T. Scopes for teaching evolution in the public schools of Dayton, Tennessee. The majority of Americans, however, were not participants in these extreme reactionary activities. They generally lived lives of hedonistic pleasure, participating in the consumerism of postwar prosperity—a life style antithetical to the ideals of progressive social reform.

Reflecting the apolitical attitudes of the Roaring Twenties, the Progressive Education Association (PEA), founded in 1919, ignored the political and social reform-oriented Progressivism of John Dewey and focused upon "creative expression" and a child-centered approach. Stanwood Cobb, a young man interested in educational reform, and a small group of upper-middle-class philanthropists, private school headmasters, and teachers created the organization based upon the following principles: "Freedom to Develop Naturally; Interest, the Motive of All Work; The Teacher a Guide, Not a Task-Master; Scientific Study of Pupil Development; Greater Attention to All that Affects the Child's Physical Development; Co-operation Between School and Home to Meet the Needs of Child-Life; and The Progressive School a Leader in Educational Movements." [47] The handbook for this popular new trend in progressive education was written by Harold Rugg and Ann Shumaker in 1928. Entitled *The Child-Centered School,* it expresses an attitude that has remained valid for one faction of the progressivist educators. The new approach to education, the authors asserted:

> assumes that every child is endowed with the capacity to express himself, and that this innate capacity is immensely worth cultivating. The pupil is placed in an atmosphere conducive to self-expression in every aspect. Some will create with words, others with light. Some will express themselves through the body in the dance; others will model, carve, shape their idea in plastic materials. Still others will find expression through oral languages and some through an integrated physical, emotional dramatic gesture. But whatever the route, the medium, the materials—each one has some capacity for expression.[48]

Rugg's first book, *Statistical Methods Applied to Education* (1917) reflected his original academic training in engineering, the behavioral sciences, and mathematics. After the war, working for Teachers College as Director of Research for the newly established Lincoln School, Rugg's interest turned to the bohemian life of Greenwich Village. There he was influenced by the romanticists, the cynics, and the disillusioned rebels who were involved in developing an elitist philosophy of freedom and protest against Puritanism, Babbittry, and materialism. Many members of this circle previously had been engaged in or had sympathized with the Progressive movement. Disillusioned with the prospects of social reform, however, they turned inward and sought the inner, spiritual freedom they associated with the creative artist. Their criticism generally reflected a contempt for the Philistinism of the masses—a contempt typified in the writings of H. L. Mencken and Irving Babbitt. In general, their critique of the American scene was cultural rather than political or economic.

The progressivists' disregard for social and political reform was one of the factors that contributed to Dewey's refusal to accept the position of the first Honorary President of the Progressive Education Association. The appointment in his stead of Charles W. Eliot, the president of Harvard, was an appropriate choice, however, at least insofar as it reflected the progressivist desire for prestige and tendency toward elitism. Eliot, as we shall see in Chapter VII, had espoused the belief that the public

[47] *Progressive Education: A Quarterly Review of the Newer Tendencies in Education* (April 1924), p. 1.
[48] Harold Rugg and Ann Shumaker, *The Child-Centered School* (New York: World Book Company, 1928), p. 63.

schools should function to "select and sort" students according to their "probable destinies," for as he saw it, the schools' role of equalizing and unifying was outmoded if not impossible. Although Eliot could not be termed a progressivist, his attitudes exemplified the Brahmin trend which, perhaps unintentionally, leaned toward elitism, showed a willingness to accept a more rigid class system, and demonstrated a marked lack of concern for economic, political, and social reform.

The apolitical ethos of the twenties was shattered by the Great Depression. Herbert Hoover, in his inaugural address of March 1929, had proclaimed, "I have no fears for the future of our country. It is bright with hope." Six months later, the stock market collapsed. Emerging from the chaos of the depression, the social reconstructionist faction of the progressive education movement expressed the need for developing a social consciousness among educators and students. Led by such progressivists as George Counts and Theodore Brameld, the social reconstructionists proposed that schools become the major institutions for directing social change and restructuring society. In his booklet *Dare the Schools Build a New Social Order?* (1932), Counts expressed his continued support of progressive education but castigated those "liberal-minded, upper-middle-class" members who had failed to adhere to any theory of social reconstruction and had accepted unquestioningly the "child-centered, creative self-expression" approach to education. Pulling no punches, he admonished,

> If Progressive Education is to be genuinely progressive it must emancipate itself from the influence of this class, face squarely and courageously every social issue, come to grips with life in all of its stark reality, establish an organic relation with the community, develop a realistic and comprehensive theory of welfare, fashion a compelling and challenging vision of human destiny, and become less frightened than it is today at the bogies of *imposition* and *indoctrination*. In a word, Progressive Education cannot place its trust in a child-centered school.[49]

The sometimes bitter conflict on the question of social involvement within the Progressive movement has never been resolved and re-emerges periodically, depending upon social conditions. The ferment of the sixties, for example, witnessed a resurgence of social reconstruction as many professional educators and students became involved in social reform activities. Many students, even those who were only moderately progressive, expressed social commitment by joining the Peace Corps and VISTA and working for political candidates. The more radical progressivists engaged in demonstrations, voter registration drives, and the establishment of po-

---

[49] George S. Counts, "Dare the School Build a New Social Order?" (1932), in *Social History of American Education,* Volume II: *1860 to the Present,* ed. Rena L. Vassar (Chicago: Rand McNally & Company, 1965), p. 277.

liticized free schools in the south. Some programs at the national conventions of educators bespoke a concern for social issues among intellectuals. The late sixties and the early seventies, however, provide a striking historical parallel with the decade following World War I, for the social reform movement of the sixties, encouraged to an extent by presidents John F. Kennedy and Lyndon B. Johnson, was shattered by America's involvement in southeast Asia. Progressivists, divided over the war, engaged in political infighting and the election of President Nixon, like the election of Harding, represented a "return to normalcy."

Numerous individuals, disillusioned by the continuance of the war and the failure to institute significant social change, have reverted to a focus upon "personal growth and development." The moderates pursue their personal interests while the more dedicated progressivisits are searching for inner freedom and creative self-expression. Indeed, sentiments remarkably similar to those expressed by Rugg and Schumacher in 1928 have become increasingly popular in the seventies as new schools, free schools, and experimental schools have emerged across the nation. Social criticism, if it exists at all, is directed toward the Puritanism of the "unliberated" lower-middle-class "straight" people. Many modern progressivists have proclaimed that the country is in the midst of a cultural revolution, an attitude that echoes the ethos of the twenties, in which cultural criticism generally replaced economic and/or political critiques. "Doing one's own thing" is hardly compatible with social reform or revolution.

From an ideological perspective, the child-centered progressivists tend toward Romanticism. Unlike their earlier counterparts, modern child-centered progressivists in private schools generally reject elements of Scientism. Those in public schools, however, accept the Scientism implicit in the study of child development, turning to it in the hope that it will provide them with an evaluative technique for accountability. The focus upon "groupism" and the acceptance of formal institutions among child-centered progressivists distinguish their attitude from the more rebellious and anti-institutional attitudes of Romanticism, for child-centered progressivists distinctly are not romanticists.

If child-centered Progressivism is often confused with Romanticism, so social-reconstruction Progressivism tends to be mistakenly equated with revolutionary Puritanism. Social reconstruction differs from Puritanism in its lack of zealousness, rigidity, and radicalism. Social reconstructionists may be social reformers but they are not revolutionaries. They generally maintain a practical political position and, working within the system, attempt to institute what they believe to be responsible and reasonable social changes. Social reconstructionists fit quite comfortably into the progressive tradition as it emerged in the late nineteenth century.

The third major function of progressive education, the life-adjustment movement, was formally organized in 1945. At the national convention of the National Society for the Promotion of Industrial Education (NSPIE), a resolution proposed by Dr. Charles Prosser was unanimously adopted. The resolution read, in part,

> . . . the vocational school of the community will be better able to prepare twenty percent of the youth of secondary school age for entrance upon desirable skilled occupations; and the high school will continue to prepare another twenty percent for entrance to college. We do not believe that the remaining sixty percent of our youth of secondary school age will receive the life adjustment training they need and to which they are entitled as American citizens—unless and until the administrators of public education with the assistance of the vocational education leaders formulate a similar program for this group.[50]

In contrast to the child-centered approach, which appealed generally to the hearts and minds of the upper-middle class whose "probable destinies" rested in the universities and the professions, the life-adjustment curriculum was directed toward those middle-class students who were destined to become bureaucratic functionaries—clerks, secretaries, and salesmen. In terms of the labor market, these previously "forgotten Americans" were to be prepared for the demands of an increasingly consumer- and service-oriented, white-collar society. In place of preparing students for factory work, the previous focus of vocational education, the life-adjustment educators directed their major effort toward the preparation of white-collar employees, individuals involved in the "people business"; that is, employees who serve and manipulate people rather than producing goods. To develop this other-directed, market-place personality the schools would stress not only the basic skills of reading and writing, but more importantly, the development of the personal characteristics that exemplify the organization man. These mannerisms include, as television commercials reiterate, the use of "proper" speech, dress, manners, cleanliness, deodorants, and oral antiseptics. As Willie Loman, the salesman in Arthur Miller's play admonished his sons, 'You have to be liked, well liked; that's what it takes to get ahead today.'

The attitudes and life style of the organization man reflect the ambiguity inherent in the newly emerging corporate society—a society in which there are more personal relationships which are increasingly impersonal. Intimate primary relationships are rapidly being replaced by superficial friendships. Such a social situation creates a demand for individuals who can "relate well with others," yet maintain a personal detachment; who can remain flexible in his personal views, yet retain a

[50] United States Office of Education, *Life Adjustment Education for Every Youth* (Washington: Office of Education, n.d.), p. 15.

sense of loyalty to his organization. As the leadership of the life-adjust-ment program asserted, "The aim of life adjustment education is to de-velop an individual who achieves reasonable compromise between his own aspiration, attainment and happiness and the welfare of society as a whole." [51]

To achieve their goal, proponents of life adjustment utilized nu-merous booklets published by Science Research Associates, Inc. Reflect-ing the attitudes espoused in Dale Carnegie's immensely popular book *How to Win Friends and Influence People* (1937), the booklets empha-sized the importance of meeting the desires of "others" by adapting one's personality to changing group pressures. Included among the many titles and maxims were the following: *Clubs Are Fun; How to Get Along With Others* ("Pretend to be interested, and listen, anyway"); *Getting Along With Others* ("Hermits and recluses have always been considered strange, abnormal"), and *Your Heredity* ("Happy, well-adjusted people are made, not born"). Sprinkled throughout this material were numerous "Friend-ship Quizzes" and "Personality Tests."

In the mid-1950s, a decade after the birth of the life-adjustment movement, this "new education" and new life style was bombarded with criticism by individuals representing a variety of viewpoints. The Soviet Union's successful launching of Sputnik provided the stimulus for intense criticism from the scientific establishment as well as from anticommunist cold warriors. Led by such men as Admiral Hyman Rickover and Max Rafferty and supported by the country's anticommunist sentiment, the critics condemned progressive education for its failure to maintain tradi-tional academic standards, its disregard for moral discipline, and its ne-glect of patriotic concern. Critics with as widely divergent sociopolitical views as Ayn Rand and David Riesman agreed in their distaste for the groupism and conformity of the life-adjustment approach. Perhaps the critics' views were best summarized in the title of Arthur Bestor's book, *Educational Wastelands*. Few critics of Progressivism, however, meant to propose a return to the stark realities of Calvinism or Social Darwinism, yet, the intransigence of some progressivists has forced some critics to adopt extreme positions. The progressivists have tended to ignore valid and insightful criticism, thus betraying the element of inflexibility inherent in their own ideology.

The influence of progressive education cannot be minimized. In-deed, the progressivist focus upon personal interaction and growth, group activity, and social responsibility was responsible, in part, for the decline of the rigid competitive individualism of nineteenth-century Puritanism.

[51] U.S. Office of Education, *Report of the Commission on Life Adjustment Educ. for Youth to the National Conference* (Washington: Federal Security Agency, 1950), p. 110.

In addition, Progressivism enhanced the emergence of the corporate, technological society. The life style of the progressivist gained national attention and popularity in the mid-1950s when books such as William H. Whyte's *The Organization Man,* David Riesman's *The Lonely Crowd,* and A. D. Spectorsky's *The Exurbanites* depicted the life style of "the man in the gray flannel suit" who inhabited the rapidly expanding suburbs. This image—part stereotype, part reality—persisted relatively unchallenged for a decade.

The civil rights movement for fair housing, attempts to create racial balance in the schools by busing, and court decisions concerning property tax are factors that have directed the society's attention toward the socioeconomic stratification of the suburbs. The inhabitants of many suburban housing developments, especially those nearest the city, are not white-collar "organization men"; many are Catholic and of Eastern European origin rather than WASPs. The majority are blue-collar working class and share the value structure generally associated with their socioeconomic class; that is, they retain many of the values associated with the Protestant Ethic. For the white steelworker who lives in an inexpensive housing development on the outskirts of Gary, Indiana, formal schooling is decidedly *not* a means of attaining creative self-expression, life adjustment, or social reconstruction. On the contrary, he supports the public (or parochial) schools because he continues to believe that they are the means through which his child will escape from the steel mills. This conflict concerning educational philosophy was noted by Arthur B. Shostak:

> School policy, the transitional suburb's most divisive controversy, separates the modernists (mostly white-collarites) from the fundamentalists (mostly blue-collarites). The area blue-collarites, already struggling with the suburb's heavy tax burden, are often willing to settle for large classes, split sessions, comparatively low salary schedules, and a traditional, non-experimental curriculum.[52]

Disagreement with the goals of progressive education has also been voiced by many blacks living in urban areas. A large number of black educators and community members view formal schooling as a preparation for their competitive struggle in "white society." The more "militant" members express a desire to developing "Black awareness" and "Black power" with the intent of controlling their destinies. Consequently, many blacks want to see the emphasis on the "three R's" and discipline rather than on finger painting and personality development.

Progressive education from its inception has been associated with the middle-class, especially the upper-middle-class, schools. Although its

[52] Arthur B. Shostak, *Blue-Collar Life* (New York: Random House, Inc., 1969), p. 120.

impact has been felt throughout the system of American public education, progressive education's greatest influence has been found in private schools or the quasi-private schools of suburbia.

### Neo-Progressivism: Issues and Education

While the spirit of Progressivism lingered in American society, it gradually was traditionalized by the inexorable pressures of institutional life. Similarly, America had changed. In the 1950s it faced a vicious technological competition with the Soviet Union, leading various patriots to call for moral, mental, and emotional discipline. The ugly head of nativism appeared during the McCarthy era to challenge educators who focused upon innovation and social planning. Progressive organizations such as the international New Education Fellowship were viewed with suspicion by superpatriots.

Progressivism in education gradually assumed a nonthreatening image as a result of the general rejection of its social reconstructionist stance. Many progressive educators changed their methods and no longer differed significantly from their traditional counterparts. The life-and-death polemical battles over the role of the school in society at large gave place in the 1950s and early sixties to moderate methodological debates concerning the nature of the structure of knowledge, the use of media in schools, techniques of teaching, and the nature of professionalism. Except for a handful of Old Progressives, who were politely applauded, and an occasional insecure neophyte professional, who was tolerantly observed, few speakers at national conventions reflected the progressive concern for child-centered education or social reconstruction.

With the social ferment of the sixties, however, the educational world reacted with uncharacteristic vigor. Progressivism re-emerged, speaking a new language. The advocates of mental and behavioral discipline, such as Admiral Rickover and Jerome Bruner, were barely audible as new critics—Neo-Progressives such as Harold Taylor and John Holt—rocked the educational world with their calls for a student-centered education that would help to democratize the social order. Taylor admonished: "There is nobility and strength in the lovely old words 'fraternity,' 'equality,' 'liberty and justice for all'—and the university is the place where these words can become names for the living experience of those within its environs. Unless the reality of that experience is to be found there, it is unlikely to be found in the larger world." [53] His statement is almost a paraphrase of Boyd Bode's call in 1933: "Consequently the school must

[53] Harold Taylor, *Students without Teachers* (New York: McGraw-Hill Book Company, 1969).

bė transformed into a place where pupils go, not primarily to acquire knowledge, but to carry on a way of life. That is, the school is to be regarded as, first of all, an ideal community in which pupils get practice in cooperation, in self-government, and in the application of intelligence to difficulties or problems that may arise." [54] Indeed, Harold Taylor's numerous popular essays concerning education in the United States reflect the concerns of the great progressivists of bygone days such as William Heard Kilpatrick, John Lawrence Childs, and Boyd Henry Bode.

Charles Frankel, in a speech honoring Kilpatrick on his ninety-third birthday, praised this spirited reformer-teacher but raised important questions concerning some of his pedagogical assumptions. Frankel's doubts are applicable to a major thread of the progressive ideology and are helpful in understanding some of the current innovations in education. He questioned Kilpatrick's automatic acceptance of cooperativeness and his rejection of competitiveness. "In fact," Frankel admonished, "neither competition nor cooperation can be called either good or bad unless the particular context in which the judgment is made is specified. Obstinacy was a virtue in Socrates, and the petty officials who carried our orders in Nazi concentration camps cannot be faulted for lack of cooperativeness." [55] He also warned against the danger of rejecting traditional views of authority while failing to appreciate the forms of group pressures that may inhibit creative individuality. What is more Frankel noted that Kilpatrick's naive view concerning the nature of integration in a group "encouraged the implausible belief that a process known as 'group thinking' can take place in which there are no elements of politics, power, leadership, and submission to senior authority. At its worst, such an idea can be simply a cloak for the manipulation of the child." [56]

The progressive strand that focuses upon group activity and cooperativeness can easily degenerate into a form of groupism and gladhandism whereby an individual's uniqueness is suppressed by group pressure. The life-adjustment movement in education during the decade between 1945 and 1955 reflected this focus upon social and psychological adjustment. Children frequently were exposed to a doctrine which questioned the value of independence and the puritan spirit of the struggle for excellence. Some youngsters were admonished to remember the happy Indian tribe that believed: "All the members of the group work together for the good of all. And any person who tries to be different by being

---

[54] Boyde Bode, "The Confusion in Present-Day Education," in *The Educational Frontier,* ed. William Kilpatrick (New York: D. Appleton-Century Company, 1933), p. 19.

[55] Charles Frankel, "Appearance and Reality in Kilpatrick's Philosophy," *Teachers College Record,* LXVI, No. 4 (1965), 355.

[56] Frankel, "Appearance and Reality in Kilpatrick's Philosophy," p. 358.

'better' is not being a good citizen." [57] In a pamphlet entitled *Getting Along with Others,* children were given the negative example of a girl named Grace: "Lacking the social skills for making friends, Grace works hard for good grades." [58]

Some of the more recent attempts to promote cooperativeness and intra group concord, labeled with such elusive phrases as "encounter group" or "sensitivity session," degenerate in the hands of inexperienced and immature leaders into a form of groupism which bestows the laudatory epithet "self-actualized" on those individuals who express syrupy and banal "lovingness," while those who are perhaps too independent or too secure to succumb to or to need this sort of gladhandism are criticized for being unable to expose their inner fears to others. Thus the encounter group attempts to impose its own rules on those who come in contact with it, and it can be every bit as authoritative as the social institutions to which it is supposed to be an alternative. Carl Rogers warned of this distortion of the encounter group process when he pointed out that members of a group tend to

> feel they have learned the "rules of the game," and they subtly or openly try to impose these rules on newcomers. Thus, instead of promoting true expressiveness and spontaneity, they endeavor to substitute new rules for old—to make members feel guilty in that they are not expressing feelings, are reluctant to voice criticism or hostility, are talking about situations outside the group relationship, or are fearful of revealing themselves. These old pros seem to be attempting to substitute a new tyranny in interpersonal relationships in the place of older, conventional restrictions. To me this is a perversion of the true group process. [59]

The same process that is going on in the relatively insulated world of encounter groups is also going on in modern corporate society at large. In such a society, characterized as it is by vast bureaucratic structures, the necessity for the management of interrelated and interdependent factions may increase to a point of obsession. Efficiency demands harmony, and the price for efficiency and harmony is quite often individual freedom. Indeed, the encounter group member often bears a striking resemblance to what Whyte calls the "organization man" and what Riesman calls the "other-directed" personality. Riesman's analysis of conformity, in fact, is applicable to all three. "This mode of keeping in touch with others," he writes, "permits a close behavioral conformity, not through

[57] National Forum Staff, *High School Life* (Chicago: National Forum Inc., 1946), p. 59.

[58] Helen Shacter, *Getting Along with Others* (Chicago: Science Research Associates, Inc., 1949).

[59] Carl R. Rogers, "The Process of the Basic Encounter Group," in *Challenges of Humanistic Psychology,* ed. James F. T. Bugental (New York: McGraw-Hill Book Company, 1967), p. 274.

drill in behavior itself, . . . but rather through an exceptional sensitivity to the actions and wishes of others." [60]

This enormous threat to individual liberty was illustrated in a frightening statement by Lawrence Tirnauer. In an article entitled "The Future of Encounter Groups," Tirnauer, a psychologist, noted the practical relationship between the "human potential movement" and corporate social life: "It is not uncommon, for example, to discover that after an encounter group session, where the need for self-aggrandizement and destructive competitiveness are low, a business group can make important decisions about policy and planning much more rapidly, and with much less of the usual hassle that goes into such decisions." [61] Looking to the future, he noted:

> There will be a questing for ways to make the growth experience (with its emphasis on honesty, directness, openness, interdependence, etc.) relevant to our total culture, community, and society. We will discover that dissension and disease in any part of our culture affect all of us adversely, and that concern for the welfare of our total population is no maudlin "humanism," but hard core pragmatics. Just as one tense individual in a group affects the morale of an entire group, so alienation in any part of our culture affects us all. [62]

The "encounter movement" is in some ways analogous to the romanticists' search for authenticity. The dilemma of the progressive orientation to creative liberation, which tries to achieve communal sharing within a democratic framework, is revealed in the encounter process, for the associative and individual aspects of a person are not easily bridged. For all its diverse emphases, the encounter movement has one consistent theme in its rejection of the puritan and technocratic view of man. Its essential dogma is its faith in the goodness of the self-actualized man and its recognition of the need to remove the dehumanizing or oppressive forces that result from the socializing process. It is not surprising that *insecure* puritans, *bland* adherents of Scientism, and *super*nationalists all have mounted campaigns against the movement, for its personalism sets it in opposition to Puritanism, Scientism, and Nationalism.

Many of the attacks on progressivism have been based on ignorance or fear, but many others have raised valid points. Thus Frankel, for example, wondered about the importance progressivism places on the processes of thinking and valuing at the expense of intellectual discipline and external authority. He warned: "When we tell our children that they are

[60] David Riesman, *The Lonely Crowd* (New Haven: Yale University Press, 1950), pp. 21–22.

[61] Lawrence Tirnauer, "The Future of Encounter Groups," *The Futurist*, V, No. 2 (1971), p. 59.

[62] Tirnauer, "The Future of Encounter Groups," pp. 59–60.

on their own and must simply work out their own system, we do not free them to think for themselves; we simply leave them without rules to guide them or limits to reassure them." [63] His observation relates directly to the observation in Chapter IV on the difference between the guilt-oriented puritan child and the anxiety-prone progressive child. Thrown into the quandary of having to make ethical choices without a sound moral foundation, progressive children may exhibit the symptoms of alienation and/or apathy. Similarly, child-centered education, if drawn to its extreme position of a felt-needs curriculum, may reveal an insensitive and possibly fatal disregard for social problems. Should a racist student, for example, who does not feel that he is a racist and who does not want to deal with the issues of racism, be allowed to leave an educational institution without confronting the issue?

Of course, all child-centered progressive educationists do not advocate a felt-needs curriculum. Some progressivists, for example, have sought to design a curriculum which would deal with the major problems confronting human beings during their development and with the relation between individual needs and the needs of the society. In *Developing a Curriculum for Modern Living*, Stratemeyer, Forkner, McKim, and Passow attempted to bridge the gap between a learner's needs and a democratic society's expectations by focusing upon the persistent life situations confronted by an individual throughout his lifetime: "A curriculum in which the learner and society are brought into relationship is one in which the daily life concerns of children and youth are seen as aspects of persistent life situations with which all members of society must be able to deal." [64]

Because the progressivists focus upon process and change in an age of technological change, they too often become victims of the cult of newness. Recent educational innovations implemented in diverse community schools, private experimental schools, and some public schools reveal that much of the innovation heralded as "new" is in fact quite similar to previous progressive educational plans. Many of these "new schools," for example, are not unlike the schools described by John and Evelyn Dewey in their book *Schools of To-Morrow*, published in 1915. Although the terminology has changed, the emphases have remained the same. The tragedy that results from the progressivists' lack of interest in the past and their disenchantment with the present is that they often are doomed to relive the errors of the past. Numerous recent educational programs, for example, are confronting unnecessary problems because pro-

[63] Frankel, "Appearance and Reality in Kilpatrick's Philosophy," p. 357.
[64] Florence B. Stratemeyer *et al.*, *Developing a Curriculum for Modern Living* (New York: Bureau of Publications, Teachers College, Columbia University, 1957), p. 117.

gram planners have failed to study previous attempts at innovation. Experimental schools were designed before the present decade—some in urban settings, others oriented to agrarian life; some focused upon social reconstruction, others emphasizing creative self-expression; some failures and some successes. Unfortunately, recent innovators generally have ignored these past experiments and noble efforts remain hidden in the archives of libraries.

The necessity of change, many progressivists believe, results from the failure of various social norms and institutions to "progress" at the same rate as technological development. This view, commonly titled the cultural lag theory and associated with the sociologist William F. Ogburn, contains the congruent elements that serve to unify the ideologies of Progressivism and Scientism. Awed by the accomplishments in technology, progressivists attempt to emulate the techniques of the physical sciences in their efforts to solve the social problems they believe are created by cultural lag. In addition, the degree of achieved technological development is used as a standard to which social conditions must adjust.

Although rapid technological change obviously creates some social disruption, the cultural lag theory tends to obscure moral and political issues implicit in such change. As C. Wright Mills insightfully observed,

> It involves a positive evaluation of Science and of orderly progressive change; in brief, it is a liberal continuation of The Enlightenment with its full rationalism, its messianic and now politically naïve admration of physical science as a model of thinking and action, and of the conception of time as progress.[65]

Because these implications are seldom examined by proponents of the cultural lag theory, technological predictions tend to become social and moral imperatives. Rather than perceiving potential technological developments as questions requiring value judgments, such developments are viewed not only as inevitable but also as worthwhile. When these developments produce problems, the problems are seen as the result of man's failure to adjust to technological inevitabilities, rather than as the result of the technology itself.

Recently, proponents of the cultural lag theory, neo-progressivists, and technocrats all have adopted the concept of futurism. In an address to the First General Assembly of the World Future Society in 1971, Ian H. Wilson revealed the close relationship between Scientism and future-oriented Progressivism (Futurism) when he admonished his listeners to avoid the pitfalls of Romanticism. Calling for definitions of goals as well as research into the processes of institutional change, he warned:

[65] C. Wright Mills, *The Sociological Imagination* (New York: Grove Press, Inc., 1959), p. 89.

The answer, my friends, is not blowin' in the wind; we will not find it in the Beatles' magical mystery tour; it will not come to us with the dawning of the Age of Aquarius or the onset of Consciousness III. Indeed, if we rely on the presumed panacea of Charles Reich's phenomenon, we shall more likely experience the groaning than the greening of America. The developing tensions in our society cannot wait that long.[66]

Wilson typifies the modern futurists who, armed with such material as Alvin Toeffler's *Future Shock, The Futurist* magazine, and *The Bulletin of Atomic Scientists*, espouse, often apocalyptically, the necessity of preparing for the adjustment to scientific and technological prophecies. Those who accept futurism are destined to inherit the new world; those who question it are branded ill-informed or hopeless reactionary. By accepting technological determinism, however, futurists fail to examine the values inherent in decisions concerning various technological developments— values that are determined by the various social, political, and economic forces in the society. In a rapidly expanding technological society, such a limited perspective of reality represents a major threat to the freedom and dignity of man.

The cultural lag theory also has been used to explain the currently acknowledged problems in the area of ecology. In fact, the ecological movement has emerged as one of the most popular issues in recent decades, in part because of its ability to appeal to a variety of ideological perspectives. For Puritanism, the ecological movement provides a concern for thrift and cleanliness; for Scientism, the potential for research and development; and, for Romanticism, a rationale for preindustrial utopianism. The ecological movement is especially attractive to neo-progressivists, for it provides the rationale for personal involvement and social activism at the same time as it evokes a demand for social responsibility. By approaching the issue of ecology in terms of personal exhortation and collective guilt, the progressivists unify the populace. Such an approach, however, generally fails to analyze the economic and political implications of ecological issues and thus fails to threaten the vested interests of the powerful corporate forces. Consequently, the ecological movement, approached from this perspective, can retain its popularity in the school systems because it is not seen as a threat by powerful vested interests. By focusing on individual, personal responsibility rather than on the inherent evils of technology or on the power of the corporate structure, the concern for ecology is reduced to a "safe" issue. And, like most "safe" issues, it is characterized by banality and superficiality.

Throughout the history of the American educational system, critics

[66] Ian H. Wilson, "The New Reformation: Changing Values and Institutional Goals," *The Futurist*, V, No. 3 (1971), p. 108.

have emerged periodically to condemn the schools for being irrelevant. With the emergence of the industrial system in the eighteenth and nineteenth centuries, it was subjects such as the classical languages of Greek and Latin which were criticized for this reason. Spokesmen for the emerging industrial middle class in the eighteenth century, such as Benjamin Franklin, severely criticized the curricula of their day because of their impracticality—that is, their lack of usefulness to individuals interested in commerce or the trades. During the latter part of the nineteenth century and the early twentieth century, similar criticism was expressed by educational activists who formed the vanguard of the Progressive movement. In their terms, the trouble with the schools was that they were authoritarian. They called for a child-centered educational program which would be designed according to the perceived needs, often viewed as felt-needs, of the students.

Pedagogical arguments concerning the relevant bases for curriculum design continue unabated to this day. The decade of the seventies began with a call by numerous educational reformers for schools to change their programs and to design curricula which would emphasize direct involvement in resolving social problems. Although few individuals within educational circles advocate the development of mental discipline or the training of the will as valid educational objectives, the call for more rigorous academic discipline has been sounded by academicians who view the neo-progressivist influence on the educational programs as an expression of anti-intellectualism and as an escape from the fundamental issues which confront man as man.

Aided by the traditional American belief in progress, the progressivists strongly enhanced the legitimacy of social change or reform, making social action a respectable, if not admirable, calling. Indeed, the Establishment is termed "liberal." Just as few politicians would campaign on a platform of maintaining the status quo or few companies would promote last year's products, few teachers or administrators would advocate holding the line on changes in school organization and curriculum. Rhetorically, at least, the overwhelming majority of educators are progressive. They prefer meaningful experiences over rote memorization, the development of the whole child as opposed to strict cognitive learning, and the need to meet individual needs and to understand individual differences.

Difficulties arise, however, when one attempts to distinguish between rhetoric and reality. Decades have passed since the philosophical foundations of progressive education were originally developed. During that period some of the theories and concepts have acquired new meanings while others have become abstract and vague. Consequently, while many teachers may adhere in principle to the tenets of progressive education, their actualization of these principles in behavior takes quite diverse forms.

### Conclusion

Since its inception, the ideology of Progressivism has been plagued by the problems engendered by such concepts as direction, progress, change, and growth. These concepts require a fixed point of reference, without which they become meaningless. Without a standard, how can one determine if the many educational innovations during the past decades were valuable or merely trite gimmicks and contrived artifices? How does one judge the educational value of an experience? It is easy enough to measure certain types of experiences quantitatively, but can they be evaluated qualitatively? How can one distinguish between superficial, irrelevant change and meaningful, significant change? These questions are further complicated by the influence of the media and the emergence of the public relations and advertising industries. These factors contribute to an increasing emphasis upon style or form with less regard to substance. Consequently change, like beauty, is likely to be in the eyes of the beholder, in addition to being in the hands of the promoter. In McLuhanesque fashion, the medium is the message. It may be as difficult to distinguish between the "new curriculum" and the "old curriculum" as it is between the new improved soap and its predecessor.

Certainly another contributing factor to the emphasis upon change and/or the appearance of change has been the immense influx of money into projects and experimental programs. Successful grantsmanship enhances the prestige of the university and furthers the careers of academic entrepreneurs. When asked how one evaluates the success or failure of projects, an experienced colleague responded that they neither succeed nor fail; they simply exist or do not exist.

The neo-progressives of the sixties and seventies differ markedly in style from their predecessors in the Progressive Era. First, their language and behavior reflect the volatile climate of their time and is often immoderate, colorful, and uncompromising. Progressivists such as Dewey, Kilpatrick, Bode, and Stratemeyer, on the other hand, reflected a remarkable degree of moderation, professionalism, and social grace. Secondly, although the old progressives attempted numerous experimental private school ventures, they preserved a faith in the public school ideal; recent neo-progressives, in contrast, generally would agree with Edgar Friedenberg's conviction that compulsory school attendance laws violate the civil liberties of the adolescent population, and would support legislation which would channel educational funds into nonpublic experimental programs.

A third major difference between the neo-progressives and the old-progressives is their pattern of alliances. Reflecting the changing character of the society, neo-progressives are prone to ally themselves with cultural nationalists and romanticists rather than with internationalists or adherents of Scientism. Few neo-progressivists are active in international organizations. Unlike their predecessors, however, many of them have actively involved themselves in the various calls for the development of ethnic identity.

A fourth difference between the two progressive movements is their psychological orientation. The Progressive Era in education following World War I reflected America's excitement concerning the importation of Freudian psychology to our shores. As Freudian psychology was popularized in the twenties, it became the puritan ideology known as Freudianism. The progressive rebellion against formalism which exploded during the sixties, however, was directed against the repressive view of man expressed by Freud. Even Erich Fromm, a neo-Freudian, popularized a view that was more hopeful and, as Friedenberg pointed out, reflected more closely the thinking of the saintly Martin Buber than that of Freud.

Latter-day progressivists generally have accepted the view of man popularized under the label "third force" psychology. The father of this humanistic psychology, Abraham H. Maslow, contrasted it with previous views when he wrote: "The key concepts in the newer dynamic psychology are spontaneity, release, naturalness, self-choice, self-acceptance, impulse-awareness, gratification of basic needs. They *used* to be control, inhibition, discipline, training, shaping, on the principle that the depths of human nature were dangerous, evil, predatory, and ravenous." [67] The neo-progressivist adherence to a Maslowian view explains why they readily imitate the behavior of romanticists. It also explains why enclaves of progressive faculty members at large universities have witnessed the institutionalization of the styles and expressions generated in the counter-culture.

Although the neo-progressives differ from their predecessors in style, their cause remains remarkably the same. Translating the old aims into "hip" language, we still can hear echoes of the felt-needs curriculum (Do your own thing), small group involvement (T-Groups), the teaching of the whole child (individualized instruction), creative self-expression (a Happening), integrated studies (the Open Classroom), social reconstruc-

---

[67] Abraham H. Maslow, *Motivation and Personality*, 2nd ed. (New York: Harper & Row, Publishers, Inc., 1970, p. 279.

tionism (community involvement), and the Project Method (action programs). Progressivism hasn't died; indeed, it hasn't even faded away.

## Suggested Readings

BECKER, CARL L. *The Heavenly City of the Eighteenth-Century Philosophers.* New Haven: Yale University Press, 1932.

BURY, J. B. *The Idea of Progress.* New York: Dover Publications, Inc., 1955.

CREMIN, LAWRENCE A. *The Transformation of the School: Progressivism in American Education, 1876–1957.* New York: Random House, Inc., 1961.

CURTI, MERLE. *The Social Ideas of American Educators.* Paterson, N.J.: Littlefield, Adams & Co., 1959.

DEWEY, JOHN. *Democracy and Education.* New York: The Macmillan Company, 1916.

——————. *Experience and Education.* New York: The Macmillan Company, 1938.

——————. *Reconstruction in Philosophy.* Boston: Beacon Press, 1948.

EDELSTEIN, LUDWIG. *The Idea of Progress in Classical Antiquity.* Baltimore: The Johns Hopkins Press, 1967.

GOLDMAN, ERIC F. *Rendezvous with Destiny.* New York: Random House, Inc., 1952.

HOFSTADTER, RICHARD. *The Age of Reform from Bryan to F.D.R.* New York: Random House, Inc., 1955.

——————. *The Progressive Movement, 1900–1915.* Englewood Cliffs, N.J.: Prentice-Hall, Inc., 1963.

KENNEDY, GAIL, ed. *Pragmatism and American Culture.* Boston: D. C. Heath and Company, 1950.

KILPATRICK, WILLIAM H., ed. *The Educational Frontier.* New York: C. Appleton-Century Company, 1933.

RIESMAN, DAVID, NATHAN GLAZER, and REUEL DENNEY. *The Lonely Crowd.* New Haven: Yale University Press, 1950.

WHITE, MORTON. *Social Thought in America: The Revolt against Formalism.* Boston: Beacon Press, 1947.

## Chapter 7

# EDUCATIONISM
## The Ideology of the Professional

### Introduction

Ideologists continuously seek to perpetuate and creatively expand their belief systems. A faithful ideologist will defend his ideology with the intensity and care a loving parent devotes to rearing a child. Defenders of ideologies will seek through various means to increase the quality of true believers as well as the quality of ideological configurations.

Various individuals in diverse realms of social activity serve to increase the complexity and richness of ideologies. Historians, scientists, artists, economists, musicians, mass media personalities, politicians, and statesmen assist in the process of initiating, perpetuating, and creatively expanding ideological systems. Of course, many ideologies begin as philosophies. Both Thomas Acquinas and Karl Marx helped to develop elaborate philosophical systems which were integrated into social doctrines and movements and then became ideological systems. When philosophies become the cement of social groupings, they become ideologies. When the arts legitimize societal goals, they too become ideological elements. Artists such as Richard Wagner, for example, have added immeasurably to emerging Nationalisms.

Various organizations and institutions also serve to research and creatively expand ideologies. Business, economic, professional, and scholarly associations, political groups, governmental agencies, and universities often function as agencies in the development of ideological materials.

Because ideologies are "social beliefs," their dissemination is essential to their effectiveness. Even though the social environment provides ample opportunity for an individual to learn the ideological patterns which prevail within his social system, ideologists prefer that intentionally devised systematic programs be utilized to disseminate and popularize belief systems. Thus, through various deliberately designed communication networks, the popular expansion of ideologies spreads and becomes the basis of social solidarity.

Various organizational forms are utilized to popularize ideologies. While the ideologies of the established order are disseminated through the major social institutions, rebel or revolutionary ideologies are spread through "underground media." In nations where freedom of the press and freedom of speech are valued, illegitimate ideologies are often the topic of popular debate. Of course, ideological systems that conflict directly with the "unquestionable verities" of the established order rarely are "aired" publicly. Anarchism and cannibalism, for example, are rarely seriously debated in most nation-states. In societies where freedom of speech is not prized, unpopular ideological systems are disseminated through clandestine meetings and, recently, through the mimeograph revolution. In the Soviet Union, where capitalistic ideological convictions are barred from the mass media, the arts are utilized to spread revisionist ideas. A major function of the arts, especially poetry, in most societies has been to spread convictions that are antithetic to those enshrined in the ideologies of the Establishment. For this reason Plato barred poets from his Republic.

In modern nation-states, mass media and schools serve as major communication networks for the dissemination of most national ideologies. As noted in Chapter III, Romanticism is popularized through the massive recording industry.

Before the advent of Nationalism, various forms besides schools and popular media served as indoctrinating systems. During the Middle Ages in Europe, for example, monastic orders, church councils, public theological debates, and Papal pronouncements added to the Roman Catholic ideology. Clergy were the primary agents through whom the expanded system was popularized. When the Protestant reformers sought to break the hold of Catholic beliefs upon the populace, they utilized "individual interpretation" as a means of altering ideological frameworks. In the former method, the dissemination of beliefs was accomplished through a carefully supervised hierarchial system in which creeds were orally communicated. Literacy was required by few individuals but church attendance was mandatory. In the Protestant form, ideological expansion depended upon maximizing literacy. If books were to serve the function of the "priest," literacy must become a moral duty.

Of course, the written word does not automatically decrease the chances of mass oppression. Illiterate peasants are notably immune to propaganda. Indeed, the twentieth century reveals that literacy has served in great measure to increase the horrors of totalitarianism. George Orwell's Big Brother was well aware that by controlling what a people reads one largely controls the people; if they were illiterate, the dictator would lose a valuable tool.

Generally, major instructional agencies within a modern society function as defenders of national ideologies. Issues do arise, however, which illustrate that conflicts can result from ideological pluralism. During the latter part of the nineteenth century, for example, the question of religionism and the secularization of schooling was a major educational issue. The religionism of the large numbers of Roman Catholic immigrants to the United States conflicted with the secular approach to education which many Americans felt was inherent in the concept of religious freedom. The various current debates concerning the allocation of public funds to private schools also reflect the importance placed upon schooling as a means of ideological dissemination within nation-states. The volatile social conflicts that are raised by educational issues such as saluting the flag, prayer in the schools, integration and busing, the teaching of ethnic languages, and compulsory education provide a good index of the centrality of public schooling in the twentieth century. With government agencies, diverse communication media, patriotic organizations, and political interest groups serving as important agencies for popularizing national ideologies, the school has assumed a central role as an ideological agency.

The need for efficient communication systems to popularize ideologies is increased in complex societies. Because extended nation-states rarely possess cultural hegemony or homogeneity, the preservation of social solidarity must of necessity become a conscious and organized effort. Indeed, effective ideological dissemination in societies characterized by cultural pluralism is the only defense against acute anomie. Without effective ideological internalization among the diverse intranational groupings, social systems either would collapse or would remain dependent upon coercive forces.

Because of the centrality of schooling in the process of perpetuating ideological systems in extended societies, the formal educational process has become a major area of study and concern. Numerous researchers, for example, have analyzed the symbiotic relationship between the school and the society, and criticism directed against schools often is based upon the argument that they do not reflect adequately the social system—hence the call for relevance. Both conservative and liberal critics have affirmed that schools fail to prepare the young for the challenges of contemporary life. Although some educators have called for schools to serve as agents for altering the social fabric, most individuals involved in the formal educational system identify schooling as a process of socialization. Schooling, therefore, is most often viewed as one of many institutions which modern societies utilize to socialize and politicize their children, youth, and adults newly arrived by migration. Because of this symbiotic relationship, schools generally have served as subsidiary agencies designed to expand upon the education which was expected to occur within the family environment. The school thus has been viewed as supplementary to the family and ancillary to the socioeconomic system. In recent years, however, alterations in the social fabric of most modern nation-states reveal that this conception of schools as a means of supporting familial education or as a means of determining the socioeconomic status which an individual may attain during his lifetime is no longer applicable.

With the rapid extension of formal schooling, reflected by the fact that 40 percent of children aged three to five attended schools in the fall of 1971 in the United States and by the fact that college enrollment has increased to over 6 million students, formal educational institutions have become central in the life of the citizenry. Where formerly they were merely central to the process of disseminating the dominant ideology, today, schooling has become an end rather than a means.

With the increase of affluence and the expansion of automation, the role of youth has altered significantly in modern nations and the changes in the status of youth has revolutionized the role of schooling. To protect the adult work force, the longevity of youth has been extended. Thus, adult responsibilities and behavior are intentionally removed from their grasp. The extension of preadult behavior and expectations is fostered by the socioeconomic structure and does not result from major alterations in the physiological or psychological makeup of man. On the contrary, the physiological development of man has been accelerated as a result of the application of the expanded knowledge concerning human growth and health. Although puberty arrives earlier in life, mating expectations are increasingly delayed. If such a development does not necessarily create the circumstances for a sexual revolution, it certainly explains the increasing influence of spokesmen who advocate the separation of human sexual expression from the childbearing and childrearing functions.

The leisure-class status of middle-class youth today does not imply liberation from economic limitations. The youth leisure class is supported by the limited funds attained through part-time jobs or by parental allowances. Unable to join the self-sustaining work force, and prevented from enjoying luxury, the youth leisure class must be provided a social outlet for its energies. Schooling provides this outlet. Without posing a threat to the work force, it serves to create "work" for the young and thus, according to the ever-present puritanical ideology, diminishes the influence and expectations of the devil or the id.

Schooling also serves the vital function of preserving and extending youthness. In all nations, formal education is structured according to familial authority patterns; indeed, inasmuch as schools are designed according to evaluative criteria, the role of the teachers remain that of an authority figure.

Because of the centrality and universality of schooling, formal education cannot be equated to other socializing patterns for schools have become a way of life. Schooling is no longer solely a socialization process, but is also an ideational configuration in its own right—a cultural framework. Willard Waller observed:

> There are, in the school, complex rituals of personal relationships, a set of folkways, mores, and irrational sanctions, a moral code based upon them. There are games, which are sublimated wars, teams, and an elaborate set of ceremonies concerning them. There are traditions, and traditionalists waging their world-old battle against innovators. There are laws, and there is the problem of enforcing them. There is *Sittlichkeit*. There are specialized societies with a rigid structure and a limited membership. There are no reproductive groups, but there are customs regulating the relations of the sexes. All these things make up a world that is different from the world of adults.[1]

Because of the increasing size as well as influence of schooling and because institutions which develop their own mores and taboos become self-perpetuating, numerous individuals function to legitimize and perpetuate schooling. These ideologists, labeled educationists, have developed and elaborated upon the ideology which is basic to formal education, Educationism. What began as a means of disseminating ideological systems has resulted in a system with its own ideology—an ideology which increasingly is popularized and upon which the modern social system rests. This chapter is an exploration of the ideological system which has as its focus the school. Because Educationism, of necessity, is expressed within the ideological framework of the society in which it is rooted, the influences of previously analyzed ideological systems upon beliefs concerning schooling also will be probed.

### Assumptions of Educationism

Educationism as an ideology rests upon the assumption that institutional and formal education is an essential element in preserving social cohesion and in maximizing individual fulfillment and self-expression. Adherents of Educationism believe that institutional and formal education, schooling, should be compulsory for all children and youth. The ideology also includes the conviction that individuals who sustain schooling—that is, educators—are bound by ethical codes that are based upon the ideal of social service and thus are to be viewed as professionals.

Thus, Educationism implies that the educational process is improved

[1] Willard Waller, *The Sociology of Teaching* (New York: John Wiley & Sons, Inc., 1965), p. 103.

by formalism, institutionalism, and professionalism. It also implies that schooling will guarantee the creative growth of cultural systems and that the abolition of formal institutional education would lead ultimately to barbarism and a "dark age" of ignorance. The schoolhouse door, according to educationists, serves as the threshold that separates modern man from savagery.

Educationism is based upon the assumption that schooling influences positively the development of an individual's potential. Thus schooling is viewed as the intentional manipulation of human growth and development, and the lack of schooling is increasingly labeled "deprivation." The fact that numerous scholars and creative artists have emerged without formal schooling throughout history is repudiated by educationists on the grounds that these cases are simply exceptions. Indeed, the numerous critics of American education who popularized the art of debunking schooling during the sixties rarely advocated the abolition of formal, institutional education.[2] Rather, they argued for alternative schooling practices and institutions. The free school movement in the sixties reflected the progressive institutional approach to reform and not the romantic anti-institution stance. The liberation which these vociferous educational critics set as their goal generally was based upon increasing the alternatives within formal institutional settings. Even the program of "deschooling" education advocated by Ivan Illich can be misleading, for Illich desires the perpetuation of organized education in decentralized forms which differ significantly from the present public system. He does not, however, advocate the abolition of intentional interference in the process of human growth and development. Indeed, critical educationists of the mid-twentieth century seek to broaden the base upon which schooling occurs. The numerous day care centers, community workshops, paraprofessional training clinics, and compensatory educational programs serve to increase the utilization of institutional and formal educational practices. Current educational changes reveal the rapid expansion of schooling rather than the disintegration often described in popular literature.

When Educationism prevails, there exists a positive correlation between levels of formal schooling and lifetime earning power. The often avowed conviction that levels of schooling *determine* lifetime earning power is, however, questionable, for the positive correlation need not imply causality. In the first place, levels of schooling generally reflect the economic status of the student's family; thus the odds are that formal

---

[2] See, for example, Harold Taylor, *Students without Teachers* (New York: McGraw-Hill Book Company, 1969); Jonathan Kozol, *Death at an Early Age* (Boston: Houghton Mifflin Co., 1968); John Holt, *How Children Fail* (New York: Pitman Publishing Co., 1964); Paul Goodman, *Compulsory Miseducation* (New York: Horizon Press, 1964); and Edgar Z. Friedenberg, *Coming of Age in America* (New York: Random House, Inc., 1965).

schooling merely illustrates the actual as well as the projected economic life of a student.[3] Secondly, the structure of the schools themselves reflects socioeconomic realities. Whether socioeconomic segregation of school-children is intentional or *de facto,* the fact remains that the community level of aggregate personal income will influence schooling practices and schooling attitudes as well as future earning power. Children who value formal schooling, whether public or alternate, also will tend to value the qualities which enhance the opportunities for economic advancement. In viewing differences in the achievement levels of children from differing social classes, individuals should heed the cautionary remarks written by George Bernard Shaw in the preface of *The Doctor's Dilemma:* "Thus it is easy to prove that the wearing of tall hats and the carrying of um-brellas enlarges the chest, prolongs life, and confers comparative im-munity from disease; for the statistics show that the classes which use these articles are bigger, healthier, and live longer than the class which never dreams of possessing such things." [4]

A third factor which explains, in part, the positive correlation be-tween formal schooling and future earning power relates to the modern practice of requiring educational credentials in order to be accepted in particular vocational or professional occupations. The credentials rather than the schooling in such cases are in positive correlation to future earn-ing power. This form of discrimination is increasingly becoming a cause for civil rights activists. The fact that numerous employers require the formal schooling of employees in areas which do not relate to their oc-cupational tasks is reflective of the importance placed upon academic credentials regardless of their relationship to learning. Despite the fact that the importance of a particular credential is diminished as it becomes easily and universally attainable, educationists readily supply a rationale for increasing the need for greater levels of schooling. The Educational Policies Commission, an agency of the National Education Association, in 1964 affirmed:

> That every American should receive education through the high school has long been a national goal. In this regard, the United States has been pacesetter for the world. Yet, as America approaches this goal, it becomes apparent that it is not enough to meet present and future demands. The Educational Policies Commission proposes that the nation now raise its sights to make available at least two years of further education, aimed primarily at intellectual growth, for all high school graduates.[5]

[3] See, for example, Patricia Sexton, *Education and Income* (New York: The Viking Press, Inc., 1961).

[4] George Bernard Shaw, *The Doctor's Dilemma* (New York: Brentano's, 1928), p. xxvii.

[5] Educational Policies Commission, *Universal Opportunity for Education Be-yond the High School* (Washington: National Education Association, 1964), p. 219.

Within the ethos of Educationism it becomes increasingly disadvantage-
ous to diminish an individual's schooling expectations. The grandparents
of many of the present school-age children often did not complete elementary school. Instead, they joined the ever-expanding work force that
supported the emerging industrial complex. Their limited formal educational experience was viewed as a minor loss in comparison to their early
entry into occupational groups and their accumulation of vocational experience and occupational longevity. Within such a society early school
leavers were often viewed as conscientious breadwinners. Today such
leavers are viewed as "dropouts" or quitters.

Ideologists generally view opposing ideologies or antithetic values
as errors or lies, and their own ideological assumptions as facts or self-
evident truths. Educationists view their value system in such a fashion.
Indeed, defenders of illiteracy are virtually nonexistent. Those who attack
formal schooling on the grounds that on-the-job training is of greater
value are labeled by educationists as vocationalists (a term of disparage-
ment) or, worse, as dupes of the profit-hungry scrooges of the business
world.

The fact that most schools are designed to popularize ideological
assumptions that are basic to the social system or to a particular social
group does not necessarily imply that ideologists view schools as centers
of indoctrination rather than free learning. Although most ideologists will
claim that schools exist to acculturate the young, they often deny any
conscious attempt on their part to subvert free thought. Schools universally
are purported to teach truth and critical thinking. Indeed, most ideologists
believe that liberal and universal education ultimately would result in
universal consensus and that peoples should agree on social, political, and
economic ends. "Indoctrination" is usually a cunning deception resorted
to by one's enemies, whereas "education" is the tool which one's friends
utilize in defeating the lies of indoctrinators. Even though ideologists do
not agree on educational aims, most would avow that their goals are to
enable man to choose that which is correct and supportive of human
good.

Educationists also defend the conception of schooling as enhancing
individual choice and social betterment. Within such a framework, however, they continually debate the issue of what goals should serve as
directions for the educational process.

### Characteristics of Educationism

Educationism implies that education which occurs through nonformal means, such as the accidental learning that results from spontaneous play among children or the teaching and learning which occurs

within the home or through the mass media, is inferior to schooling. Educationists generally admit that the tools of the mass media are useful aids in the teaching-learning process, but they nevertheless affirm that professionally designed opportunities for learning are far more valuable and effective means of educating the young.

Admittedly, the school continues to serve as a connecting agency between the family and the larger social system. This interstitial position, however, gradually has increased in scope and importance. This extension of schooling down into the young ages and up into adulthood was occasioned by the development of the *educationist* ideology. Once the Deweyan concept of the school as a society rather than as an agency preparing youth for society was popularized, the ideology of Educationism increased in importance. Indeed, the importance of the school will continue to increase in coming decades. The advent of educational parks as well as increased federal monies for education serve to alert us to the fact that schools are becoming ends as well as means. With the recent extension of the suffrage to eighteen- and nineteen-year-olds, and with the resultant political power of college students in university towns, the school eventually may assume a major political role in American life. The educational history of the United States reveals that the American student, unlike his counterpart in such nation-states as Mexico and France, rarely has played an important political role. With the late-teen suffrage, this situation seems to be changing.

Educationism implies the *conscious professional* direction of the socialization and politicization process within the schools. Although in modern nation-states this process also entails the secularization of the educational endeavor, such a development does not follow automatically from the nature of Educationalism. It results, rather, from the fact that the major controlling forces of education today are secular agencies. In the earlier history of Educationism, especially in Europe before the advent of Nationalism, educational dogma in fact was deeply rooted in religious value systems. Thus two relatively famous educationists—Ignatius of Loyola, the founder of the Society of Jesus, and L'Abbé de la Sale, the founder of the Order of Brothers of Christian Schools—devised educational patterns as a means of generating a religious and sectarian form of Educationism.

Because of the importance placed upon Educationism in modern nation-states and the consequent centrality of schooling in modern life, the school has been placed in a vulnerable position in times of social discontent. Various axe-grinders wait patiently in the wings in hopes of getting a chance to lambast the schools. Thus, as the schools increasingly took upon themselves what were formerly the family's responsibilities in the training of the young, they have opened themselves to the charge that the rising rate of juvenile delinquency is the result of their failure to provide a proper ethical environment for the young. In short, the greater the perceived influence of the school, the greater the dissatisfaction expressed against it; the more territory it claims for itself, the more territory it has to defend.

Critics of schooling are as diverse as the social issues to be found in a society. Whatever ideology a group adheres to, and in America there are thousands of ideological groupings, rarely will the group believe that its ideology is adequately taught in the schools. The adherents of Scientism, for example, have persistently called for the increase in the teaching of the scientific approach to problem solving. With the shocking announcement of the successful orbiting of Sputnik in the 1950s, their plea gained relevancy and a flurry of science programs were initiated in schools. At the same time, classicists are continuously accusing the schools of failing to teach "high culture" and intellectual discipline. During the fifties such critics as Arthur Bestor, Jacques Barzun, and Admiral Hyman Rickover gained popularity by their relentless attacks upon the public schools, which they viewed as having succumbed to an intellectual paralysis as a result of the popularization of Progressivism.[6] Then, in the sixties, criticism of the school in contrast, rotated around the concept of relevancy which usually implied that the schools had failed to teach about the defects of the social system and that academicians had failed to deal with the affective nature of man.

The nationalists have seldom been satisfied with the way in which the schools have performed their patriotic assignment. Similarly, puritans who expect schools to reflect the ideal ethical environment have denounced the secularization of schooling. Romanticists, of course, view schools as destructive of creativity in children and youth. Even the progressivists have voiced dissatisfaction with schooling practices, especially as they relate to grading, the rating of children, and the academic foci of the fragmented curriculum. Even educationists reflect dissatisfaction with the learning and teaching environment of schools. In this case, however, most of the vociferous dissatisfaction is directed against the society which educationists believe does not support the schooling systems adequately. Especially during the sixties, when a taxpayers' revolt spread across the nation and school bond levies increasingly were voted down, did educationists question whether the American public was serious about its often publicized commitment to schooling.

Even though many of the admonitions directed against schooling practices are based upon actual limitations and defects, the fact remains that the criticisms often reflect the ideological bent of the axe-grinders

6 See, for example, Jacques Barzun, *The House of Intellect* (New York: Harper & Row, Pubishers, Inc., 1959); and Arthur Bestor, *Educational Wastelands* (Urbana: University of Illinois Press, 1953).

rather than the severity of the defects within the school system. The mere fact that schools have been able to withstand the incredible pressure from ideological groups is one of their major claims to success. Moderation may be a virtue, but it rarely pleases the immoderate ideologists. Educationists, however, continue to hold their ground. And when critics accuse the schools of fostering or failing to prevent such social problems as racism, delinquency, venereal disease, and low voting patterns among Americans, the educationists can reply with the exclamation: "Thank God for schools! Imagine how bad the situation would be if the school did not exist to check the further spread of such social problems." According to educationists, the best cure for social illnesses is an increase in formal education.

Because the school has assumed such a central role in American life, teachers should anticipate that schools increasingly will become the centers of social controversy. Major dissatisfaction will continue to be vented against them, largely because educationists have convinced the public that they serve to humanize and, in America, democratize the society.

While admitting that direct and spontaneous experiences may possess important educational value, educationists believe that such random experiences can best serve the learner when they are incorporated within a systematic and formalized teaching and learning pattern. For this reason Educationism, when pushed to extremes, often results in attempts to neutralize or destroy the influences exerted upon children and youth by nonformal educational activities. Educationists, for example, sometimes tend to view parental influence upon children as detrimental to the socialization process. They often have argued, especially when analyzing the teaching of the children of the immigrants at the turn of the century or the children of ethnic ghetto minorities today, that the child suffers from deprivation resulting from his home environment. The fact that the patterns of behavior which are described as symptoms of "deprivation" are rooted in cultural differences sometimes eludes the educationist who seeks to expand the influence of schooling.

The educationists who view parental influence as a hindrance to education rather than as an assistance advocate maximizing schooling. The rapid expansion of day care centers in the United States, while reflecting the increasing demand for female labor in the work force, also reveals the influence of Educationism. Often arguing that a child's home is a center of experiential deprivation in which he languishes in a world of limited stimuli, educationists have designed professionally controlled centers where the environment is manipulated to furnish an "enriched" pattern of stimuli.

Besides extending formal schooling to earlier periods in life (some educationists are seeking to discover means of formalizing prenatal learning), educationists also seek to incorporate into the formal curricula various areas of human activity which formerly were viewed as extra-curricular in nature. The progressive relabeling of "extracurricular" to "co-curricular" is one product of this gradual evolution and extension of formal schooling. Numerous athletic events, street gang activities, and community programs, for example, increasingly have been formalized and institutionalized. The spontaneous informal community activities of di-verse neighborhood groups have been increasingly professionalized and systematized—in a manner which has all too often resulted in decreasing public interest. While furnishing work opportunities for retired profes-sionals such as former athletic stars and politicians, the formalization of the educational experiences that would occur spontaneously on the play-ground or in youth gangs often creates predictable outcomes and thus diminishes the interest of the participants. The antiseptic environment of a scientifically designed playground, for example, often fails to excite the imagination of children. The hazardous street alley or broken-down shed served many generations of youth as stimuli to their imaginations, helping them discover creative ways to deal with the physical environment. From a romanticists' frame of reference, the antiseptic playground is in fact a center of educational deprivation. Similarly, organized college debate societies and clubs rarely create the excitement of the perennial dormitory bull sessions. Indeed, many exciting but inefficient planning meetings have had organization imposed on them by the application of Robert's Rules of Order; while more efficient, such meetings ofen become weari-some, laborious, and aridly humdrum. Many democratic rights have been rejected because of the boredom that accompanies their expression in formal settings. Although critics readily lampoon the apathy of citizens in our democracy, they rarely question the causes of such apathy. In many cases, it is the rules and processes which regulate meetings and commit-tees that serve to elicit apathy. Educational apathy is a symptom rather than a cause. The inherent tendency of the progressive ideologists to structure educational environments to ensure that events will be pre-dictable often serves to create the kind of boredom which they attack in the fragmented subject matter orientation of traditional schools.

Educationists view schooling as a means of sustaining and expand-ing the complex technological base of the society and its ancillary af-fluence and "good life." Believing that any increases in formal education will result in immeasurable improvements in technology, they pursue their goal of expanding schooling. In fact, however, schooling generally has not had this effect. The industrial base of the twentieth century was estab-lished by the labor of thousands of illiterates and unschooled individuals who learned their vocation on the job and today the increase in automa-tion obviates the need for a great deal of schooling. The argument that automation results in greater complexity, thus requiring an increase in formal education, is inaccurate. In reality, the more complex the machinery, the less sophisticated the operator. Automation serves to create a technological base which is people-proof. Indeed, thinking people may be less efficient in such a system than nonthinking ones. Education, as previously noted, often serves as a means of attaining a credential rather than as a proof of learning or training.

Besides assuming that the technological society rests upon schooling, most educationists believe that public forms of schooling are preferable to private vocational programs operated by industry. Although the educationists' argument is relevant from a socialization point of view, their position is rarely realistic in view of developing operational skills. Most schools cannot keep pace financially with the need to update educational materials because of the increasingly short life span of automated tools. While schools are training operators for computers, for example, the industry has produced new generations of computers. Often, industry must retrain school-trained operators. The school as an agency for vocational training is doomed to play second fiddle to industrial training programs.

Educationists believe that literacy is a prerequisite for the operation of complex social systems. They also believe that literacy rates are an index of the "advancement" of any civilization that purports to be democratic or socialistic. On the international scene, nations often utilize international agencies as forums to compete, and much of the competition in peacetime is based upon issues such as literacy rate and formal schooling practices.

Unfortunately, educationists rarely distinguish between alphabetism and literacy. Whether those who know the alphabet do in fact read is often not questioned. The fact that numerous adults who possess the ability to deal with the written word rarely utilize this training reveals the misuse of literacy figures, for literacy rates do not reveal how literacy is utilized.

The aggrandizement of formal education has fostered a number of unexamined assumptions concerning education. For example, where educationists in the past insisted that formal education was a right—an argument that was utilized in developing the tax base for public schooling in the twentieth century—educationists today see it also as a duty. Dropouts are copouts. From such a perspective, children who do not attend school are viewed as *criminal*. Numerous reform schools are populated by children who violated the truancy laws. Indeed, the rapid increase in the numbers of children incarcerated for truancy may reveal the emergence of dual educational system in which incarcerated truants are subjected to intense resocialization. As the society increasingly becomes therapeutic, truants will be viewed as emotionally disturbed and socially deficient.

Within such a pattern of education, the misuses of schooling by the Brahmins of society becomes a major threat to democracy.

### Historical Antecedents

In primtive societies, the education of the children and youth was accomplished by observation and direct participation in the society's processes. Play, for example, served as a major socializing force. Indeed, the role of play always has been and continues to be a major socializing force. Toy manufacturers exert profound influence upon the young. Military toys, for example, prepare the young for their possible adult role as soldiers. While dolls functioned to acculturate a girl child to her future role as mother, the recent popularization of "teen-dolls" reveals that the social system is exerting pressure upon the girl-child to view herself as a future professional consumer. Notwithstanding the unchanging importance of play in the acculturation process, imitation and unplanned activities also served as major educational forces in societies which were characterized by a poorly developed ideology of Educationism. Even in primitive societies, however, the formal training of certain specialists did occur. Tribal shamans, for example, devised apprenticeship systems whereby their role could be assumed by well-trained specialists. Incipient Educationism is rooted to man's prehistoric past.

Educationism, thus began as an ideology for the few who, in most cases, directed social systems. Formal schooling in ancient Egypt, for example, was required of the priests as well as of those neophytes who aspired to the priesthood. Pharaohs and their families also received formal schooling as a means of learning the relevant religious dogmas. "The Book of the Dead" served as the Bible of these ancient social Brahmins. Similarly, the ancient Hebrew people furnished a formalized educational system for the preparation of the clergy. The ancient Hebrews utilized formal education as a means of preserving their religious ideological system, and in many cases this formal education was extended to include all of the young male children. Indeed, the Jews have remained as a symbol of perseverance, for through their adherence to schooling they have managed to preserve a heritage against odds that were both cruel and powerful. The ancient Spartans who have been scorned by historians for their failure to add creatively to the heritage of the Western world, subscribed to a version of the ideology of Educationism. They were the first people to recognize the usefulness of universal education as a means of sustaining a secular ideology and preserving social cohesion. Formal education in Sparta served to perpetuate a militaristic and collective state. At the age of seven, children became the property of the state and were taught military techniques as well as a puritanical ideology which was utilized to socialize them to a barrack's society generally devoid of aesthetic expression. Unlike most ancient peoples, the Spartans did not exclude females from schooling: girls were trained to serve as rugged mothers for militaristic sons.

In Athens, universal and compulsory education was not established. The wealthy supported education for their children, but the citizenry as a whole had no sort of formal schooling. Some ancient philosophers such as Plato did establish formal educational centers for their pupils, but for the most part education remained informal and unstructured. Nevertheless, although the Athenians often expressed dislike for those who learned from lessons rather than from experience, they provided a political environment in which numerous views of education could be explored. Thus it is from Athens rather than Sparta that various ideological forms of Educationism have been handed down.

During the Roman Empire, secular schools were established by the wealthy, such as the Imperial schools for the children of the Brahmins. Some of the Roman Emperors encouraged schooling: Vespasian granted draft deferments as well as some tax exemption to teachers and the Emperor Antonius Pius ordained that some towns should pay the salaries of teachers. While on the one hand Roman schools often focused upon preparation for the practical demands of political or business life, on the other hand it was within the Roman Empire, that an inchoate form of religious education was popularized within the rapidly growing Christian communities. In addition to the required informal education of those who desired to join the Christian community, Christians gradually devised formal school for those members of the community who would serve to minister to the faithful. These catechuminal schools designed for the formal training of clergy served as a basis for the popularization and creative expansion of Christian ideology.

During the Middle Ages, formalism in education served as a foundation for the major educational developments in the Western world. Besides the rapidly formalized apprenticeship system utilized by the medieval guilds to control the quality of craftsmanship and the quantity of craftsmen, the Roman Catholic Church developed two major forms of schooling. Designed to prepare men for the role of clergy, the monastic schools trained their students for the rigorous demands of communal life while the cathedral schools prepared clergy who would minister to the people, especially in urban centers. Gradually the monastic schools expanded their educational offerings and attracted young men who sought learning but not priesthood. Such cathedral schools, especially in large urban centers, developed into "general learning centers" and eventually became the famous European universities. The Cathedral school of

Notre Dame, for example, expanded from the Isle of La Cité to the left bank of the Seine and became the University of Paris. Because students generally spoke the language of scholars, Latin, their community became known as the "Latin Quarter," a term which today serves to capture the flavor of the bohemian way of life so common among students everywhere. Throughout the medieval period, students roamed from university to university in informal fraternities known as *Goliardi*. The songs and poems of these roaming students express the medieval version of the ideology of Romanticism. During this era, as formal university education emerged, various patterns of control were developed. In 1200, at the University of Paris, for example, the faculty, with the help of secular authority in the person of King Philip Augustus snatched control of the university from the hands of ecclesiastical authority. At the University of Bologna, which became a model for southern European universities, the students assumed control over the educational program. In both cases, universities preserved a significant amount of political autonomy, evidence of which can be seen in the numerous "town and gown" battles. Often, civil agents were prevented from arresting or placing on trial any student accused of a crime. All accusations were placed for scrutiny and trial in the hands of university faculties or students. This incredible power and political autonomy resulted from the significance of the universities in the economic life of urban centers. Numerous towns vied for such centers of potentially profitable activity, and faculties or students could threaten at any time to move the university to another town if the townspeople were not willing to grant them the "right, privileges, and immunities" to which they felt they were entitled. The recent extension of suffrage in the United States may serve, in part, to restore some of this political power to university students.

Although medieval universities differed in their curricular offerings, their curricula were formalized. From the classical patterns of the trivium (grammar, rhetoric, logic) and the quadrivium (arithmetic, geometry, astronomy, music), the universities assumed their basic design. Depending upon the university and its specialization, other "subject matter" was added. Various professional emphases were reflected in medieval universities and vocational preparation was provided for theologians, lawyers, and doctors. It was in the medieval universities that the elements of educational formalism were devised. Examinations, academic degrees, professional certification, and academic programs emerged and remain as a badge of educational formalism and professionalism.

With the advent of the Renaissance, universities gradually altered their generally religious emphasis. Secular teachers made their appearance and thus teaching became a vocation in its own right, where previously it had been viewed as an addendum to other professional activities such as the priesthood. The Protestant Reformation, with its persistent emphasis upon individual interpretation of the Bible, completed the development toward modern Educationism by enhancing the importance of literacy and encouraging universal and compulsory schooling.

If the educational patterns of twentieth-century America are rooted in traditions stretching as far back as ancient Athens, their immediate foundation can be located in the puritan past of the New England Bible State. The Puritans settled in the New World and brought with them a Utopian dream of establishing a theocracy based upon the Word of God and predicated on the assumption that disobedience to the state was treason against Jesus Christ. In establishing such a theocracy, they devised two educational patterns to ensure that their state would prevail against the call of savagery and the devil. First, to protect all children against the snares of the devil, the Brahmins of the Bible State devised numerous laws to ensure that children would learn the art of reading Holy Script. In 1642 the law ordained that compulsory education would prevail; in 1647 the law further stated that schools were to be established in all towns in which there were fifty householders. In order to ensure that the ministry would be replenished, the Puritans established Harvard College in 1636.

A century and a half later colonists' respect for formal education was expressed by the Founding Fathers of the new Republic. They believed that democracy could not prevail without an educated populace. Dedicated to secularism, men such as Jefferson waged a "crusade against ignorance." Reflecting the influence of the classical tradition, Jefferson viewed education as a means of creating a "natural aristocracy of talent" comprised of the "best geniuses" that have been "raked from the rubbish" of mankind. This natural aristocracy, developed through publicly funded formal schooling, would provide the leadership for a people determined to control their own destiny. Even though Jefferson's Bill for the More General Diffusion of Knowledge was defeated, his plans for a university were realized and resulted in the creation of the University of Virginia, which opened its doors in 1825.

In contrast to the ideology of Jeffersonian democrats, the endeavors of Benjamin Franklin typified the attitude of the rising middle-class merchants and artisans, which was characterized by an emphasis on the practical and the useful. Condemning the "cultured-gentleman" approach to education, Franklin advocated an alternative to academic formalism with its focus upon the study of classical languages, theology, and literature. He promoted the establishment of an academy in Philadelphia, later to be named the University of Pennsylvania, that would further the interests of individuals engaged in the practical necessities of building a nation.

The concept of publically funded public schooling languished in the United States until the mid-nineteenth century, when educationists such as Horace Mann and Henry Barnard began to crusade for effective public schooling. As secretary of the Board of Education in Massachusetts, Horace Mann led an educational revival that resulted in the genesis of a common school system—a system designed to promote equality and fraternity. By the latter part of the nineteenth century, a somewhat disorganized public educational system had emerged in the United States. The common school movement had multiplied student enrollment many times over, and normal schools were established to meet the increasing demand for teachers. In addition, the Morrill Acts of 1862 and 1890 created numerous land-grant universities to meet the needs of a rapidly emerging industrial society.

Growing from diverse ideological patterns and greatly influenced by regional factors, the educational system failed to develop with any consistency. Offerings in secondary school, for example, differed markedly from school to school. Admission into universities and university expectations rarely reflected actually secondary schooling practices. From 1891 to 1920 diverse national educational committees were organized to deal with the lack of integration and unity in educational patterns. Committees such as the Committee of Ten in 1891, which focused upon devising secondary programs that would serve the student who did not plan to attend a college, and the Commission on the Reorganization of Secondary Education, which deliberated from 1913 to 1920 and ended up calling for a comprehensive high school as well as a "standardization" of secondary education, functioned as national agencies for the standardization of schooling.

During the 1940s and 1950s, educational life in the United States reflected the struggle between the advocates of progressive education and the academicians. During the 1960s and continuing into the 1970s, educational history has moved into the direction of greater differentiation and less standardization. The concept of compulsory education has been called into question by the erstwhile advocates of the neo-progressive ideology. Goaded by the fact that schools often failed to adjust to the rapid socioeconomic and technological changes that characterized the United States in the last decade, neo-progressives, called for a reorganization of schooling. The educational alterations of the 1970s appear to be moving toward greater individual and group differentiation of educational patterns. Of course, educational change has not occurred as rapidly as educational literature would imply.

### Educational Conflicts

The educational world witnesses incessant changes in the jargon used to describe actual or desired educational programs. Many educationists suffer from an "open sesame syndrome" which propels them to perpetually seek a magic formula which will open the wall that separates teaching from learning. This latter-day search for a pedagogical philosopher's stone has created a naive faith in innovative educational ideas. With credence automatically given to any idea that sounds new, it is only to be expected that neologisms often serve to cloak old practices. To be sure, periodic shifts in educational concerns and emphases do occur, but on the whole, educational practices have remained relatively stable while the language describing them has changed considerably.

Such changes in educational emphasis as do occur can be described in terms of a pendulum motion whereby "traditional" educational practices and "progressive" educational programs vie with one another. Thus educationists are periodically admonished by other educationists to stress academic and behavioral discipline and periodically urged to focus upon individual needs and deformalization. For example, the mid-fifties can be characterized by a call for rigorous academic and moral discipline and dedication to national goals and pedagogical excellence. The mid-sixties, on the other hand, witnessed a demand for a form of relevance which implied action-oriented programs and individualized instruction. This educational swing mirrors a previous pattern of change from a subject matter orientation in the 1920s to an antithetic focus upon self-directed learning in the 1930s. Such a pattern of change not only reveals a persistent conflict among educationists, but also testifies to their ability to react quickly to criticism. Indeed, this linguistic agility offers a safety valve for the educatonal profession by allowing it to shift its ideological emphasis rapidly and convincingly, thus neutralizing noneducationist critics of schooling.

The process is indicative not only of pendulum like change, but also of significant growth as well. The curriculum is not condemned to repeat itself! Thus, Alice Miel proposed the metaphor of a spiral for describing the changes in educational thought. Rejecting both the simple pendulum metaphor and the educationists' claim that all educational growth is pedagogically progressive, she suggested:

> A third way of viewing the path of change in educational thought is to think of a spiral which ascends, enlarging as it climbs. In common with the pendulum swing, this view allows for renewed attention to a problem

and line of solution which have been neglected for a time. The difference in the spiral view is that it accounts for the fact that proposals made at a later point in educational history usually are much more refined, with wisdom distilled from experience at both sides of the spiral built into them. At each new point on the upward and outward spiral the concepts are clearer and the language of education is more precise.[7]

Miel's model can serve as a valuable guide to understanding the varying and conflicting proposals which are perennially forwarded, and also may provide a fitting paradigm for analyzing the gradual refinements of the ideology of Educationism. Pedagogical tracts such as Jerome Bruner's *The Process of Education* (1960) and the numerous reports concerning the "new" approaches to the teaching of academic disciplines (e.g., the "new math") have served to increase the sophistication of the rationale for a "subject matter" emphasis in schooling.[8] Similarly, latter-day research in the field of psychology, especially in the areas of behavioral modification and phenomenology (humanistic psychology), has significantly refined the child-centered educational movement.

Besides the confusion generated by the persistent creation of neologisms, a major area of disagreement among educationists relates to their differing perceptions of what constitutes an educated man. While most educationists would agree with Montaigne that education should serve to make a man rather than a scholar, they disagree as to the means of achieving such an end.

Advocates of general education believe that a curriculum should be designed for all people and should reflect the major areas of knowledge. They also argue that education should be oriented to the total development of an individual and that all students should share similar educational experiences. Advocates of general education generally view the movement toward extending the elective system as a sort of educational smorgasbord which inhibits societal cohesion and serves to deprive the student of a well-balanced orientation toward his civilization. Thus Lewis B. Mayhew observed: "One of the strengths of the English Parliament in the eighteenth and nineteenth centuries was the fact that its members were all products of the same intellectual environment, hence had a common language, a common ideology, and a commonly possessed set of symbols and allusions with which they could communicate with

---

[7] Alice Miel, "Reassessment of the Curriculum—Why?" in *A Reassessment of the Curriculum,* ed. Dwayne Huebner (New York: Bureau of Publications, Teachers College, Columbia University, 1964), p. 14.

[8] Jerome S. Bruner, *The Process of Education* (Cambridge: Harvard University Press, 1960). For a somewhat dated but broad overview of an academic discipline orientation to reform, see John I. Goodlad, *School Curriculum Reform in the United States* (New York: Fund for the Advancement of Education, 1964).

each other."[9] Although Mayhew's observations deal with education at the college level, his point is applicable today to secondary schools and in some cases to elementary education where the elective system has been developed.

Generally, educationists who are puritans and nationalists support the idea of general education whereas adherents of Scientism and Progressivism find comfort in educational programs that are tailored to meet the individual needs or interests of students. The latter groups, however, differ markedly among themselves as to their reasons for supporting individually tailored programs. Progressivists, for example, believe that the needs of the students should form the cornerstone of educational programs, and that needs of course vary with the unique experiential background of each individual. Adherents of Scientism, in contrast, advocate individualized instruction in order to facilitate early specialization which will allow a student to develop a high degree of skill in dealing with his particular vocational interests.

Although scientians and progressivists support individualized and specialized educational programming, each for their own reasons, they often fail to perceive the incongruities between such programs and their educational goals. For example, adherents of Scientism are often greatly concerned with national goals, for technocrats are prone to be politically conservative. But the early specialization which they advocate tends to weaken national cohesion, for some segments of the citizenry are not able to communicate effectively with other elements of the citizenry because of the differences in education which have been enhanced by specialization. Similarly, adherents of Progressivism also often fail to realize that individualized instruction weakens the sense of community and can create social alienation by depriving students of shared experiences and symbols which facilitate communication.

Educationists, therefore, do not agree among themselves as to the most effective ways to design formal educational patterns. Their disagreements are expressed in numerous educational journals and at the annual national meetings which serve as informational clearinghouses and attitude readjustment socials. The disagreement among educationists rests in great part upon the fact that educationists reflect the diverse ideologies that compose the national ideological fabric. Professional organizations often specialize in representing one or another of the major ideological thrusts in the educational community. The Association for Teacher Education, for example, reflects the progressive impulse in American education, whereas educators committed to Scientism join forces in the American Educational Research Association (AERA).

[9] Lewis B. Mayhew, ed., *General Education: An Account and Appraisal* (New York: Harper & Row, Publishers, Inc., 1960), p. 4.

### The Threat to the Art of Teaching

Although the educational world reflects a healthy pluralism of ideological patterns—a fact which creates a great deal of ambivalence and thus frustrates the true believers of all persuasions—one ideological strand, Romanticism, is increasingly ignored in schooling. According to the perspective of Romanticism, teaching is primarily an art and thus must reflect the authentic personality of the teacher. Conversely, learning implies experiencing the way another person, a teacher, perceives, experiences, and communicates his reality. Thus for the romanticist the issue of style rather than method is central to the educational process. Indeed, since imitation is considered a violation of the aesthetic dimension of teaching, methods courses and student teaching often are criticized as detrimental to the development of an art of teaching.

What is more, romanticists tend to feel that formalism diminishes the rugged self-expression of individuals. Institutionalism, as previously noted, is anathema to the romanticists, so that schooling comes increasingly to reflect the ways and values of nonromanticist ideological assumptions. The art of teaching is eroded rather than enhanced by the science of teaching. Artist-teachers can survive in formal systems only because of their ability to veil their individualist attitudes and to reflect when necessary the patterns demanded by formalism and institutionalism. According to the tenets of Educationism, they are pedagogically subversive.

The gradual erosion of the art of teaching—a result of the increase in educational formalism, professionalism, and institutionalism—has been accompanied by an increase in attempts to make education a people-proof process. Indeed, some educationists dedicate themselves to designing curricular patterns which can be implemented without reflecting the style of the teacher. Teaching machines and computerized programming serve to facilitate this process of destylizing the teaching-learning process. Recent suggestions such as the open classroom and individualized instruction also are utilized to diminish the role of the artist-teacher, a role which is gradually being filled by an environmental manipulator or a facilitator.

The erosion of the art of teaching is not traceable to conspiratorial planning on the part of administrators or community leaders. Rather, it results directly from the three elements of schooling—formalism, professionalism and institutionalism—which demand that individuals adjust to a complex educational environment which is designed to maximize alternatives but which necessitates adjustment to specified patterns and directives. Even though computerized programming, for example, maximizes the number of course offerings, it also demands that teachers and students follow selected paths carefully. The teacher of a mini-course on the Civil War, for example, may be more restricted within such an arrangement than he would be with the much scorned "world history" course which, while forcing the teacher to deal with extensive materials, also permitted and even required a certain degree of selection. Once prescribed paths have been designated, whether they are based on academic, psychological, or sociological considerations, they define man's behavior. Even the progressive approach to education, which maximizes self-selection within a *prescribed* framework, may serve to channel rather than liberate student potential.

Professionalism also limits the self-expression of teachers because professionalism carries with it prescribed and acceptable behavioral patterns. Codes of professionalism generally insist upon behavior according to certain ethical patterns and selected rules of etiquette. Professionals, for example, are expected to behave in a manner which will not be offensive to the community in which they serve, whereas artists rarely are required or even expected to adhere to their community's behavioral expectations. Thus most teachers succumb to social sanctions, not because of fear or cowardice but because their professionalism so dictates. As C. Wright Mills so aptly observed,

> Yet the deepest problem of freedom for teachers is not the occasional ousting of a professor, but a vague general fear—sometimes politely known as "discretion," "good taste," or "balanced judgment." It is a fear which leads to self-intimidation and finally becomes so habitual that the scholar is unaware of it. The real restraints are not so much external prohibitions as control of the insurgent by the agreements of academic gentlemen.[10]

The gradual erosion of teaching as an art form is also occasioned by the growing demands of specialization within the field of education. Expertise and specialists are increasingly called upon to fulfill the functions that were formerly integral to teaching. The fragmentation of the teaching function into such segments as counselling, moral training, testing, and academic preparation, combined with the expanding specialization and fragmentation of knowledge, have served to diminish the role of the artist-teacher, who by definition is a humanist and a generalist who deals with teaching-and-learning as integral to living-and-experiencing.

Even with the virtual disappearance of the role of the artist-teacher, the teacher's role is not easily classified. Perpetual arguments go on between academicians who seek to increase the emphasis upon the areas of knowledge to be learned and the professional educators within schools of education who are often more concerned with the educational process

[10] C. Wright Mills, "The Social Role of the Intellectual," in *Power, Politics and People* (New York: Ballantine Books, Inc., n.d.), p. 297.

itself. Of late Scientism has increased in importance, but on the whole educators continue to be eclectic in formulating their aims.

### Aims of Education—An Overview

In the field of education there is a continuous debate concerning the aims of the educational endeavor. The reasons for such persistent controversy are numerous, but central to the issue is the unalterable fact that the preservation of society rests ultimately upon the effectiveness of the education of the citizenry. Because formal schooling is held to enhance the effectiveness of the socialization process, it naturally becomes a central factor in modern societies.

The nature of the educational endeavor and the aims which give it direction depend upon the characteristics of (1) man, including the way he learns, (2) his environment, including the physical, cultural, and ideological milieu and the knowledge which is available to him in that milieu, and (3) the process of interaction between man and his environment.

Thus educational aims are determined by the capacities, limitations, and needs of the human organism. Certain skills such as walking, for example, cannot be cultivated unless certain physiological developments occur. Similarly, the environment influences the nature of educational aims insofar as education is a process which directs the individual through the intricacies of a society's cultural and ideological framework, so that he will "fit" within his physical and social environment. Man, the social animal, is also in a continuous process of interaction with his environment. Education both reflects and is this interactive process.

Although the nature of man, knowledge, the learning process, and society determines the nature of educational aims, another relevant factor is the manner in which individuals *perceive* the aforementioned ontological and epistomological elements. Inasmuch as perception is selective, as the phenomenologists have pointed out, expressed aims will reflect the nature of the selection. The degree of sophistication and the nature of the knowledge which an individual brings to his analysis of education, as well as the methods utilized in determining aims, such as historical analysis or scientific analysis of human behavior, will affect the aims expressed. Indeed, as Fischer and Thomas noted, "The same set of facts can be used differently by equally intelligent persons." [11] The diverse philosophies of education and the varied aims that are inherent in them reflect, in part, the disagreements concerning the nature of "reality."

[11] Louis Fischer and Donald R. Thomas, *Social Foundations of Educational Decisions* (Belmont, California: Wadsworth Publishing Company, Inc., 1965), p. 8.

Because ideologies channel perception, they are central factors in determining the nature of educational aims. All too often, educational aims are viewed as resulting from cohesive and objective philosophical systems. The fact that Plato, for example, devised his elitist educational system at a time when Athens was undergoing severe internal disorder cannot be ignored, for Plato, too, was influenced by ideological factors and his philosophy of necessity reflected them.

Central to the development of educational objectives and inextricably interwoven with the previously noted factors is the fact that such objectives or aims are based upon values—that is, upon an individual's perception of what the actions of man "ought" to be. Every educational system is based upon aims which reflect beliefs concerning the "ideal" type of individual and the moral ways to foster the development of such an individual.

In a pluralistic society, the selection of educational aims assumes complex proportions, for cultural pluralism leads to eclectic educational aims. But the fact that formal schooling in the United States has reflected a particular set of values not illustrative of the actual cultural makeup of the entire social system reveals that formal schooling is controlled and designed according to the ideology of only one segment of the population.

Aims have been viewed both as *directions* and as *goals*. As directions, they are expressed from the perspective provided by existing situations and with the focus upon the process of development. Dewey made this point when he noted that education has no aims—individuals have aims: "Even the most valid aims which can be put in words . . . are not aims, but rather suggestions to educators as to how to observe, how to look ahead, and how to choose in liberating and directing the energies of the concrete situations in which they find themselves." [12]

As goals, aims are expressed by focusing upon an objective to be achieved which is extrinsic to the educational process. Pius XI in the encyclical, *Divini illius Magistri*, provided an approach to this kind of orientation to an external goal when he wrote: "In fact, since education consists essentially in preparing man for what he must be and for what he must do here below, in order to attain the sublime goal for which he was created, it is clear that there can be no true education which is not wholly directed to man's last end. . . ." [13]

Notwithstanding the unresolved issue of whether aims are to be seen as directions or as goals, all educators insist that the means of

[12] John Dewey, *Democracy and Education: An Introduction to the Philosophy of Education* (New York: The Macmillan Company, 1917), p. 125.
[13] Pius XI, "Divini illius Magistri," in *Papal Teachings: Education* (Boston: Daughters of St. Paul, 1960), p. 203.

achieving them must be morally unobjectionable according to the value system implied in the aims. Means and aims are inextricably interwoven. Indeed, means may be viewed as temporary ends.

Aims may be categorized in a variety of ways. Phenix, Alexander and Saylor, and Brubacher furnish a triadic classification based upon the degree of specificity of aims.[14] These three levels of aims are (1) ultimate aims; (2) mediate (or intermediate) aims; and (3) proximate aims. Ultimate aims are the fundamental bases of the entire educational endeavor and they determine the nature of all other educational aims. When expressed, and they need not be expressed, such ultimate aims are identified in general terms such as "growth," "self-realization," "salvation," the "cultivation of the intellect," and "acculturation." Although some critics deny the existence of ultimate aims, the fact remains that such aims have been provided from the days of Aristotle to the present.

Mediate aims are intermediate between the ultimate and proximate aims. Such aims are more specific and concrete than ultimate aims and are expressed as objectives to assist in planning the variety of opportunities for learning within the schools. The "Seven Cardinal Principles of Education" are examples of mediate aims.

Proximate aims are those which the teacher utilizes as an integral part of the learning-teaching situation and which immediately influence the sequence and character of classroom activities. Phenix provided an example of proximate aims when he observed: "When a teacher confronts a class in noisy disorder, his immediate aim may be to restore some sort of order so that the intended work can continue. . . ."[15] The perennial controversy concerning the value of autocratic, laissez-faire, or democratic behavior of the teacher within the classroom does not result solely from the degree to which such behavior facilitates learning, for it also refers to the issue of proximate aims and their relationship to ultimate and/or mediate aims.

The issues raised by the variety of aims are crucial in analyzing schooling practices. Whereas ultimate aims are derived from complex philosophical systems, mediate aims are devised by attempting to reflect the social environment and proximate aims are derived from the direct acculturation of individual teachers. Generally, teachers reflect their ideological predisposition in determining proximate aims while often ignoring the ultimate aims which are basic to the school's curriculum. Phi-

[14] Philip H. Phenix, *Philosophy of Education* (New York: Holt, Rinehart & Winston, Inc., 1958), pp. 554–55; William M. Alexander and J. Galen Saylor, *Modern Secondary Education: Basic Principles and Practices* (New York: Holt, Rinehart & Winston, Inc., 1959), pp. 205–6; John S. Brubacher, *Modern Philosophies of Education* (New York: McGraw-Hill Book Company, 1962), pp. 113–19.

[15] Phenix, *Philosophy of Education*, p. 554.

losophies of education are often left at home while ideologies of education are carried in one's head. One of the reasons why the numerous analytically devised philosophies of education fail to alter educational practices is the fact that ideologies rather than philosophies direct everyday educational activities. *To change educational practices, it is necessary to alter ideological patterns rather than philosophical systems.*

The ideologies analyzed in this text may help to explain the often noted differences between a teacher's behavior and his expressed educational philosophy. The authoritarian teacher whose behavior reflects the ideology of Puritanism, for example, often adheres to an expressed belief in democracy. His behavior in the class will reflect the puritan ideology which he has internalized rather than the philosophy or the educational principles which he espouses. Teachers and future teachers must beware lest they express educational aims that are inconsistent with their ideological convictions. Numerous teachers speak of sensitivity as an educational aim, yet are willing to crush individual creativity in order to achieve it in the behavior of children. Similarly, many teachers express democratic aims of education yet behave in a manner which illustrates the effectiveness of totalitarianism in the classroom.

The plurality of educational aims is revealed in the diverse listings of aims of education expressed in the writings of philosophers, educationists, educators, laymen, and educational commissions and committees. Some of the emphases worthy of note are (1) vocational education (cf. Ben Franklin's "Proposal Relating to the Education of Youth in Philadelphia," and the Smith-Hughes Act of 1917); (2) education aimed at developing spiritual and ethical character (cf. the "Old Deluder Satan" act of 1647 and some of the writings of the Catholic philosopher Jacques Maritain); (3) education aimed at intellectual development and knowledge of "subject matter" (cf. the writings of Arthur Bestor, the reports of the Council for Basic Education, and works of such writers as Jerome Bruner, and the materials developed by the University of Illinois Committee on School Mathematics and the Physical Science Study Committee); (4) education aimed at reforming society (cf. George S. Counts' *Dare the School Build a New Social Order?* and the objectives of the John Dewey Society for the Study of Education and Culture); and (5) citizenship education (cf. publications of the National Council for the Social Studies and the writings of such men as Noah Webster.)

Although the objectives noted represent major emphases within American education, other less universal aims also are propounded. Such additional aims include: the development of a "cultural gentleman or woman" which characterizes some of the private academies and "finishing schools," the improvement of racial self-identity as expressed in some urban community schools, and the development of contemplative abilities as focused upon under the informal auspices of "guru-teachers" or within the diverse communes established by various romanticists.

The lack of consensus concerning aims, however, tends to obscure the great degree of behavioral conformity among educationists. Although an educationist may express only one specific orientation and direction, most adhere to a mixture of aims. Statements of specific aims serve to accentuate a major concern and to provide an effective "slogan" to rally diverse factions but do not necessarily imply a rejection of other concerns. The focus upon intellectual development, for example, does not necessarily imply a disregard for the socialization of the individual or the welfare of society. Arthur Bestor revealed this relationship when he wrote:

> The school does have a contribution to make to every activity of life. But it makes that contribution by doing its own particular job honestly and well. That job is to provide intellectual training in every field of activity where systematic thinking is an important component of success.[16]

While the aforementioned aims of education reveal an eclectic concern, they often betray the American focus on the practical rather than the theoretical or intellectual. Patricia Sexton observed this phenomenon in viewing the goals advocated by the 1918 NEA Commission on the Reorganization of Secondary Education: "Seven cardinal educational goals were set: health, command of fundamental processes, worthy home membership, vocation, civic education, worthy use of leisure, and ethical character. The cardinal goals did not include scholarship, thinking, inquiry, training of the mind, intelligence, or knowledge." [17]

Of course, the values expressed in the daily activities within the schools do not always derive from the stated educational aims. Teachers' lounge conversations and student concerns reflect a less sophisticated view of schooling. One of the major reasons for this discrepancy is the fact that educational aims flow from philosophical assumptions, whereas daily concerns reflect ideological realities. Similarly educational issues are human issues and thus cannot be easily classified and predicted. While educationists spend long arduous hours developing educational philosophies and aims for would-be inspectors or evaluators, school activities are generally based upon many unstated but well known assumptions.

A brief view of a few of the basic assumptions which guide both student and teacher behavior should serve to illustrate the differences between the "living realities" and the stated philosophies of education.

---

[16] Arthur Bestor, *The Restoration of Learning* (New York: Alfred A. Knopf, Inc., 1955), p. 30.

[17] Patricia Cayo Sexton, *The American School: A Sociological Analysis* (Englewood Cliffs, N.J.: Prentice-Hall, Inc., 1967), p. 84.

Teacher handbooks, for example, usually emphasize the democratic commitment of public schools and stress the belief that teacher's are servants of the public and should be committed to excellence in teaching and the growth and expansion of knowledge. They are encouraged to be creative and innovative and to readily express their concerns. Their professional growth and development is identified as a major school commitment and they are encouraged to participate in community activities as citizen-teachers.

School realities, however, often differ from the ideals expressed in teacher handbooks. Indeed, teachers are often oppressed by the tyranny of trivia as they expend many "professional" hours in such activities as collecting milk money, detention room monitoring, rest room patrol, and chaperoning various school extracurricular activities. Though labeled professionals, they often find themselves performing the duties of bureaucratic functionaries. Their confidant within the school is most likely to to be the custodian rather than the principal.

The oppression which often is reflected in the daily life of the teacher at school should not be construed as resulting from the intentional perfidy or tyranny of administrators. Indeed, school administrators are also oppressed by the triviality of their daily task. A major reason why an anticreative atmosphere pervades many schools is the fact that schools have become bureaucratized without a supporting rationale for such a hierarchial structure. Thus, although essentially democratic in philosophy, schools tend to have an oligarchical structure which often serves to prevent change. Role definitions become increasingly clear-cut and "professionals" are unwittingly forced to behave according to the exigencies of bureaucratic demands. With the proliferation of specialized roles, direct person-to-person means of resolving conflicts and devising alternatives are inhibited and educational issues are relegated to ad hoc committees for their consideration and analysis. The numerous committee reports, often reflective of professional commitment and concern for humanizing the school, are reproduced one hundred fold and serve to "bottle up" the channels of communication. With the arrival of the end of the academic year, reports, minutes of meetings, and proposals for curriculum revision are often placed in files and become part of the school's innovative but unlived history.

Although educational philosophies and school aims are designed to emphasize the community ethos which envelops educationists and students, sociological studies dealing with the student populations of schools, especially at the secondary and college levels, reveal that a student subculture exists in most schools and reflects ideological assumptions which not only differ from stated educational objectives but often are antithetic to them.[18] The events of the previous decade revealed that many secondary school and college students are assuming a militant role in relation to their status in school. The educational community often assumed to exist in schools has been eroded by the growing gap between philosophical assumptions of education and ideological and sociological realities. When the characteristics which distinguish teachers and students include such factors as race and ethnic identity, socioeconomic class, and linguistic patterns, individual discipline issues becomes the source of group antagonisms. When such group antagonisms among teachers, students, and community representatives emerge, educational aims often pale into insignificance as individuals involved become ideological agents and zealous defenders of their beliefs. Thus, even though Educationism is an eclectic ideology, it has served and will increasingly serve as a cause for conflict. When populist militants confront adherents of Educationism the conflicts may be bloody. Teachers, too, may become true believers and forget that their task is to teach, and not solely to serve as agents for the popularization of the ideology of Educationism. Indeed, their role is integrally related to the needs of society and they can serve to enhance or destroy social cohesion.

### The Citizenship Aim of Education

The citizenship aim of education is a particularly significant and central aim for it is inextricably interwoven with the general socialization process through which social cohesion is developed and sustained. This is the aim which is the focus in a majority of the controversies concerning educational issues, for education, too, is broadly defined as socialization. All educators believe that education should help an individual deal with his duties as a member of a community. Educationists believe that schooling is the best way to prepare a citizenry for their role as citizens. The debate concerning the nature of the citizenship aim of education has persisted from the time of the ancient Spartans and Athenians to the present day. The fundamental differences between these two ancient peoples and their disagreements concerning the nature of the "good citizen" provide the models for arguments on this matter through the ages. The Spartans had devised a compulsory educational system as a means of socializing its people for a military collective city state, and since their time dictators often have utilized formal schooling as a means of estab-

18 See, for example, James S. Coleman, *The Adolescent Society* (New York: The Free Press, 1961), and, for a somewhat dated but classic view of the emerging student "subculture," August B. Hollingshead, *Elmstown's Youth* (New York: Science Editions, Inc., 1961).

lishing their power. Soviet Russia, in order to overcome the loose control exerted over peoples by the czarist regime, began a crash program of public education aimed at developing a citizenry supportive of communist goals. Similarly, the Red Chinese citizen learns his duties in schools where he reads the communist form of the *New England Primer* or the *Mc-Guffey Reader,* the Little Red Book of Chairman Mao Tse-Tung.

At the other end of the spectrum, the Athenian practice of educating for citizenship in a democracy has generally served as a model for American education. The Republic's Founding Fathers, such as Washington, Jefferson, and Jay, and the political and educational leaders of twentieth-century America have expressed the Madisonian convictions that a democracy without education is "a prologue to a farce or a tragedy; or, perhaps, both." Jefferson admonished: "I think by far the most important bill in our whole code is that for the diffusion of knowledge among the people. No other sure foundation can be devised for the preservation of freedom and happiness." [19] Armed with this conviction, the citizenry, especially in the mid-twentieth century, has utilized diverse means to exert its influence in determining the foundations upon which the educational endeavor will operate.

The citizenship aim of education is extremely complex, but regardless of the specific form it takes, the political socialization of an individual into a society plays an important part in it. This process includes the development of atttudes, values, norms of behavior, and ideals which are consistent with the political creeds of the social group. The political socialization of an individual, however, cannot be easily separated from the broader process of socialization, for political socialization includes not only political learning but also the learning of social attitudes and norms of behavior which are relevant to the political community.

The NCSS handbook, *Promising Practices in Civic Education,* includes a list of educational goals which reveals the complexity of the citizenship aims of education. This list includes:

1. Knowledge and skills to assist in solving the problems of our time.
2. Awareness of the effects of science on civilization and its use to improve the quality of life.
3. Readiness for effective economic life.
4. Ability to make value judgments for effective life in a changing world.
5. Recognition that we live in an open-ended world which requires receptivity to new facts, new ideas, and new ways of life.
6. Participation in the process of decision-making through expression of views to representatives, experts, and specialists.

---

[19] Gordon E. Lee, ed., *Crusade Against Ignorance* (Richmond: William Byrd Press Inc., 1962), p. 99.

7. Belief in both liberty for the individual and equality for all, as guaranteed by the Constitution of the United States.
8. Pride in the achievements of the United States, appreciation of the contributions of other peoples, and support for international peace and cooperation.
9. Use of the creative arts to sensitize oneself to universal human experience and the uniqueness of the individual.
10. Compassion and sensitivity for the needs, feelings, and aspirations of other human beings.
11. Development of democratic principles and [their] application to daily life.[20]

The goals enumerated here reveal the extensive and varied elements of citizenship education and its close relationship to the total ideological fabric of the society. Not only do these goals reveal the complex interchange of ideological systems in the United States, but the very idea of citizenship education itself demands an understanding of the ideological aspects of one's society.

The welfare of the national society and the educational endeavor have been linked in numerous issues. Early attempts to establish a national university and the successful establishment of military schools as well as current national education programs such as the Teachers' Corps and Head Start reveal this relationship. The growth of public education and the development of national consciousness is closely related. From Noah Webster and his call for the teaching of patriotism through the efforts of Horace Mann to develop a compulsory educational system, to today's developments in national assessment, this relationship has been emphasized. Supreme Court decisions, especially those relating to the issue of integration, as well as increases in federal aid to education are illustrative of the development of a national educational system. The relationship between the school and the growth of national consciousness was concisely stated by Commager when he wrote:

> From the very beginning of our national existence, education has had very special tasks to perform in America. Democracy could not work without an enlightened electorate. The States and sections could not achieve unity without a sentiment of nationalism. The nation could not absorb tens of millions of immigrants from all parts of the globe without rapid and effective Americanization. Economic and social distinctions and privileges, severe enough to corrode democracy itself, had to be overcome.[21]

[20] National Council for the Social Studies, *Promising Practices in Civic Education,* ed. Donald W. Robinson (Washington: NCSS, 1967), pp. 16–17.
[21] Henry Steele Commager, *Living Ideas in America* (New York: Harper & Row, Publishers, 1951), p. 547.

A major element of the American creed has been the belief in "the American dream." The overwhelming majority of American citizens have believed that they inhabited "the land of opportunity," a country without king, feudal aristocracy, or rigid class system. By adhering to the puritan virtues of industry and frugality, the American citizen's opportunities for advancement were unlimited—there was always room at the top.

Speaking before a national convention in 1908, Charles W. Eliot, president of Harvard, disputed this contention and told the members of the National Society for the Promotion of Industrial Education (NSPIE): "We must get rid of the notion that some of us were brought up on, that a Yankee can turn his hand to anything. He cannot in this modern world; he positively cannot." [22] Furthermore, he asserted

> . . . we come upon a new function for the teachers in our elementary schools and in my judgement they have no function more important. The teachers ought to sort the pupils and sort them by their evident or probable destinies. [23]

Eliot's proposal represented an interesting alliance—an alliance between the Eastern Establishment Brahmins and the vocational educators. Reflecting early New England Puritanism, the Brahmin mentality emphasized the necessity of a rather rigid class system in which each individual occupied a position in the hierarchical structure. The vocational educators' acceptance of such a construct was exemplified in the expressed purpose of their organization. Henry S. Pritchard, the president of NSPIE, stated that the fundamental dilemma of American education was "that we are no longer fitting our youths for their opportunities in the way in which they must be fitted." [24]

Eliot's assertion obviously reflected a declining faith in the American Dream. With an economy increasingly dominated by giant corporations, the rags-to-riches, any-man-can-become-president mythology was viewed with growing skepticism and cynicism. Even the most ardent proponents of the "American way" expressed cautious optimism about the possibility of social mobility.

Should educationists continue to perpetuate an ideal that once provided inspiration to generations of American citizens, or should they accept the socioeconomic "realities" of the twentieth century and prepare their pupils for their "probable destinies"? Choosing the latter course, the National Guidance Association was formed in 1913 to aid in the process of "sorting and selecting." The endeavors of such educational psycholo-

[22] As quoted in Henry J. Perkinson, *The Imperfect Panacea: American Faith in Education, 1865–1965* (New York: Random House, Inc., 1968), p. 146.
[23] As quoted in Perkinson, *The Imperfect Panacea,* p. 145.
[24] As quoted in Perkinson, *The Imperfect Panacea,* p. 143.

gists as Alfred Binet and Edward L. Thorndike promoted the search to determine as accurately as possible the pupil's "probable destiny."

Although many educationists have not overtly promoted the belief in sorting and selecting, their establishment of such programs as exceptional education (special education for the gifted and the mentally retarded) and ability tracking has served to further actualize the concept. In addition, the structuring of the curriculum according to "vocational interest" (commercial, college "prep," and vocational) has served to categorize a student according to a predicted vocational slot. As a result of such systematizing and classifying, a student's future is predefined, if not predestined. Proponents of these programs are undoubtedly sincere in their concern for the maximum potentiation of their students. Indeed, those committed to such programs often express the belief that this type of tracking and sorting makes it possible for the school to meet the specific needs of the students and may be more humane than proposals that intermix students of varying abilities and interests. The less ardent proponents of these programs generally state that they are merely being "realistic."

The belief that public schooling should serve to sort and select students according to their abilities has been maintained throughout the history of American education. The first schools established by the Puritans of the Bay Colony reflected this belief. Jefferson echoed similar sentiments when he proposed a system of public schooling that would aid in the development of a "natural aristocracy of talent." More recently, such a view has been expressed by James Conant and Arthur Bestor.

Although this "sorting and selecting" procedure may be perfectly consistent with the elitism of Jeffersonian democracy, it also falls prey to the vices inherent in categorization. First, labeling often results in a self-fulfilling prophecy—that is, students labeled unteachable become unteachable, "probable destinies" tend to become inevitable destinies. Second, categorization tends to reinforce an acceptance of a class or caste system, for democratic citizens may be willing to accept a caste system if they are led to believe that it is based upon academic ability. In fact, however, the results of academic achievement and intelligence tests often reflect little more than socioeconomic status. Man's attempts to systematically discover or create philosopher kings, however, always have encountered failure.

Opponents of sorting and selecting practices generally reflect the influence of populism, Jacksonian democracy, and the common school movement. They generally believe that public school should serve to minimize differences and promote socioeconomic and political equality. These egalitarian educationists adhere to ideals of the American Dream, albeit in modified and tempered form, for they believe that public schooling should serve to enhance the potential of social mobility. They focus upon "possible destinies" rather than "probable destinies."

The conflict among educationists concerning public schooling and its relationship to social mobility and the labor market has been intensified with the emergence of two-year colleges. These junior colleges, community colleges, or branch colleges—the name depending on which state one inhabits—serve several functions. First, they provide what is called a two-year terminal education, designed for those students entering a "profession" or updating the skills required for the myriad of "new professions." Second, they serve as a feeder system, which is more or less what the world of sports calls a farm team. If an individual succeeds in the "minors," he moves up to the "majors." Upon "moving up," however, these students often discover that many four-year universities will not accept some of the college credits attained in the "minors." Consequently, they find it necessary to attain additional credits and perhaps remain in college an extra year. This additional burden is especially difficult for them inasmuch as the enrollment at the two-year colleges consists primarily of students from minority and/or lower socioeconomic groups.

As a result of the increasing demand for white-collar skills and the professionalization of numerous vocations, two-year colleges have replaced, in part, the vocational schools of the past. They have become an extension of the high school and maintain somewhat the same ethos. Consequently, although their defenders would staunchly deny it, their is an air of second-class citizenship about them; indeed, the inferiority implicit in the name "junior college" is one of the chief reasons many states have had recourse to euphemisms in labeling these institutions. It is rather ironic that many advocates of "junior colleges" seem to promote them for the children of other people, just as in the past many advocates of vocational schools, although espousing the "nobility of labor," assumed that their sons would not become auto mechanics and that their daughters would not marry laborers.

Inasmuch as enrollment figures tend to show that the student population at two-year colleges consists primarily of minority groups and/or lower socioeconomic groups, the educational disagreement between W. E. B. DuBois and Booker T. Washington remains relevant. Washington believed that the route to success for black people rested in their being "realistic," by which he meant that black people should meet white society's demand for technicians and craftsmen; he considered it unrealistic for blacks to opt for the more prestigious positions in the occupational hierarchy. In other words, he wanted them to receive training rather than education. In contrast to the practical realism of Washington, DuBois emphasized the necessity of intellectual discipline and academic scholarship. He demanded social, economic, and political equality and believed that if one is trained for second-class citizenship, one will never have more. DuBois agreed that the teaching of basic skills was a necessary function of schooling. "Nevertheless," he profoundly observed, "I insist that the object of all true education is not to make men carpenters, it is to make carpenters men. . . ." [25]

It may be too soon to adequately judge the future development of the two-year college movement. They may rapidly become three-year, then four-year colleges with prestige almost equivalent to that of the present four-year schools. They may remain two-year colleges, however, and become a significant factor in the development of a more rigid class structure, a class structure based not only upon the amount of formal education one has attained but also upon the prestige of the college one has attended.

The relationship between formal schooling and the maintenance of a social class structure can be observed in the contrasting developments of the Ivy League schools and the land grant universities. Harvard, the first of the Ivy League schools, was founded in 1636. It was, in a sense, a vocational school in that it was instituted to train the ministry for the Puritan theocracy. Of course, the difference between Harvard and what later were termed vocational schools is readily apparent. Harvard was established, maintained, and attended by the sons of eminent parents who possessed significant social and political power, and this has continued to be the case more than three centuries later.

In *The Power Elite*, C. Wright Mills noted the close interrelationships between the men of power who direct the corporations, the military complex, and the government agencies, and observed that such an elite was educated in exclusive private schools. Their colleges degrees were primarily from Ivy Lague schools, especially Harvard, Princeton, and Yale. This elite in many cases has retained its power since the heyday of the New England Brahmins. Disagreeing with Mills, however, John Kenneth Galbraith argues that power has shifted from capital to the technostructure—that is, into the hands of upper management. But this class, too, is predominantly made up of Ivy League graduates. Even though the power has shifted from the church to industry and the state, Harvard has remained for nearly 350 years the training ground for a prestigeous elite.

In contrast to the development of Ivy League schools, the public-supported university movement is usually associated with the Land-Grant or Morrill Acts of 1862 and 1890. In the words of the sponsor, Congressman Justin Morrill, a self-educated Vermonter and himself the son of a

[25] W. E. Burghardt Dubois, "The Talented Tenth," in *The Negro Problem* (New York: James Pott and Company, 1903), p. 63.

blacksmith, "The fundmental idea was to offer an opportunity in every state for a liberal and larger education to larger numbers, not merely to those destined to sedentary professions, but to those much needing higher instruction for the world's business, for the industrial pursuits and professions of life." [26] The intent was to provide educational opportunity for more individuals with a wider range of vocational choices, and thus to bridge the gap between the classical, European-type approach and the more "practical" necessities of a growing technological society. The act itself stated that each college "without excluding other scientific and classical studies, and including military tactics," would "teach such branches of learning as are related to agriculture and the mechanical arts." [27]

These universities have been and continue to be ridiculed by many individuals for being "anti-intellectual," "trade schools," and "diploma mills," but the fact remains that they have provided an educational opportunity for many middle- and lower-middle-class students and have produced many doctors, lawyers, dentists, teachers, and engineers, the bulwark of the technological society. Although some have risen in prestige, have they significantly altered the structure of power in America? Or, have they merely served to "sort and select" students according to their "probable destines"?

Answers to this question are hard to come by. When discussing the relationship between formal schooling and social mobility, it should be noted that private schooling on any level is generally not a bootstrap to success, but rather a symbol of success for those who have attained upper- or upper-middle-class socioeconomic status.[28] In like manner, the public school has been the symbol of success for the lower-middle socioeconomic levels of society. Although schools recently have come under sharp attack for failing in the education of racial and/or ethnic minority groups, it is necessary to recall that historically schools generally have failed the lower socioeconomic classes, regardless of race. As Colin Greer aptly observed, "The establishment of an ethnic middle-class was basic to entry onto a wider middle-class stage via public education. . . . [N]ot until the 1950's did the Irish begin to enter the university in large numbers, but they remain predominately 'blue-collar' in status and, like Italian high schoolers, sustain a high incidence of poor school performance." [29]

[26] Justin S. Morrill, "State Aid to the U.S. Land-Grant Colleges," in *Educational Ideas in America: A Documentary History*, ed. Alexander Rippa (New York: David McKay Company, Inc., 1969), p. 520.
[27] "The Morrill Act, 1862," in *American Higher Education: A Documentary History*, ed. Richard Hofstadter and Wilson Smith (Chicago: University of Chicago Press, 1961), II, 568–69, Document II.
[28] Evidence of this phenomena can be found in Ferdinand Lundberg, *The Rich and the Super Rich* (New York: Bantam Books, Inc., 1969).
[29] Collin Greer, "Immigrants, Negroes and the Public Schools," *The Urban Review* (January 1969), p. 11.

What creates the crisis in education for the lower socioeconomic groups is *not* that the schools are now doing a less satisfactory job than in the past. In fact, the schools probably have improved the quality of their programs. The problem generally results from the fact that students who usually do poorly in school have no other alternative but to remain in a school which is not designed for them and which would probably prefer that they drop out. This is not to deny the educational importance of the personal racism of some of the educational personnel, the institutional racism of some parts of the educational system, and the social class prejudice of some educationists. But to focus entirely on the school system is to overlook the realities of the society's political and economic structure. At best, schooling can be a doctor, but it lacks the healing powers of an omnipotent being. If the schools are a failure for a socioeconomic or a racial group, generally it is because they reflect the failures of the society. The question remains: Dare the school build a new social order?

For those individuals who do succeed in school and perhaps become elementary school teachers, computer programmers, or lab technicians (especially when such positions involve higher status than attained by their parents), questions about the power elite or the rigidity of class structure may seem of little importance. In fact, many individuals have accepted almost a deistic belief about the power elite. The elite, like God, may exist, but except for calamities, such as floods in the one case or wars in the other, neither plays more than a minor role in our everyday lives. For this reason it is easy for many educationists, as good puritans, to continue to believe that personal destiny rests in the hands of the individual.

Even though the belief in social mobility and the American Dream has been modified within this century, bureaucratization and the creation of the "new professions" have served to legitimatize the Horatio Alger stories even while drastically tempering them. The clerk who sells shoes in a department of a large chain store rarely believes that he will someday own the chain. He may believe, however, that he can become the assistant manager in the department. And he certainly believes that his children will surpass him, especially if they "get an education." This schooling, whether attained in a four-year university, a two-year college, or a vocational school, will fulfill the modest aspirations of many middle-class and working-class families. Thus it has become increasingly true, as television commercials continue to reiterate, that to fail in school is to fail in life. That this is true, however, makes education both cruel and inhuman punishment for many.

### The Emergence of Professionalism

Normal schools, the first teacher training institutions, were established to meet the increasing demand for teachers that accompanied the expansion of the common school movement. The early schools were restricted to females, and when they later became coeducational the number of male students remained small. The first normal school, a private institution promoted by the Reverend Samuel R. Hall, was established in Concord, Vermont, in 1823. In 1839, aided by the political influence of Horace Mann and Charles Brooks, the first state-supported normal school in Massachusetts was established in Lancaster. From 1860 to 1898 the number of state normal schools proliferated from eleven to 167, a growth rate that nearly equaled that of the private schools.

The ethos of the normal schools reflected the moralistic tenets of the early Puritans but lacked the puritan zeal for intellectual achievement. The focus upon neatness, cleanliness, manners, and order rather than scholarship established a priority that persists in the value orientation of many educationists. Indeed, from their inception, the normal schools were criticized for their lack of scholarship. In 1847, for example, an early educationist, David Page, the principal of the State Normal School in Albany, New York, asserted, "To be a teacher, one must first of all be a scholar. So much stress is now placed on method and on the theory of teaching that there is great danger of forgetting the supreme importance of scholarship and culture." [30]

The warning Page directed toward educationists has been reiterated frequently by numerous individuals. Indeed, some educationists themselves have reflected the concern expressed by Page. The most important condemnation, however, has emanated from liberal arts professors and has created a continuing conflict between them and the educationists. While the academicians condemn educationists for their lack of scholarly endeavor, the educationists, in turn, condemn the academicians for their lack of knowledge about the teaching and learning process.

Responding to the increasing popularity of the normal schools and the expressed interest of many academicians, liberal arts colleges became involved in the process of training teachers. In 1832, nine years after the creation of the first private normal school and seven years prior to the first state normal school, the liberal arts college of New York University began a series of lectures on the "art of teaching." Within the next

[30] As quoted in David B. Tyack, ed., *Turning Points in American Educational History* (Waltham, Mass.: Blaisdell Publishing Company, 1967), p. 412.

decade Brown University and the Universities of Michigan, Wisconsin, and Iowa also adopted this practice, and by 1870 regular professorships in teacher training were established. From their inception these positions were of lesser prestige than those of equivalent status in the liberal arts colleges; they maintained, however, much higher prestige than similar teaching positions in normal schools.

As a result of continued criticism and in spite of an enormous demand for teachers, the educationists in the normal schools became increasingly defensive about their lack of academic standards. To counter this criticism, they sought to establish a separate academic discipline for the training of teachers, By requiring a mastery of this new discipline and by controlling the certification of the graduates, educationists sought to make teaching a legitimate profession in the strict sense of the term. The founding of Teachers College (TC) at Columbia University in 1887 provided a major thrust in this direction in that it united educationists, professionally oriented progressivists, and established academicians. Nicholas Murray Butler, an Associate Professor of Philosophy in Columbia College, had taken an interest in Educationism; after numerous failures in attempting to establish an area of pedagogy in the College, Butler and Frederick A. P. Barnard, the President of Columbia, created a separate but related institution.

Teachers College not only promoted the professionalization of educationists but also further legitimized teacher training by attracting numerous well known academicians, including Edward L. Thorndike, Paul Monroe, and John Dewey. The college provided the academicians with an institution in which to further their own interests. In return, the endeavors of the academicians enhanced the image and prestige of Educationism. Their influence has been awesome. For nearly a century, Teachers College has remained a major institution engaged in the promulgation of Progressivism and Educationism.

Additional attempts to enhance the ideology of Educationism have included changing normal schools to state teachers colleges and, more recently, universities; increasing the number of schools of education within established universities; and establishing minimal requirements for teacher certification. Regardless of these efforts, however, educationists generally continue to be considered second-rate scholars if not second-class citizens of the university community.

The professionalization of education in the United States is a relatively recent phenomenon. Unlike medical doctors or lawyers, teachers generally were gleaned from the "blue-collar" classes. Until recently, they were viewed in literature and in the public press as simple (sometimes simple-minded), moral, unambitious individuals who served happily as town functionaries. Preparatory programs for teachers were locally designed and supervised and licensing practices varied throughout the country and in some cases did not exist. Even today, when some states are demanding master's degrees for teaching in certain fields, others include among the teaching ranks individuals who attended two-year normal schools or who began teaching before "requirements" were established. Today teacher education programs are evaluated by the National Council for Accreditation of Teacher Education (NCATE)—an organization which was formed in 1952 and which can trace its ancestry to the first accreditation organization, the American Association of Teachers Colleges, which began inspections of teacher education programs in 1927.

An important document reflective of the professionalization of the teaching function is the report issued by the task force on New Horizons in Teacher Education and Professional Standards, an action-oriented committee of the National Commission on Teacher Education and Professional Standards (NCTEPS). Dedicated to the professionalization of the entire spectrum of American education, the task force emphasized. "*The three essential processes of enforcement of professional standards are accreditation of preparatory programs, licensure of professional personnel, and rigorous application of standards of practice.*" [31]

Although this document is a veritable bible for the growth of professionalism in education, it also reveals the gradual erosion of community control over all aspects of the school. Professionalization implies that teachers, as professionals, must ultimately be responsible for the preparation, admission, and retention of their colleagues. Major educational associations are national in scope and thus their growth in importance serves to shift decision making from local to national groups. Thus, while educationists persistently have supported the view that professionals should join *with* the public in establishing and evaluating educational programs, they increasingly reserve the right to evaluate their personnel and the means to achieve the mutually established educational aims. Despite the fact that the movement toward community control has gained in popularity, it should be expected that it increasingly will confront the parallel movement toward professionalism. Indeed, in numerous schools, especially in areas where population shifts have occurred, professionals and the public have developed antagonisms because of their difference in perceptions concerning the teacher's role. The issue of community control and professionalization of the teaching profession will remain as a major area of conflict in the seventies.

Unfortunately, the increase in public involvement in school practices has not always served the cause of democratizing the school. In

[31] Margaret Lindsey, ed., *New Horizons for the Teaching Profession* (Washington: National Commission on Teacher Education and Professional Standards, National Education Association of the United States, 1961), p. 238.

many cases, for example, community involvement means the inordinate influence of one segment of the local population. Most American citizens seem to prefer that educators make the major educational decisions, and the call for community control has not served to engage their involvement. For this reason so-called community spokesmen often do not represent the community and serve, on the contrary, to create greater antagonisms between the school and the public by their unpopular militant position. What is more, despite the fact that community control is based upon the assumption that democracy is served when the people are directly involved in the activities of *their* schools, it often mitigates against the democratic creed. Unfortunately, many Americans are not well versed in Jeffersonian beliefs and would prefer to deprive other Americans of their civil liberties. Local control may mean local oppression!

Of course, advocates of local or community control readily counter such admonitions by reminding teachers that public schools are designed by the public, supported by the public, and built for the public, and that teachers are fundamentally civil servants—hirelings of the community. When a teacher faces the issue of violating a school ordinance, therefore, the issue may be ideologically complicated. Does a teacher have the obligation to obey rules designed by representatives of the people? Isn't the teacher who believes in the democratic charter and who was hired to teach according to the dictates of the people obliged to do their bidding or resign? What if a teacher is forbidden to mention the United Nations or to discuss racial issues? Should he obey such dictates or should he assume an attitude of "public be damned"?

Along with the local control of public schooling, a second factor serving to inhibit the emergence of professionalism in education has been the conflict between the two major education associations—the NEA, representing the advocates of professionalism, and the American Federation of Teachers (AFT), the voice for the unionization of the teaching force. The emergence of these two organizations is the focus of the following section.

Although Educationism may imply a withdrawal from community pressures, it also may serve to diminish the market orientation of schooling. Maxine Greene observed: "The market orientation, nevertheless, does much to explain why there is so much deafness in our profession and why protests are so infrequently heard. If one is in the business of marketing a commodity and satisfying those who can afford to buy, one is not likely to criticize one's customers' values or to challenge the way they live their lives." [32] Needless to add, if teachers are to assume the pro-

[32] Maxine Greene, "Values in Society and Teacher Education," in *Teacher Education: Future Directions,* ed. Margaret Lindsey (Washington: The Association of Teacher Educators, 1970), p. 67.

fessional role as teacher, with its implication of leadership and ethical responsibility, the professional preparation of teachers must include explorations in areas of leadership, value commitments, and alternative educational patterns. If the first of these areas sometimes results from activity programs, the latter two must result from intense intellectual exploration, which to Americans attuned to the value of practical activity may appear irrelevant.

The separation of theory from practice characterizes many of the debates dealing with the educational endeavor. Generally, students call for greater practice and less theory, believing that the art of teaching can best be refined with practice. While some educationists believe that the best practice is a good theory, others have succumbed to the popular American ideological conviction that the best preparation for teachers is practice. The debunking of theoretical analysis results not only from the belief that practical activity is the mother of learning, but also from the fact that theoreticians often fail to comprehend the complexity of the emotional element in schooling. Many student-teachers have been overcome by their personal inability to deal with the highly charged emotional environment within schools. What is more, future teachers are rarely prepared to assume a role of leadership—a role which teaching implies. Because the teaching profession has been viewed as "good clean work" and a "pleasant position for a young lady," many individuals who prefer non-leadership roles have been attracted to teaching. Recent militancy within schools, however, is changing this image and may serve to discourage the individual who prefers to follow rather than guide.

An additional reason for the unpopularity of dealing with theory is the fact that individual growth in dealing with theoretical issues and social maturity are not easily perceived. The development of a practical skill is visible and the process of refinement of a skill can be measured, but growth in social awareness, sensitivity, confidence, and commitment —a process often ancillary to intellectual exploration and necessary for effective teaching—is not easily measured. Often, students either fail to see their individual growth or attribute it to nonschool sources. In fact, contrary to the beliefs of many current debunkers of schooling practices, all experiences, including college experiences, influence the behavior of a teacher. If some college experiences—such as learning the teaching role by observing numerous professors who may not be artist-teachers—are detrimental to effective teaching, others serve directly or indirectly in the teacher's performance of his duties. Of course, individuals who view teaching as an art which results from the application of a "bag of tricks" are doomed to be dissatisfied with potentially meaningful theoretical analyses of the educational process. The practical value of a proven theory does not depend only upon the theory but also upon the individual who seeks to apply it!

### Professionalism, Unionism, and Control

The aggrandizement of formal education has created numerous alterations in the educational environment. A major result of the extension of schooling has been the centralization of educational patterns. From the local control of educational programs, through state control that emerged as part of the common school movement, to the present nationalization of education, educational programs have become increasingly standardized across the United States, and the recent national assessment programs reflect, in part, the gradual standardization momentum.

The movement from local town control of education toward a massive centralized national system of education has resulted from numerous phenomena. For example, the growth of schooling eventually necessitated an increase in the tax base for funding educations support. The local property tax basis for funding education has proved to be inadequate to the demands of bureaucratic and extended educational systems. State taxation and eventually federal support—often provided indirectly through such devises as monies for lunch programs or grants for improving counseling facilities—have become necessary and have served to standardize education.

The spreading of a national ideology and the development of national cohesion are aims of all national educational systems. Although such educational programs are characterized in many countries by centralization, the federal government in the United States does not participate *directly* in the development of uniformity of curricular programs. American education, however, is remarkably standardized. The reason for such uniformity are diverse, but the emergence of educational professional groupings which serve to unite the profession on the basis of national designs is certainly one of the major factors enhancing the development of such uniformity. Such national associations tend to ". . . explicitly or implicitly function to promote the development of knowledge theoretical or applied, *within their own national society.*"[33]

The major professional and national organization of teachers in the United States is the National Education Association. It boasts the largest membership of any educational association and was the first national educational association within the United States. The National Education Association was organized in 1857 as the National Teachers' Association.

[33] Florian Znaniecki, *Modern Nationalities: A Sociological Study* (Urbana: The University of Illinois Press, 1952), p. 66.

On May 15, 1857, the presidents of ten state teachers' associations called for the establishment of a national organization of teachers. "Believing that what has been done for States by State Associations may be done for the whole country by a national association," they extended an invitation for an August meeting "to all *practical teachers* in the North, the South, the East, and the West, who are willing to unite in a general effort to promote the educational welfare of our country." [34] The name which they selected, the National Teachers' Association, was changed in 1870 when the Association combined with the National Association of School Superintendents and the American Normal School Association. That decision defined the nature of the association and created the ethos of professionalism which has served to delineate the nature of teacher behavior and expectations. In 1908 it became what is presently called the National Education Association. T. W. Valentine in his call to order during the convention for organization held in Philadelphia, avowed:

> What we want is, [sic] an association that shall embrace *all* the teachers of our *whole* country, which shall hold its meetings at such central points as shall accommodate all sections and combine all interests. [35]

The original members of the NEA included representatives from Delaware, the District of Columbia, Georgia, Illinois, Indiana, Iowa, Maryland, Massachusetts, Missouri, New York, Ohio, Pennsylvania, and South Carolina. William Russell, in a speech read at the 1857 organization convention affirmed:

> For the first time in the history of our country, the teachers of youth have assembled as a distinct professional body, representing its peculiar relations to all parts of our great national Union of States. The event is a most auspicious one, as regards the intellectual and moral interests of the whole community of which, as citizens, we are members. [36]

Besides the professional emphasis of the new Association, its national composition also was a central factor influencing the direction it took. During the first annual meeting in 1858, Zalmon Richards, the first president of the National Teachers' Association, acknowledged that the Association was national in fact as well as in name: "Its friends, therefore, do not feel that they are guilty of arrogance, or of inwarrantable assumption, in giving it the cognomen of 'Nation.' . . . [F]or this Association we claim the Nation—the United States—as its field of operation." [37]

[34] "Proceedings of Convention for Organization," *Proceedings of the National Teachers' Association, 1857–1870* (Syracuse: C. W. Bardeen, Publishers, 1909), p. 2.

[35] "Proceedings of Convention for Organization," p. 12.

[36] William Russell, "National Organization of Teachers," *Proceedings of the National Teachers' Association,* p. 15.

[37] Zalmon Richards, "The Agency of the Association in Elevating the Character and Advancing the Interests in the Profession of Teaching," *Proceedings of the National Teachers' Association,* p. 49.

Zalmon saw education as a process to help develop effective citizens and to prepare those "young immortals, who, in a few days more, are to hold in their hands the destinies of our country!" [38] The Association, he asserted, will provide for the "preservation and advancement of our country's prosperity . . . while it does not claim this as its specific work, it will most essentially aid in accomplishing it." [39]

The National Education Association included at the turn of the decade a membership in excess of one million. Its NEA *Journal* has the largest circulation of any educational journal in the United States. Through the variety of its departments, committees, commissions, councils, journals, conventions, pamphlets, and lobbying in state and national legislative assemblies, it exerts a significant influence upon the educational system of the United States. Through such meetings as the Committee of Ten and the Committee on College Entrance Requirements in 1893 and 1899, respectively, it has assisted in the process of standardizing the curriculum. Its continuous call for federal funds for education and for the equalization of educational opportunity has prepared the road for greater federal involvement in schooling. Recently, its use of sanctions against particular education districts has served to equalize educational systems throughout the nation. Although the NEA does not always present a clear-cut official policy, goals, and philosophy, it has remained national in scope and has strived continuously for "professionalism" in education.

During its long history the NEA has confronted numerous crises, the first of which came during the Civil War, just a few years after the Association had been founded. At the annual meeting of 1863, the members of the National Teachers Association affirmed their unconditional loyalty to the Union. However, in the "call of the states," during the last day of the convention, representatives from the seceding states were notably absent. A significant entry reads: ". . . Major W. S. Pope, of the Army of the Miss., [sic] reported on educational matters in Tennessee, Louisiana, and Mississippi . . ." [40]

The NEA weathered the Civil War and numerous other national crises. Indeed, the greatest threat to its influence occurred in recent years with the growth of teacher militancy and the increasing appeal of the American Federation of Teachers (AFT). The relationship between professionalism and unionism has emerged as a major issue for educationists.

The concept of professionalism generally is believed to have emanated from the structure of the medieval European guilds, which in turn

---

[38] Richards, "The Agency of the Association . . . ," pp. 47–48.
[39] Richards, "The Agency of the Association . . . ," p. 48.
[40] Minutes of the Annual Meeting, 1863, *Proceedings of the National Teachers' Association, 1857–1870.*

can be traced back to the religious associations of Germanic antiquity. Prior to the Middles Ages, individuals engaged in the vocations now considered to be professions served apprenticeships that required no formal schooling. In ancient Greece and Rome, for example, "lawyers" were trained by the sophists and "doctors" generally were slaves in the households of the affluent. Architects, accountants, and engineers usually were salaried administrators employed by the state.

With the emergence of the universities in the medieval period, the concept of professionalism was formulated. Professors, reacting to the problem of job security in the student-controlled universities, organized guilds to protect their interests. These newly formed guilds demanded that students master a specific body of knowledge and pass qualifying examinations if they wished to be admitted to the guild. Once admitted, a student was required to complete his studies under the tutelage of the professors, who might then grant him a *licentia docendi* (license to teach), the earliest known form of academic degree.

With the further development of the universities, degrees were granted in law, theology, and medicine—vocations that later were titled "professions," a term first used in 1541. Thus a historical precedent emerged. Formal schooling attained at a university became a prerequisite for entrance into the professions while apprenticeships served in a guild continued to function as the prerequisite for admission into the crafts. Except for this important difference, the professions retained many of the functions previously associated with the guilds, such as "control over the work situation, regulation of relationships among colleagues, maintenance of an occupational ethic, rules governing relationships between guild member and customer [clients] and special protection by the broader community." [41]

Early in the eleventh century, guilds of merchants were organized in the European cities to determine, control, and protect prices, ethics, and standards. Following the pattern of the merchant guilds, artisans created craft guilds with similar structure and intent. In 1162 the bakers guild in France, for example, was guaranteed the exclusive right by Louis VII to prepare bread for sale—a monopoly that excluded millers and fullers, groups that previously had baked bread. Other groups, including tanners, weavers, fishers, and cordwainers eventually received official sanction for the establishment of exclusive trade arrangements. Such policies served to protect the artisan from competition with his fellow workers and to restrict competition among artisans in different cities. In addition, the policies established and controlled working hours,

[41] Sigmund Nosow and William H. Form, eds., *Man, Work, and Society* (New York: Basic Books, Inc., 1962), p. 198.

wages, methods, and quality standards. The guild itself served as a foundation for political power and societal prestige in the bourgeois social structure.

Prior to the nineteenth century, the formal recognition of professionalism remained rather limited. The "three great professions of Divinity, Law and Physick" were popularized in seventeenth-century England. Accountants gained recognition in Italy with the development of commerce, and surgeons and apoethecaries were so honored as a consequence of discoveries in science and medicine.

Similarly, in the nineteenth and twentieth centuries the rise in the number of professions paralleled the emergence of industrialization as the exponential increases in technological developments were reflected in the burgeoning number of professions. Recent developments in nuclear science, space exploration, and computer technology, for example, have created a myriad of vocations that are ranked as professions. In addition, technological growth has influenced the professionalization of many occupations previously deemed to be nonprofessional. With the addition of formal schooling as a necessary prerequisite for certification, beauticians became cosmetologists, undertakers became morticians, and laboratory employees became medical technologists.

During the past decade the controversy among educationists concerning the question of union membership has received public attention as the image of the teacher exemplified by the prudish schoolmarm and the kindly Mr. Chips has been shattered by the reality of teachers walking on picket lines. Such public displays have been especially shocking to those Americans who have accepted the traditional view of the teacher as a "self-sacrificing, gentle, kindly, self-effacing creature overworked, underpaid but never out of patience and always ready to 'give freely of her time and money' for school purposes." [42]

The stereotype of the teacher as missionary has been reinforced by various media. The old western movies portrayed the teacher as a puritanical, New England schoolmarm who journeyed westward intent upon bringing some modicum of "culture" to the crude, illiterate agrarian masses. Upon her arrival she encountered the ridicule and harassment of many unappreciative townspeople. But through dedication to her strict puritanical virtues of cleanliness, sobriety, and chastity, the schoolmarm ultimately triumphed, the townspeople came to realize the error of their ways, and she finally gained the respect she so rightly deserved.

The image of the teacher as a missionary also has been popularized by a variety of television series. Whether the teacher be the shrewd,

[42] Willard Waller, *The Sociology of Teaching* (New York: John Wiley & Sons, Inc., 1965), p. 419.

manipulative Miss Brooks, the meek, bumbling Mr. Peepers, or the sophisticated, "hip" inhabitant of "Room 222," the puritan spirit of self-sacrifice and dedication to a calling is a constant ingredient in the formula. Such a view generally has been accepted by the lay public and not totally rejected by the professional educators. Consequently, the "bread and butter" issues of unionism appear antithetical to the traditionally defined interests of those engaged in the field of education.

The public image of the teacher also has been influenced by the pervasive anti-intellectualism in this country. As Willard Waller observed, there has been a common belief among Americans, especially in the business community, "that only persons incapable of success in other lines become teachers, that teaching is a failure belt, the refuge of unsaleable men and unmarriageable women." [43] In the words of the trite slogan, "Those that can, do; those that can't, teach." Although "Yankee ingenuity" has been praised intellectual pursuits have been greeted with skepticism. Intellectualism generally has been associated with upper-class snobbery and viewed as a luxury in a society dedicated to the practical activities of country building. Henry Ford's oft-quoted phrase "you learn by doing" illustrates the mentality of the entrepreneur with its emphasis on practical experience and its equation of wisdom with financial rewards ("If your so smart, why aren't you rich?"). The business community's suspicion of, if not contempt for, intellectuals was shared by those involved in the labor movement. Union leaders often pejoratively branded intellectuals "visionaries," "radicals," and "communists," Consequently, this social ethos of anti-intellectualism has contributed greatly to the teachers' relatively low prestige and minimal financial reward. In such a social milieu teachers encounter great difficulties in their demand for higher salaries. Indeed, many taxpaying citizens consider educators overpaid.

Needless to say, the image of the teacher as a missionary and the belief that teaching is a "failure belt" have not been conducive to unionism. Missionaries are expected to be working for rewards in the next world, not this one, and "failures" can expect little in either world. Perhaps the most significant obstacle to the unionization of teachers, however, has been the teachers' own identification of themselves with professionalism. This phenomenon was noted by Richard Bruner, a union organizer. Expressing the frustration of frequent failure, he avowed:

> I believe, however, that the labor movement will not have any more than token success in bringing them into the union. The overwhelming majority of salesmen, typists, file clerks and professionals will not join because they consider it beneath their dignity, because they feel differently from

[43] Waller, *The Sociology of Teaching*, p. 379.

blue-collar workers about their jobs and their status, because they are afraid it will hurt their advancement and because the face of the labor movement seems to them cruel and exploitative.[44]

The American Federation of Teacher (AFT) developed out of the Chicago Teachers' Federation (CTF), which had been organized in 1897 to resist the domination of the public schools by the mayor of Chicago and his appointed board of education. In 1902 the CTF joined the American Federation of Labor (AFL) and fourteen years later it merged with seven other local associations to form the American Federation of Teachers.[45] *The American Teacher,* which had begun publication in 1912, became its published voice.

In contrast to the NEA, the original AFT chapter permitted only teachers to become members. This policy, revised in 1933 to generally exclude only superintendents, was based upon the labor movement principle that there is an inevitable conflict of interest between employer and employee. Although the AFT continues to accept this position, the union does not strongly emphasize it and generally submerges it in a rhetoric that is exemplified by the following statement: "Administrators are excluded from its membership not because the Federation believes that they are necessarily different or hostile to the interests of teachers, but because it recognizes that two types of responsibility are involved. . . ."[46]

Unionism is generally defined as the collective effort of a group of individuals, organized to protect and promote their own interests. From this definition one can establish four basic assumptions. First, a society consists of conflicting or competing collective interests. Second, the individual must relinquish some of his personal freedom for the common good of the collective interests. Third, groups of individuals having collective interests will actively protect and promote them. And fourth, the "common good" of the society will be enhanced by the promotion of these competing collective interests.

Unionism in America, however, in contrast to unionism in many European countries, never has been strongly ideological or principled. Indeed, American unionism has reflected many of the fundamentally bourgeois attitudes of the country as a whole. From its inception, Ameri-

---

[44] Dick Bruner, "Why White-Collar Workers Can't Be Organized," in *Man, Work, and Society,* p. 188.

[45] The eight charter locals included: The Chicago Teachers' Federation, Chicago Federation of Men Teachers, The Chicago Federation of Women High School Teachers, The Gary, Indiana Teachers' Federation, The Teachers' Union of the City of New York, The Oklahoma Teachers' Federation, The Scranton, Pennsylvania Teachers' Association, and the High School Teachers' Union of Washington, D.C.

[46] Commission on Educational Reconstruction, *Organizing the Teaching Profession* (Chicago: American Federation of Teachers, 1955), p. 140.

can unionism generally has been philosophically pragmatic. Far from being a revolutionary force in a class struggle, American unionism has been more interested in the struggle for upward mobility. Generally, it has been perceived as a means of achieving the short-range goals of such "bread and butter" issues as higher income, unemployment and retirement benefits, job security, and systematized social mobility.

Because of its relatively nonideological nature, the American version of unionism has the potential of appealing to individuals of various ideological persuasions. As noted previously, teachers generally have identified with professionalism and rejected unionism. Many teachers, reared in the lower-middle-class environment of smalltown and agrarian communities, view unionism with great suspicion. In addition, many teachers are first generation professionals; although they belong to families with union members, they consider themselves as having "risen above" union membership. Nevertheless, changing social conditions have forced teachers to re-examine the concepts of unionism.

Technological developments have eliminated, in part, the distinction between professional and nonprofessional. As the factors which have differentiated the professional from the nonprofessional become more equally distributed (e.g., formal education) or change as a result of societal influence (e.g., community sanction), the differences between these two employment categories decrease in importance. In addition, a technological society places a great deal of emphasis upon formal schooling and public services, so that the uniqueness of the teachers' role relative to that of policemen, firemen, and numerous other public servants tends to disappear. Realizing their potential prestige, they will tend to further enhance their power, and the concept of unionism may be viewed as a means to actualize their goals.

As numerous research endeavors have indicated, the most significant factor in determining an individual's propensity to accept the concept of unionism has been job dissatisfaction. Within the past several decades, job dissatisfaction among educationists has increased as a result of various changing social conditions. Reflecting the managerial revolution in the corporate structure, there has been a major increase in the number of administrative and semi-administrative positions. There also has been a vast increase in the number of specialized occupations, including guidance counselors, speech and hearing therapists, curriculum consultants, test and measurement experts, special teachers of reading, and teachers for the gifted and the disadvantaged. Individuals engaged in these occupations generally are favored over the traditional subject matter or grade-level teacher when openings occur in the administrative ranks. In addition, many administrative positions are filled by "outside" candidates who have attained the formal prerequisite credentials. Consequently, many teachers who desire to "move up" find their aspirations frustrated. The concept of unionism appeals to these teachers by providing a systematized order for job promotion.

Vertical mobility, however, is only one means of getting ahead. Another method, horizontal mobility, is perhaps a more important one, especially for teachers in large urban areas. Horizontal mobility can be viewed as a type of "moving up" if one transfers to a "better" school. As racial and socioeconomic segregation continues to increase in urban areas, many teachers fear being trapped in a "bad" or "core" school and desire to be transferred to a "better" school nearer the fringe of the city. In addition, the hostility, anxiety, and alienation felt by the teachers in their relations to the community have served to intensify the general problems faced in the school situation. The following problems were observed by Howard S. Becker:

> (1) the problem of *teaching*, producing some change in the child's skills and knowledge which can be attributed to one's own efforts; (2) the problem of *discipline*, maintaining order and control over the children's activity; and (3) the problem of what may be termed *moral acceptability*, bringing one's self to bear some traits of the children which one considers immoral and revolting.[47]

Consequently, with educationists believing that the problems have been intensified, it is not surprising to find that "a higher proportion of teachers in schools serving disadvantaged areas, are dissatisfied with their present assignments and with their students than are their counterparts in other schools." [48] Such dissatisfaction tends to enhance the appeal of unionism.

The issue of job satisfaction includes the concern for job security. With the increased emergence of "black awareness" and the demands for equal rights, members of various minority groups have demanded a greater voice in the control of the public schools. This ideological commitment was expressed by Stokely Carmichael and Charles V. Hamilton:

> Control of the ghetto schools must be taken out of the hands of "professionals," most of whom have long since demonstrated their insensitivity to the needs and problems of the black child. These "experts" bring with them middle-class biases, unsuitable techniques and materials; these are, at best, dysfunctional and at worst destructive. . . .
>
> Black parents should seek as their goal the actual control of the public schools in their community: hiring and firing of teachers, selection of teaching materials, determination of standards, etc.[49]

[47] Howard S. Becker, "The Career of the Schoolteacher," in *Man, Work, and Society*, p. 323.

[48] *Report of the National Advisory Commission on Civil Disorders*, Otto Kerner, chairman (New York: Bantam Books, 1968), p. 429.

[49] Stokely Carmichael and Charles V. Hamilton, *Black Power: The Politics of Liberation in America* (New York: Random House, Inc., 1967), pp. 166–67.

The conflict between this ideological perspective and the teacher's concern for job security resulted in a major teachers' strike in New York City in 1968. Increasing demands for community control and the decentralization of urban school systems obviously will result in the teacher's reconsideration of the concepts inherent in unionism.

Another factor that has contributed to teacher militancy has been the "flight to the suburbs." Suburban governments are faced with a rapid increase in population, a large proportion of which is strongly consumption oriented yet receiving relatively low salaries. Lacking the financial assistance of a business-industrial tax base, most suburbanites have united in a demand for "no new taxes." What is more, as a result of their increasing numbers they have gained in political power at the state level and have formed a powerful alliance with the representative of rural areas to block financial aid to the cities. Thus, educationists encounter increasing resistance to expenditures for education at a time when their prestige has risen as a result of their position in a rapidly emerging service- and credential-oriented society. Cognizant of their new importance, they are demanding higher salaries while voters increasingly reject school bond levies. Consequently, school boards can anticipate demands for collective bargaining and communities increasingly will encounter work stoppages by teachers in addition to those by policemen, firemen, and other public servants.

During the decade of the sixties the percentage of teachers enrolled in the AFT nearly doubled while that in the NEA remained relatively stable. Recognizing this factor and responding to the growing demands of the teachers, the NEA has increasingly emphasized the need for more "militant" action and a greater concern for protecting the interests of teachers. For example, the title of the main address to the 1968 national convention was "Commitment to Action," a phrase previously associated with the AFT; in this speech Braulio Alonzo, the president of the NEA, made the following statements:

> The teachers of America have a new image, a new determination. They are committed to action. . . . No longer a sleeping dragon, the NEA is an aroused, active, alert giant. . . . Professionalism does not mean acquiescence! Professionalism does not mean acceptance of the status quo! . . . Teacher militancy is having a positive effect. . . .[50]

The second speech, given by Sam Lambert, executive secretary, was entitled "Teacher Power: Key to Change." It echoed the same sentiments as the first, but with even greater intensity.

The demand for "action," "militancy," and "power" also was reflected

[50] Braulio Alonzo, "Commitment to Action," National Education Association, *Addresses and Proceedings* (Washington: National Education Association, 1968), CVI, 7.

- 8

Educationism

in the NEA's attitude toward strikes ("work stoppages"). While not openly advocating them, the NEA does not categorically deny that they may be necessary. This changing attitude was manifested during the 1967 national convention when William Carr, then stepping down as president of the association, declared:

> [the] use of strikes by the teaching profession for the economic advantage of the teacher, especially when such action is contrary to law and court order, will impair and ultimately destroy the confidence of the public in the teacher. And when that is gone, the American public school and American life will have lost something precious and irreplaceable.[51]

In contrast, Sam Lambert, the incoming executive secretary, announced that the NEA "will not encourage strikes but if one occurs after all good-faith efforts fail, we will not walk out on our local associations." At a news conference he added: "when school conditions present a serious threat to the safety and welfare of children and teachers, teachers may be justified in taking drastic action."[52] This statement was made in 1967, and during the 1967–68 school year there were 114 strikes involving more than 160,000 teachers in twenty-one states. This should be contrasted with only ninety-one strikes in the twenty-two-year period between 1940 and 1962. The vast majority of the strikes were by local teachers associations whose membership belonged not to the AFT, but to the NEA. In April 1969 the NEA urged congress to legalize teacher strikes and to require local school boards to negotiate with teachers. Thus the position of the "new NEA" is strikingly similar to that of the AFT. They both agree about the necessity of work stoppages (strikes) and professional negotiations (collective bargaining), and they are both concerned about the health and safety of the teachers ("crime in the halls").

The traditional debate about whether teachers will join the union (the AFT) or the professional association (the NEA) is of less significance now that they have become rather similar in their views and behavior. In fact, there has been increasing talk of their merger. As early as the mid-1950s Myron Lieberman discussed this possibility:

> What appears to be happening is that the NEA and the AFT are moving toward common programs. The AFT, on the defensive because of criticisms of its concentration upon teacher welfare, is trying to broaden its program to include matters not directly concerned with teacher welfare. The NEA, on the defensive for ignoring teacher welfare in the past, is giving it more attention than ever before.[53]

[51] New York Times, July 5, 1967, p. 29.
[52] New York Times, April 8, 1968, p. 33.
[53] Myron Lieberman, Education as a Profession (Englewood Cliffs, N.J.: Prentice-Hall, Inc., 1956), p. 312.

With or without merger, however, differences between the NEA and the AFT have diminished and the "great debates" entitled "Unionism vs. Professionalism" appear to have lost much of their significance.

## Conclusion

The American citizen's historic faith in education and the increasing focus upon formal schooling have served to enhance the ideology of Educationism. Indeed, the educational system has regained some of the power it held during the Middle Ages when the "teacher" knew the secrets of both writing and Holy Writ. In the future, one can anticipate further controversy between the schools and the society and among the educationists themselves. In a pluralistic society, these tensions, however, have a positive function. Although the eclectic nature of Educationism may frustrate the efficiency expert and the true believers of all persuasions, it also may serve to protect educationists from the excesses so evident in other ideological systems.

## Suggested Readings

ALLEN, DWIGHT W., and ELI SEIFMAN, ed. *The Teacher's Handbook*. Chicago: Scott, Foresman & Company, 1971).

CALLAHAN, RAYMOND E. *Education and the Cult of Efficiency*. Chicago: University of Chicago Press, 1962.

COLEMAN, JAMES S. *The Adolescent Society*. New York: The Free Press, 1961.

CONANT, JAMES BRYANT. *The Education of American Teachers*. New York: McGraw-Hill Book Company, 1963.

CURTI, MERLE. *The Social Ideas of American Educators*. New York: Charles Scribner's Sons, 1935.

DEWEY, JOHN. *Democracy and Education*. New York: The Macmillan Company, 1920.

EDWARDS, NEWTON, and HERMAN G. RICHEY. *The School in the American Social Order*. Boston: Houghton Mifflin Company, 1963.

GAGE, N. L., ed. *Handbook of Research on Teaching*. Chicago: Rand McNally & Co., 1963.

GREENE, MAXINE. *The Public School and the Private Vision*. New York: Random House, Inc., 1965.

HASKINS, CHARLES HOMER. *The Rise of Universities*. New York: Great Seal Books, 1923.

KIMBALL, SOLON T., and JAMES E. MCCLELLAN, JR. *Education and the New America*. New York: Random House, Inc., 1962.

LIEBERMAN, MYRON. *Education as a Profession*. Englewood Cliffs, N.J.: Prentice-Hall, Inc., 1956.

LINDSEY, MARGARET, ed. *New Horizons for the Teaching Profession.* Washington: National Commission on Teacher Education and Professional Standards, National Education Association of the United States, 1961.

SEXTON, PATRICIA CAYO. *The American School: A Sociological Analysis.* Englewood Cliffs, N.J.: Prentice-Hall, Inc., 1967.

SILBERMAN, CHARLES E. *Crisis in the Classroom: The Remaking of American Education.* New York: Random House, Inc., 1970.

SPINDLER, GEORGE D., ed. *Education and Culture: Anthropological Approaches.* New York: Holt, Rinehart & Winston, Inc., 1963.

TYACK, DAVID B., ed. *Turning Points in American Educational History.* Waltham, Mass.: Blaisdell Publishing Co., 1967.

WALLER, WILLARD. *The Sociology of Teaching.* New York: John Wiley & Sons, Inc., 1965.

## Epilogue

# A FINAL WORD:
# A PERSONAL VIEW

In concluding our exploration we ask the reader to linger with us briefly in our attempt to clarify and emphasize some assumptions which we feel are critical to an understanding of our intent. Our purpose in writing this epilogue is fourfold. First, we recognize that our particular ideological propensities have unwittingly found their way into our analysis and undoubtedly have distorted some of our observations. Objectivity is a myth perpetuated by Scientism! The previous exploration, although based on an attempt to do justice to the various ideological systems analyzed, inevitably reflects our own biases. Although we attempted to illustrate our conviction that various ways of perceiving reality offer creative possibilities as well as inherent dangers, we recognize that our personal beliefs have oriented our emphases and skewed our findings. Some of the following comments, therefore, are provided to clarify our opinions and thus should serve the reader as a guide in detecting the distortions that result from our ideological prism.

Secondly, we believe that this book could serve the reader—whether he be a layman, a student, a teacher, or an administrator—as an ideological gyroscope by helping him understand why he perceives and behaves in the way that he does. We hope that the reader has looked within himself during this ideological exploration and we wish in this epilogue to emphasize some cautionary observations. Even though this exploration may assist the reader in discovering channels of perception, he should avoid utilizing it as a guide for personality analysis.

Thirdly, although we noted throughout the analysis the diverse ways in which the schools relate to the world of ideology, we have attempted to avoid prescriptive statements concerning the role of the school. In this epilogue we will present briefly some admonitions which we believe *should* orient the schools of the seventies.

Our fourth purpose is to offer suggestions concerning the development of safeguards against ideological excess. These suggestions should serve as a *porte-cochère* for discussion and as a guide for those individuals in search of a shield against ideological excess.

The importance of ideologies and their centrality in the life of man cannot be diminished without dire consequences. Man cannot live meaningfully or creatively without them. They enliven his existence and enhance his capacity to dream and to see visions. His social systems depend upon them and his aesthetic awareness is intensified by them. His sanity and comfort rest upon them.

Without ideologies, physical force and psychological manipulation would be the sole means of sustaining social cohesion. With the breakdown of ideologies, societies increasingly need policemen, psychiatrists, and undercover agents. Ideologies serve the vital function of providing social cement because they furnish a society with a perceptual and communication network which binds individuals together while permitting them to find peace and exert freedom of choice within certain ideational limits. Because of the countervailing forces and diverse alternatives within them, some ideological systems enhance individual creative self-expression and ethical awareness.

Belief systems serve men by furnishing them with an ideational structure which channels their perceptions and thoughts and influences their behavior. They serve as a source for human intellectual, aesthetic, emotional, and spiritual expression. Without ideologies, man's freedom of choice would be obviated for he would lack a foundation upon which to activate his valuing processes. When ideological systems collapse, man suffers the fate of moral nihilism and behavioral atrophy. Without the security of the warm blanket of a belief system, an individual is either unable to act or fears to make the choices necessary for action. Like Meursault in Albert Camus' *The Stranger,* the individual would be a man alone wandering through the obscurity of absurdity. Social anomie creates debilitating alienation and men increasingly resort to tranquilizers, stimulants, or the call of demagogues.

Ideologies serve as guardians to a creature who sometimes appears to be overwhelmed by the reality of knowing that he knows while doubting what he knows. They serve as a comfort to creatures who ponder eternal verities but remain painfully aware that they will die. Besides providing him with solace, they function as his inheritance from his ancestors and as a legacy for his progeny. They bind him spatially and temporally with those unknown individuals who share his civilization.

A belief system also provides a vital wellspring for man's creative and spiritual energies. The eclectic ideologist may be an ideal construct for a rational pacifist but he does not serve as a referent for a creative artist. Men who have inspired others by their passionate life styles have been carriers of ideologies who have disseminated them by serving as models for their expression. Francis Bernardone, for example, would have remained a seeker of bourgeois pleasures without the ideological pressures generated by a formidable religious ideology. Christianity served as a wellspring for his spiritual energies and he lives in our memories as the gentle and humble St. Francis of Assisi. Countless artists, saints, and heroes have excelled because of the influence of ideological stimulants. The eclectic believer as well as the nihilist may be pleasant participants in a debate, but they do not inspire thought or inflame emotion.

Ideologies serve as energizers for action. Social movements reflect diverse ideological emphases and the success of any movement will depend in part upon the ability of leaders to attract individuals who adhere to various ideological systems. The women's liberation movement is a fitting example to illustrate the multi-dimensional ideological attraction of a social movement. Adherents of Scientism, for example, could see women's liberation as a means of enhancing the efficiency of the technological society. The passage of equal opportunity legislation as well as the removal of various restrictions against women in the world of work perhaps would increase the technological competency of our social system. Thus educationists might view the movement as an opportunity to increase formal schooling through the proliferation of day care centers that would be required when women have equal access to the labor market. Similarly, the progressivist, with his commitment to group process, democracy, efficiency, and social planning, might welcome the liberation of women as a means of removing the remnants of rugged individualism and role formalism that have remained rooted to the nuclear family structure.

Both romanticists and puritan revolutionaries well might see their ideologies served by the woman's liberation movement. The former could welcome it as a psychic liberation and an opportunity for devising alternative life styles, whereas the latter could utilize it as a means of weakening the family, an institution which has served as a major bulwark of the established order. Moreover, the puritan moralists could perceive it as an opportunity for the moral regeneration of a society which is structured upon sexual bigotry and the debasement of the female form that results from the utilizing of women as a lure and bait in the economic marketplace. Even the nationalists could view such a movement with delight, for the equalization of opportunity for women could strengthen national cohesion by ensuring that both men and women would serve their nation together as equal partners.

The foregoing observations concerning the possible ideological components of the woman's liberation movement should be viewed as an example of the various ways in which ideologies can be utilized. Using somewhat different arguments, we should note, each ideology also could oppose the liberation movement.

Within all societies, schooling serves as a means of acculturating neophytes into the ideological realities upon which their civilization is founded. Indeed, to fail in the task of conveying an ideological inheritance is to remove from a social system a vital link among the people and to deprive individuals of a necessary source of creative energy. To rob the ideology of a people is to enslave them to the boredom of nothingness. Thomas Merton rightfully warned about the danger of removing some of the assumptions which most human beings carry in their ideological baggage when he admonished:

> Most men cannot live fruitfully without a large portion of fiction in their thinking. If they do not have some efficacious mythology around which to organize their activities, they will regress into a less efficacious, more primitive, more chaotic set of illusions. When the ancients said that the solitary was likely to be either a god or a beast, they meant that he would either achieve a rare intellectual and spiritual independence, or sink into a more complete and brutish dependence. The solitary easily plunges into a cavern of darkness and of phantoms more horrible and more absurd than the most inane set of conventional social images. The suffering he must then face is neither salutary nor noble. It is catastrophic.[1]

If man cannot live without ideologies, he can often die and kill because of them. For every St. Francis of Assisi and Thomas Jefferson there exists a beady-eyed inquisitor in search of a religious or political heretic. Ideologies driven to excess function like an overdose of drugs—they can be fatal. While they serve to channel perception and to provide a wellspring for man's valuing processes, they easily serve as a crutch and as an escape from moral choice. The morally lax individual can kill in the name of his ideology and call it heroism rather than murder; he can give his life in its expansion and call it commitment rather than foolishness. Similarly, the intellectually indolent can be victimized by an ideology. He can forsake his freedom in its name and call it service rather than cowardice; he can avoid thought because of dogma and call it discipline rather than ignorance.

When ideologies as well as institutions become ends in themselves, man is always the loser. Although ideologies are necessary, they are also dangerous when they become ends rather than means. Man must protect himself against their excesses. Excessive Puritanism, for example, changes commitment into authoritarianism. Similarly, excessive Progressivism turns openmindedness into bland amorality. Students must learn ideologies, but they must also be taught to intellectually withdraw, if only momentarily, and to view ideologies like an anthropologist attempting to view their culture. Students must be taught to seek a referent which may emerge from their ideological systems but which extends beyond it and

[1] Thomas Merton, *Disputed Questions* (New York: The New American Library of World Literature, Inc., 1965), p. 146.

which permits them to transcend the limits imposed upon those who see solely through the prism of their social religion.

The ideologies analyzed in this book represent some of the belief systems which form the matrix labeled Americanism. Our attempts to explore them by unraveling the fabric of Americanism should be viewed as a theoretical separation. In reality, no ideology stands alone. Ideological eclecticism is the nature of man and his society. Puritanism, for example, may have dominated the ideological world of many Brahmins in the Massacuhsetts Bay Colony, but it never stood alone. It always formed part of an eclectic matrix. Similarly, despite the fact that many of the individuals noted in this text have been identified as representing certain ideological orientations, the reader should not conclude that they were ideologically unidimensional. Man is a carrier of various ideological orientations. Our premise has been that an individual has a propensity toward a specific ideological system and that he can deal more effectively with his social environment when he is aware of his ideological penchant.

Although we have emphasized ideological influences upon individuals and groups, and espouse a belief that ideological orientations serve as guides in understanding people, we wish to caution the reader against stereotyping. First and foremost, we believe that all human beings share common traits in their ability (potentially or actually) to reason, love, and laugh. Secondly, we also believe that all individuals are unique and that to understand a person it is necessary to explore his particular identity. Indeed, the preciousness of each and every human life rests ultimately upon the fact that individual human beings are unique and can never be replaced or replicated. Thirdly, human beings are in a continuous process of reaffirmation and change. To stereotype a man is to fail to recognize that he is in fact a *process*—a process which often reflects a magnificent ability to stupify would-be clinical categorizers.

With these safeguards, we believe that an understanding of ideological orientations will serve a sensitive person in partially unraveling an aspect of man which simultaneously lies at the root of human diversity and serves the cause of community.

We also wish to emphasize that ideological labels should not imply a negative or positive judgment concerning the worth of a particular orientation. We recognize that terms such as "Nationalism" and "Puritanism" have popular pejorative meanings whereas "Progressivism" and "Romanticism' are in vogue. We hope, however, that the reader will attempt to divest himself of these simplistic assumptions. To assume that ideologically different people are perverse, miseducated, or ignorant is not only cruel but also reflects a failure to comprehend the nature of ideological systems. Individuals, especially teachers, must acquaint themselves with ideological differences and learn to tolerate them. Teachers serve in an important socialization role and must possess ideological awareness. The effectiveness of their attempts to train or teach the young depends upon their ability to decipher the ideological world of their students.

Educationists continuously have admonished teachers that they should understand their students. Indeed, it is an unquestioned assumption that teaching a child must follow learning him. Unfortunately, teachers often succumb to the tendency to measure a child's ability rather than devoting their time to the necessary process of studying individual differences. Numerous teachers and students have failed in the world of schooling because of ideological orientations. Many students have been erroneously labeled "slow learners," "emotionally disturbed," and "mentally retarded" because they perceive the world through uncommon ideological lenses. Saints have been called fools and wise men have been called sinful because of ideological peculiarities. Teachers have earned the wrath of their students because they failed to comprehend the subtle but important differences in perception that result from divergent ideological systems. Ignorance concerning ideologies has been and continues to be fatal to the educational process. This book was written in the hope that it will decrease the fatality rate resulting from ideological conflict.

Because cross-ideological communication is a way of life in a modern complex society, ideological analysis must characterize the education which occurs within the schools of such a society. Schools are agencies for indoctrinating the young so that they will internalize the ideological assumptions of their society. This function requires skilled trainers and remains a fundamental and essential task of schooling. To be sure, it is not the sole function of the school, but individuals who advocate its removal fail to comprehend that ideologies are intentionally or unwittingly communicated by instructors. Training, of course, is not enough. Schools must furnish students with the tools which will enable them to transcend ideologies.

Thus, besides trainers, schools must also provide students with teachers. Trainers are valuable in indoctrinating individuals into their society's world, but teachers are the best reliance for helping students to transcend such socialization. Teaching is an art performed by a creative individual who may possess a field of specialization but who remains a generalist in the sense that he can relate his discipline to the human enterprise. He perceives aesthetic elements in knowledge and in its communication. Because he is an artist, he is not a methodologist. Style rather than method is reflected in his endeavor. Because teachers are able to place their particular tasks within the perspective of the lives of the individuals they teach, they are ideally qualified to assist others in the process of transcending ideological limitations which are imposed upon individuals by the socialization and politicization processes. Although he can serve as an effective indoctrinator, his students invariably will begin to question their training, for his artistry will encourage them to seek to express their own styles and their own views of the world.

To affirm that indoctrination and teaching are dual functions of the school should not imply that schooling should be separated into two distinct segments according to age level, subject matter, or instructors. Some ill-informed observers, for example, believe that children should be trained and adults should be taught. The advocates of training who believe that children are solely receptacles to be filled or animals to be manipulated fail to understand the subtle ways in which thinking and empathy find expression. Ethical dilemmas confront children as well as adults, for children too must choose between right and wrong, good and evil. The fears and anxieties which numerous children experience because of assumed transgressions exemplify the fact that children begin early in life with a valuing system. If children are trained into believing and not questioning, they will grow into dogmatic and authoritarian adults who will be unable to deal with human diversity.

All individuals need to be indoctrinated to the norms and values of their civilization. Their survival depends upon it. However, all individuals also need to be assisted in the process of transcending such indoctrination. Their humanness is rooted to it.

If some individuals advocate indoctrination for children and teaching for adults, others have divided the training and teaching functions according to academic disciplines. Often such proponents argue that instructors of science or mathematics must train skills into their students and do not have time for creative exploration. Co-curricular activities and some subject matters such as literature and creative writing are seen as opportunities for students to explore beyond the beliefs basic to certain disciplines, but other fields of inquiry, it is argued, require rigid methodology. In fact, however, all subject matter is the matter for teaching. The mathematical mind as well as the scientific mind is a liberated mind. The individual who cannot move beyond skills and methodology is doomed to be a technocrat and not a scientist. The trainers who seek merely to impose a methodology without conveying the liberating excitement of exploration, questioning, and doubting fail to teach the essence of knowledge regardless of their field of inquiry.

Just as schools need trainers, so they also need trainers who are teachers. The often expressed belief that some individuals are suited to train while others are equipped to teach merely confirms the misconceptions about teaching. Teaching is a transcending, performing, and practical art. It is an art which rises above training but is dependent upon it. Regardless of the knowledge to be communicated, a trainer must be a teacher to be effective. Similarly, a teacher must possess the skills of a trainer, just as an artist must first master his tools. Trainers may possess enviable skills, but only teachers can understand the subtleties of the learning process, the intricacies of psychological and environmental influences, and the complexity of human interaction. The belief that better trained trainers will solve the dilemma of schooling in America is rooted to the erroneous conviction that learning can be understood by dissecting, analyzing, and measuring the communication patterns which individuals utilize. Furthermore, such a belief indicates a naive view of the complexity and diversity of the ideological systems which nourish our society. A trainer trains, a teacher educates. Such a distinction was cogently illustrated by Eliseo Vivas:

> To begin the education of a young person is to start a radical alteration in him, and the alteration is as radical as the education is successful. But whereas we can, within reasonable limits, control the training of a person, the transformation that takes place as a man becomes educated is beyond our control. For this reason the man who undertakes to educate another assumes an awful responsibility. He may be instrumental in the production of a saint—or of a monster.[2]

Schools must be designed as centers for ideological training and for ideological transcendence. Both functions are critical and are explored in the following pages.

To function effectively within a society necessitates knowing the ideological assumptions upon which the social system rests. If an instructor within a school deliberately seeks to hide or distort the nature of his society's ideological fabric, he has failed his students and may have endangered their survival in the hostile world of ideological conflict. His foolish attempt to transmit the society's ideological matrix, regardless of the nobility of his aim, will fail, causing hardship to his misinformed or uninformed students.

The distortions that arise in the transmission of ideological systems compound the difficulties involved in humanizing societies. Dystopias invariably are based upon training systems which are deliberately structured to distort the nature of social realities. Ideological systems cannot be changed when individuals distort their content, nor can they be changed by wishful thinking, avoidance, or lies. Ignorance is never a source of strength. The avoidance of reality may be temporally soothing, but the long-range effect of such an escape will be fatal. Those individuals who are involved in the socialization and politicization processes and who believe that lying by omission or commission can serve the welfare of a society are displaying gross ignorance about the complexity and integ-

---

[2] Eliseo Vivas in Introduction to Friedrich Nietzsche, *Schopenhauer As Educator*, Gateway Editions (Chicago: Henry Regnery Company, 1965), p. xiii.

rity of man. Of course, ideological realities include both ideals and practices—two aspects which must be presented to the youth. To focus upon the ideals and to avoid identifying their applications and violations will serve as fuel for discontentment. Similarly, to focus upon violations and the inadequate implementation of ideals while avoiding the ideals themselves as well as their successful applications is to create a mythical straw man which will not serve the cause of change.

A cursory view of the schooling practices in the United States reveals that ideological training is often inadequate. The inadequacy is due primarily to poorly designed ideological programs and ineptness in their transmission. The fear that foreign ideologies are being transmitted clandestinely in American schools by a "fifth column" is not and never has been warranted. American teachers usually are well trained ideologically in schools which reflect the most moderate aspects of the American ideological fabric. Indeed, school philosophies and aims are usually drawn by committees of teachers and invariably reflect a loyalist attitude toward American institutions. In addition, teachers are drawn mainly from a new middle class, a socioeconomic class which is notably loyal to the expressed goals of national political leaders. Consequently, the schools do not reflect the total society, for they are reflective primarily of that segment of the population which adheres to the Aristotelian conviction that "moderation is the mother of virtue" and to York's admonition in *Henry VI:* "Let them obey that know not how to rule."

The failure of the schools in the process of ideological transmission is due primarily to their ideological traditionalism rather than to individual conscious acts of ideological sabotage. Schools often convey anachronistic ideological tenets which have been superceded by emerging values in the society as a whole. They are not in the vanguard of ideological change, nor do they react quickly to ideological shifts which occur in the society.

The reasons for the ideological traditionalism of schools are numerous. First, the schools exist, in great measure, precisely for the purpose of conveying the traditions and the cultural inheritance of a people. Their mission is essentially a conservative one, and because they tend to focus upon the past, the ways of the past often become for them the "oughts" of today.

Secondly, public schools are viewed as an agency of the people and as a tool which the social system utilizes to train its youth ideologically. Their legitimacy rests, as is often stated, upon the assumption that they reflect the will of the people. In a nation-state in which pluralism exists, the role of the school as a reflector of the people which it serves is not an easy one for it to fulfill. When there is a conflict of values, traditional values provide an easy haven, so that school personnel often fear to tread upon the uneasy and uncertain ground of emerging values. Whenever the accusation of "irrelevance" is forwarded, educators can always reply that schools reflect the standard virtues of the American civilization. As numerous ultraconservative critics of schools have shown, it is an easy matter to equate relevance with sin, and educators are prone to prefer the accusation that they are innocently irrelevant to the charge that they are relevant malefactors.

The ideological gap which results from the inherent traditionalism of schools, especially during periods of profound ideological change, tends to generate disillusionment among the students, and this disillusionment is the seedbed of loss of faith in the American system. When outdated ideological elements are taught as though they reflect current social practices, they serve only to undermine the foundation upon which a society rests.

Because of the rigidity of institutionalism and the often distorted manner in which American ideologies are presented within formal educational settings, values which are transmitted within the schools often are in conflict with the expectations of the social system. When such a gap is created, other informal educational agencies assume a major role in the socialization process. Thus peer groups, besides exerting their normal influence on certain age groupings, assume a major role in socialization and value transmission. Mass media such as television and the record industry have made profitable note of the importance of the peer group as a socialization agency and have catered directly to their needs and demands. The record industry, for example, once the preserve of the adult world, increasingly has become, a platform for youthful preachers. And the music heroes of the young are often members of their own age group. Ideologists for American youth are increasingly recruited from their own ranks.

Schools unwittingly seek to transmit values which are often detrimental to the stability and welfare of the social system. A few examples should serve to illustrate this dilemma. Instructors in public schools, for example, invariably emphasize the importance of thrift—a central social value during eighteenth-century America. The economic system in the United States, however, has changed radically in the past fifty years. Indeed, the puritan virtues of thrift and prudence are increasingly viewed with suspicion by a nation hopeful of conquering space while perpetuating and increasing a national deficit.

By manipulating peoples through clever advertising and built-in obsolescence, a consumer-oriented market continues to demand new products. If internalized as a value by the children and youth of today, thrift would sabotage the economic life of the United States. Thrift has changed from a social value to a social vice which threatens the economic life of the nation. Indeed, when the economy does not appear sound, the public begins to save and government officials frantically attempt to convince them to spend.

In addition to outdated economic ideals, some schools also transmit a naive view of the democratic process. The "town meeting" approach to democracy continues to be popularized in some public schools, despite the fact that its relevancy in the life of a citizenry who increasingly inhabit large metropolitan areas is diminishing if not already nonexistent. "Field trips" from large urban schools to town meetings in small neighboring towns may be a quaint educational tactic, but they often produce greater frustration than commitment. The complexity of preserving a democratic process within large urban centers remains a central dilemma that cannot be resolved through periodic escapes into traditions of the past. Sadly, schools have often failed to tackle the problem of the lack of adult interest in the political life of their cities, and it is to be hoped that the granting of suffrage to the youth of eighteen and over will serve the cause of enlivening America's democratic commitment. This hope is all the more urgent because the past reveals that if America is to witness the demise of its democratic dream, it will be because of omission rather than because of the misdeeds of tyrants.

Even though educators have often attempted to structure their schooling practices in a manner which reflects a democratic commitment, such programs often serve to undermine rather than sustain a commitment to democracy. Student governments, student courts, and innumerable committees usually are utilized to resolve unimportant issues. Democracy becomes a process whereby unimportant citizens make unimportant decisions while the Brahmins determine the directions and the rules. It is not surprising that the belief in a power elite behind all major national decisions has gained numerous adherents. Educators should reconsider the progressive conception that schools should be mini-democracies, unless they seriously desire to implement such an ideal. The tragedy is that educators believe in semi-democracies in school. Semi-democracies are not democracies at all and are, in fact, more destructive to the democratic dream than the oppressive yoke of authoritarianism.

Just as some school trainers have failed to update their ideological training programs to meet the needs of social realities, so other ideologists have distorted the American belief system by confusing the practices with the goals of society. A major tragedy in America today, a tragedy which could be fatal to the great democratic experiment, is the fact that instructors often utilize sociological analyses of existing patterns to ridicule the ideals and the goals which have sustained the American experiment. Overwhelmed by the fact that current realities do not fit the patterns devised in previous generations, some instructors dedicate themselves to debunking the democratic dream. Such a process serves to undermine the ideals which are a cornerstone of all social systems, for it forgets that men often become what they dream. Students and instructors all too often ridicule the idea of democracy because of the currently popular beliefs about the power elite and the "military-industrial complex." Similarly, many instructors misuse sociological and psychological studies to undermine their students' faith in the aspirations and abilities of the "common man," or of the newly emerged target of the would-be critic, the middle class. To debunk the democratic ideal as well as to ridicule the faith in man's ability to structure a humane society in which freedom and equality will prevail is to provide the rationale for a future totalitarian society.

To communicate properly the American ideological system implies that students must be assisted in understanding the practices as well as the assumptions, myths, dreams, rationalizations—and even the lies—which support the existing social system. The school instructor's role is to study, select, and communicate them effectively. He also must communicate the spirit that supports the ideas of his society. In an age when scientific analysis characterizes the search for truth and when men scoff readily at mythology, there is a tendency for schools to diminish the importance of dreams, visions, and faith in the life of man. The attempts to scientize life may lead to emptiness. As Pascal observed centuries ago, "The heart has reasons which reason cannot understand." Indeed, reason as well as scientific evidence do not sustain by themselves a hope in man's future. Faith ultimately sustains the pillars of civilization. Without faith or hope, charity flounders and civilizations decay.

Because of a sense of irrelevance that has gripped many American schools, the traditional training-learning and teaching-learning processes have been subject to increasing criticism. In some situations, students have been propelled into community activities and have become agents for social change. Indeed, involvement has recently become a byword of those who fail to comprehend the complexity of the learning process.

Educational progress that fails to provide the opportunity for teachers and students to analyze ideological systems and to study their influences upon human behavior is doomed to failure. Because America is a pluralistic nation and reflects diverse ideological assumptions, teachers must understand the ideological realities which prevail in the locality where they teach. A teacher assigned to teach in an area greatly influenced by the ideology of Black Nationalism, for example, should be prepared to deal with such a reality. To expect that one's personal unexamined experiences can prepare one for such a teaching assignment is to be incredibly naive.

Placing students in storefront schools, free schools, community centers, or day care centers does not automatically imply relevancy or improved education. Unexamined life experiences are useless to teachers even if they occur in "relevant" locations. The currently popular belief that school walls have been the cause of educational atrophy reveals a gross misunderstanding of the nature of teaching. The examined direct experience may have greater value than the examined indirect experience, but the unexamined experience regardless of its nature has little educational value.

Intellectual exploration is a vital aspect of education and should not be diminished in the name of relevance. Reason exists to enrich emotions and imagination, not to limit them. Action without thought or instead of thought serves to create a hidden form of deprivation. Intellectual exploration provides students with the opportunity for breaking through the temporal and spacial provincialism which usually accompanies human growth. It is through intellectual exploration of experience and the study of the intellectual exploration of others that human beings learn of the complexity of human existence. Without such efforts, Socrates would truly be dead and the past would be destroyed. It is through the study of the past as well as the study of man's Utopian dreams that we can break through the provincialism of our own time. Action programs may serve to awaken students to the realities of their immediate environment, but if such programs are utilized to replace the intellectual search beyond one's immediate temporal and spatial environment, then students will be deprived of much needed knowledge about man. What is more, the potential pleasures of the mind which await those who patiently strive through the academies would be forever barred from their grasp. It is through the process of breaking the hold of temporal and spatial provincialism that an individual discovers that wisdom rather than convention is the only humane source of authority. It is through the intellectual pursuit of truth that an individual comes to realize that the imposition of truth is a violation of truth and that ideological commitment does not necessitate dogmatism.

The instructor, of course, must continuously confront the dilemma of choosing between communicating an ideology and communicating *about* an ideology. The difference is critical in view of the fact that most ideological systems contain strands that are destructive to individual growth and are based upon anachronistic beliefs which are debilitating to society. Racism, for example, has been woven into the American ideological fabric from the inception of the nation. It was utilized as a rationale for an inhuman slavery system and continues to be utilized to support the unequal treatment of the races.

The issue that confronts all individuals who are involved in the socialization process is ideological selection. The ideology must be accurately analyzed and understood by the instructor and must be communicated honestly to his students. He also must decide which ideological elements should be inculcated and which should be analyzed and rejected. This ethical dilemma faces all those who assume the role of a socializing agent. The fact that in the name of ethical neutrality, schools often fail to prepare students for making such ethical choices is one of the dangerous characteristics of modern public education. Unless instructors can be relied upon to make mature and humane judgments in selecting ideological elements to communicate to their students, educational systems will flounder in a moral neutrality.

Not only should educators be prepared for unraveling the intricacies of the valuing process and the selection of ideological elements to be conveyed, but they also must be committed to the removal of those ideological distortions, such as racism, which they may have internalized. Self-study as well as ideological analysis must be performed continuously by those individuals who seek to train and teach the young effectively.

At the beginning of this epilogue we promised that we would furnish a few suggestions concerning means of protecting oneself from the blinding and mesmerizing appeal of ideological excess. Needless to say, shielding oneself from ideological excess requires painstaking and continuous effort. Not only must an individual become aware of his own ideological world, but he also must develop the ability to see it as others, especially his ideological antagonists, would view it. Immaculate perceptions are a myth.

Moving beyond beliefs does not imply the rejection of one's ideological commitments. Relativism and cynicism are the bedfellows of apathy and despair. Any attempt to immunize oneself against the excess of ideology must be based upon a means which does not endanger the survival of commitment. The psychic vaccine we describe as "moving beyond beliefs" is not a destroyer of ideologies but rather a control mechanism which alerts an individual when his beliefs cause him to forget his uniqueness as well as his membership in the family of man. Our vaccine is derived from our unalterable conviction that man is not *determined* by ideological forces and that he can diminish their influence if he is willing to struggle for his freedom.

Ideological transcendence, therefore, does not require that an individual forsake his beliefs, but merely that he sincerely explore them. It also requires that he possess a third eye—an eye which enables him to perceive himself perceiving. This talent may place him in an unpopular role, especially when he confronts his erstwhile allies. True believers detest marginal men who vaccilate between believing and questioning, but the man who trancends ideology must perpetually assume the task of questioning and doubting. To transcend ideological prisms, to move beyond beliefs, one must, like Nietzsche, continue to encourage the trans-valuation of values.

A major step in protecting oneself from ideological excess is to ac-quaint oneself sympathetically with the views of adherents of ideologies which are antithetic to one's own convictions. Such sympathetic explora-tion requires that an individual begin by admitting that sincere and good men may disagree. Similarly, he must attempt to see the world as his oppo-nent sees it and must try to understand why he perceives it in that way. Although most individuals prefer to acquaint themselves with materials that agree with their position, ideological transcendentalists must con-tinuously seek out materials that are supportive of positions that they oppose. They must attempt to comprehend the convictions as well as the underbelly of feelings which compose the social religions other than their own.

Ideological tourism, of course, contains pitfalls. Through persistent exploration an individual may learn to enjoy the freedom of traveling upon various ideological pathways. Such an intellectual passport could result in a partial estrangement from all beliefs. The marginality of the liberated man may cause him to suffer social alienation, and he must ensure that it does not make him withdraw from social responsibility.

The individual man who desires to shield himself from extremism also can protect himself by developing a system of beliefs which is based upon universally recognized maxims and which is designed to protect individuality within a framework of universal brotherhood. Although such a system is itself an ideology, its universality may serve to protect an individual from the snares of ideological provincialism. Again, the reader is cautioned, when such a system of beliefs becomes an end rather than a means, it too will be destructive.

The rugged ideological transcendentalist is an individual who ad-heres to an ethical system which gains its relevancy by utilizing as a goal for all human acts the welfare of mankind—not mankind viewed as an aggregate, but mankind viewed as a union of diverse human integers whose uniqueness should never be violated. Thus to our hero, the issue of where an individual's rights end is not resolved by affirming that they end at the tip of another's nose, but rather is found within the commit-ment of an individual to the betterment of mankind viewed collectively and to the preservation of the integrity of the millions of individuals who form the human family.

Our hero also will remain aware that even though the human col-lectivity may serve as a guide in determining human moral action, it can never replace the centrality of the individual in moral choice. He realizes that he is morally responsible for his actions as well as the actions of his social group—a responsibility which is greatly enhanced if he lives in a democratic society. Of course, all individuals are not necessarily equally free or responsible in the exercise of moral choice. Environment does influence human predisposition and behavior, and roles do convey particular responsibilities. Indeed, our ideological transcendentalist is aware that his transcendence carries with it grave responsibilities.

Just as our hero avoids making judgments about the culpability of particular individuals, he rejects all forms of determinism for they become self-fulfilling prophecies. Environmental determinism, childhood-determinism, or biological determinism are concepts which remove the responsibility for moral action from man's shoulders. The currently popular concept of social determinism, whereby man's societies and institutions are viewed as determining his behavior, is also rejected. Alex Comfort rightly observed: "We are living in a madhouse whenever society is allowed to become personalized and regarded as a super-individual. We are living in a madhouse now." [3]

Although many forces influence man, a mature human being is not determined by any force other than his own will in matters that relate to his ethical accountability. Of course, the degree of individual culpability remains a matter of conjecture. Inasmuch as each individual possesses a unique life pattern, freedom of will varies from person to person and within the same person at different times and during different circumstances. Indeed, the inherent danger in weakening the will of individuals through collective action remains as one of man's most dangerous characteristics. Collective actions, whether they be in the form of mob hysteria or in the deliberate actions motivated by institutional necessity, serve to diminish the individual participants' sense of responsibility. In this sense, the greatest danger inherent in modern warfare is not that individuals will seek to inflict bodily harm upon others because of their ideological differences, but rather that they will reject their responsibility and allow the massive bureaucratic institutional patterns to decide what they will do. The colossus man has constructed can be kept in check only by the efforts of individuals who assume responsibility for their acts, whether they are visible or camouflaged by the maze of bureaucracy and the call of institutional necessity.

Although all individuals must assume moral responsibility for their acts as well as the acts of their social group when such acts are performed in their name, moral responsibility is increased when one assumes a role of leadership within such a system. Individuals who assume the responsibility of teaching must weigh carefully the implications of such a choice. Too many individuals seek the role of priest or teacher as an escape from

[3] Alex Comfort, "The Ideology of Romanticism," in *Romanticism: Points of View*, ed. Robert F. Gleckner and Gerald E. Enscoe (Englewood Cliffs, N.J.: Prentice-Hall, Inc., 1970), p. 173.

life rather than as a threshold for its joy and agony. The person who seeks teaching as a career and who desires to avoid responsibility is either a fool or a fraud. The day that a person assumes the role of teacher is the day that he assumes a mantle of responsibility that cannot be removed without dire consequences for man.

Anthropologists have served a vital function in aiding human beings to understand and accept cultural differences. They have furnished us with valuable research materials which increase our capacity for cross-cultural communication. Most educated individuals, while not necessarily cultural relativists, reveal an admiration for man and the various ways in which he has adapted to his environment. International cross-cultural contacts often have proved to be meaningful and peaceful. Peace Corps workers, for example, despite occasionally being subject to the insecurity generated by cultural shock, have adjusted remarkably well to the ways of their host nations.

The previous decade has revealed that intranational cultural differences have been the source of numerous conflicts. These conflicts have resulted, in part, from man's tendency to rate cultural differences on various kinds of evaluative scales. Recent scholarly efforts, however, especially in the area of urban education, reveal that academicians and educationists are earnestly seeking means to remove cultural "blinders." Indeed, cultural pluralism has increased in popularity and educational institutions throughout the United States have initiated various kinds of programs dealing with ethnic differences. These efforts are a belated but welcome recognition that human creative growth is enhanced by cultural diversity and that educational institutions which are designed to encourage cross-cultural communication, whether international or intranational, are pedagogically superior to those which reflect a unidimensional cultural perspective.

The 1960s, therefore, were marked by a sometimes painful realization that institutional patterns in the United States often penalized individuals because of their racial or cultural differences. Indeed, the decade was characterized by numerous efforts, some violent, to readjust institutional patterns and government priorities to coincide with the realities of cultural diversity. Some Americans continue to adhere to a neolithic sense of racial superiority and to inflict their cultural arrogance on others, but most have been remarkably sincere in their attempts to adjust to the realities of cultural pluralism.

As Americans become increasingly sophisticated in dealing with cultural differences, they find, like most peoples on earth during the twentieth century, that they succumb easily to ideological excess. The major wars of the twentieth century, for example, reveal the degree to which men can distort ideological systems. Within modern societies individuals and groups battle one another incessantly because of conflicting ideologies. Many families have been torn apart because of conflicts which result from ideological pluralism. Similarly, some communities are segmented into warring factions because ideological differences are not confronted honestly and directly. Educational issues such as busing, sex education, the teaching about communism, the employment of hippies, the mention of God, the design of the curriculum, and the personal habits of teachers often become the source of hideous and vicious conflicts because individuals fail to recognize the nature of ideological idiosyncracies. As Pascal observed, "Men blaspheme what they do not know." In some social groups, ideologies have collapsed, leaving alienated individuals to wander helplessly in the grayness of anomie.

If advances in technology have served to moderate and in some cases nullify cultural differences, the expansion of knowledge generated by the popularization of information has served to increase ideological dissonance. Advances in communication, especially through the mass media, compulsory schooling, the popularization of reading by means of the mass dissemination of relatively inexpensive paperbacks, magazines, and newspapers, as well as the increase in travel made possible by affluence and decreased cost, have served to break down the provincial ideological framework which characterized most societies prior to the twentieth century. The knowledge epidemic rather than the knowledge explosion has served to alter the somewhat stable ideological world of previous centuries. The decades of the seventies and eighties promise to be an era of increased ideological pluralism. A world unprepared for such a reality could easily degenerate into a feudal darkness of petty warfare and intellectual regression. Prepared, however, it could serve to actualize man's eternal dream of a Golden Age of freedom and creativity.

# INDEX

Abélard, Peter, 14, 33
Academie Française. *See* French Academy
Acton, Lord, 252
Adam and Eve, 60
  as rebels, 139, 140
Adams, Henry, 291
Addams, Jane, 271, 305
Aeschylus, 295
AFL-CIO, 108
Afro-Americanism, 33, 38, 41, 54, 75, 239
  cultural pluralism, 253
  melting pot, 274
  romanticism, 152
  *See also* Black Capitalism; Black Christian Nationalism; Black Muslim; Black Nationalism; Black Panthers; Black Power; Black Separatism; Cultural Pluralism
Aiken, Henry D., 48
Albigensians, 38
Algur, Horatio, 190, 221, 372
Alienation, 408
  nature as cure, 172, 173
  of rebel, 162-66
Allegory of the Cave, 26, 57
Alliance for Progress, 241
Alonzo, Braulio, 387
Ambrose, Saint, 180
American Association of Teachers Colleges, 375
American Dream, 1, 221-26, 292, 367-72.
  *See also* Educationism; Puritanism
American Educational Research Association (AERA), 355
American Federation of Labor, 302, 384
American Federation of Teachers, 380, 384, 387, 388. *See also* Chicago Teachers' Federation
American Normal School Association, 379
American Revolution, 25, 76, 101, 260
  and Nationalism, 255
  and self-determination, 251
*The American Teacher,* 384

Americanism. *See* Nationalism
Americanization of immigrants, 77. *See also* Assimilation
Amish, 37, 180-81
Anabaptists, 141, 142, 189, 192, 199
Anglo-conformity, 269-70
Anomie, 29
Antigone, 129
Anti-intellectualism, 111, 362
  and business community, 382
  and Educationism, 373-74
  and Progressivism, 301-2, 322
  and Scientism, 70, 75
  and Unionism, 383
Apter, David, 25
Aquinas, St. Thomas, 64, 69, 335
Arieli, Yehoshua, 47, 237 fn, 260, 264
Aries, Philippe, 79 fn
Aristotle, 71, 360
Armstrong, Neil, 127
Assimilation
  forms, 269-77, 308
    anglo-conformity, 269-70
    cultural pluralism, 272-74, 307
    melting pot, 270-72, 307
  self-determination, 253
Association for Teacher Education, 355
Astronauts, 117, 241
Athens, 349, 359
Augustine, Saint, 65, 69, 194
Augustus, Philip King, 350
*The Autobiography of Malcolm X,* 38, 193, 217

Babbitt, Irving, 164, 318
Bach, Johann Sebastian, 55
Bacon, Francis, 26
Bacon, Roger, 296-97
Baez, Joan, 54, 153
Baker, Ray Stannard, 304
Balzac, Honoré de, 221
Bancroft, George, 263
Barabbas, 137

Barnard, Frederick A. P., 374
Barnard, Henry, 264, 277, 352
Bartley, Diana E., 284
Barzun, Jacques, 120, 148, 344
Baudelaire, Charles, 164, 167, 262
Beard, Charles A., 290-91, 314, 317
Beatles, 153, 156
Beat movement, 142
Bechmann, Johann, 70
Becker, Howard, 17, 386
Beckett, Samuel, 153
Beecher, Harriet, 208
Beethoven, Ludwig van, 55, 137, 150
Behavior modification, 114, 354
  and evolution, 84-85
Bell, Alexander Graham, 240
Bell, Wendell, 249
Benedictines, 141
Benson, Leonard C., 24
Berlioz, Hector, 167
Bernadoni, Louis C., 281
Bernard, Saint, of Clairvaux, 38
Bernstein, Leonard, 153
Bestor, Arthur, 9, 322, 344, 361, 362, 368
Bettelheim, Bruno, 116 fn
Bibbs, Willard, 75
Bill of Rights, 79, 260
Binet, Alfred, 86, 368
Bion, the Cynic, 145
Black Capitalism, 239
Black Christian Nationalism, 39
Black Muslims, 38
Black Nationalism, 7, 54, 286
Black Panthers, 7, 58, 152
Black Power, 285, 323, 386-87
Black Separatism, 239
Blake, William, 127, 166
Blue-collar workers, 223-24, 310, 312, 323, 371
Blue Laws, 30
Boaz, Frank, 272
Bode, Boyd Henry, 325, 332
Bogart, Humphrey, 114
Bonaparte, Napoleon, 137, 181
  and Nationalism, 256
Bond, James, 151
Boorstin, Daniel J., 214, 263
*The Bores,* 148
Boston Philosophical Society, 72
*The Bourgeois Gentleman,* 148
Bourne, Randolph, 305, 315
Boyer, Charles, 283
Boyle, Robert, 65
Brameld, Theodore, 319
Brandeis, Louis, 303, 314
Brandes, Georg, 164 fn
Bresnev, Leonid, 106
Brisbane, Albert, 182

British House of Parliament, 150
Brook Farm, 182
Brooks, Charles, 373
Brooks, Miss, 383
Brother Jonathan, 260
Brown, H. Rapp, 113
Brown, John, 206, 208
Brubacher, John S., 360
Bruce, Lenny, 147
Bruner, Jerome, 324, 354
Bruner, Richard, 383-84
Bruno, 69
Bryan, William Jennings, 220
Buber, Martin, 333
Budd, Billy, 174
Bumppo, Natty, 174
Bunyan, John, 192
Burke, Edmund, 291
Burroughs, Edgar Rice, 174
Bury, J. B., 295
Butler, Nicholas Murray, 374
Butler, Samuel, 243
Byrd, William, 72
Byron, Lord, 132, 138, 155, 173

Cabet, Etienne, 132, 151, 182
Cain, 140
California Renaissance, 152
Caligula, Emperor, 143
Calvinism, 189, 190, 209, 219, 299, 322
Camden, William, 255
Camhill Village, 183
Camus, Albert, 134, 135, 392
Capitalism
  and Nationalism, 257
  and rebels, 159-60
  *See also* Puritanism; American Dream
Capuchins, 141
Carmel, California, 151
Carmichael, Stokely, 53, 112 fn, 239, 273, 386
*Carmina Burana,* 141
Carnegie, Andrew, 218, 222-23
Carnegie, Dale, 322
Carr, Edward H., 241 fn, 257
Carr, William, 388
Carrol, Lewis, 44
Carver, George Washington, 113
Castro, Fidel, 113, 193, 210, 239
*Catcher in the Rye,* 151
Cathedral Schools, 349-50
Catholic Church. *See* Roman Catholic Church
Cattell, J. McKeen, 317
Caudwell, Christopher, 123, 160, 164
Caulfield, Holden, 151
Chamberlain, John, 317

Chansons de Geste, 254
Chapman, Stanley N., 275
Character formation
  dramaturgical model, 22
  Freudian model, 21-22, 164-65
  ideology and, 22
Chardin, Pierre Teilhard de, 170, 292
Charles I, of England, 141, 193
Chateaubriand, 132, 155, 164, 167
Chauvinism, 242
Cheops Pyramid, 241
Chesterton, G. K., 316
Chevalier, Michel, 159
Chicago Teachers' Federation, 384
*Childe Harold,* 173
Childs, John Lawrence, 325
Chips, Mr., 382
Civil Liberties Union, 40
Civil War, American, 208, 261, 264, 265,
  277, 357, 380
Clark, Kenneth B. Dr., 101-2
Clark, Lewis, 264
Classicism, 120, 147, 148, 157
  in art, 169-70
Clement IV, Pope, 297
Cobb, Stanwood, 317
*Cogito Ergo Sum,* 134
Cold War, 2, 94, 105
Coleman, James S., 24, 364 fn
Coleridge, Samuel Taylor, 55
  and drugs, 154, 167
  anti-revolutionary, 132, 137
  on education of children, 185, 186
  utopian, 182
Collier, John, 176
Colt, Samuel, 103
Combs, Arthur W., 282
Comfort, Alex, 165, 406
Commager, Henry Steele, 366
Commission on the Reorganization of
  Secondary Schools, 352 362
Committee of Ten, 352, 380
Common Market, 241
Common School System, 277-79
Communalism
  current forms, 181, 183
  eighteenth-century forms, 149
  Icaria, 182-83
  pantisocracy, 182
  U. S. nineteenth century, 150-51
  *See also* Essenes; Romanticism, utopian
Communism. *See* Marxism; Puritanism
Community
  and anomie, 29-31
  and ideological dissonance, 41-44
  extended groups
    elements of, 20
    ideology and, 28, 35-37

Community (*cont.*)
  Gemeinschafts and Romanticism, 121-
    22
  membership groups, 51-52
  national forms, 242-50
  primary groups, 19-20
    element of, 19
    purpose, 19-20
Community colleges. *See* Junior colleges
Conant, James, 81, 115, 368
Condon, John C. Jr., 286
Condorcet, Marquis de, 297, 298
*The Confessions of an English Opium
  Eater,* 167
*The Confessions of Jean-Jacques Rous-
  seau,* 163
Connolly, William E., 27 fn, 39, 41-42
*Conscience Collective,* 29. *See also* Ano-
  mie and Community
Conservatism, 92, 203-6, 291-92, 310-12
Constable, John, 150
Constitution of the United States, 260,
  262. *See also* Bill of Rights
Converse, Philip, 46
Cooper, James Fenimore, 150, 174, 263
Copernicus, 69
Coser, Lewis, 75
Cosmonauts, 241
Cotton, John, 194, 202-3
Council for Basic Education, 361
*The Count of Monte Cristo,* 150
Counterculture, 35
  anti-middle class, 155-57
  emergence, 6, 125, 126
  popularity of, 156-58
  *See also* Romanticism
Counts, George, 33, 319, 361
Covenant, 188, 209-10, 229
Crates, the Cynic, 145
Credentialization, 79-81
Cremin, Lawrence A., 278
Creon, King of Thebes, 129
Crockett, David, 174, 263
Cromwell, Oliver, 38, 142
Cult of the Madonna, 161
Cultural lag theory, 329-30
Cultural Nationalism
  and German identity, 176-77
  and Romanticism, 174-78
Cultural Pluralism
  Afro-Americanism, 253
  and educational aims, 10-11, 15
  and immigration, 265
  and testing, 281-83
  assimilation model, 272-74
  identity and schooling, 283-87
  in modern nation-states, 23-24, 269,
    276-77

Curie, Marie, 32
Curti, Merle, 85
Cybernetics, 102–3, 110, 127
Cynics. *See* Cynicism
Cynicism, 131, 143
    Diogenes, 144-45
    philosophy of, 128-29
    style, 144-46

Dante, 255
Darwin, Charles, 219, 220, 221, 306
    and religion, 64
    influence on psychology, 83, 84, 227
    theory of evolution, 217, 298
Daughters of the American Revolution,
    40
Day-care centers, 109-10, 228
*Death of a Salesman*, 81, 321
Debs, Eugene, 317
Declaration of Independence, 55, 161,
    264
    and self-determination, 251
Declaration of the Rights of Man, 161
De Grazia, Sebastian, 29, 39 fn, 44
Deism, 64, 211
Delacroix, Eugène, 150
Demetrius, 143
De Quincey, Thomas, 154, 167
Descartes, René, 83, 134
Destutt de Tracy, 26
Determinism
    and free will, 406-7
    environmental, 102
    genetic, 191
    in Darwinism, 298-99
    in Educationism, 346
    in Freudianism, 227-28
    in Marxism, 191
    in Progressivism, 291, 303
    in Puritanism, 102, 189, 191, 200-201,
        231
    in Scientism, 64-67, 102
Deutsch, Karl, 248
Dewey, Evelyn, 328
Dewey, John, 55, 83, 292, 294, 314, 315,
        317, 318, 332, 375
    and morality, 298, 305
    and religion, 301
    assimilation, 308
    co-operation, 39 fn, 82
    education, 262, 306, 307, 309, 310,
        328, 359
    nationalism, 280
    pragmatism, 299, 300
    war and pacifism, 305
Dickens, Charles, 75
Diderot, Denis, 38, 148, 297
Diogenes, of Sinope, 143, 144

Divine Comedy, 255
Dix, Dorothea, 97
Dominic, Saint, 38
Donald, David, 311
Drop outs, 78-80
DuBois, W. E. Burghardt, 53, 113, 369-
    70
Dudley, Donald, 144
Dumas, Alexandre, 132, 150
Duncan, Isadora, 154
Dunkers, 142
Dupree, Louis, 256
Durkeim, Emile, 29
Dvořák, Antonin, 175
Dylan, Robert, 54, 127, 153

Ecology movement, 98-99, 330
Economic Opportunity Program, 277
Edison, Thomas, 74, 75
Educational issues
    assimilation, 275, 276-79, 280
    common school, 277-79
    cultural minorities, 283-88
    desegregation, 279
    ideology and schooling, 33-35
    overview, 9-14
    romantic view, 183-86
    social change and, 11-14
    testing and Nationalism, 281-83
    training and teaching, 369
Educationism, Chapter 7
    aims of formal education, 358, 360-62,
        364-66
    and the American Dream, 367-72
    and citizenship, 364-66, 379-80
    and Professionalism, 51, 372-76, 382-
        89
    and Unionism, 380, 382-89
    assumptions of, 339-42
    characteristics of, 342-48
    historical antecedents, 348-52
Egalitarianism, 205, 367
    and anti-intellectualism, 262
    rejection of by rebels, 163
Ehrlich, Paul, 212
Einstein, Albert, 68, 75, 127
Eisenhower, President, 103, 314
Eliot, Charles W., 318, 367
Ellul, Jacques, 9, 105, 108, 131
Ely, Richard T., 223
Emerson, Ralph Waldo, 151, 182, 263,
        264
    folk culture, 175
    love, 179
    nonconformity, 160, 161, 162
    revolution, 136
    schooling, 184
*Emile*, 178

Encounter groups, 326-27. *See also* Neo-Progressivism; Progressivism
Enfantin, 149
Engles, Friedrich, 261
Enlightenment, 129, 148, 175, 255
  and science, 65
  *See also* Progressivism
*Épater le bourgeois,* 144, 154
*E pluribus unum,* 240, 277
Erikson, Erik H., 88
Essenes, 139, 180
Establishment, 54, 91, 103, 111, 158, 164, 202, 314, 336
  and counterculture, 35, 126
  as liberal, 331
  cynic attack against, 143-46
  definition, 37
  entente with Scientism, 121-22, 152
  perceptions of, 9
  romantic view, 129-30
  *See also* Power Elite
Etatism, 244, 256
  antecedent to Nationalism, 254-55
  contrast to Nationalism, 243
  definition, 243
Eugenics, 110, 219-20
Evans, David, 147, 179
Evans, Oliver, 76
Evolution, 84, 217, 291, 292, 298, 299
Ezechiel, 49-50

Fairchild, Hoxie Neale, 134, 167
Family
  extended, 75-76, 78, 110
  nuclear, 76, 78, 110
Family of the Mystic Arts, 101
Faulkner, William, 75
Faust, 134, 150, 160
Federal aid to education, 43
Federalism, 43
Fichte, Johann Gottlieb, 250, 251, 252
Fields, W. C., 114
Finn, Huck, 118, 151
Fischer, Louis, 50, 358
Fitzgerald, F. Scott, 159
Fleming, Ian, 151
Flying saucers, 50, 181
Ford, Henry, 74, 383
Form, William H., 381
Fourier, Charles, 132, 182
Francis of Assisi, Saint, 141, 393, 394
Franciscans, 141
Frankel, Charles, 291-92, 325, 327-28
Frankenstein, 60, 115, 174
Franklin, Benjamin, 297
  as author, 216-17
  autobiography, 192, 216-17
  emerging middle-class, 211

Franklin, Benjamin *(cont.)*
  on education, 331, 351, 361
  on humility, 192
  puritan values, 215
Free Speech Movement, 6, 90, 152
Freedom
  and license, 293-94
  threat against, 4-6
  *See also* Determinism
Freedom Riders, 6, 152
French Academy, 147, 225, 255
French Revolution, 148-49, 181, 251, 255
Freud, Sigmund, 69, 88, 89, 168, 226-28, 333
Friedenberg, Edgar, 8, 332-33, 340 fn
Fromm, Erich, 29, 39 fn, 88, 333
Frost, Robert, 6, 264
Frye, Northrop, 124, 164
Fugitivi, 145
Fuller, R. Buckminster, 102
Furst, Lilian, 165
*The Future of Public Education,* 51
Futurism. *See* Scientism and Progressivism

Galbraith, John Kenneth, 105, 370
Galileo, 69, 70, 103
Galton, Thomas, 219
Gandhi, Mohandas, 105
Garden of Eden, 139
Garvey, Marcus, 194
Gasset, José Ortega y, 291
Gattegnno, Caleb, 284
Gemeinschaft, 121
Generation gap, 7
George III of Great Britain, 268
Geronimo, 174
Ghettoism, 277
Gibbon, Edward, 297
Gibbons, James Cardinal, 266
Ginsberg, Allen, 25, 40, 152, 153
Glazer, Nathan, 269 fn
Glenn, John, 152
Goethe, Johann Wolfgang von, 134, 150, 154
Gogol, Nikolai, 150
Golding, William, 184
Goldwater, Barry, 229
Goliardi, 350
Goodman, Paul, 9, 153, 340 fn
Gordon, Milton M., 269
Graham, Sylvester, 207
Grant, Madison, 270
Gray, Zane, 151
*The Great Gatsby,* 159
Greene, Maxine, 376
*The Greening of America,* 163
Greenwich Village, 151, 163

Greer, Colin, 277, 278, 371
Grodzins, Morton, 35, 245 fn
Grotowski, Jerzy, 153
Group identity. *See* Character formation
Guetzkow, Harold, 245 fn
Guevara, Che, 133, 138, 158
Guilt *vs* Anxiety, 233

Haight Ashbury, 151, 163
*Hair,* 153
Hall, G. Stanley, 83, 86, 306
Hall, Rev. Samuel R., 373
Halsted, John, 149
Hamilton, Charles, 53, 273, 386
Hamlet, 160
Handman, Max Sylvius, 238 fn
Hardin, Warren G., 317
Harrington, Michael, 225 fn
Harris, Nigel, 28, 41
Harris, William T., 232
Harvard, 142, 196, 199, 211, 318, 351
Harvey, William, 65
Haseldon, Kyle, 274
Hauser, Arnold, 154, 179
Hawthorne, Nathaniel, 182, 263
Hayes, Carlton B., 177, 237 fn, 238 fn,
    242, 254
Head Start, 196, 277
Helen of Troy, 162
Hemingway, Ernest, 317
Henry VI, 399
Heraclitus, 295
Herbart, Johann, 306
Herder, Johan Gottfried von, 250
Herod of Antipas, 139
Hesiod, 296
Higham, John, 267, 269, 270
Hipparchia, 145
Hippie, 156, 157
Hitler, Adolf, 95, 177, 239, 244, 252
Hoffer, Eric, 57-58, 194
Hoffman, Abbie, 113, 132, 239
Hofstadter, Richard, 70, 111 fn, 196 fn,
    218, 303, 304-5, 313
Hollingshead, August B., 364
Holmes, Oliver Wendell, Jr., 315
Holmes, Sherlock, 95
Holt, John, 324, 340
*The Holy Barbarians,* 127
Homer, 104
Hooker, Thomas, 195
Hoover, Herbert, 312, 319
Hopkins, Mistress, 201-2
Hugo, Victor, 150, 165, 169, 174, 230
Human nature, 196-98, 207, 219, 227,
    297, 358
Hume, David, 37, 65-66, 67, 297
*The Hunchback of Notre Dame,* 150, 174

Hunt, Thomas P., 190
Hus, Jan, 38
Hutchins, Robert, 81
Hutchinson, Anne, 67, 142, 202, 229
Huxley, Aldous, 95, 98
Huxley, Julian, 292
*The Hypocrites,* 148
Hyslop, Francis E. Jr., 167 fn
Hyslop, Lois Boe, 167 fn

Icaria, 151, 182
Ideological Pluralism, 1-2, 407-8
    and communication, 396
    and schooling, 402
    defense against extremism, 58, 405-6
    in United States, 15
Ideology, Chapter 1
    activist, 55-56
    agents, 56
    and anomie, 29-31
    and community, 20-26, 42
        characteristics, 26-28
        citizenry, 24-26
        definition, 27-28
        personality, 22, 36-37, 44, 52-55
    and culture, 21-25, 31
    and human growth, 392-93
    and institutions, 31-35
    and Progressivism, 40
    and schooling, 33-35, 57-58, 396-408
    conflicts, 37-38
    dissonance, 41
    efficacy, 38-41
    extremism, 56-57, 394
        protection from, 405-6
    language of, 44-49, 127-28
    loyalty, 42-44
    parodist, 56
    perception, 49-54
    Romanticism as anti-ideology, 129-30
    symbols of identity, 42
    syncretism, 41
    theoreticians, 55
Ignatius Loyola, Saint, 38
Illich, Ivan, 340
Immigration, 265
Individualism
    and romantic love, 161-62
    Romanticism and, 158-62
    *See also* Puritanism
Indoctrination, 31, 369, 396-98
    *vs* education, 342
Industrial Revolution, 76, 91, 124
Ingsoc, 48
Institutionalism, 6
    and change, 12
    and ideology, 31-35
    and mass society, 122-25

Institutionalism (*cont.*)
  romantic rejection, 159-62
  romantic view of schooling, 122-25
Intelligence quotients, 67
Iron Mountain Report, 105
Itzkoff, Seymour W., 176, 273, 276
*Ivanhoe*, 150
Ives, Charles, 153
Ivy League Universities, 225, 314

Jacksonian Democracy, 199, 368
Jacobs, Paul, 131, 154, 155, 185
Jaeger, Werner, 295, 296
James I, of England, 141
James, William, 55, 83, 112
  pragmatism, 299, 300
Jarolimek, John, 13
Jay, John, 266, 365
Jeanne d'Arc, 38, 244
Jefferson, Thomas, 46, 394
  Enlightenment, 204, 297
  on education, 351, 365
Jeffersonian Democracy, 76, 351, 368
Jerome, Saint, 146
Jesus of Nazareth, 14, 33, 97, 147, 156,
    180, 208, 351
  as a rebel, 131, 139-40
  as anti-revolution, 137
*Jesus Christ Superstar*, 153
Jesus Freaks, 142
Jeunes-France, 149, 154
Jingoism, 242, 262
Joan of Arc. *See* Jeanne d'Arc
Job Corps, 277
John Birch Society, 40, 108
John Dewey Society, 361
John Hopkins University, 86
John the Baptist, 139, 180
Johnson, Ben, 242
Johnson, Lyndon B., 320
Junior colleges, 369

Kallen, Horace, 177, 272, 307
Kandel, I. L., 242, 249
Kant, Immanuel, 37, 250, 297
Keane, John C. Bishop, 266
Keane, Robert, 209
Keats, John, 150, 173
Kedourie, Elie, 251, 255
Kennedy, John F., 6, 152, 202, 320
Kennedy, John Pendeleton, 151
Kerouac, Jack, 6, 152, 153
Khrushchev, Nikita, 106
Kichter, Ernest, 214
Kilpatrick, William Heard, 310, 325, 332
Kimball, Solon T., 23 fn
King, Martin Luther, Jr., 8, 194
Knight, Everett, 75

Knights of Hospitallers, 141
Know-Nothing Party, 267
Knox, John, 190
Kohn Dichotomy, 256
Kohn, Hans, 254, 256, 260, 261
Koinonia Farm, 183
Kosciuszko, Tadbusz, 38
Kosygin, Alexei, 106
Kozol, Jonathan, 9, 285, 340 fn
Kubla Khan, 150
Ku Klux Klan, 42, 267, 317

Labor market, 75, 76
  and progressive education, 82-83
  and professionalism, 80-81, 385
  as alternative to schooling, 78-79, 371
  as defining childhood, 78-79, 90-91, 108
  training for, 77-78
  *See also* Progressive education, life
    adjustment
LaFollette, Robert, 312
Laissez-faire, 188, 204, 215, 218, 291,
    302
Lamarck, Jean Baptiste, 219
Lambert, Samuel, 387-88
Lamennais, Félicité, Abbé, 132 fn
Landau, Saul, 131, 154, 155, 185
Lane, Robert E., 48, 58
  on democracy and anomie, 29
  on ideology and institutions, 34-35
  on indoctrination, 31
Lasswell, Harold, 52
Latin Quarter, 350
Lawrence, Reverend William, 218-19
Leary, Timothy, 113, 127, 133, 153, 167,
    183
Leather Stocking Tales, 150, 174
Leeuwenhoek, Anton van, 65
Lemaire, Herve-B, 283
Lenin, Nikolai, 56, 193, 211, 234, 238
Lennon, John, 32, 156
*Le Sacre du Printemps*, 153
*Les Miserables*, 150
Lewis, Sinclair, 226
Liberalism, 92, 203-6, 291-92, 310-12
Liberation, 3
  and education, 13
  and ideology, 57-58
  and utopianism, 179
  in art, 150, 153
  psychological form, 163-65
  romantic view, 131-34
  transcending ideology, 403, 404-8
Liberty, 260, 261, 406
Liberty Bell, 276
*Licentia docendi*, 381
Lieberman, Myron, 51, 388

Liebniz, Gottfried Wilhelm von, 83, 297
Lincoln, Abraham, 208, 222
Lindsey, Margaret, 375 fn
Lippmann, Walter, 8
Lipset, Seymour Martin, 303
Lipton, Lawrence, 127
Literacy and alphabetism, 336, 347
Locke, John, 297
Logical positivism, 35, 166
*The Lonely Crowd,* 22
*The Lord of the Flies,* 184
Louis XIV, of France, 244
Lovell, Robert, 182
Loyalty, 15, 35-36, 245
    and group identity, 42-44
    and ideology, 35-38
    and nationalism, 244-48
    and nativism, 267-68
LSD, 154
Lucian, 145
Luther, Martin, 91, 141, 199, 229, 244
*Lyrical Ballads,* 150

McCarthy, Eugene, 312
McCarthy, Joseph, 105, 324
McCartney, Paul, 127
McClellan, James E., Jr., 23 fn
*McClures,* 304
McGuffey Readers, 74, 221-22, 256, 264, 365
McGuffey, William Holmes, 216, 264
Machiavelli, Niccoló, 179
McLuhan, Marshall, 104, 105, 112, 113, 114, 115, 116, 146, 211, 332
Madison, James, 365
Mailer, Norman, 152, 153
Maistre, Joseph de, 243
Malcolm X, 193, 217
Malthus, Thomas Robert, 221
Manifest Destiny, 268
Mann, Horace, 77, 264, 277, 352, 366, 373
Mannheim, Karl, 27 fn, 45, 118
Marcuse, Herbert, 9, 112 fn, 158, 203, 294
Maritain, Jacques, 361
Martin, James G., 53
Marx Brothers, 114
Marx, Karl, 69, 88, 89, 106, 112, 172, 194, 229, 292, 300, 335
Marxism, 30, 35, 40, 47, 123, 238, 247
    as unAmerican, 37
Maslow, Abraham H., 333
*Mass,* 153
Massachusetts Act of 1842
    compulsory school attendance, 196, 264

Massachusetts Bay Colony, 142, 189, 194, 395
Mather, Cotton, 72, 188, 193, 197, 198, 216
Mather, Eleazar, 195
Mather, Increase, 72, 192
Matthew, Saint, 135
Maui Zendo, 181
Maupassant, Guy de, 246
Mayhew, Lewis B., 354-55
Mead, Edwin, 266
Media
    movies, 113-14
    television, 98, 112-13
Meiklejohn, Alexander, 261
Melting Pot, 239, 269, 270-72, 277
*The Melting Pot,* 270
Melville, Herman, 174, 230, 263
Membership group, 51-52
Mendel, Gregor, 75
Menken, H. L., 188, 318
Mercantilism, 257
Merriam, Charles, 246
Merton, Robert K., 51
Merton, Thomas, 394
Mexican War 1846-48, 268
Michelangelo, 55
Middle Ages, 141, 146-47, 349, 381, 389
Miel, Alice, 353
Milbrook, 183
Military-industrial complex. *See* Establishment
Mill, John Stuart, 188, 204, 247, 252
Miller, Arthur, 321
Miller, Henry, 163
Miller, Perry, 209, 212-13
Mills, C. Wright, 9, 152
    bureaucracy, 115
    cultural lag theory, 329
    free enterprise, 225
    power elite, 112 fn, 314, 370
    professionalism, 51, 357
    progress, 290
    research, 100 fn
    values, 298
Milton, John, 193
Mind-body dualism, 83, 84
Minnesota Fats, 308
Minogue, K. R., 236, 243
Modernization
    definition, 126
    elements of, 14
    and Nationalism, 257-58
Molière, Jean Baptiste, 148
Monastic schools, 349
Monroe, Paul, 374
Montagnard, 54
Montesquieu, 243, 297

Mora, Jose Ferrater, 127
Morgan, Edmund S., 195-96
Mormons, 142
Morrill Acts, 277, 352, 370-71
Morrill, Justin, 370-71
Moskos, Charles C., Jr., 249
Moynihan, Daniel, 269
Mozart, Wolfgang Amadeus, 240
Muckrakers, 304
Muhammad, Elijah, 193, 194
Murdock, Kenneth, 217

Nader, Ralph, 212
Nation
  as cultural unit, 247-50
  as political unit, 243-47
  contrasted to state, 243-44
  definition, 242
Nation, Carry A., 207
National assessment, 277
National Association of Manufacturers, 108, 302
National Association of School Super-intendents, 379
National Commission on Teacher Education and Professional Standards (NCTEPS), 375
National Council for Accreditation of Teacher Education, 375
National Council for the Social Studies, 361, 365, 366
National Education Association
  and professionalism, 51, 376
  and Civil War, 380
  and Educationism, 341
  and unionism, 387-89
  on assimilation, 265, 266, 270-71
  on Nationalism, 280, 307
  origin, 378-79
National Guidance Association, 367
National self-determination, 250-53
  and ethnicity, 252-53
National Socialist Party. *See* Nazism
National Society for the Promotion of Industrial Education (NSPIE), 321, 367
Nationalism, Chapter 5
  Americanism, 15, 259-68
    bases, 259-64
    meanings, 259
    nativism, 267
  and colonialism, 256
  and democracy, 243-45
  and etatism, 254-55
  and ethnic identity, 283, 287
  and modernization, 257-58
  and schooling, 275-79
  and testing, 281-83

Nationalism, Chapter 5 (*cont.*)
  assimilation, 269-75
    anglo-conformity, 269-70
    cultural pluralism, 272-74
    melting pot, 270-72
  citizenries, 242-47
  common school, 277-79
  definitions, 239
  European antecedents, 253-59
  Kohn Dichotomy, 256
  meanings, 237-42
  national self-determination, 250-53
  nationalities, 247-50
  role of teacher, 279-87
  symbol of, 240-41
Nationalities, 247-50
  and Americanism, 259-63
  and schooling, 281-87
  bases of, 248-50
  definitions, 247-48
Nativism, 265, 267, 269-70
NATO, 239, 241
Natural law, 215, 303
  economics, 304
  science, 64-65
  social Darwinism, 291
Nazism, 29, 40, 238
  distortion of cultural Nationalism, 176-77
NEA. *See* National Education Association
Neil, A. S., 293-94
Neo-American church, 183
Neo-Progressivism, 324, 329, 332-34
  cultural lag theory, 329
  ecological movement, 330
  encounter groups, 326-27
  futurism, 329-30
  *See also* Progressivism
Newcomb, Theodore, 46
New England Primer, 74, 198, 216, 259, 263, 365
New Frontier, 181, 313
New Harmony, 55, 151
New Orleans, 151
Newton, Sir Isaac, 65
Nietzche, Friedrich, 107, 145, 191, 230, 405
  distortion of, 177
  on education, 185, 186 fn
Noble Savage, 118, 151
  examples of, 173-74
  in Romanticism, 167
Normal Schools, 373-74
  anti-intellectualism in, 373
  origin, 373
Northwest Ordinance, 277
Nosow, Sigmund, 381
*Novum Organum,* 26

Noyes, John Humphrey, 56

Ogburn, William F., 329
Old Deluder Satan Act, 361
Olympic Games, 241
Oneida Community, 56, 181
O'Neill, Eugene, 152
One World Family of the Messiah's
  World Crusade, 181
Open Sesame Syndrome, 353
Oppenheimer, J. Robert, 60
Orff, Carl, 141
Organization man typology, 42, 56, 82,
  87, 321-23, 326
  *See also* Progressivism; Progressive
  Education
Organized intelligence, 82
Orwell, George, 48-49, 93, 98, 336
Owen, Robert, 32, 55, 151, 267, 292

Pacifism, 105, 305
Page, David, 373
Paine, Thomas, 46, 297
Pan-Americanism, 258
Pantheism, 138, 142, 170
Pantisocracy, 137, 182
Parkman, Francis, 151, 263
Parmenides, 295
Parrington, Vernon L., 194
Pascal, Blaise, 408
Pasteur, Louis, 32
Patch, Richard, 257
Patriotism
  definition, 242
Peace Corps, 319
Peckham, Morse, 125
Peepers, Mr., 14, 383
People's Republic of China, 195, 214,
  215, 365
Pepi I, Pharaoh of Egypt, 147
Perception, 49-54
Perry, Ralph Barton, 189, 194, 206, 230
Pestalozzi, Johann, 306
Pétain, Henri-Philippe, 38
Petrarch, 255
Pharisaism, 229
Phenix, Philip, 360
Phenomenology, 354
Phillips, Wendel, 208
Phylogenesis, 306
Physical Science Study Committee, 361
Picasso, Pablo, 55
Pickering, John, 263
Pierce, Charles, 55, 220, 299
Pike, Zebulon M., 264
Planned Parenthood Association, 220
Plato, 26, 71, 110, 144, 296, 336, 359.
  *See also* Allegory of the Cave

Poe, Edgar Allen, 154, 167, 262
Politzer, Robert L., 284
Pontius Pilate, 137
*Poor Richard's Almanac,* 74, 83, 216
Poor Theater, 153
Pope, Alexander, 65
Pope, Major W. S., 380
Populism, 220, 302, 368
  and Progressivism, 310-11
Post, Emily, 148
Power Elite. *See* Establishment
Pragmatism. *See* Progressivism
Professionalism
  and Educationism, 350, 373-78
  and industrialization, 382
  and unionism, 383-84, 389
  as restricting influence, 357
  origin, 380-81
Professionalization
  and labor market, 80
  *See also* Professionalism
Progress
  technological, 106, 117, 290-92
  doctrine of, 218, 295-96
Progressive Education
  as middle-class phenomenum, 319-21,
    323-24
  child-centered, 316-19, 320, 321, 331
  life adjustment, 321-22
  and organization man, 321-22
  *See also* Labor market
  social reconstructionism, 319-20
  *See also* Educationism; Neo-Progres-
    sivism; Progressive Movement
Progressive Education Association, 317,
  318
Progressive Movement, 302-6
  and education, 306-10
  and the Muckrakers, 304
  and war, 305-6
  *See also* Progressivism
Progressivism, Chapter 6
  and cultural pluralism, 307-8
  and the Enlightenment, 296-99
  and groupism, 324-27
  and neo-Progressivism, 324-29, 332-34
  and politics, 310-27
  and populism, 310-11
  and Scientism, 293, 329-30, 333
  and social reform, 302-3, 311-14, 315,
    329, 332
  and pragmatism, 299-302
  and the progressive movement, 302-6
  and religion, 301
Pritchard, Henry S., 367
Prometheus, 60, 143, 295, 296
*Promising Practices in Civic Education,*
  365-66

Prosser, Charles Dr., 321
Protestant (Puritan) Ethic, 74, 208, 215, 218, 302
Protestant Reformation, 91, 189, 198, 351
and Romanticism, 141
*Proverbs from Hell*, 127
Prufrock, 160
Psychologizing, 227
Puritan Revolution
and Nationalism, 255
Puritanism, Chapter 4
and the American Dream, 221-26
and economic development, 208-11
and formal schooling, 196-201
and Freudianism, 226-28
and reform movements, 207-8, 232-33
and social Darwinism, 217-21
as revolutionary doctrine, 193-96, 211-14
individual and community, 201-7
left wing–right wing, 203, 206
literary style, 216-17
moral exemplarism, 195-96, 198
secularized and democratized, 215-17
Pushkin, Aleksander, 150

Quakers, 142
Quisling, Vidkun, 38
Quizano, David, 270

Racism, 53, 79
institutional, 93, 308, 372
personal, 93, 372
"Radical chic," 224
Rafferty, Max, 9, 81, 322
Rand, Ayn, 135, 140, 322
Raushchenbusch, Walter, 301
Raymond of Toulouse, Count, 38
Read, Herbert, 169
*Reader's Digest*, 25
Realism, 120
Redfield, Robert, 19 fn
Reference group, 51-52
Reich, Charles A., 163
Relativism, 54-55, 299-300, 307
*Remains Concerning Britaine*, 255
Renaissance, 147
Renan, Ernest, 248
*The Republic*, 26, 57, 110, 201
Revere, Paul, 264
Rexroth, Kenneth, 127, 157, 169
Richards, Zalmon, 379-80
Richman, Julia, 270
Rickover, Hyman, 9, 81, 322, 324, 344
Rieff, Philip, 227-28
Riesman, David, 22, 56, 82, 152, 322, 323, 326-27
*The Rime of the Ancient Mariner*, 150

Rivlin, Harry N., 276
Robber Barons, 303, 304
and Brahmins, 224-25
Roberts, Ron E., 181
Robert's Rules of Parliamentary Procedure, 315
Robinson, James Harvey, 314
Robinson, Crusoe, 160
Rogers, Carl, 326
Rolling Stones, 153
Roman Catholic Church, 30, 41, 91, 247, 255, 349
and American loyalty, 265-66
and Romanticism, 141
as ideological system, 37
Romantic love, 161, 162
Romanticism, Chapter 3
and drugs, 167
and eighteen-century classicism, 147-48
and individualism, 159-62
and nature, 169-74
and politics, 131-33
and Puritanism, 141-42
and revolution, 134-38, 148, 149
and schooling, 183-86
as anti-middle-class, 153-58
as artistic movement, 149-50
as rebellion, 128-34
as style, 133-34
contrasted to classicism, 169-72
contrasted to revolution, 134-38
contrasted to Scientism, 120-28
definition, 128-29
ideology of action, 134-35
in Greek mythology, 143
in "Old West," 151
melancholic Romanticism, 162-68
religious antecedents, 138-43
role of court jester, 146-47
romantic Nationalism, 174-78
secular antecedents, 143-53
synthetic hippies, 157-83
utopian Romanticism, 178-83
*See also* Counterculture; Cynicism; Romantic love
Roosevelt, Theodore, 294, 304, 311, 312
Rosenberg, Julius and Ethel, 38
Roszak, Theodore, 67, 124
Rousseau, Jean-Jacques, 55, 69, 148, 154, 156, 164, 167, 228, 306
and national self-determination, 251
on citizenship, 178
on civilization, 130
on science, 171
Royal Institute of International Affairs, 237 fn
Royal Society of England, 72
Rubin, Jerry, 112 fn, 121, 184

Rugg, Harold, 318
Russell, Bertrand, 103, 198
Russell, William, 379
Rustow, D. A., 258
Ryle, Gilbert, 84

Sacco, Nicola, 317
Saint-Marie, Buffy, 54
Saint-Simon, Comte de, 149, 159, 182
Salinger, J. D., 151
Sand, George, 154
Sanhedrin, 137
Santayana, George, 291
Sarnoff, General David, 115
Satan, 160
    as rebel in Eden, 139-40
Satre, Jean-Paul, 171, 191
Schaar, John H., 21, 245 fn
Schenk, H. G., 172
Schlegel, August, 163
Schlegel, Friedrich, 163
Schoenberg, Arnold, 153
Schubert, Franz, 175
Scientism, Chapter 2
    and Educationism, 85-87
    and futurism, 329-330
    and Progressivism, 82, 293
    and psychology, 83-88, 96-98
    and Puritanism, 72-75
    and religion, 61-64
    and social control, 88-98
    and social issues
        drugs, 108-9
        liberation movements and youth cul-
            ture, 109-14
        methodology, 98-102
        pollution, 106-7
        population control, 107-8
        war, 103-6
    and technology, 70-71
    methodology, 64-70, 98-102, 221
    natural law, 64-65
    objectivity, 67-68
Scopes, John, 32, 62, 220, 317
Scott, Walter, 132, 150
Sebba, Gregor, 48
Sectionalism, 277
*Self Reliance,* 160
*Sejanus,* 242
Seven Cardinal Principles of Education,
    360
Sexton, Patricia, 341 fn, 362
Shakers (United Society of Believers in
    Christ's Second Appearing), 142,
    181
Shakespeare, William, 75, 240
Shaman, 122

Shaw, George Bernard, 341
Shelley, Mary, 60, 174
Shelley, Percy Bysshe, 132, 150, 172, 177
Shepard, Alan B., Jr., 137
Sherif, Muzafer, 51
Shostak, Arthur B., 323
Shumaker, Ann, 318
Sibelius, Jean, 175
Silbert, K. H., 247 fn
Simon & Garfunkel, 54, 153
*Sinfonia Eroica,* 137
Skinner, B. F., 86, 95, 110, 175, 292
Slater, Samuel, 76
Smetana, Bedrich, 175
Smith, Adam, 215
Smith-Hughes Act, 361
Snygg, Donald, 282
*Social Contract,* 178
Social Darwinism, 217-21, 291, 302-3,
    322. *See also* Puritanism
Social Gospel movement, 301
Social Issues, 8-14. *See also* Scientism
Socialism, 41
    and Nationalism, 257
Social Mobility, 386-87. *See also* Ameri-
    can Dream
Socrates, 14, 33, 296, 298
Sophists, 296
Southey, Robert, 137
Soviet Union, 105-6, 110, 195, 214, 215,
    322, 365
Spanish Americanism, 54
Spanish-American War (1898), 268
Spectorsky, A. D., 323
Spencer, Herbert, 217, 218, 291
Spillane, Mickey, 151
Spindler, George D., 34
*The Spirit of the Laws,* 243
Sputnik, 39, 81, 152, 322
Stalin, Joseph, 55, 211
Steffens, Lincoln, 304
Stereotyping, 48, 395
Stockhausen, Karlheinz, 153
*The Stranger,* 392
Stratemeyer, Florence B., 328, 332
Stravinsky, Igor, 153
Students for a Democratic Society, 108.
    *See also* Weatherman
St. Vincent Millay, Edna, 152
Suez Canal, 159
Sumner, William Graham, 217, 218, 291
Supreme Court, 43, 62, 279
Swift, Jonathan, 107
Sykes, Gerald, 71
Synanon, 183
Synod of Dart, 189
Sypher, Wylie, 68, 120
Szasz, Thomas, 94, 96

Tacitus, 176
Taj Mahal, 241
Taos, N. M., 151
Tarbell, Ida, 304
Tarzan, 118, 174
Tawney, R. H., 209 fn
Tax-revolt, 344, 387
Taylor, Harold, 324-25, 340
Teacher
    as artist, 357-58, 376-78, 396-98
    as behavior modifier, 84-85
    as facilitator, 309-10, 327-28, 333-34
    as moral exemplar, 87, 195, 198
    as patriot, 279-80, 284-86
    as professional, 51, 373-89
    image of, 51, 382-83
    social mobility, 385-86
(National) Teacher Corps, 277
Teachers College, Columbia University, 310
Teaching *vs* Training, 369, 396-98
Technism, 120
Technological Anesthesia, 131
Technology
    reciprocal relationship with man, 115-16
    *See also* Scientism; Labor Market
Teresa, Saint, 141
Terman, Lewis, 86
Testing, 281-83
Theater of the Absurd, 153
Theodicy question
    definition, 130
Therapeutic state, 94-98, 347
Think tanks, 313
Third force psychology, 331, 333
Third World Nations, 104
Thomas, Donald R., 50, 358
Thomas, Dylan, 153
Thoreau, Henry David, 55, 150, 151, 180, 295
    and American character, 263, 264
    anti-establishment, 130, 161
    on nature, 163
    on technology, 171
Thorndike, Edward L., 84, 85, 86, 368, 374
*The Three Musketeers*, 150
Tirnauer, Lawrence, 327
Tocqueville, Alexis de, 112, 205, 261, 291
Toffler, Alvin, 330
Tolerance
    and ideology, 58
    and assimilation, 273-74
Tonnies, Ferdinand, 19, 121, 201
Totalitarianism, 243
Town and gown conflicts, 350

Toynbee, Arnold J., 104, 238
Transcendentalism, 151, 211
Trivoli Farm, 183
Troubadours, 161
Tse-Tung, Mao, 193, 210, 211, 215-16, 294, 365
Tubman, Harriet, 113
Turgot, Robert Jacques, 297
Turner, Frederick Jackson, 272
Turner, Joseph M. W., 150
Turner, Ralph, 46
Twain, Mark, 151, 161, 302
*The Tyranny of the Majority*, 205

Ulibarri, Horatio, 281
Ultranationalism, 242
Uncle Sam, 240, 260
Unionism
    History and function, 381-82, 384-85
    *See also* Educationism
United Nations, 239, 241
University of Bologna, 350
University of Illinois Committee on School Mathematics, 361
University of Paris, 243, 350
University of Pennsylvania, 351
University of Virginia, 351

Valentine, T. W., 379
Values
    emerging, 34
    romantic view of, 130-31
    traditional, 34
Vanderbilt, Amy, 148
Vanzetti, Bartolomeo, 317
Veblen, Thorstein, 224, 302, 314
Vespasian, Emperor, 145, 349
Viereck, Peter, 291
Vietnam War, 7, 242
Vigny, Alfred de, 168
Villon, François, 255
Vinci, Leonardo da, 103
Violence
    institutional, 92-93
    personal, 92-94
Vista, 277
Vivas, Eliseo, 398
*Volk*, 248
Voltaire, François, 148, 297
Von Braun, Wernher, 32, 75, 127

Wagner, Richard, 175, 176, 335
*Waiting for Godot*, 153
*Walden Two*, 183
Wallace, George, 113
Waller, Willard, 339, 382, 383
Walzer, Michael, 193
Warner, Charles Dudley, 302

Warren, Earl, 206
Warsaw Pact, 241
Washington, Booker T., 113, 217, 369
Washington, George, 113, 263, 365
Watson, John B., 84
Watts, Alan, 25, 127, 133, 142, 153, 156,
    166, 167
Weatherman, 152, 158
Weber, Max, 208, 209, 210, 215
Webster, Noah, 54, 366
    and Educationism, 356
    and Nationalism, 256, 263
    and Puritanism, 216
Weimar Republic, 29
Westminster Abbey, 241
Whewell, William, 70
White, Morton, 82, 314
White Collar, 51
The White Negro, 152
Whitehead, Alfred North, 64, 65, 74
Whitney, Eli, 76, 103
Whyte, William H., Jr., 51, 87 fn, 152,
    323, 326
Widmer, Kingley, 146, 157, 185
    on cynicism, 143-44, 154
    on rebel style, 135-36, 156
Wiener, Norbert, 102
Wiggin, Gladys, 239, 276
Wigglesworth, Michael, 197
Wilde, Oscar, 154

Willeford, William, 147
Williams, Roger, 67, 72, 142, 191, 202,
    229
Wilshire, Bruce, 170, 171, 172, 180
Wilson, Ian H., 329-30
Wilson, Woodrow, 239, 252, 305
Winthrop, John, 190, 195, 199, 201-2
Winthrop, John, Jr., 72
Wirth, Louis, 238 fn
The Witness, 56
Wittenberg, 141
Wolfe, Robert Paul, 273
Wolfe, Thomas, 226
Woman's liberation, 373. See also Scien-
    tism, social issues
Woodstock Nation, 30, 152, 155, 157,
    178
Wordsworth, William, 150, 170, 172
    antirevolutionary view, 132, 137
    on childhood, 183, 184
World War I, 104, 226, 305, 316, 320
World War II 70, 94, 104, 243

Yoga, 142, 181

Zangwill, Israel, 270, 272
Zarathustra, 177
Zen Buddhism, 142, 181, 294
Zionist, 40
Znaniecki, Florian, 255 fn, 378